Respondus^LE from H. K. Publishers

D0221540

Respondus^LE from H. K. Publishers

Motor Learning and Development

Motor Learning and Development

Pamela S. Haibach, PhD
College at Brockport

Greg Reid, PhD
McGill University

Douglas H. Collier, PhD
College at Brockport

Human Kinetics

Library of Congress Cataloging-in-Publication Data

Haibach, Pamela S., 1977-
    Motor learning and development / Pamela S. Haibach, Greg Reid, Douglas H. Collier.
      p. cm.
    Includes bibliographical references and index.
    ISBN-13: 978-0-7360-7374-5 (hardcover)
    ISBN-10: 0-7360-7374-4 (hardcover)
  1. Motor learning. 2. Motor ability in children. 3. Movement education. I. Reid, Greg, 1948- II. Collier, Douglas Holden, 1953- III. Title.
    BF295.H25 2011
    152.3'34--dc22

                                                                    2010053483

ISBN-10: 0-7360-7374-4 (print)
ISBN-13: 978-0-7360-7374-5 (print)

The web addresses cited in this text were current as of March 2, 2011, unless otherwise noted.

Acquisitions Editor: Myles Schrag; **Developmental Editor:** Amanda S. Ewing; **Assistant Editors:** Antoinette Pomata and Kali Cox; **Copyeditor:** Joyce Sexton; **Indexer:** Betty Frizzell; **Permissions Manager:** Martha Gullo; **Graphic Designer:** Nancy Rasmus; **Graphic Artist:** Tara Welsch; **Cover Designer:** Keith Blomberg; **Photographer (cover):** James Dusen/© Human Kinetics; **Photographs (interior):** © Human Kinetics unless otherwise noted; photo on page 47 © allOver/TPH/Blickwinkel/age fotostock; 225 Sven Simon/Imago/Icon SMI; and 299 ©Howard Lipin/San Diego Union Tribune/ZUMA Press. Chapter 5 movement photos taken by James Dusen/© Human Kinetics; **Photo Asset Manager:** Laura Fitch; **Visual Production Assistant:** Joyce Brumfield; **Photo Production Manager:** Jason Allen; **Art Manager:** Kelly Hendren; **Associate Art Manager:** Alan L. Wilborn; **Illustrations:** © Human Kinetics unless otherwise noted; **Printer:** Sheridan Books

We thank the College at Brockport in Brockport, New York, for assistance in providing the location for the photo shoot for this book.

Printed in the United States of America   10 9 8 7 6 5 4 3 2 1

The paper in this book is certified under a sustainable forestry program.

Human Kinetics
Website: www.HumanKinetics.com

United States: Human Kinetics
P.O. Box 5076
Champaign, IL 61825-5076
800-747-4457
e-mail: humank@hkusa.com

Canada: Human Kinetics
475 Devonshire Road Unit 100
Windsor, ON N8Y 2L5
800-465-7301 (in Canada only)
e-mail: info@hkcanada.com

Europe: Human Kinetics
107 Bradford Road
Stanningley
Leeds LS28 6AT, United Kingdom
+44 (0) 113 255 5665

e-mail: hk@hkeurope.com

Australia: Human Kinetics
57A Price Avenue
Lower Mitcham, South Australia 5062
08 8372 0999
e-mail: info@hkaustralia.com

New Zealand: Human Kinetics
P.O. Box 80
Torrens Park, South Australia 5062
0800 222 062
e-mail: info@hknewzealand.com

E4400

To my parents for their ongoing love and support and to my loving family, Jeff, Tristan, and Makayla, for inspiring me to write this book.

—Pam Haibach

To my family who make everything worthwhile, Carol, Drew, Tyler, Tara, Tara, and of course Jacob.

—Greg Reid

To the three women in my life, Chris, Robin, and Shannon, who, at all times, give me love and support. Love always.

—Doug Collier

CONTENTS

Contents

(Handwritten margin notes: "Nov 6|8", "Nov 13|15", "TXGive", "Nov 27·29", "Dec 4-6")

Whether it be outsmarting the opponent on the field of play or simply walking down the street, we are consistently faced with the challenge of solving movement problems. When we walk down the street, we often have to avoid obstacles or other pedestrians while keeping in mind the wet, slippery pavement. In a competitive sporting environment, we may have to consciously think about "faking out" our opponent. No matter the setting, our skill level, or our age, we cannot avoid the fact that movement is a vital part of our lives and affects us in terms of our overall physical well-being, our intellectual functioning, and the development of our social skills. These effects are ever present—and ever changing—and take place over the course of our lives.

Clearly then, how an individual develops in addition to an individual's previous movement experiences affect how we acquire new motor skills or how we refine old skills. The learning of new motor skills, and the refinement and adjustment of existing motor skills, are critical aspects of our lives—aspects that we don't always appreciate. When performing everyday movements, we often do not appreciate how difficult it is to coordinate our limbs so that we can effectively execute an activity. As an example, adults use a knife and fork to eat without giving these actions a second thought. This was a very difficult task when we were small children, however. We had to learn how to control both limbs in a coordinated fashion in order to cut meat and feed ourselves. Over time, though, this initially challenging feat became second nature, and the frustration caused by the complexity of these actions was soon forgotten. That feeling of frustration in learning those early everyday tasks returns, however, if as adults we must relearn these "basic" movements following a serious accident or medical event (such as a stroke). The intense physical and occupational therapy required to relearn even the simplest of tasks reminds us of the intricacy of motor skills. No matter the time of life—infancy through old age—the ongoing interaction between our ever-changing abilities, the environment, and the task we're solving at the moment determines how we proceed.

Motor Learning and Development provides a framework for understanding both fields and for exploring how motor learning and motor development interact with and affect each other. Having a thorough understanding of the factors that "push" the development of motor skill across the life span will better prepare you to teach movement skills effectively to learners at any chronological age and at any skill level. *Motor Learning and Development* examines the development of movement skill in humans from infancy to older adulthood (referred to as "life span motor development") and examines how having different motor, cognitive, and social abilities affects how, when, and why an individual learns motor skills. As movement educators, we must understand the complexities of teaching movement skills to individuals of various backgrounds, interests, experiences, and abilities. As we have noted, learning a motor skill (or a combination of motor skills) can be quite challenging, and many elements must be taken into consideration. *Motor Learning and Development* is a textbook that has been designed to guide the learner, in an

Intro to Course

accessible and interesting manner, into the fields of motor development and motor learning. The book includes a variety of methods to facilitate readers' learning and keep them engaged with the material.

Motor Learning and Development is an undergraduate text written for students and professionals pursuing careers in physical education, athletic training, early childhood education, gerontology, kinesiology, special education, adapted physical education, primary and secondary education, and related fields. The text presents a strong theoretical foundation for motor development and motor learning in an engaging and accessible fashion. Readers will learn how to develop, implement, and critically assess motor skill programs for learners at all developmental levels.

Although the fields of motor learning and motor development have been addressed in a variety of undergraduate texts, none have merged these two fields into one textbook. *Motor Learning and Development* fills this void and does so in an eminently readable fashion. The contents are based on the latest research in the fields of motor development and motor learning. This text also provides a framework for developing movement programs that will facilitate skill acquisition for all types of learners—from those with significant disabilities to extremely high-level learners. This book will also help prepare students for meeting national standards and Praxis exams.

Life Span Perspective

This book adopts a life span perspective. This perspective goes beyond the developmental and neuromotor changes associated with childhood and younger adulthood. Rather, a life span perspective provides an in-depth look at all ages throughout the human life span, including the many large life changes associated with younger and older adults. These changes can include leaving home, entering the workforce, getting married, and having children. We also examine the social and psychological changes associated with life transitions. Societal mores and expectations can have a huge impact on the motor development of various cohorts. For instance, in today's highly technological age, adolescents are much more likely to spend a large portion of their free time playing with cell phones, iPods, and video games than they are to be participating in physical activity. On the other hand, many adults have changed their focus to health and wellness, causing a surge of people who are eating healthier meals, giving up unhealthy habits such as cigarette smoking, and participating in more physical activity. These healthy decisions are certainly having a large impact on older adults' motor development and on slowing their rate of functional decline. However, what motivates an adolescent to participate in sport or physical activity may be of little interest to a middle-aged adult or, indeed, a child. It is important to take a broad view and consider many variables when one examines individual motor development and performance. This book details these variables in order to prepare movement educators to teach motor skills to a broad array of individuals representing many ages, developmental levels, and degrees of physical proficiency in a variety of settings, including educational, athletic, clinical, and fitness settings.

Organization

Part I, "Motor Behavior: Theory and Foundational Concepts," provides a basic understanding of the fundamental concepts in motor learning and motor development. Chapter 1 introduces the subfields of motor behavior, motor development, motor learning, and motor control, exploring major tenets and theoretical perspectives from these fields. Unidimensional and multidimensional skill classifications, as well as games classifications, are explained in chapter 2. Chapter 3 discusses motor skill progression as well as three models of motor learning stages. It is important to understand each of these models for more effective teaching and learning. Instructors who have a thorough understanding of the strengths and shortcomings of each model will have more and better-developed tools to engender positive behavioral, cognitive, and physical changes in performers. It is at this point (chapter 4), that we discuss important methodological considerations, including how to measure and assess motor learning and organize the learning experience so as to facilitate positive transfer and long-term retention.

Part II, "Motor Development: Childhood and Adolescence," provides a solid background regarding the fundamental motor skills developed during childhood and the individual constraints, both functional and structural, in childhood and adolescence. Chapter 5 discusses fundamental motor skills, including locomotor and manipulative skills. The development of fundamental movement skills is essential to the healthy development of children; and when children are given a strong movement foundation, they will have the skill sets and the confidence to be physically active with their families, with peers, and on their own. Chapter 6 discusses some of the structural factors that constrain the acquisition and development of those movements. This chapter provides readers with the knowledge of how structural constraints may interact with functional factors (the focus of the next two chapters), tasks, and environment. The potential affective, cognitive, behavioral, and psychomotor differences that affect the learning of movement skills over the life span are then examined in chapters 7 and 8.

Part III, "Motor Development: Adulthood and Aging," follows a sequence similar to that of part II, exploring physical activity and individual constraints in young, middle, and older adulthood. The discussion focuses first on physical activity in adulthood and peak athletic performance, then explores the changing movement patterns observed in older adulthood (chapter 9). With advancing age, many physiological changes occur in the body systems. Chapter 10 discusses the physiological changes that affect physical function and movement, including age-related changes in the skeletal, muscular, cardiovascular, nervous, endocrine, and sensory systems. Movement educators who work with older adults must understand the effects of aging on the physiologic systems and the impact these changes have on movement. Chapter 11 examines a variety of psychological, sociological, and cognitive variables in adulthood. It is important to distinguish psychological and sociocultural factors in adulthood from those that are present in childhood and adolescence, as they change quite considerably.

Part IV, "Motor Learning: Designing Appropriate Programs," will get readers ready to prepare, develop, and implement a developmentally appropriate movement program. This section begins by examining the physical, instructional, and affective dimensions that affect motor learning and will prepare readers to structure the environment appropriately with these factors in mind (chapter 12). Chapter 13 discusses prepractice considerations, including how to effectively set goals and introduce motor skills through the use of demonstrations, verbalizations, attention directing, and physical guidance. The effective use of these skills promotes performance and learning. In chapter 14, the discussion continues with the design and structure of effective practice sessions. Topics include practice distribution, part and whole practice, variable practice, and practice specificity. Just as practice should be designed around the individual and the task, feedback should be individualized to the learner and the task. Chapter 15 discusses the types and functions of feedback as well as effective feedback scheduling. The importance of appropriate augmented feedback cannot be emphasized enough. More often than not, movement educators provide augmented feedback too frequently or too soon without realizing the negative effects that are occurring with regard to short- and long-term retention. The book closes with a section titled "Conclusion: Devising a Plan," bringing all of the book's concepts together in the service of designing developmentally appropriate programs. Examples of developmentally appropriate programs are presented, and readers are encouraged to design programs using the case study examples provided.

Pedagogical Features

Many features throughout the book will help the students understand the concepts introduced in each chapter.

- **Opening vignette:** Each chapter opens with a vignette, a practical example, that introduces readers to one or more of the main concepts to be explored in the chapter.
- **Research Notes:** Each chapter includes sections separate from the text that present important research experiments.
- **Try This:** This feature enables students to supplement their knowledge on the course content by way of a variety of short applications that can be performed at home or at their desk. Readers are given a simple task that clarifies a concept and then are asked to answer questions that will help them think critically about the concept.
- **What Do You Think?:** Each chapter includes opportunities for students to stop and think about the material. This feature will provoke critical thinking and stimulate further thought about the material. Students can answer these questions on their own or discuss them in class.
- **Summary:** At the conclusion of each chapter, a brief summary of the key elements and concepts is provided.
- **Supplementary Activities:** Two additional activities are presented at the conclusion of every chapter. These are intended for completion either as outside activities or as classroom laboratory activities.
- **Glossary**: Key terms and concepts are printed in bold type for emphasis and are defined in the glossary at the end of the book.

LETTER TO INSTRUCTORS

Although there are many excellent books that examine motor development from a life-span perspective and books that explore the field of motor learning, there is not, to our knowledge, a book that combines the two. You will find that *Motor Learning and Development* achieves the goal of combining the two fields in an accessible and interesting fashion, allowing students to thoroughly understand how motor development and motor learning inform and intersect.

If a learner has a thorough understanding of the multiple factors that set in motion the development of motor skills from infancy to older adulthood, that learner will be in a much better position to teach movement skills efficiently and individualize the instruction. This individualization is a point of emphasis throughout the text, given the complexity of teaching learners of various backgrounds, interests, abilities, and ages. Furthermore, these learners' abilities and interests are hardly static; rather, they are very dynamic. Thus, to work with learners at all life stages, we must be continually aware of the ongoing interactions between ever-changing abilities, an ever-changing environment, and the task at hand. The intersection of these three factors determines how we proceed.

And so, this textbook—based on the latest research in the fields of motor development and motor learning—provides both the theoretical foundation and applied information for developing movement programs for *all* types of learners—from those with identifiable disabilities to those at the ultimate end of the ability spectrum.

Motor Learning and Development is divided into four parts. Part I, Motor Behavior: Theory and Foundational Concepts, lays the groundwork by outlining the fundamental concepts of motor development, motor learning, and motor control. Part II, Motor Development: Childhood and Adolescence, provides a solid background regarding not only *what* skills are developed but also *how* they are developed. This part of the text delineates the structural, functional, and environmental constraints that may, in combination, hinder or promote optimal development. Part III, Motor Development: Adulthood and Aging, follows a sequence that is similar to part II in that it explores physical activity patterns and individual constraints in young, middle, and older adulthood. The fourth and final part, Motor Learning: Designing Appropriate Programs, gives detailed information that prepares students to organize, develop, implement, and evaluate developmentally appropriate movement programs for a variety of learners. Although the material that precedes part IV has a direct bearing on the development of appropriate programs, the students need not have read every chapter of the text to benefit from part IV.

Although this book is written from a life-span perspective and details how skill is acquired over the course of one's life, a particular course may emphasize a certain time frame. If, as an example, motor development and motor learning in school-age children and adolescents were the foci of the course, parts I, II, and IV would provide the learners with excellent data-based information for this time frame. The same applies to a course examining adult development and aging. In this case, the emphasis would be on parts I, III, and IV. As can be seen from the attached syllabus, the material in *Motor Learning and Development* can be taught over the course of a 15-week semester.

Motor Learning and Development Syllabus

Week	Day	Topic	Assignments and readings
14	1	Practice	Chapter 14; Try This 2 and SA 2
	2	Detecting and correcting errors	Chapter 15; Try This 1 and SA 1
15	1	Detecting and correcting errors	Chapter 15; SA 2
	2	Conclusions	Conclusions section; case studies
16	1	Final exam	

SA = supplemental activity

Each chapter in *Motor Learning and Development* has several features that engage the students in their reading and help them to understand the concepts presented:

- **Chapter Objectives:** Each chapter begins with approximately six learning objectives that indicate what are considered to be the most important concepts. These objectives guide the students' reading and allow you to spend less class time lecturing and more time on interactive, student-focused learning activities and skill development. If, conversely, you think that the best approach to learning the material is to use the lecture as your primary teaching methodology, the chapter objectives provide a road map for both you and the students.

- **Research Notes:** Research experiments, pertinent to a given chapter, are presented throughout the text. Beyond their importance to the fields of motor learning and motor development, these research notes allow you to engage the students in debate and discussion about topics such as research design, appropriateness of the question (i.e., *why* is this a good question to ask—or is it?), what the next question might be, and how the students might design said question. Students can work on these questions and others during or outside of class, either individually or in a small-group setting. As noted, much of the research presented can lead to robust debate.

- **What Do You Think?:** This feature gives students the opportunity to think about the course content both critically and creatively. This feature might require, for example, thinking back to how the students acquired a challenging skill, how to teach a diverse group of learners, or how plasticity is demonstrated when a stroke patient regains the ability to hit a slice backhand. The key point is to stimulate critical thinking. Again, students can use this feature individually, in pairs, as a group, or as a class discussion either inside or outside of the classroom.

- **Try This:** This feature engages students in a practical application that clarifies a given concept. Students actively engage in an activity; that is, they *do* something in a physical fashion in order to attain a more thorough understanding of the concept at hand. This feature stimulates critical thinking and can be incorporated into the course either in or outside of the classroom.

- **Supplemental Activities:** At the end of each chapter, two additional activities are provided that can be completed as either classroom laboratory activities or as activities to be completed away from the school setting.

These activities intersect with the material presented in the chapter and give students a chance to deepen their understanding of the topics presented.

• **Key Terms:** As the phrase suggests, the key terms are the most important concepts in the chapter and appear in bold text in the chapter. They are defined at the end of the book.

Two ancillaries facilitate the teaching of this material:

• **Test Bank:** This ancillary includes more than 370 multiple-choice, true-or-false, and short-answer questions and their answers. These test questions can be used for building quizzes or as a supplement to your own exam questions.

• **Image Bank:** This ancillary includes most of the figures, tables, and photos from the book. Images are grouped by chapter in .jpg format. You may reuse the images in your own PowerPoint templates to create custom presentations. To help with the creation of these presentations, we have provided a blank PowerPoint template.

Both of these ancillaries are available at www.HumanKinetics.com/Motor-LearningAndDevelopment.

Hopefully, we have laid some groundwork for using *Motor Learning and Development* in your course, allowing you to teach and, more important, engage students in these essential subjects. It is important that you become familiar with the text to assist you in managing your time to cover the appropriate material for your course. Clearly, you will need to determine the amount of time required for covering a given chapter and concept. Keeping track of whether something took more time or less time than you anticipated allows you to make informed changes as you teach the class in the future.

How much time you take to cover material from the text is, of course, an individual decision and has as much to do with your pedagogical philosophy as students' characteristics. As noted, the material in *Motor Learning and Development* engages and stimulates the learners in an accessible way.

We wish you the best as you use the first textbook that combines the fields of motor learning and motor development.

Motor Behavior
Theory and Foundational Concepts

In the first part of this section, we define the three fields of *[handwritten: 3 field]* motor behavior: motor development, motor learning, and motor control. *[handwritten markings: ①, ②, ③]* The key terminology underlying each field is explained and the core areas of research in each field are introduced. We then turn to the theoretical constructs of motor behavior, as well as examine the evolution of the field of motor development from its inception in the late 18th century to the present day.

Next, we detail motor skill classification and games classification. The *[handwritten: 2 ... 3]* motor skill classifications discussed include sport skills, developmental classifications, single-dimensional classifications, and multidimensional classifications. The classification of motor skills is important for any movement educator with an interest in rehabilitation, education, or athletics, because the appropriate practice and feedback schedules are often dependent on the type of the motor skills. Following this discussion, we explain the distinction between motor skills and abilities.

Once we have examined motor skill and games classifications, we turn to an examination of developmental and motor learning stages. First, we use Clark's mountain of development to explain how skills evolve from prenatal development through the acquisition of skill proficiency. This is followed by discussion of the stages of learning, including Fitts and Posner's, Bernstein's, and Gentile's learning stages, providing a framework for categorizing the skill level of the learner from novice to expert. These models enable practitioners to assess the level of the learner and more appropriately prepare practice sessions. *[handwritten: Framework for categorizing skill levels of learners]*

Part I concludes with methodological considerations, including how to measure and assess motor learning. Indicators of motor learning beyond basic performance measures are described; the best indicator of motor learning is performance following a retention interval. Transfer of learning is also examined, as this is a critical component of learning a motor skill, including how practitioners can promote positive transfer in any setting.

[handwritten: Save for practic conditions]

Perspectives in Motor Behavior

CHAPTER OBJECTIVES

After reading this chapter, you should be able to

> define the fields of motor learning, motor control, and motor development;

> understand the evolution of motor development;

> compare and contrast the theoretical constraints in motor behavior; and

> explain why the fields of motor behavior are important for teaching and assessing motor skills in sport, physical activity, and health professions.

Choke Up On the Bat!

Makayla, an active 6-year-old child, enthusiastically attended her first baseball practice. She had not been involved in any team-affiliated activity before and was anxious to begin. The first day of practice began with skill assessment on batting, catching, and throwing. Makayla regularly played ball with her dad and older brother after school and was confident with her ability to perform these skills. After performing well on both the catching and throwing tasks, Makayla was poised going into the final task of batting. As Makayla was about to bat, the coach instructed her to choke up on the bat. Not knowing what "choking up on the bat" meant, Makayla proceeded to lift her arms higher, holding the bottom of the bat higher than the top. With this awkward position, it is not surprising that Makayla performed very poorly in the batting exercise, even though she was well practiced with batting.

As a practitioner, it is important to understand not only motor learning and motor development, but also how each influences the other. These two fields are strongly related but often separated in textbooks. This chapter provides a background for each of these fields, discussing the main motor learning and development concepts, tenets, and theoretical frameworks. Subsequent chapters use a life span perspective to explain how to prepare, implement, and assess motor skill programs for any group of individuals regardless of age, developmental level, or motor skill. In the batting example, the coach did not realize that he was not using developmentally appropriate terminology when providing feedback to Makayla, causing confusion rather than providing effective instruction.

Defining Terms in Motor Behavior

Before you can begin designing, implementing, or assessing a motor skill program, you must have a full understanding of the fields of motor behavior. **Motor behavior** is an umbrella term for the fields of motor development, motor learning, and motor control. Researchers in the field of **motor development** examine the products and underlying processes of motor behavior changes across the life span. **Motor learning** is the study of the processes involved in the acquisition of a motor skill and the factors that enhance or inhibit an individual's capability to perform a motor skill. **Motor control** researchers investigate the neural, physical, and behavioral aspects of human movement. It is important to understand all three fields—motor learning, motor development, and motor control—in order to optimize skill acquisition. (Refer to table 1.1 for a summary of each field.)

TABLE 1.1   Summary of the Fields of Motor Behavior

Field	Key points
Motor development	• Focus on performance product (outcome) • Focus on process (underlying mechanisms) • Development is successive (following in uninterrupted order) • Development is systematic (step-by-step procedures) • Development is related to, but not dependent, on age
Motor learning	• Process of acquiring a capability for producing skilled actions • Occurs as a direct result of practice and is not due to maturation or physiological changes • Cannot be observed directly • Relatively permanent changes in the capability for skilled behavior

Motor control	• Underlying processes of movement
	• Key issues include the following:
	  - Degrees of freedom problem—investigates how the system is able to constrain the number of degrees of freedom to produce a coordinated movement pattern
	  - Serial order problem—examines the sequencing and timing of movement behaviors
	  - Perceptual–motor integration problem—addresses how perception and action are incorporated

A practitioner with a strong background in each of these areas will have a solid foundation in how humans develop across the life span; be able to explain why particular behaviors have manifested themselves; and be able to design efficient programs to assess, diagnose, or teach motor skills for the purposes of instruction or rehabilitation. In this book, the term practitioner refers to any type of movement educator, including physical education teachers, clinicians, instructors, and coaches. Let's take a closer look at the fields of motor behavior.

Motor Development

Regarding motor development, two key words must be defined: **product**, the outcome of performance, and **process**, the underlying mechanisms of change. The amount of weight lifted or the distance a javelin was thrown is an example of a movement product, while the action that was performed to produce the throw is a movement process. Motor development, however, is not simply change. Motor development must be organized and systematic, such as an infant progressing through the motor milestones of raising the head, to rolling over, to crawling, and then to walking. The changes also need to be successive. In other words, the changes must occur in uninterrupted order. Motor development, therefore, is systematic and is marked by successive changes over time. Not all types of change are motor development. If a physical education teacher instructs a student to snap his wrist in a squash swing as opposed to using a solid arm swing in the tennis stroke, the resultant change would be considered motor learning. A therapist teaching alternative methods to lift objects overhead following a shoulder injury would also be dealing with motor learning rather than motor development.

Development can occur over various time scales, from changes that take place over a very long time period (phylogeny) to those that take place over the briefest of time periods in response to immediate task demands. **Phylogeny** is the evolutionary development of a species, which may take many hundreds, even thousands, of years. **Ontogeny** is development occurring over the life span of one individual. The focus throughout this book is on ontogenetic development. A third level is local biology, including physiological changes such as respiration. Task demands are imposed on an immediate time scale, which can be as short as minutes or even seconds.

Although laymen often use the terms growth and development interchangeably, each refers to something fundamentally different. **Physical growth** refers to an increase in body size or in individual parts that occurs through maturation. However, the term growth is more inclusive of overall body changes, as defined by development. The process of development is not limited to the changes occurring during infancy and childhood. Development occurs throughout the life span. All people are continually undergoing cognitive, physical, and psychosocial changes regardless of their age. This perspective, the life span perspective, is discussed in further detail later in this chapter.

The term **maturation** refers to the fixed transitions or order of progressions that enable a person to progress to higher levels of function. Maturation includes internal processes that are unaffected by external factors such as the environ- *Huh?* ment. Of course, aspects of the environment, such as learning experiences, parental influence, and physical surroundings, certainly can alter the timing

See examples next page

of developmental transitions. A child who has been given a ball during infancy is much more likely to be able to catch and throw at an earlier age than a child who was only given a doll. Not receiving a ball does not prevent the child from learning how to catch and throw but will delay the onset of these skills.

Aging refers to a process or group of processes occurring in living organisms that with the passage of time lead to a loss of adaptability, functional impairment, and eventually death (Spirduso, Francis, & MacRae, 2005). Aging is the progression of life from birth whereby an individual matures and continues through physical decline, ending with death. People are often classified by chronological age (table 1.2) to avoid confusion in defining age groups. For instance, one professional may define a 4-year-old as a child while another professional refers to a 4-year-old as a preschooler. The importance of age classifications becomes even more prominent in the upper continuums of life, where age classification discrepancies can be as much as 10 or 20 years (i.e., when does old adulthood begin?—at 55, 65, or 75 years of age?).

Motor Learning

Motor learning is the study of the processes involved in the acquisition of a motor skill and the variables that enhance or inhibit the capability to perform a motor skill. One common mistake practitioners make is not understanding the clear distinctions between performance and learning. Learning is defined as a relatively permanent change in the capability to execute a motor skill as a result of practice or experience. **Performance**, the act of executing a motor skill, is a temporary or nonpermanent change. One way to conceptualize this difference is to make an analogy of learning to the change of state in an egg (Schmidt & Lee, 2005). When an egg is boiled, there is a permanent change in the state of that egg. The egg has irreversibly transformed into a solid. To conceptualize performance we could make an analogy to water. When temperatures drop below 32 degrees Fahrenheit, water solidifies to ice. This is not a permanent

TABLE 1.2 Age Classifications

Description	Age or transition marker
Newborn	Birth to 6 weeks
Infant	Six weeks to age at walking
Toddler	Age at walking to 2 years
Preschooler	Age 3 to age at start of school
Young child	Age at start of school to 7 years
Child	Eight to 10 years
Preadolescent	Eleven years to onset of puberty
Adolescent	Onset of puberty to 20 years
Young adult	Age 21 to 40 years
Middle-aged adult	Age 41 to 60 years
Young-old adult	Age 61 to 74 years
Old adult	Age 75 to 99 years
Centenarian	Age 100+ years

change, as water will convert back into its original form if temperatures increase again to above 32 degrees Fahrenheit. The permanent change occurring as a result of boiling an egg is analogous to the permanent change in the capability to perform a particular motor skill, motor learning. The change in water resulting from temperature increases or decreases, on the other hand, is analogous to performance changes because of its lack of permanency.

Now let's return to the definition of motor learning. Recall that motor learning is the process of acquiring the capability for producing skilled actions. The first characteristic of motor learning is that a process is required to induce a change in an individual's capability to perform skillfully. A **process** is a set of events or occurrences resulting in a change in the state or end product. Dropping temperatures would be the process causing water to change form. Drills in sport are processes with the goal of leading to a change in the capability to perform skillfully. For instance, soccer juggling is a common method (*process*) to improve ball control in soccer players. The goal of conducting a process, be it altering the temperature to change the state of water or practicing drills, is to increase the strength of this state. A **capability** implies that skilled behavior may occur if the conditions are favorable. There is certainly no question that Jack Nicklaus acquired the capability to play the game of golf. However, even Nicklaus had his off days, although, his "off"-day skills in golf most likely still far exceed many, if not all, of our golf skills. Certain variables can prevent optimal performance even when the capability is attained, such as external conditions (rain, snow, sleet, cold, wind, etc.), motivation, wellness, or fatigue.

The second distinct characteristic of motor learning is that it must occur as a direct result of practice. Motor learning is not due to maturation or physiological training. A change that occurs owing to maturation is motor development change. For instance, learning to walk is motor development, not motor learning, because it is a motor skill that all humans acquire; in contrast, learning to shoot a basketball requires practice and is due to motor learning. Third, motor learning cannot be observed directly. It can only be assumed based on long-term performance changes. Motor learning, like love or success, is a construct. It cannot be seen, but is assumed to have occurred when relatively permanent changes in the capability of skilled behavior are observed through performance changes. Motor learning is assumed to produce positive, irreversible effects in the capability for skilled behavior, meaning that these changes are not temporary, as reflected in the saying "It's like learning how to ride a bicycle."

Motor Control

Motor control researchers study the neural, physical, and behavioral aspects of human movement. One area of much study for motor control researchers is the role of the neurological system in the function of the body. Some researchers examine reaction time as an indicator of processing speed and nerve conduction velocities under varying conditions. Researchers in the field of motor control also investigate how the system moves in a controlled and coordinated fashion. Even fundamental skills and movements are quite complex. The number of movement possibilities is nearly infinite because of the degrees of freedom available to the individual. The field of motor control deals with three core issues: the degrees of freedom problem, the serial order problem, and the perceptual–motor integration problem. This section provides a brief overview of each of these motor control problems.

Compare to Kinesiology
Expand this

A Joint level
Axes of rotation

B 100's of muscles

C Palsy Gait Parkinson's

Define "Constraining"

Ex:

Degrees of Freedom Problem

Degrees of freedom are the number of independent elements that must be constrained in order to produce coordinated motion (Bernstein, 1967). At the joint level, there are dozens of possibilities just to reach for a glass. Minimally, the wrist, elbow, and shoulder are involved in the reach, each with multiple axes of rotation. If the individual was standing during the reach, the hips, knees, and ankles would also be involved in the coordination of the movement. At the muscular level, the number of movement possibilities, or degrees of freedom, would be increased to hundreds. If extended to the neuronal level, there could be millions, if not billions, of movement possibilities.

Coordination involves constraining the number of degrees of freedom in order to decrease the complexity of the movement task so as to produce a movement pattern and achieve a task goal (Sparrow, 1992). Coordination involves the bringing together of parts into proper relation (Turvey, 1990). Increased coordination leads to a more positive task outcome. But not only is it important to be able to coordinate the body parts; tasks must also be completed with **control**. The mover must be able to manipulate the movements in such a way as to meet the demands of the task. For instance, a dancer can coordinate her body parts such that she is executing all of the correct steps; however, what distinguishes her as a dancer is her ability to accentuate certain movements while also moving with style and grace, making each movement appear seamless and effortless. A softball pitcher must also constrain his degrees of freedom, as in deciding when to initiate the pitch and the speed of the pitch. The timing of the pitch, the initiation and release, and the speed of the pitch are all variables of control.

Serial Order Problem

The **serial order problem** refers to the sequencing and order of movement behaviors. The timing and order of an activity are critical for nearly every movement we produce. Think about the importance of the sequence of sounds in speech or the movements in walking, running, or throwing. In speech, if the order is changed, then the sounds and meaning of the words and sentences have changed. For example, a speech error would occur if you misspoke by saying "dirthbay" instead of "birthday." Making errors in speech sounds by exchanging letters in adjacent words has been termed **spoonerisms** after an Oxford professor, Professor William Spooner, who was known to often make speech errors (Rosenbaum, 2010). He has been quoted as having made the slip "You hissed all my mystery lectures" instead of "You missed all my history lectures." In general, these sequencing errors occur in a specific way. Consonants switch with other consonants, vowels with other vowels, and even nouns with nouns and verbs with verbs.

These errors are not limited to speech. People make performance related-action errors all the time too. For example, have you ever put something away in an obviously wrong place, such as silverware in the trash instead of the dishwasher, or poured orange juice instead of milk into your cereal? These errors occur when we are not paying attention to what we are doing. With these errors, we clearly know what we are intending to do. The problem arises because we are mindlessly thinking about the action rather than the specifics of the task. We can visually identify milk and orange juice, but we are more focused on the goal of pouring the liquid into a bowl of cereal and not on what we are actually pouring. This causes us to make an **action slip**.

Coffee on cereal add moring person slips (keys)

Everyone makes some of these errors from time to time. So, why are they particularly interesting? These examples indicate that people prepare an action plan in advance, rather than planning and then executing one thought at a time (Lashley, 1951); this allows us to be much more efficient with our actions.

The serial order problem has also been found in the production of correct, or accurate, movements through coarticulation. **Coarticulation** is the simultaneous motions that occur in sequential tasks (Rosenbaum, 2010). This means that we are preparing for subsequent movements rather than completing one movement before preparing for the next. Coarticulation suggests that we preplan activities, allowing us to move more efficiently. Preparing simultaneous movements enables faster typing or speaking or faster transportation of objects. A typist's fingers prepare for future key presses by moving to the position of the next key press even while another finger is pressing a different key (Rumelhart & Norman, 1982). Coarticulation also occurs in grasping. The position we use to grasp an object depends on where we are going to move the object. In a study by Cohen and Rosenbaum (2004), participants were asked to grasp a plunger and place it to either a high or a low final position. The position of the grasp changed based on the final position, high or low. Participants grasped the plunger high when they were going to place the plunger in a low position, and conversely, grasped low when placing it in a high position. Refer to the "Try This" activity for a speech example of coarticulation.

[Handwritten margin notes:]
We prepare the sequence before completing the movement
Type
Grasp
Do the plunger lab.
Baseball bat storage — rack or shelf
Dumbbells?

Try This

Look in the mirror and say the word "twilight." Did you notice that your lips rounded prior to producing the "t" sound? Look at your lips as you say the words "gold" and "cupid." Did you notice the same thing? These examples indicate that there is an action plan for the entire word prior to the utterance of the first sound. If each sound were planned separately, then your mouth would not have changed shape until after the "t," "g," or "c" sounds.

1. What are some other words for which you can notice a preparatory action plan?
2. Provide examples of performances other than typing and grasping in which movements are prepared in advance.

Perceptual–Motor Integration Problem

The third major issue in motor control is the perceptual–motor integration problem. As the name implies, this problem addresses how perception and motor control are integrated, for example how movement is affected by perception and, conversely, how perception is affected by movement. This is not a *which came first*, the chicken or the egg, kind of problem. Instead, perception and movement work together, continuously influencing one another. You may move closer to an object to see it better or closer to a sound to hear it better. In this manner, movement improves perception.

Movement can also inform perception. Our perception is affected by our actual or intended actions. In an experiment by Proffitt, Bhalla, Gossweiler, and Midgett (1995), two groups of participants (people in one group wearing a heavy backpack) were asked to estimate the steepness of a hill. The group wearing the backpacks estimated the hill to be steeper when indicating the level of

[Handwritten margin notes:]
Hunting (moving)
Punting (stationary)
Treadmill Example
Heavy backpack vs no " " applied to treadmill grade

Represent the ∡ by positioning the hand @ the slope's ∡

steepness by the angle of their hands. When the groups were asked to estimate the steepness verbally, there were no differences between them. These results indicate that the participants estimated the steepness based on the amount of effort that would be required to climb it. Their perception was affected by the movement characteristics necessary to perform the task. This topic is discussed further in the next section on theoretical constructs.

Neurophysiological research has provided further insights into the perceptual–motor integration problem. It was discovered that the same motor neurons fired when macaque monkeys watched an activity being performed as when they were actually producing the movement themselves. This observation occurred by chance when one of the researchers picked up some food and ate it. The researcher noticed that the same neurons were firing that would be firing if the monkey was picking up food and eating it himself. These neurons are referred to as mirror neurons because they fire when individuals witness an action that they could perform themselves. Research on mirror neurons was conducted with ballet and capoeira dancers (Calvo-Merino, Glaser, Grezes, Passingham, & Haggard, 2005). The brain activity of the dancers was higher when they watched others performing the dances that they were skilled in (e.g., ballet dancers had more brain activity when watching ballet, and capoeira dancers had more brain activity when watching capoeira). The results further indicate that learning new motor skills can change the amount of firing during observations of those motor skills.

The Evolution of Motor Development

The field of motor development combines biology, which is the study of growth and maturation of living organisms, and psychology, the study of human behavior (Clark & Whitall, 1989). However, because the study of motor development must involve living humans, the research tends to focus more on the behavioral aspects and so is more aligned with psychology than with biology. The history of the field of motor development has commonly been divided into four periods: the precursor period, the maturational period, the normative period, and the process-oriented period (Clark & Whitall, 1989) (table 1.3).

TABLE 1.3 Periods in the Evolution of the Field of Motor Development

Period	Characteristics
Precursor (1787-1928)	Focus on product development Nature versus nurture argument
Maturational (1928-1946)	Focus on maturation
Normative (1946-1970)	Focus on movement skills in school-age children
Process-oriented (1970-present)	Hypothesis-driven research Emergence of information processing, ecological psychology, and dynamic systems theory

Precursor Period (1787-1928)

The field of motor development has its roots in the precursor period, beginning in the late 18th century. During this time, the main method for studying motor development was through descriptive observations, with the focus on the product or outcome of development. It was also during the precursor period that Charles Darwin came up with one of the main arguments for understanding the processes of motor development, the nature versus nurture argument. The perspective that development occurs as a function of nature assumes that maturation occurs as a result of genetic or internal factors (Gesell, 1928, 1954). This view, known as the **maturational perspective**, became quite popular in the 1930s during the maturational period. On the flip side, the **environmentalism perspective** assumes the converse: It is not heredity that molds the maturational process; rather, humans are nurtured by their environment. This argument would ensue for many decades and continues to some degree even today. Charles Darwin did not believe that nature or nurture favors one developmental process over another. Instead, the environment (nurture) and genetic factors (nature) interact. Maturationists assume that a child born with the underlying abilities to excel at certain sports will eventually exhibit excellence in those sports. However, environmentalists propose that even basic skills must be developed. Either individuals who are not given the appropriate equipment or environment to learn such skills will be delayed in developing them, or the skills may never materialize.

Charles Darwin's work was seminal in the study of motor development. It provided insights into the effect of the environment on the animal. Darwin theorized about how animals must adapt to changing environments and discussed developmental sequences found across species (Darwin, 1859, 1871, 1872). He also wrote about the importance of studying both the product of the behavior and the process.

Maturational Period (1928-1946)

A boom in motor development studies occurred in the 1930s following the emergence of the field of developmental psychology. As the name of this period implies, the main focus was on maturation. Arnold Gesell led the maturationist movement, asserting that infant maturity is genetically predetermined, meaning the infant moves from one developmental cycle to the next under the control of the central nervous system. The central nervous system is composed of the brain and the spinal cord. Each cycle occurs in a very orderly and predetermined fashion; for example, infants roll over at around 5 months, sit up at 6 months, and stand at 8 months. Maturationists assume that these transitions are set and controlled by nature. Children progress to the next step when they are "ready." External influences are not included in these transitions; an internal clock, so to speak, simply determines precisely when the infant will progress. More recent research has shown that the environment can certainly influence the onset of these transitions. For instance, a child who never lies on his belly will crawl much later than a child who receives regular "belly time." The child's environment has delayed this transition because the infant was not given the opportunity to strengthen the arm, leg, and core muscles necessary for crawling. Children who are blind have been found to be significantly delayed in reaching many of these milestones (Fazzi et al., 2002; Ribadi, Rider, & Toole, 1987), taking on average an additional five months to crawl and an additional eight months to walk in comparison with their sighted peers. It is doubtful that the delay is genetically predetermined. Rather, it is more likely that the delay results from the lack of visual stimuli that would motivate the infants to reach objects of interest.

Esther Thelen's research on the infant stepping reflex and walking was seminal in this area. According to the maturation perspective, infants do not walk following the disappearance of the stepping reflex until neuronal paths mature. The persistence of the stepping reflex had been viewed as an indication of a developmental delay. Thelen examined the effects of body build and arousal on infant stepping and found that the disappearance of the stepping reflex was due to increased body mass in proportion to strength (Thelen, Fisher, Ridley-Johnson, & Griffin, 1982). Infants decrease their number of steps simply because they do not have the muscle strength to lift their heavy legs.

Gesell also discussed fetal growth patterns. Growth occurs in a **cephalocaudal** direction, meaning that the head develops first and distal structures grow more slowly. Essentially, growth occurs from the head to the foot. An infant can control movements of the head much earlier than movements of the trunk or limbs. For instance, the eyes and mouth develop more quickly than the hands and feet. Controlled eye movements can be seen postnatally at very early ages. On a personal note, when my first child was born, I was shocked to discover that only minutes after birth he was able to track our eye movements. While in my husband's arms, our newborn would lie quietly if eye contact was maintained but would scream immediately when eye contact was removed even for just a moment. It seemed amazing that he was not only wide-eyed and alert but also very aware of his surroundings. It was also quite clear that although he was able to control his eye movements, it would be quite some time before he could control his head, neck, trunk, and limb movements.

While growth is occurring in a cephalocaudal direction, it is concurrently developing in a **proximodistal** direction, such that as the body is growing from head to foot, the trunk is advancing at a faster rate than the limbs. This can be examined in the prehension or grasping stages in infants. Initially, infants attempt to grasp an object with the whole palm. As they mature, they begin to use three fingers and then finally add their thumb and forefinger.

A secondary focus during the maturational period was on motor learning (McGraw, 1935). McGraw explained that "maturation and learning are not different processes, merely different facets of the fundamental process of growth" (McGraw 1945/1969, pp. 130-131). Comparing the development of twins in a study in which one twin was taught motor skills and the other merely matured, McGraw found not only that the environment has a strong influence on motor development, but also that there appear to be critical periods in which improvement can be optimized through advanced opportunities and instruction (McGraw, 1935, 1940).

Normative Period (1946-1970)

Following World War II, the study of motor development was largely influenced by several physical educators, with a focus on movement skills in school-age children. The focus was less on cognitive development and more on the physical aspects of development, which caused a shift from process- to product-oriented research. Physical educators and researchers were also interested in anthropometric measures (growth measures) through childhood and the role of maturation and strength changes in children (Clark & Whitall, 1989, p. 189). Part of this shift was due to physical educators' interests at the time. They wanted to improve motor skill instruction through understanding changes in motor performance (Halverson, 1970). Motor learning researchers focused on the processes underlying performance changes when new simple motor skills are learned and on the evaluation of such performances. Unfortunately, it was not until the 1980s that motor developmentalists and motor learning and control researchers began appreciating the value of each others' work (Clark & Whitall, 1989).

Process-Oriented Period (1970-Present)

A reemergence of motor development research occurred in the early 1970s as psychologists developed renewed interest in the field and much study focused on hypothesis-driven research. During this period, three theoretical constructs emerged, each of which is still prominent today: the information processing approach, ecological psychology, and dynamic systems theory. It is important to have a basic understanding of the theories that drive research in motor development and motor learning in order to understand and interpret experimental findings in these fields.

Theoretical Constructs in Motor Behavior

The three theoretical constructs that were developed during the early part of the process-oriented period—information processing theory, ecological psychology, and dynamic systems theory—are all still used today. These theories differ in the manner in which they define development and learning as well as in how behavior is examined. According to the **information processing approach**, the brain receives, processes, and interprets information in order to send signals to produce skilled coordinated movements, similarly to how a computer functions. Proponents of the **ecological psychology perspective**, however, state that movement is much more complex than a simple input–output relay of information from the brain to the other systems. Instead, actions are determined by many internal (e.g., goals and capabilities of the individual) and external factors (e.g., what is available in the environment). The third theoretical perspective, **dynamic systems theory**, has been viewed as a perspective that has branched off from ecological psychology. In this perspective, movement does not occur due to a specific set of instructions but rather as an interaction between the task, the environment, and the individual. Movement is "softly" assembled, meaning that movement emerges as a result of these three constraints.

Information Processing Approach

The basis of the information processing approach is the idea that the brain acts like a computer, working as a receiver and processor of information (Fitts & Posner, 1967; Keele, 1973; Marteniuk, 1976; Schmidt, 1975a). A key area of this research addressed the processes involved in movement behavior. Although

[Handwritten margin notes: Reaction Time lab set up (light + Timer); Stop cell phones watches!! Electronic Motion Sensors; Cone r (small) stacking cup (Importance High); cone + tennis ball; phone; cup 3/30 10]

the process of development was a key area of interest in earlier research, there was a shift from investigating ontogenetic (life span) changes to processes of change within a life span such as memory, feedback, attention, and perception (Clark & Whitall, 1989).

The **generalized motor program (GMP)**, defined as a representation of a pattern of movements that are modifiable to produce a movement outcome, provided an explanation for the production of skilled movement for the information processing approach. A GMP can be thought of as a set of instructions that are stored in the brain. When an individual performs a particular skill, she retrieves this set of instructions, sending the message to the necessary muscles. The time necessary to organize a motor program is dependent on the complexity of the task, with more complex tasks requiring more time to organize than less complex tasks. Henry and Rogers (1960) illustrated this by measuring reaction time for three tasks varying in complexity. Reaction time, the time from the onset of a stimulus to the initiation of the response, increased with increasing complexity. When participants were to simply lift their finger from a switch, reaction time was only 165 milliseconds; but it went up to 199 milliseconds when the task increased in complexity to lifting the finger from the switch and then grasping a hanging tennis ball, and up to 212 milliseconds for lifting the finger, striking the ball, pushing a button, and grasping another ball. These results indicate that movements are in fact planned prior to the initiation of a response, since more time is required to prepare a motor program for more complex tasks.

In order to be classified into a particular GMP, an action had to include some **invariant features**, variables that could not be modified between one attempt and another attempt. Invariant features are unique to their GMP much as the features of an individual's signature are unique. If you were asked to write your name under varying conditions (e.g., with your dominant hand, with your nondominant hand, in large print or small print, or even with your feet), the general stroke and structure of your signature would be the same. Of course the writing may be a bit sloppier with your feet, but it will still have the same general features as your signature with your dominant limb. The main difference between the signatures is the effect of experience and reduced coordination and control in the nondominant limb, not the structure of the letters. A classic example that illustrates the effect of invariant features is shown in figure 1.1.

Research Notes: Monkey Business

Polit and Bizzi (1978) investigated the notion of the GMP by deafferenting monkeys. Deafferentation is a technique whereby the sensory receptors are severed so that no proprioceptive feedback can be received. In other words, there is no longer any feeling in the deafferented limb. Polit and Bizzi trained several monkeys to perform pointing tasks. The monkeys were later deafferented, and their vision was blocked so that they could not see or feel where their deafferented limb was located. Following deafferentation, the monkeys were still able to accurately point to the target, without sensory feedback. These findings provide support for the notion of the motor program and the information processing approach.

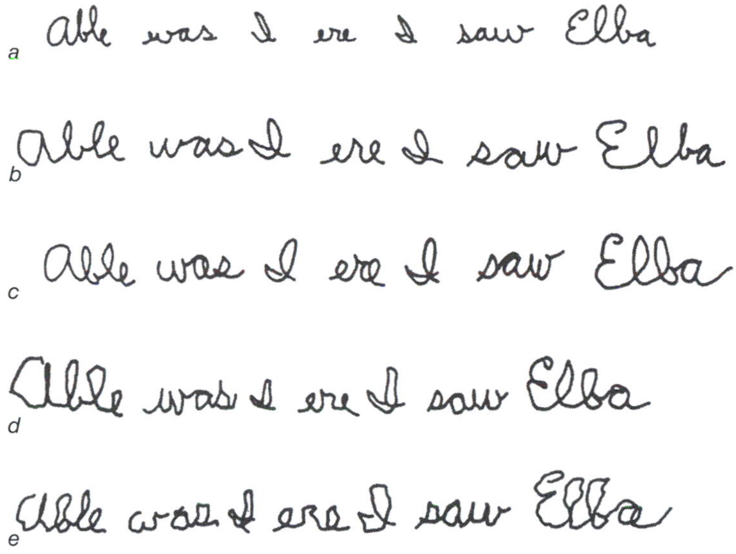

a Able was I ere I saw Elba

b Able was I ere I saw Elba

c Able was I ere I saw Elba

d Able was I ere I saw Elba

e Able was I ere I saw Elba

FIGURE 1.1 Invariant features affected this person's ability to write *(a)* with the right (dominant hand), *(b)* with the wrist immobilized, *(c)* with the left hand, *(d)* with the pen gripped in the teeth, and *(e)* with the pen taped to the foot.

Reprinted, by permission, from M.H. Raibert, 1977, "Motor control and learning by the state space model," *Technical Report AI-TR-439* (Cambridge, MA: MIT Artificial Intelligence Laboratory), 50.

[handwritten margin note: Classroom activity.]

[handwritten margin note: Adequate Examples of Invariant features + parameters]

The three invariant features are the sequence of actions, relative timing, and relative force. In punting a football, the sequence of actions includes the approach, the catch, the drop, and the kick. If the sequence of actions is altered in any manner, such as kick, catch, approach, drop, then the movement pattern is no longer a football punt. If proportionally more time is spent in any one of these actions, the overall movement pattern will also be compromised. For instance, during walking, 60% of the time is spent during stance phase, and 40% is spent during swing phase. The stance phase can even be broken down further into two double-support phases (10% of the gait cycle each) and single-limb support between double-leg support (40% of the gait cycle). An individual can walk at many different speeds; however, this relative timing will always remain the same unless the person transitions to running. The same is found for relative force. In order to kick a ball harder, an athlete must proportionately increase the amount of force produced when planting the nondominant foot, in the backswing of the foot, and during the forward swing and contact with the ball. *[handwritten note: Why is this kid not selected as the team punter]*

The features that can be modified during the execution of a movement pattern are called **parameters**. This allows adaptability of a response, such as walking at different speeds, shooting basketballs from different positions on the basketball court, and kicking with more or less force. The three parameters are muscle selection, overall duration, and overall force. In the signature example, similar features were found for writing with the dominant and with the nondominant limb. Writing with a different limb is a parameter change, not an invariant feature change, because of the use of different muscle groups. Quarterbacks can throw a short pass to a running back or throw much farther for a "Hail Mary" pass to a wide receiver 50 yards away. The GMP used will be the same whether you are unscrewing a very tight lid or a loose one, or whether you are kicking a penalty kick from the right or the left side of the goal.

As a reminder, GMPs are defined by their invariant features (nonflexible features) and parameters (flexible features). It is important to recognize the differences between invariant features and parameters; here is a quick recap of each:

Invariant Features

- Sequence of actions
- Relative timing
- Relative force

Parameters

- Muscle selection
- Overall duration
- Overall force

? What Do You Think?

Place kick football, playground soccerball

1. Provide three examples of invariant features for a movement skill of your choice. Discuss why these features would place this movement into a different GMP.
2. Now provide three examples of how you could vary this skill without compromising the movement pattern (parameters).
3. If a variation in a motor skill caused a change in the invariant features, should the learner practice under these conditions? Why or why not?

homework

▶ Try This

In early theories of motor programs, separate motor programs were required every time a task was changed. A new program was required to catch a tennis ball versus a softball, or to throw a ball 10 feet rather than 15 feet. If a new program was required for every variation of a movement, an immense amount of space in memory would be needed for all the information. A theory of generalized motor programs was developed to account for these variations. As long as a new coordination pattern was not required to perform a motor skill, it could be controlled by the same generalized motor program. To test this, try the following variations of tossing a ball in the air and catching it. If you have a partner, you could instead toss the ball back and forth.

- Toss a ball in the air and catch it.
- Toss the ball much higher and catch it.
- Toss the ball much lower and catch it.
- Toss the ball with your nondominant limb and catch it with your nondominant limb.
- Crinkle a piece of paper into a ball. Toss it up into the air and catch it.

Answer the following questions based on your observations:

1. Would the action of tossing the ball and the paper ball be controlled by the same generalized motor program?
2. Were you manipulating invariant features or parameters?
3. What features were flexible (parameters)?
4. What features were not flexible (invariant features)?

Ecological Theories

The line of research known as the ecological approach to perception contrasts sharply with the information processing approach (Gibson, 1966). According to this view, perception and action occur at the same time. This perspective was known as the direct perception approach because it holds that cognitive mediation is not necessary to provide meaning to objects or events in the environment. In contrast, the information processing approach holds that action occurs as an indirect process of perception, such that in order to act upon the environment, an organism must go through a series of steps. For instance, if a person were to come across a steaming hot cup of coffee, he must first perceive the cup of coffee by locating memory stores of a cup of coffee. Upon perceiving the cup of coffee as such, he would then decide if he wanted to drink the coffee. If he was interested in drinking it, a message would be sent from the brain to the limbs to reach for the cup of coffee. An example of this can be seen in figure 1.2.

Ecological psychologists explain that an organism does not go through a long series of processes to complete a task such as drinking a cup of coffee (refer to figure 1.2). Rather the individual acts upon the environment in the manner afforded by the object. One cannot move without perceiving, just as one cannot perceive without acting. For example, a hiker walking through the woods who sees a fallen log will not see the log, perceive what it is, decide how to act upon it, then act upon it. Instead, the log will "afford" the hiker a place to sit. The perception and action are one and the same. **Affordances** are the action possibilities of the environment and task in relation to the perceiver's own capabilities (Gibson, 1977, 1979). Perceiving and acting is guided by body-scaled ratios. For example, the leg length of an individual affects how the person climbs a set of stairs. Toddlers have much shorter leg lengths and must compensate for a reduced ratio between their leg length and the action space of the step height (Warren, 1984). Children are tuned in to this body-scaled ratio such that they do not have to learn a new movement pattern due to growth and maturational changes. Depending on individual differences and goals, action possibilities for a particular object can vary quite widely. A chair will most often afford an individual a place to sit; however, an individual who needs to reach for a high object may use a chair as a stool. A stool may afford small children a seat due

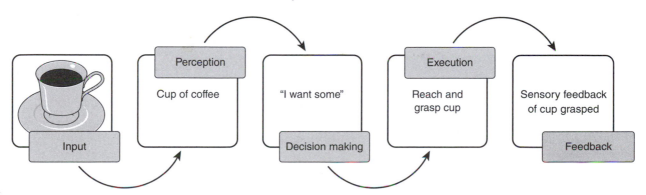

FIGURE 1.2 Example of an indirect process of action and perception as viewed by the information processing approach: The individual must perceive first, and then act upon the environment.

Example Developmentally @ locomotor stage

 Research Notes: Watch Out for the Slope!

Karen Adolph and colleagues (1993) conducted a study to investigate infants' perception of affordances on slopes ranging from 10 degrees to 40 degrees. Two age groups were assessed (14-month-old toddlers and 8.5-month-old crawling infants) on ascending and descending a sloping walkway. The findings showed that the locomotor stage influenced how the infant approached the task. Both groups overestimated their ability to ascend the slopes, but only the toddlers altered their movement pattern during the steeper descents. The toddlers often switched to a sliding movement, while the infants continued to crawl headfirst down the steep descents, often resulting in a fall. The infants hesitated only prior to the steeper descents, but they did not attempt an alternate means of negotiating the slope. The toddlers, on the other hand, hesitated on the lower slopes and then switched to the more stable sliding method for the steeper slopes. These findings indicate that the perception of affordances (the degree to which a surface is walkable or not) is influenced by the locomotor skills of the infant. Children must learn how to perceive locomotion affordances through movement exploration.

What Do You Think?

Affordances relate to action possibilities for an individual and a particular environment. Movement patterns are specified by body-scaled ratios between the piece of equipment or elements in the environment and the size of the individual. For each of the following examples, explain how the size of the individual will affect the person's movement pattern.

1. If an adult was going to teach a 6-year-old child the basics of tennis, how do you expect their grips (both the adult's and the child's) to be affected if both were using the same size racket? Discuss in terms of affordances.

2. How would you expect children of various ages (2, 4, and 8 years) to catch a beach ball? A soccer ball? A Koosh ball?

to their shorter height and leg length; however, an adult might not be able to sit comfortably on a stool.

The ecological approach (rejects) the idea that there is a need to search for memory stores for object representations. Instead, the acts of perceiving and moving occur simultaneously (Michaels & Carello, 1981). Objects are used to suit particular goals or needs (direct perception), not because there is a prior memory of using that object (indirect perception).

The Dynamic Systems Theory

During the early 1980s, the dynamic systems theory was introduced (Kugler, Kelso, & Turvey, 1982). The dynamic systems theory emphasizes that movements are controlled by more than just the central nervous system; movements are also controlled by interactions within various body systems as well as with the environment. The information processing theory asserts that functioning occurs in a hierarchical manner such that all signals must go to the brain and the brain issues commands to be sent to the muscles. However, the information processing theory does not account for the continuous interaction of the

Weakens tenants of GMP approach

organism with the environment. Proponents of the dynamic systems theory contend that coordinated behavior occurs as a result of many variables that are continuously interacting with one another to constrain movement, while researchers who favor the maturational perspective suggest that there is a predetermined plan specifying the sequence of movement behaviors. They suggest that movement is hardwired and preset, whereas the dynamic systems theorists suggest that instead, movement *emerges* as a function of the individual, the task, and the environment.

The dynamic systems theory characterizes movement as a self-organizing process. **Self-organization** is the system's ability to change states or acquire a new structure or pattern by itself. This perspective defines movement and coordination as a complex and evolving process. The system is constantly looking for stable states, or **attractors**. When the system is perturbed enough, for example if locomotor speed has increased or an injury has occurred, the system will be disrupted and pushed into a new attractor, or stable, state (Thelen & Ulrich, 1991). An example of disruption because of injury might be seen in a racquetball player who suddenly cannot grip the racquet tightly because of a strained ring finger. Interestingly, this looser grip results in a more mechanically efficient swing that leads to more accuracy and velocity. Once the injured finger heals, the player, realizing the benefits, stays with the new (and improved) grip. The finger injury "perturbed" his physical status (the system), pushing him into a new way of hitting the ball (a new attractor state).

Basic developmental phases such as sitting, creeping, and crawling can also be viewed as attractor states. During development in infants, new attractors emerge as they mature and increase strength and coordination, causing former attractor states to disappear. When infants are first learning to walk, they often switch back to their more comfortable state of crawling. However, after they have been walking for several months, they will have lost the attractor state of crawling and will most likely not be seen crawling except on rare occasions to negotiate the environment.

The stability of attractors has been compared to the depth of a basin or well; the deeper the well, the more stable the behavior (Ennis, 1992). Very stable patterns are quite difficult to change, such as a movement skill or pattern that is well learned, while shallow wells are volatile and very susceptible to switching into a new attractor state. A swimmer who has learned an unorthodox method for performing the butterfly may have a difficult time when introduced to the correct technique by a new instructor. The swimmer most likely will go through a period of slower sprint times and uncomfortable movement patterns before

What Do You Think?

What would cause a change in self-organization in each of these examples?

1. Compare hiking in the woods—encountering branches, fallen logs, and so on—to hiking in deep snow.
2. Compare dancing in a crowded club to dancing on an open floor.
3. Compare bench pressing at 60% of your max to bench pressing at 95% of your max.

Phase shifts *(handwritten margin note)*

a phase shift will push her movement pattern into a new attractor state. **Phase shifts** are the change in a state that *cause a shift or reorganization to a new attractor state.*

Control parameters are the variables that induce a shift to a new attractor state. Speed, injuries, weight, force, and sensory information can all act as control parameters. In the example of the racquetball player, the finger injury was the control parameter that caused a phase shift to a new grip. Increasing the speed on a treadmill can be a control parameter that causes an individual to transition from walking to running. Control parameters can also limit or hinder performance. When this occurs, the control parameter is referred to as a **rate limiter**. Fear is a common rate limiter, as it often causes individuals to alter their movement patterns. A toddler who is afraid of being hurt by a thrown ball will likely close his eyes and protect his face rather than place his hands out in preparation to catch the ball. A bowling ball or a bat that is too heavy could also act as a rate limiter. Physical and occupational therapists work with patients to resolve some of the changes resulting from rate limiters. For example, a physical therapist may work with a stroke patient who must relearn how to walk or even pick up objects with the affected limb. Injuries and arthritis are other examples of rate limiters that physical or occupational therapists often encounter. Figure 1.3 presents each of these terms along with a brief description and practical example. Bench pressing with a comfortable weight would be a strong attractor. As the amount of weight is increased (control parameter), this state will become progressively less stable until at some point the person will change form to be able to continue to lift. The amount of increased weight that causes this change to poor form is an example of a rate limiter. The change from good form to bad form is an example of a phase shift.

In the 1980s, Kugler and colleagues (1982) proposed that coordination is developed by changing constraints imposed by the interaction of the organism with the environment—the **constraints model**. Newell (1986) asserted that movement is constrained by boundaries that limit movement possibilities. These boundaries are termed **constraints**. Individuals choose movement patterns based on the interaction of the individual, the task, and the environmental constraints (figure 1.4).

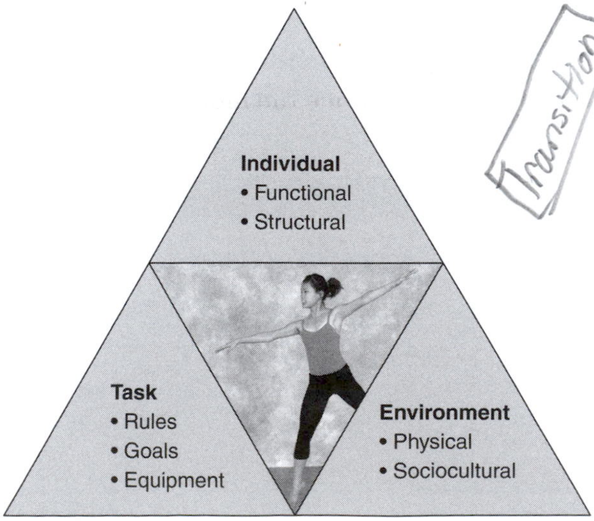

FIGURE 1.3 Description and practical example of key terms in dynamic systems theory.

Attractor	Control Parameters
• Stable states • Ex. Bench pressing with good form	• The cause of the change • Ex. Increasing weight

Rate Limiters	Phase Shifts
• The cause of a negative change • Ex. Increasing weight beyond capability	• The change • Ex. Too much weight can lead to a change in correct form

FIGURE 1.4 Model of the three constraints: individual, task, and environment.

Individual
• Functional
• Structural

Transition (handwritten note)

Task
• Rules
• Goals
• Equipment

Environment
• Physical
• Sociocultural

 What Do You Think?

Since it is the goal of any motor skill program to promote increased proficiency in motor skill performance, it is important for practitioners to understand what may potentially be limiting the progression of a skill. For the following examples, list the potential rate limiters that are preventing or delaying progression in the particular motor skill.

1. An older adult is able to walk and climb stairs normally, but when descending must go down backward. What rate limiter is preventing him from stepping downstairs forward? *Define → Cause – knee arthritis*
2. An infant is not able to hold her body upright to stand without supporting herself with a solid stationary object. What is preventing her from standing without support?
3. A 4-year-old is able to hit a ball from a tee but is unable to make contact with the ball when it is pitched to him. What are the rate limiters preventing him from hitting a moving ball?
4. What was the rate limiter for Makayla in the scenario about choking up on the bat at the beginning of the chapter?

Individual Constraints

Individual constraints are divided into two categories, structural and functional. **Structural constraints** include physical characteristics such as gender, height, weight, and body makeup. One would expect a 6-foot, 5-inch man to perform very differently on a basketball court than a 4-foot, 7-inch female. We would also expect the tall male to move differently from the petite female on the dance floor or simply when walking down the street. **Functional constraints** include psychological and cognitive variables, such as motivation, arousal, and *fear* intellect. That same female may perform her dance routine with more small errors when under much stress, illness, or fatigue, even though her structural constraints have not changed.

Task Constraints

Task constraints include (1) the goals of the movement, (2) rules, and (3) equipment (Newell, 1986). All movement tasks are constrained by the goal of the movement. The goal of basketball is to outscore your opponent by shooting basketballs through a regulation-sized hoop while the other team is attempting to steal the ball. Because of this goal, athletes practice the motor skill of jump shooting. The rules of basketball also govern the body movements. Basketball players are allowed to take only one step after they have stopped dribbling. This rule adds to the complexity of the sport, preventing athletes from simply running up and down the court and requiring them to outsmart their opponents while dribbling. Finally, implements constrain movement possibilities. If the ball used in basketball was changed from a regulation size of 30 inches to 12 inches (76 to 30 centimeters), athletes would certainly have to alter their shots to accommodate this new task constraint.

Environmental Constraints

Environmental constraints are constraints that are external to the mover. These constraints can either be physical or sociocultural. **Physical environmental**

constraints include external conditions such as weather, temperature, lighting, floor surface, and step height. Tennis players alter their game play during matches on a grass court versus a clay or concrete court. Football strategies are changed to shorter passes during rainy games due to increased difficulty of grasping the wet ball. **Sociocultural environmental constraints** are imposed by social and cultural norms and pressures. For instance, young women in India are less likely to be regularly participating in sport as compared to young women in the United States because "sporty" females are considered less attractive than thin, "weak" women. In the United States, women's participation in sport is rivaling that of the men. This was not always the case, however. It was not until the passage of Title IX in 1972 that the gender gap in sport participation began to close. Prior to this educational amendment, women were given far fewer opportunities for sport participation.

 Try This

INDIVIDUAL CONSTRAINTS

Place one hand over and behind your head and the other hand behind your back. Now reach each arm and attempt to grasp your fingers.

1. Were you able to accomplish this task? If not, what prevented you from being able to grasp your fingers?
2. Would this be considered a structural or a functional constraint?

TASK CONSTRAINTS

Using a crumpled-up piece of paper, throw the paper ball into a basket (wastebasket if need be). Now throw a racquetball into the same basket from the same distance. Place the basket on top of a table or even higher, on a shelf. Throw each ball into the basket again.

1. Did you use the same movement pattern for each ball?
2. Did you use the same movement pattern for each basket height?
3. What are the three types of task constraints?

ENVIRONMENTAL CONSTRAINTS

Shoot your paper ball and the racquetball into the basket again, this time with a fan blowing across the basket.

1. Did the added influence of wind influence the accuracy of your shot?
2. Did it affect both the paper ball and the racquetball?
3. Did you alter your movement pattern to overcome the increased airflow produced by the fan?

What Do You Think?

1. Categorize each of the following list items as either an individual, environment, or task constraint.
   - An athlete with the flu
   - Running into the wind
   - Brushing your teeth with an electric toothbrush rather than a regular toothbrush
   - An older adult with stiff joints
   - Shooting hoops with the goals changed (i.e., playing P-I-G instead of a conventional game)
   - Hiking through rough terrain

2. Categorize each of the following list items as either a structural or functional constraint.
   - Lack of motivation
   - Broken leg
   - A 5-foot, 10-inch (178-centimeter) 12-year-old child
   - Poor flexibility
   - Fatigue

Summary

This chapter provided a background for the fields of motor development, motor learning, and motor control. It is important to understand the similarities and differences among these fields of knowledge and to appreciate the importance of bringing them together when planning a motor skill program for learners of any age, developmental level, or background. It is also critical to understand the differences between growth and development and between learning and performance, as these differences are very often overlooked. Growth generally refers to physical growth. All individuals stop growing at some point in time but never stop developing. Many people falsely assume that development is confined to infancy and childhood; however, development occurs throughout the life span. Another common misconception is that performance changes equate to learning changes, but this is often not the case. Learning results in a permanent change in the ability to perform skilled movement, while performance changes are the observable products of movement. Shooting a one-time half-court shot for a million dollars and shooting a free throw shot the next day are examples of performance. In a moment of extreme luck, an individual could make the million-dollar shot but not be able to make a foul shot the following day. This person's performance would not reflect learning because a permanent change in the capability to shoot a basketball has not occurred.

The chapter also presented an overview of the emergence of the field of motor development, including a description of each of the major theoretical constructs. These perspectives all differ not only in the manner in which they define development and learning, but also in how they examine behavior.

Some perspectives focus on particular age groups (maturational) while others compare age differences (information processing) or examine how movement transitions emerge (dynamic systems and ecological psychology). Students are encouraged to compare and contrast these theories and to examine development and learning from the theoretical perspective they find the most compelling.

Supplemental Activities

1. Manipulating task and environmental constraints is a very effective strategy to improve a learner's performance. The equipment can be changed so that it is appropriate for young learners or beginners. The rules can be adjusted so learners can understand the basics without being overwhelmed. Activities can also be practiced in more predictable environments to enhance performance during acquisition.

    a. Choose an activity and discuss several ways in which you could manipulate the environment and task (including the rules, goals, and equipment) to increase successful performances in beginning learners.

    b. Discuss how you would progressively manipulate these constraints as the learner improves.

    c. When could manipulating these constraints be ineffective and potentially even detrimental to skill learning?

2. Search the Internet for products related to motor development. Devise a list of a few of these products. Who are these products targeted toward? What age range are they designed for? Describe how the products are expected to help infants or children develop. Do you think these products will help infants or children develop the abilities or skills they are intended to develop? Why or why not?

CHAPTER TWO

Classifying Motor Skills

Found also in MaGill

CHAPTER OBJECTIVES

After reading this chapter, you should be able to

> explain the importance of motor skill classification,

> classify motor skills using unidimensional and multidimensional classifications,

> distinguish between motor skills and abilities,

> classify games and activities using a problem-solving theme as defined in this chapter, and

> understand Fleishman's taxonomy.

Don't Choke Under Pressure

Chris spends many hours per week practicing his golf swing at his local driving range, mastering techniques such as his grip, posture, and the basics of the swing. Although he can perfect his swing on a practice tee, he experiences problems when transferring to a golf course. Why can he perform so well at the driving range, yet have problems when playing on a course?

The answer to this question is relatively simple. While golf is performed in a somewhat predictable environment when compared to team sports, golfers can benefit from practicing with added pressure or the element of surprise. Golf is often practiced in a very controlled and predictable facility (i.e., driving range), then played in a much less predictable environment (i.e., golf course). Golfers are often not prepared for playing under the increased pressure and environmental conditions they may face during a match. Tiger Woods has exceptional focus even under intense pressure but didn't become a highly skilled professional golfer by practicing only in controlled environments. Earl, Tiger's father, was a Green Beret who learned to shoot a rifle performing simulated war games rather than practicing in controlled, predictable environments. When Tiger was a young child, Earl prepared him for unpredictable situations by distracting him during golf rounds. Tiger would play under various weather conditions, night or day. At times, Earl would talk during Tiger's swing. These distractions taught him how to tune out environmental influences, preparing him to play championship golf matches under unpredictable and often distracting circumstances.

Golf affords only one example of how manipulating the environment can assist the learner to perform more effectively. Amateurs of any sport or recreational activity may believe that they simply "choked" under pressure, although there are methods to minimize this potential occurrence. Most often, amateurs do not have experience in a more stressful, competitive environment, whereas professionals are very familiar with varied conditions and pressure situations. In order to prepare the learning environment, a practitioner must understand the fundamental differences across various game and motor tasks.

Children and adults receiving occupational or physical therapy may also notice that they perform better in the therapy setting than at home. To facilitate the transition from the clinic to home and continue the benefits of therapy outside of the facility, therapists often teach patients activities that can be practiced at home. For example, school occupational therapists help children with fine motor delays to improve skills such as writing, typing, or cutting. To continue the improvements when school is not in session or when the therapist is not available, the therapist should encourage students to create art projects that require fine motor control, such as drawing, cutting, or painting, and to work on their writing or typing as a form of at-home occupational therapy.

This chapter explains how to classify motor skills using both unidimensional and multidimensional classifications. Classifications of motor skills are important for both physical educators and health professionals who design and implement motor skill programs, as certain practice designs are more appropriate for particular skill classifications. The chapter also discusses games classification, which is particularly important for physical educators including teachers, coaches, and instructors. The games in a given classification have similar play rules, performance measures, and scoring. Previous experience in a game or activity in a particular classification will benefit the individual learning another game or activity in that same classification.

Skills Classification

Skills are the learned ability to bring about predetermined results with maximum certainty, often with minimum outlay of time or energy (Knapp, 1963).

An athlete or performer is considered ==skillful== if he has achieved a criterion of excellence and is capable of performing at a high level the majority of the time. Motor skills have also been defined as activities that require a chain of sensory (vision, hearing, touch, smell), central (brain and nervous systems), and motor mechanisms whereby the performer is able to maintain constant control of the sensory input and in accordance with the goal of the movement (Argyle & Kendon, 1967). Physical activities can be classified into particular categories. Each individual activity is unique with respect to the structure of the task, task goals, and obstacles. Although there are many unique qualities of physical activities, there are also commonalities across different activities, such that proficiency in one skill can lead to increased proficiency in another (i.e., positive transfer of learning).

Skill classification can be tricky, because many skills do not solidly fit into only one category. However, classifying skills is a useful tool for effective teaching and learning. Practitioners who are able to appropriately classify skills are better able to adapt the learning experience to a changing environment, enabling more efficient program design and maximizing motor learning. As discussed in chapters 13 and 14, practice sessions should be specifically designed for particular skill classifications. The following section examines motor skill classifications including sport skills, developmental taxonomies, unidimensional classifications, and Gentile's multidimensional classification system.

Sport Skills

Skill in sport has been separated into three categories: cognitive skills, perceptual skills, and motor skills (Honeybourne, 2006). **Cognitive skills** include the intellectual skills of the mover. These are the skills that enable a performer to make decisions and problem solve. Cognitive skills such as decision-making speed are critical for a quarterback to make quick, effective decisions. **Perceptual skills** involve interpreting and integrating sensory information to determine the best movement outcome. Attention and previous movement experiences also affect perceptual skills. For example, a soccer player assesses the position of defenders and teammates to determine whether to pass the ball to an open player or continue dribbling toward the goal. The speed and direction of the athlete's movements are dependent on the perceptual information that she receives regarding the current situation. **Motor skills** include the physical elements that enable the movement. To put it simply, the activity could not be completed without the learned ability to coordinate the limbs to produce the action.

At young ages, basic skills provide the foundation for activities with much more complicated sport-specific motor skills. These basic skills are termed **fundamental motor skills** and include activities such as the overhand throw, jumping, catching, kicking, and striking. By building a basis with these fundamental motor skills, a learner is able to perform a wide array of similar activities. For instance, a child who has learned jumping, hopping, and skipping will be better able to perform more sport-specific activities like the long jump, the high jump, or even a basketball layup. The fundamental skill of striking is useful for many sports, including hockey, golf, racket sports, and baseball. Chapter 5 discusses the developmental progressions for several fundamental motor skills.

Developmental Taxonomies

A **developmental taxonomy** provides a framework for grouping motor skills into themes for teaching fundamental motor skills (Gallahue & Ozmun, 2006). **Taxonomies** are classifications of objects or events according to a common theme. In the developmental taxonomy, motor skills can be broken down into three groups: nonlocomotor stability, locomotor skills, and manipulative skills.

- *Nonlocomotor stability.* **Stability** is the ability to maintain body position against forces of gravity, which may include other circumstances that increase the difficulty of the task (Gallahue & Ozmun, 2006). Gymnasts must be able to maintain body position while holding the body's entire weight upright between two rings or while completing a balance beam routine; figure skaters must be able to maintain a static position while gliding across the ice; and divers must be able to hold a vertical position while entering the water. Maintaining stability is fundamental for not only most sport-related motor skills, but also many functional skills. It is critical to maintain your stability while reaching high for a can in a cupboard or when you unexpectedly step onto ice.

- *Locomotor skills.* **Locomotor skills** are gross motor skills in which the goal of the movement is body transport. Locomotor skills cannot be developed separately from stability. People must be able to stabilize their body before they are able to perform a proficient locomotor pattern. Body transport can occur when a person is moving the body from point A to point B, but also is present during sporting activities, such as a racquetball match, a gymnastics routine, or a soccer game. Typically developing infants progress through a developmental sequence of body transport. When they are very young, they are not strong or coordinated enough to be able to locomote using their feet, so they learn other methods for transporting their bodies from one point to another. Young infants begin body transport by learning how to roll over. This usually begins around 3 months of age, when most infants can roll from their back or stomach onto their side. Infants then progress to using their arms and knees to transport their bodies by crawling (body drag) at 6 to 8 months and by creeping (quadruped movement, abdomen off the floor) around age 8 to 10 months. After infants have increased their abdominal and leg strength as well as their coordination, they can pull to a standing position (7-9 months), walk with assistance (9-10 months), and then finally perform bipedal walking alone (12-14 months).

- *Manipulative skills.* **Manipulative skills** use smaller muscle groups and are classified as fine motor skills. Manipulative skills enable individuals to explore the world, bringing objects closer and feeling their size and texture in order to identify them. Some physical activities are specifically geared toward the manipulation of objects, as in archery or marksmanship. In these tasks, even slight adjustments to the movement can compromise the performance outcome considerably. Infants begin reaching and grasping as newborns; however, this motion is spontaneous and reflexive. At approximately 4 months, typically developing infants begin voluntary reaching and grasping. The palmar grasp, which appears at birth when objects are placed and stroked in the infant's palm, is still present at this age. The infant then grasps the object with a strong but unpredictable grip. By 5 to 6 months of age, the palmar grasp disappears and the infant is able to grasp objects with smooth and controlled movements.

By 8 months, infants can pick up multiple objects at a time. The pincer grasp (thumb and forefinger) appears at around 9 to 10 months of age. By 14 months, infants are able to reach and grasp similarly to adults, but they are not able to effectively release objects until around 18 months.

Although tasks can be classified as manipulative or locomotor, they rarely occur as one or the other in complete isolation during recreation or sporting activities; most advanced motor skills require the ability to control all three of the skill elements, while fundamental motor skills focus more on individual elements. For example, a basketball player is manipulating the basketball while also transporting the body closer to the basket; a bowler manipulates the bowling ball, adjusting the amount of spin and force at the release point, while also transporting the body closer toward the pins; and even in billiards, while players are eyeing up the point of contact for the stick, they must also transport their body to that position. When one is designing a practice sequence or teaching a new skill, especially to a young child or an individual with few movement experiences, it is best to simplify the task by focusing on only one aspect of the movement at a time and to take each of the three developmental taxonomies into consideration. The sequence should begin with a stable task; as the performer increases in proficiency, more difficulty can be added, such as increased locomotion and manipulation of an implement. Table 2.1 presents an example of teaching a child how to kick a ball using the developmental taxonomy.

TABLE 2.1 Developmental Taxonomy Progression for Kicking a Ball

Step 1	Kick a stationary ball into a goal while standing still
Step 2	Take a step and kick a stationary ball into a goal
Step 3	Run and kick a stationary ball into a goal
Step 4	Dribble the ball and kick into a goal
Step 5	Dribble the ball and kick into a goal that is being guarded

Single-Dimensional Classifications

The first step in learning a new motor skill is to understand the basic elements and order of the movements. Movements can be broken down into particular situations, including game strategies, rules, and goals. It is also important to break the activity down further into simple units, or the basic skills. In this section, skills are classified into movement precision, environmental predictability, time constraint taxonomy, and the nature of the skill.

Movement Precision

Motor skills can be classified according to the level of movement precision. Skills in which large muscle groups produce the movement, such as the quadriceps, hamstrings, and gluteus maximus, tend to be much larger, less precise movements. These motor skills are classified as **gross motor skills**. Skills in which precise movements are critical to perform the skill with increased accuracy and control use smaller muscle groups and are categorized as **fine motor**

skills. Dialing a phone number, playing the piano, and marksmanship are skills that require precise movements of smaller muscle groups. This classification is important for developmental sequencing. Children are generally less able to control smaller muscle groups and are thus taught activities that involve larger muscle groups, such as running and jumping, before they are taught how to coordinate their limbs to perform fine motor skills as in drawing, writing, and playing games (e.g., jacks or marbles). Practitioners should keep this in mind when preparing a motor skill program for very young children.

Environmental Predictability

Skills can also be classified by the predictability of the environment. Skills used in a task that takes place in a stable environment in which objects or events are also stationary are considered **closed skills**. With closed skills, the performer's goal is to learn how to perform the movement successfully and then replicate this action; an example is performing a foul shot in basketball. Foul shots are not constrained by time or space, and the environment is stable. The shooter does not have to pay attention to defenders trying to steal the ball or block the shot, and the distance to the hoop and the height of the hoop are going to remain stable. On the other hand, **open skills** occur in an ever-changing environment where objects, people, and events are constantly varying. These skills require that the mover be much more attentive to the environment, constantly monitoring the situation for changing conditions. A hockey slap shot is considered an open skill, as the environment is highly unpredictable.

Skills classified according to the predictability of the environment occupy a continuum. There are no skills that are entirely closed, because there are always some conditions that will change; however, for closed skills, the predictability is much greater than for open skills. Bowling would be placed more toward the closed end of the continuum because the skill is completed inside of a building, and the pins are placed in the same position for each frame and remain stationary. Gutters are the only obstacle, and they too remain stable. The only condition that will vary is the number of pins that remain after each attempt and perhaps the amount of background noise, which will be presumably much less than during a Division 1 collegiate football game. Figure 2.1 provides several examples of motor skills on the open–closed continuum.

An additional element of environmental predictability is intertrial variability. **Intertrial variability** includes any change that occurs between trials, with a trial defined as a practice attempt. A skill with intertrial variability has aspects that change with every performance attempt. Intertrial variability can be present in either open or closed skills. The closed skill of batting in T-ball has no intertrial variability, while a pitch in baseball has intertrial variability. Each pitch is unique, requiring the batter to be able to adapt to the changing condi-

FIGURE 2.1 Examples of skills on the open–closed continuum. Many motor skills fit somewhere between the extremes of open versus closed skills. For instance, no skills are entirely closed skills. Every skill has at least some aspects that are somewhat variable or unpredictable.

tions. The key to success of batting in T-ball is consistency. Functional tasks can also have varying levels of intertrial variability. Functional activities such as walking up the stairs in your home or across the room should have relatively low intertrial variability, while walking on the busy sidewalks in Manhattan would have high intertrial variability. Every day your exact path would change because you would need to avoid bumping into people or objects along the way.

While open skills always include at least some intertrial variability, most closed skills have little to no intertrial variability. They are often performed in a stable environment in which most factors are predictable. There are some closed skills in which intertrial variability adds to the challenge of the task, as in golf. After each golf putt, the distance, angle, and position of the ball in relation to the hole changes. There are no defenders or other variable conditions except for weather conditions. The terrain may also change with differing obstructions (man-made) and impediments (natural) across the course. This variability adds to the complexity of the task, making it more challenging and interesting to the performer and the observer.

Time Constraint Taxonomy

The difficulty of a task can be determined by the movement pacing of the task. Tasks in which there are no time constraints are less complex than tasks in which there are time constraints. **Self-paced tasks** begin when initiated by the mover and as such when the mover chooses, as in golf, darts, or archery. A basketball player shooting a foul shot often has a preliminary routine prior to the shot. Players adopt a routine because the shot is not constrained by time; instead, accuracy is the key. Other skills do not have the luxury of self-pacing. A pitcher determines when to initiate the pitch, so the pitch is self-paced. The batter's movements are **externally paced tasks** because the batter is responding to the pitched ball. The batter cannot swing when he is interested in swinging. Instead, he must swing when the ball reaches the plate, which is determined by the release of the pitch and the speed and trajectory of the pitch. Kicking a penalty kick in soccer is another example of a self-paced movement. The goalie's response is externally paced by the kicker. Most functional tasks and physical and occupational therapy treatments are internally paced, such as writing, brushing your teeth, and muscle strengthening exercises. Driving, on the other hand, is a combination of the two. You choose your speed, to some degree, and your route; but you must stop at red lights awaiting the green, and then go ahead.

What Do You Think?

1. What components in racket sports are self-paced? What components are externally paced?
2. Name a game or sport that is entirely self-paced.
3. Are there any games or sports that are entirely externally paced? If so, which?
4. What are some everyday or functional tasks that are internally paced? Name one or two that are externally paced.

Nature of the Skill

A fourth method for defining skills is by the nature of the task. Fitts and Posner (1967) defined tasks by the beginning and end points of the movements. A **discrete motor skill** is one in which the beginning and end points are clearly defined. These movements are generally short in duration and have a distinct difference between their initiation and termination. A photograph taken during the beginning of the movement for a discrete skill would be qualitatively different from a photograph taken at the conclusion of the movement (see figure 2.2). The two photographs would illustrate something undoubtedly different. An observer would also easily be able to determine which photograph was taken at the beginning of the movement and which was taken at the end. Another key component of discrete skills is a period of time that must elapse before a subsequent movement must occur. For instance, a quarterback must wait for a ball to be thrown to him before he can pass. Some examples of discrete skills are throwing, kicking, punching, shooting, and catching.

Continuous motor skills do not have a clearly defined beginning or ending point. These tasks are longer in duration, and the mover is in constant motion (Fitts & Posner, 1967). Continuous tasks appear as repetitive movements. The movements are generally simple and are continuously repeated as in running, swimming, cross-country skiing, or bicycling. If a picture is taken of a child riding a bicycle, it will be difficult to determine whether she is at the beginning or end of the movement. **Serial motor skills** are motor skills that include a series of discrete skills that must occur in a specific sequence. If the order of the movements can be altered, the task would not be classified as a serial task. The triple jump, consisting of a sprint, hop, skip, and jump, is an example of a closed serial skill. If the sequence were altered to a hop, sprint, jump, skip, the jump would no longer be considered the triple jump. A football punt, consisting of a catch, approach, drop, and kick, is an example of an open serial skill. Serial skills can be thought of as a string of beads. Each component of the serial skill can be performed separately as a discrete skill, such as hopping, skipping, or jumping. Serial skills require not only that the performer be skillful at the discrete skills independently, but also that he transition from one movement to the next in the proper sequence.

FIGURE 2.2
The movement at the beginning of a throw is qualitatively different from the end of the motor skill.

What Do You Think?

1. Provide one example of each of the following classifications of skills.
   - Discrete open skill
   - Discrete closed skill
   - Continuous open skill
   - Continuous closed skill
   - Serial open skill
   - Serial closed skill
2. Define each of your examples as either self-paced or externally paced.

Multidimensional Classification

Practitioners lead learners through a progression of movements in order to perform an open skill proficiently. It is best to place learners in a closed environment in which much of the task can be simplified and controlled before progressing to a more challenging and adaptable open environment. Gentile (2000) designed a classification system for gradual progressions from closed to open environments. Gentile's taxonomy is a useful tool for individualizing motor skill progressions. Gentile's taxonomy uses two main categories to assist practitioners in program development: the environmental context and the action requirements. Gentile's classification system was developed for physical therapists, but is widely used as a tool for physical educators and coaches as well.

Environmental Context

The environmental context consists of two factors: regulatory conditions and intertrial variability. **Regulatory conditions** are the environmental factors specific to a particular skill or sport. For example, some of the regulatory conditions in soccer are the size of the soccer field, the height and width of the goal, and the size and weight of the ball. These conditions typically remain the same for any soccer game regardless of where it is played. Regulatory conditions standardize how a person must adapt to a given situation to produce a successful outcome. Gentile (2000) classified regulatory conditions as either in motion or stationary. Skills for which the regulatory conditions are stationary, such as the pins in bowling, are considerably less complex than skills for which the regulatory conditions are in motion, such as the clay targets in skeet shooting. Stationary regulatory conditions and the absence of intertrial variability represent a closed skill, while moving regulatory conditions and intertrial variability would be considered to require a moderately closed skill. Figure 2.3 gives an example of a motor skill in each of the four categories. The complexity of T-ball is lower than that of batting with a machine because the regulatory

	Regulatory Conditions	
Intertrial Variability	Stationary	Moving
Consistent	T-ball	Batting with a machine
Variable	Hitting a ball hanging on a rope	Swinging at a pitched ball

FIGURE 2.3 Examples of the environmental context of Gentile's (2000) multidimensional classification system.

conditions are stable and there is no intertrial variability—the ball will be in the same position for every attempt. A ball that is hanging on a rope will be in a different position every time, but the regulatory conditions will be stationary. The most complex task is batting a pitched ball. The ball will be moving, and the trials will be variable.

Action Requirements

Gentile (2000) used two classifications to define the action requirements of a skill: body orientation and manipulation (figure 2.4). **Body orientation** is classified as either body transport, as during sporting activities such as a basketball layup or triple jump, or body stability, as in archery shooting. Body orientation is an important component in exercises used in therapy settings. Body transport activities include locomotor exercises, such as crawling, walking, or jumping, while body stability includes many balance exercises. Activities that require body transport are higher in complexity than activities that can be completed in a stable body position. When an individual must manipulate an object, such as a racket, a ball, or an opponent, the task is considered higher in complexity. The individual not only must adjust or maintain her body posture and position (or both) but also must manipulate and control an implement (e.g., tennis) or person (e.g., judo).

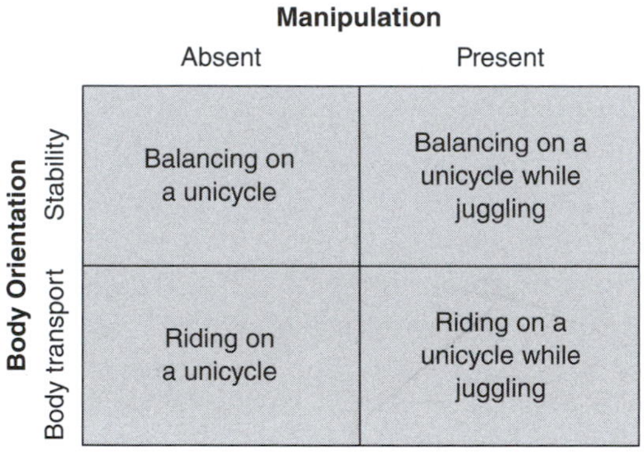

FIGURE 2.4

Examples of the action requirements of Gentile's (2000) multidimensional classification system.

	Manipulation	
Body Orientation	**Absent**	**Present**
Stability	Balancing on a unicycle	Balancing on a unicycle while juggling
Body transport	Riding on a unicycle	Riding on a unicycle while juggling

Gentile's taxonomy combines the four classifications for the environmental context with the four classifications of the action requirements to compose a 16-category system for classifying motor skills. An example of a motor skill for each category is depicted in figure 2.5. Motor skills become increasingly complex from the upper left quadrant of the taxonomy to the lower right quadrant. The push-up, in the first quadrant (upper left), is the task lowest in complexity compared to all the other tasks. There is little variability in performing a push-up from trial to trial. When performing successive push-ups, the performer simply needs to repeat the previous movement until either reaching muscle failure or achieving a goal. No body transport or object manipulation is required. Throwing a football pass, in the last quadrant (lower right), is considered highest in complexity. A quarterback must be able to anticipate the receiver's position and the time and location of the pass. A successful quarterback must also be able to adapt to different environmental conditions with each performance attempt while transporting his body and manipulating the ball.

Activities could be planned for all 16 categories for a particular motor skill. However, it is not always necessary to include all 16. A performer who can complete the fundamental movement pattern consistently and under variable conditions is prepared to begin at the ninth category, which is for a motor skill that is moving, consistent, and does not have body transport or object manipulation. If the motor skill is a closed skill, then the practice should be designed for only the first eight categories. Gentile's taxonomy enables an instructor to implement a precise skill progression appropriate for learners of all developmental levels to enable them to progress to their desired level of difficulty.

Stability   *Locomotor (Transport)*   *Kick (leg) Throw, shoot (Arms)* *Object involves limbs*

Action Requirements

		No body transport or object manipulation	Object manipulation but no body transport	Body transport but no object manipulation	Both body transport and object manipulation
Closed skills	Stationary and consistent	Push-up	Decline sit-ups with a medicine ball	Triple jump	Javelin throw
Moderately closed skills	Stationary and variable	Balancing on one foot with different shoes on	Playing cricket with darts	Completing an obstacle course	Salsa dancing in an empty dance studio
Moderately open skills	Moving and consistent	Sitting on an exercise ball	Hitting a tennis ball served from a pitching machine	Running in the woods	Kicking a ball to an unguarded goal
Open skills	Moving and variable	Doing a push-up on an exercise ball	Skeet shooting	Dancing in a crowded club	Throwing a football pass

Environmental Conditions →

Increasing complexity →

—Increasing complexity—

FIGURE 2.5   Examples of motor skills in each category of Gentile's (2000) multidimensional classification system.

What Do You Think?

Choose one motor skill and explain how you can modify it to fit into eight of Gentile's categories.

Action Requirements

		No body transport or object manipulation	Object manipulation but no body transport	Body transport but no object manipulation	Both body transport and object manipulation
Closed skills	Stationary and consistent				
Moderately closed skills	Stationary and variable				
Moderately open skills	Moving and consistent				
Open skills	Moving and variable				

Environmental Conditions →

Increasing complexity →

—Increasing complexity—

Distinction Between Skill and Ability

Abilities are genetically predetermined characteristics that affect movement performance such as agility, coordination, strength, and flexibility. Abilities are enduring and as such, difficult to change in adults. Abilities differ from skills in the sense that skills are learned, whereas abilities are a product of both learning and genetic factors (Fleishman, 1964). Skills are a level of proficiency on a specific motor task, while abilities are part of an individual's traits that affect her capability to become skillful when learning a new motor task. For example, abilities that are required for a skilled race car driver include rate control, manual dexterity, stamina, control precision, and reaction time; a typist needs to have abilities in aiming and finger dexterity; a surgeon requires arm–hand steadiness and multilimb coordination; and a figure skater performing the triple axel requires abilities such as explosive strength, dynamic flexibility, gross body coordination, and multilimb coordination (refer to table 2.2 on p. 38 for the description of each motor ability).

Factors Affecting Abilities

An individual's abilities are shaped by biological and physiological factors (Fleishman, 1964). The composition of an individual's muscular tissue is certainly going to affect his physical proficiency motor abilities such as strength, endurance, and flexibility. Physiological deficits in the development of rods and cones would also limit an individual's perceptual–motor abilities, potentially affecting reaction time. Abilities are also affected by environmental factors. For example, children who are afforded formal education will continue to develop their verbal and reasoning abilities throughout their academic years, just as

 Research Notes: What Abilities Most Influence Soccer Performance?

A research study was conducted to examine the motor abilities that most strongly influence technique and performance in soccer (Talvoć, Hodžić, Bajramović, Jeleškovíc, & Alić, 2009). Soccer was chosen because it is a unique sport in that it is generally considered an aerobic sport due to the size of the field and the duration of the game, 90 minutes. Yet soccer also has anaerobic elements, such as sprints and jumps. In the study, 88 participants between the ages of 12 and 14 years completed 18 variables for motor abilities, such as foot tapping on the wall, body lift-ups from lying, forward bend on the bench; two variables for functional abilities, a 12-minute run and six 50 meter runs; and 15 variables on soccer technique performance, such as inside foot receiving ball, rolling dribbling, and heading.

So the question is, What abilities most influence soccer performance? The results revealed a strong influence of all of the abilities as a whole, indicating that soccer is a complex sport that may require the interaction of many underlying abilities for highly proficient performance. Moving beyond this general finding, the authors examined each ability at a one-variant level and found that the most important abilities were coordination, dynamic strength, and explosive strength. These results indicate that physical proficiency abilities may be more influential on soccer technique performance than perceptual–motor abilities, specifically those related to strength, endurance, and coordination.

children who participate in physical fitness- or sport-related programs will develop their motor abilities. The rate at which abilities develop varies across childhood and adolescence, both within individuals and across individuals. This is largely due to growth and maturation changes. The rate of development levels out between the ages of 18 and 22 years, remaining relatively stable throughout adulthood (Fleishman, 1964).

Motor Ability Hypotheses

Initial researchers in the area of motor abilities hypothesized the existence of only one **general motor ability** (Brace, 1927). This hypothesis was based on observations of accomplished athletes who were adept at many athletic events and also able to quickly learn new and unfamiliar motor skills. It is likely that you know of athletes in your age group who fit this description. Perhaps the star quarterback from your high school, who led the basketball team to state championships and held the school batting average record, comes to mind. It may appear that there are many athletes who are capable of performing very skillfully across many different motor skills.

Research examining individuals' performances across different activities supports the notion that every motor skill requires very specific abilities for skillful performance. This has been termed the **specificity hypothesis** (Henry, 1968). Henry proposed that each individual has a large number of separate and independent abilities. Fleishman (1962) developed a taxonomy to identify each ability and separated abilities into two main categories, perceptual–motor abilities and physical proficiency abilities (table 2.2). Although it is doubtful that **Fleishman's taxonomy** is an exhaustive list of motor abilities, it does provide a framework to assess individual differences.

 What Do You Think?

1a. Choose one motor skill that you are proficient in.

1b. Name five of the motor abilities that would be most important to be able to perform skillfully at that motor skill.

1c. For each motor ability, personally rank yourself from 1 (very low ability) to 5 (very high ability).

2a. Choose a motor skill that you are not skillful in.

2b. Name five of the motor abilities that would be most important to be able to perform skillfully at that motor skill.

2c. For each motor ability, personally rank yourself from 1 (very low ability) to 5 (very high ability).

3. Did you notice a difference in your rankings for an activity that you are proficient in comparison to one in which you are not?

4. Do you think your underlying abilities influence the sports and activities you choose to engage in? What about the sports and activities you generally avoid? Explain your answer.

TABLE 2.2 Fleishman's Taxonomy of Motor Abilities

PERCEPTUAL–MOTOR ABILITIES	
Control precision	Ability to make highly controlled movements with larger muscle groups (e.g., hockey puck handling)
Rate control	Ability to make continuous anticipatory adjustments in relation to a moving target (e.g., Formula 1 racing)
Aiming	Ability to make accurate hand movements directed at small targets (e.g., texting)
Response orientation	Ability to make a quick decision with multiple response options; choice reaction time (e.g., quarterback)
Reaction time	Ability to react as quickly as possible to gain an advantage; simple reaction time (e.g., sprinter)
Manual dexterity	Ability to manipulate large objects with hands (e.g., dribbling a basketball)
Finger dexterity	Ability to manipulate small objects with fingers (e.g., typing)
Arm–hand steadiness	Ability to precisely move the hand and fingers without regard to strength or speed (e.g., surgical procedures)
Wrist and finger speed	Ability to rapidly move the fingers and wrist (e.g., speed stacking)
PHYSICAL PROFICIENCY ABILITIES	
Strength	
Explosive strength	Ability to exert maximum energy in one explosive act; power (e.g., standing long jump)
Static strength	Ability to exert maximum force against an immovable or heavy object (e.g., dynamometer)
Trunk strength	Ability to exert repeated strength using the core muscles (e.g., pole vaulting)
Flexibility and speed	
Extent flexibility	Ability to move the body through a large range of motion (e.g., yoga)
Dynamic flexibility	Ability to make repeated flexing movements (e.g., squat thrusts)
Speed of limb movement	Ability to make fast, gross, and discrete limb movements without regard to accuracy (e.g., throwing a javelin)
Balance	
Static balance	Ability to maintain body equilibrium in one position (e.g., standing still on one foot)
Dynamic balance	Ability to maintain balance while changing position (e.g., gymnastics)
Balancing objects	Ability to balance an external object (e.g., circus clown balancing a stick on his nose)
Coordination	
Multilimb coordination	Ability to coordinate movements of more than one limb simultaneously without movement of the whole body (e.g., driving a manual car)
Gross body coordination	Ability to coordinate gross motor activity of the whole body (e.g., hurdling)
Endurance	
Stamina	Ability to prolong exertions of the entire body; cardiovascular endurance (e.g., marathon)
Dynamic strength	Ability to exert repeated force; muscular endurance (e.g., kayaking)

Presentations [handwritten]

Games Classification

With a vast number of different sporting activities, classification schemes are necessary to generalize similarities across games, increasing opportunities for positive transfer across games from the same classification. When introducing games in physical education classes, physical educators have insufficient time to adequately teach all games and cannot offer an extensive variety of games. Students do not have enough time to become skillful in these activities within such a short time frame. By classifying games, teachers can introduce one game from the classification group and then build on the students' understanding by adding a second game from the same classification. The instructor is then able to compare and contrast the two games while also improving proficiency on similar skills (Werner & Almond, 1990).

A **game** is "any form of playful competition whose outcome is determined by physical skill, strategy or chance employed singly or in a combination" (Loy, 1968, p. 1). It is important to note from this definition that games arise out of play, are competitive, and require physical skill, strategy, or chance (Siedentop, 2007). Each game has its own defining set of rules and strategies. The rules that characterize the play of the game and how the game is won are the **primary rules** (Almond, 1986). Games can be modified to be developmentally appropriate. Rules that can be modified without changing the nature of the game are termed **secondary rules**. For example, National Basketball Association (NBA) regulations have extended the 3-point shot from 19 feet, 9 inches (6 meters) to 23 feet, 6 inches (7.2 meters). Changing this regulation has not changed the play of the game. However, it has made it more challenging for professional basketball players to score a 3-point basket. Other secondary rules in basketball include the size of the ball (women vs. men), the 3-second zone rule, and the 10-second half-court rule.

Classifying games became popular in the 1970s and 1980s, providing instructors with a framework for a more balanced curriculum based on the tactics of the games (Hopper & Bell, 1999). For classifying games, a problem-solving theme was employed that used six criteria: the purpose of the game, the initiation and conclusion of the game, game play rules, skill requirements, and game scoring (table 2.3). In this section, we discuss games using Thorpe, Bunker, and Almond's (1986) games classification system. The five game categories include *target games*, where the goal is accuracy (e.g., golf and archery); *fielding/run scoring games* with the essential skills of throwing, striking, and receiving the ball (e.g., cricket and baseball); *net/wall games,* with the essential skills of striking and controlling the placement of the ball (e.g., tennis and volleyball); *invasion games*, which require sending away, retrieving, and retaining the ball (e.g., basketball and football); and *personal performance games*, which are self-contests (e.g., track and field and gymnastics) (figure 2.6).

That which must be learned – (taught) [handwritten margin note]

Invasion Games

With **invasion games**, players are divided into two opposing teams separated by sides on the playing field. During the game, the teams "invade" each other's territory. Invasion games can be subdivided into games that have a focused target, such as basketball or soccer, or games in which a line must be crossed to

TABLE 2.3 Table of Classification Scheme for Each Game Category

	Purpose	Start of game	End of game	Rules	Skills	Scoring
Invasion	Invade the opposing team's territory and score points.	Players begin on their own half of the field and play begins with players moving to the opponent's side.	Play is stopped after a certain period of time has elapsed.	Rules often include restrictions on body contact and ball handling restrictions.	Skills are separated into offensive skills and defensive skills.	Number of points scored from invading other team's territory and scoring (shots, goals, touchdowns).
Net or wall	Keep the ball in play and outsmart opponent by positioning the ball such that it cannot be returned.	Play begins when one player serves the ball either across the net or at the wall.	Play is ended after a certain score has been achieved by one team.	Rules include contact with net and boundary and serving violations.	Accuracy and control of the ball	Points are scored when the serving team prevents the opponents from returning the serve or hits.
Target	Be the individual or team who is able to perform more accurately than the opponent(s).	Play begins when initiated by one of the players; then play occurs alternately from one team to the other.	Play ends after all performers have had equal performance attempts.	Rules regulate where and how the object can be propelled and what defines accuracy.	Accuracy and control of the object.	Score is determined by a measure of accuracy.
Fielding	The batting team's aim is to score as many runs as possible while the fielding team is trying to get the batter out.	Play begins following the opening pitch.	Play ends after each team has had a certain number of opportunities to score runs; no time constraints.	Rules include boundary restrictions on ball trajectory, batting, and pitching.	Temporal and spatial skills; fielding, catching, and throwing skills.	Score is number of runs.
Personal performance	Often a self-contest in which the performer competes alone, striving for peak performance.	These sports begin when initiated by the performer or by an external stimulus (starter's gun).	Play ends after all performers have completed the activity.	Rules regulate the movement type and equipment used.	Specific skills for each individual activity, which requires specific equipment.	Each individual's performance is ranked after the performer has completed the activity.

Adapted from P. Werner and L. Almond, 1990, "Models of games education," *Journal of Physical Education, Recreation and Dance* 61(4): 23-27.

Games Classifications

Invasion		Net or Wall		Target		Fielding	Personal Performance
Focused Target	Open End Target	Divided Court	Shared Court	Opposed	Indirectly Opposed		
• Basketball • Lacrosse • Ice hockey • Soccer • Water polo	• Ultimate frisbee • Football • Rugby • Speedball	• Volleyball • Tennis • Badminton	• Racquetball • Handball • Squash	• Croquet • Horseshoes • Shuffleboard	• Archery • Bowling • Golf	• Baseball • Kickball • Cricket • Rounders • Softball	• Wrestling • Gymnastics • Track and field • Swimming • X sports

FIGURE 2.6 Games classification system.

score (open-end target), such as football or Ultimate Frisbee (Thorpe, Bunker, & Almond, 1986). The offensive goal of invasion games is to maintain possession of the ball and score, while the defensive objective is to obtain possession of the ball and defend the goal area to stop the other team from scoring. Taking the ball from the opponent serves two purposes: preventing the opponent from scoring and taking possession of the ball, thus giving the team a chance to score. Examples of invasion games are basketball, hockey, soccer, American football, rugby, and lacrosse. Play is broken down into timed segments. Invasion games are won by the team with the highest score at the conclusion of a set time period. The final score represents the team that is most successful at invading the opposing team's territory and scoring. These games have similar tactical problems; however, they differ in the task constraints imposed, including specific rules, equipment, and goals and different environmental regulations (e.g., terrain, weather, indoor vs. outdoor play).

Net or Wall Games

Net or **wall games** are games in which the object of play is to serve or return the ball strategically so that the opponent is unable to sustain the play of the ball. These games separate opposing players by a net (e.g., volleyball, tennis, badminton), or may use a wall, with players alternating hits (handball, squash, racquetball). Players gain points each time they serve the ball and are able to prevent their opponent from returning the ball. The contest has ended when a certain number of points have been achieved by one player or team. One key component in skill proficiency in net or wall sports is accuracy. The player must manipulate the speed and angle of the hit to control the ball position and the pace of the game. The ball must land within designated lines for each sport. Tactical understanding in net and wall games is to outsmart the opponent by placing shots where they cannot be returned, and the rules are geared toward boundary restrictions and serving. Most net and wall games use an implement to strike the ball (e.g., table tennis, badminton, racquetball); however, some require use of the hand (e.g., volleyball or handball). Net and wall games are subdivided into games in which opposing teams are separated by a court (e.g., volleyball, tennis, badminton) or share the court (e.g., racquetball, handball, squash).

Target Games

Target games include activities during which the performer competes without direct body contact or physical confrontation during the competition. The main goal of target games is accuracy. During target games, competitors wait until the activity has been completed by other performers before beginning their attempts (e.g., golf, archery, and billiards). The focus of target games is self-testing. The winner is generally the performer with the highest score (except in golf). Target games are subdivided by the positioning of the teams with respect to one another, directly opposing (e.g., croquet) or indirectly opposing (e.g., archery).

Fielding Games

Fielding games are team games in which the contest begins with one team occupying positions throughout the field (the fielders) or with one player who throws the ball (pitcher) toward a player on the opposing team. Examples of fielding sports include softball, baseball, rounders, cricket, and kickball. All fielding games use a striking implement except for kickball. A team scores points by the number of runs counterclockwise around bases only when batting or kicking. The offensive team strikes the ball into the defensive team's territory. The defensive team fields, throws, and catches the ball in an effort to prevent the offensive team from scoring runs. Generally, fielding games have no time restrictions. Instead, each team has a set number of opportunities to bat or kick and score runs. The team with the most runs wins the contest.

Personal Performance Games

There are many games in which individuals attempt to outperform their opponents, exceed their personal best performance measures, or both. **Personal performance games** can include racing activities such as cycling, running, and swimming; combative activities such as wrestling, judo, and boxing; and games with subjective performance measures such as diving and gymnastics. In recent decades many new performance games have emerged that are often referred to as "X Games" because of their extreme nature. Each of these activities requires unique skills and equipment, in addition to much intrinsic motivation and drive, as the games not only challenge individuals to compete against competitors but also with themselves.

Teaching Games for Transfer

When teaching games, the practitioner should emphasize movement concepts, principles, and strategies that will transfer from one game to another game in the same classification. Movement concepts are cognitive ideas, such as a particular pattern of movement (Rink, 1998). The concept of the overhand throwing pattern would be expected to transfer to some extent to throwing other implements (e.g., javelin) or to performing an overhand serve. When teaching a movement concept, an instructor should focus on key action words that can transfer from one situation to another. When teaching learners how to strike, an instructor can provide many different opportunities for striking an object. The instructor can focus on where to apply the force on the object and how

List all of the games you have participated in for each of the classifications.

	Invasion	Net or wall	Target	Fielding	Personal performance
Number of games					
Percentage					

Count the number of games you have participated under each classification and mark beside the "Number of games" row. Divide these numbers by the total number of games in all columns and multiply by 100%. Write these percentages in the percentage row.

1. Do you participate in one classification of games more than the others? If yes, what in particular interests you about these games?
2. Which categories have you to some extent avoided? Why do you think you have avoided these activities?
3. Provide some examples of games in which you have modified the secondary rules.
4. What did you modify and why?
5. Choose a game and discuss how you could modify it for one of the following:
   - An elderly person with some shoulder and wrist arthritis
   - A child with a sensory impairment (such as a visual or hearing impairment)
   - An elite athlete

this affects the trajectory of the object. The student should be able to apply the information learned from one experience, such as striking a ball with a bat, to striking with a racket.

Movement skills can also transfer from one game to another in the same games classification. Movement tactics include stealing the ball in defensive play in invasion games and how to control the ball in net or wall games. Movement strategies—ideas related to how movement is used in cooperative and competitive relationships with others (Rink, 1998)—such as offensively faking defensive players to gain an advantage are similar in basketball and hockey. Zone defensives are similar for many invasion games as well. Movement concepts, tactics, and strategies will transfer best if they are clearly explained and the learners are given a wide array of opportunities to apply them.

Summary

Skills are classified unidimensionally, according to movement precision, environmental predictability, time constraints, and the nature of the skill, as well as through a multidimensional classification system, Gentile's classification system. Skills with precise movements are classified as fine motor skills, while skills with large, less precise movements are gross motor skills. Motor skills that are performed in an unpredictable and variable environment are considered open skills, while those performed in a predictable and consistent environment are classified as closed skills. According to the initiation and pacing of the task, externally paced skills are skills that are controlled by an external stimulus, such as the start of a sprint, while self-paced skills are initiated and controlled by the individual. The nature of the movement is another method for classifying a task. Motor skills with clearly defined beginning and end points are discrete tasks (e.g., throwing). Continuous tasks, on the other hand, do not have a clearly defined beginning or end point. These movements are generally less complex and are continually repeated (e.g., cycling). Skills that require several discrete skills and that must occur in a specific order are serial skills (e.g., triple jump).

Gentile developed a multidimensional classification system (2000) that classifies motor skills by their regulatory and action requirements. The environmental context consists of regulatory conditions and intertrial variability. Two questions are asked about the environment. Are the environmental conditions stationary, or are they moving? Are the environmental conditions consistent or variable? The action requirements specify the movement characteristics of the performer. Is body transport required? Does the motor skill require an object or person to be manipulated? Practitioners who use a multidimensional system, such as Gentile's, will be able to individualize practice sessions for learners at various skill levels. More complex motor skills require an individual to be able to combine fundamental motor skills. By progressing through these stages, individuals are able to gradually increase the difficulty of the task until they are ready for full complexity of the motor skill.

This chapter explained the difference between motor skills and abilities. Abilities are genetically predetermined characteristics, while motor skills are learned and are therefore controlled by external factors. Motor skills can be acquired only if the learner has the underlying abilities; however, an individual can have the underlying abilities but not be skillful in a particular motor skill. Fleishman developed a taxonomy for abilities, separating each ability into one of two categories, physical proficiency motor abilities and perceptual–motor abilities.

Games were classified into six categories including: the purpose of the game, the start of the game, end of the game, rules, skill requirements, and scoring. Invasion games are games in which two teams attempt to invade the opposing team's territory in an effort to score points. Net and wall games include games that are either divided by a net or are played against a wall, with the goal of placing the ball in a position on the court such that it that cannot be returned by the opponent. Target games are played as a self-contest with the goal of accuracy and outperforming oneself and opponents. Fielding games are games in which the offensive team strikes a ball, invading the opponent's territory, and the defensive team fields the ball in an attempt to decrease the number of runs. Personal performance games are games in which performers participate individually in an effort to outperform themselves and opponents.

Games in each category have similar goals, purposes, and often similar skills. For example, offensive and defensive strategies in hockey can be learned much more quickly by learners who are familiar with basketball or soccer. Many strategies, tactics, and skills will transfer from one game to another in the same game classification, enabling quicker learning of the new game and better retention of the initial game.

Supplemental Activities

1. Conduct a web search on a game that you have never played before. You can choose a game that may be more popular in other countries than in the United States, such as cricket, curling, squash, or kabaddi. Classify the game. Describe the purpose of the game, how the game starts and ends, the basic rules of the game, the equipment, the skills required to perform the game, and how the game is scored. Name a game you are familiar with that is most similar to this game. Compare the two games; how are they similar and how are they different?

2a. Choose a game and name three primary and three secondary rules associated with that game. Devise three more secondary rules you could implement. (You can use the chart on page 46 to record your thoughts.) Describe how these rules would change the game.

2b. Play the game with your new secondary rules. Describe how these rule changes affected the game.

GAME			
	Primary rules	**Secondary rules**	**Your secondary rules**	**Game play changes**
1				
2				
3				

Stages of Skill Acquisition

CHAPTER OBJECTIVES

After reading this chapter, you should be able to

> describe how motor skills progress through each period in the mountain of motor development;

> compare and contrast three learning models—Fitts and Posner's, Gentile's, and Bernstein's;

> explain the learner's behavioral characteristics for the stages of each learning model; and

> understand the role of the practitioner for each of the learning stages.

It's Never Too Late to Learn How to Swim!

Henry is a 67-year-old fit and active retiree. Although Henry is an avid cyclist, tennis player, and golfer, he has never learned to swim. At an early age, Henry developed a fear of the water following a tragic boating accident. Now that Henry is retired and has more free time to enjoy life, he has decided to take swimming lessons and overcome his fear. During his first lesson, Henry's instructor notes that Henry has very little arm action. When Henry does use his arms, he moves with short downward thrusts in an effort to produce forward movement; however, this assists Henry only in staying afloat. His leg action appears more like a "bicycling" motion than a straight-leg flutter as performed by skilled swimmers. Henry's body position is at about 75 degrees, placing him in a more vertical position as opposed to a horizontal position that allows for fluid forward propulsion. These characteristics are found in all novice swimmers. Although Henry is an active, older man, his movements appear very similar to those of a young inexperienced child.

This example is certainly not unique to swimming. When learning a new motor skill, individuals progress through a series of stages, regardless of the motor skill. Several models, discussed in this chapter, address stages of learning and provide a framework for categorizing the skill level of the learner from novice to expert. These models enable practitioners to assess the level of the learner and more appropriately prepare practice sessions. When working with children, it is also important to understand motor skill development from infancy to adolescence. This chapter also examines how skills progress from prenatal development through skill proficiency using Clark's mountain of development.

Mountain of Motor Development

There is a misconception that maturation drives infant and child motor skill development (Clark, 2007). Although it may appear that a child has developed a new motor skill overnight, such as running, jumping, hopping, or catching, these skills do not magically appear. They must be taught and practiced. Children move the way they do because of individual and environmental constraints. Humans sit upright because of the biomechanical constraints of the human body and the gravitational forces imposed upon the body. If gravitational forces were removed (as in outer space), it is unlikely that infants would acquire the ability to sit upright. Humans are born with "preadapted" motor behaviors that predispose particular reflexes and actions; nonetheless, these are either reinforced or modified by constraints in the environment. These preadapted motor behaviors prepare the infant for acquiring basic motor skills that generally develop during the first year of life. The acquisition of these motor skills does not occur through maturation alone; rather these skills are honed by adaptations to changing constraints and through a learning process (Clark, 2007). As a normally developing infant continues to grow, he is able to use these developmental skills to perform increasingly complex skills such as many sport-specific skills.

Clark and Metcalfe (2002) developed a life span view of motor skill development. In this framework, separate periods were defined in which typical patterns of motor skill development occur in a particular order (figure 3.1). Clark and Metcalfe labeled this framework the mountain of motor development because each period builds on the previous period. This model describes motor skill development from birth to death, breaking down the development of skills into five periods.

The base of the mountain is the **prenatal period**, consisting of the last two trimesters of pregnancy. During this time, there is much movement of the fetus in the womb. The initial stage, the **reflexive period**, occurs following birth and lasts only two weeks. As suggested by the title of the stage, movements are reflexive as the newborn is adjusting to many sensory changes such as bright lights and sounds. Following the first two weeks, the **preadapted period** begins. Infants start interacting with the environment by making goal-directed movements. During this period, phylogenetic motor behaviors prevail, such as sitting up, standing, crawling, and walking. When the infant is able to independently walk

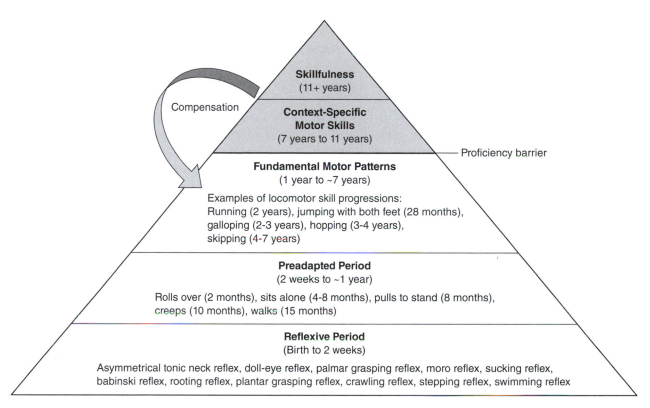

FIGURE 3.1   The mountain of motor development. *Note:* These ages are approximations. Each individual is unique and progresses at his own rate.

Adapted, by permission, from J.E. Clark and J.M. Metcalfe, 2002, The mountain of motor development: A metaphor. In *Motor development: Research and reviews*, vol. 2, edited by J.E. Clark and J.H. Humphrey (Reston, VA: National Association for Sport and Physical Education), 163-190.

and self-feed, that is, perform the two fundamental skills necessary for basic survival, the infant has progressed to **fundamental motor patterns**. Fundamental motor patterns are basic movements such as throwing, catching, hopping, and jumping that form a base for more complex sport-specific movement patterns. These patterns are mature or well developed around the age of 7 years (Clark & Metcalfe, 2002).

From here, children begin to refine these fundamental motor patterns to movements specific for sports or other movement forms (e.g., a striking pattern may be modified for racket sports, baseball, or golf). This period is termed the **context-specific motor skills period**. The period at the peak of the mountain is the **skillfulness period**. This period does not separate individuals of different skill levels (junior varsity, varsity, college, professional). To reach this period, an individual needs to be skilled at the movement. Those who aspire to reach the very peak of the mountain must understand that this is a very long and demanding journey. If an individual has incurred an injury or must make some other adaptation due to declines resulting from aging, she has entered the **compensation period**. If she is able to fully recover from the injury, she may return to the former level of skillfulness. However, biological changes due to permanent injuries or aging effects may cause the individual to remain at a lower position on the mountain.

What Do You Think?

Choose two specific motor skills. Define how the motor skill is performed skillfully. For example, an experienced basketball player can perform a layup even when faced with a defender or increased game pressure, while a novice basketball player is unable to dribble to the basket and shoot. The novice must then focus on the fundamental motor skill, such as dribbling and jumping. Work backward and describe the underlying motor skills and patterns that are required for your selected skills from the preadapted period to the skillfulness period.

Motor skill	Skillfulness	Context-specific motor skills	Fundamental motor skills	Preadapted period
Basketball layup	Right, left, jump, shoot; pattern is performed well in spite of external influences (e.g., defenders)	• Basketball shooting • Stepping and shooting	• Jumping • Dribbling	• Pull to stand • Stand alone • Walk with and then without assistance

Motor Learning Stages

Learners progress through a series of stages when improving motor skill proficiency, whether they are learning how to throw a ball, ride a unicycle, or type on a keyboard. By knowing and understanding the characteristics of each stage, practitioners are better prepared to meet the needs of the learner. There are several models that address the behavioral features of these stages and provide a unique perspective on the behavioral aspects of each stage.

Fitts and Posner's Learning Stages

Fitts and Posner (1967) proposed a three-stage learning model (figure 3.2). Regardless of age or skill, all learners go through each of these stages when advancing from a novice to an expert level. This model classifies the stages

Cognitive Stage (Beginner)

How do I produce this movement pattern?

Performer's Behavior

- Learning the fundamental movement patterns
- High cognitive activity (attention to movement and self-talk)
- Inconsistent performance
- Many gross errors
- Greatest performance improvements occur during this stage

Practitioner's Role

- Assisting the learner in understanding the movement pattern
- Teaching strategies are most effective during this stage (e.g., verbal instruction, demonstrations, modeling, etc.)

Associative Stage (Intermediate)

I've got it! Now, how do I get to the next level?

Performer's Behavior

- More consistent performance
- Fewer errors
- Fewer attentional demands
- More gradual performance improvements
- Motor stage

Practitioner's Role

- Practice design
- Facilitating error detection and correction

Autonomous Stage (Advanced)

I'm on top! How do I stay here?

Performer's Role

- High level of skill proficiency
- Performance largely automatic
- Very few errors
- Very consistent
- Focus on strategies

Practitioner's Role

- Practice design
- Refining performance
- Motivating the performer

FIGURE 3.2

The progression from beginner to advanced level using Fitts and Posner's learning stages.

around behavioral changes that can be observed in the performer. Practitioners have distinct roles at each level of learning.

Cognitive Stage

During the first stage, the **cognitive stage**, the learner's main goal is to understand the basic components of the motor skill movement pattern. This stage is termed the cognitive stage because learners require a considerable amount of mental activity to be able to understand the movement pattern and appropriately coordinate the limbs. Novice learners often mentally verbalize their movements (e.g., a dancer may count the beats of the steps, or a triple jumper may say "left, right, left, jump" to help reinforce the movements until the movement pattern has been learned). During the cognitive stage, the learner often is easily confused and has many questions. If you were water skiing for the first time, you might have questions like these: How do I position my feet? Do I bend my knees? How fast do I stand up when I'm being pulled out of the water? Although experienced water skiers do not even think about how to get out of the water, novice water skiers must attend to the position of their body segments and the timing of their movements. Although attending to their movements is a necessary process in learning any skill, it often causes movements to appear choppy, uncoordinated, and awkward.

During the initial stages of learning, individuals must attempt various techniques in a sort of trial-and-error process until they have achieved a certain level of success. It is not surprising, then, that the use of verbal instruction, feedback, modeling, and other teaching strategies is most effective during the cognitive stage. The largest gains in learning occur during the cognitive stage compared to any other stage. The learners are beginning with very little knowledge of the motor skill and make rapid gains in performance as they learn the basics of the task.

Associative Stage

Once learners have a basic understanding of the task and have shown significant improvement in the movement pattern, they have progressed to the **associative stage** of learning. In the associative stage, the goal of the task has shifted to refining the movement as opposed to learning how to solve the movement problem. Performance improvements are more gradual than the rapid gains observed during the cognitive stage. The learner, however, is able to perform more consistently and focus on error detection and correction. The individual no longer requires as much attention to the production of the movement and is able to attend to other sources of information. The verbal component ("self-talk") that was prominent in the cognitive stage is no longer present in the production of the movement pattern, as it is no longer necessary or beneficial.

The role of the instructor has shifted when the learner is in the associative stage from instruction to designing appropriate and effective practice sessions (refer to chapters 13 and 14). The learner understands the basic movement pattern, but will still benefit from instructor feedback regarding his errors and fine-tuning his movements.

Autonomous Stage

The final stage of learning in the Fitts and Posner model is the **autonomous stage**. For learners to progress to the final stage, they must practice for an extended period of time, often many years. Most people do not make it to the

What Do You Think?

Choose a motor skill in which you are moderately to highly skilled. Discuss the behavioral aspects of the performance for an individual in each of Fitts and Posner's three learning stages and develop strategies for instructing a learner in each stage (practitioner's role). An example is provided for the motor skill of juggling.

BEHAVIORAL ASPECTS			
Motor skill	**Cognitive**	**Associative**	**Autonomous**
Juggling	• Can make very few catches • Self-talk • Much attention required • Does not know how to compensate for poor tosses • Fast improvement after movement pattern is learned • Visually tracks ball movements	• More confidence • Can make many more catches • Attention shifted to apex of the juggling trajectory • Can detect errors but cannot always correct them while juggling	• Very confident • Can perform multiple activities while juggling • Can sustain pattern for a long duration
PRACTITIONER'S ROLE			

	• Demonstrate
	• Provide verbal instructions
	• Discuss the juggling pattern and the movement of the limbs
	• Answer questions
	• Provide a lot of feedback
		• Some feedback
		• Increase challenges of the task
		• Motivate the learner
		• Design practice sessions
			• Further increase challenge
			  - Add distractions
			  - Add secondary task
			  - Try more difficult task (e.g., juggling with clubs or more balls)
			• Motivate the learner

BEHAVIORAL ASPECTS			
Motor skill	**Cognitive**	**Associative**	**Autonomous**
PRACTITIONER'S ROLE			

autonomous stage of learning. During this stage, the performer is so skilled that the movement appears automatic, or without thought. The individual can perform the task with very little effort and is able to perform an additional task at the same time; an example is a circus performer riding a unicycle on a high wire while simultaneously juggling. In this stage, the mover is able to focus on decision-making strategies, which are critical for high-level performance in open skills such as wrestling or rugby. This stage is reserved for very skilled performers and is considered the highest skill level. Performers in the autonomous stage consistently perform very well and are confident in their performance capabilities.

Although performers who reach this stage may be at the top of their game, this does not mean that instructors no longer play an important role. Although the amount of improvement may appear quite minimal, performers can continue to fine-tune their performance (Coker, 2003). It is also important for instructors to assist in the maintenance of the performer's level of skill. Practitioners should focus on the details of the movement pattern and motivating the performer. It is not only difficult to reach the top; it is challenging to stay there!

Try This

Go to an open gym, court, or field and observe the people playing a pickup game. Try to find the most and least skilled players. Describe specific behavioral characteristics about each of these players. Explain why you categorized these players as most and least skilled.

Bernstein's Learning Stages

Another view of the learning stages is based on the degrees of freedom problem. Bernstein (1967) identified the challenge of organizing a complex structure of joints and muscles to produce smooth goal-oriented movement as the degrees of freedom problem. **Degrees of freedom** are the number of functional units that are required to solve a movement problem. Degrees of freedom can be thought of as the number of possible solutions to a performance task. A movement that requires only the motion of the arm would include seven degrees of freedom at the joint level (three degrees of freedom at the shoulder, one at the elbow, two at the wrist, and one at the radioulnar joint). However, the movement possibilities of the arm are also controlled by numerous muscles, which increases the degrees of freedom. If we were to take into consideration the degrees of freedom at the neuronal level, the number would increase exponentially. Keep in mind that very few movements involve only one body segment. Many movements require whole body coordination. That would equate to a nearly endless number of possibilities to produce even a seemingly simple movement such as taking a step. Using the notion of the degrees of freedom problem, Vereijken (1991) proposed a three-stage learning model.

Stage 1: Freezing the Limbs

In order to perform a novel task, novices simplify the movement problem of having to control an overwhelming number of degrees of freedom by eliminating some. The novice does not understand the optimal method of managing these degrees of freedom in order to perform the new movement pattern, so the individual reduces these options into a more controllable number (Vereijken, van Emmerik, Whiting, & Newell, 1992). Vereijken described this process as "freezing the limbs." This is accomplished by keeping certain joint angles rigid throughout the movement or by temporarily coupling multiple joints together such that they move as one segment. Although freezing the degrees of freedom simplifies the task, the movement appears very rigid in its execution, and the novice's ability to adapt to any unexpected changes is poor. For example, when a young child throws a ball, she uses only her arm. The legs and trunk are not used to assist in the throw as they are in more advanced throwers. Inexperienced throwers also eliminate the backswing. The throw is completed almost exclusively at the elbow joint.

To assist a beginner during the freezing the limbs stage, practitioners should simplify the task. By simplifying the task, the practitioner is encouraging learners to focus on fewer degrees of freedom and increasing their opportunities for success. For example, in instructing learners how to juggle a soccer ball, it would be more effective to have them attempt to keep the ball in the air by hitting the ball only with one leg than to encourage them to control the ball in the air with both legs, chest, shoulder, and head. Clinicians should begin rehabilitation exercises that require only one plane of motion, fewer joints, or both. As learners or patients improve, one can increase the difficulty of the task by encouraging movements that require more degrees of freedom.

 ## Research Notes: You're Staying Too Still!

A study completed several decades ago comparing novice and expert pistol shooters revealed that while novices tightly lock the degrees of freedom in their arms, expert shooters do not show any locking of their upper limb degrees of freedom (Arutyunyan, Gurfinkel, & Mirskii, 1968, 1969). Instead, expert pistol shooters use compensatory actions in the arm, allowing them to perform with more arm control and less pistol motion. As suggested by Bernstein's learning model, novices are simplifying the task by freezing their limbs.

Stage 2: Releasing the Limbs

As learners become more comfortable with the basic movement pattern, they are able to gradually release the constraints imposed on the degrees of freedom. This enables the movement to appear more fluid and allows the learner to gain more control over the production of the movement pattern. At this point, the degrees of freedom become incorporated into larger functional units of action, termed **coordinative structures**. Coordinative structures are formed by constraining or limiting potential options (e.g., muscles and joints) appropriately for a particular movement pattern. For instance, pole-vaulters form coordinative structures to be able to swing their trail leg forward and row their arms down while also keeping both arms and their left leg straight. Some coordinative structures appear at birth, providing the groundwork for phylogenetic motor behaviors (e.g., grasping, walking) that will be developed later with growth and maturation.

If you've ever watched people ice skate for the first time, you probably noticed how they stiffen their knees and move each leg as if it were a single segment. Their movements are very rigid and deliberate. Experienced ice skaters tend to move fluidly across the ice. Professional ice skaters are able to exploit the environment by propelling their bodies into the air, completing multiple turns and landing smoothly.

In the chapter opening vignette, Henry reduced the degrees of freedom of his movement when learning how to swim. Rather than freely moving his arms and legs, Henry moved his arms in a short downward pushing motion and his legs in a bicycle pattern, causing him to produce more of a doggy paddle than a fluid, advanced formal stroke. Stiffening his limb movements caused his body to be in an upright vertical position, preventing him from producing much forward propulsion.

Think of two other activities in which Bernstein's learning stages are noticeably visible. Describe how the learner's movements appear in each of the three stages.

Motor skill	Stage 1: Freezing the limbs	Stage 2: Releasing the limbs	Stage 3: Exploiting the environment
Swimming	• Little to no arm or leg action occurs. • Arm action that does occur is a simple, short downward push. • Leg action that does occur is a circular bicycling action. • Overall, little to no forward propulsion occurs.	• More arm and leg action • Arms: long push-pull • Legs: bent-knee flutter kick • Overall: rudimentary crawl	• Arms: lift propulsion and bent elbow; over-arm • Legs: straight-leg flutter • Overall: advanced crawl, rhythmic breathing

Once learners have gained a basic level of proficiency, they use significantly more degrees of freedom than when they began practicing the motor skill. The practitioner should continue to encourage learners to increase their range of motion and, depending on the skill, the speed of the movement as the learner's movements become smoother and more controlled.

Stage 3: Exploiting the Environment

During the final stage of learning, the learner continues releasing degrees of freedom until all of the degrees of freedom necessary to accomplish the task have been released. At this point the performer is maximizing muscular efficiency through the use of the optimal number of degrees of freedom and is able to exploit environmental passive forces (i.e., gravity or inertia). Learners at this stage would be considered experts. It is at this stage that figure skaters can land impressive jumps, wide receivers can make unbelievable catches while leaping into the air and avoiding defenders, and tennis players can maintain complete control of the flight patterns of the ball.

The main role of a practitioner with a learner in stage 3 is to design variable practice sessions that push performers to continue extending their capabilities. A practitioner must keep the task interesting and fresh for performers so that they continue to stay motivated.

Evidence for Bernstein's Learning Stages

Researchers in one investigation examined the degrees of freedom by teaching participants how to operate a ski simulator apparatus. Initially, the participants moved very rigidly, fixing their lower limb joints (Vereijken et al., 1992). This enabled them to move with relatively high frequency (quick movements), but low amplitude (small side-to-side movements). The cross correlations were very high between joints during the early stages of learning. With practice, the cross correlations (couplings between joints) decreased, indicating that the degrees of freedom were being released. At this point, the participants were moving with more amplitude (further distance covered), but this came at the cost of frequency, meaning they were unable to move back and forth at the same rate. As practice continued, the cross correlations continued to decrease and movement frequency continually increased, until the performers were able to move with the same or greater frequency as in the initial practice trials while maintaining large movement amplitudes. Again, these results indicate that initially learners freeze their degrees of freedom in order to gain control over the movement. They "freeze" degrees of freedom because they are afraid of falling! As the learners' confidence and familiarity with the task increase with practice, the number of degrees of freedom also increases.

Another research study compared dominant limb movements with nondominant limb movements during handwriting to investigate whether there was a difference in the number of degrees of freedom involved in the two limbs (Newell & van Emmerik, 1989). Limb dominance provides an opportunity to compare the effect of skill acquisition within the same participant. The investigators found that the nondominant limb used fewer degrees of freedom than the dominant limb. These findings provide more evidence in support of Bernstein's (1967) learning stages by demonstrating that the degrees of freedom were released in the more practiced, dominant limb as opposed to the nondominant limb. These results were observed through high correlations between the joints in the nondominant limb. The authors also evaluated the independence between multiple joints. Cross correlations reveal the independence of two variables, with high cross correlations indicating that the variables are highly interdependent. In this case, if one body segment moved, such as the shoulder, then movement of another body segment such as the elbow joint would occur. When the participants were writing with their nondominant limb, they were freezing their degrees of freedom. In contrast, when they were writing with their dominant limb, each body segment was moving independently.

Evidence Against Bernstein's Learning Stages

In more recent years, the Bernstein learning stages have been challenged because they do not consider all influencing factors inherent in the performance of the motor skill. Completion of a motor skill occurs as the learner's characteristics (including structural constraints, such as height and weight, and functional constraints such as motivation and movement experience), the task (goals, equipment, and rules), and the environment (physical and socio-cultural factors) interact. It was proposed that the order of the learning stages is dependent on the task goal and the constraints of an individual.

To examine how changing the constraints of the task affects behavioral characteristics of the learning stages, researchers had participants practice maintaining balance on a moving platform that oscillated in an anteroposterior direction (Ko, Challis, & Newell, 2003). In contrast to what happened in the study by Vereijken and colleagues, participants produced large ranges of motion at all joints, including the neck, hip, knee, and ankle. With practice, rather than increasing the amount of motion, the participants decreased their joint motion. The learners were gradually freezing the degrees of freedom that were not essential for that task. Learners decreased motion in some degrees of freedom, but not in others.

It appears that the participants were initially decreasing their degrees of freedom in an effort to find a new coordination mode, one that was more efficient and stable (Newell, Kugler, van Emmerik, & McDonald, 1989). This new movement pattern would have a stronger attractor state (refer to chapter 1). The main suggestion from this research is that there are many methods of solving a movement task. The most appropriate method for learning a new motor skill is determined by the interaction between the structural and functional constraints of the learner; the goals, equipment, and rules of the task; and the environmental constraints imposed upon the learner.

Try This

Throw a ball five to 10 times with as much force as you can using your dominant limb. Then switch limbs and throw five to 10 times with your nondominant limb. It is most likely that you were not able to throw the ball with as much distance or velocity with the nondominant limb, but what about the movement characteristics of your throws? Describe what was different about the kinematics of your throws with your dominant versus nondominant limb. You may find it easier to observe the differences when watching a friend throw with his dominant and nondominant arms. Which limb used more degrees of freedom (e.g., contralateral step, increased range of motion of the arm)? Explain why there is a difference in the number of degrees of freedom used in each limb to accomplish the same task.

Gentile's Learning Stages

A two-stage learning model was proposed by Gentile (1972, 1987, 2000). Gentile's learning stages were developed to assist practitioners by not only describing the nature of the movement, but also providing instructional strategies for each learning stage.

Stage 1: Getting the Idea of the Movement

The first stage of learning is the "**getting the idea of the movement**" **stage**. The getting the idea of the movement stage is similar to Fitts and Posner's cognitive stage of learning. During this stage the learner has two main goals: to understand the movement coordination required to perform the movement task and to determine the regulatory and nonregulatory conditions of the movement. Gentile used the term **regulatory conditions** to refer to those conditions that provide relevant information for a motor skill. Regulatory conditions for the game of basketball would include the ball, the positions of opponents and teammates, and the position of the player relative to the basket. In order to perform proficiently at the game of basketball, a player must selectively attend to these important aspects. To produce a successful outcome, an individual's movements are dependent on the external environment (Luria, 1966). Regulatory conditions for a simple motor skill such as walking down the street would include the surface of support (concrete, ice, gravel, etc.), other pedestrians, and objects along the path. A more complex motor skill such as hitting a baseball with a bat requires the player to make contact with the ball; to do this, the player must understand both the positional (spatial) and the time (temporal) characteristics of the ball (Gentile, 2000). For the batting example, there is a much greater margin of error than for the walking example. If the batter anticipates or misjudges the pitch, then the bat will not make contact with the ball. The movement pattern executed by the batter will depend on the spatial and temporal characteristics of the environment and the batter's spatial–temporal skills.

It is perhaps even more important for a learner to ignore nonrelevant cues, which Gentile refers to as **nonregulatory conditions**. Nonregulatory conditions distract the learner from important relevant cues, preventing the learner from performing skillfully or even accomplishing the goal at all. Practitioners should emphasize the regulatory conditions during early skill acquisition to help learners avoid the acquisition of bad habits and to maximize learning during practice sessions. Learners who are more easily distracted, especially children, should frequently be redirected toward the regulatory conditions. The learner must not only be able to selectively attend to the relevant cues (regulatory conditions) but must also be able to ignore the irrelevant cues (nonregulatory conditions). A basketball player shooting a free throw must focus on the release of the ball and the rim of the basket while ignoring the sounds of the crowd screaming and stomping their feet on the bleachers. Most often, those distractions are not present during practice. The pedestrian needs to focus on oncoming traffic and traffic signals when crossing a busy street and avoid distractions from cell phone conversations, music, or other external noise. However, it is important for learners to practice under varying nonregulatory conditions to be better prepared for performances or real-world situations.

It is also critical to note that during the first stage of learning, the emphasis cannot be solely on the movement. It is essential that learners recognize how

Tennis

to identify and select the regulatory conditions that influence their movement. This information is necessary for organizing a successful movement pattern.

The practitioner's role during Gentile's getting the idea of the movement stage (stage 1) is to clearly and concisely instruct the learner how to perform the movement pattern. The practitioner should emphasize the basics of the task, such as the task goals and objectives, through demonstrations and verbal instructions. The learner's attention should be directed toward the relevant stimuli in the environment. For example, a batter should be told to focus on the pitcher's release point during the pitcher's windup. Novice batters often alter their visual focus between the release point and the pitcher's head, whereas experts maintain a steady focus on the release point (Shank & Haywood, 1987). By focusing on the relevant stimulus (the release point), experts were able to accurately assess the pitch nearly 100% of the time, while novices who fluctuated between the head and the release point during the windup could accurately identify only a little more than half of the pitches. Altering their visual focus caused the novices to miss critical components of the pitch, which decreased their chances of making contact with the ball.

Stage 2: Fixation and Diversification

Once learners understand the basic movement pattern, they advance to the second learning stage, the fixation and diversification stage. The key element during this stage is refining the movement pattern (similar to what occurs in Fitts and Posner's stage 2, the associative stage) and maintaining consistent performance (similar to what occurs in Fitts and Posner's stage 3, the autonomous stage). Gentile separates the stage into two subcomponents dependent on the predictability of the environment and the skill level of the individual (figure 3.3).

- *Fixation.* When one is learning a closed skill, such as performing a power clean or playing billiards, the focus should be on consistency. The learner must refine the movement by determining how to most accurately perform the motor skill and then reliably replicate the same action time and time again. Learners who are performing a routine, as in gymnastics, figure skating, or dance, practice

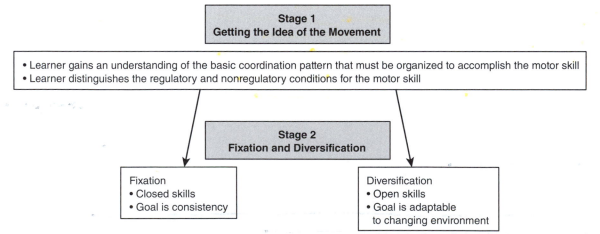

FIGURE 3.3 Gentile's two-stage learning model.

and refine the movements until they are able to consistently perform the movement sequence well. For rehabilitation settings, therapists first assist patients in performing exercises under very controlled settings. Gentile refers to this as fixation, because the learners are focusing on consistently reproducing the same movement pattern. If, however, this was all they did, the performances would be very boring to watch.

- *Diversification.* Open skills, such as passing the puck to a teammate during a hockey game, are performed in an unpredictable environment. Successful performers of open skills must be very adaptable. Performers cannot predict how the opposing team is going to respond to their play and so must alter their response to accommodate such a change. When learning an open skill, learners must focus on diversifying their movement pattern by practicing the motor skill under many different conditions. For learning a closed motor skill, the main objective is consistency, or in Gentile's terms, fixation. The objective in open motor skills is adaptability, or diversification. Learners who can perform a motor skill very consistently under predictable conditions will not be prepared when the environment unexpectedly changes, so they must be able to make quick decisions and adapt their movement pattern to accommodate such variations. Patients undergoing physical or occupational therapy must not only learn how to perform the exercises in the controlled setting of the clinic, but more importantly, must learn how to adapt the exercises so that they can perform them at home. Furthermore, the activities or motor skills they are learning or relearning must enable them to circumvent many different obstacles and adjust to varying surfaces, slopes, and objects.

Once the learner has progressed to the second stage of learning, the fixation and diversification stage, instructional strategies should focus on refining the movement pattern until the performer is able to complete the movement pattern consistently. Gentile refers to this as fixation. The movement pattern should be practiced repeatedly under similar regulatory conditions, while nonregulatory conditions should be varied. For example, during a closed skill such as bowling, the regulatory conditions (i.e., length of lane, size of gutters, number of pins, size of pins, etc.) should not be changed, while the nonregulatory conditions (i.e., crowd noise, level of fatigue, motivation level, number of pins remaining, etc.) should be varied.

If the motor skill is an open skill, the practitioner will advance to a diversification strategy after, and only after, the learner is proficient at performing the motor skill consistently by using the fixation strategy. Again, the fixation strategy includes teaching under similar regulatory conditions and variable nonregulatory conditions. Regardless of whether the motor skill is open or closed, instructional strategies will be similar during stage 1, getting the idea of the movement, and then progress to stage 2, fixation. When practicing closed skills, the learner will continue using the fixation strategy. For open skills, the practitioner should vary both the regulatory and nonregulatory conditions (diversification strategy) only after the learner can proficiently perform under stable regulatory conditions and variable nonregulatory conditions. For example, a punter should be able to punt the ball consistently without defenders prior to punting with defenders. Table 3.1 presents an example of teaching a learner how to shoot a basketball using Gentile's learning stages.

TABLE 3.1 Example of Practitioner's Role in Using Gentile's Learning Stages to Teach Shooting a Basketball

Stage 1: Getting the idea of the movement	• Teach the goal of a basketball shot. • Provide a demonstration—you could use a common method such as BEEF (**B**alance, **E**yes on rim, **E**lbow, **F**ollow-through). • Allow the learner to practice from the same position on the court repeatedly before moving onto a different position. • Provide feedback regarding the shot—such as "shoot with more arc," "increase the bend of your knees," "don't forget to follow through."
Stage 2a: Fixation	• Have learners practice shots without defenders at the foul line. • Have them practice when fatigued. • Have them practice under various motivation levels. • Have learners practice with crowd noise. • Have them practice under various levels of stress (e.g., provide incentives or punishments for missed shots, altering the importance of the shot).
Stage 2b: Diversification	• Have learners practice shots with the previous fixation conditions varied while also practicing at different positions on the court with defenders.

 Research Notes: Link to Dynamic Systems Theory

The dynamic systems perspective supports the changing dynamics and coordination patterns discussed in each of the three learning models. According to the dynamic systems perspective, learners begin producing a pattern of movement that is familiar to them, such as one from a similar motor skill (Zanone & Kelso, 1994). For instance, a skilled tennis player who has never played racquetball will likely swing at the racquetball with very little snap of the wrist. In order to control the ball in tennis, players are often initially taught to hit forehand and backhand with the whole arm from the shoulder. In racquetball, there is no need to hit the ball above a net, into a court. Rather, the player can strategically hit the ball with great force onto the wall, whereas in tennis, the player must clear the net and land inside the boundaries of the court. Racquetball players can generate more force and power by snapping the elbow and wrist when swinging at the ball. Swinging with the whole arm is a coordination pattern that has been well developed by a tennis player. This pattern would "work" in the racquetball court, but not as effectively. This coordination pattern would be a strong attractor state with a deep basin for a tennis player. As the player practices and progresses with the new game of racquetball, she is likely to vary her swing to accommodate the changing constraints of the enclosed court and the different elastic properties of the ball and the strings of the racket. With practice and instruction, the learner's swing would transition from the initial preferred coordination pattern of swinging with the whole arm to a new attractor state of swinging with more elbow and wrist action.

It is important to consider prior movement experiences before instructing a new motor skill. Prior movement experiences will strongly influence the coordination patterns that a learner adopts, for better or worse. A practitioner should be aware of the learner's prior movement experiences and adjust teaching strategies accordingly to maximize the learner's rate of learning.

What Do You Think?

Refer to the tennis and racquetball example just discussed in Research Notes: Link to Dynamic Systems Theory on page 62.

1. What is the rate limiter (refer back to chapter 1) for the tennis player who is learning how to play racquetball?
2. For tennis, at what stage (using Fitts and Posner's learning model) would you classify the athlete? Explain why.
3. How would you classify the racquetball athlete using Fitts and Posner's learning stages? Explain why.
4. What instructional strategies would be most appropriate for the athlete in tennis?
5. What instructional strategies would be most appropriate for the athlete in racquetball? (*Hint:* The instructional strategies should be dependent on the learner's stage of learning for each motor skill.)

Practical Use of the Learning Models

These three learning models provide the practitioner with a multilevel perspective on motor learning (Rose & Christina, 2006). An emphasis on the impact the environment has on the learning process is stressed in both Bernstein's learning stages and Gentile's learning stages. In Bernstein's learning model, the individual's perception is affected by the changing dynamics of the environment. Gentile emphasized how instruction should be designed based on the predictability of environmental influences. Fitts and Posner's learning model defined cognitive and behavior processes across the skill level of the performer. A practitioner who understands how the environment affects the learning process will be able to manipulate the environment to optimize learning.

When one is providing learners with initial instruction, the focus should be on the organization of the learner and then goal of the task. The practitioner should provide learners with adequate instruction to get them started performing the movement task, with the goal of allowing them to explore movement options while attempting to produce the basic coordination pattern. During this time period, movement errors can be seen as positive because learners are discovering the patterns of movement that work and discarding those that do not work. Novice performers should be expected to show rapid improvements in performance. This rate of improvement will gradually taper off with continuing practice.

Learners who are able to perform the basic movement pattern should then focus on refining the movement with the goal of increasing their probability of success. Once the learner is able to consistently produce a movement pattern, he can focus on adapting the movement pattern. This will enable him to produce the movement pattern under various internal (i.e., fatigue levels, motivation levels, importance of outcome, etc.) and external conditions (crowd noise; position, angle, and distance of movement; positions of other players, etc.).

These three models provide the practitioner with a multilevel perspective on the learning progression. They provide a background to the cognitive and physical components of the learning stages as well as instructional strategies appropriate for each stage. A practitioner who fully understands the learning process will have the skills necessary to properly manipulate the learning environment and the learner (Rose & Christina, 2006).

Summary

Many models have been proposed to describe the acquisition of motor skills. Each of these models contributes to our understanding of how individuals learn motor skills and helps the practitioner structure, design, and implement practice sessions with the goal of maximizing motor learning. It is important for practitioners to keep in mind the task to be completed and the individuality of the learner when structuring each practice session.

Motor skill progression was defined developmentally by Clark and Metcalf's (2002) mountain of motor development. These stages used the analogy between developing skill and climbing a mountain. The climb begins at birth (reflexive period) and continues through skillfulness. Although all individuals develop at different rates, the mountain of motor development illustrates how individuals progress from one stage to another and even incorporates descent down the mountain (although unintentional) following injury and declines due to aging (compensation).

Fitts and Posner (1967) developed a three-stage model for the acquisition of any motor skill. The first stage, the cognitive stage, is marked by many errors, inconsistencies, and self-talk. Once learners have learned the basic components of the task, they progress to the associative stage in which the errors are few in number and less gross. The final stage, which many people may never reach, is the autonomous stage. At this stage the motor skill appears effortless.

Vereijken (1991) proposed a three-stage model from the notion of the degrees of freedom problem. In the first stage, novices tend to freeze their limbs in an effort to simplify the movement. Freezing the limbs causes the movements to appear very stiff and deliberate, but it reduces the learner's risk for error. As learners progress, they increase the number of degrees of freedom, allowing their movements to be much more fluid. It is during the second stage of learning that the learner is releasing the degrees of freedom. When learners have achieved a high level of proficiency, they have reached the third stage, exploitation of the environment. In this stage the learner has released all of the degrees of freedom necessary to execute the movement pattern.

The third learning model, proposed by Gentile (1972, 1987, 2000), was intended to provide instructional strategies to practitioners. During the first stage, the "getting the idea of the movement" stage, the learner focuses on the movement basics. During this stage, learners are not focused solely on producing the movement pattern. They must also learn the regulatory and nonregulatory conditions specific to a given movement pattern. After learners have acquired a basic concept of the movement pattern, they progress to the fixation and diversification stage. Regardless of whether the motor skill is an open or a closed skill, learners must first attempt to increase the consistency of the movement. They accomplish this by practicing the motor skill under the same regulatory conditions but under varying nonregulatory conditions. If the motor skill is an open skill, the learner will eventually need to learn a multitude of variations of the movement patterns. After learners have achieved a high level of consistency by fixating on the same regulatory conditions, the practice sessions should be designed to provide practice on a large number of movement modifications to prepare them for an unpredictable environment.

It is important to understand each of these models for effective teaching and learning. By using a multilevel perspective, an instructor will have more tools to manipulate the environment to accommodate behavioral, cognitive, and physical changes in the performer with increased skillfulness.

Supplemental Activities

1. Bernstein's learning stages: YouTube has become a popular portal for searching for videos, from educational videos to cartoons to homemade videos. Many individuals are very proud of their skills and post videos of themselves performing these skills. See if you can search YouTube to find three skill levels of soccer jugglers. Soccer juggling is an excellent example of Bernstein's learning stages because beginners generally limit their juggling to the use of only one leg, sometimes only the foot or the knee. As learners increase their skill level, they begin to use more and more degrees of freedom by introducing more and more limb segments into their juggling.

- Were you able to find three soccer jugglers you would classify as being in stages 1, 2, and 3 of Bernstein's learning stages? Explain your rationale for these classifications. Describe the jugglers' behavioral characteristics.
- Try to search other motor skills (e.g., ice skating, throwing a ball, skateboarding) that you could classify into Bernstein's three learning stages. Describe how performance of these skills fits into each of these classifications.

2. Mountain of motor development: Choose a motor skill you would describe yourself as skillful in. Working backward down the mountain of motor development, explain what prior skills and experiences led you to achieve your level of proficiency at that motor skill.

- At what age did you become skillful?
- What context-specific skills, which were critical to developing the level of skill you have attained now, did you practice at an earlier age?
- Step back to fundamental motor skills. What fundamental motor skills were critical? Explain why these were essential.
- Talk to your parents. Ask them if they did anything during the pre-adapted period that may have helped you advance your manipulative skills, postural skills, and locomotor skills.

Methodological Considerations

CHAPTER OBJECTIVES

After reading this chapter, you should be able to

> describe multiple indicators of motor learning;

> label performance curves and explain the limitations;

> understand transfer, including types of transfer, how to measure transfer, and how to foster positive transfer; and

> calculate retention and transfer measures.

If You Don't at First Succeed, Try, Try Again

Kalil moved to the United States from India when he was 12 years old. Kalil considered himself a versatile athlete until he moved to the United States and was introduced to some new sports that were very different from the sports he had played in India. At first, he had difficulty not only with the movement patterns but also with the rules and strategies, as they were so different. Initially, he took particular interest in baseball because it was similar to one of the sports he had played, cricket. This previous movement experience in cricket helped him to quickly learn the game of baseball. Kalil was also interested in basketball. With no previous movement experiences in basketball or a related sport, he had a lot of difficulty at first with the mechanics of his shot. He shot the ball with both hands, and his shots were very erratic. Although Kalil's initial performances were poor, he remained very motivated and quickly excelled not only with shooting but also with controlling the ball. He was able to consistently make shots from many spots on the basketball court, including in the lane, beyond the arc, and midrange. With Kalil's increased improvement with the ball, he was then able to focus more on strategizing during ball play, and keeping defenders off balance through shot fakes before and after the drive.

Although it is quite evident through his sustained improvement that Kalil had learned the motor skills of basketball shooting and ball handling, motor learning is not always so transparent. Instructors may only have limited time with their learners, making it especially challenging to assess the amount of motor learning that has occurred. Physical educators and health professionals are an essential component of childhood and adolescent motor development. Teachers, physical therapists, and coaches engage their students in fitness activities, sports, games, and other activities, teaching fundamental motor skills that are critical to motor development. Practitioners may assist a delayed infant in learning how to crawl; they may help a child learn how to throw a ball, a young athlete learn how to serve a volleyball, or an adult learn how to properly bench press. It is not only important to properly instruct motor skills, but also to appropriately measure and assess the learner's movement patterns.

Kalil also experienced transfer of learning from cricket to baseball. Previous movement experiences can greatly influence an individual's performance for a similar movement pattern. Some previous movement patterns can benefit performances while others can be detrimental when someone is performing a new movement pattern. This chapter discusses transfer of learning, including the types of transfer and how to foster positive transfer, in addition to assessment of motor learning and retention.

We can take many performance characteristics into consideration to determine whether students are learning motor skills, such as improved coordination patterns, increased consistency, and reduced mental and physical effort, to name a few. These are all important in assessing improved performance, but the key to determining the level of learning attained is to assess the permanency of the motor skill. Think about an occupational therapist who is teaching a stroke patient how to brush her teeth or write her name again, or a physical therapist who is teaching a victim of a car accident how to walk again. What characteristics of the learner's performance assure the instructor that the learner is actually learning the movement and not simply showing improved performance? Just as math, science, and English teachers assess learning through an examination that covers the material, retention tests must be administered for motor skills. Physical educators and movement clinicians assume that students have learned the material if they are able to perform at or near the same level as their previous performance following a break.

Indicators of Motor Skill Learning

Learning takes time. It is important for the practitioner to understand and accept this fact. Classrooms are based on the premise that the learning of some basic concepts will adequately prepare students for the next step in their career, be that college or their first professional job. Physical education classrooms assume that practicing basic movement patterns will transfer to other more complex activities. Sporting practices are centered on the assumption that drills will positively reflect upon game day performances. However, there are many factors that must be addressed in skill transfer. Motor learning is defined *as a relatively permanent change in the capability to execute a motor skill as a result of practice or experience.* This section discusses how motor learning is

Keep these measures brief + examples from ES P.E.

assessed and how to facilitate positive transfer and prolonged retention. The following are some movement characteristics that can be used to indicate that motor learning has occurred:

- **Performance improvement.** Are observable performance changes shown across practice?
- **Consistency or stability.** Is the learner able to sustain a higher level of performance over time?
- **Persistence.** Is the learner able to perform the motor skill proficiently following a break in practice or performance?
- **Effort.** Is the learner performing with less physical or mental effort across practice?
- **Attention.** Does the learner require less attention to perform the motor skill?
- **Adaptability.** Is the learner becoming increasingly adaptable with increased motor skill proficiency?

Performance Improvement

Several behavioral characteristics are indicative of motor skill learning. The most intuitive behavioral characteristic of learning a motor skill is performance improvement. **Performance improvement** is an increase in the overall performance outcome. Let's refer back to the discussion of performance and learning in chapter 1. Performance is the act of executing a motor skill at a particular time. Learning is the result of *permanent* changes, while performance is a temporary, *nonpermanent* change. Performance is observable, while learning is a construct. It can be assumed that someone has learned only when performance changes have been monitored over a period of time.

Performance improvement is the most common indicator of learning simply because it is the most obvious. We make inferences every day based on our observations; for example, we look for signs of a person's mood in his face. People often assume that someone is in a good mood because he is smiling, even though he may actually be sad or angry and is just smiling to hide his true feelings.

Although performance measures do not necessarily exhibit motor learning at any particular point in time, assessing performance provides a good indicator of learning if it occurs across an extended period of time and if the results are combined with other factors, such as consistency, persistence, and coordination stability. Depending on the performance measure, improvement may be marked by a decrease, as with error or speed. It is often assumed (although sometimes incorrectly) that individuals are learning when there are significant gains in performance. In order to assess whether motor learning has occurred, one must assess performance following a break in practice.

Improved performance may also result from the acquisition of bad habits. Learners can adopt bad habits when they are focusing on the outcome or product of the movement as opposed to the coordination patterns involved in moving skillfully. For example, when learning how to throw the discus, athletes must learn some movements that may feel unnatural to them until they become proficient. They must learn the rhythm of the throw, how to turn the lower body in a whipping motion with a relaxed upper body and with the lower body movement trailing. They must keep their heels off the ground throughout the movement. It is important to note that as with all motor skills, the precise technique and style of the throwing pattern is going to be unique to every thrower, individualized by that athlete's structural and functional constraints. Novices who are learning the throwing pattern may have a tendency to tighten the upper body, which initially may allow them to throw farther because of the increased power behind the throw; but ultimately, this same movement will prevent them from reaching their full potential. The more athletes practice this throwing pattern, the more difficult it is going to be for them to develop proper technique. A similar problem could result from continuing practice when one is ill or under prolonged fatigue.

Humans are competitive by nature, so practitioners should eliminate movement outcomes when teaching a novice the basic movement patterns to prevent them from adopting unorthodox movement patterns, or bad habits. To prevent a thrower from focusing on the outcome of her throw, such as the distance the object traveled, one could have her throw into a net. Basketball players could take practice shots on the wall, so they are focused on their form and not on whether they made the shot. Once a bad habit is formed, it can be very challenging to overcome. Using dynamic systems terminology (refer to chapter 1), this results when the system becomes trapped in a very deep and stable attractor state that has enabled the individual to perform at an adequate level, even though other more effective states should be found.

What Do You Think?

Have you ever learned a bad habit you had to later overcome to move more effectively? Explain what the bad habit was and how you overcame it. How long did it take you to eliminate the bad habit and move more proficiently?

Performance Curves

Not only is it important to evaluate a learner's progress through subjective evaluations, it is also important to obtain and record objective performance measures over time. When deciding to quantify performance, the instructor must first decide what performance measure would be most appropriate to record. This decision is completely task dependent and may be driven by the resources available. For quantifying many motor skills, a measure of performance magnitude may be most appropriate, such as the distance of a throw, the height of a high jump, or the amount of weight benched. Recording error is a good performance measure for motor skills in which the objective is accuracy. Instructors who have access to more technology may be interested in quantifying the kinematics of the movement, for example by measuring joint angle changes through high-speed video cameras and motion detectors. If the instructor is interested in assessing the amount of effort required to perform the task, then measuring heart rates throughout the performance may be useful. By quantifying performance, an instructor is able to document performance changes over time and examine the effectiveness of instructional techniques or strategies.

One can generate performance curves by collecting a performance measure across a period of time—for instance, the number of catches made each day in juggling or the number of foul shots made each practice session. Figure 4.1 illustrates the maximum distance jumped per week for a long jumper. The dis-

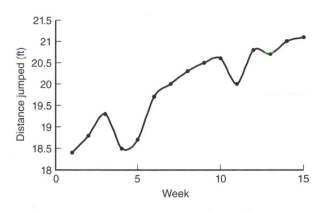

FIGURE 4.1
Fabricated performance curve of mean distance jumped in the long jump per week across 15 weeks.

tance jumped in feet is plotted on the y-axis, and the weeks are plotted on the x-axis. This allows the performer and instructor to see the gradual progress across the season.

Types of Performance Curves

There are four main types of performance curves (figure 4.2). The most common type is known as the **negatively accelerating curve**. This performance curve illustrates a very rapid initial rate of improvement followed by a gradual

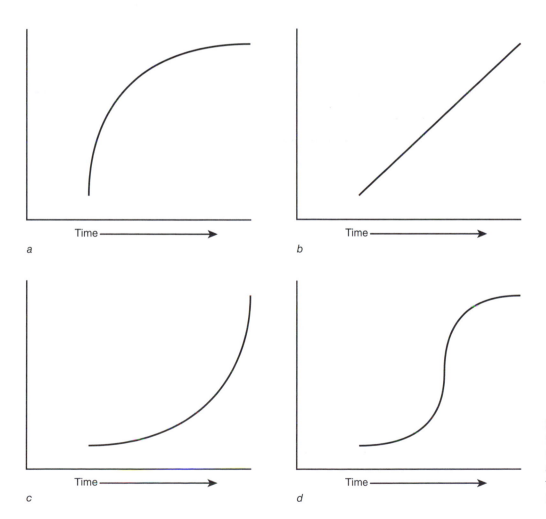

FIGURE 4.2
Performance curves. (a) Negatively accelerating, (b) linear, (c) positively accelerating, and (d) S-shaped.

71

reduction in the rate of improvement. This rate of change is so common that it has been assigned a mathematical law known as the **power law of practice** (Snoddy, 1926; Newell & Rosenbloom, 1981). Negatively accelerating curves are common because performance gains occur much more rapidly during early practice when a learner is essentially starting a motor skill from scratch. Initially, the learner will experience rapid improvements because there is much room for improvement; however, this rate of improvement is impossible to maintain. As the learner continues practicing, the room for improvement decreases, so further improvement becomes increasingly difficult to obtain.

A **positively accelerating curve** is illustrated by small initial gains, but this rate of improvement increases with every practice session. Learners may exhibit a positively accelerating curve when performing a challenging task such as juggling. Initially, learners may have difficulty improving, making only two to four catches per attempt. At some point, the learner will figure out the task and experience rapid gains in improvement. A **linear curve** indicates that there is a direct relationship between the performance measure and time. A perfectly linear curve would be found for an individual who shows the exact same gain in performance with every practice session or performance attempt. For example, a juggler makes one catch on day 1, two catches on day 2, three catches on day 3, and so on. The juggler improves at the same rate every day. On average, the individual is performing proportionately better each week. Finally, the **S-shaped curve** combines the rates of improvement found in the positively and negatively shaped curves. The learner initially takes some time to learn the motor skill. After a period of time, the learner experiences his "aha" moment and can perform the movement pattern much more successfully, similar to the positively accelerating curve. Performance then follows a gradual decline in the rate of improvement, such as the negatively accelerating curve.

A final important note: Keep in mind that the direction of the performance curve is dependent on the performance variable being measured. A thrower would be concerned with increasing the distance of the throw, but a sprinter would be focused on decreasing the duration of the sprint. In the latter case, the performance curve would illustrate a downward trend. The same would be expected for a target shooter who is measuring error.

 Research Notes: How Do I Balance on This Thing?

The power law of practice was demonstrated in an experiment using a pedalo (Chen, Liu, Mayer-Kress, & Newell, 1995). A pedalo is a simple device that has two pedals connecting four wheels. There is nothing for the hands to grasp to assist with maintaining balance and steering, so the individual must simply pedal either forward or backward to propel the pedalo. Four participants were tested across seven days on their ability to propel the pedalo a specified distance. The goal of the task was to move as quickly and smoothly as possible. Movement times and kinematics were examined to assess the consistency of the performance and improvements in coordination. As expected based on the power law of practice, the movement time decreased rapidly over the initial days of practice, but decreased less with increasing practice.

Performance Curves "mask" cognitive improvement (Stage 1 Fitts & Posner)

Soft Psyche Cessation / Ex

Limitations of Performance Curves

Although performance curves are a very useful objective method of measuring and assessing performance, it is important to understand that performance curves represent only temporary effects. Performance does not always indicate that learning has occurred, so assessing learning through performance curves may falsely imply that an individual has learned, even if the effects are not permanent. Performance curves may also mask learning effects when there are no observable performance changes, when in fact a learner may have *gained* some learning. For example, if several learners are attempting the unicycle, some may progress very rapidly, some may progress slowly at first, and others may not ever show observable improvements. Learners who are still averaging only two or three catches per attempt in juggling after many practice sessions may have learned the overall movement pattern of the hands in relation to the balls, or a better technique to toss the balls through trial and error and observation, or both. These individuals may have poorer hand–eye coordination, making the motor skill more challenging for them to perform. They have gained some learning even though their performance curves are flat.

Performance curves also provide only a limited perspective. For example, when one is averaging across participants, individual trends are often lost. An averaged performance curve may indicate that participants have learned a motor skill very quickly when it is possible that only one individual learned very quickly while others showed a very small amount of improvement. Figure 4.3*a* shows a performance graph of the individual performances for four jugglers across 10 practice sessions. Juggler 1 progressed very quickly, while Jugglers 2, 3, and 4 progressed at a much slower rate, and none of these three performed at nearly as high a level as Juggler 1. It is difficult to even notice that Juggler 4 became proficient with cascade juggling, averaging 15 catches by practice session 10. Although Juggler 4's score doesn't compare to 250 catches, it does show that the juggler has acquired the basic coordination pattern of this complex motor skill. Examining figure 4.3*a,* we may infer that only one juggler was able to learn the motor skill of juggling. Now take a look at figure 4.3*b,* which exhibits the mean performance across the four jugglers. If we examined

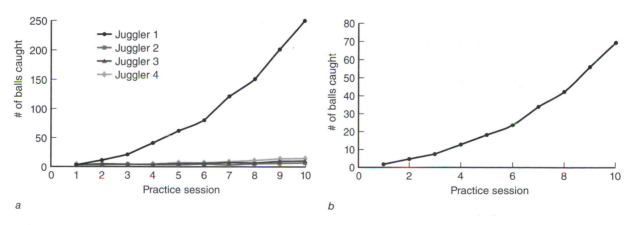

FIGURE 4.3   (a) Individual performance curves for four jugglers. (b) Mean performance across the four jugglers.

only figure 4.3*b*, it would appear that all jugglers most likely learned cascade juggling because the rates of learning are lost when performances are averaged across participants.

There are also limitations to averaging across trials for an *individual's* data. A graph that depicts only the average performance per session, as in figure 4.3*a*, does not provide any information about the consistency of an individual's performance. The consistency of an individual's performance provides important information regarding the learning process. As discussed in chapter 3, learners in the cognitive stage are inconsistent in comparison to learners in the associative and autonomous stages. Analyzing individual trials can also provide information regarding the effects of a warm-up decrement. A **warm-up decrement** is a reduction in performance due to a period of inactivity. These effects are generally short in duration. It is important to assess the amount of performance that is generally lost due to the warm-up decrement and the length of time or number of attempts required to overcome the warm-up decrement. This can be valuable information when people are preparing for a competition or event.

Consistency

The consistency of performance is another important indicator of motor skill learning. A consistent performer is capable of sustaining a higher level of performance over time. Although it is often assumed that consistency implies learning, this is not always the case. Let's refer back to the definition of motor learning. Motor learning has been defined as the relatively permanent change in the learner's capability to execute a motor skill as a result of practice. Although the performance appears permanent because it is consistent, instructors must be careful not to use this as the only measure of motor learning, because it does not necessarily mean that the motor skill has actually been learned.

The consistency of a movement pattern from the dynamic systems perspective indicates the stability of the movement pattern, in other words, the depth of the attractor basin. Again, it is possible that the learner has adopted a bad habit and is consistently performing less skillfully because she has become trapped in a strong attractor state. Sometimes these attractor states can become *too* stable, making it very difficult for learners to change their movement pattern. At this point, it is best for the instructor to force the learner out of the stable pattern. It will take time for the learner to be able to become consistent with the new movement pattern; but it is better to be inconsistently producing the desirable movement pattern than consistently performing the flawed movement pattern. Learners may feel uncomfortable producing this new movement pattern for a while, but it is important to encourage them to continue pushing through this potentially awkward stage. For example, body posture is a very important element in ballroom dance, but it is common for dancers to have poor body postures such as curved shoulders or a forward head position. The more a ballroom dancer has practiced with these bad habits, the more challenging they are to overcome. It is easy for dancers to focus on the steps and forget about maintaining their posture. When they are focusing on maintaining their posture, it is likely that they will mess up their steps or make some other error. Over time, the bad habit will be eliminated without detriment to their overall performance.

Persistence

Learning can also be measured by an increased amount of persistence in the performance of a motor skill. With practice, the learner will gain the capability to perform following longer and longer durations of time without practice, as reflected in the saying, *It's like learning to ride a bike.* When initially learning a motor skill, people need to practice regularly; however, with increased practice, skill proficiency is maintained for longer periods of time, extending from days and weeks to months and even years. Of course, it can be expected that some losses will occur due to forgetting or to physical changes with the passage of time, but a sustained relative permanency should be present. This performance characteristic is central to the definition of motor learning (a relatively *permanent* change in the capability to perform a motor skill).

Effort

Another method of measuring performance or learning changes is by assessing effort. Experts perform challenging feats effortlessly. BMX bikers can complete phenomenal jumps; outfielders can leap into the air to make amazing catches; and dancers can complete incredible lifts in what appears to be an effortless, seamless movement. Novice performers, on the other hand, can expend a lot of mental and physical effort in order to perform just a simplified version of the coordination pattern. Many learners expend a great deal of energy producing an inefficient movement pattern because they have not learned the correct muscles to activate, or the correct sequence for activating the muscles, or both. This causes them to exert much more effort than is necessary to perform the task. Learners can become quickly fatigued and frustrated through this process.

Novice swimmers, young or old, initially have their body in a more vertical position, which is very inefficient for swimming yet seemingly more comfortable for the inexperienced swimmer. This vertical positioning forces the swimmer to expend much energy to produce little if any forward propulsion. This can lead to frustration, and in an attempt to increase forward propulsion, the swimmer will kick harder and use more arm motion. He is exerting a great deal of effort but only tiring himself out without gaining much forward motion. This effort just fatigues and frustrates the swimmer more. With practice, swimmers become increasingly comfortable in the water, and their body position gradually becomes more and more horizontal. This change in body position enables them to produce a more fluid motion with less overall energy expended.

Research Notes: Learning to Creep

Sparrow and Newell (1994) investigated how energy expenditure changes across practice when people are learning a new task. Three healthy young males were tested on walking and creeping (walking on hands and feet) on a treadmill at various grades ranging from +29% incline to −18% decline. Metabolic energy expenditure was examined via oxygen consumption and heart rate. The authors found that the participants reduced their heart rate and oxygen consumption with practice when task conditions remained constant. These results indicated that participants learned how to produce the movement pattern with increased mechanical efficiency with practice.

Attention

The amount of conscious attention required to perform a motor skill significantly decreases with practice and skill level. Novices require focused attention on the overall mechanics of the movement. Because novices are so focused on the coordination patterns of producing the movement, they are not able to attend to game playing strategies. Instead, they are focused on the technical components of the movement. With the development of skill, the learner attends to the specifics of the movement pattern less and less. If learners practice long enough to reach the autonomous stage, they can perform the skill with essentially no conscious attention devoted to the production of the movement pattern. This is termed **automaticity**. The following are the primary criteria of automaticity: (1) No processing capacity is required for the task; (2) the task is performed independently or without the performer's intentional control (involuntarily); and (3) the movement is not produced with consciousness or introspection (Neumann, 1984).

Since novices cannot perform the movement pattern efficiently and require much conscious attention when performing, their movements appear deliberate and choppy. Not only can experts produce the movement fluidly, but their attentional resources are freed up, allowing them to focus on strategic elements of the game or task. For instance, a skilled soccer player does not have to focus on foot position and ball control; instead she can focus on positions of teammates and defenders as well as strategies and game plays. By attending to these other game elements, the soccer player is able to respond quickly to changing environmental conditions.

Once automaticity is achieved, attention drawn back to the production of the movement pattern can have a negative impact on performance. Attention directed toward the production of a well-learned performance may interfere with the processes that have become automatic in a skilled performer, disrupting the production of the skilled movement (Beilock, Bertenthal, McCoy, & Carr, 2004). Skilled performance is unconsciously controlled (Anderson, 1993; Fitts & Posner, 1967), while novice performances are produced with a focus on

Try This

We do many activities without thinking, such as walking, taking a shower, and locking the door. You are probably also capable of doing some skillful activities automatically, such as typing on a keyboard, throwing a ball, or riding a bicycle. If you are a skilled typist, try typing while paying more attention to exactly what you're typing. It is likely that when you attended to your typing, you slowed down. Even breathing rate can be altered if you focus on your breathing. Try counting your breaths. Did you feel as though you were controlling your breathing rate? Do you think you may have slowed down or sped up your breathing rate?

On the other hand, the benefit of performing a motor skill with little attention is that you can focus on other things; for example, you can talk while you are walking. What are some other examples of activities you can perform at the same time you are performing another functional task (i.e., multitasking)? Provide some sport-related examples.

declarative knowledge and the production of the coordination patterns. Drawing an expert's attention to the production of the movement pattern distracts the performer, disrupting the skillful performance. This may also explain why some skilled athletes "choke under pressure." The athlete may be able to perform very skillfully under most conditions but under intense pressure may shift his attention to the production of the movement, which distracts him just enough to degrade the performance.

good

Adaptability

Another method of assessing performance is to measure adaptability. **Adaptability** is the capability to make movement adjustments to fit the changing demands of the task and environmental conditions. The adaptability required for a particular movement is situation and skill dependent. For example, the catching capabilities of an outfielder will likely extend to catching other objects besides baseballs. A tennis player's experience with striking a ball with a racket will increase her capability to play other racket sports. Adaptability is especially critical for open skills, which test an individual's ability to adapt to constantly changing environmental demands, such as returning the ball with a forehand or backhand, at various positions on the court, with variable force, or some combination of these. Although closed skills do not require split-second adjustments necessarily, it is also essential to be adaptable in closed skills because every movement is variable. There are always at least some changes in the environment or the context of the movement itself (individual constraints) or the task.

Individuals become increasingly adaptable with increased motor skill proficiency. The reason is that the performer is now comfortable with the movement pattern and is no longer required to focus attention on internal processes. The individual can alter his strategies for changing weather conditions, plays, or stressors such as the importance of a game or situation.

Performance and Learning Tests

Performance curves can provide a means to evaluate changes in performance measures over time. A simple method of measuring performance changes is to compare performance on a **pretest**, a test conducted prior to the practice sessions, with a **posttest**, a test conducted at the end of the practice sessions. This method allows inferences of learning, but does not reveal the persistence of the improved performance, retention. To assess the persistent capability to perform a motor skill, a retention test must be administered. A **retention test** is given following a break from practice. Retention tests allow practitioners to determine whether the change in skill level is temporary (performance) or permanent (learning). If the effects are only temporary, it is unlikely they will be reproduced following the retention interval. The amount of time between the last practice session or posttest and the retention test is called the **retention interval**. The appropriate length of the retention interval depends on the duration and complexity of the motor skill and how often the motor skill is practiced. A motor skill that is practiced regularly, such as every day or even multiple times per day, could be assessed following a retention interval of only a day or two. A motor skill that is practiced less frequently will require a longer retention interval for adequate assessment of the persistence of that capability.

It is important to understand the difference between learning and retention. Measures of performance during the acquisition phase allow inferences about learning, such as the mechanics, processes, and outcomes of learning (Rose & Christina, 2006). Measures of performance following a retention interval allow practitioners to make inferences about memory and forgetting processes by assessing what was maintained or lost following the retention interval.

Another test that examines the permanence of motor skill acquisition is a transfer test. The difference between a transfer test and a retention test is that a retention test assesses performance on the *same* task following the break, while a transfer test assesses performance on a *similar, but different* task following the break. **Transfer tests** measure the adaptability between the practiced motor skill and the related motor skill or performance situation. For example, a transfer test could examine how the experience of snowboarding in the winter affects wakeboarding performance in the summer. While a retention test would simply examine an individual's snowboarding performance following a retention interval, a transfer test would measure an individual's performance on a similar motor skill, such as wakeboarding, following the retention interval. Table 4.1 provides a breakdown of the different types of performance and learning tests.

TABLE 4.1 Comparison of Pre- and Posttests With Retention and Transfer Tests

Type of test	Definition	Measurement
Pre-	Test prior to practice of a motor skill	
Post-	Test following practice of a motor skill	Performance (may or may not reveal learning)
Retention	Test following a retention interval; conditions are same as in acquisition	Retention (memory and forgetting)
Transfer	Test following a retention interval; conditions are different from but also similar to those in acquisition	Adaptability

Measuring Retention

There are several methods of measuring retention. The simplest method measures absolute retention. **Absolute retention** is merely the learner's performance immediately following the retention interval. This value is limited and does not provide information about how learners did in comparison to their prior performance levels.

Two other basic methods of measuring retention provide a comparative measure relative to performance during the original learning period. There are two main types of relative retention. The first is the difference score. To calculate the **difference score**, one subtracts the absolute retention score from the last score during the acquisition phase (original learning). This score is the change in performance following the retention interval. It represents the amount of performance that was lost following the break. This score is still somewhat limited because it does not inform the learner as to how much was lost relative to the change in the original learning. The **percentage score** is the most informative measure of retention. This score is interpreted as the percentage of performance that was lost (or gained) following the retention interval. To calculate the percentage score, one divides the difference score by the change in original learning and then multiplies by 100%. To calculate the change in original learning, one subtracts the performance on the first session (or trial) from the performance on the last session (or trial) of the original learning trials. Refer to figure 4.4; in this pursuit rotor example, the participant is timed on how long he or she can track the movement. In this example, the absolute retention is 60 seconds because the learner's time on target was 60 seconds during the first trial following the retention interval of one week. To calculate the difference score (40 seconds), the absolute score (60 seconds) was subtracted from the last score of the original session (100 seconds). To calculate the percentage score, the difference score (40 seconds) was divided by the change in original learning (100 seconds – 30 seconds) and multiplied by 100%. The percentage score is calculated as 57.14%, which can be interpreted to mean that 57.14% of the original improvement was lost over the retention interval, or 42.86% was retained.

Another useful retention measure is the retention savings score. The **retention savings score** reflects how much time is required to return to the same level of performance as compared to the time required to reach this level during the original practice sessions (figure 4.4). During the original sessions, the learner took 10 sessions to reach his peak of 100 seconds. However, following the retention interval, the learner reached this same level in only three practice sessions. The retention savings score is the difference between these two values, so seven sessions were saved in reaching the same level of performance following the retention interval.

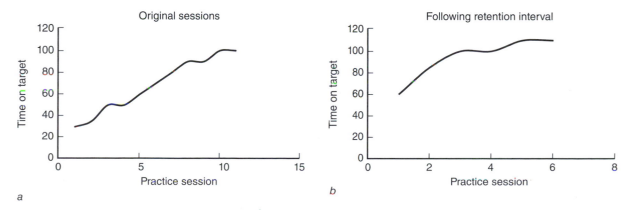

FIGURE 4.4 (a) Time on target was measured across 11 sessions. The goal of the task was to stay on target for as long as possible. (b) Following 11 sessions, the learner took one week off (retention interval) and then practiced for an additional six sessions.

Types of Transfer

Previous movement experiences influence an individual's ability to perform a new motor skill. This is referred to as **transfer of learning**. There are three types of transfer, positive, negative, and zero; the type depends on the direction of the transfer. **Positive transfer** occurs when the learning of a previous motor skill enhances the performance of another motor skill. You may have experienced positive transfer if you were experienced with one racket sport and then tried to play a new racket sport. A tennis player will likely experience an advantage when learning how to play racquetball because of the similarities in making contact with a ball and racket. Positive transfer generally occurs only in beginners to a sport or activity. An experienced tennis player is likely to experience negative transfer after playing racquetball for a while due to adoption of a different swing technique. When a previous movement experience hinders performance, then **negative transfer** has occurred. Players who switch from baseball to softball can experience negative transfer because there are differences in tracking the ball following the pitch. In baseball, the ball is released high and then moves down because it is pitched overhand; in softball, pitchers use an underhand pitch, causing the ball to approach the plate moving from a low position to a high position (Coker, 2003). This previous experience could cause temporary negative transfer with batting when the player switches from softball to baseball. When the previous movement experience does not change performance, then **zero transfer** has occurred. This occurs when the two motor skills are unrelated, such as hurdling and fencing, or football punting and the backstroke.

Practitioners should be aware of learners' previous movement experiences because initial poor performance may be caused by negative transfer from prior experience in a similar skill. Luckily, when negative transfer does occur, as in batting in softball after prior experience with batting in baseball, it is generally temporary. On the other hand, learners often capitalize on previous movement experiences that provide positive transfer. In general, *most transfer effects are*

 Research Notes: Does Cascade Juggling Transfer to Bounce Juggling?

A research group investigated the transfer effects of cascade juggling (the typical figure-8 pattern of juggling in which the balls are tossed up in the air) experience on learning bounce juggling (juggling in which the ball is bounced on the floor rather than thrown in the air) (Bebko, Demark, Im-Bolter, & MacKewn, 2005). Four experienced cascade jugglers and five novice jugglers learned to bounce juggle for a period of five weeks. The experienced jugglers had an initial advantage of approximately seven days over the novice jugglers at the start of the study and by the end of the study were about 10 days ahead of the novice jugglers. The lag in performance in the novice jugglers did not occur because the novice learners did not perform well or acquire the task of bounce juggling, since each learner was able to make at least 20 consecutive catches by the end of the practice sessions. Instead, it appears that previous cascade juggling experience provided positive transfer to bounce juggling, enabling the experienced jugglers to pick up the skill of bounce juggling faster and improve further than the novice jugglers.

small and positive. The more movement experiences learners gain, the more likely they are to pick up new motor skills more quickly.

Some of the strongest evidence for the persistence of negative transfer is found when individuals learn a second language (Asher, 1964; Figueredo, 2006). The production of speech sounds necessary for speaking a particular language strongly influences how the individual will produce the speech sounds for English, for example. This is why German and Chinese natives have very different accents. The negative transfer is causing nonnative speakers to have difficulty with pronouncing certain sounds. For example, native Japanese speakers confuse the letter *l* with the letter *r,* so they often pronounce "salary" as "sarary" (Cook, 1997). French speakers have difficulty pronouncing *h,* saying "ouse" for "house" (Morris, 2001). These accents are so persistent that it is generally easy to differentiate the nationality of speakers simply from hearing their pronunciation. People who learn a second language can spend years or even decades speaking another language while being immersed in the newer culture but still maintain their very distinct accents.

 What Do You Think?

1. Choose a motor skill. Give one example of a motor skill that would likely produce positive transfer to that skill, one motor skill that would likely produce negative transfer to that skill, and one that would likely produce zero transfer. Explain why you would expect these effects for each example.

2. Explain how you could eliminate the effects of negative transfer in your example of negative transfer?

Transfer Tests

Sometimes practitioners want to assess the adaptability of a motor skill. The capability to quickly adapt to unpredictable changes in the environment is especially important when people are performing open skills. Transfer tests are a method of assessing adaptability. Transfer tests are very similar to retention tests; however, rather than assessing performance on the same motor skill, they assess performance on a very similar skill following the retention interval. For example, a learner could practice racquetball for several months and then be tested on squash. Both are racket sports played inside a court with four walls and a ceiling. The main difference between the two sports is the size and elasticity of the balls and rackets. Squash balls are much smaller and less bouncy than racquetballs. When switching from racquetball to squash, racquetball players are generally quite surprised to find that they must move to the ball because it is not going to bounce to them.

Practitioners often make context changes in transfer tests rather than assessing different sports or games. For instance, a regulatory condition that can vary in some activities is the surface, as in football (grass or Astroturf) or tennis (grass, clay, acrylic, or asphalt). Other regulatory conditions remain constant from location to location, such as the size of the field or court and the height and length of the net. A transfer test could assess tennis performance on a different surface. A transfer test could also assess performance under varying nonregulatory conditions, such as changing the importance of the situation. For instance, if a learner is preparing for a competition, it is useful to test while she is under increased emotional stress.

It is useful to assess performance with varying regulatory and nonregulatory conditions. This enables the practitioner to assess not only the adaptability of the learner, but also the stability of the performance. A performer should not be limited to performing skillfully during controlled conditions, but should be able to adapt to changing situations and environmental conditions. This is important not only in physical education classes and sport, but also in rehabilitation. The role of rehabilitation is to prepare patients to be functional outside of the rehabilitation clinic. Rehabilitation specialists design movement activities with the expectation that these learned patterns will assist with producing functional movement patterns. For example, when treating stroke patients with hemiplegia (paralysis on one half of the body), it is recommended that specialists have the patient practice moving in the supine and sitting positions to relearn how to walk (Sawner & LaVigne, 1992). Movements that are practiced diagonally, however, are considered much more beneficial for locomoting throughout the environment and for sports (Voss, Ionta, & Myers, 1985) because diagonal movements are so commonly produced when it is necessary to avoid obstacles. Although diagonal limb patterns may be more beneficial, they are not used as often in rehabilitation because it is simply more convenient for specialists to manipulate the limbs in a supine or sitting position (Mount, 1996). It is always important when designing an activity either for a sporting drill or for rehabilitation to focus on the similarities between the tasks. Tasks must be very similar in order to produce positive transfer.

 ## Research Notes: Transfer of Throwing Positions

Mount (1996) investigated the effect of transfer between throwing with varying postural demands, sitting versus reclining. The task was to throw a dart to a target with a fixed elbow in an extended position. The prediction was that participants who practiced throwing the dart in one position would perform the skill in the same position better than those who practiced in a different position.

Forty right-handed female participants aged 20 to 34 years participated in the study. The two conditions were sitting on a Balans chair and reclining on a table at a 45-degree angle. Participants were randomly separated into four groups: (1) Control group 1 used the chair during both the practice and transfer sessions; (2) control group 2 used the table during both sessions; (3) experimental group 1 practiced with the chair and tested with the table; (4) experimental group 2 practiced with the table and tested with the chair. Participants practiced four sets of five throws. Following the practice session, participants were given a 5-minute break before completing four sets of five throws for the test.

Negative transfer occurred between the two positional conditions even though the task was the same. Mount's interpretation was that this negative transfer occurred because of a strong linkage between the first position learned and the movement of the arm. When the participants then switched positions, they had to adjust to the new body position with the motion of the arm throw. These results indicate the importance of taking into consideration an individual's body position prior to practicing a motor skill to avoid bad habits resulting in prolonged learning periods and poorer performances.

Theories of Transfer

The **identical elements theory** asserts that the amount and direction of transfer are dependent on the number of identical elements between two motor skills (Thorndike, 1914). It would be expected, then, that transfer would occur if two motor skills involved similar equipment and movements, such as the example at the beginning of this chapter of Kalil experiencing positive transfer from cricket to baseball. Playing different types of racket sports would also be expected to transfer, while sports and games that have similar strategies but very different movement patterns, such as football and Ultimate Frisbee, would be expected to have zero transfer. Ultimate Frisbee and football are both outdoor sports played on a rectangular field with two end zones. The object is to keep passing the ball or Frisbee until it gets into the end zone. In both sports, play begins with two teams lined up opposing one another. The main difference between the two sports is that in Ultimate Frisbee the players cannot run.

Although the movement patterns necessary to throw and catch a Frisbee versus a football are very different, there are many similarities in the strategies and conceptual aspects. According to the **transfer-appropriate processing theory**, movements or games that require similar cognitive processing can positively transfer (Bransford, Franks, Morris, & Stein, 1979). Activities that require learners to engage in similar problem-solving strategies promote positive transfer (Coker, 2003). For instance, the strategy of faking an opponent is employed in many different sports and games, such as basketball, hockey, and football. A skilled basketball player is going to be much better at reading an opponent's intentions even when switching to a different sport, such as hockey, in comparison to someone who has not had experiences with opponents, like a gymnast or diver.

One common method of implementing transfer into an instructional design is to simplify the task using progressions. Instructors simplify a task expecting that the simpler versions will transfer to the more complex motor skill. For instance, preschoolers often first learn how to bat by using a tee. This allows the child to learn the fundamental movement pattern without the temporal component of making contact with the ball, changing the motor skill from externally paced to self-paced. The spatial component of the motor skill is also less challenging because the ball position is stationary, which changes the initiation of the skill to self-paced. Learners may then progress to batting a ball that is hung from a string, then a balloon or a large light ball that is pitched, and finally a regular ball. It is expected that positive transfer is occurring during each transition, enabling the child to learn how to bat more quickly and safely. Skill progressions are often used for activities that are complex or for lead-up activities. Lead-up activities are activities that carry a risk of injury, such as gymnastics, figure skating jumps, or diving.

Promoting Positive Transfer

The first step in promoting positive transfer is to analyze the transfer task. A successful practitioner is one who can effectively analyze skills when designing drills and activities. Positive transfer is dependent on the similarities between the two tasks. These similarities can be either the fundamental movement pattern, as proposed by the identical elements theory, or the strategies and concepts of the tasks, as asserted by the transfer-appropriate processing theory. Skills that involve striking have similar fundamental movement patterns. A learner who has experience with cricket will have an advantage in playing softball or baseball. Both skills have temporal and spatial elements. The bat must make contact with the ball at a specific time and position. The strategic and conceptual components of the skills can also provide positive transfer. For instance, the fundamental movement patterns in kickball and baseball are very different and even require the use of different limbs. However, there are similarities between the strategies of the game. For both games, one team has possession of the ball, the fielding team, while the other team, the batting team, is attempting to hit or kick it. Each side has a very specific role that does not change until one team has acquired a certain number of outs. Games are classified by their similar strategies and concepts (refer to chapter 2), so positive transfer would be expected for learners who play multiple games in the same classification.

Understanding how to effectively analyze motor skills not only is important in designing practices, but also can assist in maximizing positive transfer from the learner's past experiences. You can gain positive transfer from your learner's previous experiences. Learners will understand the new skill more quickly when comparisons are made with skills they are familiar with. For instance, baseball and cricket have a similar "defensive" component that occurs in parallel with the offensive component of scoring runs. In baseball, the batter defends the strike zone, while in cricket it is the wicket that is defended. Highlighting the differences can be just as beneficial to the learner as pointing out the similarities. Some of the many differences between cricket and baseball include the terminology for similar positions such as a bowler versus a pitcher, wicket-keeper versus catcher, or batsman versus batter. Another big difference between cricket and baseball is the batting stance. In cricket, the handle of the bat is held in a vertical direction with the end of the bat towards the ground, while in baseball the bat is held upward and cocked behind the head.

Comparing two motor skills or pointing out analogies between them can be helpful to learners. For example, when teaching a learner how to swing a bat, one can compare the lead arm position to that in throwing a Frisbee. The back arm moves right through the movement with the elbow in, similar to the action of skipping a rock across a pond. It is important to be sure that the learner has experience with the skill one is comparing to the new skill. A learner with very little experience with the skill being referred to may actually perform worse after receiving comparative information (Coker, 2003).

Another factor that should be considered in promoting positive transfer is the skill level of the learner. Novices gain more benefit from transfer in comparison to individuals at higher skill levels. For example, an individual learning how to play racquetball will gain more advantages from his or her previous tennis experience than an experienced tennis player will gain from playing racquetball in his or her off-season. Learners in the associative or the autonomous stage will benefit much less because they are able to produce the fundamental movement pattern and are now focusing on much more specific movements involved in the given motor skill. In these cases, some negative transfer may occur for the higher level players because the previous movement experiences (transfer) can alter some of their techniques.

Measuring Transfer

Before progressions or drills are incorporated into a practice design, the cost–benefit trade-off should be examined. To determine the cost–benefit trade-off, practitioners must assess how much practice is necessary to obtain positive transfer. If more practice is required for the transfer task than for the primary task, then the cost outweighs the benefit. Two methods of measuring the cost–benefit trade-off are to calculate the percentage transfer score and the savings score. The percentage score is the gain in performance as a result of experience on the transfer task as a percentage of the total amount learned (Schmidt & Lee, 2005). To measure the benefits of transfer, the practitioner must assess two groups—a control group, which practices only the primary task, and a transfer group, which practices a transfer task before practicing the primary task. To calculate percentage transfer, complete these steps:

1. Mark the control group on the graph with an X.
2. Take the difference between the two groups' (control group, transfer group) initial scores.
3. Divide this difference by the difference across the sessions for the control group (subtract the score from the last session from the score of the first session).
4. Multiply by 100%.

Figure 4.5 is an example of a transfer design assessing the transfer effect of prior tennis practice on racquetball performance. Group A practiced tennis three times a week for four weeks. Following the four weeks of tennis practice, groups A and B practiced racquetball three times per week for four weeks. To calculate the percentage transfer in this example, the difference between the two groups' initial performance (Z – X) is divided by the amount of improvement in the control group (Z – Y), where X = 15, Y = 25, and Z = 3. The formula for percentage transfer is (Z – X) / (Z – Y) × 100. The percentage score for this example would be 54.5%. The interpretation would be that 54.5% improvement occurred in racquetball as a result of prior tennis practice. A score of 0% would indicate that the two groups playing racquetball began at the same level. A negative score would imply that negative transfer had occurred.

The amount of practice that the transfer group required to gain the initial advantage should also be taken into consideration. If more practice was required for the transfer task than for the primary task alone, then the cost would outweigh the benefit.

The savings score is a calculation of the amount of practice time saved by previous practice of the transfer task. The savings score is

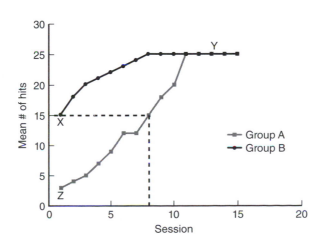

FIGURE 4.5
Performances in racquetball for group A, which had prior tennis experience, and group B, which had no prior experience (control). If group A performs better than group B, than positive transfer from tennis to racquetball has occurred. If group B outperforms group A, then negative transfer has occurred.

simply the number of practice sessions or trials required with the primary task (control group) to reach the same level that the transfer group began at. A horizontal dotted line can be drawn from X to the group B data line. In this example, eight practice sessions were saved because of the prior tennis practice. The amount of practice saved should then be compared with the amount of practice of the transfer task. In this case, 12 tennis practice sessions were required for the initial positive transfer of 54.5%. This initial performance improvement saved eight practice sessions in racquetball. However, the total amount of practice was more for the transfer group because the transfer group practiced for 12 practice sessions, while the control group only needed eight racquetball practice sessions to reach the same level.

 What Do You Think?

Refer back to figure 4.5. How would the transfer percentage score change if groups A and B were switched, with group A becoming the control group and group B becoming the transfer group?

1. Is the transfer positive, negative, or zero?
2. Calculate the percentage transfer score.
3. Interpret the percentage transfer score.

Key Points in Transfer

The previous sections have outlined many factors related to transfer, but here are the key points to take away:

- Transfer is generally small and positive.
- Transfer is dependent on the number of similarities between the two motor skills.
- Negative transfer is generally temporary.
- Previous movement experiences often provide some transfer.
- Most positive transfer effects are found in early acquisition.

Summary

This chapter discussed how to measure and assess motor learning. The many indicators of motor learning include consistency of performance, permanence of the movement production, decreased effort, reduced attentional demands, and increased adaptability. Learners who have acquired the capability to perform a motor skill can *consistently* perform at a higher level. Their performance is also sustainable and *permanent* over long periods of time. Skilled learners can also perform the motor skill with less cognitive and physical *effort* than they could when they were initially learning the motor skill. They also need to devote less *attention* to the movement production, allowing them to focus on strategies rather than on producing the coordination pattern. Finally, improved performance can be measured by the *adaptability* of the learner, meaning that learners can perform similar and related motor skills at a higher level due to their experience with another task.

The true test of motor learning is sustained performance following a period away from regular practice, also known as a *retention interval*. Motor learning is a *permanent change in the capability to produce a skilled movement*; so if learners lose their capability to produce a particular movement pattern following the passage of time, then the motor skill has not been learned. In this case, only performance (temporary) changes have occurred.

The chapter also discussed transfer of learning. Understanding transfer, including types of transfer, how to measure transfer, and how to foster positive transfer is of critical importance to practitioners in school, athletic, and rehabilitation settings. Educators in school settings must design appropriate activities that will promote both the transfer and retention of fundamental movement skills and sport-specific skills. Coaches must focus on drills that will positively transfer to the sport, preparing the athletes for competitive situations. Structuring the environment and the task so that they are as realistic as possible is critical in order for clinicians to promote transfer from the rehabilitation setting to patients' homes.

Supplemental Activities

Transfer of Learning

Other than being able to recall material or a skill you have previously practiced, the only way to demonstrate learning is to apply what you have practiced to a new situation. Transfer is the application of previously acquired skills and knowledge to new situations. You may have varying degrees of familiarity with the situations in this supplemental activity, squash and racquetball. These two activities have similar elements (ball and racket) and action plans (serves and drives). The challenge is in the different elastic properties of the ball and strings of the racket, as well as the varying shapes. These properties cause the response to vary among the parameters of speed, direction, and force. Your goal is to continue hitting the ball as many times as possible, up to a maximum of 50 hits.

Instructions

In this activity you will perform racquetball serves and then squash serves. Stand in the service box holding the racket in your dominant hand and the ball in the other. When you are ready, serve the ball to the wall so it rebounds to you in the manner appropriate for the sport. Continue to hit the ball until you lose control of it, it bounces twice, or until you've reached the maximum number of hits (50 hits). For each activity, record your number of hits for five trials. Your score is the total number of times the ball hits the wall for each trial. The lowest score you could get is 1 hit.

Have one of your friends complete the same activity, only beginning with squash for five trials and then switching to racquetball for five trials.

Participant 1

	TRIALS					
	1	2	3	4	5	Mean
Racquetball						
Squash						

Participant 2

	TRIALS					
	1	2	3	4	5	Mean
Squash						
Racquetball						

Questions

1. Consider your experience when you initially performed the second task.
   a. What did it feel like?
   b. Did you think it was easier or harder to do because of the previous activity?
2. After completing this supplemental activity, would you expect positive, negative, or zero transfer from squash to racquetball? Explain your answer (i.e., elastic properties and size of the ball, size and strings of the racket, etc.).
3. Would you expect positive, negative, or zero transfer from racquetball to squash? Explain your answer (i.e., elastic properties and size of the ball, size and strings of the racket, etc.).

Performance Curves and Retention Project

Choose a motor skill that requires you to produce a movement pattern that you have not produced before (e.g., juggling, speed stacking, standing on an exercise ball, one-handed push-up, handstand, etc.). Practice the skill every day for 10 days for a set period of time (e.g., 5 minutes per day). Record your performances every day. Following 10 days of practice, wait for a week (one-week retention interval) and then perform a retention test. Record your performance on the retention test.

1. Make a performance curve exhibiting your performance changes across the 10-day practice sessions.
2. What type of performance curve is this graph?
3. Calculate your retention scores, including the absolute retention, the difference score, and the percentage savings score.
4. Did you *learn* the motor skill?

Motor Development
Childhood and Adolescence

This section of the book presents an overview of motor development in childhood and adolescence. While part I addresses some of the basic principles, terminology, and theoretical approaches in motor development, this section expands upon this knowledge with a focus on growth and development during the first two decades of life. The discussion begins by examining the reflexive behavior and spontaneous movements that are present prior to the development of fundamental motor skills in childhood. This is followed by an extensive examination of the fundamental movement skills that appear and are refined between the ages of 2 and 6 years. The development of fundamental movement skills is emphasized in this section because they are absolutely essential to the healthy development of children in all domains. Readers need a solid foundation with respect to how and when these fundamentals are achieved.

Next, the emphasis turns to the structural and functional constraints present in both childhood and adolescence. The structural constraints—physical growth and the changing dynamics of the body systems (including the skeletal, nervous, endocrine, and sensory systems)—are explored. The focus is on structural factors that constrain, that is, promote or limit, the acquisition and performance of both fundamental and skillful movements, providing readers with knowledge of how these structural constraints may interact with functional factors, tasks, and the environment. Two chapters on the development of functional constraints during childhood and adolescence—those that influence motor learning and performance—follow the discussion of structural constraints. The first of these chapters addresses cognitive development, knowledge, and the changing dynamics of attention and memory, while the second addresses psychosocial-affective development. Learners have different abilities with regard to cognition, knowledge, personal skills, attention, and memory—abilities that affect them in a motor learning and performance situation. The powerful impact of self-esteem, motivation, and emotion on learning and performance cannot be overstated. A strong knowledge base with regard to the development of structural and functional constraints will help readers appreciate the individual differences in a class of children or adolescents, better enabling them to design developmentally appropriate programs as discussed in part IV.

Fundamental Skills in Childhood

CHAPTER OBJECTIVES

After reading this chapter, you should be able to

> understand the term fundamental movement skills;

> identify different levels of competency in selected fundamental movement skills;

> understand what factors facilitate the acquisition of high-level fundamental movement skills;

> understand what factors interfere with the development of skilled fundamental movements;

> understand the important interactions between motor development, cognitive development, and affective development; and

> appreciate how researchers study the emergence of fundamental movement skills.

Molly at the Playground

For Molly, things were getting better and better, and she was starting to have fun in first grade. It had been hard when she first arrived at the school because everyone seemed to know each other and was good at playing games. The other children could hit pretty well, and the ball always went to the right place; when the ball came to them, they could usually catch it. At the beginning, when it was Molly's turn to get up to bat, she would get nervous and usually miss hitting the ball completely. The same kind of thing happened when she tried to jump rope. When it was her turn to jump in, she would freeze up and the rope would get tangled up in her feet. But she had had time to practice these activities much more than at her other school and with this extra practice, she started to do a lot better. Also, friends in class genuinely seemed to want her

to do well, which made Molly feel good and helped her feel less nervous when she participated in games or jumped rope. She realized that her teacher knew a lot about hitting balls, catching well, skipping, and jumping and was patient with her when she had to try things a few extra times. Now she liked going out to recess and playing, whereas before, she hadn't liked it much.

As children begin to spend more and more time in school settings, moving well and being able to play competently, both independently and with their peers, becomes tremendously important. Indeed, having successful early experiences—as Molly was beginning to have—is very important with regard to involvement in physical activity over the life span. As well, there are many ancillary cognitive and social benefits to being a skilled mover, especially in the United States, where physical skill is often rewarded. This chapter discusses the important fundamental movement skills that emerge over the first six years of life, as well as how and why they emerge. It also addresses how skilled (and less skilled) movement affects a child's development in the cognitive and social–affective domains.

Fundamental Movement Skills

During the first two years of life, amazing motor skills emerge, allowing developing infants to interact with their environments in meaningful ways. They are now able to explore somewhat capably and to act on their environments by walking in and around objects and by reaching for, grasping, manipulating, and then—if they feel like it—releasing an item of interest. No longer are they prisoners of gravity; rather, they can maintain and change their postures while lying, sitting, standing, and moving. While no one would argue that typically developing children 2 years of age or younger are not necessarily *skillful* movers, they have progressed systematically at a tremendously rapid rate and have developed an important array of rudimentary movement abilities. At the age of 2 years, they are acting upon (and are acted upon by) their physical and emotional worlds in such a way that the amount they are learning is truly amazing. This time of rapid and observable motor development is studied extensively. Researchers interested in early, preverbal cognitive and affective development are able to conduct elegant experiments that make use of observable motor acts as a window into their areas of interest (Fagan & Rovee Collier, 1983; Rovee Collier, Sullivan, Enright, Lucas, & Fagen, 1980). As we know, a picture—or in this case an action—is worth a thousand words.

The past three decades have also seen a rekindling of interest in the underlying processes that lead to developmental change in the motor domain. This renewed interest coincides with the advent of the ecological (Adolph, 1997; Gibson, 1977; Adolph, Vereijken, & Shrout, 2003; Newell, 1986) and dynamic systems (Clark & Whitall, 1989; Thelen, 1995; Thelen & Smith, 1994; Thelen & Ulrich, 1991) approaches to how perception and action develop (and influence each other) over time. These related approaches to development have been discussed extensively in earlier chapters and will provide the theoretical underpinnings as we explore the development of fundamental skills in early

Ecological approaches

childhood. To briefly recap, from the ecological and dynamic systems perspectives, movement skill emerges, and becomes refined over time, through changes in individual constraints, as well as environmental, and task-related constraints "imposed on the organism-environment system" (Savelsbergh, Davids, van der Kamp, & Bennett, 2003, p. 6). One or more of these constraints—at a particular point in developmental time—may act in a *rate-limiting* capacity, potentially inhibiting the emergence of new skills, slowing the development of existing skills, or even causing an individual to regress (i.e., to return to a less skillful level). An example of regression due to individual constraints was seen in the world-class gymnast Aurelia Dobre. Before she turned 15, Dobre was the world gymnastics champion, but she was unable to retain that incredibly high level of performance because of a combination of growth spurts and injury. She retired from international competition before she turned 19 years of age.

So, with respect to motor development, what goes on during that interesting time period following infancy we refer to as early childhood? It has been noted (Whitall, 2003) that regarding movement skill, the primary goal during early childhood has changed from acquiring movement skills to becoming an adept or proficient mover. Into and during adulthood, people's developmental goals change to maintenance of skills and finally to functional adaptations to the aging process. In a nutshell, between the ages of 2 and 6 years, some new and important movement abilities appear while existing skills become more

 ## What Do You Think?

Can you identify two highly skilled athletes who, because of changes in individual constraints, regressed, or became less skillful? This regression could be due to injury, changes in body type (morphology), or changes in movement pattern (either planned or unplanned).

Athlete	Type of individual constraint	Result

Slide

refined, flexible, and functional. Preservice physical education teachers, physical therapists, and movement scientists must be knowledgeable about (a) the fundamental movement skills that emerge during this time period, (b) how researchers study these skills, (c) what factors lead to skilled movement, (d) what factors interfere with the development of skilled movement, (e) how we can facilitate skill acquisition, and finally, (f) why we should care.

Infant Motor Skills

The primary aim of this chapter is to discuss the development of fundamental movement skills in children between the ages of 2 and 6 years. However, we must acknowledge and briefly discuss the critically important motoric developments that take place prior to the emergence of these fundamental skills. Readers are encouraged to consult a text that focuses on *motor development* for further information about the acquisition of motoric skills during infancy. In brief, during this exciting and rapidly changing time frame, three relatively distinct types of movements occur. Although authors may use slightly different terminology, these movements types are (a) reflexive behavior (some reflexes observed as early as the second or third month of fetal life until 4 months of age); (b) spontaneous movements, also referred to as rhythmical stereotypies (from 4 to 10 months of age, peaking between 6 and 10 months); and (c) voluntary movements (motor milestones) that appear and are generally refined between birth and 2 years of age.

Reflexive behaviors are thought to be automatic, involuntary responses to stimuli that are controlled at a subcortical level. That is, the higher brain centers are not involved in these movements. Generally, reflexive behaviors are broken down into three distinct categories: primitive reflexes, postural reactions, and locomotor reflexes. It is hypothesized that primitive reflexes serve the functions of protection (e.g., the startle reflex) and securing nourishment (e.g., the sucking reflex) and should disappear within a specific time frame. For example, the sucking reflex is present from birth to 3 months of age. If a particular reflex is still present beyond the typical time period, this may indicate an underlying neurological problem. Postural reactions (e.g., the parachute reflex) automatically maintain the appropriate posture in a changing environment (Haywood & Getchell, 2005). Locomotor reflexes (e.g., the stepping reflex) are thought by some theorists (Thelen, 1995; Ulrich, Ulrich, & Collier, 1992) to be precursors to voluntary locomotion and serve, at some level, as practice for these later abilities. Reflexive behaviors are not voluntary but are critical to the initial survival and later development of the young infant.

Although less often discussed than the earlier reflexive movements and the exciting motor milestones to come, spontaneous movements (rhythmical stereotypies) are frequently exhibited and are of great importance to the developing infant (figure 5.1). If you've ever watched an infant kick his legs in a rhythmical manner, thrust his arms into the air, or extend his fingers, you have observed spontaneous movements. Although they do not appear to be goal directed, these seemingly random movements are thought to have a purpose for the developing infant. These movements (both of the arms and of the legs) appear to have coordination patterns similar to those of later voluntary, goal-directed behavior. This thinking, as well as the supporting research, suggests that rhythmical stereotypies could be fundamental building blocks of the voluntary movement skills to come.

These early, voluntary movement skills are the motor milestones that mothers and fathers the world over look forward to. As exciting as it is for parents to see their infant sit up unassisted for the first time, it is even more exciting to see her

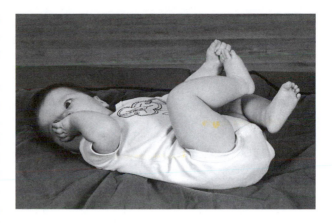

FIGURE 5.1 Early rhythmic behavior is demonstrated in an infant (approximately 5 months of age) kicking in a supine position.

take her first steps. These cortically controlled movements (contrasted with the subcortically controlled reflexes) follow a fairly predictable sequence, although individuals may vary widely in terms of when a given skill will appear. Following a cephalocaudal–proximodistal direction with regard to movement development, infants first control the head and then the upper body, which allows them over time to sit unassisted. This is followed by standing independently and exploring the environment through a variety of ambulatory patterns including crawling, creeping, cruising, and walking. The hands and arms are critical throughout this time; over the course of the first two years of life, undifferentiated and reflexive reaching becomes a relatively smooth and coordinated effort leading to exploration of the environment through reaching, grasping, and, when appropriate, releasing the object of interest. Obviously, much is in place that allows for fundamental movement skills to develop.

Breakdown of Fundamental Movement Skills

To best understand how, between 2 and 6 years of age, **fundamental movement skills** develop and why they are so important to the developing child, we must first be clear about what skills we are talking about. Referred to at times as the movement foundation (Gabbard, 2008) because of their importance in the subsequent development of more complex skill combinations used in sport, gymnastics, and dance, fundamental movement skills can be divided into the following three general groupings: **stability skills** (also referred to as nonlocomotor skills), **locomotor skills,** and **manipulative skills** (also referred to as **object control skills**). Stability skills refer to axial movements—movements around the axis of the body such as bending, stretching, swinging, swaying, pushing, pulling, turning, and twisting—that are done with little or no movement of the base of support. Locomotor skills, in contrast, transport an individual from one place to the next. The Merriam-Webster dictionary defines locomotion as the "act of moving from place to place." Although human beings most commonly move by walking or running, locomotor activities also include jumping, hopping, galloping, and skipping. These less common ways to move are nevertheless often used in sporting events (e.g., gymnastics, track and field, fencing, court games, and combative activities) and in dance as the child gets older.

The third grouping, the manipulative skills, includes an array of abilities: overarm and underarm throwing, rolling, striking, heading, kicking, punting, catching, and trapping. If we examine manipulative skills more closely, a number of issues become apparent. To begin with, they can involve either the upper body (arms or head) or the lower body; they can also involve either imparting force to an object and moving it *away* from the body or positioning a part of the body in front of an oncoming object in order to deflect or stop it. Gallahue and Ozmun (2005) have referred to these actions as propulsive and absorptive, respectively. A third issue involves the use of an implement to either impart force to an object or absorb the force of an object. Common examples of implements are rackets, bats, and gloves. Obviously, implements may or may not be used depending on the skill level of the individual, the rules of the game, or both.

A later section of the chapter revisits some of these locomotor and manipulative skills, examining what research and practice have shown about how children become competent in their execution over developmental and chronological time. At this point, though, we will consider why it is important for prospective teachers and therapists to understand the development of fundamental movement skills.

What Do You Think?

As children (and adults) become more skilled, they combine different fundamental movement skills as they engage in different sporting activities. In fielding a ground ball during a softball game, for example, a right-handed player has to slide to her right (locomotor skill), bend and turn her body as she prepares to field the ball (axial movements), field the ball with a backhand motion (absorptive manipulative skill, using an implement), and then throw the ball to first base (propulsive manipulative skill). Come up with two movement combinations that involve axial, locomotor, and manipulative skills. These combinations could be used within a game context (e.g., a team game or a racket sport) or an individual pursuit (e.g., cycling or rock climbing).

Activity	Axial skill(s) involved	Locomotor skills(s) involved	Manipulative skill(s) involved

Importance of Understanding Fundamental Movement Skills

Researchers and practitioners, as well as social critics, have addressed why the timely and appropriate acquisition of fundamental movement skills is crucial to the development of young children. From a scientific vantage point, Whitall (2003), as noted earlier, has suggested that careful study of motoric skillfulness in the young child offers a window into the development of perceptual, cognitive, and affective processes. There are also clinical reasons for careful study, as a significant number of young children struggle with their movement skills. An understanding of the level of movement skill development that should be expected of children of a given chronological age helps us to develop individualized, educative programs for students who struggle with their movement skills.

Across all societal groups, people have become more sedentary over the past two decades, with a concomitant increase in obesity and the host of health risks that accompany obesity (Mokdad et al., 1999). Teasing out the relative contributions and interactions of diet and physical inactivity, as well as genetic predispositions to obesity remains challenging; however, it is clear that inactivity plays a significant role in reducing healthful living. An important task, therefore, is to identify the factors that are likely to maintain appropriate physical activity levels throughout the life span. An array of motor developmentalists (Clark & Metcalfe, 2002; Gallahue & Ozmun, 2005; Whitall, 2003) have argued strongly that competence in fundamental motor skills is essential if individuals are to remain active over the course of their lives. Regarding the importance of establishing strong foundational skills, Clark and Metcalfe (2002) note that an inability to perform fundamental locomotor and object control (manipulative) skills will result in limited opportunities for physical activity as children age because the prerequisite skills will not be adequately developed.

With poorly developed stability, locomotor, and manipulative skills, young learners are clearly at a disadvantage when it comes to taking part in games and activities. Before too long, the requirements of play become more demanding. Movements have to be done more quickly; decisions regarding which pattern to use become more complicated; and the consequences of making the wrong play, or choosing the right play but making an error, become more important. It is little wonder that so many children stop moving. They see no reason to participate in activities that they are not good at and that lead to derision on the part of peers, often in very public ways. As Wall (personal communication, September 15, 1973) has pointed out, when a student struggles with reading, a good teacher likely will not embarrass him by having him read aloud to his classmates. When it comes to physical activities, there often is no choice. In a high-stakes game of kickball at recess, when the ball comes to a child and bounces off her hands, the result is public humiliation. The child sees no reason to endure this if she does not have to. Clark and Metcalfe (2002) noted that the acquisition of a solid base of fundamental movement skills was a prerequisite to enjoying the multiple benefits of sport and lifetime activities. In essence, in order for physical activity to become an integral part of one's life—with the concomitant physical and psychological health benefits—it is imperative to have a solid base of fundamental movement skills. This is in addition to the more general but still tremendously important benefits of movement as it relates to the acquisition of cognitive and affective information about one's place in the environment and how one relates to that place.

Gabbard (2008) noted that *how* children acquire and develop fundamental motor skills has likely been the most carefully studied area in motor development. Indeed, beginning with Wild's seminal work on overarm throwing (Wild, 1938), researchers and practitioners have been intrigued with the apparent age-related changes in fundamental motor skills, as well as the components that make up a particular skill. Whereas much of the earlier work focused on cataloging age-related (as well as gender related) changes in fundamental movement skills from a **quantitative** or *product* perspective (that is, how fast, how far, or how high), more recent work has attended to the **qualitative** or *process*-related changes in fundamental movement skills over time (Gallahue and Ozmun, 2005). It should be intuitively clear that if a child's form (that is, his mechanics) is closer to a mature level of execution, the outcome will be better. As an example, if Juan is in right field and takes a long contralateral step, pointing his toe at his target, he will likely throw the baseball farther and more accurately than if he did not take a step. The stepping action would be considered to be at a mature level, while not stepping would be considered to be at the initial stage. If, on the other hand, Juan was playing darts, taking a contralateral step would hinder his performance; he would be much better off taking a small step, if any, with the leg on his throwing side (an ipsilateral step). Gallahue and Cleland-Donnelley (2003) have suggested that practitioners use a three-tiered system to classify the level of development for a given fundamental motor skill; the tiers are initial, elementary, and mature. As discussed later, the manner in which researchers and practitioners examine qualitative changes in movement skills has been an area of debate over the past five decades.

What Do You Think?

In the example just given, Juan might have thrown the baseball skillfully, with the long contralateral step, or at an unskilled or initial level with no step. Think about a soccer player who is just learning the game. Imagine him standing in front of the goalie trying to score on a penalty kick. What does the kick look like? Now imagine the legendary Ronaldo or some other soccer superstar. What does his penalty kick look like? In the following table, describe in a qualitative manner what each kick looks like. Describe the kick as a whole, but keep in mind all parts of the body—legs, torso, arms, and head.

Novice kicker	Qualitative description of the kick
Expert kicker	Qualitative description of the kick

Whole Body Approach Versus Component Approach

When Wild (1938) did her classic cross-sectional research on the overarm throw for force, she concluded that children move through relatively invariant stages of development for the entire body. That is, in the example of Juan, if he was at a beginning (initial) stage with regard to his foot (stepping) action, he would also be at the initial stage with regard to all of the other body components involved in the throw. These would include the trunk (pelvis and spine), upper arm (humerus), and forearm. As Juan's performance improved qualitatively in one component, it would improve in all of the other components. Roberton and her colleagues, however (Roberton, 1977; Roberton & Konczak, 2001), took issue with the **whole body approach** to the development of fundamental movement skills. Their longitudinal and cross-sectional research indicated that rather than all components becoming qualitatively more advanced (that is, moving toward the mature form) at more or less the same time, different components improved at different times. Roberton referred to this perspective as the **component approach**. In this view, Juan's foot action might be at a mature level with the long contralateral step while his trunk action, with a forward–backward movement, might be at the initial level, often referred to by practitioners as an immature level.

Fundamental Locomotor and Manipulative Skills

As discussed earlier in the chapter, the development of fundamental movement skills allows the child to explore and act upon her environment in a progressively more adept fashion. At the same time, this steady improvement results in concomitant gains in the intellectual and social arenas. This section examines the development of fundamental locomotor and manipulative skills. The locomotor skills discussed are walking, running, jumping, and hopping; the manipulative skills include overarm throwing, kicking, and striking. A considerable body of research has been devoted to understanding and accurately assessing the development of fundamental movement skills; knowledge of this area will help practitioners develop the tools necessary to work effectively with young children in the motor arena.

 What Do You Think?

Take a moment and think back to when you were developing the fundamental movement skills. For some of them (running, for example) it may be difficult to remember how and when you realized, "Hey, I'm pretty good at this!" But for others, such as catching a ball, you might have a stronger memory. As you look back, think about (a) how you knew that you had mastered the skill and (b) how you arrived at that point. For example, was it by playing around with your friends in the driveway? Practicing with your mom? Playing on a travel team? Or was it through some other avenue?

Locomotor Skills

Although locomotor skills have been described simply as movements that transport people from one physical location to another (Gabbard, 2008), and although their development seems to be relatively automatic, they received considerable attention over the course of the 20th century. That this attention came from fields as diverse as biomechanics, physical therapy, and medicine suggests that efficiently moving through space may be a more complex undertaking than meets the eye. The truth is that the developing child must commandeer a dizzying array of body systems (many that are changing rapidly) and use them in a controlled and coordinated way to navigate through changing physical environments. Four-year-old Jose might be walking along a level and firm pathway and suddenly find that there is a steeply angled dip and also that the ground becomes spongier and less firm. If he doesn't speed up—that is, run downhill—he'll land flat on his face. Suddenly he has to deal with a change in angle and surface characteristics, and all at once there is a need for a new locomotor pattern, from a calm walk to a somewhat frenzied run. As noted by Gallahue and Ozmun (2005), flexibility is needed because Jose has to solve specific movement tasks that often require different skills. At one point he might be running downhill, and at another he might be playing hide and seek and need to look out for others as he moves.

When examined in more depth, the requirements for Jose to efficiently navigate his way from point A to point B seem quite remarkable. As noted earlier, the development of efficient and effective locomotor skills takes place as a variety of constraints interact one with another. A child's weight and height, as well as the length of arms and legs, are undergoing radical anthropometric changes, and at the same time, societal values influence how motivated a child might be (for example, boys don't skip) (Haywood & Getchell, 2005). Thus, in dynamic systems terms, as children develop a variety of forms of locomotion, they must do so while dealing with physical and cultural constraints that are constantly interacting with one another.

In the following sections, we'll look at the locomotor skills of walking, running, jumping, and hopping. Although jumping and hopping have not received the amount of empirical attention that walking and running have, these movements have been carefully examined by researchers, therapists, and physical education teachers. Most of the work has focused on the development of these skills during childhood (Haywood & Getchell, 2005).

Walking

More than three-quarters of a century ago, the eminent developmentalist Mary Shirley (1931) suggested that the emergence of independent walking was the most important and certainly the most impressive of the developmental milestones. Few parents who delight at their children's first uncertain steps would disagree. Although up to now, the child has been able to locomote through his environment by crawling (moving on hands and stomach), creeping (moving on hands and knees), and cruising (moving sideways so both hands and feet can be used to aid balance), the arrival of independent walking frees up the hands to further explore the changing environment. While we often think of walking as a highly automatic skill that, once learned, changes little over the course of our lives, this perception is not necessarily true. As people's physical abilities change (e.g., in arthritis) or their confidence wavers (e.g., after a serious fall), their technique might change. Environmental variables might also play a role. Vacationers walking on a sandy beach are likely to slow down their pace. People in a cold climate in the winter who encounter heavy snow or slick ice will likely modify their cadence, their trunk angle, and the amount of force used. Logic would suggest that 36-year-old Dan, dealing with early-onset arthritis of the hip and navigating an icy parking lot, would walk in a very different way than his cousin, 29-year-old Louis, enjoying perfect health and walking his dog in 75-degree Fahrenheit weather. Other factors that potentially influence walking patterns include (a) moving while handling an object (e.g., dribbling a basketball); (b) performing activities that require a great deal of balance and stability (e.g., traversing a balance beam) (Gallahue & Ozmun, 2005); and (c) walking with an external load (e.g., carrying a backpack) (Payne & Isaacs, 2008).

A number of motor developmentalists (Gabbard, 2008; Haywood & Getchell, 2005; Wickstrom, 1983) have noted, with reference to walking, that what does remain constant over the life span is the underlying timing of the act. During walking, weight shifts from the left to the right foot, with one foot in contact with the ground at all times. Generally, the initial contact of the foot occurs halfway through the gait cycle. This is referred to as a 50% phasing between the legs. A walking cycle (also referred to as a gait cycle) is made up of a support phase and a swing phase. The swing phase begins when the toes of one foot (or the whole foot) leave the ground and ends when the heel of that foot (or the whole foot) returns to the ground. The support phase of the gait cycle takes place when one foot is in contact with the ground. Therefore, when one foot is in the swing phase, the other is in the support phase. When both feet are in contact with the ground, the walker is in the double-support phase. Although early walking has been called a "precarious adventure" (Wickstrom, 1983) with frequent falls, the young walker over the next two to six years becomes an accomplished mover whose gait resembles that of a mature adult. Table 5.1 outlines the whole body approach for walking (Gabbard, 2008; Gallahue & Ozmun, 2005; Haywood & Getchell, 2005; Payne & Issacs, 2008; Wickstrom, 1983).

While the ability to perform an alternating movement pattern is present from birth (Thelen, Ulrich, & Jenson, 1989), the beginning walker must deal with a lack of both balance and strength (referred to as rate controllers or rate limiters). In order to move around the environment without falling too often, the developing walker must take short "baby" steps while using a wide stance with the toes pointing slightly outward. With the hands held in a high guard position to protect against falls, the beginning walker moves tentatively with little trunk rotation, landing on a flat foot. The pelvis tilts slightly, and the ankles are pretty well locked. Although this walking pattern is, at one level of analysis, immature, it allows for relatively stable ambulation. What it does not allow for is efficient movement with the ability to change direction smoothly and quickly. Haywood and Getchell (2005) have observed that proficient walking involves the individual's "exploiting biomechanical principles as body dimensions change" (p. 87). As a more mature gait gradually emerges (generally by

TABLE 5.1 Whole Body Approach for Walking

Initial stage

- Wide base of support
- Flat footed contact
- Toes pointed outwards
- Short steps
- Quick, rigid steps
- No trunk rotation
- Single knee lock position
- Flexed knee at contact followed by rapid knee extension
- Significant hip flexion
- Slight forward pelvic tilt
- Arms held in high guard position
- Arms held rigidly with little or no movement

Elementary stage

- Narrowing of the base of support
- Out toeing occurs less frequently
- Increase in pelvic rotation
- Heel strike becomes apparent
- Increase in stride length
- Reduction in hip flexion
- Reduction in forward pelvic tilt

Mature stage

- Significantly narrowed base of support
- Foot contact becomes heel–toe as opposed to flat footed
- Single knee lock pattern is replaced by double knee lock pattern
- Increased step and stride length
- Increased walking speed and step frequency
- Oppositional arm swing apparent

age 4 or 5), the following characteristics are seen (Haywood & Getchell, 2005; Gabbard, 2008):

- **Base of support and foot angle.** The dynamic base of support (that is, the base of support during moving) is reduced to approximately the width of the individual's trunk. This narrowing generally takes place 4.5 months after independent walking begins, allowing for more efficient movement (Gabbard, 2008). With regard to foot angle, the beginning walker tends to move with the toes out (toeing out). This pattern disappears at approximately the same time the base of support narrows, with the foot becoming aligned in a straight fore–aft position. Both the narrowing of the base of support and the disappearance of toeing out result in application of forces in a forward–backward plane (Haywood & Getchell, 2005), a significantly more efficient movement pattern. In-toeing (commonly referred to as a pigeon-toed gait) is not a normal pattern and is seen only infrequently.

- **Foot contact.** As walkers develop, they move from the flat footfall to a heel–toe pattern, resulting in an increased range of motion. Toe walking is often seen in young children and is not a cause for concern; however, if it persists beyond 3 years of age it should be examined.

- **Step and stride length.** Between ages 1 and 7 years, step and stride length almost doubles. This is due, for the most part, to significant increases in force and leg extension at push-off. Secondarily, children's stride length increases because of increased leg length.

- **Walking speed and step frequency.** As walking develops, speed increases while step frequency (steps per minute) decreases. Sutherland (1997) has hypothesized that increased neuromuscular control in older walkers is primarily responsible for the decreased step frequency. Fundamentally, younger walkers lack the postural control to increase speed through longer strides and thus must take more frequent steps.

- **Double knee lock.** As walking improves, children increase their range of motion through the double knee-lock pattern. The knee is extended at heel strike, flexed slightly as body weight shifts over the support leg, and extended once more at push-off.

- **Pelvic rotation.** By 14 months of age, pelvic rotation is apparent, allowing for full range of motion as well as oppositional movements of the upper and lower body.

- **Oppositional arm swing.** As noted earlier, beginning walkers have their arms in a high guard position with elbows slightly flexed and abducted. Over the ensuing months, this position is gradually replaced by a mechanically efficient oppositional arm swing. Initially, the arm swing may not be coordinated, with the arms sometimes coming forward in unison. Over time, oppositional arm swing becomes established, and the opposite arm and leg come forward and backward at the same time. As this reciprocal movement is refined, the arm swing becomes relaxed, with slight movement at both the shoulder and the elbow (Haywood & Getchell, 2005).

As noted previously, the development of proficient walking not only allows children to explore their environment capably but also provides a stable and effective base for more advanced locomotor skills.

Running

Randy looked down at his watch and realized that dinner would be on the table in 6 minutes and he had a long way to go before he got home. Walking would not get him there on time, and a light jog wouldn't do it either. Even though the terrain was uneven, he launched into a smooth run. Randy made it to the dinner table with minutes to spare. Running has been characterized as an extension of walking, and certainly the two forms of locomotion have much in common—the reciprocal arm and leg action as well as the alternating leg action. However, there are clear differences; primary among these is that running does not have a double-support phase. Instead there is a flight phase during which neither foot is in contact with the ground. Randy's running wasn't always as smooth as on that evening. When he began to run (approximately 6 to 7 months after beginning to walk independently), he had to develop enough strength to become airborne, as well as the balance to catch himself on one leg and maintain balance on that leg while moving forward. Thus, developing adequate strength and balance is imperative, and these factors may act as *rate limiters* for the developing runner. Table 5.2 presents a hypothesized developmental sequence for running, including both leg and arm action (Gabbard, 2008; Gallahue & Ozmun, 2005; Haywood & Getchell, 2005; Payne & Issacs, 2008; Wickstrom, 1983).

As children mature physically (specifically, gain in measures of body size and strength as well as coordination) and get more practice, they show concomitant improvements in both process and product measures related to running. With regard to product measures, they run more quickly and increase the amount of time spent in the flight phase. With respect to the running process, the following positive changes take place over developmental time, resulting in a mature run pattern (Wickstrom, 1983; Haywood & Getchell, 2005):

1. A slight forward lean is maintained throughout the stride.
2. The arms swing in a synchronized pattern in opposition to the leg pattern, with the elbows held at approximately 90 degrees.
3. The support foot makes contact with the ground approximately under the center of gravity in a flat-footed fashion.
4. The knee of the support leg bends slightly after the foot contacts the ground.
5. The body is moved forward and upward (into the nonsupport phase) through forceful extension of the support leg at the ankle, knee, and hip.
6. The recovery knee moves forcefully to a high knee raise while the lower leg simultaneously flexes, bringing the heel close to the buttock.
7. Out-toeing is eliminated and the base of support is narrowed.
8. Trunk rotation increases, leading to greater stride length as well as improved arm–leg opposition.

For typically developing children, learning to run proficiently occurs fairly automatically. However, if more advanced maneuvers are being taught (i.e., chasing, fleeing, or changing direction quickly) or an increase in absolute speed is the aim, effective teaching techniques (based on the student's developmental age) should be used.

TABLE 5.2 Whole Body Approach for Running

Initial stage

- Exaggerated movements of legs and feet
- Minimal flight period
- Flat footed contact, generally (although some children run on tiptoes)
- Wide base of support
- Arms held in either a middle or high guard position
- Arms move to the sides as opposed to back and forth

Elementary stage

- Hip, knee, and ankle extension is increased at takeoff
- Increased height of the forward knee at takeoff
- Length of running stride is increased
- Speed of running is increased
- Flight period is increased
- Horizontal arm swing is increased

Mature stage

- Narrowed base of support
- Length of running stride increased further
- Greater application of force
- Slight forward lean of trunk
- Arms move in a large arc, in opposition to the leg movements
- Arms are bent at the elbows at approximately 90°
- Recovery knee is raised high and swings forward quickly
- Support leg bends slightly at contact and subsequently extends quickly and completely

Jumping

A child who can run has the essential ingredients needed to be a jumper; and from the age of 2, children begin to explore and develop ways of moving the body through space other than walking and running. As Gabbard (2008) has pointed out, "Jumping is one of the most diverse and fundamental of all motor skills" (p. 271). The family of jumps is a large one; it is made up of leaping (a one-foot takeoff followed by a landing on the opposite foot), hopping (jumping from one foot to the same foot in a rhythmic fashion), the vertical jump for height (two-foot takeoff with a two-foot landing), and the standing long jump or horizontal jump for distance (two-foot takeoff with a two-foot landing).

Developing proficiency in this assortment of jumps allowed Randy in our example not only to speed along quickly and fluidly but also to keep his brand-new shoes dry by jumping over a narrow stream. As he got closer to home and knew that he had time to spare, Randy gathered himself, jumped high in the air, and grabbed an apple from a tree. As Randy became older, all the jumping skills he had developed helped him with the activities he liked—hitting a volleyball, making a layup, and running the steeplechase. Jumping is a fundamental movement skill whereby an individual projects the body into the air by the force generated by either one or both legs, subsequently landing on one or both feet. This broad definition includes leaping, hopping, the vertical jump, and the horizontal jump. Jumping can be done in a forward, backward, or sideways direction. Although related to walking and running (the leap is actually an exaggerated running step), jumping is a more challenging movement skill for children to master. They need adequate strength to get the body into the air, postural control and coordination while in the air, and balance upon landing. When it comes to hopping, strength is particularly important as the one-foot-to-one-foot pattern is done repeatedly. Wickstrom (1983) has observed that, beyond the significant physical requirements of jumping, there are confidence requirements. Jumping from heights, in particular, requires a certain level of bravery. In an early investigation, Gutteridge (1939) noted that when children had to jump from an increased height or were introduced to a new type of jump, they reverted back to an earlier form of jumping.

Gutteridge's and Wickstrom's observations lead to an interesting question that motor developmentalists must answer, regardless of the skill being considered: How do we measure improvement? Haywood and Getchell (2005) have suggested the three following methods:

- Use of age norms: Comparing when an individual acquires a skill to when most individuals acquire the skill
- Quantitative measures: Determining how much of something is present; for jumping, determining the height or the distance of the jump
- Qualitative measures: Observing the pattern or form of the movement

Along with these three methods, Wickstrom's perspective regarding courage or confidence should be considered. Although this is more difficult to evaluate objectively, how sure a child is of her skill level has a considerable bearing on how well she performs.

With respect to the age at which preschool children typically learn various types of jumps, early scholars in the area of motor development (Bayley, 1935; McCaskill & Wellman, 1938) have assigned approximate ages. Wickstrom (1983) stressed that these are approximate because of the wide range of scores observed. These normative data are shown in table 5.3. As there have clearly been changes in the size and strength of people of all ages over the past century (referred to as a *secular trend*), the likelihood is strong that children born in the 21st century will achieve these jumping landmarks at somewhat younger ages.

Skill development in children involves the gradual refinement of movement abilities over time. Indeed, researchers examining the acquisition of movement skill from a dynamic systems perspective (Ulrich et al., 1992) have noted that children who refine their movement patterns appear better able to take advantage of the principles of motion. These observations clearly apply to the acquisition of jumping skill. With respect to the refinement over time of movement abilities, Haywood and Getchell (2005) have noted that even if beginning jumpers intend to perform a long jump, because of limitations in their form (the qualitative components of the jump) they end up doing a vertical jump. This is largely due to posture that is too erect. By 3 years of age, however, the developing child is able to modify the trunk angle to perform either a vertical or horizontal jump—that is, the one that they want to do (Clark, Phillips, & Peterson, 1989). Early jumps, for either height or distance, are characterized by a preparatory crouch that is shallow. That is, the hip, knees, and ankles are not flexed enough to generate a significant amount of force. Additionally, the legs remain slightly flexed at takeoff. Beginning jumpers often use a one-foot takeoff (also referred to as a step-out), as well as a landing during which one foot touches down before the other. Because of the one-foot takeoff, the legs are frequently asymmetrical during flight. Adopting a two-foot takeoff, with an appropriate body lean, generally keeps the legs symmetrical and thus more aerodynamic during flight.

Although to this point the discussion has concentrated on the lower body, how the arms are used can help or hinder jumping. Beginning jumpers often demonstrate arm actions that are not beneficial when it comes to performing a skillful long jump or vertical jump. The arms may be used asymmetrically, may be held stationary (at the jumper's sides), or may be held in a high guard position for protection in case of a fall.

TABLE 5.3   Jumping Achievements of Preschool Children

Achievement	Motor age (months)	Source
Jump from 12-inch height; one foot ahead	24	M and W
Jump off floor; both feet	28	B
Jump from 18-inch height; one foot ahead	31	M and W
Jump from chair 26 centimeters high; both feet	32	B
Jump from 8-inch height; both feet	33	M and W
Jump from 12-inch height; both feet	34	M and W
Jump from 18-inch height; both feet	37	M and W
Jump from 30-centimeter height; both feet	37.1	B
Jump forward 10 to 35 centimeters from 30-centimeter height; both feet	37.3	B
Hop on two feet one to three times	38	M and W
Jump over rope 5 to 20 centimeters high; both feet	41.5	B
Hop on one foot one to three times	43	M and W

Reprinted, by permission, from R.L. Wickstrom, 1983, *Fundamental motor patterns* (Philadelphia: Lea & Febiger), 68. Adapted from information in studies by Bayley (B) (1935) and McCaskill and Wellman (M and W) (1938).

Despite these inauspicious beginnings, most children learn to jump effectively by the time they begin school. Movement toward the mature jumps outlined earlier depends on the opportunity to practice in varied environments as well as normal growth in body size and strength. While consistent quantitative changes in jump distance (average increases of 3 to 5 inches [7.6 to 12.7 centimeters] a year during the elementary years) and height (average increases of 2 inches [5 centimeters] per year during the elementary years) have been cataloged (DeOreo & Keogh, 1980), qualitative changes are more varied (Haywood & Getchell, 2005).

As discussed earlier and demonstrated for the skill of running in table 5.2, changes in movement skill have been presented by researchers as developmental sequences that capture the qualitative changes in the critical features of a skill. Both the whole body approach and the component approach identify the steps children go through in moving from inefficient movements to more skillful patterns. Tables 5.4 and 5.5, present developmental characteristics of the standing long jump and the vertical jump, respectively, utilizing the whole body approach (Gabbard, 2008; Gallahue & Ozmun, 2005; Haywood & Getchell, 2005; Payne & Issacs, 2008; Wickstrom, 1983).

The standing long jump (also referred to as the horizontal jump or broad jump) and the vertical jump have much in common. Both jumps have easily identifiable preparatory, takeoff, flight, and landing phases, and the takeoffs and landings are two footed. However, the standing long jump presents more movement challenges than the vertical jump. Because the jumper is moving his body both upward and outward, the center of gravity must be slightly in front of the base of support at takeoff. Proficient jumping requires a takeoff angle of approximately 45°. This is a challenge for developing jumpers, and thus they frequently step out in order to maintain their balance (Gabbard, 2008). A second significant movement challenge for long jumpers is swinging their legs from behind the center of gravity (at takeoff) forward and under the trunk in preparation for landing. Because the vertical jump does not require the body to tip forward or the legs to swing forward, it is an easier jump to perform and master compared to the long jump.

Hopping

A hop takes place when an individual takes off and lands on the same foot. As discussed earlier, this movement requires considerable strength and balance. The proficient hopper demonstrates certain characteristics (Haywood & Getchell, 2005, p. 100):

1. The swing leg leads the hip.
2. The support leg extends fully.
3. The arms move in opposition to the legs.
4. The support leg flexes at landing to absorb the force of the landing and to prepare for extension at the next takeoff.

Both a component developmental sequence (Halverson & Williams, 1985) and a whole body developmental sequence (Gallahue & Ozmun, 2005) for the hop have been developed. Table 5.6 presents a whole body sequence (Gabbard, 2008; Gallahue & Ozmun, 2005; Haywood & Getchell, 2005; Payne & Issacs, 2008; Wickstrom, 1983).

TABLE 5.4 Whole Body Approach for the Standing Long Jump

Initial stage

- Limited and inconsistent preparatory crouch
- Trunk lean is less than 30°
- Minimal extension of the hips and knees at takeoff and during flight
- Minimal and ineffective arm swing (arms held rigidly at the sides with elbows flexed or arms held in winged position)
- Legs are positioned asymmetrically during flight
- Vertical force is generally greater than horizontal force leading to an upward rather than a forward jump
- An inability to flex the hips and knees during the jump leads to an abrupt landing

Elementary stage

- Preparatory crouch becomes deeper and more consistent
- Extension of hip and knees is increased
- Forward swing of arms (in the anteroposterior plane) is increased
- Total body extension at takeoff is increased
- Increase in thigh flexion during flight

Mature stage

- Deep preparatory crouch with flexion of the hips, knees, and ankles
- Trunk lean is at least 30°
- Arms are swung backwards simultaneously in a smooth fashion
- Heels come off of the ground before knee extension
- Rapid and vigorous extension, at takeoff, of the hips and knees in the direction of travel
- Arms vigorously swing forward and upwards
- Both knees are flexed with the thighs brought forward, parallel to the ground during flight
- Lower legs swing forward for a two footed landing

TABLE 5.5 Whole Body Approach for Vertical Jumping

Initial stage

- Form is variable and unpredictable
- Limited and inconsistent preparatory crouch
- Legs are not fully extended at takeoff
- Very quick flexion of hips and knees (the legs are tucked under the body)
- Sideways elevation of the arms and shoulders
- Forward flexion of the head

Elementary stage

- Form becomes less variable and more predictable
- Preparatory crouch becomes deeper (with increased knee bend)
- A two foot takeoff takes place
- Arms are used to aid in flight and balance, but often unequally
- Body does not extend completely during flight

Mature stage

- Deep preparatory crouch with flexion of the hips, knees, and ankles
- Hips, knees, and ankles extend completely upon takeoff
- Very quick flexion of hips and knees (the legs are tucked under the body)
- Arms are swung forward and up
- One hand continues up while the other comes down resulting in an effective tipping of the shoulder girdle near the peak of the jump
- Backward (dorsi) flexion of the head
- Extension of the trunk at the crest of the reach
- Landing is on the balls of the feet with the hips and knees flexed

  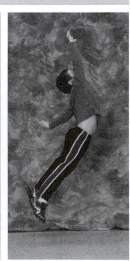

TABLE 5.6 Whole Body Approach for Hopping

Initial stage

- Little forward movement
- Little elevation
- Movement is jerky
- Support leg is lifted by flexion rather than by forceful extension
- Nonsupport (swing) leg is generally held high and is largely inactive
- Minimal arm action; any action is minimal or inconsistent
- Arms are held in the high guard position and to the sides for balance
- Flat footed landings

Elementary stage

- Increased forward movement
- Increased elevation
- Support leg is lifted by minimal knee and ankle extension because of slight body lean
- Nonsupport (swing) leg moves forward and upward
- Arms begin to be used (bilaterally) for thrust rather than for balance

Mature stage

- Weight is transferred smoothly, upon landing, to the ball of the foot of the support leg before the ankle and knee extend
- The support leg reaches almost full extension upon takeoff
- Swing leg leads movement, pumping upwards and downwards
- The pumping action of the swing leg increases such that, when viewed from the side, it passes behind the support leg
- Arm opposite the swing leg moves in an upward and forward direction in synchrony with the upward and forward movement of the swing leg
- The other arm moves in a direction opposite to that of the swing leg
- A vigorous swinging action may not be present unless there are speed and/or distance requirements

Manipulative Skills

When children are able to walk in and around their immediate environment independently, their hands (and feet) are suddenly available to explore even more thoroughly. All of a sudden, they can impart force to an object and watch it move through the environment. They can also receive objects projected toward them. Gallahue and Ozmun (2005) have observed that manipulative skills (also referred to as object control skills) generally involve a combination of at least two movements and are performed in concert with other types of movements. For example, in striking a ball with a bat, stepping, turning, swinging, and stretching occur. Fundamental manipulative skills include overarm throwing, catching with one or both hands, and kicking and striking objects (with or without an implement). This section discusses the development of the ballistic skills of overarm throwing, kicking, and striking.

Overarm Throwing

Objects can be thrown from a variety of positions including, but not limited to, underhand, sidearm, and overarm (also referred to as overhand) throws. The pattern chosen by the individual has much to do with the task to be performed, that is, (a) what the thrower hopes to accomplish and (b) specific constraints of the task as defined by the size, shape, and weight of the implement to be thrown (e.g., regulation-size football vs. a basketball). From a biomechanical (technique) perspective, the three throws have much in common. Here we concentrate on the overarm throw, as it is frequently used in sports (e.g., softball, European handball, football) and has been extensively studied over the past 70 years (Halverson, Roberton, & Langendorfer, 1982; Haubenstricker, Branta, & Seefeldt, 1983; McCleneghan & Gallahue, 1978; Wild, 1938; Roberton & Konczak, 2001). As with all fundamental motor skills, overarm throwing can be examined in a number of ways. If researchers use a quantitative or product approach, they focus on such outcomes as ball velocity, distance thrown, or accuracy. Researchers have, since Wild's initial work in 1938, also looked at throwing from a qualitative or process approach. Haywood and Getchell (2005) persuasively argue for the usefulness of rigorously examining the quality of the movement. Coaches, parents, and physical education teachers will be of most use to developing throwers if they become skilled at (a) assessing *how* the individual throws and (b) setting up the task and environment so that throwing improves and the learner is engaged in and excited about the activities.

Children first demonstrate a rudimentary overarm throw when they are approximately 6 months of age and in a sitting position (Eckert, 1987). Although a majority of children demonstrate a mature overarm throwing pattern by 6 years of age, a significant number remain unskilled into adulthood (this is particularly true for girls, an observation that has garnered a large amount of research attention over the past four decades). A study by Halverson and colleagues (1982) supports observations that many children remain unskilled throwers well into their middle school years and that many more girls remain unskilled compared to boys. The authors observed the development of overarm throwing in a sample of both boys and girls from kindergarten through grade 7. Using this longitudinal approach, the authors noted that by the seventh grade, 80% of males had reached the mature level of upper arm action while only 29% of females had done so. Other studies (see, for example, Leme & Shambes, 1978) indicate that many women never achieve a mature throw. Indeed, it has been repeatedly demonstrated that men outperform women in overarm throwing at all ages (Butterfield & Loovis, 1993; Halverson et al., 1982; Rehling, 1996). It was hypothesized that with the advent of Title IX, the gap between boys and girls would narrow; however, more recent work by Runion, Roberton, and Langendorfer (2003) on throw velocity suggests that significant quantitative differences between the genders remain. Irrespective of gender differences, the route to a mature throwing pattern appears to be a circuitous one, and considerable variability in movement patterns is a consistent observation (Wickstrom, 1983). By being aware of what elements are involved in an excellent throw, practitioners and parents become more attuned to what is missing given a more immature attempt.

As presented earlier in this chapter, changes in throwing proficiency can be cataloged through either a component or a whole body approach. Both approaches precisely delineate changes in competency as the developing child moves toward throwing proficiency. Table 5.7 presents the hypothesized whole body developmental sequence for the overarm throw for distance (Gabbard, 2008; Gallahue & Ozmun, 2005; Haywood & Getchell, 2005; Payne & Issacs, 2008; Wickstrom, 1983).

Try This

Stand 20 feet (6 meters) away from a target located at head height. Throw a tennis ball at the target 10 times with your dominant hand, keeping track of the number of times you hit the target. As well, think about how you're throwing, that is, the quality of the throw. Now, throw the tennis ball 10 times with your nondominant hand, again keeping track of how many times you hit the target and the quality of the throw. After completing this exercise, write down the differences you experienced both quantitatively (how many times you hit the target) and qualitatively. Having done this exercise independently, have a partner observe you doing the same thing. Compare their qualitative observations with your own. Which observations would you consider the most accurate, and why?

Research Notes: Do Men and Women Differ in Darts?

Much has been written about differences in the throwing abilities of young and adult males and females. Usually, though, the type of throw examined is the overarm throw for distance, accuracy, or both. Duffy and her colleagues (Duffy, Eriksson, & Baluch, 2007) took a detailed look at the accuracy of male and female competitive dart players and reported that the least-skilled male dart players (competing at a club level) were significantly more accomplished than the international-level female players in their sample. The average score of the 15 best female dart players was 15.6, while the average score of the 15 best men was 22.6. This is an extremely large difference between the genders (statistically significant at the .001 level) and prompts the question: Why? The authors, citing research from not only the athletic arena, but also music, ballet, and chess, note that when it came to the development of elite performers, practice generally started at a very early age. Both male and female dart throwers, however, rarely began their training when they were young; instead they began their training at 18 to 20 years of age. In their discussion, Duffy and her colleagues wonder whether or not beginning systematic practice at a much earlier age would decrease the differences in ability between the genders. They point out that many difficult questions must be studied more thoroughly before we will be able to understand, in adequate depth, the benefits (and shortcomings) of such early intervention.

TABLE 5.7 Whole Body Approach for the Overarm Throw for Distance

Initial stage

- Throw tends to result from arm action only
- No preparatory backswing; rather, the hand is brought back with the elbow up
- Throw is completed by releasing the ball following elbow extension
- Follow through occurs in a forward direction, if present
- There is either little or no trunk action; if trunk action takes place, it does so in a forward-backward direction
- Body weight may shift slightly to the rear in order to maintain balance
- There is no step taken

Elementary stage

- Trunk and shoulders rotate toward throwing side to prepare for the throw
- A sideward and backward swing of the arm then brings the ball to a position behind the head with the elbow flexed
- The arm is swung forward, high over the shoulder
- The forearm extends before the ball is released
- A forward shift in body weight is evident
- An ipsilateral step (same-side step) is taken during the throw

Mature stage

- Body pivots to the throwing side with the weight on the foot of the throwing side
- Throwing arm swings back in a circular downward direction
- Elbow of nonthrowing arm is raised for balance
- Elbow of the throwing arm is bent at approximately a right angle
- A long contralateral (opposite side) step is taken in the direction of the target
- There is differentiated trunk rotation; that is, the pelvis begins to rotate before the upper spine in the initiation of trunk rotation
- Throwing elbow moves forward horizontally as it extends
- The forearm lags behind at the moment the shoulders are front facing
- The ball is released just forward of the head; at this point, the arm is extended at the elbow
- The arm follows through across the body after ball release

Kicking

As with throwing, a kick imparts force to an object. However, with the kick, the individual strikes the object as opposed to hurling it. To kick proficiently, the individual must have, as prerequisites, adequate perceptual abilities along with eye–foot coordination. As with throwing, children kick in a number of different ways. Gallahue and Ozmun (2005) have postulated that the kick chosen is based on the desired trajectory and how high the ball is when contacted. A third consideration, in the playing of a sport, is what techniques the rules allow. For example, in soccer, the goaltender may hold the ball in the hands, drop it, and then kick it; other players may not contact the ball with the hands, which means that a different type of kicking technique is necessary.

As with the other fundamental movement skills, an advanced kick has certain critical features. In this section we consider the place kick, a kick that is performed when the ball is either on the ground or on a kicking tee.

As with throwing, immature kickers do not sequence their actions; rather, the kick is a single action, and the force imparted to the ball is inadequate. The action is more of a push, with the kicking leg often remaining bent on contact. The development of kicking skill has not been carefully examined with regard to the qualitative changes needed for proficiency. Given that only 10% of the 7.5- to 9.0-year-old children studied by Haubenstricker, Seefeldt, and Branta (1983) were proficient kickers, it appears that more careful examination of developmental changes in this fundamental movement skill is imperative. Initial work has been done on the validation of a whole body developmental sequence for place kicking (Haubenstricker, Seefeldt, Fountain, & Sapp, 1981; Seefeldt & Haubenstricker, 1975). Table 5.8 shows the hypothesized whole body developmental sequence (Gabbard, 2008; Gallahue & Ozmun, 2005; Haywood & Getchell, 2005; Payne & Issacs, 2008; Wickstrom, 1983).

Try This

As you did with throwing, stand 20 feet (6 meters) away from a target located at head height. Kick a soccer ball with your dominant leg at the target 10 times, keeping track of the number of times you hit the target. As well, think about how you're kicking, that is, the quality of the kick. Now, kick the soccer ball 10 times with your nondominant leg, again keeping track of how many times you hit the target and the quality of the kick. Then write down the differences you experienced both quantitatively and qualitatively. Have a partner observe you doing the same thing. Compare their qualitative observations with your own. Which observations would you consider the most accurate, and why?

TABLE 5.8 Whole Body Approach for Place Kicking

Initial stage

- A simple pushing of the ball with the foot
- Straight pendular motion of kicking leg
- Very limited range of motion; minimal backswing and follow through
- No step forward with the nonkicking leg
- Trunk remains upright with no rotation present; there is very limited movement of the upper body
- The knee of the kicking leg is often bent at contact
- Arms are held out to the sides to aid in the maintenance of balance

Elementary stage

- The range of motion of the kicking leg (backswing and follow through) increases at the hip and knee
- The kicker takes one or more deliberate steps while approaching the ball
- The kicker tends to start farther behind the ball and move his or her body forward into the kick
- The support leg is placed slightly to the side of the ball
- Kicking leg is in a cocked position and tends to remain bent throughout the kick
- The kicking leg often retracts after completing the kick; that is, there is minimal follow through
- There is an increase in compensatory trunk lean and arm opposition

Mature stage

- Following one or more deliberate steps, the kicker becomes airborne immediately before contacting the ball allowing appropriate hyperextension of the hip and flexion of the knee
- The trunk is rotated to the side and the knee of the kicking leg is flexed
- The knee of the kicking leg extends rapidly just prior to contacting the ball
- The arms are used in opposition to the legs during the kick
- The trunk bends at the waist during follow-through
- If there is sufficient forward momentum, the kicker will either hop on the support leg or scissor the legs while in the air, thus allowing a landing on the kicking foot

Striking

Striking is a skill that is used in many different sporting activities, employing many different configurations. It can be done with an implement (e.g., bat, racket, golf club) or with a body part (e.g., head, hand, foot). It can be performed in a variety of orientations—swinging a bat sidearm, spiking a volleyball overhand, hitting an overhead smash in tennis, or driving a golf ball underhand. Striking can also be done with either one or two hands (e.g., one-handed backhand or two-handed backhand in tennis). With such an array of orientations, implements, and sporting activities, one would think that this fundamental motor skill would have been studied extensively. It has not. Haywood and Getchell (2005) have suggested that the dearth of research may be a result of the difficulty of the task. Indeed, the perceptual judgments needed to make effective contact with a projectile, often a moving one, are tremendously challenging. As many frustrated golfers know, making contact with a stationary ball can also be more than a little challenging. Because the developing child generally lacks the ability to strike a moving object, teachers and researchers adapt the task by making the ball stationary. As the child becomes more adept, a slowly moving ball with a smooth trajectory can be used. The size and shape of the object to be struck can be modified, as can the length and weight of the object used to do the striking. As with jumping for height and jumping for distance, different configurations for striking (e.g., overarm, sidearm) have certain commonalities. These commonalities, for the inexperienced as well as the advanced striker, are presented in table 5.9.

Although the research base for striking is sparse, Seefeldt and Haubenstricker (1976) have hypothesized a whole body developmental sequence for striking with a bat. The sequence has not been validated, but it provides practitioners with fundamental and important information regarding the development of mature striking. Table 5.10 presents a hypothesized whole body developmental sequence for sidearm striking (Gabbard, 2008; Gallahue & Ozmun, 2005; Haywood & Getchell, 2005; Payne & Issacs, 2008; Wickstrom, 1983).

TABLE 5.9 Characteristics of General Striking Development

Inexperienced striker	Advanced striker
1. Generally, the striker does not take a step. If a step is taken, it is with the ipsilateral leg. 2. The striker uses an up or down chopping motion. 3. There is very little backswing with the implement or the striking arm. 4. There is no trunk or hip rotation. 5. Little or no wrist snap is apparent when striking is done with a racket or a bat. The striker generally holds the arms rigidly.	1. The striker takes a forward step with the foot opposite the striking arm or striking side (contralateral). 2. The striker swings the implement in a horizontal plane. 3. An appropriate backswing is used. 4. Differentiated trunk rotation is used. 5. In the two-handed striking pattern, the arms are relaxed, and a coordinated wrist snap is present when a bat is swung.

Adapted, by permission, from V.G. Payne and L.D. Isaacs, 2008, *Human motor development: A lifespan approach*, 7th ed. (New York: McGraw-Hill), 349. ©The McGraw-Hill Companies, Inc.

TABLE 5.10 Whole Body Approach for Sidearm Striking

Initial stage

- Early attempts to strike are similar to the immature throwing motion with the racket being swung in a vertical (chopping) motion
- Motion is from back to front with a slight bend at the waist
- The striker flexes and extends his forearm to chop at the ball while the trunk directly faces the direction of the tossed ball
- There is minimal involvement of the trunk and legs and the feet are, generally, stationary
- There is minimal or no weight transfer
- Arms are held rigidly, with little or no wrist snap

Elementary stage

- Striker stands sideways to the ball
- Striker transfers his weight from the rear foot to the front foot by taking a step forward
- Differentiated (hip then shoulder) rotation is apparent
- The plane of the swing changes from the vertical chop to an oblique plane to a horizontal plane
- The elbows are held away from the sides allowing for extension of the arms before contact resulting in increased force productions

Mature stage

- Trunk is turned to the side in anticipation of a thrown ball
- Weight is shifted to the back foot with the trunk and hips, subsequently, rotating before ball contact
- The striker uses a full range of motion and strikes the ball in the horizontal plane
- Weight shifts to forward foot at contact
- The striker's arms are relaxed

Summary

The development of fundamental movement skills is absolutely essential to the healthy development of children. Children given a strong movement foundation will have the skill set—and the confidence—to be physically active on their own, with their families, and with their peers. Whether the child ultimately decides to participate in more formalized athletic events or is content to play more recreationally is of course up to the individual. What is evident, though, is that carefully designed movement environments and progressive educational experiences that are well thought through are essential for early and sustained success. This chapter has laid a solid foundation with respect to how and when these fundamentals are achieved. Practitioners can take the concepts that have been presented and build upon them through practical experiences, focused research, or a combination of the two.

Supplemental Activities

Activity 1: Accurately Observing and Assessing Fundamental Locomotor Skills

It is imperative that you be able to accurately assess, qualitatively, how skillfully individuals move through space. Accurate assessment requires frequent, well thought out observations. From the internet (YouTube or another video sharing website), access video clips of novice and expert runners (one of each) and, using the component approach to running discussed in this chapter, assess their proficiency. Watch each video clip at least five times. Use the following checklist in completing the assignment.

	Novice Age: Gender:	Expert Age: Gender:
Leg action Step 1: Minimal flight		
Step 2: Crossover swing		
Step 3: Direct projection		
Arm action Step 1: Middle guard		
Step 2: Oblique arm swing		
Step 3: Opposition, sagittal		

Discussion Questions

1. Were some components more difficult to observe than others?
2. Did the observations become easier the more you viewed the video clip?
3. Was it easier to rate the expert runner? Why or why not?

Activity 2: Observing Gender Differences in Overarm Throwing or Kicking

For this activity you are to watch elementary-age students playing either soccer or softball, depending on the time of year. Go to a local sports complex, recreational facility, or school, at which you are allowed to observe. Choose two male players and two female players and watch them throughout the contest. Using the whole body approach as outlined in this chapter, assess the proficiency level of four players. If you are watching soccer, assess kicking; if you are watching softball, assess the overarm throw.

Discussion Questions

1. Did you observe differences in the proficiency levels that broke down along gender lines?
2. If so, why do you think this was the case? If there were no gender differences, why not?
3. Do you feel you became more proficient with regard to accurately assessing kicking or throwing as you had more experience observing?
4. Were the individuals consistent in their attempts, or was there considerable variability?

Structural Constraints in Childhood and Adolescence

CHAPTER OBJECTIVES

After reading this chapter, you should be able to

> understand the role of genes and environment in motor learning and development;

> discuss distance and velocity curves as well as relative growth;

> discuss key developmental changes in skeletal, nervous, endocrine, and adipose systems; and

> understand the developmental changes in three sensory systems.

Great Diversity

Chelsea just completed her kinesiology degree and has been hired by the local fitness club. On Saturday, she meets a group of 12-year-old children for a "Fun and Fit" class. She recalls her university professor speaking about individual differences such as height. Of course people are different; she did not have to attend a university to know that the class would vary in such things as height. But as she interacts with the group, she notices that other physical features distinguish children in the class. Many of the girls are taller than the boys, and some look more like mature women. While many of the boys are barely 5 feet (152 centimeters) and still have young voices, a couple of them are approaching 6 feet (183 centimeters) and have some facial hair. There also appear to be large differences in strength and body shape. And oh yes, there are huge differences in movement skill that become evident as she directs a few games. Chelsea wonders how these physical factors will affect fitness and whether genetic differences largely explain the vast range of skill.

Define constraints

Boundaries that limit a person's movement capabilities

As dynamic

As dynamic systems and ecological theories predict, intrinsic dynamics are constraints that affect observable motor patterns and the learning or refinement of new motor skills. We hinted in chapter 1 that the size and shape of an individual are important constraints but did not explain developmental changes in height, weight, or physique—nor did we describe other structural differences in individuals such as bone growth and development, muscular development, or changes in sensory systems such as vision or spatial awareness. This chapter explains how both genetic and environmental factors may affect motor learning and development. It then deals with the important and fascinating growth changes in height and weight and outlines the developmental changes in systems—the skeletal, nervous, endocrine, and adipose systems as well as the sensory systems of vision, audition, and kinesthesis. All of these systems can function as constraints to learning and development. This discussion should assist professionals concerned with the learning and development of physical skills. The next chapter deals with the functional constraints of learners that would further help Chelsea understand the vast differences in her group of 12-year-olds.

Perhaps the famed cartoonist Charles Schultz summed up the essence of this chapter with his insightful cartoon (figure 6.1). There is motivation to throw that basketball, but also the realization that size and strength have to wait for time to pass. Growth in height and gains in strength are important structural constraints in children and adolescents. Other examples of structural constraints include spinal cord damage that restricts or eliminates lower limb movement, and hearing and visual problems. Such individuals can be very independent, but they perform tasks in unique ways, with wheelchairs, hearing aids or sign language, and canes or a guide dog, respectively.

Nature and Nurture

We are amazed by truly exceptional performance, whether it is Beethoven or Mozart in music or Tiger Woods, Derek Jeter, or Roger Federer in sport. Their brilliance seems to defy practice and learning as the primary explanations of their achievements and innovations, so we often turn to some inborn talent or gift to explain their excellence. Recent research identifying specific genes in

FIGURE 6.1 Individual structural constraint.

DNA may have produced the illusion that it is only a matter of time before one or more genes are linked to exceptionality. Ericsson (2007) suggests that the complete genetic account of superior abilities is exceedingly complex and that an environmental perspective of extensive practice is better able to account for exceptional abilities. The relative contribution of genes (nature) and environment (nurture) to individual differences that we observe in everyday life has been the topic of one of the most energetic scientific debates for over 135 years (Baker & Davids, 2007).

There is much to be learned about the role of genetic constraints in living organisms. Genetic factors are almost the sole determinant of characteristics such as height, blood type, and hair color in humans. Genes largely control the timing of growth, such as the onset of the adolescent growth spurt and loss of muscular strength later in life. However, growth can be significantly affected by extrinsic factors; poor prenatal nutrition, ingestion of the wrong drugs, or exposure to X-rays can negatively affect the growing embryo or fetus. Good nutrition and exercise can positively affect growth and development across the lifespan. Therefore, motor learning and motor development most certainly are affected by both genetic and environmental constraints, but the precise manner of their interplay is not well known. More often than not, we simply read about the interaction of genes and experience as contributing to sport performance or academic learning, as if this fully explains the relationship. There is some truth to this idea, but the interaction is exceedingly complex and influenced by one's theoretical viewpoint of genetic action (Davids & Baker, 2007).

The impact of genes and extrinsic influences on human behavior is often studied with **monozygotic** and **dizygotic** twins (Klissouras, Geladas, & Koskolou, 2007). Human beings receive genes from both parents in a random fashion, which results in a unique genetic makeup, or genotype. Monozygotic twins have identical genotypes, while dizygotic (fraternal) twins share half their genes like ordinary siblings. Twin research can compare monozygotic and dizygotic twins. Occasionally twin research provides one of the monozygotic twins with some special treatment to determine the impact of heredity or environment in producing the phenotype, that is, an observable characteristic or behavior such as height, personality, or fitness. Since these twins are genetically identical, a positive impact from the special treatment suggests that the characteristic or phenotype is modifiable by the environment (e.g., gain in $\dot{V}O_2$max or motor skills). Thus the characteristic or phenotype is not completely determined by the genotype. Twin studies also include situations in which monozygotic twins are reared apart. In this case it is assumed that the nurturing life experiences of the two twins are different. If they have a similar phenotype after many years apart, it is usually concluded that the phenotype was largely determined by the genes rather than environment.

Nature–nurture research attempts to explain differences in individuals in a population as a function of genetics, extrinsic factors, or both; it cannot explain how much of *your* weight is controlled by *your* genes or *your* exercise and *your* eating habits, nor can it predict how much improvement *you* might expect as a function of training or practice. It can only explain differences among a group of people. Suppose a group of 40 was requested to practice a juggling task until each person reached a criterion of 10 consecutive tosses without dropping a ball. Assume that an average of 200 trials was required to reach that criterion.

Research Notes: A Classic Nature–Nurture Study in Motor Development

McGraw (1935) conducted an early and classic longitudinal study on the impact of environment on the acquisition of motor skills, specifically, to determine if a stimulating and challenging movement environment would alter motor development. Twins Johnny and Jimmy were involved for several years in the research. McGraw began observing them soon after birth, but Johnny began receiving stimulation and practice on several motor activities at about 1 year that were not offered to Jimmy. At various times Johnny was exposed to climbing, jumping, tricycles, swimming, jumping, and roller skating. If motor development was "fixed" and determined largely by the maturation of the central nervous system, as most theorists at that time believed, the extra exposure and practice received by Johnny should not have had any positive influence on his acquisition of motor skills. Nature would have scored a point over nurture. Support for the impact of nurturing by practice in a stimulating environment would have resulted if Johnny's motor development excelled that of Jimmy. Unfortunately, the results of the study were equivocal. In some movement skills, such as climbing, Johnny demonstrated superiority over Jimmy, which supported the nurture perspective. In other activities there seemed to be no evidence of difference between the twins, supporting a nature explanation. Of course, this type of twin research requires monozygotic twins, which unfortunately was not the case, as it was later revealed that Johnny and Jimmy were dizygotic twins. This fact may have influenced the results of McGraw's research.

The quickest individual in the group needed 150 trials, while the slowest needed 250. Genetic research attempts to explain how much of the 100-trial difference among the group of 40 is due to genetic factors. A statistic called **heritability** can be calculated (see Klissouras et al., 2007, for more details and other estimates of genetic influence). A heritability score closer to 1 is interpreted as a strong genetic influence in producing differences among individuals, but it has no meaning for the abilities of an individual. A high heritability score of 0.9 does not mean that an individual's $\dot{V}O_2$max score is due to 90% genetic and 10% training factors. Nor should such a high score be interpreted as suggesting that the environment has almost no impact. The 0.9 does mean that "after individuals have reached the upper limits of their $\dot{V}O_2$max, with appropriate training, there will still be wide interindividual variability which is genetic in origin" (Klissouras et al., 2007, p. 52).

Heritability scores are often quite high for physical fitness measures, body mass index, physique, height, and somatotype, as well as personality and cognitive abilities (Klissouras et al., 2007). Investigations have explored individual differences in motor learning, but the studies are fewer and the overall findings remain mixed. Fox, Hershberger, and Bouchard (1996) used both monozygotic and dizygotic twins reared apart to investigate individual differences in motor performance in a pursuit rotor tracking task for 75 trials. They concluded that differences among individuals in performance did reflect genetic influence. It is important to remember that the authors did not discount the role of practice; they asserted simply that there is a significant genetic impact on the outcome of practice. Marisi (1977) also used the pursuit rotor task with twins but found that the genetic influence diminished over trials. Generally these findings support the impact of genetic factors on motor learning and are consistent with the views of Klissouras, Bouchard, and their colleagues in physical fitness (Bouchard et al., 1999; Klissouras et al., 2007). In the domain of musical talent, Howe, Davidson, and Sloboda (1998) concluded that "individual differences in some special abilities may indeed have partly genetic origins" (p. 407). Thus, they accept the notion that genetic endowment can constrain ultimate skill level, acting as a ceiling of performance. Geladas, Koskolou, and Klissouras (2007) stated, "It seems that training will never erase individual differences that are due to innate abilities. Training can exert its . . . profound effect only within the fixed limits of heredity" (p. 125). Thus training and practice, true environmental factors, are considered critical even if genetics determines a ceiling of performance. It is important to remember that these statements say nothing about the extent of improvement or the ultimate level of performance for a specific individual. Parents, teachers, and therapists can justifiably remain optimistic about the motor learning of each child and adolescent.

Ericsson (2003, 2007) advances an opposing viewpoint in the context of explaining expert performance. He acknowledges that genes are important in developing physiological adaptations of the body and nervous system but maintains that they place no limits on performance of healthy individuals. He argues that genetic differences in innate talent cannot explain the remarkable improvement in training research because "the DNA stored in the nucleus of each cell of a person is the same before and after training" (Ericsson, 2007, p. 6). Deliberate practice is a proposed theoretic explanation. Deliberate practice is specific practice requiring much effort, without an immediate reward, motivated by performance improvement, and is not necessarily enjoyable. Through the lengthy process of deliberate practice and the accompanying changes in cognitive activity, any healthy individual can become an expert. To state this differently, deliberate practice, rather than genetic endowment, can explain individual differences among individuals who have access to instruction, training, and social support necessary for high levels of achievement. Most people do not become experts in part because they cannot sustain the intensity and effort of the required practice. The only exceptions to the deliberate practice hypothesis acknowledged by Ericsson are height and body size. Neither has been shown to be influenced by training and practice. These can be viewed therefore as influenced primarily by genes.

Galton made the distinction between nature and nurture in 1874 as an explanation for individual differences. Thus began the nature–nurture debate in science. Much of the debate has centered around which one is most important for a specific domain, such as movements skills. Some scientists have expressed frustration over this debate because the two are inextricably linked so that it is impossible to separate "what is nature" and "what is nurture" (Baker &

> ## Try This
>
> Let us look at the complexity of heritability a bit further. Find a person in your class (maybe yourself) who has achieved a reasonably high level of athletic success (e.g., college or high school varsity). Ask if this person's mom or dad was athletic at a young age. Or perhaps an aunt or uncle? Was it in the same sport as the person in your class? Are physical characteristics like height important in this sport?

Davids, 2007). Kimble (1993 as cited by Baker & Davids, 2007) suggested that trying to determine if individual differences in behavior are caused by heredity or environment is like asking if the area of a rectangle is determined more by its width or its length. While the precise impact of genes and environment on skill acquisition is not clear, there is certainly no evidence of a physical skill acquisition gene (Davids & Baker, 2007). Individual differences in motor learning and development are no doubt influenced by many genes interacting with many extrinsic factors, from types of practice, to amount of practice, to social support mechanisms, to motivation, to personal value beliefs, and to cultural influences.

A final closing note may be helpful. While many current theories of development and learning adopt a genetic–environment interaction perspective, dynamic systems theory minimizes the privileged status of genetic influence on conceptual grounds (Thelen & Smith, 1994). According to this argument, a key issue in development is the respective impact of many systems, and genes are only one system. The continued search for the genetic impact may be slowing the search for more important explanations of development.

What Do You Think?

1. Has the previous section of the chapter challenged your views of instruction in physical education? Is it fair to view students as "naturally talented"? Explain.
2. Pick two sports. Describe how students' ability to play these sports may be influenced by both nature and nurture.

Physical Growth and Maturation

The size and shape of children and adolescents change as they grow, and these structural realities affect how they coordinate their movements and learn motor skills. Most certainly a small child will throw a 7-inch (18-centimeter) playground ball with two hands because the ball is almost impossible to balance on one hand, while a teenager may use a one-handed throw because of a larger hand. Older adults might change how they perform physical skills because of loss of strength or arthritis. Thus, motor performance and learning will be affected by changes during growth and aging in skeletal, muscular, and nervous systems (Haywood & Getchell, 2009).

The rate of physical growth in the first year of life is remarkable. A newborn infant may be 7.5 pounds and 20 inches (3.4 kilograms and 51 centimeters) long, but by her first birthday will be 22.5 pounds and 30 inches (10.2 kilograms and 76 centimeters) long. This represents a 200% gain in weight and a 50% gain in height. Never again does the body change so much in a year. In fact, if the **rate of change** in the first year after birth continued until age 20 years, the individual would be 1,150 feet tall and weigh nearly 50 million pounds (Krogman, 1972). Many new motor skills are acquired in the first year of life, such as sitting, standing, crawling, and walking; and the child's rapidly changing weight and length constraints must be coordinated with changing task and environmental constraints.

Growth Curves

Stature (height) growth curves for males and females are shown in figure 6.2, *a* and *b*. Other common body size measures in growth research include weight; sitting height; leg length; limb and head circumferences; and breadth of shoulders, hips, and knees (Malina, Bouchard, & Bar-Or, 2004). The pattern of change for height and weight is called a **sigmoid curve** after the Greek letter for *s*. The rapid change after birth and again at adolescence make the sigmoid shape curvilinear rather than straight. Since the values on the y-axis are accumulated heights, this type of curve is also called a **distance curve**. These curves also include percentile rankings. The 50th percentile is the average for the age group; half the children score above this height or weight and half fall below these figures. A child who falls at the 75th percentile is taller at this age than 75 percent of his chronological-age peers.

These growth charts show whether a particular individual is short, tall, light, or heavy for his age. A group of adolescents of the same age can vary greatly in height and weight. A parent may be concerned if a child is at the 50th percentile for height but at the 80th percentile for weight, suggesting extra weight for a given height. Pediatricians monitor the extremes of stature and weight as possible indicators of growth pathology.

A youngster could be relatively short for her age due to genetic factors or a problem with growth. Additional assessment would be required to determine which one of these is the prime reason for the short stature. Much to the disappointment of parents of a big newborn child, perhaps, size at birth is not an accurate predictor of final height or weight. By age 2 or 3 years, children tend to remain in their percentile position compared to others (Haywood & Getchell, 2009; Malina et al., 2004). Thus, a male at 4 years of age who is at the 90th **percentile** for height (taller than 90 percent of the 4-year-old boys) is likely to be a tall adult, and a male at the 30th percentile will likely be shorter than the typical adult male. This relative stability in growth can be used for clinical evaluation, since a child would not be expected to be at the 80th percentile at one age and the 30th at a subsequent age. Such dramatic changes might be an indication of unhealthy growth and reason for further assessment.

Distance curves show only the extent of growth and hide whether children are growing fast one year and slower the next. The sigmoid distance curves are created by averaging the heights of many children, and they also hide the dramatic changes that can occur in an individual. Notice that the **velocity curve** for height shown in figure 6.3 looks very different from the distance curve for height. A velocity curve describes *change* in height (centimeters per year) over 18 years. Think of centimeters per year like miles per hour. A change from 60 to 40 miles per hour is described as decelerating, that is, slowing down. Forward movement is still occurring, just more slowly. The same thing happens in height over the first five years; each year less height is gained compared to the previous year, and therefore the velocity of height gain is *decelerating*. The individual is getting taller each year, just not as fast as the previous year.

Figure 6.3 shows that height velocity continues to slow slightly from age 5 years until the initiation of the adolescent growth spurt, at which time height gain accelerates for about two years. Notice that the **peak height velocity** is the time when gain in height is the fastest since the first year of life.

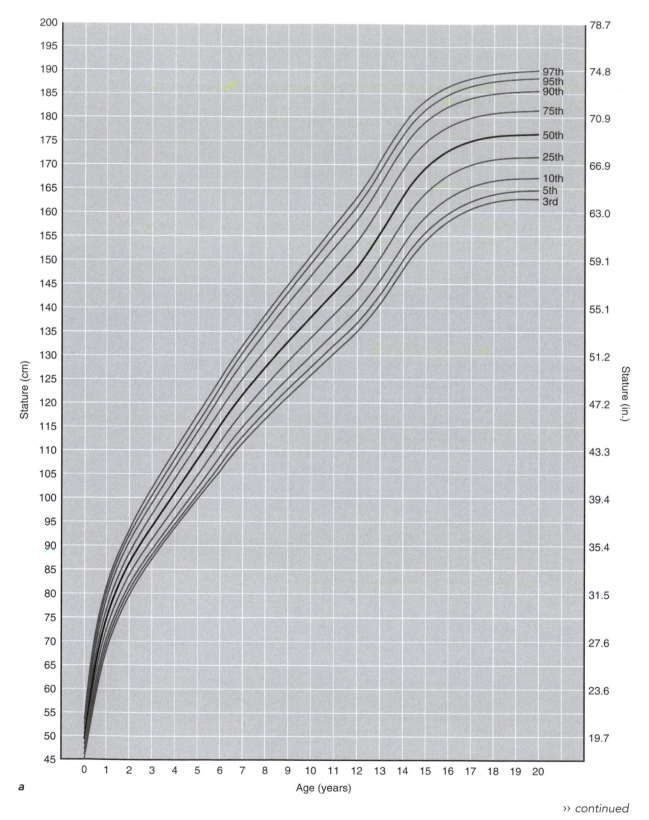

›› continued

FIGURE 6.2 *(a)* Stature (standing height) by age percentiles for boys. Note the sigmoid, or S-shape, of the curves.

Adapted from R.J. Kuczmarski, C.L. Ogden, S.S. Guo, et al., 2002, "2000 CDC growth charts for the United States: Methods and development," *Vital and Health Statistics* 11(246): 29-30. [Online]. Available: www.cdc.gov/nchs/data/series/sr_11/sr11_246.pdf [January 3, 2011].

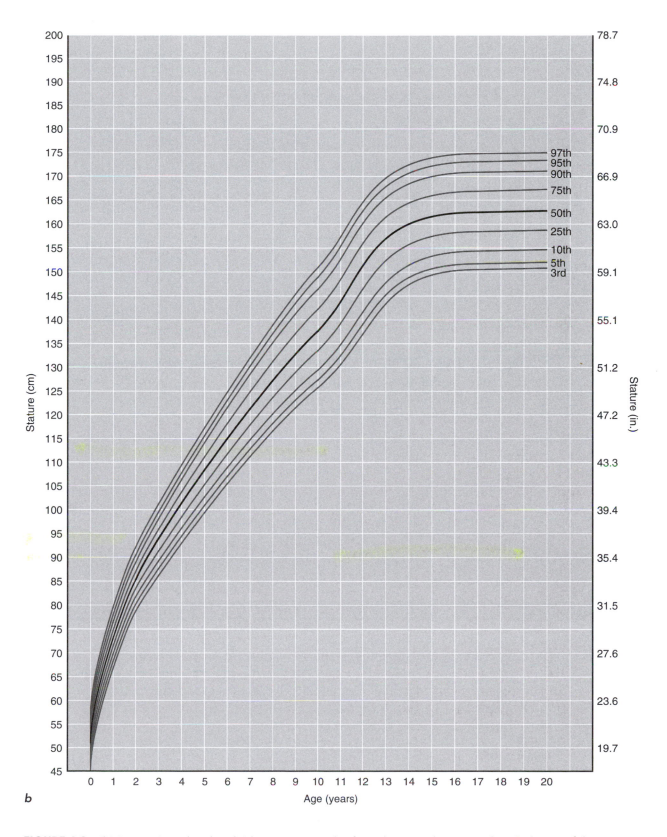

FIGURE 6.2 *(b)* Stature (standing height) by age percentiles for girls. Note the sigmoid, or S-shape, of the curves.

FIGURE 6.3 Velocity curves.

Reprinted, by permission, from K.M. Haywood and N. Getchell, 2005, *Life span motor development*, 4th ed. (Champaign, IL: Human Kinetics), 39. Adapted from J.M. Tanner, R.H. Whitehouse, and M.Takaishi, 1966, "Standards from birth to maturity for height, weight, height velocity, and weight velocity: British children, 1965, part II," *Archives of Disease in Childhood* 41(220): 613-635.

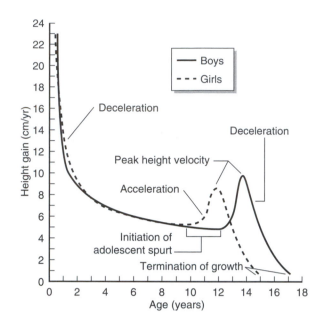

The peak height velocity corresponds to the dramatic change in stature that most adolescents experience. For females this may be 8.5 centimeters (3.4 inches) per year, for males 10 centimeters (3.9 inches) per year. It is small wonder that individuals may experience some awkwardness as they attempt to incorporate rapidly changing limb lengths into personal movement. The velocity curves also demonstrate that females enter the adolescent growth spurt and puberty about two years before males—9 and 11 years, respectively. As shown in figure 6.3, females also stop growing two years before males. The difference in adult height between the sexes is largely due to females' lower peak height velocity and their cessation of growth two years prior to the males (Haywood & Getchell, 2009; Malina et al., 2004).

The motor learning of children and adolescents is affected not only by changes in overall stature and weight, but also by changes in **body proportions** or form. Figure 6.4 demonstrates postnatal changes in body proportions, a phenomenon called relative growth (Haywood & Getchell, 2009). In essence, body parts and tissues have different rates of growth. The head grows more than the legs during prenatal months. At birth, the head is about one-fourth of the infant's length, but it contributes only one-eighth to the height of an adult. It is clear that a child is not a miniature adult. One of the movement problems of the first year

Research Notes: Environmental Constraints Can Affect Height

Did you know that the tallest people in the world are the Dutch? How they became the tallest is an interesting story of human plasticity over many generations (Bogin, 1998). In the mid-1800s, Americans were the tallest males in the world at an average 5 feet, 6 inches (168 centimeters) while the Dutch stood at 5 feet, 4 inches (163 centimeters). At the turn of the 21st century, the Dutch were 5 feet, 10 inches (178 centimeters) while the typical American male was 5 feet, 8 inches (173 centimeters). Bogin argues that over the last 150 years, the Dutch have profited in stature from societal changes that include purifying drinking water, installing sewer systems, regulating the safety of food, and providing public health care and diets to children. The Dutch children responded to the changing environment by growing taller. While these changes are available to many Americans, those who are poor may lack adequate housing, sanitation, and health care. This scenario demonstrates the plasticity of stature over generations if people's life conditions improve, showing that height, while influenced almost completely by the genes inherited from parents, can change over generations.

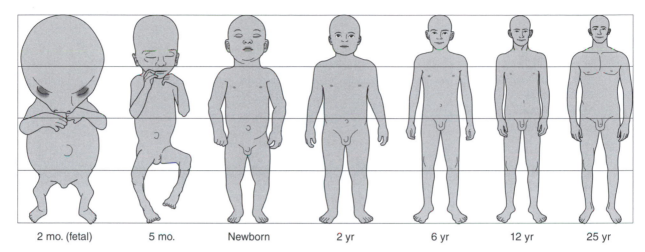

| 2 mo. (fetal) | 5 mo. | Newborn | 2 yr | 6 yr | 12 yr | 25 yr |

FIGURE 6.4 Changes in body form: relative growth.

of life is how to balance a large head on a relatively small body. The legs are about three-eighths of height at birth and one-half when growth terminates. In other words, from birth to adulthood, the legs grow faster than the head.

Thus, while adults are obviously taller than young children, adults have a distinctly different form. Newell (1984) argued that these changes are biomechanical constraints that affect coordination. As children grow, their movement patterns must include a constantly changing body shape. In some cases, performance is affected. For example, as elite female gymnasts progress through puberty, they may not maintain sufficient strength to compensate for their longer and heavier limbs, resulting in a decline in skill (see case of Aurelia Dobre on page 93).

Limitations to Growth Curves

Distance and velocity curves describe average patterns of change, but individuals have very unique timing of these events. This is illustrated clearly by those who mature early and late. The initiation of the adolescent growth spurt may differ by several years. An early-maturing male may begin to accelerate in growth at 9 years of age while his late-maturing counterpart may be delayed until age 15 years. Peak strength velocity follows within a year of the peak height velocity, and therefore it is not surprising that the early maturer will be taller and stronger than most of his peers for a few years despite being the same chronological age. Since stature and strength are structural constraints, the early maturer may be more coordinated than same-aged peers and hence enjoy an athletic advantage. Early-maturing adolescents may ultimately be shorter than later-maturing peers if they terminate growth earlier and therefore do not grow for as many years as their later-maturing peers. It is not uncommon for athletically talented children who mature early to be very successful as a 12-year-old (girl) or 14-year-old (male) yet lose relative placement in their peer group when peers begin and proceed through maturation. Early maturers do not suddenly become poorly coordinated or uninterested; the later-maturing athletes catch up and possibly surpass them in size and strength. In this adolescent growth period of rapid change in size and strength, it is difficult to predict future athletic success.

Try This

Assume that a female is 150 centimeters tall. Look at figure 6.2. How old is the girl if 150 centimeters places her at the 90th percentile? How old is she if 150 centimeters places her at the 50th and 5th percentiles? Those three ages represent quite a wide range. Which of the ages leads you to think she is an early maturer? What other information is necessary to support your prediction?

What Do You Think?

1. How will the age at which an individual experiences a growth spurt influence his performance in sport? What other factors (e.g., social) must be considered?

2. Describe growth differences and similarities between the genders from birth to adulthood.

3. One day you may teach students in late elementary school. What factors do you have to take into consideration (in terms of physical growth and maturation) when planning and implementing activities?

Body System Constraints

Motor learning and development can theoretically be constrained by any body system. The systems that most affect movement and performance are the skeletal, muscular, nervous, respiratory, endocrine, adipose, and sensory systems. Just as with relative growth as shown in figure 6.4, these systems do not change at a constant rate. The developing child and adolescent must learn to incorporate changing limb size, muscle mass, and visual capabilities into new and old movement patterns. Once again, the changes described next underscore the notion that children are not miniature adults.

Skeletal System

The skeleton is the structural support system of the body and provides a lever for muscles, enabling movement. Large developmental changes occur in bone size and structure from birth through adolescence, as previously discussed. Bone changes do not end following the cessation of growth during late adolescence. Bone is a living and growing tissue. Old bone is removed (resorption) while new bone is continually being formed. Through this process termed remodeling, an entire skeleton is replaced every 10 years. During childhood, bone building occurs at a much faster rate than bone resorption, allowing for increases in bone size to occur.

Our previous discussion of stature dealt with typical development of the skeletal system, but there are some difficulties with skeletal growth. **Osgood-Schlatter** disease is a painful disruption in growth of the upper shinbone where the patella tendon attaches. **Legg-Calvé-Perthes** is an irritation of the femur where it inserts into the hip. These are childhood problems that restrict weight-bearing activities and make movement painful. In the case of limb amputation, the individual will perform some movements in unique ways to compensate for the loss of the limb.

Muscular System

The muscular system follows a sigmoid growth curve similar to that for weight (Haywood & Getchell, 2009). Muscle mass becomes a relatively larger component of overall body weight with development. It is about 25% of total body weight at birth but 54% for men and 45% for women at maturity. It has been suggested that a critical level of strength is an important rate limiter for independent walking (Ulrich, Ulrich, Angulo-Kinzler, & Yun, 2001). This helps explain why heavier babies might not walk as early as leaner babies, more strength being necessary to move a larger mass. Strength is important for many motor skills and is influenced by the amount of muscle mass, maturation, and recruitment of muscle fibers, as well as extrinsic factors such as nutrition and exercise.

Strength

A growth in muscle mass can occur through an increase in the number of muscle fibers **(hyperplasia)** or through an increase in the relative size, or volume, of the muscle fibers **(hypertrophy)**. Muscle fibers increase by both hyperplasia and hypertrophy prenatally and for a short time postnatally. Then, muscle mass can be increased only by hypertrophy. Gender differences in muscle mass are small until adolescence when both genders have a rapid gain in muscle mass. However, the spurt in muscle mass continues in girls only until age 13 years, while in boys the rapid increase continues until age 17 years (Malina, 1978). Following maturity, muscle mass can be changed only through hypertrophy (increase in size of muscle fibers) or through atrophy (decrease in size of muscle fibers) (Gollnick, Timson, Moore, & Riedy, 1981). Muscle fibers increase in both diameter and length during growth and development. Increases in muscle length occur in conjunction with increases in bone length, while increases in the diameter of a muscle fiber result from physical activity (Malina & Bouchard, 1991).

What Do You Think?

Provide an example of how strength can be a rate limiter for the following.

- A 4-month-old infant learning to crawl
- An 8-year-old male baseball pitcher
- An 11-year-old female tennis player

Flexibility

Flexibility is the ability to move body parts through a range of motion without strain (Gabbard, 2008). Flexibility is necessary to perform well athletically and prevent muscular injury, as well as to perform activities of daily living from dressing oneself to climbing in and out of a car (Shephard, 1998). The sit and reach test is one of the most commonly used measures of flexibility. This test assesses the flexibility of the hamstrings, lower back, and hip flexors.

Gender differences exist in flexibility, with females tending to be more flexible than males. Flexibility increases in both males and females until approximately the age of 10 years for males and 12 years for females (Clarke, 1975). Females tend to be more flexible than males from the age of 5 years through adulthood (Haubenstricker, Wisner, Seefeldt, & Branta, 1997). The gender differences have been attributed to body size and composition, hormone levels, and physical activities (Gabbard, 2008). Individuals with larger body sizes generally have poorer flexibility. Females also participate in physical activities that promote increased range of motion more often than males, such as dance and gymnastics. Flexibility changes occur at specific joints rather than across the body as a whole and are greatly affected by physical activity.

 What Do You Think?

Females participate in physical activities that promote flexibility more often than males. Why? List ways in which you could encourage male students (of all ages) to increase their flexibility.

Cardiovascular System

The simplest cardiovascular measure is monitoring the heart rate. Heart rates are a convenient measure of cardiac effort at rest, during moderate exercise (submaximal heart rate), and during maximal effort (maximal heart rate) (Gabbard, 2008). Heart rates provide an indicator of both cardiac output (amount of blood pumped) and maximal oxygen consumption. On average, resting heart rates decrease with age (Lowrey, 1986). At birth, resting heart rates are very high, averaging 140 beats per minute. By age 2 years, resting heart rates have decreased to about 105 beats per minute; and by age 20 years they have declined to approximately 66 beats per minute. The increase in heart rates in infancy and childhood is a physiological compensation for smaller heart sizes. With a smaller heart, the stroke volume (volume of blood pumped during each contraction) is decreased. To compensate, the heart rate increases. For this same reason, females average about 5 beats per minute more than males.

$\dot{V}O_2$max is considered the best measure of aerobic capacity and cardiovascular fitness. $\dot{V}O_2$max is the maximum amount of oxygen that can be transported and used during exercise. Endurance performance and $\dot{V}O_2$max are highly correlated (Joyner, 1993); however, this does not mean that an individual's $\dot{V}O_2$max is set. $\dot{V}O_2$max can be greatly increased with endurance training. Athletes' $\dot{V}O_2$max increases as they are able to run farther and faster because $\dot{V}O_2$max is determined by the maximum amount of oxygen that is required. An individual who is running faster requires more oxygen than someone who is running more slowly. This increase continues until the runner is not capable of running any faster. Some highly trained competitive athletes have reached as much as 8 liters per minute. In general, $\dot{V}O_2$max increases for both males and females at the same rate throughout childhood. At the age of 12 years, boys and girls have similar $\dot{V}O_2$max measures. Girls continue to increase their $\dot{V}O_2$max until about the age of 14 years, and boys continue to increase their $\dot{V}O_2$max until 18 years of age (Gabbard, 2008). The increase in $\dot{V}O_2$max in boys is a result of continued growth through a later age.

Nervous System

The nervous system undergoes change throughout life. As many as 100 billion neurons are formed, most by the third or fourth prenatal week. Later in the pre-natal period and early in the first postnatal year, the neurons fire and establish **synapses** (connections) with other neurons. At birth the brain is 25% of its adult weight, and by 5 years it is 90% (Keogh & Sugden, 1985; Piek, 2006). Beyond the rapid development of the number of neurons, which may continue until age 6 years (Piek, 2006), learning and life experiences will alter the nervous system throughout life. Motor learning produces synapses between motor and sensory neurons. In fact, one account of motor control proposed that muscle synergies, the synchrony of motor neurons, produce coordinated movement patterns. Practicing new motor skills results in hundreds of thousands of new groups of synapses. Neuromotor difficulties can severely affect coordination, for example in **cerebral palsy**. In this case, an extrinsic factor such as loss of oxygen to the developing brain, prenatally or during birth, may damage brain tissue needed in coordination. Severe malnutrition can also hinder optimal function in the brain.

Endocrine System

The **endocrine system** controls the hormones in body tissue. For example, **pituitary** growth hormones and **thyroid** hormones are largely responsible for skeletal growth. In some cases, shorter stature may be related to a deficiency of these hormones and may be a structural constraint. Hormones from the tes-ticles or ovaries and adrenal glands, primarily estrogen and androgens (e.g., testosterone), are responsible for the growth spurt and for epiphyseal fusion of the long bones, which terminates growth.

Adipose Tissue

The age-related changes in fat-free mass resemble the sigmoid curves of height and weight. Adipose tissue develops rapidly in the last three months of preg-nancy. Babies born prematurely often have a skinny appearance because they have not remained long enough in the womb during this important period of adipose tissue formation. As figure 6.5 demonstrates, adipose tissue continues to develop rapidly during the first 6 to 12 postnatal months (Malina et al., 2004) when fat constitutes as much as 30% of body weight. When adipose tissue is expressed as a percentage of body weight, there is a decline in both sexes after a peak at about age 1 until the adolescent growth spurt. However, if body fat is expressed as an absolute value in pounds or kilograms, adipose tissue continues to develop from 12 months to 20 years. The absolute amount of adiposity will increase during childhood and adolescence, like skeletal or muscular tissue, but this is simply due to the fact that children and adolescents are still growing and getting bigger. Compare a 50-pound child to one at 100 pounds. We would expect the 100-pound child to have more adipose tissue than the 50-pound child because of the difference in weight. The average adult female possesses about 70% of the fat-free mass of her male counterpart, largely because males at adulthood are taller than females and gained more muscle mass during adolescence than females.

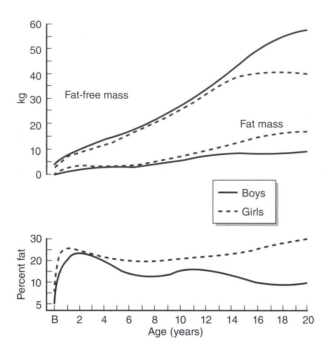

FIGURE 6.5 Growth curves for fat-free mass, fat mass, and relative fatness derived from measurements of total body water.

Reprinted, by permission, from R.M. Malina, C. Bouchard, and O. Bar-Or, 2004, *Growth, maturation, and physical activity*, 2nd ed. (Champaign, IL: Human Kinetics), 113. Data from Malina, 1989, pp. 223-265, and Malina, Bouchard, and Beunen, 1988, pp. 187-219.

At least since 1990, there has been an epidemic of childhood obesity in developed and developing countries caused in part by inactivity. Obesity is associated with many health issues but is also a structural constraint during performance because greater energy expenditure is necessary to move the additional weight. Obesity is associated with sedentary behaviors, and perhaps not surprisingly, there is evidence that obesity is associated with poor motor skills (Marshall & Bouffard, 1994, 1997). Malina and colleagues (2004) concluded that after 6 years of age, the fattest children have a higher risk of remaining fat until adolescence and adulthood. Variation is large, and there are certainly individuals who are fat as children and not obese as adults, while some lean children become fat in adolescence or adulthood. It appears that professionals and parents should be very concerned with children after 6 years of age who carry too much body fat.

Sensory Systems

Many developmental changes occur in the sensory systems. Sensory system development is of particular importance to motor development and motor learning, as it has many implications for skillful performance. Movement is dependent on and intricately related to perception. Our movements are based on what we see, hear, and feel. A child's sensory development can greatly affect how she performs. Practitioners should take developmental changes in vision, audition, and kinesthesis into consideration when designing programs. Equipment and the tasks should be modified according to not only the physical capabilities of children or adolescents but also to their perceptual capabilities.

Vision

Vision is the predominant sensory system, with an estimated 70% of sensory receptors residing in the eyes. Vision provides information about the environment with respect to the position of the head. In order to perceive a visual image, three functions occur. First, light enters the eye and passes to a light-sensitive membrane called the retina, forming an image. The image is then converted into nerve signals by light-sensitive cells called photoreceptors. The two types of photoreceptors are rods and cones. Rods and cones differ in their structure and function:

Rods	**Cones**
More numerous	Fewer and more dense
Ambient vision	Visual acuity
Movement detection	Best operation in bright lighting
Night vision (shades of grey)	Color vision

Second, the nerve signals are transmitted from the eye through the optic tract to the visual cortex of the brain. The nerve signals are actually sent to the opposite side of the brain, crossing the optic chiasm (figure 6.6), such that nerve signals from the right side of the visual field go to the left side of the visual cortex and nerve signals from the left side of the visual field are sent to the right side of the visual cortex. Third, the brain then interprets the nerve signals.

Structurally, the eye is completely intact at birth; however, all visual structures change following birth (Gabbard, 2008). The eye of a newborn is not smaller in overall size, but the depth is shorter and the distance between the retina and the lens is less, causing farsight-edness (difficulty seeing close objects) in newborns. The structure of the retina changes rapidly over the first year. Retinas in newborns are thicker and the fovea is not well formed, making it difficult for them to see images clearly (Gabbard, 2008). Infants also have difficulty focusing on objects (astigmatisms) due to their weaker ciliary muscles. Structural differences between adult and newborn eyes are shown in figure 6.7.

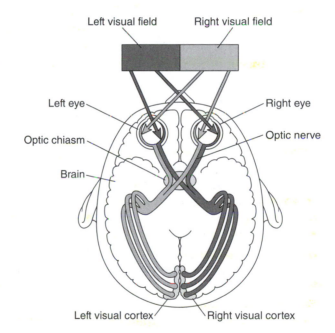

FIGURE 6.6 Light enters the eye through the pupil and moves to the retina, where a visual image is formed. Photoreceptors convert the image into nerve signals, which are sent through the optic nerve and cross over the optic chiasm to the visual cortex to be interpreted.

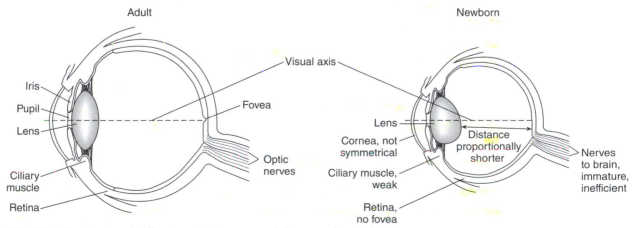

FIGURE 6.7 Structural differences between an adult eye and a newborn eye.

Gabbard, Carl P., *Lifelong Motor Development*, 5th ed., © 2008. Printed and electronically reproduced by permission of Pearson Education, Inc., Upper Saddle River, New Jersey.

Among the many visual functions, we focus only on those that are of particular importance to moving skillfully, including visual acuity, visuomotor coordination, depth perception, and figure–ground perception. **Visual acuity** is the sharpness of vision. Visual acuity allows one to see an image clearly, such as a face or words on a page. There are two types of visual acuity, static and dynamic. **Static visual acuity** is the ability to clearly see an image that is stationary; it is most commonly assessed using the Snellen eye chart. Normal vision is considered 20/20, meaning that the image can be clearly seen from 20 feet (6 meters) away. At birth, visual acuity is approximately 20/400, meaning that the newborn could distinguish at 20 feet what individuals with normal vision could see at 400 feet (122 meters). Newborns can clearly see images only if they are less than 1.5 feet (.46 meters) away (Kellman & Arterberry, 1998). Visual acuity improves rapidly throughout the first year and then continues to improve at a slower rate to a 20/20 rating by the age of 10 years (Williams, 1983).

Dynamic visual acuity is the ability to distinguish objects that are moving. Dynamic visual acuity is particularly important for athletes who must track an object or the position of an opponent. Dynamic visual acuity develops at a later age than static visual acuity, reaching adult levels at around age 15 years (Schrauf, Wist, & Ehrenstein, 1999). Girls tend to have poorer static and dynamic visual acuity than boys, which could have an impact on performance in sports. Visual acuity differences for both age and gender should be taken into consideration when programs are developed. Poorer dynamic visual acuity most notably affects activities in which a moving object must be tracked. Delayed development of dynamic visual acuity may be factor in the reduced participation of girls in some of these sports (Gallahue & Ozmun, 2006).

The perception of motion is a particularly important factor in motor development and motor learning. Motion is visually perceived in newborns, but young infants are unable to perceive the direction of motion until approximately 8 weeks of age (Wattam-Bell, 1996). **Visuomotor coordination**, the ability to visually track a moving object and guide the body or limbs (or both) to intercept the object, improves with the infant's active exploration of the environment, by playing with the hands, toys, and eventually throwing. One of the reasons young children have difficulty with catching is underdeveloped visual–motor coordination. Children cannot accurately track a moving object, such as a tossed ball, until approximately the age of 5 or 6 years (Morris, 1980). Parents often throw balls with a high arc to children to allow them more time to prepare for a catch; however, it is even more challenging for children to catch a ball thrown in a high arc because they cannot visually track objects in two planes until they are approximately 8 or 9 years of age. Movement perception continues to develop until approximately age 12 years (Williams, 1983).

These are only a few of the developmental changes in vision. It is also important to consider that children have difficulty separating an object from the background. The ability to do this is referred to as **figure–ground perception**. Figure–ground perception improves through childhood and adolescence until approximately age 18 years. The ability to distinguish the object from its surroundings is of critical importance to many sports and activities. A ball that is not easily discernible apart from the environment is much less likely to be caught or struck. **Depth perception**, the ability to see in three dimensions, is also a critical component in intercepting an object. Depth perception arises partly from the **retinal disparity** of the two eyes. Since the eyes are in different

What Do You Think?

Provide an example of how vision can be a rate limiter for the following populations based on visual development.

- A 4-month-old infant learning to crawl
- An 8-year-old male baseball pitcher
- An 11-year-old female tennis player

locations, they see images at different visual angles. The development of depth perception is affected by the development of visual acuity because depth perception is dependent on the clarity of the image to each eye, allowing a better comparison. Many factors affect the perception of depth of an approaching ball, such as the ball's size, color, speed, and trajectory of motion (Payne & Isaacs, 2008). It is essential that the child be able to clearly distinguish the ball from the background and use all depth cues in order to make a successful catch.

Audition

The importance of auditory information is often overlooked in skillful movement; however, it is a component critical to both learning a movement pattern and performing skillfully. One of the most common methods of teaching a motor skill is using verbal instruction. Think about it. Have you ever been taught a motor skill without the use of verbal cues, or at least some form of verbal instruction? Skilled performers also often use auditory signals during an activity to enable them to react more quickly or to use a frame of reference. For instance, a racquetball player may know the direction and speed of the ball simply from hearing the location and pitch of the ball bounce; a basketball makes a different sound depending on whether it hits the rim or the backboard or just the net (swoosh!); and a softball sounds different when it is caught in the palm of the glove rather than the pocket. Sounds can indicate the rhythm of the movement as well. The rhythmic movement of a golf swing can be heard. Devices have even been made to assist golfers in learning the timing and rhythm of the golf swing through listening to a music file composed from the rhythm of skilled golfers.

The development of the inner ear occurs prior to that of the middle and outer ear. The inner ear contains the main components primarily responsible for sound detection (Gabbard, 2008). By birth, most of the ear structures are completed (Timiras, 1972), with the exception of some structures including the drum membrane, the length of the ear canal, and the Eustachian tube. Infants, who are able to hear prior to and following birth, often turn their heads in the direction of sound. Infants under 4 months of age can differentiate both non-speech sounds (Vouloumanos & Werker, 2004) and speech sounds (Eimas, 1975). By 6 months of age, infants can differentiate native languages from nonnative languages (Kuhl, Williams, Lacerda, Stevens, & Lindblom, 1992) and become increasingly interested in listening to native languages as they are beginning to understand that these sounds are associated with meaning.

Children are able to effectively locate sound by the age of 3 years. The ability to localize sound continues to improve through the teens. The ability to localize sounds is especially important in sporting contexts, such as knowing the location of an oncoming ball based on the sound it made when hitting a wall in racquetball or the position of other players relative to one another in invasion sports. Localizing sound is also very important for driving, allowing the driver to appropriately react after hearing sirens, horns, or other sounds.

Young children are able to differentiate similar speech sounds, such as *b* and *d*. Differentiating *b* and *d* becomes quite important when learning how to read and write. A child who cannot discern the difference will have difficulty correctly spelling or pronouncing words with these letters because they cannot hear the difference. The ability to differentiate similar sounds amidst noisy background sounds is particularly challenging for children. Improvements in the ability to discriminate speech sounds in noisy environments continue through late childhood (Neuman & Hochberg, 1983). The ability to ignore background noise while attending to particular sounds is **auditory figure–ground perception**. Although it appears that some children have more difficulty with figure–ground perception than others, it is not well known how figure–ground perception changes during childhood as there has been little research conducted in this area.

What Do You Think?

Choose two activities. As an instructor, how would you include auditory information to enhance student learning? Would this change if you were instructing children versus adolescents? Explain.

Kinesthetic Perception

The kinesthetic system provides us with our sense of body position, and it is supported by muscle, tendons, joints, and skin receptors as well as the inner ear and eyes. Because of the kinesthetic system we are able to move our body and know where our hands, limbs, and feet are positioned with respect to one another without looking at them. Poor kinesthetic perception has been linked to clumsiness in adolescents (Visser & Geuze, 2000). The kinesthetic system is critical to performing skillfully, enabling fluid movements by providing information regarding the relative positions of body parts to one another and in space and the movements of the body (Haywood & Getchell, 2009). To fully develop the kinesthetic system, children must experience a wide variety of activities. In today's society, many children lack such experiences due to increased sedentary lifestyles and more urban environments. Children are spending less and less time playing outside and more time with passive activities such as watching television and playing video games. Limited active experiences can delay kinesthetic development and hinder their ability to learn more complex motor skills as they get older (Gallahue & Ozmun, 2006). Kinesthetically, some of the most important aspects to develop include body and spatial awareness.

Body Awareness   **Body awareness** is an individual's sense of the body, such as knowledge of the different body parts, and body image. Body awareness includes being able to locate body parts, knowing the movement of the body parts, and knowing how to efficiently move the body parts (Gallahue & Ozmun, 2006). The development of body awareness begins at birth and continues through childhood. Infants are born with an unconscious sense that enables them to orient themselves toward pleasant sensory experiences. The initial discovery of their own hands can be very exciting to infants. Infants can spend much time simply staring at their hands, opening them and closing them and watching them move closer and farther away. This discovery becomes even more exciting when they shake a rattle. They are beginning to understand the relationship between their movements to other objects, as well as the placement of their body parts with respect to other body parts. Through active exploration, older infants learn how to propel themselves by understanding the relationship between their feet and leg movements with respect to the ground. Preschoolers, aged 3 and 4 years, continue to develop their body awareness through active experiences in relation to their own bodies, as seen in the following example:

> While they are eating a snack together, 4 year old Joseph's teacher says to him, "You have the longest eyelashes!" Looking straight ahead, Joseph asks, "Do they reach all the way out to the juice pitcher?" The teacher laughs and replies, "Not that far." Curious, Joseph wonders aloud, "Then how far?" Spontaneously, he holds up his finger and moves it slowly toward his eye until he feels it gently touch his lashes. Delighted with his experiment, he shares, "Now I can see and feel how far!" Later, Joseph and his friends have more fun checking out their eyelash length in a mirror (Poole, Miller, & Booth Church, 2006).

Joseph not only further developed his body awareness, but also gained a better sense of distance and size. By comparing the feeling of his eyelashes with the image he saw in the mirror, he was also gaining a better understanding of the link between visual and kinesthetic perception. When instructing young children, practitioners should help them to become more aware of their bodies by asking them where their body parts are and what the body parts do.

Spatial Awareness Spatial awareness is the awareness of the size of the body and the position of the body in relation to others and external objects. Toddlers are very interested in spatial concepts. A favorite activity of toddlers is to place small objects into and take them out of boxes or containers. They learn about size and dimensions by filling open containers with smaller objects. Toddlers are also gaining a sense of **object permanence**, the concept that an object still exists even if it can no longer be seen. They learn that the ball they put in a box is still inside the box even if the lid has been placed on top. Children learn spatial awareness through active exploration. They need a wide variety of experiences in manipulating objects and interacting with other children and adults. Preschoolers relate the positioning of objects to their own personal space. At this age, children are very **egocentric**, meaning that they perceive the world only in terms of themselves. By age 5 or 6 years, children learn spatial orientation and the words associated with orientation, such as "near" and "far," "left" and "right," and "front" and "back" (Poole, Miller, & Booth Church, 2006). Children learn much better through active experiences than through observations or verbal instruction. By the age of 6 years, children are less egocentric and their spatial awareness is much more established. They also have a stronger sense of "personal space" and are able to locate objects relative to other objects and general space (Gallahue & Ozmun, 2006). Activities that encourage various movements through space, such as obstacle courses, are especially helpful for young children.

What Do You Think?

Describe specific activities you could implement to assist children in developing kinesthetic perception.

Summary

Chapter 5 outlined changes in movement skills during childhood and adolescence. Those are the products of movement and sequences through which most of us pass if our environment encourages motor development (Clark, 2007). This chapter explored some of the structural factors that constrain, that is, promote or limit, the acquisition and form of those movements. Chelsea now appreciates the vast range of structural differences in her "Fun and Fit" group of 12-year-olds. Parents, therapists, and leaders like Chelsea need to understand how structural constraints may interact with functional factors (the focus of the next chapter), tasks, and the environment. For example, the difficulty many youngsters have with catching is understood in a new light if one knows that tracking and movement perception are rather late to develop.

The structural systems we have described change at very different rates; for example, the rapid growth in stature during the first year of life decelerates in subsequent years until the growth spurt of puberty. The endocrine system is rather quiet until puberty when its influence on skeletal and muscle tissue becomes dramatic. While systems change at different rates, change among individuals is extremely variable as well. Our discussion of early and late maturers underscores this fact. The discussion of relative growth, both in stature and in percentage of muscle mass from birth to adolescence, reminds us that structural changes provide challenges and new opportunities for coordination, and that children are not miniature adults. Finally, gender differences in structure are generally minimal until puberty, and thus motor development and learning differences between girls and boys prior to adolescence are likely influenced largely by environment constraints.

Supplemental Activities

1. It seems that almost weekly we read about a new research study that indicates more and more children are becoming obese. This is a significant challenge for our society and for the professions associated with kinesiology or physical education. A good professional should keep up to date on statistics such as those on obesity. Search the website of the Centers for Disease Control in Atlanta to find the most recent statistics and recommendations for practice.

2. Are athletic injuries in developing children and adolescents detrimental to optimal growth? Are some sports (e.g., football or long-distance running) associated with injuries to such an extent that parents or professionals should place restrictions on the kids playing them? Search the Internet for information on this topic.

Functional Constraints of Thinking, Knowing, and Processing

CHAPTER OBJECTIVES

After reading this chapter, you should be able to

> explain Piaget's four stages of intellectual development;

> discuss the differences among declarative, procedural, and metacognitive knowledge and skill execution;

> describe the developmental relationship between knowing and doing;

> discuss distinguishing features of an expert;

> understand the development of attention and information processing; and

> describe the relationship between memory and knowledge and ways to improve memory for movements.

Even People the Same Age Are All Different

In the previous chapter's opening vignette, Chelsea met her fitness class of 12-year-old children and was not sure if they were children or adolescents. In fact, she had both, even if the common factor was age. She noticed the wide differences in body size and shape. These were among the structural constraints discussed in that chapter. As she directed a couple of basketball activities, she observed individual differences in skill level. Chelsea did not expect everyone to be at the same level of basketball, but she was not ready for such vast differences. One youngster could barely bounce a basketball more than a couple of times while watching the ball, but another ran while dribbling

with alternating hands and never glanced at the ball. In fact, Chelsea noted that this girl was actually better skilled in dribbling than she. As the "Fun and Fit" class progressed, some children responded quickly to her feedback by showing immediate improvement in skill and appearing enthused by her motivational comments; others had difficulty with the skills and still others did not even seem interested in basketball, the game she loved. What was going on?

This chapter explores the developmental changes in functional constraints that affect learning of physical skills; these include cognitive development, knowledge development, attention, and memory. We also briefly explain what it means to be an "expert" in sport. Awareness of these functional factors will help to explain the skill and learning differences in a group of 12-year-olds. From birth, children move through phases of cognitive development—the ability to understand, think, and conceptualize. This development is quicker for some children than for others, and it extends well into adolescence. It is not surprising that all 12-year-olds may not comprehend the subtle aspects of instruction or team play. Also, sport-specific knowledge is likely to assist performance, and some keen youngsters have acquired an almost encyclopedic knowledge of their favorite sport. Moreover, children experience an important development of attention to detail and the ability to focus on two things at the same time, and these interact in intriguing ways with physical skills. Finally, you may not have thought that we have a memory of movement, but the ability of older people to ride a bicycle after not doing so for many years suggests that we do. How can we assist learners with their memory of the physical skills we are instructing? In this chapter we will explore the functional constraints related to thinking and learning.

Cognitive Development

Jean Piaget was a brilliant Swiss child psychologist who published his first paper at age 10 and received his doctorate at 21 (Crain, 1985). His passion was the origin of knowledge, which led to his developmental studies of children's thinking. Experimentally, he observed youngsters in spontaneous activities and discussed with them their logic in arriving at "wrong" answers. Younger children's cognition was not wrong, but it was quite different from the cognition of those who were more mature. In addition, Piaget recorded in great detail, and interpreted, the activities of his three children. His theory of cognitive development emerged from this body of work.

Piaget's theory of cognitive development proposed four general periods (table 7.1) to describe the qualitatively different ways children and adolescents think from birth to maturity (Crain, 1985; Ginsburg & Opper, 1969; Shaffer, 1999). He proposed that children develop structures called **schemes** or schema for thoughts and action. The schemes are the result of children's actively constructing understandings of the world based on their experiences (Shaffer, 1999). Cognitive experiences early in life are movement generated, and thus movement development and cognitive development are interacting processes. Let's take a quick look at the four periods Piaget proposed.

TABLE 7.1   Piaget's Four Stages of Intellectual Development

Stage and age	Description
Sensorimotor (0-2 years)	Sensory experience and movement are coordinated to act upon the world and generate knowledge.
Preoperational (2-7 years)	Thinking is symbolic but egocentric and often illogical from an adult perspective.
Concrete operations (7-11 years)	Thinking is logical but restricted to events experienced, seen, or heard.
Formal operations (11-12 years and beyond)	Logical thinking can now extend to ideas and hypotheses.

- In the first month of the **sensorimotor period**, newborn schemes are based on reflexes, according to Piaget. By one month, children learn to self-initiate a movement that is similar to a reflex, for example a sucking action in anticipation of a nipple. This would be referred to as a sucking scheme. By four months, they repeat actions they enjoy, such as bringing their hand into view to watch it. These actions occur very close to the body. In this early development period, infants learn that their actions have an effect on their own bodies. From 4 to 10 months, this cause-and-effect link is extended outside the body; for example, the infant realizes that shaking a rattle results in a unique sound and that actions such as a crude throw of food produce a curious "splat" and interesting reactions on the part of parents. By one year, children are experimenting with a host of actions that produce many fascinating outcomes. A rattle can be seen, reached for, grasped, and shook. They also become aware that an object removed from vision still exists **(object permanence)**. They find the object by thoughtfully searching around barriers and under coverings. By two years, children demonstrate some time lag before acting on a problem. While the outcome remains a motor act, there appears to be a thought process that precedes the action. Of course, by age 2, children understand many words and requests and have been experimenting with expressive language for almost a year.

- **Preoperational thought** is characterized by the use of symbols such as images and words. Language can reconstruct a previous event, explain the present, or predict the future. Children at this stage initiate pretend play, and through action finally develop logical thinking. In most cases, however, children are not logical thinkers like adults. In Piaget's famous experiment on **conservation of liquids**, children were presented with two identical glasses that contained the same amount of water (Crain, 1985). When water from one glass was placed into a taller glass, the child was asked which glass now had the most water. He often responded that the taller glass had more water, suggesting that the child's logic was based on only one dimension, in this case height. It is not surprising that parents, therapists, or teachers who attempt to use adult logic with a child find minimal understanding. In social situations children are often **egocentric** in their thinking until quite late in preoperational thinking. "Egocentric" does not imply selfishness, only that they are unable to view the world from another perspective. Thus, it makes little sense to the child to spread out on a playing field in the hope that someone will pass him the ball, or even to wait his turn on a playground. The child who tells the teacher on a

Monday morning that her parents had a big fight during the weekend over the time she should go to bed cannot understand that sharing the "fight" story with the teacher is not desirable from the viewpoint of her parents. This period is also the time when children move from **parallel play** (playing alongside peers but not really interacting) to **cooperative play**, when two youngsters assume a common goal like building a sandcastle.

- **Concrete operations** are a much more logical use of thinking, albeit regarding real objects or events based on experience. Children can now master the conservation of liquid problem as well as other conservation problems; for example, they are aware that objects have more than one dimension. In sport, the child can begin to think strategically about the intent of an opponent and what personal action is required to counter such tactics (Payne & Isaacs, 2008). They also develop a less egocentric view of the world during this period, as they find that they must adopt the perspective of others if they want to be understood. Thus, they consider what they are saying and the needs of the listener. Rules of games that were unchangeable and were determined by adults can now be viewed as plastic, modifiable to suit the needs of several people and the group.

- **Formal operations** begin at about age 11 years and develop until adulthood, according to Piaget. Thinking is no longer restricted to concrete objects but can deal with abstractions. In the conservation of liquid problem, the child understands that water can be repoured into the original glasses and knows the outcome without actually performing the action. This affects a wide array of cognitions, in areas from science to sport to social values. The child can deal with science problems systematically by exploring many possibilities and hypotheses. A defensive player in a team sport can picture the oncoming players, predict potential outcomes, and decide on a defensive strategy. Formal operations enable adolescents to ponder questions of the future and their own aspirations. In relation to this thinking, they can begin to set longer-term goals and realize that certain actions are needed now for the ultimate goal. As we will see in the context of social development, prior to the formal operations period a child might brag about a parent as tall, athletic, and rich; during the formal operations period, concepts of honesty, thoughtfulness, and integrity develop. Some aspects of egocentrism may reappear as adolescents ponder the vast array of life's possibilities. Eventually, experience and adult-like thinking enable self-realization as older adolescents learn their own limits and cognitive abilities.

Piaget's theory helps us appreciate the cognitive functioning of children and adolescents. Piaget advocated neither a strict maturational or environmental position. Rather than viewing knowledge as something to be provided by the teacher or parent, he believed that true learning comes from active discovery. Materials of interest to the child are critical but should be tailored to her stage of cognition so that she is drawn to them. The ages associated with Piaget's four stages vary with each child. Some of the 12-year-old youngsters described at the beginning of the chapter may still be functioning in the concrete operational stage while others may be well into formal operations. Thus, students in this class will vary a great deal in how they think and view the social and academic world. Piaget was primarily concerned with qualitative changes in children's thinking as they developed. But children also gain knowledge; they know things as they develop. We turn to this topic next.

What Do You Think?

Movement development and cognitive development are interacting processes. How might a child's stage of cognitive development influence his movement abilities in the following situations?

- Playing a game of soccer with modified rules
- Jumping rope with a partner

Types of Knowledge

Influential papers by Chase and Simon (1973) and Chi (1978) prompted the exploration of knowledge and its relationship to memory and development. Chase and Simon asked people to look at a chess board and to remember the position of the chess pieces, and then to re-place the pieces in their identical spots on the board after they had been removed. Not surprisingly perhaps, the chess experts remembered the position of the pieces better than nonexperts. However, this excellent memory was apparent only when the chess pieces represented real patterns seen in a game. When the chess pieces were randomly placed on the board, the chess experts could not recall their positions any better than novice chess players. The experts did not have any advantage in basic abilities or mental "hardware" (Ericsson, 2003), but their extensive knowledge of the game was responsible for their remarkable memory of real chess patterns. This result has been replicated in studies in which expert athletes recalled patterns of actual game play in sports such as basketball, volleyball, and field hockey more effectively than sport novices (Starkes & Allard, 1991).

Chi (1978) extended this thinking about the role of knowledge by challenging the long-held assumption that the memory of adults always exceeds that of children. She used the chess task and demonstrated that children who were chess experts could recall more chess positions than adults who were novices in chess. Children can outperform adults when their knowledge is more extensive than that of the adults. This supported the impact of domain-specific knowledge on memory and led researchers to compare experts and novices in a wide range of areas such as chess, sport and refereeing, music, and science as a means to gain insight into knowledge development and performance (Starkes & Ericsson, 2003). We will focus on knowledge in physical activity and sport (see table 7.2). Different types of knowledge have been identified and include declarative, procedural, and metacognitive (e.g., Brown, 1975; Chi, 1981; Wall, McClements, Bouffard, Findlay, & Taylor, 1985).

- **Declarative knowledge** about action is factual and conceptual information stored in memory that can influence development and execution of skilled movement (Wall, Reid, & Harvey, 2007). Factual knowledge includes knowing the difference between a softball (which is not really soft) and a nerf ball (which is actually soft) or an underhand versus an overhead throw. Factual knowledge begins to develop in preschool and is acquired through experience and facilitated by language. Conceptual knowledge is developed by athletes and sport enthusiasts and involves knowledge of the rules, equipment, and

TABLE 7.2 Knowledge Influences on Movement Performance

Types of knowledge	Description
Declarative knowledge	Factual knowledge stored in memory: *The shortstop usually stands to the left of second base, so I should move to that location.* **A**
Procedural knowledge	Knowledge underlying action such as decision making: *If the ball rolls slowly to me at third base and the runner on first is fast and has a good lead, I will throw to first base instead of second to get the sure out.* **B**
Metacognitive knowledge	A higher level of declarative knowledge about how one learns: *I really want to make this team but my attention can wander, so I had better place myself in the front of the other players where I can see the coach.* **A**
Metacognitive skills	A higher level of procedural knowledge about how one performs: *I am not doing very well in this race at the moment, but I will not stay with the leaders because I think they are going too fast and I know my strength is the final "kick."* **B**

tactics of the game. This is affected by cultural norms, as Canadians often have extensive knowledge of ice hockey, as do the British about cricket. Declarative knowledge is often assessed by written or verbal tests.

- **Procedural knowledge** is about how to do something. It underlies an action and includes anticipation and prediction, decision-making, and response selection aspects of information processing (Wall et al., 2007). Catching a ball will be influenced by perceptual knowledge of the trajectory, speed, and size of the ball; cues from the thrower; and the position of the catcher in relation to the environment. Experts pick up cues earlier than nonexperts for perceptual processing (Abernethy, 1991; Wall et al., 2007), and children from 5 to 12 years show improvement in the use of cues to predict the direction of a ball (Lefebvre & Reid, 1998). One researcher assessed the procedural knowledge of gymnastics judges by showing video clips of gymnasts performing with errors and requesting the judges to describe the error, as well as by monitoring their eye movements to determine where they were focused and for how long (Ste-Marie, 2003). French and Thomas (1987) studied decision making in basketball with an observation instrument that recorded whether the child shot, passed, or dribbled after receiving the ball; while French, Spurgeon, and Nevett (1995) conducted a similar study in baseball.

The relationship between execution of movement, declarative knowledge, and procedural knowledge is complicated. In chess, declarative knowledge is information about the game quite apart from actually playing. One would assess procedural knowledge by having people play the game to determine the extent of knowing how to play. In chess, researchers are not typically concerned with the act of reaching and grasping the chess pieces and moving them to a new location. But movement scientists are very much interested in the act of reaching and grasping, not just declarative and procedural knowledge. While some argue that procedural knowledge is synonymous with skill execution, it is probably wise to differentiate between movement execution, declarative knowledge, and procedural knowledge (e.g., French & Thomas, 1987; Kourtessis & Reid, 1997). If you have ever made a decision to execute a particular movement (procedural) but failed to actually accomplish it (execution)—didn't do what you meant to do—then you understand the distinction between procedural knowledge and execution.

- "Meta" is a prefix that refers to a higher level. In the context of knowledge, it is a higher level of understanding of one's knowledge. It is not just more knowledge but personal reflection on one's knowledge, awareness of how one acquires knowledge, and awareness of one's strengths and weaknesses. University students demonstrate **metacognitive knowledge** when they realize that they must study in a quiet environment to be successful or when they find it easier to learn subject A than subject B. Wall and colleagues (2007) distinguished between metacognitive knowledge, a higher level of declarative knowledge, and **metacognitive skill**, a higher level of procedural knowledge. A swimmer may know that her kick in the breaststroke is fine but that more work is needed on the arm action; this is an example of metacognitive knowledge about action. With development, metacognitive knowledge becomes more "organized, coherent, and accessible" (Wall et al., 2007, p. 267). Metacognitive knowledge is self-awareness of one's strengths and weaknesses. Metacognitive skills are especially important in selecting and planning goal-directed learning (Wall et al., 2007). Much of what we describe later as self-regulation could be viewed as metacognitive skills. A budding athlete who intentionally continues to problem solve to push personal performance limits is demonstrating metacognitive or self-regulatory skill.

Try This

Establish a group with one or two of your classmates. In your group, pick an area of knowledge within movement (e.g., specific sport, playing a musical instrument). It is best if you feel quite knowledgeable about this area. Your first task is to list specific examples of declarative knowledge, procedural knowledge, metacognitive knowledge, and metacognitive skill that are important in your sport or activity. For procedural knowledge, focus on decision making rather than actual skill execution. Second, can you think of professional players or other highly skilled athletes or musicians who are recognized as particularly strong in one of the types of knowledge?

Development of Knowledge

The development of declarative, procedural, and metacognitive knowledge likely follows that order (Brown, 1975, 1978; Wall et al., 1985). As children acquire language in the preschool years, they demonstrate factual declarative knowledge of early movements. Evidence of declarative knowledge and procedural knowledge then emerges. However, these knowledge types are related to quite specific actions (i.e., domain-specific knowledge), and therefore the extent of knowledge is based largely on experience rather than age. One of the children in the grade 7 class mentioned at the beginning of this chapter might have extensive procedural and declarative knowledge of basketball because of playing the game so frequently. Therefore, just like the chess experts in the experiment of Chi (1978) who could remember the placement of pieces better than adults, this basketball player may possess more declarative and procedural knowledge of basketball—not only beyond that of her age peers, but also beyond that of her teacher. Metacognitive knowledge is the last to develop and requires Piaget's formal operations but much experience as well.

Knowing and Doing

Perhaps it does not surprise anyone that sport-specific declarative, procedural, and metacognitive knowledge are more extensive in people who participate extensively in a given sport. Is it really unexpected that people who play baseball might know more about baseball than those who do not? But what about the "armchair quarterback" who might have much declarative knowledge about the game but limited playing ability? "Knowing" and "doing" are obviously related, but precisely how they are related and how they change over time is not clear; the relationship is quite complex because knowledge and performance are dynamic, ever-changing factors.

Research Notes: Basketball Skills and Knowledge

French and Thomas (1987) published two studies that began to explore knowing and doing in basketball. In the first study, they examined declarative knowledge, skill development, and expertise. The participants were basketball players in age groups 8 to 10 and 11 to 12. The coaches completed a questionnaire to rate each player's basketball ability and designated the top third of each age group as experts, while the bottom third were termed novices. All players completed a 50-item multiple-choice declarative knowledge test and a skills test of basketball. In addition, an observational instrument was used during real games to assess control, decision making, and execution. Control referred to whether the player made a successful or unsuccessful catch. Decision making involved whether the player held the ball, passed, shot, or dribbled. Execution related to the success of the decision. The findings showed that the experts in both groups possessed more shooting skill and basketball knowledge and made more correct decisions than novices. The authors concluded that "development of sport-specific declarative knowledge is related to the development of cognitive decision-making skills or procedural knowledge, whereas development of shooting skill and dribbling skill are related to motor execution components of control and execution" (French & Thomas, 1987, p. 24).

The second study explored change in declarative knowledge, skills, and basketball performance (observational instrument) over a seven-week season—and also included a control group from physical education classes from a middle school. Basketball knowledge, cognitive decision making, and control components of performance improved; but performance on the skills test did not change significantly, nor did the execution component of performance. Since cognitive knowledge and decision making improved, the authors concluded that "children are learning what to do in certain basketball situations faster than they are acquiring the motor skills to carry out the action" (p. 30).

That children might learn appropriate actions before attaining the ability to execute them was supported by Kourtessis and Reid (1997), who demonstrated that fundamental knowledge of catching preceded actual performance. In contrast, French and colleagues (1995) showed that skill contributed to expertise in baseball players 7 to 10 years of age more than decision-making skills, possibly because baseball is a low-strategy sport compared to basketball. If sport experts have more declarative knowledge than novices, is it simply because the experts have more experience with the sport, or because they have more skill? Williams and Davids (1995) tried to distinguish between **game experience** and **skill** by comparing high-skilled soccer players, low-skilled soccer players, and spectators who had a physical disability and therefore had never played the game but reported having watched hundreds of games. Arguably the latter group had much experience with the game but minimal skill. Overall, the results showed that the high-skilled players had the most extensive declarative knowledge about soccer, suggesting that playing the sport was an important factor in developing declarative knowledge. It seems that declarative knowledge is part of skill rather than only a by-product of experience. Clearly, the relationship between knowing and doing is not simple, and at times knowing might be advanced compared to doing; but more research is needed to determine the best combination of cognitive and motor instruction.

 What Do You Think?

How will students' declarative knowledge, procedural knowledge, and metacognitive knowledge influence their ability to learn motor skills?

Attention

Attention has been investigated for over a hundred years by scholars interested in motor performance and learning. Bicyclists navigating a busy street, students learning in a noisy environment, typists in an open office, and trauma patients trying to reacquire lost skills understand the need to pay attention. But there are different meanings of attention and several theories, as well as insights about its development. We now turn to these topics.

Meaning of Attention

Attention has several meanings (Schmidt & Lee, 2005). Abernethy, Maxwell, Masters, Van der Kamp, and Jackson (2007) propose three common roles of attention in skill learning. First, attention is related to limited information processing capacities while people are attempting to perform two or more tasks simultaneously. Secondly, attention relates to alertness and readiness to respond to stimuli when they occur. This may be a very brief time period as in waiting for the sound of the starter's gun or quite long as in waiting in left field for a ball hit to that area. Third, selective attention refers to selecting essential information for processing, such as external visual or auditory cues or internal kinesthetic cues, that is necessary for performance.

Attention as Limited Information Processing

Multitasking refers to executing multiple tasks simultaneously, like pecking away on a keyboard, listening to music, and watching TV, consistent with the first meaning of attention. Attention in the context of simultaneous task performance is central to the current controversy about whether or not using handheld telephones should be legal in cars. In a sport context, limited information processing capacities are critical to understanding the importance of automaticity of performance. As some skills become automatized, the player can attend to other aspects of the environment. For example, a basketball player must learn to dribble without looking at the ball before she is able to simultaneously dribble, run, view the positions of teammates and opponents, and contemplate the next move of passing, shooting, or continuing to dribble. Leavitt (1979) conducted a study many years ago with ice hockey players of different ages and experience as they skated for speed and performed one, two, or three simultaneous tasks. It is clear from the results in figure 7.1 that the skating speed of young players decreased more than that of older and more experienced players when they were required to stick handle with a puck and simultaneously perform other tasks. Years of playing had provided the older players with a greater degree of automaticity of skating and even stick handling so that they were minimally affected by a visual identification task of naming geometric shapes projected onto a screen.

In research, **dual-task paradigms** are often used to formally explore simultaneous performance on two tasks. Participants are asked to focus on the **primary task**, such as ice skating for speed or listening for their name on an audiotape. At the same time, they must attend to a **secondary task**, such as stick handling or a visual presentation of geometric shapes. The researchers are usually interested first and foremost in the attention demands of the primary task. Attention limits have not been reached if the two tasks can be managed together as effectively as apart. If performance on the primary task suffers, it

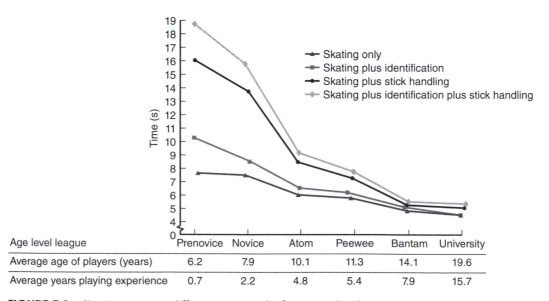

FIGURE 7.1 Skating times at different ages and information loads.

Reprinted, by permission, from J. Leavitt, 1979, "Cognitive demands of skating and stickhandling in ice hockey," *Canadian Journal of Applied Sport Science* 4: 46-55.

is assumed that performing the secondary task either exceeds the processing limits of the person or requires the same mechanism as the primary task. It has been recognized for over a century that attention has limits; regardless of how automatic some skills become, we have limits in multitasking. Loeb (1890, as cited by Magill, 2007) demonstrated that pressure exerted on a hand dynamometer decreased while a person engaged in mental work.

Attention as Being Alert

Alertness and sustained attention is the second meaning of attention. Parents who have watched their child on a baseball or soccer field know that alertness can waver in young children. If the play is not near, grass or flowers may gain their attention. At other times children can become engrossed in activities that are particularly interesting and motivational. Most children improve in alertness with age, experience with the activity, and motivation to engage in the activity.

Attention as Selective

Selective attention is the third perspective of attention. With selective attention, not only does relevant information gain access to limited processing capabilities, but irrelevant information is restricted from access. It is assumed that this latter type of information impedes performance (Abernethy et al., 2007). Development of selective attention is discussed later in this chapter, and the impact of verbal and visual cues from teachers and coaches to direct selective attention is discussed in chapter 13.

Theories of Attention

Most theories of attention propose that people have a **central limited capacity** when performing simultaneous activities (Magill, 2007; Schmidt and Lee, 2005). In other words, the brain and central nervous system do not have a bottomless pit of space. If you have ever felt overloaded by visual and auditory information, you realize that attention is limited. But the theories differ with regard to the extent and location of the limits. **Single-channel filter theories** propose that tasks are accomplished in serial order and that a bottleneck occurs at some point in information processing at which the system can process only one task at a time. If the bottleneck occurred with information detection, two tasks that rely greatly on detecting information (as might be necessary for an air traffic controller) could not be performed simultaneously without many errors. On the other hand, a task that required information detection might be more easily accomplished along with a task not depending on information detection, such as watching for a signal on a monitor while riding a stationary bike.

Alternatively, Kahneman (1973) proposed a **central-resource capacity theory**. This is a more flexible system in which information processing capacity could expand on the basis of conditions related to the individual, the task, and the situation. Kahneman asserted that attention is cognitive effort. There is no particular bottleneck but a more general pool of effort that can be strategically allocated to the activities. The individual evaluates the amount of attention (e.g., cognitive effort) necessary to perform the various tasks to determine if she can do them simultaneously. The expansion and flexibility of the processing are not unlimited, and at some critical point, performance of one or more of the tasks will be adversely affected. Finally, **multiple-resource theories**

contend that we have several attention mechanisms, each with limited capacity (Magill 2007). Wickens (1980, 1992) posits that the mechanisms might be modalities (e.g., movement and speech), stages of information processing (e.g., perception or decision making), and codes of processing information (e.g., verbal codes or spatial codes). If tasks require a common mechanism they will be difficult to perform simultaneously, while tasks based on separate mechanisms can be performed simultaneously, much as suggested by central-resource theories, but each mechanism has its own capacity limitations.

Development of Attention

Management of limited information processing develops with age; there would seem to be little doubt that children are less able than adults to perform simultaneous tasks. The intriguing developmental question is why adults are more capable. The simple explanation is that overall capacity increases with age. The person is analogous to a container that changes over time from a pint to a gallon. This capacity-increase view has generally not received much support (Thomas, Thomas, & Gallagher, 1993). Rather, it is more likely, as Wickens and Benel (1982) concluded, that automation and deployment of attention skills explain developmental changes. Automation is the autonomous phase of learning described by Fitts and Posner (1967)—the point at which motor skills can be executed with almost no attention. This occurs after considerable practice, and thus automation is not limited solely by age or maturation, but also by specific experience with the task. Think of the excellent downhill skier, young or older, who requires thoughtful attention only if he finds himself suddenly on dangerous terrain. Attention skills are strategies employed during the learning and performance of tasks that improve with age and experience. Later in this chapter we will see that children's memories improve if they intentionally engage in rehearsal strategies, such as rehearsal of a telephone number presented to them verbally.

Thomas and colleagues (1993) presented a review of the development of selective attention for motor skills. Ross (1976, as cited by Thomas et al.) described overexclusive, overinclusive, and selective attention. Children 5 or 6 years of age are likely to be overexclusive, that is, attend to a limited number of cues regardless of their task importance. Between 6 to 7 and 11 to 12 years, the child becomes overinclusive, directing attention to the complete display rather than focusing on task-relevant cues. Children older than 11 years begin to selectively attend to the task-important cues and ignore the task-irrelevant cues. Teachers and coaches can help children focus on relevant cues, as explained in chapter 13.

Developmental Changes in Speed of Information Processing

Speed of information processing also shows clear developmental trends. In a **simple reaction time** experiment, individuals remove a finger from a response key when a light comes on. Adults outperform children, or to put this more positively, children improve with age. In a more complex situation called **choice reaction time**, the finger is lifted from the key and moved to a second response key under two or more lights. The act of removing the finger from the initial response key is the same act in either simple or choice reaction time. Yet choice reaction time is longer than simple reaction time presumably because the decision to move to a specific response key is processed before the lifting of the finger. Hick (1952) demonstrated that reaction time increases as more choices are presented, although he used the term "information load" as a more general term for number of choices. Choice reaction time improves with age and is particularly slower in children than in adults at higher loads of information (Keogh & Sugden, 1985). Information processing speed also improves with age on tasks involving feedback processing and decision making (Thomas et al., 1993). Children process information more slowly and less efficiently than adults.

As in the case of attention, the intriguing question is why children are slower on information processing tasks. It is unlikely that children have reduced nerve impulse conduction speed or capacity of the motor system compared to adults (Thomas et al., 1993). Central information processing mechanisms may account for age difference in speed of processing. Keogh and Sugden (1985) suggest that this may occur in any part of the processing chain (e.g., perception, recognition, decision making). More research is necessary to determine if slower reactions of children are due to slower perception or slower decision making. It is also possible that children lack task-specific strategies and knowledge, which reduces their speed of processing (Thomas et al., 1993). Finally, several noncentral factors might be involved, for example attentiveness, incentive, and practice. That is, perhaps children do not perform as well on such speed tasks because they are not attentive enough during testing or have no great motivation to perform well.

 What Do You Think?

Consider the aforementioned theories of attention. How do these theories make you rethink how you will effectively teach your future students?

Memory

Memory is the ability to recall things and allows us to benefit from experience. When someone gives you a telephone number for later use, your first impulse is to list it quickly in your cell phone directory, or to write it on piece of paper if your phone is not handy. If neither is available, you rehearse the number several times with the hope of recalling it later; that is, you commit it to your memory. These three activities are conscious strategies you use because you realize the failings of the memory system. This section outlines some important ideas about how memory works. First, we explore short- and long-term memory, types of memory with which you are likely familiar. Today memory researchers usually use the term *working memory* instead of short-term memory, but they share some similarities. Then we move to the relationship between memory and knowledge. This becomes a bit more complicated because some people believe that memory and knowledge cannot be separated, while others argue that different types of memory recall different forms of knowledge. At this point we also introduce the idea that individuals can engage in deliberate attempts to remember, and then outline ways to improve memory of movements.

Working and Long-Term Memory

If you could dial the telephone number immediately, you would do so quickly, knowing that it will remain with you for a only a few more seconds before you forget it. Older models of memory distinguished between **short-term** and **long-term memory** (e.g., Atkinson & Shiffrin, 1968). In early computer terminology, these memory structures were described as the hardware of memory. Information moved from short-term to long-term memory via control processes like rehearsal or practice. Control processes were considered the software of memory. Short-term memory was used when you dialed the number immediately. If you rehearse the number frequently and use it often, the number eventually finds its way to long-term memory, a permanent store. Long-term memory is reflected in the saying about riding a bicycle with reference to performing a task not attempted for many years. Adults actually do ride a bicycle (and perform other skills) successfully after many years of not riding. How are they able to do this? Quite simply, the movement skills of riding remain in the long-term memory store.

A more recent model of memory proposed by Baddeley (1986, 1995) had two structures: working memory and long-term memory.

Working memory has some similarities to short-term memory, but the term "working" underscores the more active role of the control processes beyond those typically described under the term short-term memory. Working memory performs a number of functions, including temporarily storing recently presented material. It also retrieves information from long-term storage to influence current problem solving, decision making, and movement production. Working memory is the structure in which memory control processes work to transfer information to long-term memory. One can think of working memory as a cognitive workspace (Magill, 2007). Just before a hitter comes to the plate, the player at second base might review the batter's hitting tendencies stored in her long-term memory, couple that information with knowledge that a runner is on first base, and review her options if the ball is hit either slowly or sharply to her. Many of these cognitive activities are similar to the self-regulation and attention processes previously described.

Working memory has been described in terms of both duration and capacity. Its duration is limited to 20 to 30 seconds. Adams and Dijkstra (1966) required blindfolded participants to move the handle of an apparatus on a trackway until it was physically blocked. After a retention interval, the person tried to recall the movement by moving the handle back to the same point on the trackway. Results demonstrated that arm movements could be recalled very accurately if the retention interval was very short, but performance declined substantially in only 20 seconds.

It has long been argued that the capacity of working memory is seven items, plus or minus two (Miller, 1956). Depending on the content and the person, capacity is between five and nine. Adults can usually remember a series of seven numbers without too much effort. Beyond that, there will be severe challenges to the memory system. When researchers asked young gymnasts (Ille & Cadopi, 1999) and dancers (Starkes, Deakin, Lindley, & Crisp, 1987) to recall a movement sequence, the participants showed limits of six items and eight items, respectively. They were relatively experienced in the activity and could remember only a few movements in the correct order. Thus, practitioners should avoid lengthy sequential lists when teaching children.

Information that is practiced and used often will find its way into long-term memory. Long-term memory contains memory of past events and our general knowledge. In terms of movement, knowledge includes the ability to perform physical skills such as swimming, bicycling, and skiing as well as declarative, procedural, and metacognitive knowledge discussed earlier in this chapter. The capacity and duration of long-term memory are often considered to be unlimited, and long-term memory is relatively permanent.

Memory and Knowledge

Since long-term memory is our personal knowledge, memory and knowledge have been categorized in a number of similar ways. Piaget believed that understanding, knowledge, and memory were inseparable. Tulving (1985, 2002) distinguished between **episodic** and **semantic memory**. The former refers to remembering personal events, going back in time, such as your first day at a university. You might recall details of your feelings, reactions of parents, the people you met, and your first class. Semantic memory refers to general knowledge built from life experiences and learning. Semantic memory includes everything from the concept of school to the name of the country north of the United States. Tulving (1985) also included procedural knowledge, knowing how to do something. He viewed motor skills as a form of procedural knowledge that allows us to achieve goals in our environment, not just talk about what to do. The point was made in this chapter that skilled movement performance should be differentiated from procedural knowledge of that skilled movement.

Developmental psychologist Brown (1975) described memory as three types of knowledge: knowing, knowing how to know, and knowing about knowing. **Knowing** is our knowledge base, which others have called semantic memory or declarative knowledge. From a developmental perspective, younger children are not expected to perform as well on memory recall tasks as older children, because the younger ones have a less detailed knowledge that new information can be related to. If practitioners can build links with previous knowledge, learners will benefit: "Remember how you learned to step forward when throwing a ball? With the football, you have to do the same thing." **Knowing how to know** refers to control processes and strategies that are used for deliberate learning. These activities move information or action from working memory to long-term memory. Strategies include rehearsing information, naming (attaching a verbal label to stimuli), grouping information (e.g., tennis instructors may suggest you scratch your back with the racket rather than provide a lengthy list of actions), and searching long-term memory. Much learning, and hence knowledge, is dependent on strategic learning, according to Brown. Her research has demonstrated that young children and those with intellectual disabilities must learn to use strategies and become more active learners. Therefore, games that intentionally teach strategies such as getting into the open for a pass are important. Likewise, the common reminder in teaching the breaststroke, "arms, legs, glide," specifies the important coordination sequences and is a strategy that learners can use on their own.

Finally, **knowing about knowing** is metamemory, or metacognition; it is the knowledge of how our personal memory functions. If young children are asked if they can recall a list of 14 foods provided verbally by the teacher, they are likely to say yes. Adolescents know that 14 items will exceed their memory capacity (seven plus or minus two). The teenagers know more about how memory works. They realize that they can recall a list of 14 only if they use a memory strategy, like writing the list on paper or grouping a food list, for example, into fruits, vegetables, and grains. In a movement context, the person with excellent metamemory might know that she needs to read about a skill to learn the verbal labels and to gain some declarative knowledge, then practice alone to get the idea of the movements and rehearse the declarative knowledge, and then to seek out a teacher to provide feedback after some trials. Others might know they learn best by going to an instructor at the beginning. *Knowing how to know* develops after *knowing about knowing* and *knowing.*

Memory for Movements

Memory for movements may be assisted by visual imagery, verbal labels, rehearsal, intention to remember, and subjective organization (Magill, 2007). First, memory is influenced by the **meaningfulness** of the movement. This is not meaningfulness in a motivational context of how important the movement is for the person. Rather, it refers to the similarity of new movements to previous ones. Movements have space and time constraints. A meaningful movement is one that the learner can relate to because the new movement is similar to something already known. Meaningfulness can be assisted by **visual imagery** and **verbal labels**. A swimming instructor could describe the biomechanics of the arm pull of the side stroke or provide an image for the learner of picking an apple from a tree, bringing the apple down, and putting it into a basket. The visual image is preferable. If the new movement skill is similar to a previously learned skill, the instructor can provide that link for learners.

Verbal labels can also improve meaningfulness. Research indicates that learners can remember the end location of movements and the distance of the movement. A verbal label for the end locations of movements, such as the position of the golf club driver at backswing, can be used to improve memory of the swing. And the moon walk is assisted if learners remember that the knee is straight when the leg begins to slide backward. Verbal labels for movements that match something well known are also effective, such as "Move your arm to the 2 o'clock position." Winther and Thomas (1981) and Weiss (1983) have shown that children as young as 5 years can benefit from use of labels. Magill offered four reasons why images and verbal labels are effective. They reduce the complexity of verbal instructions needed to describe all movements, assist in making an abstract movement more concrete, promote a focus on the intended outcome of the movements rather than the movements themselves, and assist movement planning by retrieval of memory for previously learned movements. Verbal labels and cues are discussed further in chapter 13.

Most children begin to use deliberate rehearsal strategies between 5 and 7 years of age and over the childhood and early adolescent years become more efficient and intentional in their use (Ornstein & Naus, 1978). Conscious rehearsal of movements is also developmental (Reid, 1980a; Sugden, 1978). Young children often do not spontaneously rehearse, but when they are instructed to use a memory strategy, performance usually improves. With a sequence of movements to be remembered, 5- and 7-year-old children who were taught to rehearse a subset of the movements (rather than perform instance-by-instance practicing)

Try This

We do not often think about memory for movements we perform. But vision, the vestibular apparatus, and kinesthesis permit us to replicate movements we have experienced. Form pairs with classmates. One pair should volunteer to go to the front of the class and do a quick demonstration that proves we can replicate previously experienced movements. One student stands facing the class with eyes closed. His partner lifts one of his arms to form an angle (45 or 90 degrees) to the side of the body, then lowers the arm and asks him to return to the previous angle. The angle will not be perfect, but it will approximate the angle experienced.

After you have seen the demonstration, face your partner, with each of you at a desk. One of you places your elbow and forearm on the desk so that the forearm crosses the chest. Close your eyes. Your partner should slowly move your hand around an arc with the elbow as a pivot point (really a curvilinear path of the hand). After 20 seconds, your partner will ask you to go back to the same spot. Your partner will select five distances to move your arm, such as 30, 60, 90, 120, and 150 degrees. Thus, there will be five trials consisting of (a) a movement, (b) 20 seconds, and (c) replicating the movement. After five trials, switch positions.

After each person has had five trials, discuss with your partner how you remembered the movements. Discuss whether you used any of these strategies: visual imagery, verbal labels, rehearsal, intention to remember, or subjective organization. Did you use techniques other than these?

---

improved compared to those not receiving instruction (Gallagher & Thomas, 1984). Memory strategy instruction is also effective for those with intellectual disabilities and learning problems (Reid, 1980b; Hoover & Wade, 1985).

Another way to help memory for movements is to tell learners explicitly that they will be required to remember the movement. While incidental memory, or nonintentional recall, occurs, being aware that a "test" of memory will happen at a later time should promote use of personal intentional memory strategies: "We will use this sliding action in the folk dance we will learn tomorrow." Memory can also be enhanced if participants are allowed to develop **subjective organization**. This is particularly useful in remembering a series of movements in sequence, such as dance steps or gymnastics moves. When novices are faced with a sequence, they are likely to view the sequence as a long list of individual movements (Magill, 2007). If there are 20 movements, the novice becomes overwhelmed. With practice, two or three separate movements might become organized into one, thus reducing the number of movements to remember from 20 to 7 or even less. Experts might view the sequence of 20 as only parts, and it is no wonder that they can remember the list more easily than novices. Their knowledge of dance makes it easier because they really have less to remember. In the study of dancers by Starkes and colleagues (1987), the expert dancers recalled the eight steps of the sequence almost perfectly, while the novices recalled about half correctly. And as in the chess study by Chase and Simon (1973), when the dance sequences did not conform to typical and expected dance sequences, the experts were no better able to recall the sequences than the novices.

Research Notes: Rehearsal of Movements by Children

Gallagher and Thomas (1984) had four participant age groups (approximate ages 5, 7, 11, and 19 years) in a study of rehearsal of movements. The experimenters compared three rehearsal conditions: mature, child-like, and self-determined. The participants were required to grasp a handle that supported their arm and to move the handle in different angles and distance combinations. Specifically, the angles were parallel, 15 degrees, and 30 degrees, and the distances were 10 to 45 centimeters. The distances and angles were determined by the experimenters. This is an example of a positioning task, typical of much of the research in that era. Essentially, participants make an initial movement that is constrained by the experimenter, remain at the end location, and then return to the starting point and independently move the handle to the end location once again. In other words, they try to remember the first movement and then try to reproduce it in the recall trial. Distance from the end location on the recall trial is considered an error in such motor memory research.

Gallagher and Thomas' participants were presented with a series of eight movements to recall, but in any order they chose. The child-like rehearsal condition, considered passive, involved remaining at each of the eight movements for 8 seconds. The mature or adult-like condition was more active; participants remained at the first movement end location for 8 seconds. At the end of the second movement, they remained for 3 seconds, but then moved to the first end location for 3 seconds followed by the second location for an additional 2 seconds. Subsequent new movements were rehearsed for 2 seconds and the previous two movements for 2 seconds each, followed by 2 seconds at the new movement. Thus rehearsal was more active than in the passive child-like condition, but rehearsal time was a constant 8 seconds. The self-determined condition had participants move to the end point of a movement for 2 seconds and allowed them to use the remaining 6 seconds in any way they wished. The results showed that the youngest children remembered the eight movements as well as the 7- and 11-year-old children when forced to rehearse like an adult. In addition, participants using the mature strategy tended to recall movements from short to long, while the child-like rehearsal group was more likely to recall in random order. Thus, imposing an organizational strategy was effective. Overall, active rehearsal was shown to be important in recall of movements.

What Do You Think?

1. Distinguish between short-term, long-term, and working memory.
2. What role does memory play in learning movements? How can you help students remember movements?

Sport Expertise

The study of sport expertise provides important insights into the nature of differences among sport participants but less information on how expertise is developed. **Expert performance** in sport has been defined as "consistent superior athletic performance over an extended period" (Starkes, 1993, as cited by Janelle & Hillman, 2003, p. 21). Janelle and Hillman suggested that experts are distinguished by excellence in four domains: physiological, technical, cognitive, and emotional/psychological (table 7.3). One of the factors that lead to expert performance is (quite unsurprisingly) practice. It is often noted that expertise in sport and other domains requires 10-plus years and 10,000-plus hours of practice. But, as we will see in chapter 12, this is not just a matter of practice itself, but something called deliberate practice. We mention sport expertise in this chapter on functional constraints because children and adolescents come to a learning or practice context with varying levels of skill, as well as declarative, procedural, and metacognitive knowledge. Simple observation of any physical education class attests to the existence of a wide range of skill. Some of the

TABLE 7.3 Sport Expertise

Domain	Distinguishing features of the expert
Physiological	Anaerobic power and aerobic capacity, muscle fiber type, body morphology and body segment size, height, and flexibility; requirements are unique to each sport
Technical	Sensorimotor coordination for refined, efficient, and effective patterns of movement; artistic and aesthetic values as required for the specific activity; movement becomes automatic after years of extended and deliberate practice
Cognitive	Extensive base of knowledge to do such things as recognize structured game situations and match appropriate strategies and tactics to game situation; extracts the most relevant cues in the sport environment, avoids distracting cues, uses effective visual search strategies and signal detection, is able to make fast decisions
Emotional and psychological	Ability to regulate emotions and anxiety, motivation regulation; sets realistic goals, maintains confidence and positive attitude, uses effective imagery and mental training, can self-regulate and possesses metacognitive strategies

Data from C.M. Janelle and C.H. Hillman, 2003, Expert performance in sport: Current perspectives and critical issues. In *Expert performance in sports: Advances in research on sport expertise*, edited by J.L. Starkes and K.A. Ericsson (Champaign, IL: Human Kinetics), 19-47.

 What Do You Think?

As a physical education teacher, you may not have the time or resources to assist every student in becoming an expert. However, you can place your students on the path to expertise. Make a list of external factors that can contribute to expertise and provide strategies you can implement.

External factor	Teaching strategy
Deliberate practice	• Provide social support and feedback. • Provide students with many opportunities to practice skills of choice.

youngsters, particularly adolescents, may be more skilled in a particular sport than the instructor because they have spent many hours practicing the sport skills. They might not be an expert like the professional athlete or Olympian, but they are highly skilled compared to their age peers and are referred to as "experts" in research studies, although they have not achieved the 10-plus years or 10,000-plus hours of practice.

Summary

This chapter outlined several functional constraints related to thinking and learning that help define a person at one point in time. As discussed in the chapter, learners have different abilities in cognition, knowledge, personal skills, attention, and memory that affect them in a motor learning and performance situation. These functional constraints help anyone interested in learning to appreciate individual differences in a class of children or adolescents. No one is the same as an age peer in cognition or knowledge. Some young people have acquired a number of intentional memory strategies, and some have not. Experiences in a given domain or sport vary enormously, as the sport expertise literature demonstrates. Functional constraints in attention are also influential. To complicate matters even further, the functional constraints described in this chapter each change over developmental time within an individual during the phases or stages of development outlined. Children are rather immature learners compared to adults. As children develop, their knowledge base increases; attention to relevant cues becomes more precise; skills become more automatized; decisions are made more quickly; and learning is more strategic and intentional. Thus, the wide individual differences noted by most instructors in a class of 30 students results from the structural constraints discussed in the previous chapter as well as from functional constraints that change over developmental time (e.g., cognition) or learning time (e.g., skill as a function of practice). The diversity of the "Fun and Fit" class of 12-year-olds described at the beginning of this chapter can now be understood in new light. They may differ on many other factors that influence their skill, enjoyment, and attention in a setting.

Supplemental Activities

1. Arrange an interview with an accomplished occupational, physical, or athletic therapist. Ask him or her to reflect on declarative knowledge, procedural knowledge, metacognitive skills, and metacognitive knowledge. Your interviewee might not use the terms per se, but can he see his daily work reflected in this conceptualization of knowledge? Do areas of his work exist that do not fit into the knowledge perspective?

2. There are many popular books on memory and means to improve it. Find one and see what is suggested. Are some of the recommended strategies consistent with the contents of this chapter? Are some different?

Functional Constraints of Psychosocial-Affective Development

CHAPTER OBJECTIVES

After reading this chapter, you should be able to

> discuss the developmental changes in Erikson's stages of psychosocial development,

> discuss the developmental changes in how we view ourselves as a person as identified by Harter,

> identify how self-efficacy develops and how professionals can promote it,

> describe self-determined motivation and how it develops,

> explain the relationship between emotional development and physical activity, and

> describe self-regulation and its relationship to physical activity.

Beyond Physical Dimensions

Robert is an 18-year-old high school football lineman who weighs 200 pounds (about 91 kilograms) and hopes to obtain an athletic scholarship at a university after achieving all-star status for two years. His friend, Jordan, is also an 18-year-old lineman who weighs 270 pounds (about 122 kilograms) but does not want to attend a university to play football. What is happening? Would not every young man with a chance to play college football jump at the chance? Jordan's size appears to be an important structural constraint that would lead to an athletic scholarship; and while not a league all-star, he has been a starter since his freshman year, so we have to assume he has some key skills.

Participating in a sport is certainly influenced by structure (chapter 6) and functional constraints like cognition, knowledge, attention, and memory (chapter 7) but also by whether you view yourself primarily as an athlete or scholar, how competent you perceive yourself as an athlete or scholar, the extent of your motivation to become a college athlete, your awareness of emotional factors in this quest, and your ability to regulate much of your learning. These thoughts and feelings are largely shaped by psychological factors such as motivation; they have strong social and emotional influences and have roots in development from a very early age. These powerful forces and experiences have influenced Jordan's desire to study law at college rather than focus on football. This chapter is an extension of the previous chapter on functional constraints, but it outlines psychosocial–affective functional constraints such as self-esteem, competence motivation, self-efficacy, self-determination, socialization into physical activity, arousal, anxiety, and self-regulation.

Psychosocial Constraints

How individuals come to view themselves is largely affected by their social experiences. We live in a social world from birth. Our initial interactions with our immediate caregivers are followed by interactions with extended families, friends of our parents, and eventually our own friends and schoolmates. The increasingly extensive social networks influence our uniqueness as a person, our sense of self, and how well we manage in the world. To explore these psychosocial factors more completely, we will look at development of psychosocial conflict as conceptualized by Erikson, self-perception and competence according to Harter, self-efficacy viewed by Bandura, and self-determination motivation from Deci, Ryan, and Vallerand.

Erikson's Psychosocial Development Theory: Childhood and Adolescent Stages

Erik Erikson was born in 1902 out of wedlock and was abandoned by his father at birth. He became an artist, teacher, and psychoanalyst but eventually fled Europe for the United States when the Nazis gained power. He received an appointment at Harvard Medical School and went on to practice childhood psychoanalysis in Boston. While he had studied Freudian psychoanalysis, he was also greatly influenced by work with Indian communities in South Dakota and California, civil rights groups, and combat soldiers (Crain, 1985; Shaffer, 1999). His views of psychosocial development became more social and more culturally influenced than Freud's. Erikson also stressed that children are active explorers of their world rather than simply passive reactors to biological urges; his research and experience culminated in 1950 with the first edition of his classic text *Childhood and Society*. He adopted a life span perspective in his work that was unusual for the mid-20th century; his eight life stages extended into adulthood and old age. Each stage was viewed from the standpoint of a psychosocial crisis or conflict that had to be resolved in order to move to the next stage. Table 8.1 outlines the eight stages and their approximate ages (Erikson, 1963). We discuss the first five stages in this chapter and leave the last three stages to chapter 11 on functional constraints of adults. Erikson described the stages very well and influenced

Key figures
Erikson
Harter
Bandura

TABLE 8.1 Erikson's Stages of Psychosocial Development

Approximate age	Stage of psychosocial conflict
Birth to 1 year	Basic trust versus mistrust
1 to 3 years	Autonomy versus shame and doubt
3 to 6 years	Initiative versus guilt
6 to 12 years	Industry versus inferiority
12 to 20 years	Identity versus role confusion
20 to 40 years	Intimacy versus isolation
40 to 65 years	Generativity versus stagnation
65 and over	Ego integrity versus despair

Adapted from E.H. Erickson, 1963, *Childhood and society*, 2nd ed. (New York: W.W. Norton), 247-269.

thinking about social and emotional development as well as **self-esteem**. He has been criticized for not explaining the types of experiences that might resolve the conflicts and promote development (Shaffer, 1999).

- *Basic trust versus mistrust.* Basic trust for infants emerges from interactions with primary caregivers. If parents attend to feeding, cleaning, and comforting of infants, the babies learn to expect consistency and predictability in their world. The reliability and sameness of parent action produce a feeling of trust. Erikson (1963) claims that "The infant's first social achievement . . . is his willingness to let the mother out of sight without undue anxiety or rage, because she has an inner certainty as well as outer predictability" (p. 247). An unreliable parent will foster a general sense of mistrust. But if infants experience some degree of mistrust, this will actually strengthen the understanding of trust. Babies must also learn to trust themselves. Erikson suggests that babies may have an urge to bite while teething, but a grasp of the nipple rather than a bite is a sign of their trustworthiness. As they develop a sense of being trustworthy in a context of predictability, infants will form a sense of identity and of "being 'all right,' of being oneself" (p. 249). One can see the social impact of self-concept very early in life.

- *Autonomy versus shame and doubt.* The basic conflict in this stage is to become autonomous in action but within social regulations. Children from 1 to 3 years learn to stand on their own two feet (literally and figuratively), dress and feed themselves, and express their needs and wants with language. Their autonomy grows from within, according to Erikson. Their explorations of the world and growing independence are sources of cognitive development (see discussion of Piaget in the previous chapter) but also awareness of social and cultural expectations. The 12-month-old will make a mess as she tries to feed herself, and parents are likely to accept "messiness" as part of the process of gaining autonomy. At 3 years, however, parents are likely to insist on some degree of tidiness during eating; this is an early social regulation that is being imposed on the child. Social expectations should not be acquired through shame and doubt. Shame is the conscious feeling that one is exposed and does not look good to others, while doubt refers to a sense of loss of personal control. Parents are primary social agents who attempt to carefully guide the learning of social behaviors without promoting lasting shame and doubt. They realize

avoid shaming & doubt

165

that "from a sense of self-control without loss of self-esteem comes a lasting sense of good will and pride" (Erikson, 1963, p. 254).

- *Initiative versus guilt.* At 3 years of age, enjoyment of new physical and mental powers propels the child to action. Behaviors can be goal directed and very imaginative. As the child makes plans and tries to realize them, some plans will come into conflict with others because the consequences of the actions are often unknown to the child and certainly not considered. There might be physically aggressive acts toward siblings or parents, as well as infantile jealousy and rivalry for parental attention. This may produce guilt. In other cases, the initial plan is beyond the child's capacities and his autonomy is challenged by failure. As in the previous stage, the child must learn social regulations but now is ready with the assistance of parents and siblings to accept these as internal guides through self-observation, self-control, and self-punishment.

- *Industry versus inferiority.* This stage occurs in the elementary school years when teachers and peers become important social agents. Past hopes and wishes important in the family context are forgotten as children learn to win recognition by producing things in the wider culture of school. The need to produce mobilizes children beyond play and to acquire cognitive skills such as reading and writing, as well as social skills appropriate to the culture. They learn to cooperate with others to achieve shared goals. While Erikson does not mention physical skills, fundamental motor skills and game performance are valued in Western cultures and are sources of self-assuredness. In school, children can compare themselves to peers as never before. The danger is a feeling of inferiority that may result such that the child "considers himself doomed to mediocrity or inadequacy" (Erikson, 1963, p. 260). Teachers and coaches can contribute to resolving this conflict by truly valuing all students, encouraging a focus on personal improvement rather than comparison to others, and counseling those who are struggling to find niches of skilled performance.

- *Identity versus role confusion.* This stage of adolescence is characterized largely by a new search for "ego identity" or "who am I?" in the social world (Erikson, 1963; Shaffer, 1999). The crisis that must be resolved is role identity versus role confusion. This conflict occurs in the context of a rapidly changing body and sexual awakening. Erikson contends that adolescents seek a new sense of continuity and sameness and will refight some of the battles of earlier years as they combat this confusion. The sameness and continuity that are sought relate primarily to social and occupational identities. Peer influence is significant, and teenagers worry about meeting others' expectations and the career role they will assume as an adult. Their ego identity is a social matter as they wonder about how they are perceived by others and about their social role in a larger social world. Countless work and social options may result in overidentifying with heroes, cliques, and "in groups," or customs. The conflict of "who am I" is resolved in part by identifying with others who appeal to us, celebrating personal accomplishments, and engaging in the sometimes challenging acceptance of one's uniqueness with strengths and weaknesses.

A number of themes are apparent in Erikson's model of psychosocial development: trust, competency, autonomy, self-concept, self-control, social regulation, and a sense of "who am I." While Erikson quite appropriately underscored the conflict in adolescence of self-identity, the development of "who am I," or the sense of self, actually begins much earlier and is captured more completely by Harter's (1999) descriptions of change in self-representation in childhood and adolescence.

Harter's Self-Representation Stages

Harter (1999) viewed development of self as a cognitive and social process, thus influenced by the interaction of the individual thinking about and evaluating himself and feedback from caregivers, siblings, peers, teachers, and coaches. She acknowledges that distinctions between self-descriptions ("*What* I am") and self-evaluations ("How *good* I am") have been proposed, but most research deals with assessments of self-evaluations. The more common terms for self-evaluation are self-esteem and self-worth (Harter, 1999; Shaffer, 1999). Harter's six descriptive periods are outlined in table 8.2.

[*How good am I* < *broken parents*

TABLE 8.2 Change in Self-Representation

Age period	Exemplary quotes
Very early childhood B – 3	"I'm 3 years old and I live in a big house with my mother and father . . . I have blue eyes . . . I can run real fast, I like pizza, and I have a nice teacher at pre-school. I can count to 100 . . . I'm always happy. I have brown hair."
Early to middle childhood 3 – 6	"I can run fast, and I can climb high, a lot higher than I could when I was little . . . I am going to be on some kind of team when I am older. If you are good at things you can't be bad at things, at least not at the same time . . . My parents are real proud of me when I do good things."
Middle to late childhood 6 – 12	"I'm pretty popular, at least with the girls. That's because I'm nice to people and helpful and can keep most secrets . . . if I get into a bad mood, I sometimes say something that can be a little mean. I'm feeling pretty smart in . . . language arts and social studies . . . but pretty dumb in math . . . I still like myself as a person even though math and science are just not that important to me. I also like myself because I know my parents like me and so do other kids."
Early adolescence 10 – 14	"I'm an extrovert with my friends . . . I'm fairly good looking if I do say so . . . I like myself a lot when I'm around my friends. With my parents, I'm more depressed . . . and also hopeless about ever pleasing them . . . I'm curious about learning new things and . . . creative when it comes to solving problems . . . I worry about what they must think of me, probably that I'm a total dork."
Middle adolescence 14 – 18	"What am I like as a person? You're probably not going to understand. I'm complicated! With my really close friends, I am very tolerant. With a group of friends, I'm rowdier . . . I'm studious every now and again . . . if you are too studious, you won't be popular . . . My parents expect me to get all A's. So I am pretty stressed-out at home . . . When you are 15, are you still a kid or an adult? I'm very responsible at work, which makes me feel good about myself."
Late adolescence 18 – ?	"I'm a pretty conscientious person . . . I plan to go to college next year . . . eventually to law school . . . so developing good study habits and getting top grades are both essential . . . I've also become more religious as I have gotten older . . . I would like to be an ethical person. I am pretty upbeat and optimistic . . . I've never been very athletic, but you can't be good at everything. You have to be adaptive . . . It would be pretty weird to be the same kind of person on a date as with my friends at a football game . . . I'm looking forward to leaving home and going to college, where I can be more independent, although I'm a little ambivalent. I love my parents and really want to stay connected."

Quotes reprinted, by permission, from S. Harter, 1999, *The construction of the self: A developmental perspective* (New York: Guilford Press), 28-88.

One of the developmental themes is the structure of self.

- *Very young children* may view themselves as a good jumper or runner, but do not generalize this to viewing themselves as a good athlete or good at sports. They do not have a judgment of overall self-esteem and do not distinguish among competence domains such as academic, social, or physical appearance. When they are aware of specific behaviors (e.g., jumping or speaking) they are usually unrealistically positive about themselves.

- As they enter school in *early childhood*, they continue to overestimate their abilities and remain positive about themselves, in part because they are not comparing themselves with others. They do become aware that others are evaluating them; they can be good in several domains and are capable of personal comparisons over time, for example, "Last year I could not swim the length of the pool, but now I can."

- As children move toward *later childhood*, they are able to differentiate among additional competence domains such as academic, athletic, social, physical appearance, and behavior conduct. With the aid of language and increased cognitive functioning, they are now aware of social comparisons as they interact with others in school and sport. They know others have an opinion of them, which will influence their own self-esteem. They distinguish competence within domains; that is, they can be a good swimmer but a poor baseball player. At this point children have a more balanced and accurate view of self. A global evaluation of self-esteem begins to emerge: for example, "Overall, I am a talented person."

- In *early adolescence*, domains of self continue to expand and include competence with romantic partners and close friends and in work. Early adolescents may have multiple selves, as the adolescent can be "cheerful and rowdy with friends, depressed and sarcastic with parents" (Harter, 1999, p. 62). However, they do not give these seemingly inconsistent descriptions of the self much thought. In addition, they are very sensitive to the opinions and standards of people in different contexts.

- By *mid-adolescence*, they are making even finer discriminations that now include self with close friends, self with a group of friends, or self with mother versus self with father. A sport example is increased self-awareness of competence in basketball that suggests, for example, one is outstanding in dribbling and shooting, but one's passing and decision making are average. Adolescents at this stage remain greatly occupied by what others, particularly peers, think of them. Much as in Erikson's identity and role confusion stage, adolescents struggle with different levels of self-worth in various domains, potential conflict and confusion from perceptions of self versus others, and discrepancies between real and ideal self-concepts.

- Finally, *late adolescence* is characterized by a clearer sense of direction as personal beliefs, values, and standards are internalized. The older adolescent better understands her strengths, weaknesses, and potential and is less influenced by the opinions of others. Some conflict with parents may remain if parent expectations and future hopes conflict with those of the adolescent or young adult. Self-knowledge becomes internally rather than externally driven.

Conflict - athlete, but boys made fun of me - lead to lifelong desire to "be as good or better than any ole boy."

Couldn't find a peer group - just BFF

Emerging as popular in school - dating - Boys liked me.

Always feared academic weakness (Friends so smart) but thrived in Sports

NO

> ## Try This
>
> Age is not always a perfect predictor of behaviors or thinking. However, let's play a game about the self-representation age periods. Form groups of two, with both individuals having access to table 8.2. One person makes a self-statement like the examples in table 8.2 that represents one of the time periods. The other person has to determine which age period was represented by the statement. Try three statements each.

OMIT

Competence Motivation (HARTER)

Development of self-representation deals with emerging self-esteem and related competence in different domains. Harter, in 1978, proposed a specific competence motivation theory based on a concept of effectance proposed by White (1959). White believed that individuals are naturally motivated to have an effect on the environment and seek out opportunities to demonstrate mastery or competence. The young toddler demonstrates an intrinsic interest in mastery of his world by spending hours playing with blocks, stacking them, lining them up, or placing them into and taking them out of a container. As success is achieved, feelings of competence and control develop. Harter extended White's thinking into a model of competence motivation (figure 8.1).

The shaded oval in figure 8.1, competence motivation, represents the fundamental desire of humans to be competent. This desire leads to participation in a domain (e.g., physical activities or a specific sport); such participation is referred to more formally as mastery attempts. Optimal challenges should exist in the skills to be mastered; ones that are difficult but realistic with respect to improvement with practice are preferred over those that are too hard or too easy. Individuals very low in competence motivation may choose not to be involved, that is, make no attempts at mastery, and they will remain inactive. If a person is successful in an attempt at mastery, an increase in perceptions of competence and control should result, as well as an increase in positive affect such as pride

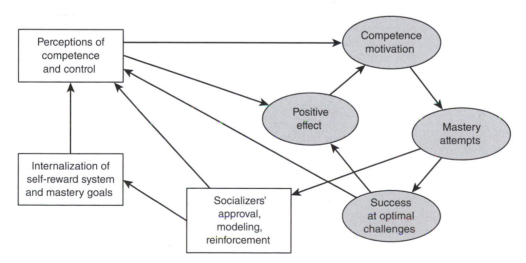

FIGURE 8.1 Harter's model of competence motivation. (White's [1959] original model is in the shaded boxes.)

Adapted, by permission, from M.R. Weiss and A.J. Amorose, 2008, Motivational orientations and sport behavior. In *Advances in sport psychology*, 3rd ed., edited by T.S. Horn (Champaign, IL: Human Kinetics), 171.

and happiness. If significant others such as parents or peers approve and reinforce such mastery attempts, perceptions of competence and control will be enhanced as well. One of the consequences of heightened self-perceptions is the seeking of further mastery attempts with effort and persistence. If I believe I am improving in an activity valued by Mom, Dad, and myself, I will tend to practice further with considerable enjoyment and persist in achieving my goals in the face of a setback.

As Weiss and Williams (2004) argue, competence motivation theory is appealing because it contains key ingredients of what is known about motivation for children in achievement situations, such as competence at optimal challenges, **perceived competence**, social acceptance and influence, and positive affect or enjoyment. These authors offer an overview of some of the critical developmental changes related to competence motivation. For example, experience in a domain and maturation will affect mastery attempts. The 10-year-old child from an athletic family may be very eager to participate in baseball if her peers are also involved, while at 15 years she may find academic and social activities more desirable as she becomes aware that her baseball abilities are quite average compared to her peers and recognizes that she wants to attend university.

Developmental change in perceived competence will be affected by the differentiation of competence domains, level and accuracy of perceived competence, and information sources used to judge competence (Weiss & Williams, 2004). The differentiation of competence domains was discussed earlier in the context of self-representation development. Toddlers have no sense of general self-esteem but can recognize skill in specific activities ("I am a good jumper"); school-aged children are aware of competence in social, academic, and athletic domains and begin to view themselves with a general self-esteem, while older adolescents recognize domains such as romantic involvement and employment.

Level and accuracy of perceived competence relate to whether perceptions are high or low (level) and the relationship between perceived and actual competence (accuracy). Young children are notoriously inaccurate in their perceptions of competence but become more realistic by the end of elementary school. Perceived competence in academic areas generally increases with age, but research is equivocal with respect to perceived physical competence; some studies show a positive increase with age and others a decline, and some demonstrate stability over childhood and adolescence. Among the reasons offered by Weiss and Williams (2004) for these contradictions are the public nature of physical performance and the unusual transition pattern through sport levels. Unlike most academic performance, physical skills can be viewed by anyone. As one practices in the gymnasium, performance is a public exercise. Moving through academic levels is standardized for all ages, for example middle school to high school. Transition through sport levels is dependent largely on skill as well as a desire to devote more time to the activity; three 11-year-old boys can be playing at three different levels soccer (recreation, select, travel). Thus their comparison groups are very different, and this may influence perceived competence.

Developmental changes in perceived competence may also be due to changes in information sources used to judge competence. Information sources include parent feedback, coach evaluation, peer comparison and evaluation, spectator feedback, performance statistics, and skill improvement (Weiss & Williams,

Research Notes: Information Sources for Perceived Competence Change With Age

One of the studies that showed an increase in accuracy of perceived physical competence and changes in social information sources over age was conducted by McKiddie and Maynard (1997). They had 80 males and 80 females from two age groups (11-12 and 14-15 years old) fill out two forms. The first, the Athletic and General Competence subscales from Harter's Self-Perception Profile for Children, measured physical competence in physical education classes. The second was the Sport Competence Information Scale (from Horn & Hasbrook, 1986), which determines sources of information young people use in arriving at a sense of physical competence. In addition, actual physical competence of the 160 participants was measured with a rating scale completed by the physical education teachers. The first purpose of the study was to determine age differences in the accuracy of judgments of physical competence. The correlation between perceived and actual competence was 0.22 and 0.88 for the children and adolescents, respectively. This indicates that the perceived physical competence of the younger children was not closely related to actual competence while the adolescents were quite accurate regarding their physical competence as rated by the their teachers. The second purpose of the study was to determine developmental changes in social sources of information about physical competence. The information scale measured sources such as peer comments, comparison to classmates, teacher evaluation, parent judgment and feedback, attraction to physical education, and enjoyment of sport. The findings showed that the 11- and 12-year-old children used feedback from important adults and their attraction to sport to arrive at a level of perceived physical competence, while the adolescents were more reliant on peer comparison and peer evaluation. Thus, developmental changes in information sources of perceived physical competence are evident.

2004). Children under 10 years of age tend to rely on parents, game outcome, and spectator feedback, while those from 10 to 15 years of age use comparison and evaluation of peers and coach feedback more than younger athletes. Older adolescents (aged 16-18 years) report greater use of self-referenced information such as skill improvement and attraction to the sport than younger adolescents. This is consistent with the development of self-representation discussed earlier as well as Harter's (1978) assertion that self-regulation (self-judgment, self-goals, self-reinforcement) develops over time when parents and coaches encourage mastery performance and independence in learning. Self-regulation was described more completely in the previous chapter.

Role of parents + coaches

Ch 7

Self-Efficacy

Bandura (1997) defined perceived **self-efficacy** as "beliefs in one's capabilities to organize and execute the courses of action required to produce given attainments" (p. 3). It is a belief that you can accomplish a specific task. Can you jump over that high jump pole at 6 feet? Self-efficacy beliefs (I can high jump 6 feet) are more specific than perceived competence beliefs (In general, I am a good at track and field compared to my peers). Bandura argues that there is little incentive to engage in an activity without the belief that you can achieve desired outcomes. One of your authors admits that a 6-foot jump is beyond his capabilities, and this lack of self-efficacy is motivation to remain on the couch rather than to jump.

Young infants have little sense of who they are and must learn that their actions have consequences. The previous chapter reviewed Piaget's position that in the first four months of life, infants begin to recognize that the hand in front of their eyes is being controlled by themselves. A few months later, this same hand is capable of successful grasps and throws. The sense of self continues to improve as children understand language and realize that others refer to them by a specific name. As children age, parents and family members, followed by peers, and then school activities have major impacts on their sense of personal capabilities. Bandura lists four sources of self-efficacy: past mastery experiences (successful actions, which increase self-efficacy), vicarious experiences (viewing others and comparing oneself to them, which may enhance or diminish self-efficacy), verbal persuasion (having others express faith in one's abilities), and physiological and affective states (personal judgment of arousal, fatigue, mood states).

Much of the research on self-efficacy and movement behavior has occurred in the sport domain. Feltz, Short, and Sullivan (2008) have provided practitioners with five techniques to increase self-efficacy in young novice athletes (table 8.3). Interested readers can consult this reference for additional ideas for more advanced athletes and teams.

TABLE 8.3 Promoting Self-Efficacy in Novice Athletes

Technique	Description
Instructional strategies and performance aids	Break down skills, modify equipment, use physical guidance and performance aids to ensure some initial success. Gradually remove aids so that learner takes some ownership for success.
Providing feedback	Give feedback based on personal skill acquisition, not in comparison to others. Provide realistic verbal persuasion about ability.
Modeling	Peer models can convey skill, attitudes, and behaviors (see chapter 13).
Imagery	Encourage imaging or rehearsing successful performance once the individual has developed the concept of the movement.
Goal setting	Establish specific, measurable, and realistic goals. This provides objective evidence of increased competence on a specific task (see chapter 13).

Adapted from D.L. Feltz, S.E. Short, and P.J. Sullivan, 2008, *Self-efficacy in sport* (Champaign, IL: Human Kinetics), 183-198.

What Do You Think?

How can you assist your students in developing self-esteem, self-efficacy, and perceived competence? How will each of these qualities influence individual performance?

Self-Determined Motivation

Motivation to learn and participate in physical activity is obviously important. It influences whether or not people even begin an activity and how long they persist. Self-motivation is an important forethought dimension in self-regulation. As noted in the discussion of competence motivation, preschoolers and young children engage in play seemingly for no other reason than the sheer joy of participating. The 2-year-old may play with pots and pans for hours, stacking, banging, and rearranging. Piaget's theory would argue that the children are learning important cause-and-effect relationships, linking language to actions, and creating and refining action schemes of exploring objects with the hands or perceptual schemes of circles and rectangles. Harter (1978) suggested that they are motivated to have an effect on their environment and develop perceptions of competence. The notion of competence was also central to the thinking of Deci and colleagues (Deci & Flaste, 1995; Deci & Ryan, 1985; Ryan & Deci, 2000), who were fascinated with such behavior of young children and proposed self-determination theory as an explanation. The theory has been expanded as a hierarchical model of intrinsic and extrinsic motivation by Vallerand (1997, 2007).

Self-determination theory includes three types of motivation:

- **Intrinsically motivated behaviors** are those that provide pleasure and satisfaction from participating in the absence of material rewards or constraints. The long-distance runner who enjoys the peace and tranquility of the outdoors is an example of someone who is intrinsically motivated.

- **Extrinsically motivated behaviors** are those that provide a means to an end and are not engaged in for their own sake. Extrinsic motivation explains a host of behaviors, from completing additional fitness workouts as a way to make a team, remaining on the job after 5:00 to impress a boss, or engaging in rehabilitation exercises to please a partner.

- **Amotivation** is present when an individual does not see any relationship between outcomes and actions. In other words, people feel that whatever they do, nothing positive will result, so why should they bother? Amotivated behaviors are neither intrinsically nor extrinsically motivated: They are not motivated at all and generally lack intention to act. We certainly do not want children or adolescents to be amotivated toward physical activity.

Self-determination theory postulates that humans have basic needs to feel **competent**, **autonomous**, and **related**; the latter refers to being connected with other people. When these needs are met, psychological health is promoted; but when they are not met, psychological health is undermined (Vallerand, 2007). People engage in activities to satisfy needs. For example, children who spend hours in free play do it of their own accord (autonomy); they gradually become more skilled at tasks (competent) and particularly enjoy the time if parents join in (relatedness). To the extent that play provides satisfaction of the three needs, it is referred to as intrinsically motivated behavior. Maintaining a learning environment that emphasizes play and fun will likely keep children motivated to participate and to learn new skills. On the other hand, think of a child who begins snow skiing because he is told he must, whose initial attempts result in frequent falls and embarrassment, and who sees no one in the future with whom to ski. Without some intervention in the form of excellent instruction and support, this child is destined to become a drop-out because his needs are not being met, and a state of amotivation may be a consequence.

When children and adolescents sample several activities and sports, a strong emphasis on intrinsic motivation is desirable. Coaches and teachers should promote choice of activity and achievable goal setting, emphasize personal improvement, and provide positive feedback. These ideas are explored further in chapters 13, 14, and 15. Of course, participation can be influenced by both intrinsic and extrinsic reasons. For example, someone can feel competent and also really want that team jacket. If extrinsic reasons dominate as children become older, the chances of their dropping out of sport increase. Côté, Baker, and Abernethy (2003) reported that highly skilled sport experts recall early practice activities connected with fun and experimenting with new ways of solving movement problems; as practitioners and parents we should be very careful not to turn fun practice into dreadful work for children.

Weiss and Williams (2004) proposed a number of reasons children and adolescents participate in sport. These include physical competence (e.g., learn skills, achieve goals), social acceptance (e.g., be with friends, social status), and enjoyment (e.g., have fun, excitement). One can see competence and relatedness dimensions of self-determination in those reasons for participation. Teachers, coaches, and parents should always remember *fun* because it is mentioned in almost all research as a reason for children's participation in sport. Saying that *fun* is a reason is another way of saying that intrinsically motivated behaviors provide enjoyment and pleasure. While more research is required, it appears that reasons to participate may be different at various ages (Haywood & Getchell, 2009). For example, late teens and young adults may place more emphasis on social status and fitness reasons to participate in sport than younger children or older adults. Fitness is a major reason for middle-aged adults to participate in sport but not for children and older adults.

 What Do You Think?

1. Name specific ways in which you can facilitate self-determination among your students or clients.

2. How can self-determination theory assist in understanding clients who do not want to engage in rehabilitation exercises?

3. Provide examples of times you were intrinsically motivated, extrinsically motivated, and amotivated to engage in physical activity. How did your approach differ in each of these situations?

Social–Affective Constraints

A newborn is not likely to have a sense of self separate from the environment. But Piaget demonstrated that infants in the first two months begin to repeat pleasurable acts centered on their own bodies and to understand that they are responsible for some of the events that fascinate them (Shaffer, 1999). Their social world is primarily limited to immediate family members, and their crying as early as 7 to 9 months when held by strangers suggests that they distinguish among friendly folk and "unknowns." They can recognize themselves in a mirror by 18 months, and by 2 or 3 years, may issue self-concept statements like "I am a big boy, not a baby" (Shaffer, 1999). The impact of their social world is powerfully demonstrated by the emergence of language early in the second year of life. Yet they may remain egocentric thinkers until the end of the preoperational stage (ages 2 to 7 years), unable to imagine that their world view is different from others' and thus have difficulty realizing that others in their world have different needs and desires. As outlined in the sections on self-representation and competence motivation, children are affected by an increasing number of social agents over time that change in their relative impact; they develop a self-esteem that can be strongly affected by physical competence; and they develop a repertoire of emotional reactions. We turn next to these functional constraints.

Socialization of Sport and Physical Activity

Haywood and Getchell (2009) list three elements in the socialization of people into sport and physical activity: **socializing agents** such as family, peers, coaches, and teachers; **social situations** such as play environments and toys; and **personal attributes** such as perceived sport ability. The child's immediate social network of parents and siblings and the availability of social environments such as playgrounds will influence physical activity participation in preschoolers (Haywood, & Getchell, 2009) and children (Fredricks & Eccles, 2004). Parents who value swimming are likely to take their child to the pool, enroll them in swim lessons, and play in the water as a family. Likewise, a backyard or basement with balls, swings, and tricycles provides opportunities for movement competence to grow. The young child may watch parents and older siblings participate in physical activities, listen to them talk about such activities, or both. Ultimately, this will influence the child's initial selection of activities and contribute to what they come to value.

Côté and colleagues (2003) have shown that expert athletes recall their parents as supportive in allowing them freedom to practice, formally or not. The experts recalled participating as children in several sports and physical activities while parents were often coaches, chauffeurs, and sometimes coparticipants. As dedication to a particular sport began, the parents were seldom coaches but remained supportive by helping the athlete structure practice routines, joining a fitness club, or setting up a weight room at home. As the experts made a commitment to one sport, the parents' direct role diminished; they may have continued to assist in practice, but most often their role became relegated to financial support.

As a child begins school, peers are added to the list of socializing agents and will continue to influence physical activity participation into the adult years (Weiss & Stuntz, 2004). Like parents, peers can encourage or discourage participation in specific activities. Coaches and teachers, although not as influential as parents, siblings, and peers, also have a significant socializing influence in childhood. The actions of adults other than parents can have a detrimental impact on participation if they place too much emphasis on winning, embarrass and criticize children, or create tasks and challenges that are too difficult. Fredricks and Eccles (2004) wisely suggest that parents have the most positive impact on sport participation of their children if they maintain a moderate level of involvement and are neither disinterested nor overinvolved. In adolescence, the role of parents as a socializing agent decreases as the impact of peers and coaches increases (Fredricks & Eccles, 2004). Likewise, peers and coaches become a source of information about physical competency after age 10, while younger children rely more on parents (Weiss & Williams, 2004).

Great strides have been made in recent decades in encouraging young girls to participate in sport. Many parents equally support participation of both sexes. Yet research still suggests that parents continue to endorse beliefs that sports are more suited to boys than girls and to encourage gender-stereotypic sports, for example, gymnastics and figure skating for girls rather than ice hockey or rugby (Fredricks & Eccles, 2004). Practitioners should recognize that these beliefs still exist and attempt to counteract them by providing equal opportunity and encouragement to girls and boys.

Try This

Parents and teachers are significant social forces that affect physical activity participation levels of children and adolescents. Form groups of three, with each person trying to remember past actions of parents, teachers, coaches, or peers that were positive or negative with regard to influencing physical activity. These may be actions that you or your friends were exposed to.

What Do You Think?

1. As teacher or coach, what role will you play in the socialization process of your students or athletes?
2. What are some ways in which socializing agents, social situations, and perceived attributes can positively influence the socialization process?

Emotional Development and Physical Activity

Participating in physical activities and sport competition is often a significant emotional experience—pride, anger, satisfaction, and happiness can be experienced and expressed (Crocker, Hoar, McDonough, Kowalski, & Niefer, 2004). The model of competence motivation suggests that positive affect is an outcome of success at challenging activities and is related to competence motivation. Young athletes must also learn to control and express emotions that are socially appropriate and regulate them for optimal performance (Crocker et al., 2004). In the first six months of life, if not earlier, children demonstrate primary emotions such as interest, distress, anger, fear, joy, sadness, and surprise (Shaffer, 1999). Later, in the second year, they may display guilt, pride, envy, and embarrassment. Yet despite the honesty of a young infant's emotions, each society has "**emotional display rules**" (Shaffer, 1999, p. 394) that determine the circumstances under which emotions should or should not be expressed.

Infants and toddlers begin to learn how to regulate their emotions. A strategy adopted from 2 to 6 years is closing the eyes to control an unpleasant emotional arousal, as when one is looking at a scary shark. Another important aspect of emotional development is recognizing the emotions of others, which facilitates social interaction. Family conversations about emotions can help children deal with their feelings and to become aware of others. Children aged 3 and over begin to show awareness, and by 5 years can offer reasons why a playmate is happy or sad. It may not be until age 6 or later that children know another can experience more than one emotion at a given time.

Attributions

Attribution theory (Weiner, 1985) has implications for understanding emotion and motivation in achievement situations (Crocker et al., 2004). According to Weiner, emotion is a function of the outcome in achievement attempts (i.e., success or failure) as well as of people's attributions for outcomes. Positive emotions such as happiness are influenced by success, but also by attributions for the success. Attributions are explanations of why things turned out as they did. Common attributions are personal ability, effort, task difficulty, and luck, or more specifically in sport, teamwork, injury, and referee decisions.

Weiner (1985) suggested that causal attributions have three dimensions: locus of control, stability, and control. Locus of control can be internal or external, the former referring to causes related to one's own behavior and the latter to causes that are beyond one's personal control such as a "lucky bounce" or a teammate's play. The stability dimension can be stable or unstable. If the attributions or factors influencing outcomes are stable from situation to situation, such as ability, they are considered stable. Unstable factors would include luck and effort. Effort is considered unstable because one can try very hard and expend considerable energy one day but become much less involved on another day. The control factor refers to whether people perceive that they control the factors influencing outcomes (If I work harder and obtain a personal trainer, I can make the team) or whether results are uncontrollable (Nothing I can do will influence my success). People who believe there is no relationship between effort and outcome, that is, that success or failure is unrelated to whatever they do, have developed *learned helplessness*, according to Seligman (1975). The person has minimal motivation to engage in the activity, but if forced to do so experiences anxiety and expected frustration. Learned helplessness may be domain specific; one of your authors concedes that car problems are totally beyond his control and will not even open the hood if his car breaks down. Teachers and coaches can influence positive, internal, and controllable attributions by enhancing successful experiences, even small success, and helping the learner take credit for the outcome. "You are working very hard, Charles, and you are getting faster on the track, you have improved by 5 seconds." Horn (1987) also recommends emphasizing improvement with effort and practice, goal setting, and accurate feedback.

In general, positive emotions such as joy and pride will occur with success in a valued activity that is attributed to personal factors (Crocker et al., 2004). Consistent with the competence motivation model of Harter, the positive affect resulting from achievement success will enhance competence motivation. Differentiating among ability, effort, luck, and task difficulty and hence making accurate attributions is developmental. Children who are 5 years old see no difference between effort and ability. By 7 years of age, children may be capable of causal explanation in some situations (Caprara, Pastorelli, & Weiner, 1997). Even at 11 years, they are limited in knowledge, ability to process information, and reasoning (Crocker et al., 2004; and see Piaget and discussion of information processing in chapter 7). While clear developmental trends have not been identified (Crocker et al., 2004; Haywood & Getchell, 2009), attributions in achievement situation emerge more clearly and are more accurate during the high school years.

Arousal and Anxiety

One of the most important tasks of an athlete, or anyone learning a movement skill, is to control the emotions evident in competition or during practice. Optimal performance is unlikely for someone who is anxious, nervous, afraid of making a mistake, or worried about not being successful. Heightened arousal (getting up for the game) is usually beneficial to some extent. **Arousal** is different from **anxiety**. Anxiety refers to an emotional response to perceived threat and can involve cognitive concerns or physiological reactions (Crocker et al., 2004). There is widespread agreement that high anxiety in youth sport has a number of negative consequences, including avoidance of sport, burnout, and reduced enjoyment; and most agree that it negatively influences performance (Crocker et al., 2004). On the other hand, arousal is a general state of activation or excitability (Magill, 2007; Schmidt & Wrisberg, 2008).

The difference between arousal and anxiety was recognized over 100 years ago by Yerkes and Dodson (1908), who studied the relationship between performance and electric shock intensity in mice. Mild forms of shock produced an increase in performance, but at some point, increasing the intensity of the shock resulted in a decrease in performance. Optimal performance was assumed to be at a moderate level of arousal. This idea, which became known as the **inverted-U principle of arousal**, has been studied extensively in motor learning (Schmidt & Lee, 2005). Coaches use "pep talks" to arouse players with the expectation that these will aid performance. However, if a player is too aroused or anxious, the likelihood is that performance will be adversely affected, according to the inverted-U principle. The inverted-U principle has been criticized (Schmidt & Lee) for its simplicity, and it has been proposed that some athletes require a very high level of arousal for best performance while others perform optimally with more modest arousal. Thus, individual differences are expected, and optimal arousal may be influenced by the nature of the task and environmental conditions. To the beginning learner of motor skills, modest arousal with a desire to perform (motivation) would seem to be beneficial.

Self-Regulation

Guidance and feedback from therapists, teachers, and coaches is important for those in rehabilitation, recreational participants, and expert performers. However, learning and performance of motor skills also occur through self-regulation, that is, practice and play without formal instruction. This begins at a young age, as infants and preschoolers learn that their actions can affect the environment and that they can learn new skills by watching others. As a student, have you ever decided to read or study for 60 minutes before you take a break and call a friend? If so, you have engaged in two dimensions of self-regulation, goal setting (60 minutes) and self-reinforcement (call to a friend). As a fitness enthusiast, have you recorded your times on 10-kilometer runs over a season, or listed the dates and duration of your workouts? These are examples of self-monitoring.

Zimmerman (2000) suggests that self-regulation is an inherently human endeavor since it permits adaptation to our environment. While similar to metacognition, self-regulation also includes knowledge of one's motivation (self-motivation beliefs) and emotional reactions. More formally, self-regulation "refers to the self-generated thoughts, feelings, and actions that are planned and cyclically adapted to the attainment of personal goals" (Zimmerman, 2000, p. 14). One must set goals for self-regulation to function. Then thoughts, feelings, and behaviors are planned to attain the goals but are monitored en route to the goal and changed as necessary if one gets off course. Self-regulation is thus an attractive concept in motor learning and development. For example, a runner might set a specific time for a long race but recognize during the race that she feels great and the humidity is low, and thus decide to increase her goal and shoot for a personal best. Zimmerman proposes a three-phase cyclical model of self-regulation consisting of forethought, performance or volitional control, and self-reflection (figure 8.2). In a movement context, the participant plans an action (forethought), executes it (volitional control), and reflects on its success (self-reflection). The self-reflection processes provide information for the forethought phase of the next trial, for a discrete motor skill like batting a ball, or later in the activity for a continuous motor skill like swimming. Table 8.4 lists the dimensions of self-regulation within the three cyclical phases.

Forethought consists of task analysis and self-motivation beliefs. **Task analysis** includes setting of personal goals for achievement and

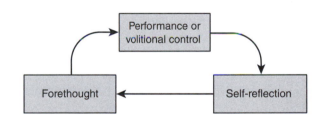

FIGURE 8.2
Cyclical phases of self-regulation.

Reprinted, by permission, from D.H. Schunk and B.J. Zimmerman, 1998, *Self-regulated learning: From teaching to self-reflective practice* (New York: Guilford Press), 3.

TABLE 8.4 Self-Regulatory Phases

Forethought	Performance or volitional control	Self-reflection
Task analysis	Self-control	Self-judgment
• Goal setting	• Self-instruction	• Self-evaluation
• Strategic planning	• Imagery	• Causal attribution
Self-motivational beliefs	• Attention focusing	Self-reaction
• Self-efficacy	• Task strategies	• Self-satisfaction
• Outcome expectation	Self-observation	• Adaptive-defensive
• Intrinsic interest or value	• Self-recording	
• Goal orientation	• Self-experimentation	

Reprinted from *Handbook of Self-Regulation*, edited by M. Boekaerts, P.R. Pintrich, and M. Zeidner, chapter 2, Attaining Self-Regulation: A Social Cognitive Perspective, by B.J. Zimmerman, pp. 13-39, Copyright 2000, with permission from Elsevier.

general strategies for how to achieve those goals. The **self-motivation beliefs** refer to the perceived value of the activity for the individual, the degree of intrinsic interest in the activity, the degree of self-efficacy or belief that one is capable of achieving the goal, and outcome expectation or awareness of what benefits will occur if the goal is attained. **Performance control** and **volitional control** are the self-regulation strategies that can be applied during the learning trials or performance. **Self-control** includes self-instruction such as reminding oneself while swimming a length that the left arm must come farther out of the water, or focusing on your own motivations when you realize you might be attending to the noise of the crowd cheering for your opponents. Imagery of performance, or imagining oneself performing an action, is a common technique for divers and gymnasts just prior to performance, while task strategies are those that can be altered during the game or event. **Self-observation** guides one's progress toward a goal, particularly self-recording of things such as percentage of successful free throws during a basketball season, types of food consumed during training, or independent steps accomplished in rehabilitation. Self-experimentation is a self-discovery type of activity in which a new approach to performance or learning is attempted and given sufficient time to provide a fair evaluation. Finally, self-regulated learners engage in **self-reflection** at some point: following a trial, a set of trials, a game, or a season. Self-evaluation involves assessing the degree to which one's goals were achieved. Causal attributions are explanations for why goals were met or not. What did you think led most to goal success? Did you exert sufficient effort? Did you try to accomplish the task without enough coaching? Finally, a self-reflective person is aware of her degree of overall self-satisfaction. Even if the goal was not attained, were you satisfied with your performance, with what you learned, and with the effort expended?

Is self-regulation important for learning and performance? Attentive readers may see some overlap between the components of self-regulation just described and the distinguishing features of expertise in table 7.3. Experts are more likely to engage in self-regulation than novices (Cleary & Zimmerman, 2001; Kitsantas & Zimmerman, 1998). Singer (2002) has suggested that self-regulation is just as important as skill in performance. Self-regulation in motor learning studies has produced positive effects when participants chose when to receive knowledge of results (Chiviacowsky & Wulf, 2005; Janelle, Barba, Frehlich, Tennant, & Cauraugh, 1997), physical guidance (Wulf & Toole, 1999), and blocked versus random practice (Keetch & Lee, 2007). Ten-year-old children were provided the opportunity to determine when they would receive knowledge of results on a nondominant hand throwing task (Chiviacowsky, Wulf, de Medeiros, Kaefer, & Tani, 2008). They threw beanbags to a concentric-circle target. Benefits generally favored self-selected knowledge of results compared to an equal number of feedback trials that participants did not specifically request. The children tended to request feedback after good trials, and the authors suggested that feedback after poor trials may be ineffective and that self-selected feedback appears to have a motivational influence.

There is also evidence that novices and those with learning difficulties show few signs of self-directed learning (Lloyd, Reid, & Bouffard, 2006; Zimmerman, 2000), so self-regulation is assumed to be very important in the learning process. It is also encouraging that research demonstrates that self-regulation can be improved through instruction (Kitsantas & Zimmerman, 1998; Zimmerman & Kitsantas, 1997).

How does self-regulation develop? There is not much research available on this question, but a developmental model from Zimmerman (2000) has proved helpful. He proposes a social–cognitive model (table 8.5) in which new skills are initially acquired via social means and then progress through steps that represent increasing metacognitive, motivational, and behavioral regulation.

TABLE 8.5   Development of Self-Regulation

Developmental level	Distinguishing features
Observation	Observing and listening to proficient models for major features of the skill
Emulation	Mimicking the model's style and skill with social assistance
Self-control	Mastery of the skill of a model in structured settings
Self-regulation	Adaptive use of the skill across changing environments and interpersonal states

Adapted from B.J. Zimmerman, 2000, Attaining self-regulation: A social cognitive perspective. In *Handbook of self-regulation,* edited by M. Boekaerts, P.R. Pintrich, and M. Zeidner (San Diego: Academic Press), 13-39.

Research Notes: Self-Regulation and Developmental Coordination Disorder

Lloyd and colleagues (2006) explored self-regulation of children with and without developmental coordination disorder (DCD). Developmental coordination disorder is a formal diagnostic term for those who have considerable difficulty performing movement skills at age-expected levels but not due to factors such as cerebral palsy or intellectual disability. Some authors have described these persons as awkward or clumsy. Developmental coordination disorder is associated with low self-concept and withdrawal from physical activity. The authors postulated that DCD might be related to poor self-regulation. Therefore, they compared a group of 10 boys without DCD to 10 boys with DCD. The mean age of the boys was 11.5 years. The investigators used two tasks: a sport-specific problem-solving task of shooting indoors at a hockey net with a rubber puck and an educational problem-solving task of peg solitaire in which to goal was to remove all wooden pegs from the holes on the board by jumping over a peg and then picking it up. Participants were taught to use a think-aloud verbal report in which they articulated their thought processes during the activity. Their thoughts were transcribed and then categorized into self-regulation categories such as goals, knowledge, monitoring, emotion, and evaluation. Among the salient results was the finding that the boys with DCD expressed less quality of knowledge about the shooting task, fewer error correction plans, more total emotion and negative emotion, and 25% fewer action plans. On the peg solitaire task, the only difference was less planning ahead by the boys with DCD. The authors concluded that the results were consistent with a self-regulation deficit in children with DCD and that with the exception of planning, the difficulties did not appear on nonmotor tasks.

Try This

In groups of two or three, review table 8.4 and identify strategies in each of the three phases of self-regulation that might improve studying behaviors. The identified strategies might be ones you currently use or might potentially use.

Observation, the first level in the development of self-regulation, includes witnessing skills of peers or older children or hearing about them from teachers. These are largely vicarious experiences that provide an image of the skills and awareness of rewards received by models. Thus, the child may be motivated to engage in the activity, say, jumping down from a height, skiing, or roller skating, and will maintain some persistence during initial learning trials. Observational learning is described more fully in chapter 13. **Emulation**, the second level, refers to adopting a model's style of skill rather than mimicking exact response components. Thus, the learner performs a skill but in his own unique manner and using self-regulatory skills. The motivated 4-year-old will ice skate at the rink with a fairly upright posture and minimal glide on the skates. This style maintains stability, but with practice, the body lean and glide will increase. As we will see in chapter 13, research has demonstrated that children who fear water can benefit from exposure to models by emulating the coping strategies of the model (Weiss, McCullagh, Smith, & Berlant, 1998). According to Zimmerman (2000), this produces sensorimotor feedback and internal standards of correct performance that are necessary for the next two steps. This process is similar to the creation of a generalized motor program, which has a recall dimension for initiating movements but also a recognition dimension for evaluating the movement based on expected sensory consequences.

Self-control refers to the use of one's own strategy as a planned and self-monitored process. Individuals practice by themselves without a model physically present. Their personal representation or image of the skill is their guide, and their motivation is largely self-rewards and personal reactions to attaining standards. Hence they may go to the gym and shoot at the basketball net while focusing on how they are performing, such as on placement of feet, arms, and hands or on how many baskets they get. The highest form is **self-regulation**, through which skills can be adapted to changing environmental demands (such as a hostile crowd, or rain during a track meet) and interpersonal states. At this level, individuals need not focus on how they are performing but on their performance outcomes, such as how many of their shots are successful. With experience at this level, self-efficacy and self-motivation toward mastery should increase.

Research has demonstrated with motor and other skills that students can be taught more effective self-regulation and that they do progress through the four levels of self-regulation (Zimmerman & Kitsantas, 1997, 1999; Kitsantas & Zimmerman, 1998). The use of self-regulation processes, much like development of expertise and knowledge, is primarily task dependent. The following recommendations may enhance self-regulation by children and adolescents (in part from Petlichkoff, 2004):

- Promote self-observation, which includes self-monitoring progress toward a goal and monitoring behavioral outcomes and processes like cognitive strategies generated internally and available from models.
- Set process goals before outcome goals. This means promoting a focus on skill improvement rather than on a specific outcome like 10 points in a game.
- When skills become automatic, shift to outcome goals that are within reach of the learner.

- To assist in self-judgment processes, children and novices should be exposed to peer coping models rather than expert models (see chapter 13) and should be encouraged to focus on personal improvement (self-comparison) rather than comparison to peers. With use of these procedures they are likely to view themselves favorably.
- Teachers, coaches, and parents should model self-regulatory strategies such as self-instruction and goal setting.
- Demonstrate and promote problem solving for tasks that have more than one movement solution, such as guarding an opponent one-on-one or executing an offensive two-on-one situation.
- Encourage self-reinforcement.
- Discuss attributions of success and failure. What influenced the outcome? What can be done immediately to counteract a failure? What factors should be considered in the longer term?

 What Do You Think?

1. Imagine you are teaching an elementary school physical education class. Provide specific examples of how you could help your students develop self-regulation. Now imagine you are teaching a high school physical education class. How would you facilitate self-regulation among these students? Do your ideas differ for these two groups? Explain. If you are an occupational or physical therapist, how might you include self-regulation into your intervention?

2. Define the term self-regulation in your own words. Provide at least three examples of times when you used self-regulation to be successful in sport or physical activity.

Summary

This chapter outlined several functional individual constraints that people bring with them to a motor learning and performance situation. The constraints included psychosocial and affective constraints as well as those having to do with self-regulation. The psychosocial model of Erikson (1963) outlined the development of autonomy, initiation, and identity while simultaneously coming to terms with social expectations and regulations. Identity, or self-representation, was also the focus of Harter's description of self-esteem. There are many individual differences in the timing and ultimate level of achievement of Erikson's and Harter's phases, and thus children and adolescents demonstrate considerable heterogeneity with regard to perceptions of self. Also, based on experiences with a host of social agents and environmental factors, self-efficacy, competence motivation, and intrinsic motivation will vary in children and adolescence. In a physical activity context, some learners show behaviors consistent with seeking competence motivation experiences and intrinsic motivation, while others will have little interest in learning or participating in physical activity because their previous experiences and social influences have been negative.

Jordan was the 270-pound (122-kilogram) talented football player who did not want to play college football. Can you see some reasons for his decision now?

He does not have any role confusion; he aspires to be a lawyer. This aspiration was influenced initially by parents but very much reinforced by teachers and counselors in high school due to his outstanding scholastic achievement. Jordan understands that college football will include deliberate practice and a huge time commitment, and he is self-regulated sufficiently to question his intrinsic motivation toward football. He has the structural constraints to play, but not the functional ones.

Supplemental Activities

1. Have a chat with a youngster. Spend some time talking to an elementary school-aged child—a younger sibling, a cousin, or the child across the street. Ask the child to describe him- or herself (see table 8.2 for ideas). See which age period of self-representation most closely matches your interviewee's comments. Even better, then talk with an older person, perhaps an adolescent, to confirm development in self-representation.

2. Self-determination is a major motivational theory as described in this chapter. But it has other meanings. Search the Internet and look for pre-20th-century philosophical interpretations of self-determination; then find political meanings of self-determination important in the early 20th century.

III

Motor Development
Adulthood and Aging

To many people, the term *aging* is synonymous with time, but even though everyone does age, we do not age the same. Environmental factors and behavioral lifestyle factors play a large role in an individual's health and well-being, and these effects compound every year. These factors contribute to the large variability across adults, with some performing at elite levels into late adulthood and others quickly declining in middle adulthood. Because people age so differently, assumptions about an individual's physiological function based solely on a simple measure of age with respect to time, *chronological age*, are not very accurate. For example, active older adults have been found to outperform sedentary young adults on many fitness tests. Due to this high variability in motor behavior across adulthood, this part of the book focuses on *primary aging*, age-related changes that are not due to disease or poor behavioral practices such as obesity, smoking, and sedentary lifestyles.

This section begins by examining movement and physical activity in adults ranging from young to older adulthood, including factors that affect participation in physical activity in adults. The exercise–aging cycle is presented as a model for illustrating the detrimental effects of a sedentary lifestyle. We then turn to peak athletic performance using Olympic performances as the age measure. We compare Olympic performances with masters athletes' records to consider how peak performance declines with advancing age. Examining elite athletes provides a clearer picture of age-related peak performance changes because elite athletes' performance changes are less likely to be affected by chronic disease or long periods of physical inactivity and disuse. Next is a summary of some changing movement patterns, including locomotor patterns, fundamental movement patterns, and movements during functional activities.

We then turn to age-related changes in the body systems, including the skeletal, muscular, cardiovascular, nervous, endocrine, and sensory systems. Again, the focus is primarily upon normal age-related changes; however, we include some discussion of secondary aging. We then extend the examination of functional constraints from chapters 7 and 8 to adulthood, including psychosocial constraints, sociocultural constraints, and changing cognitive function across adulthood. It is important to distinguish psychological and sociocultural factors in adulthood from childhood and adolescence, as they can differ quite considerably. Adults show wider variability than do children and adolescents, and this variability increases with age. Because of the combination of experiences and age-related structural and functional changes, adults become increasingly unique with age.

Movement
in Adulthood

CHAPTER OBJECTIVES

After reading this chapter, you should be able to

> define aging, contrasting biological and chronological aging;
> explain the exercise–aging cycle;
> compare peak athletic performance for various sports and activities;
> discuss how peak performance changes from young to older adulthood; and
> describe how movement patterns change from young to older adulthood in locomotor movements, fundamental movement patterns, and functional activities.

The Wake-Up Call

Sophia is not your typical great-grandmother. She is more active than most young and middle-aged adults, regularly competing in triathlons across the country. On a typical day, Sophia wakes up at 5 a.m. and swims 1 mile in the lake across the street from her home. At 11 a.m. she takes Cooper, her very energetic Vizsla, for a 2-mile walk and then finishes her day with either a bike ride or a run. Although today Sophia is a picture of health, she wasn't always so fit and active. At the age of 42 years, Sophia was diagnosed with type 2 diabetes. Sophia had never exercised or been a member of any athletic or recreational team, but she decided she needed to make a drastic change in her life in order to control her diabetes. Sophia started slowly, only jogging a block down the street and walking home. She gradually increased her distance and watched her weight drop off and her health

dramatically improve. By the age of 44 years, Sophia was in the best shape of her life and had never felt better. At 48, she was running anywhere from 5 to 15 miles a day, six or seven days per week.

It was around then that Sophia developed tendinitis in the posterior tibial tendon on her foot, likely caused by a combination of overpronation of the foot and the increased mileage. Sophia took some time off of running and placed sport orthotics in her shoes. This helped her for a while, but whenever she tried to increase her running to get back to the same level as before, an overuse injury resulted. Rather than putting up her running shoes, Sophia decided to cross train, switching from one activity to another when a new pain arose. Cross training led Sophia to her love of triathlons by enabling her to avoid injuries while maintaining a very active lifestyle. Now at the age of 81, Sophia runs more slowly than she did 30 years ago, but she is still able to run with the same movement characteristics as a young female track athlete and has gone 15 years injury free.

Older adults are becoming increasingly physically active, participating in physical recreational activities, fitness activities, and even competitive sports. Today, more and more older people are joining gyms, fitness groups, or even running in races. This increased attraction toward physical activity is seen in both genders. Every year, more seniors compete in races, triathalons, golf, and tennis. Some older adults are going extreme, competing in marathons and even Ironman triathalons. The Ironman is an ultimate testament to physical human capabilities, with a 2.4-mile swim (3.9 kilometers), a 112-mile bike ride (180 kilometers), and a 26.2-mile run (42 kilometers). In just the past decade, the number of Ironman competitors at Kona over the age of 70 years increased threefold, from only 11 in 1997 to 37 in 2007. Now, more than ever, adults are aware of the importance of physical activity and the role that fitness plays in their lives. With today's medical advances, changing technology, and increased press on the benefits of good nutrition and physical activity, we can only expect this trend to continue.

Adults advance through many stages throughout life, which affect not only the activities they are involved in but also *how* they move. Young adults are at their physical peak, yet some avoid an active lifestyle for various reasons. Older adults, on the other hand, can avoid many age-related declines by maintaining a healthy and active lifestyle. This chapter discusses movement from young adulthood through older adulthood. Peak athletic performance is discussed for both the younger and older adults, as well as changing movement patterns including locomotor skills, fundamental motor skills, and functional activities.

Aging

In the minds of many, the term aging refers to declining physical function. Aging is generally thought of as something that occurs during later life, in older adulthood. However, in its simplest terms, aging is the number of time units over which an organism has existed following birth (Spirduso, Francis, &

MacRae, 2005). When aging is defined this way, it becomes synonymous with time. The biological changes that are associated with infancy and childhood are referred to as developmental, while changes that occur due to declining functional systems are referred to as aging (Spirduso et al., 2005). Since aging does not have a definitive onset, it is helpful to define **aging** as a process or group of processes occurring in living organisms that with the passage of time lead to a loss of adaptability and functional impairment, and eventually death (Spirduso et al., 2005).

Although everyone ages, we do not all age in the same way. We age differently and at different rates. Functional impairments cannot be predicted because there are so many factors that affect how we age, such as environmental, lifestyle and cultural factors, and heredity. Individual differences are even greater for older adults than they are for young adults or children, allowing for wide variability across individuals. Older adults range from the frail elderly to masters athletes competing in marathons. At the age of 81 years, Fauja Singh became serious about his running, and he began running marathons at the age of 89 years. Now at the age of 94 years, he has run seven marathons and has been picked up by the Adidas "Impossible Is Nothing" campaign, along with David Beckham (soccer player who played for the England National team and currently plays for Major League Soccer's Los Angeles Galaxy) and Jonny Wilkinson (English rugby player known as one of the world's best).

In general, when we refer to a person's age, we are referring to **chronological age**. This is simply the number of years the person has been alive since birth. This age does not take into account any biological or health factors, such as the individual's overall well-being, fitness levels, and health. **Biological aging** refers to the physiological adaptations that are occurring within the body due to the passage of time. An individual's biological age can be markedly different from his chronological age. For example, a very active, healthy individual may have a very low biological age in comparison to his chronological age. The situation could be the opposite in an overweight sedentary individual who smokes and drinks. Currently there is disagreement on how to most accurately measure biological age (Ries, 1994).

Assessing biological age is rather complicated, as the many biological systems each age at different rates. For example, Comfort's biological age index (1979) includes anthropometric measures (body mass, graying of hair, and so on), physiological scores (vital capacity, tidal volume, blood volume, heart size, grip strength, etc.), bone and connective tissue integrity (skin elasticity, nail calcium, osteoporotic index), sensory tests (audiometry, visual acuity), biochemical data (serum cholesterol, copper, albumin, elastase, RNAase), cellular characteristics, intelligence tests, and psychomotor tests (reaction time and light extinction tests). Although a thorough biological aging examination is complex, one should take biological age, rather than chronological age, into consideration when assessing an individual's fitness, whether the purpose relates to fitness for a job, exercise program, or skill learning (Shephard, 1998). Active older adults have been found to outperform sedentary young adults on many fitness tests. An extreme example is the incredible fitness level of Jack LaLanne, the well-known father of fitness who died in 2011 at the age of 96 years. At age 90 years, Jack still performed better than an average 30-year-old on physical fitness tests.

Physical Activity

Refer to table 1.2 on age classifications and note that young adulthood generally includes the period from the early third decade to the beginning of the fifth decade (ages 21-40 years). Middle adulthood is classified as the fifth through sixth decades (approximately 41-60 years). It is during young adulthood and halfway through adulthood that both biological function and physical performance are at their peak (Shephard, 1998). During the later part of adulthood (ages 61-99 years), as energy is generally devoted to the demands of a family and a career, most individuals significantly reduce their participation in physical activity and accumulate an average of about 11 to 22 pounds (5 to 10 kilograms) of body fat.

During middle-aged adulthood (ages 41-60 years), physical activity tends to decline further in the majority of individuals as women go through menopause and men experience a reduction in sex hormones (Shephard, 1998). Physically active adults in the United States over the age of 55 years most commonly participate in walking, gardening, cycling, golf, and aerobics (DiPietro, Williamson, Caspersen, & Eaker, 1993). Not until adults reach retirement age (young-old adults, ages 61-74 years) is there is an increase in physical activity, with most walking, swimming, cycling, and dancing (Stephens & Craig, 1990).

Physical activity levels decline again during old adulthood (ages 75-99 years) and beyond as many adults develop physical disabilities. Approximately 35% of males and 45% of females have two or more chronic diseases between the ages of 60 and 69 years. By the age of 80 years, approximately 53% of males and 70% of females have two or more chronic diseases (Guralnik & Simonsick, 1993). Figure 9.1 illustrates the physical activity levels, from inactive to regular

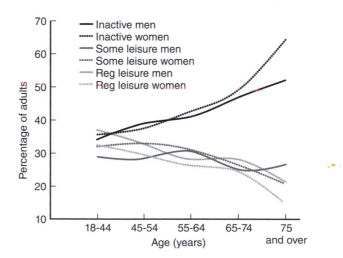

FIGURE 9.1 Percentage of adults who are inactive or who perform some leisure-time activity or regular leisure-time activity across age and gender. Adults who reported no sessions of light to moderate or vigorous leisure-time activity with a minimum duration of 10 minutes were classified as inactive. Adults who reported at least one session of light, moderate, or vigorous activity were classified as performing some leisure-time activity. Adults who participated in three or more sessions per week of vigorous activity lasting a minimum of 20 minutes, or five or more sessions per week of light to moderate activity lasting at least 30 minutes, were classified as performing regular leisure-time activity.

Source: C.A. Schoenborn and P.M. Barnes, 2002, "Liesure-time physical activity among adults: United States, 1977-98," *Advance Data From Vital and Health Statistics* no. 325 (Hyattsville, MD: National Center for Health Statistics).

leisure-time activity (20 minutes of vigorous activity five times per week or 30 minutes of light to moderate activity), of adults ages 18 and up.

Although in some Eastern cultures aging is revered, in the Western Hemisphere, aging is often associated with many negative stereotypes. Stereotyping of persons based on aging has become so common that it is referred to as **ageism**. As with racism (stereotyping based on an individual's race) or sexism (stereotyping associated with gender), ageism can have a severely negative impact on individuals. Older adults can be discriminated against for jobs or social activities. Ageism can have a serious impact on participation in physical activities. Aging adults are assumed to be less fit than others and less able to perform physical activities. In light of these attitudes, it is not surprising that many adults progressively limit their physical activity levels. When adults buy into these negative attitudes, they often decrease their involvement in physical activity, and the attitudes turn into a self-fulfilling prophecy (Berger & McInman, 1993). Decreasing physical activity levels based on age is referred to as **age grading**.

Participation in physical activity often begins its descent as young adults approach middle adulthood, facing increasing responsibilities with finances and growing families (Payne & Isaacs, 2008). Single parents find it particularly difficult to fit exercise into their schedules. Retired adults have increased free time but often limit participation in physical activity due to reduced financial means, limited means of transportation, and an apprehension about initiating involvement in many physical activities after so many years of not participating. As adults age, many decrease their involvement in exercise-related activities. These changes affect body composition and athletic abilities. It is often emotionally difficult for adults to deal with their changing bodies and abilities, and this affects their self-esteem and increases anxiety and stress. These changes cause people to become even less interested in physical activity, which in turn further impairs them physiologically. This phenomenon is known as the **exercise–aging cycle** (Berger & Hecht, 1989).

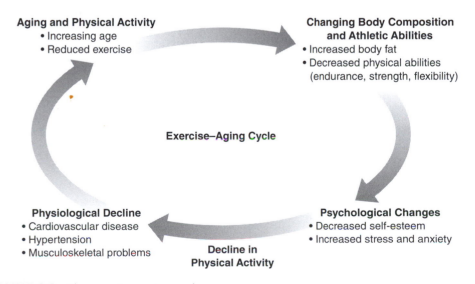

FIGURE 9.2 The exercise–aging cycle.

Adapted from B.G. Berger and L.M. Hecht, 1989, Exercise, aging, and psychological well-being: The mind-body question. In *Aging and motor behavior*, edited by A.C. Ostrow (Indianapolis, IN: Benchmark Press).

The current public health recommendations are to participate in moderate-intensity aerobic physical activity for at least 150 minutes per week or vigorous-intensity physical activity for 75 minutes per week. For additional benefits, adults should engage in physical activity beyond these minimums and incorporate muscle strengthening activities that are moderate or high in intensity, involving all major muscle groups, two or more days per week (U.S. Department of Health and Human Services, 2008). Approximately 40% of U.S. adults reported being insufficiently physically active, defined as participating in more than 10 minutes total per week of moderate- to vigorous-intensity activity but less than the recommended amount of physical activity. These activities can include leisure-time pursuits, household chores, or transportation. Twenty-five percent reported no leisure-time activity, and 15% were labeled as inactive, participating in less than 10 minutes per week in moderate- to vigorous-intensity *lifestyle* activities (Centers for Disease Control and Prevention, n.d.).

Peak Athletic Performance

One of the most intriguing issues in human motor development is the connection between chronological age and physical performance. In general, research on highly skilled athletes indicates that peak athletic performance occurs between the ages of 25 and 35 years (Gabbard, 2004). It is certainly rare for a 12-year-old to achieve a world record, and for a 75-year-old adult to break a world record would perhaps be even less expected. The main limiting factor for the 12-year-old or the 75-year-old is not motivation or behavior; rather, it is biological (Schulz & Curnow, 1988). During adolescence, many growth and developmental changes are still occurring, and the systems are not capable of working together for maximum function until early adulthood. On the other end of the spectrum, the biological capacity of older adults is declining, limiting their physiological capacity and peak performance ability.

The simplest way to measure the age of peak athletic performance in humans is to compare the ages of world record holders (Hill, 1925). Most sport records, for example in running, swimming, cycling, and weightlifting, are achieved by individuals who are in their late 20s or early 30s (Wilmore & Costill, 1994). This would indicate that humans are in their physical prime during this age range.

The age of peak athletic performance is dependent on the most important physiological element for a specific sport (table 9.1) (Shephard, 1998). In gymnastics, the key element is the ratio of strength to body mass. This becomes a large structural constraint for females when they become young adults, as they gain fat in the breasts and hips, which in part may explain why so many female gymnasts reach their peak prior to puberty. For aerobic activities, such as swimming and running, the average velocities for 100-meter and 10-kilometer runs and the 100-meter front crawl decrease by a rate of about 1% per year after the age of 25 years. The rates of decline are approximately the same for both sprints and distance performances. Muscular strength generally increases up to approximately age 25 to 35 years, decreasing by a rate of about 1.8% per year thereafter.

TABLE 9.1 Peak Performance Age for Some Sport Activities

Age	Males	Females
17		Gymnastics
18		Swimming
19		
20	Swimming	
21		Diving
22	Wrestling, diving	Running short distance
23	Running short distance, cycling	
24	Jumping, boxing, running medium distance, tennis	Running medium distance, tennis, rowing
25	Gymnastics, rowing	
26		Shot put
27	Running long distance	Running long distance
28	Baseball, weightlifting	
29	Shot put	
30		Golf
31	Golf	

GABBARD, CARL P., *LIFELONG MOTOR DEVELOPMENT*, 5th, © 2008. Printed and electronically reproduced by permission of Pearson Education, Inc., Upper Saddle River, New Jersey. Data from R. Schulz and C. Curnow, 1988, "Peak performance and age among superathletes: Track and field, swimming, baseball, tennis, and golf," *Journal of Gerontology* 43(5): 113-120, and K. Hirata, 1979, *Selection of Olympic champions*, vol. 1 (Santa Barbara: Institute of Environmental Stress).

Performances in Olympic Events

The ages of peak athletic performances in track and field events range in the lower to mid-20s, with women reaching their peak approximately one year sooner than men in most events (Schultz & Curnow, 1988). For the running events, the average age for peak athletic performance tends to be dependent on the distance of the run. The mean ages for sprints are younger than for distance running, ranging from a mean age of 22 years for the 100- and 200-meter sprints to 27 years for the 5,000 and 10,000 meter and marathon. Interestingly, this trend was not observed for swimming events. The mean age for peak athletic performance was 20 years for men and 18 years for women. The age remained the same for men regardless of the swimming event. For women, the age was younger for longer distances, opposite the trend for running events. This is well illustrated by the world record–breaking performances in 1987 by Janet Evans at the age of 15 years in the 400-, 800-, and 1,500-meter freestyle.

Surprisingly, the age of peak athletic performances from the standpoint of gold medals and world records changed very little across a period of 90 years (Schulz & Curnow, 1988), even though the performances themselves have improved quite dramatically (refer to table 9.2). For example, the age of the 1,500-meter gold medalist in 1896 was 22 years, and 90 years later the gold medalist was 24 years old, yet a 37.8% improvement was seen in the men's marathon over

TABLE 9.2 Percentage Improvement in Olympic Medal Performances in Track and Field and Swimming Events

Event	Men's % improvement	Women's % improvement
Track		
100 meter	17.50	
200 meter	12.40	9.70
800 meter	21.00	17.10
1,500 meter	21.30	
5,000 meter	10.60	
10,000 meter	13.00	
Marathon	37.80	
50-kilometer walk	20.90	
Field		
High jump	33.00	23.90
Long jump	40.10	24.00
Shot put	90.10	63.00
Swimming (freestyle)		
100 meter	33.30	
400 meter	53.00	31.30
800 meter		9.80
1,500 meter	52.00	

Reprinted, by permission, from R. Schulz and C. Curnow, 1988, "Peak performance and age among superathletes: Track and field, swimming, baseball, tennis, and golf," *Journal of Gerontology* 43(5): 113-120.

this 90-year period of time. In 1896, the fastest marathon time was 2:58.50; it decreased dramatically to 2:11:03 in 1980. The greatest percentage of improvement was found in the men's shot put—at an increase of 90%! Although there were huge improvements across this period of time, performances have stabilized in more recent years.

With the vast improvements in training programs, equipment, technology, diets, and other factors, it is not surprising that elite performance has improved quite significantly. Yet it is surprising that the age at which elite performance occurs has not changed. The simple fact that the age of peak athletic performance remained consistent over a century among all of these large scientific advancements leads to the assumption that the major factor affecting age at peak athletic performance is biological. The only exception to the stability of age at optimal performance is golf. Schulz and Curnow (1988) suggest that the higher age variability at elite levels seen in complex tasks is affected by variables additional to the biological factors that strongly affect motor skills and that rely heavily on endurance, strength, or both. Biological developmental factors do not seem to affect skills with a higher cognitive component. World chess champions tend to be significantly older than track and field athletes, with a mean age of 38 years. Similarly, productivity in the arts and sciences does not peak until the late 30s to early 40s (Belsky, 1984).

Performances in Selected Sports

Assessing the age of peak athletic performance in a sport such as baseball is more complicated than in track and field or swimming because of the complexity of the game and the large number of performance measurements compiled. To assess the age of peak athletic performance in baseball, Schulz and Curnow (1988) analyzed 10 categories for nonpitchers (runs, hits, doubles, triples, home runs, RBIs, walks, strikeouts, stolen bases, and batting average) and six categories for pitchers (wins, win–loss percentage, strikeouts, earned run average, shutouts, and saves). Although many categories were assessed, the mean age of peak athletic performance remained very consistent at age 27 to 28 years.

To examine the age at peak athletic performance for two other complex games, tennis and golf, the age of the number one–ranking athlete per year was recorded. In tennis, the mean age was 25.43 years for men and 24.46 years for women. Mean ages for golfers were significantly higher, at approximately 33 years, with women averaging one year younger than men. A trend toward younger golf champions began in the late 60s and certainly continues with the current golf sensation, Tiger Woods. In 1997, at the age of 21 years, Woods became the youngest Masters winner, won three other PGA events, and achieved the number-one world ranking all within 42 weeks of becoming a pro.

What Do You Think?

Since the age of peak athletic performance remained consistent over a period of 90 years even though performance improved substantially (sometimes as much as 90%), it can be concluded that there are biological limitations to performing at a peak level. Using this information for a sport of your interest, answer the following questions:

1. How could you use this information to maximize the performance of an athlete who is above the mean age for peak athletic performance for your sport?

2. Would you use this information to assist you in identifying talent (would you use age as a factor when selecting your team and athletes)? Why or why not?

Performance Changes in Older Adults

In general, regardless of sport or activity, performance declines tend to occur at a fairly slow to moderate rate until the age of about 70 to 75 years, after which the rate of decline accelerates (Reider, 2008). A sharp decline in athletic performance at the age of 70 years has been found in masters athletes in running events, both sprints and endurance (Wright & Perricelli, 2008), weightlifting (Meltzer, 1994), and swimming (Donato et al., 2003). It is as if these older adults are pushing a boulder up a hill that is getting steeper and steeper (Reider, 2008) as they fight with age-related physiological changes such as decreasing muscle mass, reduced size of type II muscle fibers, lower maximum oxygen volumes and heart rates, and stiffening connective tissues. It is important for rehabilitation specialists and geriatric instructors to be aware of this sharp decline in elderly adults. Although the decline is inevitable, interventions with endurance training (Coggan et al., 1992) and strength training (Fiatarone et al., 1990) can help elderly adults maximize their functional potential.

Research Notes: Senior Athletic Track and Field Performances

To examine age-related changes in peak athletic performance among elite senior athletes, researchers looked at track and field senior Olympians over the age of 50 years who participated in the 2001 National Senior Olympic Games (Wright & Perricelli, 2008). Examining elite athletes provides a clearer picture of age-related peak performance changes as these are less likely to be affected by chronic disease or long periods of physical inactivity and disuse. Age-related changes were determined from the mean winning performance times in various track and field events, and age and gender differences were compared. Performance times significantly increased for both sprints and endurance events for both males and females. Performances declined slowly until the age of 75 years and then declined dramatically. Figure 9.3 illustrates the percentage change for the 100-meter sprint across age. Men declined at a similar rate for sprints and endurance events, while women declined at a higher rate for sprints than for endurance events. Senior elite athletes provide an excellent example of what the aging human body can achieve. They demonstrate that aging alone should not prevent an individual from participating in physical activity or from competing in high-level contests. Even though significant declines in peak athletic performance are found, most notably beyond the age of 75, these individuals are delaying the onset of chronic disease and are maintaining a high sense of both physical and mental well-being.

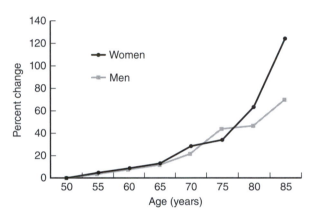

FIGURE 9.3 Percentage 100-meter performance change for men and women by age.

V.J. Wright and B.C. Perricelli, *The American Journal of Sports Medicine* 36(3): 443-450, copyright © 2008 by The American Orthopaedic Society for Sports Medicine. Reprinted by permission of SAGE Publications.

Movement Patterns

Age-related declines in strength, flexibility, and processing speed all contribute to changing movement patterns in older adults. Older adults are also much more likely to have secondary factors such as disease or injury that can compound age-related movement changes. This section focuses on the factors affecting healthy aging in relation to locomotor skills (running and jumping), fundamental motor skills (throwing and striking), and functional activities (handwriting and driving).

Changes in Locomotion

Changes in gait have been associated with the aging process. Reduced gait speed is one of the most significant changes seen in healthy older adults in comparison to healthy young adults, with older adults walking on average 20% more slowly than young adults (Spirduso et al., 2005). The reduction in gait speed is surprisingly not due to decreased stride frequency (the number of strides per unit of time). Rather, it is largely due to a reduced stride length (the distance traveled between right foot contact and the subsequent right foot contact). A reduced stride length negatively affects many other aspects of the gait, resulting in reduced joint rotation in the lower extremities, increased double-support time (time during which both feet are in contact with the ground), reduced arm swing, and a more flat-footed contact with the ground (Elble, 1997). Older adults have also been found to have less push-off power than young adults (Winter, Patla, Frank, & Walt, 1990) and increased out-toeing (Murray, Kory, & Sepic, 1970). Out-toeing is a strategy used to improve lateral stability (Gabbard, 2004). Locomotion becomes even more challenging when older adults are faced with obstacles, as when they have to step up over a curb or step around a chair (Steffen, Hacker, & Mollinger, 2002). Every day we avoid many obstacles without even noticing these behaviors. However, the ability to negotiate many different obstacles while traveling from point A to point B is an important component of independent living.

Age-related changes in gait occur as a result of many factors, including muscular weakness in the hip abductors, hip extensors, knee extensors, plantarflexors, and dorsiflexors, as well as sensory impairments in the visual, somatosensory, and vestibular systems. Spirduso and colleagues (2005) found 10 age-related gait changes:

Temporal and distance variables

- Decreased velocity
- Decreased step length (distance traveled of alternate feet)
- Decreased step frequency (walking cadence)
- Decreased stride length (distance traveled of same foot)
- Increased stride width (distance between the two feet)
- Increased stance phase (begins when the first foot contacts the ground)
- Increased time in double support (time when both feet are in contact with the ground)
- Decreased time in swing phase (begins as the foot leaves the ground)

Kinematic variables

- Flatter foot–floor pattern
- Reduced arm swing

Gait changes may not be limited to physiological age-related changes. Evidence supports the possibility that many older adults alter their gait due to a fear of falling. Older adults adopt a "safer" gait by taking shorter steps, with more time in double stance, in an effort to decrease their risk of falling. Willmott (1986) proposed this after finding that older adults walked significantly faster on carpet than on vinyl.

Try This

Take a trip to a mall or other location where many people are walking around in a leisurely fashion. Notice the kinematic, temporal, and distance variables of the people walking. Compare adults of various ages: young adults, middle-aged adults, and older adults. Describe each of their walking patterns. What are some variables other than age that may cause some of the differences in gait that you observe?

Running

The movement pattern characteristics (kinematics) of older adults up to age 80 years have been found to be the same as those of female university track athletes (Adrian & Cooper, 1995). On the other hand, few similarities were seen when sprinting kinematics were compared between older females and young athletes. Young athletes use longer strides and generate more force through greater flexion and extension. This enables them to take fewer strides. It is also not surprising that older adults show a steady decline in both jogging and running speeds in comparison to young adults (Nelson, 1981).

Jumping

Research on jumping has revealed age-related differences in the kinematics of vertical jumping. Young adult males (18-year-olds) have been compared with males in their mid 60s on vertical jumping (Wang, 2008). Older adults had significantly less strength in the knee and hip, which can affect the ability to perform other activities of daily living. During the jump, older adults decreased their hip flexion and extension but showed no differences in the knee. The decreased hip joint angles enabled them to maintain hip angular stiffness. Joint angular stiffness provides benefits to joint stability by resisting sudden angular displacements of the hip (Flanagan & Harrison, 2007), which can cause damage to the cartilage and ligaments (Butler, Crowell, & Davis, 2003).

Changes in Fundamental Movement Patterns

Unfortunately, very little is known about the movement patterns of older adults in any of the fundamental or sport-specific motor skills (Williams, Haywood, & VanSant, 1991). Most research studies have instead focused on functional activities such as walking, running, or rising from a sit to a stand position. Research on movements using maximal force is also quite limited, as most studies have focused on performing the movements at "preferred speeds." Although research is limited in this area, this section discusses fundamental movement patterns in older adulthood for throwing and striking.

Throwing

The developmental sequence for the overarm throw for force has been divided into either three or four categories for each of four body segment actions including the trunk, humerus, forearm, and foot action components (Roberton & Halverson, 1984). Adults over the age of 70 years have been found to use moderately advanced movement patterns (Williams, Haywood, & VanSant, 1990, 1991). Very few older adults threw with developmentally advanced actions for any of the body segment actions (refer to table 9.3). Older adults also threw with reduced range of motion and took smaller steps. Gender differences were reported, as women threw with significantly fewer developmentally advanced actions of the forearm and humerus in comparison to the men (Williams et al., 1991).

When the throwing velocities of the older adults were compared to those of children and adolescents tested by Halverson and colleagues (1982), the older adults' speeds were comparable to those of third grade children (figure 9.4). Throwing velocities were higher for males of all age groups than for females, which is likely due to the more advanced movement patterns produced by the males. The developmental level of movement patterns has been found to predict ball velocities in children (Roberton & Konczak, 2001).

TABLE 9.3 Developmental Sequences for Movement Components of the Overarm Throw for Force

	Developmental sequences	Percentage of older adults in each category
	Trunk action component	
Level 1	No trunk action or forward–backward action	0%
Level 2	Upper trunk rotation or trunk "block" rotation	100%
Level 3	Differentiated rotation	0%
	Humerus action component	
Level 1	Humerus oblique	48.10%
Level 2	Humerus aligned but independent	40.50%
Level 3	Humerus lags	11.40%
	Forearm action component	
Level 1	No forearm	51.90%
Level 2	Forearm lag	48.10%
Level 3	Delayed lag	0%
	Foot action component	
Level 1	No foot action	0%
Level 2	Ipsilateral foot action	3.80%
Level 3	Contralateral foot action, short step	92.40%
Level 4	Contralateral foot action, long step	3.80%

Reprinted with permission from *Research Quarterly for Exercise and Sport*, Vol. 69, No. 1, 1-10, Copyright 1998 by the American Alliance for Health, Physical Education, Recreation and Dance, 1900 Association Drive, Reston, VA 20191.

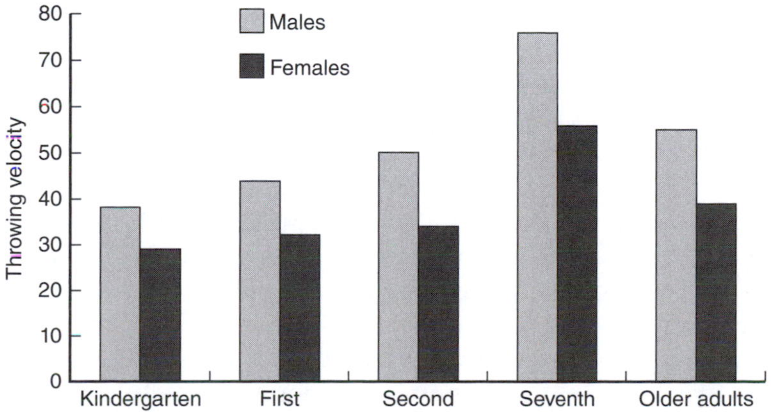

FIGURE 9.4 Overhand throwing velocities (feet/second) for children in kindergarten through seventh grade and older adults.

Data from K. Williams, K. Haywood, and A. VanSant, 1991, "Throwing patterns of older adults: A follow-up investigation," *International Journal of Aging and Human Development* 33(4): 279-294.

Research Notes: Maybe Older Adults Aren't So Bad at Throwing

Williams, Haywood, and VanSant (1998) conducted a longitudinal study on overhand throwing in adults between the ages of 62 and 77 years. Over a period of seven years, eight older adults were videotaped from the sagittal plane (side view) as they threw a tennis ball. The results indicated that many of the age-related differences found in older adults may actually be the result of the study design, since previous studies on overarm throwing were cohort studies, comparing individuals of different ages rather than the same individuals across time. The developmental levels were the same across the seven years 90% of the time, indicating that only small changes in the coordination patterns occurred in the older adults during this time period. The older adults coordinated their movements similarly to younger throwers with the exception of the control of the overarm throw, the amount of trunk rotation, and range of shoulder motion. The changes seen in movement control are likely the result of various factors, such as chronic disuse (Spirduso et al., 2005), osteoarthritis, and losses in balance (Thapa, Gideon, Fought, Kormicki, & Ray, 1994).

The researchers also found that older adults coordinated their backswings differently than younger throwers. Due to the different movement patterns performed by the older adults with their backswing, two new steps were added to the developmental sequence (levels 3 and 5):

Level 1   No backswing

Level 2   Elbow and humeral flexion

Level 3   *Humeral lateral rotation*

Level 4   Circular, upward backswing

Level 5   *Shortcut circular, downward backswing*

Level 6   Circular, downward backswing

The older adults threw using these two new steps more than any other preparatory backswing step. These movements are likely adaptations resulting from changes in the range of motion at the shoulder.

Striking

The fundamental movement pattern of striking is a coincident timing skill that requires an individual to make contact with a ball by manipulating an object such as a racket, bat, or club. Striking skills can vary quite considerably. The planes of motion—overhand (e.g., tennis serve), sidearm (e.g., batting), and underhand (e.g., golf, hockey)—vary from sport to sport, as do the size and elasticity of the ball and the implement (e.g., tennis racket, baseball bat, golf club).

Slower extension velocities have been found in the striking patterns of the tennis backhand and batting in older adults (Klinger, Masataka, Adrian, & Smith, 1980), but not in the golf swing for a short shot (Jagacinski, Greenberg, & Liao, 1997). Although no differences were found between young and older adults in the tempo of the golf swing or the overall speed of the swing, marked group differences were observed in the rhythm of the swing, or the speeding up and slowing down within a shot. The older adults actually reached their peak downswing force earlier than the young adults. Young adults reached this peak just prior to making contact with the ball. These results may indicate that older adults have reduced control during the swing compared to young adults. The older adults also exerted more effort, although most of them performed as well as the young adults.

Age-related effects on movement performances have been shown to be reduced in active adults (Klinger et al., 1980; Gabbard, 2004). In general, active older adults can maintain their movement patterns at a level similar to that achieved during young adulthood. Movement speed and range of motion are affected to a lesser degree in active adults compared to inactive adults.

Changes in Functional Activities

With the many physical changes that accompany aging, it is important to understand how these changes affect older adults' abilities to perform functional tasks such as driving and handwriting. These two activities are very important for quality of life and independence. Older adults who lose the ability to drive become dependent on either public transportation or friends and family for transportation. Public transportation can be limited for adults who do not live in a metropolitan area, forcing them to rely on others to drive them. Handwriting is also an important everyday functional task and is a strong indicator of cognitive and physical declines.

Driving

The primary mode of transportation for older adults is driving (Jette & Branch, 1992). "Driving an automobile is a source of independence, freedom, socialization, and self-esteem for many older individuals" (Johnson, 2003). Driving provides an increased quality of life for many adults, allowing them to pursue activities they could not engage in if they were not permitted to drive. Policy makers often suggest public transportation as the solution. However, older adults do not perceive public transportation as a viable alternative to driving. Some do not have access to public transportation, some don't like using it, and some cannot physically walk the distance necessary to access the system (Donorfio, Mohyde, Coughlin, & D'Ambrosio, 2008).

The number of drivers over the age of 60 years is increasing as the baby boomer generation joins this age group and as people are living longer life spans. And not only are there more older adult drivers, but it is expected that the older drivers will dramatically increase their driving miles (Castro, Martínez, & Tornay, 2005). With the growing older population and increased mileage, the number of vehicle fatalities in adults over 70 years increased 10% from 1990 to 2000 and is expected to increase 25% by 2030 (National Highway Traffic Safety Administration, 2000). In general, older adults are safer drivers and are less likely to be involved in accidents than younger adults. Yet because of their physical declines, older adults involved in an accident are much more likely to sustain serious injuries or die (Braver & Trempel, 2003).

Older adults are generally aware of their functional declines, both physical (i.e., eyesight, hearing, reflexes, neck/shoulder mobility) and psychological (i.e., confidence, enjoyment, ability to concentrate, trust of other drivers, independence, and ability to drive in stressful environments). Due to this heightened awareness in relation to driving abilities, they tend to compensate with strategies such as an increased awareness of their own performance, the driving behaviors of other drivers, their vehicle, and road rules (Donorfio et al., 2008). Driving shifts from an activity that is largely automatic and becomes a chore, requiring more planning and increased concentration and cautiousness.

Policy making for older adults is challenging. Older drivers often have physical declines, but positive alterations in their driving behaviors allow them to drive more safely than younger adults. Older adults are also quite variable, so rating driving ability solely on the basis of age would not be efficient. Some older adults can drive competently in their 90s while others show significant impairment in their 60s or 70s.

Medical conditions that are more prevalent in older adults have been found to be associated with increased accident risk (Marshall, 2008). Cardiovascular disease, cerebrovascular disease, depression, diabetes, medication use, musculoskeletal disorders, and visual deficit have been shown to cause a slight to moderate increase in crash risk. Alcohol abuse and dependence, dementia, epilepsy, schizophrenia, and sleep apnea, on the other hand, are associated with a moderate to high increase in crash risk. The accident risk fluctuates according to the severity of the condition, which varies considerably across individuals.

 What Do You Think?

What are the implications of aging for driving? What declines could affect driving ability? Do you feel that drivers should be assessed and or lose their driving privileges (or both) after they reach a certain age? If so, at what age? If not, why not? Weigh the pros and cons of implementing a policy on the cessation of driving in older adults. Think about the physical, psychological, and cognitive changes in older adults. Also think about the effects that driving cessation would have on an individual (i.e., emotional effects, impact on social life).

Handwriting

Handwriting is one of the most common daily activities. It is necessary for not only professional activities, but also leisure activities (Dixon, Kurzman, & Friesen, 1993). Handwriting is a complex activity involving eye–hand coordination, dexterity, motor planning, visual and kinesthetic perception, and manual skills (Tseng & Cermak, 1993); and many years are needed to acquire the skill. Hand function has been found to decrease with increasing age due to reduced physical activity levels and neuromuscular decline in hand strength, speed, and coordination (Cole, Rotella, & Harper, 1999).

Older adults report having no impairment in handwriting, but research has shown that they write significantly more slowly and with less pressure than young adults (Rosenblum & Werner, 2005). The decreased pressure is likely due to decreased hand strength (Fried, Storer, King, & Lodder, 1991), including reduced finger-pinch strength, and steady precision finger-pinch posture (Ranganathan, Siemionow, Sahgal, Liu, & Yue, 2001). The decreased handwriting speed was not simply the result of slower movements, but also of increased air time—the time during writing in which the pen or pencil is not making marks on the paper (Rosenblum & Werner, 2005). Unlike for other tasks requiring muscular strength, no gender differences are found with age for handwriting (Rosenblum & Werner, 2005; Shiffman, 1992).

Summary

The term aging tends to refer to physical changes that occur later in life as opposed to development, which refers to growth and maturation throughout infancy, childhood, and adolescence. Chronological age is the most commonly used indicator of age. However, this age marker is limiting, as adults can vary markedly in physiological adaptations and physical function. Two individuals can be the same chronological age but decades apart in their biological age.

Although the current public health recommendations are for adults to maintain moderate- to vigorous-intensity physical activity for a minimum of 30 minutes per day, five days per week, many adults are insufficiently physically active. Aging stereotypes and age grading contribute to negative stereotypes of older adults in Western cultures. These stereotypes have a serious impact on physical activity participation. This often leads to the exercise–aging cycle of decreased function due to decreased physical activity, leading to further decreased function and so on.

There is a strong connection between chronological age and peak athletic performance. The age of peak athletic performance is between 25 and 35 years with very few exceptions. Even with vast improvements in technology, training programs, and nutrition, it is surprising that although performances have dramatically improved in all sports, the age at which these elite performances are achieved has not. Performance declines can be minimized by continued practice in the sport, although large performance declines tend to occur after the age of 75 years regardless of sport or activity.

Older adults exhibit age-related gait changes including decreased velocity, step length, step frequency, stride length, and time in swing phase. Age-related changes in the coordination patterns of fundamental motor skills also occur in older adults. These changes can be minimized with continued practice.

Age-related changes are seen in the functional activities of driving and handwriting. Driving provides a means of independence and freedom for adults and is considered an important component in the maintenance of enhanced quality of life for many seniors. Handwriting is also an important everyday function. Both of these tasks require eye–hand coordination, sensory perception, and motor planning, all of which decline with aging. Although many physiological declines affect both of these tasks, some older adults can competently continue to write and safely drive into their 90s and beyond.

Supplemental Activities

1. Talk with older adults. How much time have you spent with an older adult—not your grandmother, grandfather, or another older relative, but an unrelated older adult? It is likely that unless you work with older adults, you haven't often sat down and had an extended conversation with an older adult. For this supplemental activity, visit a senior center or an assisted-living facility and spend some time with an older adult. Ask about the physical activities the person participated in as a child, an adolescent, a young adult, a middle-aged adult, and an old adult. Ask why the individual participated in those activities and why he or she may have dropped out of certain activities or taken up different activities as an older person.

2a. Choose a sport and search for the record performances in that sport across time (e.g., what were the records for the sport in the 1930s, 1950s, 1970s, 1990s, and today?). How have they changed? Did they change significantly more over one period of time than during others? Explain what may have caused this more significant change with regard to this sport. Why do you think performances are better now than they were in previous decades (e.g., new techniques, technological advances, diet changes)?

2b. Now search for record performance times across ages (e.g., 20s, 30s 40s, 50s, 60s, 70s). Graph the performance changes across these ages. Discuss your findings.

Structural Constraints in Adulthood

CHAPTER OBJECTIVES

After reading this chapter, you should be able to

› describe peak physiological function;

› explain age-related changes in the skeletal, muscular, nervous, cardiovascular, and sensory systems;

› compare the effects of a physically active lifestyle and a sedentary lifestyle in each of these systems; and

› understand the effects of normal aging on aerobic capacity and body composition, as well as any benefits of a physically active lifestyle on each.

Old Age and Treachery Beat Youth and Vitality Every Time!

At the age of 48 years, Leo still loves to play basketball. He no longer plays as often as he used to in part because of knee troubles, but when he does play, he's still able to leave his younger competitors struggling to keep up! Over the years, Leo has adapted his game to compensate for losses in speed and agility, enabling him to still play at a high level of skill. These younger players have some pretty swift moves, but Leo can read and anticipate them. He plays off of his man to make up for his reduced lateral quickness. He uses his body and wide shoulders to clear space for his shot because he can no longer get up higher than a defender to shoot. In basketball, some refer to such strategies as "veterans' tricks," because older players use them to keep up with the younger, quicker, more athletic players. Many of Leo's age-related changes were in his skeletal and muscular systems, but his reduced quickness is also likely due to changes in his cardiovascular system as well as body composition changes. Rather than allowing these age-related changes to limit his game, Leo uses his advanced knowledge and experience in basketball to outsmart his opponents and beat them at their own game.

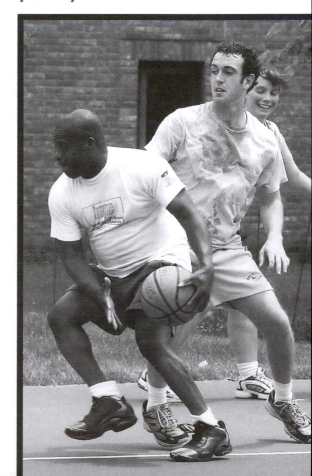

With old age, humans experience many declines, including cardiorespiratory function, muscular strength, and behavioral speed, to name a few. This chapter discusses these as well as other age-related body system changes, including skeletal, muscular, cardiovascular, nervous, endocrine, and sensory system changes. Although many age-related declines are associated with aging, older adults have discovered that by maintaining an active and healthy lifestyle, they are able to reduce many age-related declines. Thus they can maintain much of their function for years longer than their sedentary counterparts, allowing them to live a higher quality of life into old adulthood, with reduced secondary diseases and improved physical and cognitive function. It is essential for all practitioners who work with older adults to understand these aging effects on the physiologic systems, the impact the changes have on movement, and the effect of physically active lifestyles on physiologic systems.

Human peak physiological function occurs between the ages of 25 and 30 years (McArdle, Katch, & Katch, 2001). It is during these years of peak physiological function that the greatest gender differences are found with women maturing earlier and reaching their peak physiological function between the ages of 22 and 25 years and men maturing later, reaching their peak between 28 and 30 years (Gabbard, 2004). Peak athletic performance parallels peak physiological function, as muscular strength, cardiorespiratory efficiency, and reaction time are at their maximum.

How an individual moves or learns a motor skill is greatly affected by the changes occurring in the body systems. Chapter 6 discussed the development of body systems from birth through adolescence. Changes in body systems do not cease following growth and maturation. Profound age-related changes occur in the body systems across the life span. When aging is combined with environmental and behavioral factors, such as diet and physical activity, even more variability is found in the body systems across individuals of the same age and gender. When one is designing programs, the structural constraints are among the most important factors to consider. A practitioner must understand how aging affects these systems and its impact on movement. It is also important to understand the wide variability seen across adults. Because adults vary considerably more than children and adolescents, it is essential to individualize programs.

Skeletal System

Peak bone mass occurs around the age of 30 years for both males and females (Spirduso, Francis, & MacRae, 2005). Physical activities that individuals participate in during adolescence and young adulthood help determine the size and strength of their bones. Those who participate in more resistance training activities or activities that require much physical stress and load (e.g., weightlifters and powerlifters) develop stronger and thicker bones than endurance athletes (e.g., runners or cyclists). Because swimming is not a weight-bearing activity, swimmers will have weaker, less dense bones than runners (Nillsson & Westlin, 1971). The size and strength of bones acquired during youth and young adulthood provide lifelong benefits. It has been suggested that the bone mass of an individual may delay the onset of microfractures in older adulthood

(Schultheis, 1991). Bone health in adulthood is determined by **peak bone mass** (the highest bone mass acquired before the age of 30 years) and age-related rate of bone loss (Spirduso et al., 2005).

Osteoporosis

Bone tissue is eventually lost in older adulthood, causing bones to become so weak that they may fracture from mild falls or even coughing (Shephard, 1998). Fractures, especially hip fractures, in adulthood can seriously affect an individual's independent lifestyle. The threat of bone fractures is increased even further in individuals with osteoporosis. **Osteoporosis** is a crippling disease, resulting from low bone mass and poor structural bone quality. From a structural viewpoint, the vertebrae may be damaged and the person assumes a stooped posture, which affects execution of well-learned skills. Motivationally, a person with osteoporosis may be reluctant to learn new motor skills or use former motor skills for fear of falling and fracturing a limb.

The risk of osteoporosis increases with age but can occur at any age (Spirduso et al., 2005). Due to decreased peak bone mass and increased rate of bone loss, women are at a much higher risk of osteoporosis than men. One out of every two women, and one out of every eight men, will experience a fracture due to osteoporosis in their lifetime (National Institutes of Health, 2007). Thin-framed women and women under 127 pounds (58 kilograms) are at an increased risk of osteoporosis. Ethnicity has also been linked to osteoporosis risk, with Caucasian and Asian women at highest risk and African American women at lowest risk (Finkelstein et al., 2002). Women have an increased risk of microfractures and osteoporosis than men because they generally attain a peak bone mass that is 10% below the average man's peak bone mass (Shephard, 1998). Bone loss is also much higher in women during menopause, increasing from an average of 0.7% to 1% loss per year to between 2% and 3% loss per year after menopause over a 5- to 10-year period. During menopause, women can lose between 30% and 50% of their bone mineral density. Bone loss then increases in both men and women during old adulthood, between the 9th and 10th decades (Spirduso et al., 2005).

Many of the risk factors for osteoporosis are modifiable (see table 10.1). Participating in regular load-bearing exercise such as resistance training or running can decrease or even reverse bone mineral loss even throughout older adulthood (Shephard, 1998). Increasing calcium intake to 1,500 milligrams per day can also help decrease bone loss. Other modifiable risk factors include cigarette smoking, alcohol, low estrogen (modifiable by estrogen therapy), and anorexia.

TABLE 10.1 Osteoporosis Risk Factors

	Nonmodifiable risk factors
Gender	Women have a higher risk.
Age	Bones become thinner and weaker with age.
Body size	Thin-framed women are at highest risk.
Ethnicity	Caucasian and Asian women are at highest risk.
Family history	Heredity can increase risk.

» *continued*

TABLE 10.1 ›› *continued*

	Modifiable risk factors
Lifestyle	Increase weight-bearing physical activity to decrease risk.
Calcium and vitamin D	Increase calcium and vitamin D intake.
Sex hormones	Low estrogen or low testosterone can increase risk.
Medications	Glucocorticoids and some anticonvulsants can lead to loss of bone density.
Anorexia	Serious reduction in food intake and body weight increases risk.
Cigarette smoking	Quit smoking.
Excessive alcohol intake	Decrease alcohol consumption.

Adapted from National Institutes of Health, Osteoporosis and Related Bone Diseases National Resource Center, 2010, Osteoporosis overview. [Online]. Available: www.niams.nih.gov/Health_Info/Bone/Osteoporosis/overview.asp#c [January 18, 2011].

Body Stature

With age, there is a general trend toward a decrease in standing height (Shephard, 1997), starting around the age of 40 years. Women lose height at a faster rate than men. A cross-sectional study (study of different people at different ages) showed that men aged 65 to 74 years were on average 61 millimeters (2.4 inches) shorter and women were 50 millimeters (about 2 inches) shorter than young adults (U.S. National Center for Health Statistics, 1981). Losses in height accelerate after age 70 years, to an average of 2 millimeters per year in both genders (Svänborg, Eden, & Mellstrom, 1991). Decreases in height largely result from a progressive compression of the intervertebral discs (Shephard, 1997).

This compression shortens the spine and can cause kyphosis. **Kyphosis** is the curvature of the upper spine (figure 10.1) and can also be the result of years of poor posture, weak back muscles, senile osteoporosis, and osteoarthritis of the vertebrae. **Osteoarthritis** is a very common degenerative joint disease affecting approximately 80% of adults over the age of 65 years. Osteoarthritis can affect any joint but most often affects the hips, vertebrae, feet, and knees. Arthritis cripples millions of Americans, impairing their ability to move fluidly and comfortably. Fortunately, many of the symptoms of arthritis can be controlled through non-weight-bearing exercise such as swimming and cycling, flexibility training, and light resistance training (Van Norman, 1995).

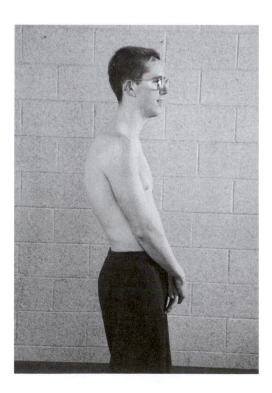

FIGURE 10.1
Kyphosis.

What Do You Think?

1. You are an instructor or clinician working with an 82-year-old female who has osteoporosis. She is frail and relatively sedentary. What are some exercises that you would prescribe? Explain why you chose these exercises. What are some exercises that this person should avoid? What are some warnings (signs and symptoms) for a frail woman with osteoporosis?

2. What activities would you prescribe for her if she also had osteoarthritis in her knees and ankles? What activities should a person with arthritis avoid? Explain why developing a program for someone with both osteoporosis and osteoarthritis would be particularly challenging.

Muscular System

The muscular system works in concert with the skeletal system to allow the body to move. Large changes in body composition occur in adulthood, resulting in a progressive loss of lean body mass. The loss of lean body mass results more from an increase in body fat than from a reduction in muscle mass (Haywood & Getchell, 2005). Losses in muscle mass are small until around the age of 50 years, after which they accelerate. People can avoid much of this loss in muscle mass by maintaining moderate to high physical activity levels and good nutrition (Shephard, 1998).

Strength

Maximum strength correlates with the muscular cross-sectional area, which is largest during the 20s and plateaus until the age of 35 to 40 years (Shephard, 1998). Strength declines generally begin at the age of 40 years, but can begin earlier for sedentary individuals. A loss of between 30% and 50% of skeletal muscle mass occurs between the ages of 40 and 80 years, thus contributing to a decline in motor performance (Akima et al., 2001). Subsequent declines in strength and power generally parallel, but are often greater than, the rate of skeletal muscle mass decline (Goodpaster et al., 2006; Bassey et al., 1992). Increases in muscle weakness and fatigability also result from decreased muscle mass (Faulkner & Brooks, 1995). Declines in maximum strength are greater in the legs than the arms (Shephard, 1998). This may be attributed to reduced use of the legs with age.

Most adults experience a reduction in muscle mass as a result of heredity, decreased levels of physical activity, and other factors (Lexell, Taylor, & Sjostrom, 1988). The number of muscle fibers decreases around the age of 50 years, so losses in muscle mass at a younger age occur as a result of a sedentary lifestyle (Faulkner, Larkin, Claflin, & Brooks, 2007).

The changes in muscle mass occur as a function of the muscle fiber type. There appears to be an age-related decline in fast-twitch, or type II fibers, while slow-twitch, type I fibers can be maintained with a physically active lifestyle even through old age (Lexell et al., 1988). **Slow-twitch fibers** have a slower contraction–relaxation cycle than fast-twitch fibers and are best suited for endurance activities; **fast-twitch fibers** with their much quicker contraction–relaxation cycle are better suited for short-duration, high-intensity activities such as sprinting or powerlifting. Although a loss of fast-twitch fibers appears inevitable, the amount and rate of decline are greatly affected by the frequency and intensity of physical activity. It is not only possible for older adults to reduce this rate of decline; they can even experience hypertrophy in the muscle fibers that remain (Lexell, 1995). The type II fibers tend to decrease while the type I fibers are maintained. This tendency remains even with frequent and intense physical activity (Shephard, 1998).

The loss of muscular strength in older adults can be quite significant, affecting their ability to maintain independence. Activities many people take for granted such as carrying a bag of groceries, climbing steps, or even opening a medicine bottle can be very challenging for an older adult with significant losses in strength (Shephard, 1991). Losses in muscular strength are exacerbated by long-term physical inactivity leading to frailty. **Frailty** is a condition in which an individual exhibits severe limitations in mobility, strength, balance, and endurance, resulting from weak and highly fatigable muscles, often due to a long-term inactive lifestyle (Faulkner et al., 2007). It is often difficult for the frail elderly to reverse their condition. A long-term inactive lifestyle combined with genetic factors, disease, injury, or aging (or some combination of these) causes muscular atrophy, decreasing strength, and increased fatigability, leading to frailty (figure 10.2). Frail individuals experience impaired mobility and balance and are at an increased risk of falls. With declining fitness, health, and quality of life, the frail elderly often spiral downward, participating in less physical activity. This in turn further reduces their strength and mobility, continually worsening their condition by limiting their physical activity and activities of daily living (ADLs) even more. By further limiting their physical activity, they experience more muscle wasting (atrophy), resulting in a worsening condition.

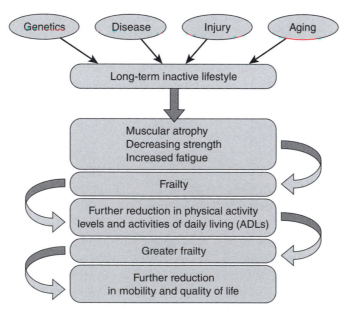

FIGURE 10.2 Downward spiral of physical inactivity leading to frailty and reduced mobility

Flexibility

The elasticity of the tendons and ligaments and the condition of the synovial fluid enable smooth body and limb movements (Gabbard, 2004). With age, flexibility decreases as cross-linkages between collagen fibrils develop and synovial fluid degrades. The cross-linkages reduce the elasticity of the tendons, ligaments, and joint capsules (Shephard, 1998). Through middle age, adults lose approximately 8 to 10 centimeters (3 to 4 inches) of flexibility of the lower back, hip, and hamstring as assessed by the sit and reach test (Shephard, 1998). Declines in flexibility accelerate at a faster rate following middle age. To mitigate the aging effects on flexibility, the joints must be taken through their full range of motion. Stretching exercises with warm muscles and yoga are beneficial in maintaining flexibility and reducing the effects of aging.

Aerobic Capacity

A progressive age-related decline in aerobic capacity is found in adults from age 25 to 65 years (Shephard, 1997). Similar to losses in strength, age-related losses in aerobic capacity accelerate at the age of 70 years and over (Shephard, 1998). It is difficult to separate age-related losses in function from changes due to other factors such as reduced regular physical activity and intensity of physical activity bouts. Although some research has suggested that aerobic capacity can be maintained with regular intense training (Kasch, Wallace, Van Camp, & Verity, 1988), most research has found this to only be a short-lived training response. Following the initial training response, the rate of age-related declines in aerobic power follows a pattern similar to that in nontraining individuals (Shephard, 1998). Some of the factors of an age-related decline in aerobic power are maximum aerobic capacity, lactate threshold, and exercise economy.

Maximum Aerobic Capacity

Maximum aerobic capacity, often referred to as $\dot{V}O_2$max, begins to decline following young adulthood. Although $\dot{V}O_2$max is highly correlated with endurance, the decline in $\dot{V}O_2$max throughout adulthood tends to be greater than performance declines. Endurance training can increase $\dot{V}O_2$max by 5% to 20% in children and adults (Gabbard, 2004). One would expect endurance-trained older athletes to experience a decreased rate of decline compared to sedentary individuals, yet recent studies have not found this to be true. Longitudinal studies have indicated that endurance-trained older women decline at twice the rate as sedentary women (Eskurza, Donato, Moreau, Seals, & Tanaka, 2002), but endurance-trained and sedentary men decline at the same rate (Wilson & Tanaka, 2000). Keep in mind that these comparisons are with the individuals' $\dot{V}O_2$max at an earlier age, not with that of the average younger adult, so the endurance-trained adults had more $\dot{V}O_2$max to lose than sedentary adults because of their higher initial levels. Secondly, many of the older women had significantly reduced their training volume, which would decrease their $\dot{V}O_2$max. Declines in the rate of $\dot{V}O_2$max are similar in endurance-trained and sedentary adults, but the endurance-trained adults have a much higher $\dot{V}O_2$max because they start at a much higher level.

$\dot{V}O_2$max gender differences in adults are quite large, due to lean body mass and overall body weight differences across genders. Men generally have a $\dot{V}O_2$max that is 40% to 60% greater than that of women (Hyde & Gengenbach, 2007). An untrained male averages approximately 3.5 liters per minute, while an untrained female averages 1.5 liters per minute less.

Lactate Threshold

Aerobic performance can also be determined by lactate threshold. **Lactate threshold** occurs at the exercise intensity at which blood lactate begins to accumulate significantly above baseline levels in the bloodstream (Tanaka & Seals, 2003). Lactate threshold declines with increasing age, resulting in reduced overall performance. Although reductions in endurance performance are largely affected by declining lactate threshold in young and middle-aged adults, reduced endurance performance is more affected by reductions in $\dot{V}O_2$max in older adulthood (Evans, Davy, Stevenson, & Seals, 1995).

Exercise Economy

The oxygen cost of exercise at a particular velocity is known as **exercise economy** (Tanaka & Seals, 2003). Exercise economy is a strong indicator of endurance ability (Morgan & Craig, 1992). Although only a few studies have addressed the affects of age on exercise economy, aging does not appear to have such an effect. So, the reductions in endurance performance found with aging are largely the result of declines in $\dot{V}O_2$max and lactate threshold.

What Do You Think?

1. Define maximum aerobic capacity, lactate threshold, and exercise economy.
2. Which is the strongest indicator of endurance ability?
3. Which is most affected by aging?
4. What types of activities increase aerobic capacity?

Cardiovascular System

The cardiovascular system declines by approximately 30% between the ages of 30 and 70 years (Spirduso et al., 2005). Heart rates, most notably heart rates during maximum exertion (maximum heart rates), decrease across the lifetime. Declines in stroke volume are also seen with aging. Increases in arterio–venous oxygen difference occur in older adults, although little difference is found in older adults who regularly exercise. Furthermore, blood pressure tends to increase in older adults. Note that these changes occur in healthy adults. Some individuals may exhibit some form of cardiovascular disease resulting from heredity and lifestyle behaviors. It is important to evaluate individuals' cardiovascular fitness level prior to their involvement in a fitness program or teaching a motor skill as it will greatly affect their ability to perform aerobic exercise.

Heart Rates

Resting heart rates exhibit only small changes with age throughout adulthood (Fagard, Thijs, & Amery, 1993). Heart rates during submaximal exercise tend to be lower in older adults than young adults (Sachs, Hamberger, & Kaijser, 1985), because heart rates not only increase at a faster rate in young adults, but also continue to increase to higher levels than in older adults during submaximal exercise (Paterson, Cunningham, & Babcock, 1989). The largest age-related change in heart rates are found during maximum physical effort. A simple and common formula for computing maximal heart rate is to subtract a person's age in years from 220 beats per minute. For instance, a 50-year-old's maximum heart rate would be 170 beats per minute. Although a maximal heart rate of around 190 beats per minute would be expected for a 30-year-old adult, this formula does not always hold for fit and healthy older adults. Some older adults have been found to reach maximal heart rates 20 beats per minute higher than would be expected based on the formula (Dempsey & Seals, 1995).

Stroke Volume

Stroke volume is the amount of blood that is pumped through one ventricle of the heart during one contraction. Not all of the blood is pumped out during a contraction. Approximately one-third of the blood remains in the left ventricle. Stroke volume is dependent on the size of the heart, the duration of the contraction, preload (the amount of ventricle stretching prior to the contraction), and afterload (aortic pressure during the contraction). In general, men tend to have higher stroke volumes than women because of their larger heart sizes. Stroke volume can be increased through aerobic training, which can also result in lower resting heart rates.

The human heart is quite flexible, enabling heart volume to be well maintained until very old ages (Shephard, 1997). Older adults can have higher stroke volumes than younger adults during submaximal exercise; however, increased stroke volume is difficult for older adults to maintain even with increased exercise intensity toward maximal effort (Niinimaa & Shephard, 1978). As older adults approach maximal effort, many actually exhibit declines in stroke volume, whereas young adults exhibit a gradual increase in stroke volume when approaching maximal effort (Tate, Hyek, & Taffet, 1994).

Arterio-Venous Oxygen Difference

The **arterio–venous oxygen difference** is the difference in oxygen content between arterial and venous blood. The mean arterio–venous oxygen difference determines the volume of oxygen that is transported to the tissues following a contraction (Shephard, 1997). Physically active men are able to sustain the arterio–venous oxygen difference during rest and submaximal exercise. The largest arterio–venous oxygen differences are found in sedentary women, up to 20 to 50 milliliters per liter greater (Dempsey & Seals, 1995). In very healthy and fit older adults, the maximal arterio–venous oxygen difference can remain the same, but it generally decreases by approximately 20 milliliters per liter (Shephard, 1998). This change is due in part to a larger distribution of the cardiac output to regions, such as the skin and internal organs, with age (Shephard, 1993).

Blood Pressure

Blood pressure changes are common with age (figure 10.3). Older adults are more prone to both orthostatic hypotension (periods of low blood pressure) and hypertension (Shephard, 1997). Older adults are less able to respond to changes in body position or heat than young adults. Sharp drops in blood pressure can occur when an older adult moves from a lying position to standing or when stepping out of a swimming pool. These drops in blood pressure may also occur following an exercise bout. Orthostatic hypotension induces dizziness, confusion, and even fainting (Fagard et al., 1993).

Clinical hypertension can rise as much as 35 mmHg (millimeters of mercury) or more across a life span (Kannel, Sorlie, & Gordon, 1980). This rise in hypertension is generally found in people living in developed countries, while indigenous community dwellers show little to no increase in hypertension across age (DeStefano, Coulehan, & Wiant, 1979). This cultural change is largely attributed to lifestyle differences between urban community dwellers and many indigenous people, such as the Navajo and the Pacific Islanders. Some behavioral factors have been found to increase blood pressure such as sedentary lifestyles, excessive body weight, and sodium intake, while others can decrease blood pressure including the intake of omega-3 fatty acids (Rode, Shephard, Vloshinsky, & Kuksis, 1995).

Blood pressure tends to increase during physical exercise regardless of age. These increases are even larger for individuals with higher resting blood pressures (Zerzawy, 1987). Elderly men have averaged 37 mmHg higher than young adults, and elderly women have averaged 26 mmHg higher (Shephard, 1997). Continued regular or vigorous exercise (or both) can decrease resting, submaximal, and maximal blood pressure in young and older adults, bringing them back down to a level similar to that of young adults over time.

Hypertensive individuals should not participate in high-intensity exercise, as it will further increase blood pressure, placing the individual at risk for cardiac problems (Hagberg, 1988). Low- to moderate-intensity exercise (40-65% of maximum) is quite beneficial and can actually decrease blood pressure. Weight training is also favorable; however, high resistance with low repetitions should be replaced with lower resistance and higher repetitions. Because some people tend to hold their breath during repetitions, it is very important to encourage breathing during the movements to avoid further increases in blood pressure (Van Norman, 1995).

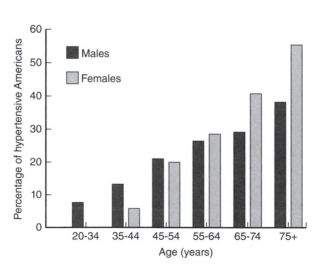

FIGURE 10.3 Rates of hypertension in adult men and women in the United States, 2003-2006.

Data from National Center for Health Statistics, 2010, *Health, United States, 2009: With special feature on medical technology*, p. 293. [Online]. Available: www.cdc.gov/nchs/data/hus/hus09.pdf [January 18, 2011].

What Do You Think?

You are an instructor or clinician working with a 72-year-old hypertensive male with arthritis in his knees and hips. Your client was an athlete as a young adult but did not continue a physically active lifestyle beyond his 30s. He held a sedentary job for 40 years and has been obese for about 30 years. What are some exercises you would prescribe for him? Explain why you chose these activities. What are some exercises that this person should avoid? What are some warnings (signs and symptoms) for an obese hypertensive older adult with arthritis?

Nervous System

The central nervous system is composed of the brain and the spinal cord. There are approximately 100 billion neurons in the brain, giving rise to a very complex neuronal network. The neuron consists of the cell body, axon, and dendrite. With age, the dendrites and axons gradually wither away. The brain also experiences a gradual loss in the number of neurons, losing thousands each day that are not replaced. These changes contribute to the reduced size and weight of the brain. Even though the structure of the brain undergoes substantial losses, generally only small functional losses result.

The brain is capable of recovering from much of these losses through a process termed **neural plasticity**. Plasticity refers to the brain's ability to actually rewire itself to compensate for such changes. The brain restructures itself based on past experiences and what it learns. Neuronal connections increase for areas of the brain that receive information more frequently than areas of the brain that are used less frequently. For instance, a soccer player would have more of his cortex devoted to the feet, and a violinist would have more cortex devoted to the fingers. Neural plasticity can occur at any age, but is most adaptable during childhood. The incredible ability of the brain to adapt does decline with age, but it can be strengthened through both cognitive and physical activity.

Aging is associated with an increase in abnormal formations such as neurofibrillary tangles and senile plaques. **Neurofibrillary tangles** occur when the fibers of a neuron become twisted with one another. These tangles can lead to the death of the neuron and are thought to contribute to the slowing of central nervous system responsiveness (Gallahue & Ozmun, 2006). **Senile plaques** form on the outside of neurons and have been related to memory loss. Plaques and tangles are found, to some degree, in the majority of adults over the age of 80 years (Saxon, Etten, & Perkins, 2010), and many are found in adults with dementia.

Older adults require more time to learn motor skills than young adults. This could partly be affected by memory losses associated with aging (Shephard, 1997). Losses occur in long-term memory recall and short-term memory in older adults (Benham & Heston, 1989; Abourezk, 1989). People can slow many age-related cognitive losses by maintaining moderate physical activity levels and keeping the mind sharp through mental activities such as word puzzles, reading, and writing.

Research Notes: An Idle Mind is the Devil's Plaything

The benefits of neural plasticity may be best evidenced by a longitudinal study on the effects of aging and brain health conducted on a group of 678 nuns in Mankato, Minnesota (Snowdon, 2003). Snowdon studied nuns because they are a unique population in the sense that they are a much more homogeneous than the general population. Nuns have very little to no drug or alcohol use, live in similar environments, and have similar reproductive histories. This group is also particularly interesting because, on average, they live much longer than the general population, many into their 90s and 100s. Not only do the nuns live longer lives, but they also suffer dementia at a much lower rate; and those that do suffer dementia generally have milder cases than the average population. Dementia is a substantial loss in the cognitive ability of an individual above normal age-related declines.

After following these nuns for years, Snowdon believed that the reason for their prolonged length and quality of life was their belief that "an idle mind is the devil's plaything" (Ratey, 2001). The nuns continued to mentally challenge themselves even in their 90s and beyond, keeping their minds actively engaged with puzzles, debates, weekly seminars, vocabulary quizzes, and daily journal writing; and some even continued working in their late 90s. Sister Matthia, featured in *National Geographic* at the age of 103 years, was one of the first nuns to participate in the study and became a model for healthy aging. Her postmortem neuropathologic evaluation revealed that she had no signs of brain pathologies, which is very rare for an individual over the age of 90 years (Snowdon, 2003).

The education level of the nuns and the jobs they held greatly affected both their brain health and their length of life. The nuns with college degrees who continued to challenge themselves lived longer and had less dementia than the nuns who held more mundane positions such as housecleaning and food preparation. The sisters who continually challenged themselves mentally had more neural connections, enabling them to recover from disease and stay healthier and active longer (Ratey, 2001).

 Try This

Performing simple activities that cause a mental conflict or require the opposing sides of the body to perform opposite or different activities is mentally challenging. The following are samples of exercises designed to integrate both sides of the brain while providing challenging movements for the whole body. With practice, they become easier. Try each of these activities. They can be performed in a seated position or standing.

- Repeatedly say the word "yes" while turning your head back and forth from left to right (as if you were saying "no").
- Do the same activity but saying the word "no" and nodding your head up and down.
- Swing your arms up and down while at the same time shaking your head "no" and saying the word "yes."
- Move your arms forward and backward while nodding your head up and down and saying the word "no."
- Move one of your shoulders up and down while moving the other one forward and backward.
- Move your shoulders in circles going in opposite directions.

- Move one shoulder in a circle while you are moving the other shoulder forward and backward.
- Do regular jumping jacks, then switch to feet apart while arms are together.
- Try alternating from feet apart while arms are together to feet together while arms are together.

Were you surprised at the difficulty of performing some of these "simple" activities? It probably required more time for you to adjust to each change. Can you think of other activities that would also challenge the brain?

Endocrine System

The endocrine system signals hormones through an integrated system of organs including the pineal gland, pituitary gland, thyroid gland, thymus, adrenal gland, pancreas, ovary, and testes. Much like the nervous system, the endocrine system is an information signaling system. The main roles of the endocrine system are regulation of metabolism, tissue function, growth, and mood influences.

Age-related changes in the endocrine system include declines in thyroid function, decreasing gonadal hormone levels, and declining neural and hormonal control systems (Shephard, 1997). The thyroid hormone has a role in increasing basal metabolic rate and thermoregulation in extended cold exposure. Changes in basal metabolic rate across a lifetime are more greatly affected by a decrease in lean body mass than by changes in the thyroid. Gonadal hormone changes can increase muscular atrophy and osteoporosis. Hormonal regulatory systems also play an important role in the maintenance of homeostasis during exercise. Hormones are particularly important during vigorous exercise, affecting cardiovascular regulation in warm environments, fuel mobilization, and the synthesis of new protein (Shephard, 1997).

Body Composition

Body weight tends to increase in adults until the age of 60 years and decreases thereafter. The increase in body weight is largely due to an increase in fat mass (FM). In conjunction with the increase in FM with age is a redistribution of body fat. With age, body fat tends to be redistributed from the limbs to the abdominal area (Spirduso, 2005). Intra-abdominal fat accumulation begins in the 20s and increases through the 60s (Schwartz, 1990). Abdominal obesity, associated with an apple-shaped body, is associated with a high risk for cardiovascular disease.

While FM increases with age, fat-free mass (FFM) decreases with age. Fat-free mass, including the nonfat components of the body such as organs, muscle, bone, and skin, peaks in the 20s and 30s and then gradually declines. The decline in FFM is largely attributed to muscle atrophy, or wasting of the muscle. Decreases in FFM are a result of reduced physical activity, osteopenia (bone loss), hormonal changes, and diet changes (Spirduso, 1995).

Exercise is the best defense against age-related changes in body composition. Physical activity can increase muscle mass while decreasing FM, increase resting metabolism, and improve mood state. Although dieting in addition to physical activity is preferred, it is detrimental to replace physical activity with dieting alone. Dieting alone often leads to a loss in body mass as a result of decreased muscle mass, a reduction in resting metabolism, and a depressed mood state (Shephard, 1997).

Sensory Systems

Human movement is profoundly affected by our ability to receive and interpret sensory information. How we move is in response to the sensory information we receive. Infants who are blind take significantly longer to crawl, stand, or walk because they lack the incentive that infants with vision are provided (Fazzi et al., 2002). Similarly, older adults who have progressive vision loss tend to walk with slower, more deliberate steps. Sensory losses begin in the 30s. These losses generally do not affect everyday function until older adulthood but do affect athletic performances in many sports. Although we receive sensory information from smells and tastes, it is vision, audition, and proprioception (kinesthetic perception) that are essential in motor performance.

Visual System

With age, many anatomical and physiologic changes occur in the visual system. Age-related changes, some of which begin in the 20s, result in reduced function, which can greatly affect skillful performance, the learning of new motor skills, and can even have an impact on independent living in older adults. Older adults have increased difficulty with visual cues, which affects driving ability and walking across the street without assistance.

Physiologic and Anatomical Changes

The many age-related physiologic and anatomical changes in vision include changes in the cornea, iris, lens, and retina. The cornea increases in thickness, resulting in decreased corneal sensitivity (Millodot, 1977), to approximately one-half the levels in 20- and 30-year-old adults. The iris also undergoes many changes, including decreased thickness, increased rigidity, and reduced pigmentation, causing a degraded retinal image due to an increased amount of stray light (Weale, 1963). The pupil begins decreasing in size in the teens. The lens grows throughout life and begins to become less compliant in adulthood. Changes in the lens reduce visual accommodation and the ability to focus clearly on close objects. **Accommodation** is the process that enables the eye to adjust and focus, producing a clearer image. The retina also increases in thickness, affecting **peripheral vision**, vision outside of the center of gaze. The rods and cones experience age-related changes that affect vision in light and darkness, as well as color sensitivity. Changes also occur in the primary visual cortex, the area of the brain responsible for interpreting visual images.

Functional Changes

Functional changes result from the many anatomic and physiological age-related changes. Young adults are quite accurate in discriminating colors; they are able to see differences in up to 100,000 colors (Garzia & Trick, 1992). With age, color and brightness sensitivity declines, affecting the eye's ability to adapt to changing levels of light and dark. Older adults may find it particularly challenging to find open seats in a theater because it takes longer for their eyes to adjust.

One of the most common measures of vision is the Snellen chart, used to assess visual acuity, the sharpness of vision, through accurate discrimination of high-contrast letters. Visual acuity remains relatively stable until the late 60s (Weymouth, 1960). Although visual acuity is the most common method of assessing vision, contrast sensitivity provides a better overall assessment of an individual's vision (Garzia & Trick, 1992). **Contrast sensitivity** is the amount of contrast necessary to discriminate between an image and its background. Contrast sensitivity peaks at age 20 years and declines thereafter. Contrast sensitivity is an important factor for many motor skills. An individual who requires more time to detect the position of a ball will likely not make contact with it.

Eye movement control also declines with age, causing further difficulty with tracking moving objects and **visual search**, the act of directing attention towards important cues in the environment. Visual search is an important factor in moving skillfully. Skilled performers' decision-making abilities and reaction time are dependent on their visual search strategies. Effective visual search strategies can be developed. Instruction and feedback should direct the learner to the most important critical cues. For example, experts tend to fixate their visual gaze on the most important aspect of the movement, while novices tend to alter their visual gaze. **Fixation** is the focusing of visual attention on an object (Coker, 2009). By looking at unimportant cues, people can often miss important information. Shank and Haywood (1987) found that during the windup of a baseball pitch, expert baseball players fixated on the release point while novices alternated between the release point and the head. Experts were able to identify the pitch nearly 100% of the time, while novices identified the pitch only 60% of the time. It is important to focus on the critical cues, such as the release point, but just as important to ignore irrelevant cues such as the head (Coker, 2009). With age, visual search can become increasingly difficult, not only compromising skillful performance, but also affecting everyday activities such as identifying street signs or locating house numbers (Garzia & Trick, 1992).

Older adults begin to experience difficulty with driving and mobility. Driving at nighttime can be particularly challenging for an older adult due to increased problems with glare and night vision. The issue of driving in old adulthood has evoked a lot of controversy, as driving provides the primary mode of transportation for most Americans. Although driving ability is a complex motor skill dependent on many factors including attentional focus, coordination, reaction time, processing speed, and sensory information, vision is one of the most important factors affecting driving performance. Twice as many older adults with peripheral deficits experienced accidents and conviction rates as older drivers without peripheral field deficits. Dynamic visual acuity is also a risk factor for driving accidents in older adults (Owsley & Ball, 1993).

Try This

The Amsler grid screening test is used to detect diseases of the retina such as macular degeneration. Macular degeneration causes a loss of vision in the central visual field due to damage to the retina. This loss can make facial recognition or reading nearly impossible. When taking the test, wear glasses or contacts if you typically wear them. Here's how to take this test:

1. In a well-lit room, hold up the book with the picture of the Amsler grid at eye level approximately 15 inches (38 centimeters) away.
2. Look at the dot in the center of the grid.
3. While maintaining your gaze, cover your right eye and continue to look at the dot.
4. Repeat this test covering the left eye.

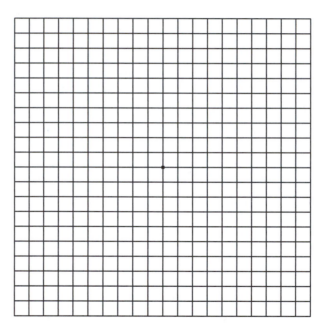

Did you notice any changes, such as the dot disappearing or the squares blurring or changing shape? A yes answer to any of these questions would indicate damage to the retina and possible macular degeneration. Macular degeneration is a serious condition that could result in legal blindness if not treated.

Auditory System

Hearing losses generally begin in the mid-30s but can occur earlier or can be exacerbated by an overexposure to environmental noise. Hearing loss that occurs from environmental noise is termed noise-induced hearing loss (NIHL). Losses of higher-pitch tones are very common and begin to occur in adults as early as age 18 years. This loss, termed **presbycusis**, occurs as a result of hardening auditory nerve cells. High-pitched ring tones, such as the mosquito ring tone Teen Buzz, have been designed specifically for teenagers, and most adults over the age of 20 years (including their teachers) cannot hear them.

Females tend to have markedly better hearing than males beginning at the age of 40 years (Schieber, 1992). This gender difference may be due in part to increased environmental noise in many male-dominated occupations. Hearing loss continues in both males and females throughout middle and older adulthood. Many older adults experience an inability to hear not only high-pitch tones but also some lower-pitch tones, making it increasingly difficult for them to maintain conversations in noisy environments.

Kinesthetic Perception

Unlike the situation with the visual system, knowledge on the extent of age-related changes in kinesthetic perception is limited. There is conflicting evidence on the changes in body and spatial awareness with age, with some reports showing age-related declines and others not (Gabbard, 2004). One common change in kinesthetic perception is a reduction in tactile sensitivity. The lower extremities tend to be more affected than the upper extremities (Corso, 1987); however, reduced sensitivity in the lower extremities may be attributed to other factors such diabetes, circulatory functions, or injuries (Gabbard, 2004). The loss of tactile sensitivity is due to an age-related decline in the number of touch receptors in the skin. A progressive loss of sensitivity to pain and temperature also occurs with age (Kenshalo, 1977). Reduced vestibular function, which negatively impacts balance, begins in the 30s. The vestibular system, located in the middle ear, provides information regarding head position and movement. Deficits in the vestibular system can cause dizziness and **vertigo**, a balance disorder that can vary from dizziness and vomiting to difficulties with standing and walking.

Summary

Aging is a unique experience for every individual. It is affected by genetic factors, behavioral lifestyle, and past experiences. These factors interact, causing each individual to age at a different rate. And not only do adults age differently from one another; their physiological systems age at different rates. Adults may experience faster rates of decline in their cardiovascular system than in their endocrine or nervous system.

This chapter outlined age-related body system changes in the skeletal, muscular, cardiovascular, nervous, endocrine, and sensory systems. These are physiological changes that are due to healthy aging (primary aging) and not the result of disease or the effects of the environment (secondary aging). Although a physically active lifestyle can slow or delay many of these age-related declines, they are inevitable. The rate of decline in many areas increases at the age of 75 years. Healthy, physically active adults experience similar rates of decline beyond this age in most areas but are starting at higher levels, enabling them to maintain their physical function much longer than their sedentary peers.

Maintaining a physically active lifestyle is a key ingredient in sustaining a higher quality of life. Regardless of a person's age, a physically active lifestyle reduces an individual's risk of many secondary diseases, decreases the symptoms of secondary diseases, and improves physical and cognitive function. Clinicians, physical educators, fitness instructors, and coaches who work with older adults must understand the effects of aging on the physiologic systems and the impact that these changes have on movement. There is much more variability across individuals in older populations than in children and adolescents, so it is perhaps even more important for programs to be individualized for older than for younger adults.

Supplemental Activities

1. Experience what it's like to live with some of the age-related changes discussed in this chapter.

- To induce visual deficits, wear dark sunglasses or a blindfold. Wear them for one full hour, preferably in the morning, and try to go about your normal routine—dressing, brushing your teeth, eating, and so on.

- Wear earplugs to induce common age-related hearing deficits. Call your friend on the phone. Watch television.

- Many older adults experience reduced sensation, tingling, or pain in their feet. Place popcorn kernels in your shoes to experience reduced sensation and possible tingling in your feet. Go for a walk with the kernels in your shoes. Walk up and down steps. See how this can affect your normal routine. How did it affect your gait?

- Place your hands in very cold water until they feel comfortably numb. Take them out and try to feed yourself. Try to pour yourself a drink. Write your name.

- Wrap your knees and elbows with athletic tape prewrap. Do not wrap so tightly that you lose sensation or cannot move your limbs, but tightly enough that your range of motion is limited but not painful. Do a variety of exercises with the prewrap on, such as arm curl, squat, military press, and flexibility exercises.

Describe your experiences with each. What surprised you about each? What would you do to adapt to these changes if they were permanent?

2. Our visual system is so dominant that we must compromise vision in order to force the use of other sensory systems to contribute to our balance. Ways to compromise vision include decreasing the lighting in a room or turning off the lights completely, or wearing dark sunglasses or a blindfold. Ways to distract people's vision include having them watch a moving object and requiring them to read aloud or catch objects. Activities that force individuals to use their somatosensory system can be very beneficial to those who have somatosensory deficits such as a progressive or permanent loss of sensation in the feet. Try the following exercises. To force the system to focus on somatosensory information, perform these activities on a broad, firm surface, and compromise your vision (e.g., wear a blindfold, be in a dark room, read something, and so on).

- Sit on a balance ball while extending arms out to the sides. Keep your feet hip-width apart and feet flat on the ground. With eyes closed, focus on the pressure in the buttocks and feet.

- Move your trunk in a circular motion, leaning as far as possible in all directions with eyes closed. Notice the changing pressure in the buttocks and feet.

- Throw various objects to someone else while the person is moving in a circular pattern on the balance ball.
- Stand on one foot with your heel raised, the other foot resting behind your knee, and your arms at your hips. How long can you maintain this position with your eyes open? How long can you maintain this position with your eyes closed?

3. Research one of the following conditions: osteoporosis, arthritis, cardio-vascular disease, hypertension, or stroke. In an essay, describe this condition and how it differs from primary aging—age-related changes that are not due to disease or poor behavioral practices such as smoking, sedentary lifestyles, or obesity. Explain if and how this condition could have been prevented through behavioral changes.

CHAPTER ELEVEN

Functional Constraints in Adulthood

CHAPTER OBJECTIVES

After reading this chapter, you should be able to

> explain psychosocial constraints in adulthood;

> identify the adulthood stages in Erikson's psychosocial development theory;

> demonstrate an understanding of self-regulation, including Kirschenbaum's self-regulation model and self-regulation strategies;

> identify psychological and sociocultural factors of development in adulthood; and

> describe age-related changes in cognitive function.

Winning Is a State of Mind

"As [Bjorn] Borg took his position for the fifth set, he said to himself, 'This is terrible. I'm going to lose.' But then thought, 'If you lose a match like this, the Wimbledon final, after all those chances, you will not forget it for a long, long time. That could be very hard.' It was his serve to start the last set. He lost the first two points. 'But then,' Borg recalls, 'I say to myself, "I have to forget. I have to keep trying, try to win".' He served the next point and won. And again and again" (Deford, 1980).

The mind can have a very powerful influence on performance. Negative thoughts can not only prevent improvement but can be the downfall of even the most skilled athletes. Maintaining positive thinking and clearing the mind can provide athletes with large advantages. Performance in adulthood is affected by many functional constraints, including psychological, sociological, and cognitive factors. This chapter extends the functional constraints discussed in chapters 7 and 8 to adulthood, including several important psychosocial constraints: self-efficacy, self-regulation, motivation, Erik Erikson's psychosocial development theory (adulthood stages), sociocultural factors and social support, and age-related changes in cognitive function including attention and memory.

Psychosocial Constraints

Changing self-perceptions and declining physical abilities related to aging can affect social interaction and social approval, which can, in turn, significantly affect mental health and well-being. There is much evidence to support the benefits of physical exercise for adults, physically, psychologically, and socially (Spirduso, Francis, & MacRae, 2005). Participation in group physical activities can be particularly beneficial, improving fitness levels, sense of well-being, and mood (Biddle, Fox, & Boutcher, 2000). Many of these health benefits result from the psychosocial benefits of participating in recreational physical activity and sport.

Psychological Factors

Numerous psychological factors interact with the physical domain. Most of the research has focused on exercise adherence, including intention to exercise, self-efficacy, and locus of control. Older adults experience different barriers to exercise than children and adolescents. Motivational factors also change throughout adulthood from a focus on weight management and appearance to health and the maintenance of physical function.

Intention to Exercise

One of the greatest factors affecting exercise adherence is simply an individual's *intention* to exercise. According to the **theory of planned behavior (TBA)**, attitudes toward a behavior are dependent on two factors, (1) the belief that the behavior will produce a specified outcome and (2) the individual's desire for attaining the specified outcome (Ajzen, 1985). Adults who do not place much value and importance on exercise are much less likely to adhere to a regular exercise program (Jette et al., 1998; Michels & Kugler, 1998). This is particularly important in older adults, as positive attitudes toward exercise behavior decreases with age (Wilcox & Storandt, 1996). In a survey conducted by Stephens and Craig (1990), 58% of adults over the age of 65 years indicated that nothing could cause them to increase their exercise behavior. For health care and especially fitness professionals, this is a disheartening statistic. Since many older adults express no intentions of changing their exercise behavior, improving older adults' attitudes toward physical activity is a critical factor in improving exercise behavior (Hausenblas, Carron, & Mack, 1997).

Self-Efficacy

Self-efficacy is also one of the most important factors when people adopt an exercise program (McAuley, 1992). **Self-efficacy**, which is very similar to a "situation-specific form of self-confidence" (Weinberg & Gould, 2003, p. 316), is the belief that an individual has the capability to perform a desired behavior leading to anticipated outcomes (Bandura, 1997). According to **Bandura's social cognitive theory**, self-efficacy determines (1) if an individual is even going to attempt a task; (2) how persistent an individual will be amid challenges; and (3) the final outcome, successful maintenance of an exercise program or failure to adhere to the program. Older adults have significantly lower self-efficacy than young adults, many perceiving reduced control in exercise behavior (Dishman, 1994) and increased fear of injury resulting from physical activity (Stephens & Craig, 1990).

Locus of Control

Locus of control is "the extent to which people believe that they have control over their own fate" (Thomas, Sorensen, & Abby, 2006, p. 1057). Individuals who believe they have some personal control over their health are more likely to adhere to an exercise program. Correlational research on older women and men has indicated that an internal locus of control is positively related to hours of exercise (Bonds, 1980). Individuals with an **internal locus of control** believe that their actions affect the environment, whereas individuals with an **external locus of control** believe that their actions do not affect the environment and that events happen by chance. It is not surprising, then, that individuals with an external locus of control are less likely to adhere to an exercise program. If they do not believe exercise can change the way they look and feel, why would they continue?

Barriers to Exercise

Adults have reported many barriers to exercise in American surveys (Dishman, Sallis, & Orenstein, 1985). The most commonly reported barriers were the same for both exercisers and nonexercisers, including lack of time, laziness, and work responsibilities. Since those who exercise and those who do not reported the same most common exercise barriers, it is likely that these findings reflect *perceived* barriers, such as personal priorities, rather than *actual* barriers. Adults who place a higher priority on exercise or do not perceive the barriers to be insurmountable are much more likely to continue exercising in spite of them. Adults who do not make exercise a priority may be using these external barriers as a method to avoid a physically active lifestyle (Valois, Shephard, & Godin, 1986). Women have been found to report more barriers than men (Stephens & Craig, 1990). It is likely that these barriers were perceived rather than actual barriers. Although women reported that health and physical activity were a high priority, the reasons for the importance of physical activity varied. Older women reported that the social aspects of exercise were more important, while young women were generally more concerned with exercise as a method to control weight. Older adults also reported accessibility, exertion, and safety as barriers to exercise (Shephard, 1994) and were less interested in challenging or competitive activities (Stephens & Craig, 1990).

To implement a successful exercise program, it is important to understand the greatest barriers to exercise. If practitioners focus older adults' attention on the benefits of exercise and reduce their perception of exercise barriers, older adults are more likely to maintain a physically active lifestyle (Rhodes et al., 1999).

What Do You Think?

For each of the following examples, list (1) several possible barriers to exercise and (2) strategies for removing these barriers.

- A 25-year-old female with little previous movement experience who does not exercise
- A 44-year-old male who played a lot of sports in high school and college but has not exercised or participated in sports since college
- A 70-year-old female who exhibits interest in going to the gym but is intimidated by all of the equipment

Motivation

Motivation is a set of reasons that determines an individual's behavior. Motivation is not necessarily present or not. It isn't just turned on or off like a light switch. It exists along a continuum (figure 11.1), including amotivation, non-self-determined extrinsic motivation, self-determined extrinsic motivation, and intrinsic motivation (Dacey, Baltzell, & Zalchkowsky, 2008). **Amotivation** is a complete lack of motivation. An individual who has no desire to engage in any type of exercise or physical activity would be considered amotivated. **Nonself-determined extrinsic motivation** is present when an individual's behavior is based on avoiding immediate negative consequences. An individual may exercise intensely for a short period of time to look good on the beach but quit exercising following the trip. **Self-determined extrinsic motivation** is characterized by behavior that is performed for extrinsic reasons. The main difference between non-self-determined motivation and self-determined extrinsic motivation is that the extrinsic reasons are personally valued and the outcomes are generally viewed as favorable or positive, as when someone practices yoga to reduce stress. With **intrinsic motivation**, behaviors are performed for the personal interest in and enjoyment of engaging in the activity.

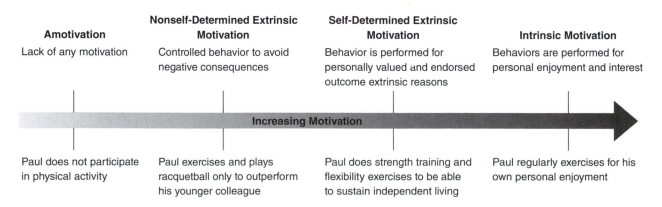

FIGURE 11.1 Motivation continuum showing an example of an older adult's motivation for participating in physical activity.

Dacey and colleagues (2008) found that the amount of physical activity older adults engage in is affected by their type of motivation for exercise. Intrinsic and self-determined extrinsic motivation is positively correlated with increased physical activity. Self-determined extrinsic motivators included health and fitness, stress management, and social–emotional benefits. Weight management and appearance were considered non-self-determined extrinsic motivators as they reflect a desire to attain social approval or an enhancement of the ego. The results of this study revealed that appearance and weight management were unaffected by the amount of motivation and that appearance became less important with advancing age, indicating that weight management and appearance are the least likely motivators to induce long-term behavior change. Better motivators for an older adult to increase physical activity levels could include the social benefits of a game of tennis with a friend or a group exercise class, or the fitness benefits of increasing flexibility through stretching exercises.

 What Do You Think?

Classify each of the following adults according to their type of motivation toward physical activity (amotivation, nonself-determined extrinsic motivation, self-determined extrinsic motivation, intrinsic motivation).

- Harvey is a 53-year-old male who regularly plays racquetball games at the local recreation center. Even though the games are noncompetitive, Harvey is very competitive when he plays. Outside of racquetball games, Harvey does not participate in any form of regular physical activity or exercise.

- Jessica is an extremely active 32-year-old who exercises six or seven times per week and regularly competes in local and regional races. She thoroughly enjoys the "highs" she feels from both her workouts and the competitions.

- Peter is a 68-year-old man who has recently started an exercise program incorporating resistance training, cardio, and stretching. Peter began the exercise program so that he could maintain his functionality and reduce age-related physical declines.

- Devise an example of an individual who would fit the fourth type of motivation.

Self-Regulation

All adults, regardless of age, health, or fitness levels, need self-regulation skills. The importance of self-regulatory skills is not limited to athletic adults trying to improve or maintain their skills. These skills are also important for the inactive adult who is trying to initiate and adhere to an exercise program or for the injured adult who is going through rehabilitation. **Self-regulation** is "a complex process whereby athletes, patients, or exercisers engage in voluntary goal-directed behaviors over time and context by initiating, monitoring, sustaining, and achieving certain thoughts, feelings, and behaviors" (Weiss, 2004, p. 385). Through management of short- and long-term goals, adults self-regulate their behavior in both exercise and sport. Adults who decide to start an exercise program, improve their skills, or recover from an injury through a rehabilitation program go through a series of steps, as depicted in Kirschenbaum's self-regulation process, to achieve the necessary self-regulation skills. It is important for practitioners to understand these steps to help facilitate self-regulation skills in their students, patients, or athletes.

Research Notes: What Do Experts Do Differently?

A study was conducted to compare the self-regulatory processes of novice, nonexpert, and expert volleyball players (Kitsantas & Zimmerman, 2002). Thirty female university students participated in the study. The experts were university varsity volleyball team players; the nonexperts played in a volleyball club; and the novices had played volleyball only informally. The experts used more self-control strategies, such as self-instruction, imagery, attention focusing, and task-specific strategies than the nonexperts and the novices. Experts prepared their serves with more forethought and set more specific process goals than the other two groups. The novices did not even report any goals. Focusing on technique as exhibited in the expert players can be beneficial to the learner in decreasing the amount of time required to learn a motor skill (Locke & Latham, 1990).

More time was spent on self-reflection in the experts than the nonexperts or the novices. Self-reflection is essential to improve performance of a motor skill. The experts were much more likely to attribute their errors to improper form or technique (e.g., "It was a bad toss"), enabling them to appropriately self-correct for the subsequent serve. Only half of the nonexperts and none of the novices attributed their errors to form or technique, instead attributing their poor serves to insufficient power.

Experts also spent more time preparing for the serves, including three components in their preparation: warm-ups, pepper drills, and specific skill training. Nonexperts included only one of these components, and novices did not include any. Experts spent significantly more time reflecting on their performances and were more likely to adapt their serves than the other two groups. Furthermore, the experts were more likely to seek assistance from coaches or teammates. It is perhaps not surprising that the novices were unlikely to seek assistance. Even the nonexperts, who played on a team through a club, were only moderately likely to seek help. Seeking help is not a sign of weakness on the part of the athlete; rather, it is an essential element of self-regulation. Athletes must focus on their errors and self-initiate assistance.

Understanding how experts, nonexperts, and novices differ in their self-regulatory behavior can help instructors preparing self-directed practice. At minimum, instructors should encourage their learners to set specific goals and self-reflect on their performances. They should also be encouraged to seek assistance when they notice errors that they cannot correct.

Kirschenbaum's Self-Regulation Process Kirschenbaum (1984) developed a five-stage model of self-regulation (figure 11.2). The first stage is the **problem identification stage**. During this stage, adults must not only identify the problem, such as a need to improve their softball game or to start an exercise program, but also decide whether the change is possible and worth the effort. It is during stage 1 that the individual must be willing to take responsibility for solving the problem. Stage 2 is the **commitment stage**. The person must be willing to make the sacrifices that are necessary to persevere through the process.

Once a commitment has been made, the individual moves to the **execution stage**. Stage 3 is the active stage of behavioral change. During this stage, individuals must develop self-expectancies for success through goal setting and continually self-evaluate and self-monitor their performance with respect to these goals. In addition to goal setting, they should plan methods to reinforce continued improvement and potentially even punishment for deviating from goal attainment. An athlete trying to improve his swim for triathlons might set a goal to swim 40 minutes, four times per week, or to decrease his swim time by 10% by the next competition. He could log when he swims and the duration and distance of each swim. If his goals are met, he could reward himself by buying new gear or an athletic watch. In therapy settings, physical and occupational therapists work closely with their patients during the execution phase, developing goals with them and continually evaluating their progress.

The fourth stage is the **environmental management stage**. In this stage, adults prepare strategies to deal with potential environmental or social barriers that may prevent them from attaining their goals. The triathlete may schedule some practices in open water but have an indoor pool option as a backup during inclement weather. Social barriers could also affect performances or practices. For instance, if an individual relies on a friend for moral support to exercise, she could lose motivation when her friend decides to cancel a workout session. Having backup plans, such as other people to walk with or group exercise classes to participate in, could help prevent this change from affecting one's exercise routine. Therapists must also work with patients to help set up their home environment, providing them with the knowledge and equipment they need to continue their treatments at home.

Stage 5 is the **generalization stage**. During this stage individuals focus on sustaining their efforts for long periods of time. They may change some of their goals. For instance, the triathlete may start to notice that his swim times have improved but may need to focus on his run. Or he may want to increase his strength and then begin a weightlifting program. An adult who has successfully adhered to her exercise program may want to shift her focus to improving her diet while continuing her exercise program. Therapists may help patients develop an at-home plan to continue their treatments after their program has been completed.

The five stages in Kirschenbaum's (1984) model interact with one another. Each stage is flexible in that the stages are continually changing and evolving with the individual. Kirschenbaum emphasizes the importance of self-monitoring in self-regulation. People must continually evaluate their performance and progress with their goals. Self-regulation is also strongly influenced by personality styles and dispositions. Optimistic individuals with high self-esteem are much more stable and likely to continue self-regulatory behavior, while pessimistic people with low self-esteem are more likely to see changing social and environmental conditions as barriers to continuing with the program (Waschall & Kernis, 1996).

Stage 1: Problem Identification Stage
Sierra needs to improve her golf drive.

Stage 2: Commitment Stage
Sierra is willing to make the sacrifices necessary to relearn how to perform a drive in golf.

Stage 3: Execution Stage
Sierra sets goals and monitors her progress.

Stage 4: Environmental Management Stage
Alternative practice locations are found for possible inclement weather.

Stage 5: Generalization Stage
Goals are reevaluated. Sierra may now focus on other aspects of her game.

FIGURE 11.2
Kirschenbaum's five-stage model of self-regulation.

What Do You Think?

1. How would a recreational hockey goalie likely differ in his self-regulatory strategies from a Division I hockey goalie?
2. What self-regulatory skills would you encourage the novice to focus on?

Self-Regulation Strategies   Although there are many self-regulation strategies, the most commonly used are self-monitoring, goal setting, self-talk, and imagery (Weiss, 2004). Self-monitoring and goal setting are critical skills in self-regulation, as they keep individuals focused to attain their desired performance change. We are almost constantly engaging in some form of self-talk. Therefore, regulating self-talk has a strong influence on all of our behaviors, from sport performance to social situations. Imagery can also be a powerful form of self-regulation. It can improve performance and assist in controlling emotion.

- *Self-monitoring.* Self-monitoring is the systematic observation of oneself (Kirschenbaum, 1987). Methods of self-monitoring include recording behaviors or performances and making self-observations. Performances can also be self-monitored through the use of a tangible item, as when someone puts a nickel into a jar for every mistake. The purpose of self-monitoring is to make one more aware of one's behaviors, which can not only help improve performance but also decrease anxiety and boost confidence (Crews, Lochbaum, & Karoly, 2000). Self-monitoring can be either positive or negative. Positive self-monitoring requires individuals to record successful performances, while negative self-monitoring is the recording of poor performances. Research has shown that positive self-monitoring is beneficial for difficult tasks, enhancing the performer's expectancies and improving performance. Well-learned or simple tasks benefit more from negative self-monitoring, such as focusing on failures and mistakes (Kirschenbaum, 1987).

- *Goal setting.* Perhaps the most critical self-regulation skill is goal setting. Setting goals focuses the learner's attention on attaining a set level of proficiency. It is especially important to set specific and measurable goals that must be achieved by a predetermined time point; for example, an athlete may set a goal of throwing 10% farther by the first meet of the track and field season. Goals that either are not specific or cannot be measured are ineffective. Goals are further discussed in chapter 13.

- *Self-talk.* Another useful self-regulation skill is the management of self-talk. Considering that people engage in a lot of self-talk every day, it is not surprising that managing self-talk can assist in regulating behavior. Athletes may say to themselves "I can't do this," "I am the worst player," or "I'm going to mess this up." On the flip side, athletes may engage in positive self-talk, as Borg did in the example at the beginning of this chapter: "I have to forget. I have to keep trying, try to win." Managing self-talk can help divert individuals from negative, unproductive thoughts to productive positive thinking. Positive self-talk can have many benefits, including improving confidence, increasing motivation, correcting bad habits, and focusing attention (Williams & Leffingwell, 1996). Self-talk management strategies include stopping self-talk that is negative or irrational; changing negative self-talk to positive self-talk; internally reasoning to counter negative self-talk; and "reframing," which is changing one's perspective on a situation (Zinsser, Bunker, & Williams, 2001).

- ***Imagery.* Imagery** is the visualization or cognitive rehearsal of a movement. It has been found to be a very effective self-regulation skill and performance enhancer. Imagery provides additional rehearsal of the movement pattern and can be implemented as part of a regular practice schedule. Imagery benefits self-regulation in a variety of ways. Imagery training helps direct attention to the movement, promotes self-monitoring, and assists with positive self-reinforcement (Kirschenbaum, 1987). Chapter 14 further discusses imagery, including basic guidelines for effective imagery training.

 Try This

VISUALIZING SIMPLE OBJECTS

The ability to visualize images and scenes takes time and practice. When you first attempt imagery, it is best to simply practice visualizing stationary objects. For instance, look closely at an object in the room. Familiarize yourself with the characteristics of this object, including its size, shape, color, and texture. Now close your eyes and try to visualize the object. Try to replicate all of the details that you noticed with your eyes open. Then open your eyes and compare your image with the object. Were you able to easily visualize this object? Were there details that you missed? Next, try visualizing an object in another room without looking at it first. After visualizing the object, go into that room and compare your image with the actual object. Did your visualization closely resemble the object?

VISUALIZING YOURSELF COMPLETING DAILY ACTIVITIES

The next step in imagery training is to practice controlling images of your movements in the environment. It is best to start with simple activities such as your morning routine. Close your eyes and imagine yourself lying in your bed. You then hear your alarm sound. What does it sound like? How does your body react to the alarm? Then follow your normal morning routine in your mind. What do you do next? Be sure to include all of your senses. What does your shampoo smell like? How does the water feel on your skin? Can you hear the sound of the shower?

VISUALIZING YOURSELF IN A COMPETITIVE EVENT

Once you can control images in a simpler environment, you can practice imagery for a more complex environment such as a competitive event. During this practice, begin by imagining the entire scene before the competition even begins. What are the sights, sounds, and smells? Continue through the entire event. Try to control the outcome. It is important that you visualize yourself performing well, as this will increase confidence and motivation. If you find yourself having difficulties with controlling the images or if you seem to visualize poor performances, go back and practice visualizing simple objects and movements. Imagery is a learned skill, and developing this capability may take some practice.

Questions

1. How vivid were your images? Which details seemed vivid? Which aspects were not part of the image?
2. Did you incorporate all of your senses (sight, sound, smell, touch)?
3. Were you able to control your movements and the outcome?
4. Did you use internal imagery or external imagery? You use **internal imagery** when you view things as though through your own eyes. You use **external imagery** when you imagine you are an external observer watching yourself.

Sociocultural Factors

Social and cultural influences on physical activity behaviors continue across the life span. Many sociocultural expectations are still present throughout adulthood. Prior to adulthood, the primary socializing factors are from home and school settings. The dominant socializing influences during adulthood include the media; significant others; friends; and community members, including instructors and health professionals (Gabbard, 2004). Physical activity and sport participation are also largely affected by life cycle changes including marriage, children, careers, retirement, and other transitions (Mihalik, O'Leary, Mcguire, & Dottavio, 1989).

The media continues to have a powerful influence on young and middle-aged adults. During young adulthood, peak performance is attained. It is common for many adults to continually test their physical abilities during this stage. On the other hand, many adults do not engage in physical activities because they feel they are already very healthy. They are not concerned with the lifelong benefits of physical activity. Once this attitude is established, it can be difficult to overcome, especially as adults begin to decline physically (Gabbard, 2004). When adults begin to approach middle adulthood, around the age of 35 to 40 years, many become increasingly concerned with their physical abilities and appearance. One of the main causes of these heightened concerns is the media, which often emphasizes youth, beauty, and vitality. On a positive note, the media has also flooded society with educational information on healthy behaviors through advertisements, websites, and community medical professionals and clinics. This increased promotion of healthy behaviors and focus on youthful appearance have had a very positive impact on young and middle-aged adults' attitudes toward physical activity. Now more than ever before, people are realizing the benefits of a physically active lifestyle, including decreased risks for cardiovascular disease, high cholesterol, high blood pressure, and type 2 diabetes.

Unfortunately, a certain level of ageism still exists (refer to chapter 9) in today's society. Ageism, the stereotyping of older adults based on their age, includes decreased expectations of older adults professionally, physically, or cognitively. These negative perceptions devalue older adults, often affecting their opportunities, choices, and lifestyles. An older adult who is expected to become increasingly sedentary with age is likely to fulfill that prophecy.

Social Theories of Aging

There are two main theories of aging: activity theory and disengagement theory. **Activity theory** suggests that adults who maintain social interactions and active lifestyles can not only maintain their life satisfaction but may even increase it (Schaie & Willis, 1991; Rook, 2000). **Disengagement theory** asserts that older adults must gradually withdraw from society by participating in fewer activities and decreasing their personal relationships. Disengagement theory suggests that it is important for older adults to separate themselves from society in order to maintain their integrity by accepting their changing status and physical decline. Since participation in physical activity often involves different forms of social interaction, increased physical activity would be considered counterproductive according to the disengagement theory because it asserts that older adults need to *decrease* personal relationships. Activity theory, however, suggests that active and productive lifestyles are necessary to sustain happy and satisfying lives. Physical activity often involves social interaction, helping older adults to remain attached rather than detaching from society (Gallahue & Ozmun, 2005). Activity theory also asserts that adults should continue their roles throughout their lifetime. If they discontinue a particular activity, for example when they retire, they should find other activities to replace it.

Social Support

Perceived social support of family, friends, and community members is a significant factor in older adults' exercise adherence (Chogahara, O'Brien Cousins, & Wankel, 1998). Individuals who provide social support and affect

Research Notes: My Friend Laura

The role of social influences is unquestionably important in older adults' adherence to exercise. However, as previously mentioned, many older adults do not receive much, if any, social support. Many live alone and are fairly isolated from society. With today's technology, it is not surprising that computer-animated images have been designed to interact with adults to motivate them to increase their daily physical activity. These computer-animated images, termed relational agents, are designed to not only motivate the user but also to build long-term social–emotional relationships with users.

Bickmore and colleagues (2005) conducted a two-month study with 21 adults between the ages of 62 and 84 years to examine whether a relational agent would be effective in increasing the daily number of steps walked versus the number in a control group. The relational agent maintained conversations with the participants, encouraged them to be physically active, and discussed their progress. The results revealed that the relational agent, Laura, was effective in increasing the older adults' physical activity levels. According to some of the participants, not only was Laura effective in motivating them to increase their physical activity, but they also formed a social bond with her. The relational agent "may be an ideal platform to provide an effective automated health educator with unbounded patience and empathy for . . . patients" (Bickmore et al., 2005, p. 733).

The following is part of a sample conversation between a user (U) and the relational agent (A):

A: Hello, Bertha. Great to see you.

U: Hi, Laura.

A: How are you feeling today?

U: I'm not feeling so great.

A: I am sorry to hear that. Tell me more about how you are feeling.

U: I'm tired.

A: How tired are you feeling?

U: I'm pretty beat.

A: Good grief, I hope you're not getting sick. Can you get some rest soon?

U: I think so.

A: That is great. I hope you come back feeling refreshed.

U: Me too!

A: So, are you from the East Coast originally?

an individual's adherence to a healthy lifestyle, including physical activity, are termed **socializing agents**. Socializing agents change across the lifespan, with parents being the primary socializing agents during infancy and childhood, and peers being the primary socializing agents for adults. When compared to younger adults, older adults have a poor social network (Stephens & Craig, 1990). Ageism may contribute to reduced social support from the family, and peers are often less active themselves. Due to the decreased support of older adults, it is especially important to encourage physical activities that involve social interaction. Older adults with mutual interest in a particular activity are more likely to encourage each other and feel compelled to continue participating.

 What Do You Think?

Using this chart, write down the three biggest sociocultural influences (i.e., primary socializing agents) that affected your physical activity participation, with 1 being the most important socializing agent. Examples: parents, teachers, coaches, peers, media, significant others, community members (doctors, medical professionals, instructors). Discuss your primary socializing agents during your childhood, adolescence, and those that most influence you currently. Then try to predict who will be your biggest sociocultural influences 30 years from now.

	Childhood	Adolescence	Currently	In 30 years
1.				
2.				
3.				

Compare these socializing agents.

- How did they change with increasing age?
- Do you think your answers are specific to your generation? Explain.
- Would you expect them to have been different 100 years ago? Explain your answer.
- Do you expect socializing agents to change for future generations?

Erikson's Psychosocial Development Theory: Adulthood Stages

As discussed in chapter 8, Erik Erikson's psychosocial theory (1963, 1980) on human development consists of eight stages. Each stage is represented by a conflict that must be resolved before the individual may advance to the next stage. It is unlikely that people will "perfect" a stage, yet resolving each stage increases their likelihood for further progress with advanced stages. Table 11.1 provides a summary of Erik Erikson's last three stages of psychosocial development (Erikson, 1963). (See table 8.1 on p. 165 for all eight stages.) The first five stages, which have to do with psychosocial development from infancy to early adolescence, were discussed in chapter 8. This section describes the final

TABLE 11.1 Erikson's Psychosocial Stages of Development

Approximate age	Stage of psychosocial conflict
20 to 40 years	Intimacy versus isolation
40 to 65 years	Generativity versus stagnation
65 and over	Ego integrity versus despair

Adapted from E.H. Erikson, 1963, *Childhood and society*, 2nd ed. (New York: W.W. Norton), 263-269.

three stages of psychosocial development during adulthood, beginning in late adolescence. We also consider implications for motor development.

- ***Intimacy versus isolation.*** Erikson believed that during young adulthood (ages 19-40 years), people focus on exploring personal relationships. During this stage of life, it is vital for people to form personal and committed relationships. Young adulthood is a transitional period of time. Young adults acquire more responsibilities and liberties than they had during childhood and early adolescence, moving out of their parents' homes and making their own decisions. This experience is often quite liberating and allows young adults to better understand who they are as individuals and how they fit with and influence other people. Young adults also form relationships through group recreational and sporting experiences. Individuals who cannot work cooperatively in a team may feel a sense of isolation, whereas those who can develop relationships with the team or group members will likely feel a greater sense of intimacy with the group. Keep in mind that Erikson's psychosocial stages are like building blocks. One must be in place before the next one is formed. Individuals must form their own identity, during adolescence, stage 5, before they will be able to develop intimate relationships. Young adults who have not developed a strong sense of self will have less committed relationships and are likely to feel lonely and isolated.

- ***Generativity versus stagnation.*** During adulthood (ages 40-65 years), Erikson believes that people's focus shifts to career and family. Adults during this stage are less interested in their own problems and more interested in how they can affect future generations, either by nurturing their own children, by helping other children through education or other support, or by having a positive influence on society. Adults interested in movement and physical activity may focus on improving society by increasing physical fitness, or by passing on to their peers or even future generations the self-fulfillment of involvement in physical activities including recreation and sport. Adults who shift their concentration from self-interests to the interests of others during this stage will feel fulfilled in that they have contributed to future generations either through their home or community or globally. Successful adults will experience feelings of usefulness and accomplishment, while adults who fail during this stage will have a shallow sense of self. Self-absorbed adults will experience increased difficulties dealing with their changing capabilities through middle and old adulthood.

- ***Integrity versus despair.*** The final Erikson psychosocial stage occurs during late adulthood (beyond 65 years). This stage is marked by individuals' reflection on their lives. Successful adults in this stage are able to reflect back with a sense of fulfillment while adults who fail at this stage experience much regret, leaving them feeling bitterness and despair. Adults who are able to reflect on their life with a feeling of accomplishment and sense of satisfaction will attain a sense of integrity. Successful adults at this stage will also gain a sense of wisdom reaching beyond their own life. In the movement domain, those who are successful can adapt their movements to their changing capabilities, enabling them to sustain an independent lifestyle. Rather than feeling despair about their declining functional capabilities, they maintain an active lifestyle, continuing to walk, swim, play tennis, or stay involved in other recreational or sport activities. This allows them a much greater freedom and enjoyment of life. Adults who sustain active lifestyles have accepted their changing physical capabilities and maintain their competence rather than feeling despair about their declining physical bodies. Furthermore, adults who feel despair often limit their physical activities, causing further physical declines.

Cognitive Function

There are many age-related structural changes in the brain, including a daily loss of thousands of brain cells that progressively decreases the size and weight of the brain. Also many detrimental changes occur within the neurons, including plaques and tangles (refer to chapter 10), affecting cognitive function. In light of the many large structural changes that occur in adulthood, cognition is much less affected. The two most affected cognitive functions by age are attention and memory. Age-related changes in attention and memory are not uniform; some areas are well maintained in older adulthood, while others exhibit substantial declines. Deficits in these areas can have significant effects on sport performance. Older adults may be able to adapt to maintain their performance levels during training sessions but have more difficulties when performing with increased arousal, as during a competition, because their capacities are already impaired.

Attention

Humans are limited by the amount of information they can process at any given period of time. This is referred to as **attentional capacity**. We can attend to or concentrate on only one thing at any moment in time. If people try to process more information than their capacity can hold, **interference** occurs. When an individual attempts to perform two activities at the same time, whether it is juggling while unicycling or simply holding a conversation while walking, interference will occur if attentional capacity is exceeded.

Interference can be either cognitive or structural. When physical structure limits an individual's actions, **structural interference** has occurred. Humans have two hands, which limits the number of activities they can do at any given time with their hands. For instance, typing while catching a ball would cause structural interference. The performance of one activity would be impaired, most likely in this case the typing. The person would have to briefly stop typing to catch and toss the ball before resuming typing. We are also structurally limited by our eyes. We can visually focus on only one thing at a time. It would not be possible for someone to see a pass happening behind him if he was focusing on the defender in front of him. These limitations are not due to attentional capacity but are imposed by our physical body.

If multiple activities can be performed given these structural limitations, then a decrement that occurs is due to a limitation in central capacity, termed **cognitive interference**. Attentional capacity, although limited, is flexible. With practice and increasing skill levels, the attentional capacity necessary to perform a particular skill progressively increases. You may have observed this if you have walked with older adults and noticed that they slowed down their pace when engaged in conversation. Most younger adults can hold conversations while walking without interference, but if the task becomes increasingly difficult, such as answering a difficult question while walking, even young adults' attentional capacities may be exceeded, causing them to either slow down or take longer to answer the question.

 Try This

Ask a friend mathematical questions while you are walking beside him or her. Start out with simple math questions such as simple addition or subtraction. Progressively increase the difficulty of the questions. You will likely notice that your friend decreases his or her pace as the difficulty of the questions increase.

Attention is also selective. **Selective attention** is the ability to focus on selected sensory information while ignoring irrelevant information (Määttä, Pääkkönnen, Saavalainen, & Partanen, 2005). Selective attention can be either intentional or incidental (Eimer, Nattkemper, Schröger, & Prinz, 1996). We can choose to attend to something **(intentional attention)**, such as reading a paper, holding a conversation, or learning to juggle, or our attention is unexpectedly directed to something **(incidental attention)** such as a phone ringing, our name being called, or the sound of the referee's whistle.

Age-Related Changes in Selective Attention

Intentional attention declines with increasing age due to age-related reductions in attentional capacity (Lustig, Hasher, & Tonev, 2001). Because of this reduced attentional capacity, older adults have been referred to as "cognitive misers" because they often focus specifically on one component of a task while ignoring others (Hess, Follett, & McGee, 1998). This is a compensation mechanism. Older adults realize that they have fewer cognitive resources than when they were younger and must focus only on the most relevant information. Older adults' ability to attend is also affected by the time of day; it is significantly worse in the morning than in the afternoon (Lustig & Meck, 2001). For instance, older adults may perform worse in a morning game of tennis than an afternoon game as they are more easily distracted; they attend to irrelevant cues rather than focusing on relevant cues such as the ball speed, the position of the opponent, and the angles of the hits.

What Do You Think?

Looking at the illustration, list all of the activities that the "multitasker" is completing. Give two examples of structural and cognitive interference that are affecting his performance on one or more of these tasks at any given period of time.

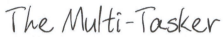

© Copyright Bonnie Mincu, Certified ADHD Coach. Bonnie Mincu is the founder of www.ThrivewithADD.com, a website of resources for Attention Deficit Disorder Adults. (Illustrator: Peter Fasolino, www.pfasolino.com).

Arousal and Attention

There is a strong relationship between arousal and attention. This is explained by the **cue-utilization hypothesis** (Easterbrook, 1959). This hypothesis states that attentional focus progressively decreases with increasing levels of arousal. With low arousal levels, attentional focus is very broad. This is detrimental because it causes individuals to be easily distracted. For example, a cornerback with a very broad attentional focus could be easily distracted by players on the sidelines, the crowd, or other environmental noise (irrelevant stimuli) rather than focusing on the movements and positions of the quarterback and receiver (relevant stimuli). As arousal levels increase, attentional focus becomes progressively narrower. At a moderate arousal level, irrelevant cues are avoided and the individual can solely focus on task-relevant stimuli. You may have referred to this as being "in the zone." If arousal levels continue to increase, attentional focus will become too narrow, and relevant cues will be lost. The cornerback whose arousal levels are too high may miss a cue from the quarterback, preventing him from blocking a pass. This progressive reduction in attentional focus is termed **perceptual narrowing**.

The cue-utilization hypothesis can serve as an explanation for the inverted-U principle of arousal (refer to chapter 8) with regard to performance and arousal levels. When arousal levels are too low, the individual is distracted by irrelevant stimuli. Attention becomes progressively narrower with increased arousal. Performance initially improves with increasing arousal because irrelevant cues are being eliminated, helping the performer to focus on the relevant cues and not be distracted by irrelevant cues. Performance peaks at a moderate level of arousal. (The optimal level of arousal is task dependent.) If arousal levels continue to increase, the performer will begin to miss relevant cues. When arousal levels become too high, performance is degraded because perception is too narrow to include all of the task-relevant cues necessary to perform the task proficiently. Once task-relevant cues begin to be eliminated, performance worsens (refer to figure 11.3).

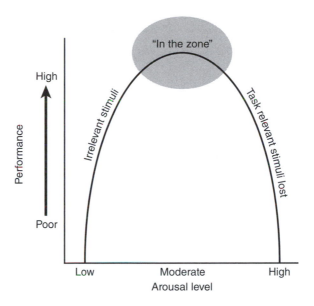

FIGURE 11.3 Effects of perceptual narrowing and the inverted-U hypothesis.

Age-Related Changes in Arousal and Attentional Capacity

Age-related differences are found with increases in arousal. Studies have shown that young, middle-aged, and older adults exhibit parallel increases in arousal levels when performing in a competitive event in comparison to relaxed settings as measured by heart rates and subjective anxiety ratings (Molander & Bäckman, 1994, 1989). While the young adults performed similarly or even better with increased arousal levels, middle-aged and older adults performed significantly worse during competitive events than during training (Molander & Bäckman, 1994).

Molander and Bäckman (1994) examined the effect of age and increased arousal in miniature golf. Young adults were able to perform well in competitive environments, while the middle-aged and older adults performed significantly worse. Even though all age groups showed a similar increase in arousal levels from training sessions to competition, the middle-aged and older adults may have experienced declines in their performance because they had higher arousal levels during training than the younger adults. It is possible that they were already "in the zone" during training, so further increases in arousal led to declines in their performance (Molander & Bäckman, 1994). When their arousal levels increased even further during the competitive events, they were losing task-relevant stimuli. Since the young adults had lower arousal levels during training, the increase in arousal levels may have either kept them in the zone or brought them up to the zone.

The results of the Molander and Bäckman (1994) study also indicate that age-related changes in performance as a result of stress (arousal levels) occur during middle age and that no further declines are found in older age. They explain that this change may be due to a shift from an external attentional focus in young adulthood to an internal (self-reflective) attentional focus. Middle-aged and older adults reported being distracted more than the younger adults and spent significantly less time concentrating prior to swinging. This is especially surprising since miniature golf is a self-paced motor skill and there was no pressure to initiate the swing early. Furthermore, while the young adults increased their concentration time in increasingly stressful situations, middle-aged and older adults decreased their concentration time. This may also be explained by reduced attentional capacity under stressful conditions with increasing age.

Research Notes: Can Older Adults Improve Their Attentional Capacities With Training?

Older adults perform significantly worse in dual tasks, or performing two tasks concurrently, than younger adults. This is not surprising since older adults have significantly reduced attentional capacities, including selective attention and **divided attention**, the ability to attend to more than one sensory input at the same time (Verhaeghen, Steitz, Sliwinski, & Cerella, 2003). Bherer and colleagues (2008) investigated whether dual-task training would improve older adults' performances in dual tasks. Eighty-eight adults (44 younger adults and 44 older adults) performed a dual task involving two visual tasks (color discrimination, yellow or green, and letter discrimination, B or C) with two motor responses. Participants were given one of three instructions on how to prioritize their responses: (1) Respond to the color first; (2) respond as fast as you can on both tasks; (3) respond to the letter first. Each instruction was given two times per session. The results revealed that both younger and older adults significantly improved their performances on the dual tasks. Both groups also performed well on a similar but different task, indicating that this training program was generalizable. The authors suggested that **cognitive plasticity**, changes in the organization of the brain as a result of experience, in attentional capacities is possible at any age through training.

Memory

Memory is often divided into short-term memory and long-term memory. **Short-term memory** stores information for only approximately 20 seconds, while **long-term memory** is seemingly limitless. Information in short-term memory can become stored in long-term memory through rehearsing the information and through associating the information with meaning. For instance, associating someone's name with a name from your favorite movie will assist in moving this information into long-term memory.

Short-Term Memory

Short-term memory can be subdivided into primary memory and working memory. Both are responsible for holding small amounts of memory for short durations, but information that is also manipulated is in **working memory**. Simply recalling a list of words is an example of using **primary memory**. Very little decline is seen in primary memory with age. Reorganizing the list of words alphabetically is an example of using working memory because the individual must not only recall the list but be able to manipulate the order of the words. Working memory does decline with advancing age (Luo & Craik, 2008). This is likely due to the increased effort that is required to be able to remember and manipulate information.

Long-Term Memory

Long-term memory can be subdivided into declarative and procedural memory. **Declarative memory** refers to memories that are consciously available through recollection or recall. Declarative memory includes episodic and semantic memory. **Episodic memory** refers to memories that are associated with a time, such as the tragic events of September 11, 2000. It is likely that you not only remember what this date refers to, but even specifically remember where you were and what you were doing when you heard that the Twin Towers had been hit by airplanes. **Semantic memories** refer to general knowledge and memories that are not associated with time, such as knowing your school colors, the function of scissors, or personal experiences. **Procedural memories** refer to memories about how to perform a particular task such as tying shoes, starting a car, or shooting a layup.

Memory changes occur as a result of age, although some types of memory are more affected than others. Procedural memory, the type of memory that enables the acquisition and performance of motor skills, shows little change with age. This is likely because procedural memory is largely automatic and cannot be verbalized (Luo & Craik, 2008). In general, semantic memory also holds up well with age; however, certain things like remembering names become impaired. The greatest age-related decline in memory is found in episodic memory, such as remembering personal experiences.

Recall and recognition are both long-term memory processes, but only one is affected by aging. **Recall** refers to retrieving long-term memories with very few cues, which requires much conscious effort. **Recognition** requires both conscious and unconscious processes and is considered easier than recall because it provides environmental support (Craik, 1986), as when one chooses a word from a list rather than remembering it without any cues. An intense memory search is not required for recognition as it is for recall (Zelinski & Kennison, 2001). Memory tasks that are strategic or effortful are more difficult for older adults, such as recalling a particular word, a person's name, or items on a grocery list (Zelinski & Kennison, 2001). However, older adults are very good at recognizing items or names.

Adults can use many strategies to help improve long-term memory.

- *Group it.* People can memorize up to about seven items fairly well. The key to memorizing larger amounts of information is to group or "chunk" items. For instance, if you have a grocery list, group the vegetables, the meats, and the dairy. It will be much easier to remember 15 items if you knew you had five in each of the three categories. It's also much easier to remember a phone number if you are already familiar with the area code.
- *Repeat, repeat, repeat.* For information to move from short-term memory to long-term memory, it must be rehearsed. This is why it is so easy to forget the name of a person you just met. If someone says her name but you do not repeat it in your head or repeat it back to her, it will likely be lost. By simply

repeating the name in your head once or twice or associating it with a sentence or something or someone familiar, you will be much more likely to remember it.

• **Make a jingle.** If you are able to make a tune out of the information or associate it with a familiar tune, you are much more likely to retain the information. For instance, if you have just met someone and know a song with the person's name in the title, you will probably not forget the name if you sing the song in your head. Think about it. You probably still sing the alphabet song when you need to alphabetize something!

• **Concentrate.** If nothing else, simply concentrate when you are receiving the information. It's a no-brainer that if you are not focused, you are simply not going to remember.

Summary

This chapter discussed functional constraints in adulthood including psychological factors, sociocultural factors, and cognitive changes. It is important to distinguish psychological and sociocultural factors in adulthood from those in childhood, as they can change quite considerably. Adults have different intentions and barriers with respect to exercise. Older adults generally place less value on exercise and perceive more barriers. Socializing agents change throughout adulthood as well. Young adults are more likely to have a strong social structure that can have a very positive influence on their attitudes toward physical activities and their motivations to engage in them. These are important factors to consider when developing a program for adults.

It is important to remember that adults vary widely and that this variability increases with age. Adults are more different from one another than adolescents or children. With increasing age, adults are affected by more and more experiences and at the same time dealing with age-related structural changes. These experiences and physical changes combine to make adults increasingly unique with age. To further complicate matters, cognitive function declines at different rates. The greatest basic cognitive changes occur in attention and memory; however, attention and memory are not uniformly affected. Some types of attention and memory are largely unaffected while others significantly decline. And again, the amount of decline is dependent on the individual. Some people maintain most of these abilities through late adulthood, while others show decline decades earlier. It is perhaps even more important to assess adults on an individual basis than it is for children or adolescents.

Supplemental Activities

Memory Tests

1. Conduct a web search on memory tests, both long- and short-term tests. Complete at least two of these tests. Describe the tests and how well you performed on them. Do you believe these tests are valid? Explain your answer.

2. Conduct a web search for strategies to improve memory. Describe at least two of these strategies. Do you believe these strategies would be effective for improving memory? Explain your answer.

Anxiety Lab

State anxiety is the anxiety that you have at a particular point in time, while trait anxiety is the amount of anxiety you have on average. Trait anxiety is much more stable than state anxiety. For example, if your professor unexpectedly told you to clear your desk because you were going to take a pop quiz, your state anxiety would probably increase dramatically over what it was 5 minutes earlier. However, this level of anxiety is probably not typical for you. Perhaps in general you are a very calm and laid-back person who only occasionally experiences sharp increases in anxiety levels.

Spielberger's State Anxiety Inventory was developed to examine state anxiety levels. The inventory includes 20 questions regarding how an individual is feeling "right now." For this supplementary activity, you are going to take the inventory (located on page 246) three different times to examine how your anxiety levels vary over the course of a day or less. Choose a particular event that you expect will be at least moderately stressful for you, such as a performance, a competition, or an exam. Take your first anxiety inventory the day prior to the event. Complete the second inventory within an hour prior to the event. Complete the third inventory within an hour following the event.

For each, rate your level of anxiety using this scale:

a = Very much so; b = Moderately so; c = Somewhat; d = Not at all
You'll also need to assign a score to your level of anxiety using these scales:

For questions 1, 2, 5, 8, 10, 11, 15, 16, 19, and 20, score 1 point for a, 2 points for b, 3 points for c, and 4 points for d.

For questions 3, 4, 6, 7, 9, 12, 13, 14, 17, and 18, score 4 points for a, 3 points for b, 2 points for c, and 1 point for d.

Once you've completed the inventory, add your points to determine your anxiety level:

Low, 20 to 29 points

Moderately low, 30 to 39 points

Moderate, 40 to 49 points

Moderately high, 50 to 59 points

High, 60 to 69 points

Through the roof! >70 points

1. Did your anxiety levels vary enough across these three tests to alter your anxiety level index? Are you surprised by how much your anxiety levels changed?

2. Do you think your anxiety levels increased so high that your performance may have been impaired?

3. Using the cue-utilization hypothesis, describe how perceptual narrowing may have affected your performance.

	Day _____		Event _____		Time after event _____	
	Test 1		Test 2		Test 3	
	Letter	Score	Letter	Score	Letter	Score
1. I feel calm						
2. I feel secure						
3. I am tense						
4. I am regretful						
5. I feel at ease						
6. I feel upset						
7. I am presently worrying over possible misfortunes						
8. I feel rested						
9. I feel anxious						
10. I feel comfortable						
11. I feel self-confident						
12. I feel nervous						
13. I feel jittery						
14. I feel "high strung"						
15. I am relaxed						
16. I feel confident						
17. I am worried						
18. I feel overexcited and rattled						
19. I feel joyful						
20. I feel pleasant						
Total Score						
Anxiety Level Index						

www.psych.uncc.edu/pagoolka/StateAnxiety-intro.html

IV

Motor Learning
Designing Appropriate Programs

Now that you understand the foundational concepts in motor learning and motor development and have explored motor development from childhood to older adulthood, you are ready to learn how to design appropriate programs. In this section, we strongly encourage you to use the knowledge about motor development that you have gained to individualize programs for each learner.

Practitioners must learn how to manipulate the constraints to encourage the appropriate movement pattern. Before implementing a program, they must make many instructional decisions, including adopting a teaching style, planning to optimize motivation, and considering how to develop tactical skills and decision making. In this section, we begin by describing how to structure the environment, including physical factors, affective factors, and instructional factors. Then we explore several prepractice variables that affect performance and learning, such as goal setting, demonstrations, verbal instruction, directing attention, and physical guidance. Of course this is only the beginning of the role of the practitioner. The practitioner must also arrange physical practice and make decisions on the provision of feedback.

It is quite clear that practice is essential to acquire a motor skill, but how much practice is necessary and how practice should be organized is probably much less obvious. This section explores key factors in arranging practice, both physical and mental practice. Practice schedules are a complex topic. Variables such as age, experience, and type of skill affect whether or not a particular form of practice actually accelerates learning. We consider when and how to use variable, part, and whole practice and also discuss distribution of practice. Next, we consider the provision of feedback. Feedback helps to guide the performer toward executing the proper movement pattern, motivates the learner, and reinforces successful performances. It is perhaps obvious that the provision of feedback is critical when people are learning a new motor skill, especially complex motor skills; but just as with practice, many considerations come into play. Each of these issues is examined, including the type of feedback, the frequency, and the timing of provision of feedback. This part of the book concludes with case studies, providing readers with the opportunity to apply the knowledge obtained from this book to practical examples. These case studies present real-life examples on a variety of topics, ranging from physical education and adapted physical education to instruction of older adults and rehabilitation.

Physical, Affective, and Instructional Factors

CHAPTER OBJECTIVES

After reading this chapter, you should be able to

> give reasons why instructors should incorporate problem solving,
> explain physical factors that instructors can manipulate,
> describe affective factors that might influence instruction,
> identify ways to enhance motivation of learners,
> explain differences between learning and competitive environments, and
> describe ways in which instructors can promote decision making.

[Handwritten margin notes:]
Cognitive
Psychomotor
Affective
Intro - gold standard (avoid theories)
① Cognitive
②
3
4 Affective
✱ minimize
GMP + Dynamic Syst Theory

How Will I Keep Their Interest?

Fred has been asked to coach his 10-year-old daughter's soccer team because he played varsity many years ago in high school. As a foreman of 30 workers at the town factory, he knows a bit about leadership, but the thought of keeping the attention of 15 girls is daunting. In his training to be foreman, Fred learned about motivation, creating a positive environment, managing competition among workers, and promoting decision making and initiative among the workers. He also remembers a former coach, a rather relaxed fellow, who did not insist on everyone's dribbling and kicking the ball in exactly the same way. Fred liked that attitude, and the coach also used lots of fun drills such as keep-away and one-on-one challenges rather than repetitive line drills. Was that coach ahead of his time? As Fred thinks about planning practices, he realizes that the 15 girls will be very different in terms of individual soccer skills but each will want to have a fun time.

This chapter explores thoughts about attempting to have all players demonstrate an identical motor pattern, for example with kicking. Should practices have much repetition and reminders of a "gold standard" for kicking? Or, should the coach expect that each child will develop a slightly different kick and be satisfied as long as the goal of getting the soccer ball to a teammate is achieved, and therefore plan practices with considerable self-discovery and self-direction? How can the coach prepare the learning environment in terms of equipment, and what impact does this have on learning motor skills? The emotional side of learning is often neglected, so we attempt to address it in this chapter. Teachers and coaches have many instructional decisions to make, some of which they can make prior to instruction, including adopting a teaching style, optimizing motivation, and considering how to develop tactical skills and decision making. We explore these issues in the chapter.

Gold Standards Versus Variability

Instruction of physical skills is sometimes done with a template in mind. The template might be a movement pattern of a highly skilled athlete. After all, does it not make sense to imitate the best? The skiing instructor encourages each of her students to emulate the style of the last Olympic champion, and the track coach highlights the running pattern of Usain Bolt. The assumption is that everyone should strive for the gold standard and the instructor's feedback should be directed at making everyone similar. However, motor learning theories challenge this gold standard thinking.

Most motor learning theorists agree that if every movement were stored in memory as a simple motor program, humans would have a **storage problem**. For example, a different motor program would be needed for kicking the soccer ball low, high, from the corner, and so on, and so on. An almost unlimited variation of movements would need to be stored in long-term memory as simple motor programs. This would likely result in a storage problem. In addition, the single motor program idea does not provide a logical or theoretical explanation of how **novel movements** are produced. All of us are able to create new movements never before practiced as we go about our daily lives and participate in physical activity. And novel movements are the trademark of exceptional sport performers. These athletes do things we simply do not anticipate, and presumably neither do their opponents. The storage challenge and novel movements led to the notion of a generalized motor program (refer to chapter 1) (Schmidt, 1975a).

The generalized motor program is argued to contain the skeleton or abstraction of a movement pattern rather than a specific movement. For example, an overhead throwing action, as described in chapter 5, might be a motor program that contains feet placement, arm flexion, sequential trunk rotation, weight transfer, arm follow-through, and visual contact with a target. As previously described, the generalized motor program likely includes information about the sequence and relative timing and force of actions. Performers use that program when the task calls for an overhead throw, but it can be modified to meet specific environmental demands. Thus, the second baseman throws the ball to first base with less arm flexion than the third baseman because the distance of the throw is shorter, and both know to "hurry the throw" when the runner is particularly quick. These situations require variations of the generalized motor program and produce different movement skills that can accomplish the task goal of ensuring the ball reaches the first baseman before the runner. Teachers and coaches need to plan variation of throwing experiences in their practice to develop generalized motor programs that can respond to different movement situations.

Supporters of ecological and dynamic systems thinking also promote variation of movement patterns in practice but for different theoretical reasons than advocates of information processing. Variability is viewed in dynamic systems in very positive terms because each person has a unique signature or style in most motor patterns. Due to different intrinsic dynamics, such as body size, strength, or experience (chapters 6 and 7) and the self-organizing nature of systems, it is expected that each person will solve movement challenges in different ways. For example, basketball players have been shown to have quite distinct shooting patterns (Button, MacLeod, Sanders, & Coleman, 2003). Those with cerebral palsy will certainly walk or reach differently than others, even those peers who also have cerebral palsy. Observation of ice hockey players skating quickly reveals unique patterns even to the naked eye. Practice experiences must recognize these differences by presenting opportunities for learners to build on their personal and current capabilities. The instructor may demonstrate one way to shoot a basketball, reach, or ice skate, but should anticipate that various patterns will naturally emerge. At other times, an instructor may watch a class and determine that a very direct comment about performance is necessary, perhaps because some of the learners are struggling. There are also times when a more direct approach is necessary because safety is an issue in activities such as gymnastics, skiing, or diving. While guided discovery has many benefits, the skilled instructor knows when to become more direct.

Variability in practice is also viewed in positive terms by ecological and dynamic systems thinkers because it mirrors the real situation in games and sport. Particularly in open sports, participants must frequently adapt their movements to their opponent's actions. Constant practice of the bounce pass in basketball without movement and opponents will not prepare the player to lean left and pass around a moving opponent. More formally, if the attractor state for a bounce pass in basketball is too stable, the player will have difficulty with the phase shift necessary to solve the dynamics of the game. Similarly, for physical and occupational therapists who may be concerned with improving walking, it is important to ensure that practice occurs on different surfaces that vary in size and slope. Variation should be incorporated into practice.

Davids, Button, and Bennett (2008) summarize these thoughts about variability in stating: "Practitioners' traditional emphasis on reducing errors during skill practice by encouraging consistency in motor patterns should be revised to acknowledge the valuable goal of variability in moment-to-moment control as well as long-term learning" (p. 151). According to Davids and colleagues, less time should be devoted to teacher-directed promotion of identical motor patterns and more time to problem solving, discovery learning, and self-regulation. As noted previously, this does not mean that a more direct instructional approach is never appropriate. Davids and colleagues propose the term **nonlinear pedagogy** as the foundation of instruction based on dynamic

Dynamic Systems Theory

Interplay of task, environment, personal constraints.

constraint changes?? How?

systems—"nonlinear" because of findings that learning is often characterized by rather sudden changes in performance (for example, to new and more mature motor patterns) rather than by linear increments as traditionally proposed by most other learning theorists. Consistent with the principles of dynamic systems, nonlinear practitioners recognize that a learner's solution to a movement challenge is a unique coordination pattern resulting from self-organization of numerous body systems. Variability among people is a natural consequence, and therapists, teachers, and coaches should design practices with this in mind. Also, by changing task, environment, and person constraints, one can nudge people to a new level of performance and can better replicate in practice the dynamics that exist in a real game or life context. Of course, in some circumstances a therapist or instructor will intervene with a particular person and suggest a change in movement pattern, but this is quite different from expecting everyone to perform skills in identical ways.

Davids and colleagues (2008) also propose that teachers and coaches be called **hands-off practitioners** to reflect a new role consistent with dynamic systems theory. The hands-off practitioner is just as involved as the traditional practitioner, only in different ways. Davids and colleagues suggest that traditional methods present drills to perfect a gold standard of performance for all, use practice skills outside the real context of performance, provide too much instruction and feedback, and overly manage the learner's practice environment. The hands-off practitioner creates "a learning environment for the discovery of optimal solutions by manipulating constraints, interpreting movement variability, and nurturing learners in their search activities" (p. 100). Since there is no one movement solution for all learners, the hands-off teacher or therapist allows greater opportunity for each learner to find appropriate personal motor patterns within practice. Allowing variability in performance during practice, as opposed to always reinforcing a stable movement pattern, is a good thing. It prepares the participant to deal with changing dynamics in real performance situations. This is particularly true for open sports and games. But even in more closed activities such as bowling or golf, movement patterns must change subtly to accommodate changes in the physical environment or in psychological functioning.

While the theoretical explanations differ, problem solving, discovery learning, and self-regulation are consistent with dynamic systems thinking as well as generalized motor programs theory and knowledge-based perspectives (Wall et al., 2007). Even thoughtful educational philosophers (e.g., Dewey, 1916) have acknowledged for many years that the most effective learning occurs through discovery and problem-based activities. So, how can the physical, affective, and instruction dimensions of the learning environment be manipulated to encourage problem solving, discovery learning, and self-regulation?

It might not need stating, but just in case—the learning environment for motor skills should be structured to promote fun. Children, adolescents, and adults list other reasons to participate in sport and physical activity (Gould, Feltz, & Weiss, 1985; Weiss & Williams, 2004), but fun is often at the top of the list. Recall that intrinsic motivation is motivation based on the pure joy of participating, and fun activities would seem to be part of intrinsic motivation. If you have seen a toddler playing with toys, making noise and repeating actions, or if you have seen an elementary school gymnasium during a class, you begin to realize the value of fun and the notion of intrinsic motivation.

3 — *GMP = skeleton*

❓ What Do You Think?

1. You just read about generalized motor programs. Choose two skills and complete the table. — *yes*

2. Describe the role of the practitioner consistent with dynamic systems theory. — *yes*

3. It is important to consider your own beliefs associated with teaching and coaching. This chapter presents a new role of teachers and coaches that you were likely not exposed to as a child. Will you adopt this role easily, or will you be tempted to take on a more traditional role? For example, will you provide opportunities for students to make choices based on their interests, or would you prefer to be in control? Explain and justify. — *discussion*

Skill	Description of motor program	Task goal	Variations to motor program
Overhand throw	Foot placement, arm flexion, sequential trunk rotation, weight transfer, arm follow-through, and visual contact with a target	Getting ball to first base before runner — *from fielding @ 2nd or short vs 3rd base*	Increased arm flexion to throw far; decreased arm flexion to throw a short distance
Swing a bat	*Stationary (Closed)*	*Open – fastball*	
Stationary shot		*z. defender*	

Environmental Constraints
Physical Factors — *How to create variability in practice*

Preferred state of stability a spontaneous shift

There are many physical factors of the environment that constrain movement patterns; some can be easily manipulated to produce variability in practice and promote discovery learning and problem solving, while others are more difficult to modify. The physical factors are control parameters that may cause a change in an attractor state. Wind, temperature, and humidity cannot be easily changed but surely influence performance. A runner racing with a strong wind in her face will likely alter her motor pattern by leaning a bit more forward than is typical, and will not expect a personal best time. These environmental constraints are difficult for a teacher or coach to manipulate. One might

Environment

consider moving indoors if that is possible. However, if weather conditions might be a factor on "game day," it is best to practice under such conditions. Factors such as humidity, altitude, and pollutants necessitate that athletes train under similar conditions or acclimatize for some time at the event site, or both, before the competition.

Therapists and teachers can rather easily manipulate physical factors such as hardness, shape, or size of the surface. Placing a mat on the floor immediately changes the dynamics of jumping, landing, or walking. A teacher who wants the children to look up while dribbling a basketball or during stick handling in ice hockey may decide to move everyone into a half or a quarter of the playing surface. To avoid bumping into others in the small space, the players have to lift their heads. Of course they might lose the ball or puck, but that is part of the fun. The game manipulates a control parameter (lifting of the head), which should force the player to focus on haptic sensations for dribbling. With time, a new attractor state of dribbling without visual contact with the ball is acquired.

One of most important task constraints, and one that is quite easily manipulated, is the size and mass of equipment relative to the person. This is often referred to as **body-scaled** equipment (Davids et al., 2008; Haywood & Getchell, 2009). Think of a young T-ball player swinging a bat the size and weight of a bat used by a professional baseball player. "Swinging" is probably the wrong word, because the child would likely hold the bat with hands many inches apart and "push" the bat forward to hit the ball. The bat is simply too heavy and too long to grasp and swing with a movement pattern approximating that of a baseball player. By changing to a smaller and lighter bat, the T-ball player is able to swing at the ball with a very different movement pattern than with the larger bat. In other words, the child is capable of producing a swing action while holding the bat at one end with both hands, but only with a bat that is scaled to his size and strength. Simply by changing equipment size relative to the learner (control parameters), practitioners can modify movement patterns and attractor states. Yet the length of the child's limbs, arm strength, experience, and the size of bat relative to the child are factors that may make Doug's swing pattern look different from Billy's. If balls and bats are far too large and heavy, it is possible that skill acquisition may be adversely affected.

The ideal learning environment will have sufficient equipment and targets of different sizes, shapes, and textures, and participants will be encouraged to explore. One of your authors challenged a group of fourth graders with the following task: Choose a ball, find a space, and throw the ball as high as you can as long as you are able to catch it. The choice of ball led to the selection of small

▶ Try This

For this activity, you will need a tennis ball or a small three-colored rubber ball, as well as a larger playground ball. Continuously bounce the small ball. Now try it without looking at the ball. Are you bouncing the ball differently than you would bounce a standard-size basketball? How is it different? Do you think that the size of the ball in relation to the size of your hand has an impact on how you bounce it? If so, what specific impact? Now let some of the air out of the larger playground ball. Try to bounce this ball continuously. How has the size of the ball and the amount of air affected how you bounce?

balls, soft nerf balls, and larger playground balls. Some students threw with one hand and others with two, and throwing technique varied widely. Skilled youngsters tossed the ball almost to the gymnasium ceiling, and others achieved more modest heights. Children were encouraged to change balls as they saw fit, and occasionally, the activity was stopped and some of the children were asked to demonstrate to their peers. With new ideas and another ball, they then began anew with the task. This is a simple example of a task with a specific goal (throw the ball up and catch it yourself) that can be accomplished in many different ways by children of diverse skill levels. Also, children were encouraged to challenge themselves at their own level of skill and explore new throws and equipment. This produced variability in throws, and they had multiple trials of practice. An information processing advocate would say that a generalized motor program was being learned, while the dynamic systems thinker would argue that the changes in task constraints were control parameters that pushed the participants into a new attractor state as the perceptual–motor landscape was explored—and better prepared them for a game context that would require them to solve a movement problem.

Almost any equipment can be modified to introduce new physical task constraints to the learning equation. Targets can change in size, amount of movement, and color. Lower the basketball net and see the difference; 5-year-old children will now be able to use a two-handed underarm throw and reach the net, while 12-year-old children will try to dunk. Balance beams can be wide or narrow or inclined, with or without obstacles. Racket handles can be long or short, narrow or thick. Gymnastics equipment can be lowered. In rehabilitation settings, the incline of a slope can be changed when physical therapists are working with infants and toddlers learning to crawl or walk, or the height of the steps can be body scaled to the individual.

Research Notes: Children Selecting Equipment for Children

Beak, Davids, and Bennett (2000) described an interesting study in which 10-year-old children showed remarkable ability to select equipment that was best for them. The researchers compared three groups, 10-year-old children inexperienced in tennis, young adults who were also inexperienced, and adults who were experienced in tennis. By placing a 50-gram weight at various points along the longitudinal axis, the researchers manipulated the moment of inertia of six rackets. The moment of inertia is the resistance of the racket to being rotated. The task goal was to select the racket that would allow the participants to swing and hit a sponge tennis ball a maximum distance with a forehand drive. Each of the three groups wielded the rackets with and without vision for as long as they wished. Vision of the rackets was occluded by having the participants place their arm through a screen to grasp the racket. Thus, the participants swung the six rackets before making their selection of their preferred racket to hit the sponge tennis ball. Generally, the children selected rackets with the weight nearer the lower end of the handle and thus less moment of inertia. In other words, they were sensitive to their own intrinsic dynamics and could reliably pick the best racket for their own body. In fact, the children showed less variability in their choices without vision, that is, when they handled the racket and relied only on haptic cues. It seems they had difficulty integrating visual and haptic cues. The authors suggested that if novice children are to become skilled at picking up haptic cues, to which they appear quite sensitive, they need to explore a variety of tennis rackets.

The results from Beak and colleagues (2000) and the story of the instructor allowing children to select their own ball with a task goal in mind provide support for structuring the learning environment with many variations of size and shape of equipment. The instructor will be better able to accommodate a wide variety of skill levels and be able to promote self-discovery and exploration of movement patterns.

What Do You Think?

1. Think of your favorite activity or sport. Using the following example as a guide, name the environmental, task, and individual constraints involved.

Sport or activity	Environmental constraints	Task constraints	Individual constraints
Dribbling a basketball	Temperature, amount of light, floor surface	Size of the ball, shooting at a large versus small target	Height, limb length, strength, motivation

2. In the vignette at the beginning of the chapter, Fred was concerned about creating soccer practices for 10-year-old girls. How could he modify task, environmental, and individual constraints to optimize fun and success? As the girls become more skilled over the season, what additional changes could he make, if any?

Team players	Environmental constraints	Task constraints	Individual constraints
Inexperienced			
Experienced			

In this section, we have stressed how manipulations of control parameters in the physical environment may produce a phase shift in the attractor state or movement pattern. The environment can also affect attention and memory. Wide-open, busy, and noisy environments make it difficult for children to attend to the key elements of a lesson if they have not learned selective attention skills and use of memory strategies. In addition, instructors can manipulate the environment to reduce the difficulty of open skills (e.g., T-ball removes the need to predict the flight of a pitch) or to add challenge and difficulty to a skill practiced in a closed manner (e.g., soccer dribbling around a person who offers token resistance and forces you to react after dribbling the width of the field without obstructions).

Affective Factors *Children*

A learning environment also has emotional factors. Think of a situation in which you felt at least somewhat confident of success if you persisted, aware that if you made an error it would not be embarrassing to you, and in which you were encouraged to solve movement problems and the focus was on your personal improvement and performance rather than comparisons with other folks. Think of another situation in which you had little confidence of success, failure would be public and perhaps embarrassing, and the instructor clearly dictated all class activities and expected your movements to conform to everyone else's. Learners of all ages approach movement tasks with a variety of emotional reactions, and it is not surprising that the stress of the second scenario will adversely affect learning.

Schmidt and Wrisberg (2008) promote familiarization and open communication early in the learning experience. Familiarization with the physical environment and the instructor's expectations and style should help to alleviate individual concerns and open up communication between the instructor and learners. Collier (2005) also reminds us that a learning environment is more than a space with equipment; it also possesses emotional dimensions. A positive emotional environment is one where everyone belongs, is valued, and is treated with dignity. Activities occur in positive, affirming ways so as to embrace individual differences. This is not restricted to respectful treatment of all learners by the instructor in a top-down manner. A positive emotional environment is also characterized by behaviors among the learners themselves and behaviors of the learners toward the instructor. Mutual respect should be acknowledged and practiced.

Hellison's teaching personal and social responsibility model (table 12.1) may provide guidance for promoting a respectful learning environment (Hellison, 2003). It was originally designed for youth at risk who demonstrated little interest in school, physical activity, or respect for others (Hellison, 1995). The five-level model places greater emphasis on values of self-respect, personal control, self-direction, and respect and caring for others than traditional curricula of skill and fitness.

Five general strategies help move learners through these levels. **Awareness talks** remind learners about the levels of responsibility, which have been explicitly discussed and posted on the walls. During the lesson itself,

TABLE 12.1 Social Responsibility Model

Level	Focus
1. Respecting rights and feelings of others	Students are taught self-control and personal responsibility to prevent physical and psychological harm to others and to respect feelings of classmates. Conflict resolution and the right to be included are also components.
2. Participation and effort	Emphasis is on physical activity participation rather than nonparticipation and assuming responsibility for self-motivation. Students are encouraged to determine if effort is related to improvement and not to give up. Success as a personal accomplishment or degree of effort is explored.
3. Self-direction	Students take more responsibility for their choices and independence with task involvement when not supervised. They establish their own goals and plans to achieve the goals and evaluate the plans. With stronger self-identity, peer pressure will be resisted.
4. Helping others and leadership	Students are encouraged to support and to assist others with compassion and sensitivity, helping those who want help, including conflict resolution. They take leadership roles such as reciprocal teaching and develop inner strength to make decisions that might not be popular.
5. Outside the gym	Students are encouraged to transfer responsibility for learning in their physical education classes to other areas such as teaching younger students, participating in service projects, and being a role model for others.

Adapted from D. Hellison, 2003, *Teaching responsibility through physical activity* (Champaign, IL: Human Kinetics), 29-36.

responsibility is taught; for example, a cooperative game may be appropriate for a level 1 learner while a level 4 learner is encouraged to help others. **Individual decision making** is the second strategy and is used at each level. A learner at level 1 who senses that she is frustrated and that she might hit someone in a game decides instead to sit on a bench. A level 5 learner might decide to volunteer at a local Saturday morning community activity program. A **group meeting** encourages discussion of what constitutes self-control and responsibility and establishes self-control rules. The students are central to this discussion and arrive at fundamental rules in the gymnasium that all are prepared to accept. **Reflection time** occurs at the end of each lesson, at which point learners contemplate what went well or not so well in the session. They are encouraged to write in a personal journal, complete checklists, and engage in discussion with others. The final strategy is called **counseling time**, time devoted to discussion of problems identified by the teacher or learners. For example, the instructor or therapist might observe that little effort is being expended by some learners during the physical education class, athletic practice, or therapy session, which is part of level 2. He wants to reinforce the goals the students have established for themselves and communicate that their expenditure of time and effort is not likely sufficient to reach these goals.

Structuring a positive affective environment of mutual respect among learners and teacher or the patient and clinician is necessary for productive motor learning. Individuals who are highly anxious about the session, fear for their physical or psychological safety, and have little hope of success are not likely to enjoy the lesson or learn very much. A positive emotional atmosphere conducive to learning involves acceptance of individual differences in skill and an opportunity for students to make decisions, set goals, and self-direct some aspects of learning, all the while knowing that effort and personal improvement will be rewarded.

What Do You Think?

Review Hellison's model. For each level of the model, provide specific examples of how you could move learners through that level.

Level	Example
1. Respect rights and feelings of others	
2. Participation and effort	
3. Self-direction	
4. Helping others and leadership	
5. Outside the gym	

Instructional Factors

There are a number of instructional factors to consider when one is structuring the learning environment. We consider teaching style, motivation, concepts ranging from free play to deliberate practice, learning and competitive environments, and promoting a decision-making and tactical learning environment.

Teaching Styles

Most pedagogical authorities agree that effective movement educators possess a number of teaching styles. A teaching style "refers to how the teacher organizes and delivers instruction to learners" (Collier, 2005, p. 118). Table 12.2 includes a summary of the teaching styles outlined by Mosston and Ashworth (2002), arranged along a spectrum of decisions made by the teacher and the learner. In teacher-mediated formats, most of the decisions regarding what to achieve, how to achieve it, and how long to spend are made by the movement educator. These are also called reproductive styles because learners are expected to reproduce a particular movement form. The learner-mediated instruction formats are designed to engage the learner in discovery of movement forms that will solve a movement problem, such as how to throw a baseball under some given game conditions. Learner-mediated instruction is also consistent with non-linear pedagogy.

[handwritten notes in margin: good term movement educator; reproductive vs discovery style; non-linear pedagogy]

[handwritten: What is non-linear pedagogy]

There is no one best style for all situations despite the emphasis in this chapter on problem solving, discovery learning, and self-regulation, which are consistent with the student-mediated instructional formats of table 12.2. Collier (2005) pointed out that an effective movement educator modifies instruction with respect to variables such as personal skills and preferences, nature of the content, characteristics of the learners, and context of the teaching. Movement

259

TABLE 12.2 Teaching Styles

Teaching style	Description
TEACHER-MEDIATED INSTRUCTION	
Command	Movement educator makes all decisions and the learner responds on cue, reproducing a performance.
Practice	Learner is allowed to work individually and privately on the task selected by the movement educator, who provides individual feedback to the learner as time permits.
Reciprocal	Learners work on task selected by movement educator but provide feedback to each other based on criteria offered by movement educator.
Self-check	Learners work on task selected by movement educator but provide their own feedback based on criteria offered by movement educator.
Inclusion	Movement educator presents several tasks that differ in difficulty. Learners select the level that is self-challenging and decide when to move to the next level of difficulty.
STUDENT-MEDIATED INSTRUCTION	
Guided discovery	Learner is guided to discover a concept by responding to a sequence of movement educator questions. The concept is predetermined by the movement educator.
Convergent discovery	Movement educator presents a question that has a single correct answer. Learners engage in reasoning and critical thinking to discover the answer.
Divergent discovery	Movement educator presents a question and learners engage in producing multiple responses, which are then assessed as feasible and desirable outcomes.
Learner designed	The learner designs, develops, and performs a series of tasks in a personal program. This is done in concert with the movement educator, who has selected the general subject matter.
Learner initiated	The learner independently initiates the learning experience as well as evaluation decisions. The movement educator supports and accepts the learners' decisions.
Self-teaching	The learner has a clear desire to learn and makes all decisions about this learning experience. This would not occur in a classroom with a movement educator but in other situations in which tenacity and intrinsic motivation to learn are evident.

Adapted from M. Mosston and S. Ashworth, 2002, *Teaching physical education*, 5th ed. (Boston: Benjamin Cummings).

educators may feel more comfortable with a particular style and hence perform better with that style (Siedentop & Tannehill, 2000), although they should experiment with a variety of styles as professionals concerned with new ways of delivering instruction to maximize learning. It is possible that content and objectives call for one method over another. Collier provides a good example. The movement educator may decide to use a command style to specifically teach the flick motion for a disc (backhand motion followed by a forearm motion). Later in the session, the objective is to decide which throwing motion to use for the particular defense confronting the players. In this case, a convergent discovery style might be most effective. Learner characteristics may enter the

What Do You Think?

1. List the pros and cons of implementing the selected teaching styles (see table 12.2) during Fred's first practice with his daughter's soccer team.
2. Pick two sports. Describe which teaching styles you would implement for each sport. Will the age of the students influence your decisions? Explain.

Teacher-mediated instruction formats	Pros	Cons
Command	The girls are relatively young learners and not particularly skilled; they may benefit from exact demonstration.	Limits opportunities to explore the skill.
Reciprocal		
Self-check		
Inclusion		

Student-mediated instruction formats	Pros	Cons
Guided discovery		
Convergent discovery		
Divergent discovery		
Self-teaching		

equation of which style to use. Because of their active nature, children and adolescents with attention deficit hyperactivity disorder (ADHD) might benefit from more teacher-directed methods, particularly when they are new to a learning situation. It is not suggested that children with ADHD or any other disability should not participate in student-mediated styles, only that skilled movement educators must evaluate the situation and act in the best interests of the individual and the group. Finally, the teaching context is also important. Some tasks, such as throwing the discus, springboard diving, or using an axe, pose more safety concerns than others. In these cases, the movement educator must ensure that unsafe procedures or movements are not permitted.

Davids and colleagues (2008) provide some helpful suggestions for organizing learner-paced and reflective practices when one is working with a group. Obviously, these lie on the student-mediated end of the styles of teaching identified by Mosston and Ashworth (2002). Some of the responsibility for practice organization is delegated to the learners. One way is to encourage self-reflection during breaks in the practice. If a goal was set to throw a ball as high as possible without dropping it, the learners are asked to consider why they are successful or not. For those who were successful, what could they do to make the task more difficult but still catch the ball? For those who were unsuccessful, why do they think they dropped the ball, and how might the task be changed to improve the number of balls caught? In a team context, a natural break in the game (e.g., scoring a goal) might be followed by intentional discussion of why one team lost possession of the ball. Such discussion breaks are easily found in rehabilitation contexts where the therapist and client are working as a pair. A second suggestion, beyond self-reflection, is to allow augmented feedback to be student driven. Davids and coworkers describe a research study by Janelle, Barba, Frehlich, Tennant, and Cauraugh (1997) in which one group of students selected when to receive visual feedback about their throwing technique while the other group had no choice of feedback schedule. The first group asked for feedback on only 11% of the trials yet retained the skill better than the second group. Thus, a movement educator does not have to be concerned about not providing augmented feedback on every trial and may even have students providing some feedback to others.

Davids and colleagues (2008) also encourage practitioners to engage learners with problem-solving opportunities. They suggest that a simple strategy such as asking children to create three different ways of throwing a ball to a target encourages unique ways to solve a problem. The instructor might also ask students to demonstrate their methods to the class to reinforce creative solutions and encourage discussion. A final strategy is one that might be familiar to movement educators, having small-sided games and opportunities for dialog. While basketball is a five-on-five game played on a large court, a one-on-one or two-on-two game provides more involvement for all participants to develop skill and discuss strategy.

Motivation

The learning environment must be structured with motivation in mind. Motivation influences activity initiation and persistence. Self-motivation is also an important dimension in the forethought phase of self-regulation (Zimmerman, 2000). Motivational ideas for practitioners emerge from competence motivation theory (Harter 1978, 1981), self-determination theory (Deci & Ryan, 1985, 2000; Vallerand, 1997, 2007), self-efficacy theory (Bandura, 1997), and achievement goal theory (Nicholls, 1989). Teachers, therapists, and exercise leaders can enhance and maintain participation in physical activity by following the steps explained next (Kilpatrick, Hebert, & Jacobsen, 2002; Ntoumanis, 2001; Vallerand, 2007). Developmental differences are noted as appropriate. Many of the recommendations are cast in self-determination theory because teachers and therapists can influence factors such as achievement and choice. An extensive body of research supports these factors as affecting perceived competence, autonomy, and relatedness, the three needs posited in self-determination theory. In other words, these factors increase or decrease intrinsic motivation via modifying perceived competence, autonomy, and relatedness (Vallerand, 2007).

- *Promote achievement.* The learning environment should provide much opportunity for successful experiences. Not surprisingly, positive past achievements enhance personal self-efficacy and competence as an important mediator of intrinsic motivation. Success can be increased by professionals who create the positive affective environment discussed earlier, who manipulate environmental and task constraints, and who encourage learners to be actively involved in the discovery learning process. This does not mean that the environment should be manipulated to avoid failure on all attempts or trials, for learning can result from analyzing why something went wrong and trying a new way. But repeated failure is destined to decrease motivation and result in little interest in the form of physical activity that produced the failure. Learners seek out opportunities to demonstrate their competence and are usually intrinsically motivated to learn physical skills. Even observing someone succeed who is similar to oneself can have a positive impact on self-efficacy and performance (Bandura, 1997).

- *Promote a mastery climate.* A **mastery climate** encourages participants to improve their skills, and success is judged by a positive change in one's performance, not in comparison to others. This contrasts with an **ego-involved climate**, which encourages participants to improve their skills to outperform others. In the ego-involved climate, success is defined in comparison to other people in the group or some idealized model. Generally speaking, before children begin school they are largely unaware of how they compare to others in terms of movement skills. Most children are intrinsically motivated to move and are eager to explore and learn. The elementary school years produce many opportunities for comparison in physical education classes or community sport and physical activity programs. If the star athlete is always held up as the idealized example of performance, the underlying message is that others should aspire to such skill levels. If the children adopt this perspective as truth, many will generate a sense of incompetence and have reduced intrinsic motivation. The mastery climate champions personal improvement as the important yardstick of success. Teachers, fitness professionals, and clinicians who point out improvement, regardless of how others perform, are creating a mastery climate that is conducive to self-determined forms of motivation.

- *Provide positive feedback.* Positive feedback to learners promotes learning, intrinsic motivation, and self-confidence with the given task. As we will see in chapter 15, there is no need to provide positive feedback on every trial, but in general, most people of all ages appreciate the therapist or parent saying "Good effort, I see you are working hard" or "Yes, you have it, that step with the throw really added distance." If verbal feedback or encouragement is not realistic, learners will quickly become aware that their capabilities do not match the words of others. Negative feedback is usually associated with a decrease in intrinsic motivation. Henderlong and Lepper (2002) cogently pointed out that other dimensions of praise can have unexpected consequences. For example, if the praise is not considered sincere, it can have the effect of negative feedback. Also, the style in which the feedback is presented is important. If the words convey autonomy (e.g., You should do this to improve performance), the participant will feel in control. On the other hand, if the message is controlling (e.g., You have no choice but to do this), intrinsic motivation will likely decrease.

- *Provide choice.* Choice facilitates intrinsic motivation. Allow participants to select their own music to accompany exercise; the size, color, or texture of a ball; or in some cases the task. ("When the music stops, move to the locomotor skill station of your choice and practice the activities on the task card") (Kilpatrick et al., 2002). Choice promotes autonomy and intrinsic motivation. Physical education teachers and therapists may be constrained to some extent by required curricula or traditional practice, but choice can still be afforded the students or patients within the required activities. With adults, every effort should be made to include participants in a broader decision-making process of actually selecting the activities, as well as amount of time for instruction, self-directed practice, or play.

- *Promote goal setting.* Preschool children will not require goal setting since they generally play and practice for intrinsic reasons. As instructors sense that younger school-aged children might benefit from setting goals as a means to promote activity and provide a barometer of success, the children will need assistance in selecting realistic and specific goals. "You swim the length of the pool with the backstroke in 40 seconds, do you want to aim for 35 seconds?" Goal setting is consistent with a mastery climate in which personal improvement is emphasized and is supported as a means to improve performance (Kyllo & Landers, 1995). Participants should be encouraged to set moderately difficult personal goals, and adults may benefit from both short-term and long-term goals. The instructor may say, "Yes, I agree that you should try to bump the volleyball six times to yourself today, but 10 times with Fred can probably wait for a few sessions." Setting one's goals is consistent with autonomy. The achieved goals provide a sense of self-satisfaction, competence, and hence intrinsic motivation. We will discuss goal setting further in chapter 13.

- *Use competition wisely.* Competition with others will arise at some point in many physical activity programs. Readers are cautioned against thinking that competition must be a huge part of all programs; think of practice that emphasizes personal skill improvement in swimming, skiing, or gymnastics quite outside the context of competition. A run can be conceived as a personal method of having a good workout or as a race against others. Realistically, however, competition will be part of units of track or basketball, since even one-on-one "drills" are inherently competitive. The early motivation literature with physical tasks showed that competition had a detrimental effect on intrinsic motivation. The sport literature confirmed this finding in those who lost. For winners, or those who did well, intrinsic motivation was enhanced (Vallerand, 2007). Practitioners are cautioned against using too much competition or placing too much emphasis on the outcome when only a few can "win."

A series of basketball studies by Tauer and Harackiewicz (2004) is informative. The researchers assessed the impact of competition, cooperation, and intergroup competition on enjoyment by children with a basketball free throw task. In the competitive situation, enjoyment increased for the winners but decreased in losers. This was consistent with the intrinsic motivation literature. It was expected from earlier research that cooperation would lead to more enjoyment than competition, but competition and cooperation did not differ in this respect. In fact, intergroup competition resulted in the highest levels of enjoyment. Even though intrinsic motivation and enjoyment are different constructs (although related), Vallerand (2007) tried to explain these surprising findings by postulating that "trying to do well" was emphasized by the researchers. Perhaps the children did not perceive the competitive environment as one of "win at all costs" and thus did not perceive a controlling dimension, so enjoyment was not reduced. In summary, practitioners should be mindful that too much competition in a program and excessive importance placed on winning may be viewed as controlling and therefore reduce intrinsic motivation for that activity in many of the participants. Rather, learners should view competition as one way to extend their skills, recognizing that competitors who try their best against them will make them a better player.

- ***Provide a rationale for activities.*** Providing reasons for some activities ("Many of our activities today are designed to help improve range of motion in your knee and will speed up your recovery") should provide knowledge about the activities and facilitate a sense of competence and autonomy (Kilpatrick et al., 2002). Therapists and instructors should encourage questions and discussion about the rationale of activities.

- ***Promote social interactions.*** The desire to be with friends and make new friends is a motive mentioned often by children for participating in sport (Weiss & Williams, 2004). Social interaction or relatedness is also a need postulated by Deci and Ryan (1985) in self-determination theory. It is expected that creating social relationships in physical activity environments will enhance enjoyment of the activity. Ways to accomplish this include partner and small-group activities that promote new interactions among people.

- ***Use rewards wisely.*** The use of rewards has been extensively researched in laboratory tasks (e.g., Deci, Koestner, & Ryan, 1999, 2000). Rewards are things like trophies or other tangible items rather than positive verbal feedback. In these situations, rewards decrease intrinsic motivation if they are presented for participating or completing an activity or for reaching a certain level of performance. They undermine autonomy. If the rewards are unexpected and not related to task achievement, they do not decrease intrinsic motivation. Thus, a participant trophy or certificate of practice given to all team members at the end of the year is unlikely to undermine intrinsic motivation if it is unexpected. However, if people participate in sport or exercise to receive a trophy or money from parents, intrinsic motivation toward that activity will likely decrease. This effect is even greater in children than in college-age students (Vallerand, 2007). Likely reasons are that children begin at a higher level of intrinsic motivation or that because of inexperience they do not expect any reward for something they enjoy. Rewards may be useful when a person is reluctant to participate; and our hope is that once the person attempts the activity, it will become appealing in itself. More research is needed on this issue, but the thoughtful

Recommendations for enhancing intrinsic motivation are listed in the bulleted paragraphs on pages 263-265. In groups of three, select a sport or physical activity and generate specific examples of how you could use each of these recommendations in teaching and coaching settings.

Enhancing intrinsic motivation	Example
Promoting achievement	Consider task, individual, and environmental constraints.
Promoting a mastery climate	
Providing positive feedback	
Providing choice	
Promoting goal setting	
Using competition wisely	
Providing a rationale for activities	
Promoting social interactions	
Using rewards wisely	

therapist, teacher, or coach should use rewards sparingly and with awareness that rewards may detrimentally affect intrinsic motivation, which in turn will lead to a decrease in participation.

Play, Learning, and Competitive Environments

In this chapter, we have discussed many factors that one can consider in structuring an optimal learning environment. While the role of competition was downplayed as a motivational technique during the acquisition of movement skills, there are certainly times when competition is at the heart of the activity, and participants need to be prepared for all aspects of the competitive event or game. The learning and practice environment of an athlete will be quite different from that of novice participants struggling with learning a new movement pattern.

Côté (1999; Côté, Baker, Abernethy, 2003) proposed a developmental framework of sport expertise inspired by Bloom (1985), whose pioneering research in science, art, and athletics determined the antecedents of experts' high level of skill. It appears that sport experts progress toward excellence in much the same way as musicians, chess players, and scholars (Janelle & Hillman, 2003). Similar to Bloom, Côté and colleagues (2003) identified three phases of development: the **sampling years** (ages 6-12), the **specializing years** (ages 13-15), and the **investment years** (16 plus).

The sampling years are characterized by exposure to many fundamental motor skills (chapter 5) and a wide range of sports with an emphasis on fun and excitement. In the specializing years, the young adolescent begins to spend more time on one or two sporting activities. Development of skill takes on a higher priority than during the sampling years, but fun remains a critical component. Côté and colleagues (2003) suggest that the activities pursued at this point are a function of "positive experiences with a coach, encouragement from an older sibling, success, and simple enjoyment of the activity" (p. 93). Adolescents who move into the investment years want to achieve elite levels of performance. The main focus is strategic, competitive, and skill development within a context of deliberate practice directed and assisted by a coach.

Côté and colleagues (2003) propose that the sampling, specializing, and investment years in sport are anchored in the concepts of **free play**, **deliberate play**, **structured practice**, and **deliberate practice**. Table 12.3 provides a comparison of these four types of physical activity participation across six dimensions. Briefly, children move from the free play of infancy and early childhood to deliberate play in which some rules are established and monitored by children or adults, then to structured practice of a sport in which improvement in skill assumes a higher priority than in deliberate play, and finally to deliberate practice for some highly motivated adolescents.

Figure 12.1 displays the results from a study in young professional ice hockey players on the number of hours of participation in various forms of physical activity. Consistent with predictions, many hours were devoted to deliberate play during the sampling years, which began to decline in the specializing years. Hours devoted to deliberate practice increased during the investment years, and there was less involvement in other games. Other research with athletes who perform at outstanding levels supports the value of sampling and specialization prior to significant investment. Overemphasis on one sport at a young age is not usually desirable.

TABLE 12.3   Comparison of Free Play, Deliberate Play, Structured Practice, and Deliberate Practice Activities

Dimensions	Free play	Deliberate play	Structured practice	Deliberate practice
Goal	Fun	Fun	Improve performance	Improve performance
Perspective	Process (means)	Process—experimentation	Outcome (ends)	Outcome (ends)
Monitored	Not monitored	Loosely monitored	Monitored	Carefully monitored
Correction	No correction	No focus on immediate correction	Focus on correction (often through discovery learning)	Focus on immediate correction
Gratification	Immediate	Immediate	Immediate and delayed	Delayed
Sources of enjoyment	Inherent	Predominantly inherent	Predominantly extrinsic	Extrinsic

Reprinted, by permission, from J. Côté, J. Baker, and B. Abernethy, 2003, From play to practice: A developmental framework for the acquisition of expertise in team sports. In *Expert performance in sports: Advances in research on sport expertise*, edited by J.L. Starkes and K.A. Ericsson (Champaign, IL: Human Kinetics), 95.

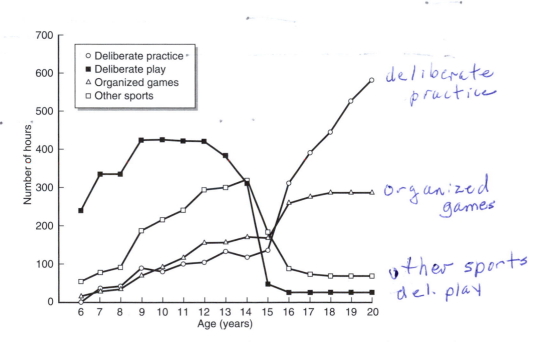

FIGURE 12.1   Hours spent per year in deliberate play, deliberate practice, organized games, and other sports.

Reprinted, by permission, from J. Côté, J. Baker, and B. Abernethy, 2003, From play to practice: A developmental framework for the acquisition of expertise in team sports. In *Expert performance in sports: Advances in research on sport expertise*, edited by J.L. Starkes and K.A. Ericsson (Champaign, IL: Human Kinetics), 102.

Research Notes: Memories of Elite Athletes

Investigating the time devoted to organized sport, deliberate play, and deliberate practice is a difficult task since it requires excellent athletes to look back in time. Such a retrospective study was conducted by Soberlak and Côté (2003), who interviewed four 20-year-old athletes who had signed contracts to play in the National Hockey League. Arguably, these were elite athletes. The in-depth interviews of the four players were corroborated by three of the parents to ensure validity of the athletes' recollection of other sports played and time devoted to them. The researchers explored the type of sporting activity, age and level of initial involvement, hours per week and months of the year participating in the activity, and age when participation ended. Among the findings were high engagement in deliberate play (hours per week) during the sampling period, a reduction during the specializing period, and decline to little or no deliberate play during specialization. As expected, deliberate practice increased in time over the sampling, investment, and specializing periods. During the sampling period of 6 to 12 years of age, the athletes actually increased the number of sports played (from three to six), but they decreased to about three sports in the investment period. The athletes remained at two or three sports in the specializing period, but in addition to ice hockey, participation in recreational activities such as golf or water skiing was typical. Overall, the results supported the three periods of sport development proposed by Côté and colleagues (2003) and suggested that early sport specialization was not necessary to reach elite levels of achievement.

Ericsson (2003) proposed an extension to Fitts and Posner's three-stage motor learning model (described in chapter 3) to explain one of the mechanisms of expert performance. He asserts that most individuals arrive at the autonomous level of performance rather easily (50 or so hours of training and experience) and are satisfied with this level of performance because they have no need to continue working hard—their performance is quite stable, and they can thoroughly enjoy recreational activities. Those aspiring to expert levels of performance, however, are not satisfied with the autonomous stage but remain in a cognitive phase that advances the features of expertise described in chapter 7. In other words, they deliberately try to find better ways to perform the tasks required in their sport. Usually with the help of a teacher or coach, the person practices with the primary goal of improving performance; this is deliberate practice (Ericsson, 2003). Such practice requires effort, without an immediate reward and motivated by the goal of performance improvement, and may not be enjoyable (Côté et al., 2003). The idea of lack of enjoyment during practice may seem disturbing to potential teachers, coaches, parents, and psychologists. The authors of this text are not suggesting that practitioners adopt such deliberate practice as regular methodology and go out of their way to make practice and training unpleasant. In fact, it seems that in the sport context, as opposed to the musical world, practice for most participants seeking expertise remains rather fun (Deakin & Cobley, 2003).

Free play, deliberate play, structured practice, and deliberate practice share features with three types of environments proposed by Wall and colleagues (2007) to promote a greater depth of knowledge and performance in physical activity. These three environments are instructional, practice, and competitive and are designated to capture the additional challenges and social pressure one experiences in moving from an environment for novices to one for athletes.

"The instructional, practice, and competitive environments can be viewed as a continuum; seeing them this way underscores the need to recognize and assess the performance capabilities of learners in different performance environments" (Wall et al., 2007, p. 270).

• **Instructional environments** are relatively closed and supportive environments with instruction, feedback, and encouragement of children to explore their movement options. Such instructional learning environments are typically present in physical education where ample practice opportunities, with manipulation of the physical factors noted earlier, are provided. Students are encouraged to move to progressively more difficult tasks and environmental conditions. In instructional settings, novice learners can practice basic skills alone, with peers, or in a small group under minimal social pressure. They have sufficient time to organize their initial attempts and use some self-regulation skills. The less skilled learner has the opportunity to acquire sufficient skill to participate in more demanding settings. Learners may play the basketball-type game of "donkey" with considerable enjoyment but may be overwhelmed in a five-on-five lead-up game during physical education.

• **Practice environments** are a more demanding learning environment because more emphasis is on proper execution of specific skills under increasingly demanding space and time constraints. An instructor or leader controls the practice session by determining the number of players involved, the player roles, the equipment, and the space. Lead-up games and practice drills consistent with the principles in the next section on tactical learning will take place in a more demanding learning environment. Successful individual performance plays a greater role in the practice environment than in the instructional environment because the participants have some interest in winning, if the activity has a competitive element.

• In **competitive environments**, the performance expectations and social pressure increase as individuals or teams compete against each other. The performance expectations are lower in younger recreational settings than in older and more elite settings, where expectations can be very high. Aspects of deliberate practice may be present in elite contexts with older participants. Recall that deliberate practice includes more control by the coach, the goal of improving performance, and more effort in practice. In competitive environments, there may be the stress of evaluative fans, and outcomes may be linked to social prestige and future opportunities in the sport.

Decision-Making and Tactical Learning Environments

Physical activities require decision making, which can vary from a simplistic, yes or no decision to the complexity of choices inherent in competitive situations. At a minimum, Grehaigne, Godbout, and Bouthier (2001) argue that any voluntary action involves the decision of whether or not to initiate the action. Thus, do I go for a walk or do I remain in front of the TV? Exercise psychologists are very much concerned with factors that compel us to move. Grehaigne and colleagues (2001) offer an interesting example in a more complex life situation. You make a decision to move a heavy object, but you then have to decide how you want to move it—pull, push, carry in the arms or in a wheelbarrow. This decision will be based on such factors as perception of personal strength, the form of the object, availability of helpers, and characteristics of the surroundings. Children's play includes many decisions such as which climbing apparatus to use and how to move along those with wall bars.

In the competitive sport context, important decisions are made even if you are not simultaneously competing with your competitors. Divers must decide which dives to execute given degrees of difficulty, confidence in performing a dive well, perceived ability of competitors, current scores of competitors, and so on. The golfer must select the club and decide on subtle mechanics of the shot with factors such as the wind and shape of the fairway in mind. In dual sports such as tennis, one plays directly against an opponent, although in many cases the opponents remain on the other side of a net or the rules restrict the degree of deliberate interference. Decisions are made to win the point: Should I return the ball with topspin, place it deep, or place it to her backhand? Many of these decisions are made in the context of the next couple of volleys; that is, the impact of this shot is not to win the point but to place my opponent in a vulnerable position on which I will capitalize in a shot or two. Finally, team sports may involve the most complex decisions, because many have open environments where players can go almost everywhere on the playing surface and intercept or block balls and pucks. There are broader team tactical decisions, such as zone or man-to-man coverage in basketball, that can be made prior to a game; but there are also countless times during actual play when players (individually or with a teammate or two) decide to execute a play because of the placement of opponents, their perception of an opponent's strength or weakness, or time and score of the game.

Tactics are organized actions by individuals, pairs, or groups intended to acquire an advantage over an opponent. In the context of soccer, these might include actions to defend a goal or open space, moving to a passing lane to receive the ball, maintaining possession of the ball, or supporting the dribbler, as well as offensive and defensive strategies. **Decision making** is the selection from a variety of choices knowing the consequences of the choice. Examples of decisions in various physical activity and sport contexts underscore the simple fact that choosing the correct course of action at the correct time is as much a part of success as executing the action with efficiency. High-strategy team or dual sports involve many critical decisions prior to and during competition; decisions are also involved in activities such as downhill leisure skiing as one navigates around other people, adjusts to snow and ice conditions, and manages a safe speed. Awareness is growing that decision making and tactics should be directly taught (Davids et al., 2008; Grehaigne et al., 2001; McPherson & Kernodle, 2003; Vickers, 2007). Skilled movement execution and physiological readiness are important, but so is decision making. Practices should be constructed with decision making in mind.

How to include decision making and tactics as part of instruction is a matter of some debate. Traditionally, coaches and teachers have focused on ensuring that participants possess the movement techniques of the activity, that is, the correct motor patterns, before introducing tactical skills. For example, the bounce pass in basketball is often taught with much repetition, feedback from the instructor, and minimal promotion of thought on the part of the learner about when the pass will be used. In addition, the drills are often rather static;

the game-like context is intentionally removed on the assumption one cannot be tactical without appropriate techniques. Only after the technique is well developed are tactics and decision making introduced in the actual game. Teachers or coaches who express great disappointment during a game—"They could do it in practice!"—may have used this traditional approach. The approach has come in for some criticism; critics claim that children achieve little success due to emphasis on technique, that they know little about game strategy, that skilled players are too inflexible and make poor decisions, and that players rely too much on the coach or teacher (Holt, Strean, & Bengoechea, 2002; Werner, Thorpe, & Bunker, 1996). In the context of teaching sport, an alternative to this approach exists, called teaching games for understanding, or TGfU (Bunker & Thorpe, 1986; Butler, Griffin, Lombardo, & Nastasi, 2003; Griffin, Brooker, & Patton, 2005; Werner et al., 1996).

Advocates of TGfU argue that game tactics and decisions are best taught in modified games prior to movement techniques, which will emerge to some extent through the games designed to teach the tactics. The modified games are designed to enhance game tactics and skill as learners are prepared for real game play. Teaching games for understanding conceptualizes four types of games; target (e.g., bowling and golf), striking/running (e.g., baseball and cricket), net/wall (badminton and squash), and invasion (e.g., basketball, football, water polo). In each category, the tactics may be quite similar across the sports. The techniques can be explicitly taught after the tactics, and learners may be more receptive to learning techniques when they understand the context in which a technique might be required.

In contrast to traditional methods, TGfU encourages students to solve problems and make decisions inherent in the actual game. Let us return to the bounce pass in basketball. It is used to pass the ball to a teammate in the real game; and that real game will always present an opponent who will try to intercept the ball. The teammate without the ball cannot stand behind an opponent, for the ball will surely be intercepted. Rather, he must understand the game sufficiently to find an open space to receive a pass. And the passer must direct the ball with sufficient force and accuracy, and quickly enough, to avoid an interception. Therefore, the TGfU teacher selects a monkey-in-the-middle game played in a restricted area on the playing surface. The goal of getting the ball to the teammate with a bounce is explained and the children begin to play. After a period of time, players change positions, and after additional time the instructor stops the play and asks the players to discuss what circumstances led to successful passes and unsuccessful passes. The players are developing their tactical knowledge, knowledge of what to do under what particular circumstances. They are certain to discover that two-hand passes and one-hand passes, sometimes thrown off balance, can achieve the goal. Also, the common beginner problem of the thrower "telegraphing the play" is surely to surface.

Despite the enthusiasm on the part of TGfU supporters, the research evidence is not sufficient to support the claim that traditional teaching techniques should be abandoned in favor of TGfU. However, some estimates indicate that games constitute more than 50% of school physical education curriculum time and that it behooves instructors to be prepared to structure the learning environment to promote games learning. Most motor learning discussions ignore tactics and relegate decision making to information processing models of performance

What Do You Think?

You just read about teaching games for understanding (TGfU). Choose two skills and describe how you would teach each using TGfU and traditional methods.

Skill	Traditional	TGfU
Bounce pass	Implement drills, many repetitions of skill. Avoid game context. Provide instructor feedback.	Implement modified games (e.g., monkey in the middle; encourage changes in positions). Encourage decision making. Discuss problems and solutions (e.g., What can you do to avoid having the ball intercepted? Find open space to pass the ball!).

rather than within the context of games. While TGfU is certainly not a direct outgrowth of dynamic systems and ecological theory, many of its suggestions about problem solving are consistent with nonlinear pedagogy.

Ecological Task Analysis

Traditional task analysis is a method of analyzing movement performance by comparing the movement pattern to a correct model. There are several problems with this approach. The main problem is that comparing learners with a particular model, or correct form, assumes that the structural constraints of the learner are similar enough to that of the model, meaning that the learner is capable of moving in the same manner as the model. The model is also problematic because everyone is placed on a continuum of performance ranging from incorrect to correct. The instructor observes the learner and corrects the movements that deviate from the correct form. The traditional task analysis model does not account for the interaction between the task and the environment either.

The **ecological task analysis model**, on the other hand, provides a method of designing appropriate programs by accounting for individual differences. This is accomplished by manipulating the environment and task on a progression of complexity, allowing learners to increase their level of complexity on one or more levels of a motor skill at a time. Davis and Burton (1991) identified four major steps for designing an ecological task analysis model.

- *Step 1.* The instructor selects the task goal and structures the environmental constraints around the task goal. An important component in the ecological task model is the involvement of the learner in this process.

- *Step 2.* The instructor should provide the learners with movement options rather than constrain their movement by instructing them to complete the movement pattern a particular way as in the traditional task analysis model. The instructor could even provide equipment options, such as different-sized balls. Learners can decide for themselves whether to make the task more or less challenging, depending on the size or bounciness of the ball (Mitchell & Oslin, 2007). When learners are presented with choices, they are likely to take more ownership in the learning process and will likely stay more motivated.

- *Step 3.* After the learner has attempted the movement pattern, the instructor should manipulate the environment, task, or both in an effort to enhance performance.

- *Step 4.* The instructor should then provide augmented feedback to the learner.

Creating an ecological task analysis model for a motor skill involves three steps. First, make a list of all the individual constraints associated with performing the motor skill. For playing basketball, important individual constraints include coordination, balance, agility, strength, and control. Second, once the individual constraints have been established, list the interactions with the task and the environment. In other words, how can the task of playing basketball be simplified? The equipment can be modified for smaller children, such as a smaller or lighter ball, to account for individual constraints such as height or strength. The hoop could be lowered and the court size could be decreased. A beginner would likely practice shooting balls while remaining stationary to decrease the balance and coordination constraints. The final step is to develop a range from simple to complex for each task and environmental constraint. It is important to note that large changes in performance can result from small variations in a constraint (Haywood & Getchell, 2009).

Task analysis can be a useful way for both instructors and learners to easily manipulate the task and environment, and enables individualized programs even in group settings. For instance, one learner could be at the simplest level, perhaps using the lowest level for all six factors in the catching example (figure 12.2), while another is using a medium-sized, heavy ball that is traveling at a slow speed (relatively complex catching task). If some control is given to learners, such that they can manipulate the task conditions, they will likely find the activity more interesting and rewarding.

Factors	Size of object being caught	Distance for object being thrown	Weight of object being caught	Speed at which ball is coming	Predictability of trajectory of object being caught	Anticipation of ball coming and getting hands ready
Levels						
Simple	Large	Short	Light	Slow	Along the ground Straight down an incline	Hands up when it gets close
	Medium	Medium	Moderate	Moderate	Bounced along the ground	Hands up when it's on its way
Complex	Small	Long	Heavy	Fast	In the air	Hands up before ball is thrown

FIGURE 12.2   Example of an ecological task analysis for catching.

Ecological task analysis is a method of outlining several possible task and environmental constraints at various levels of difficulty. Once an ecological task analysis is developed, it can become a tool for both the instructor and the learner to use to manipulate the complexity of the task and assess the level of the learner. Ecological task analysis allows for easy comparisons across individuals through comparison of the learner's level for each factor rather than through evaluation of product outcomes (e.g., distance or accuracy). Product outcomes are limiting in that some learners may adopt unorthodox techniques in an effort to throw farther. For example, a learner could catch more balls than another (product outcome) but may be using his chest to assist him with the catch (poor technique).

 What Do You Think? Ecological Task Analysis

1. Design an ecological task analysis for a sport-specific motor skill of your choice. Include at least five factors and vary them in difficulty from simple to complex using at least three different levels.

2. Design an ecological task analysis for a fundamental motor skill. Include at least five factors and vary them in difficulty from simple to complex using at least three different levels.

Summary

Fred, in the opening scenario, was challenged by the soccer coaching duties for his daughter's team. This chapter would have assisted him in understanding the pros and cons of aspiring for gold standards for soccer skills for the girls and in understanding how to structure the physical, affective, and instructional environment to enhance their enjoyment and learning. We discussed the need of learners to be exposed to variability in practice so that they can respond in novel ways if the performance situation dictates. Chapter 13 returns to the issue of variability. We then discussed a number of ways in which the physical environment, including equipment, can be manipulated to modify performance. Then we highlighted the affective factors that contribute to a positive learning environment. Many instructional decisions are to be made, and we provided an overview of teaching styles, motivation, and competitive and instructional environments. We finished by arguing that promoting decision making and tactical learning should be given greater emphasis within the motor learning context.

Supplemental Activities

1. Arrange an interview with an accomplished athlete. Ask your interviewee about her or his early years in the sport. Did she participate in many activities before she began to specialize in her current sport? What role did Mom and Dad play? Does her current practice reflect "deliberate" practice? Estimate the number of hours she has devoted to her sport. Is it close to 10,000 hours?

2. Motivation is such an important topic in human performance that the Internet is full of images, quotes, and tips pertaining to motivation. Search for these and see if you can find a quote or image to match our list of motivation topics; also see if you can add to the list of motivations to extend it.

CHAPTER THREE

Prepractice Considerations

CHAPTER OBJECTIVES

After reading this chapter, you should be able to

> describe three types of goals and principles of goal setting,

> describe when demonstrations will be effective or not effective and why,

> explain the pros and cons of expert and learning models,

> discuss the relationships between verbal instruction and both implicit and explicit learning,

> describe guidelines for using verbal cues, and

> explain attention as broad or narrow and as external or internal.

Challenging Traditional Thinking

Brittany is a thoughtful coach of the peewee ice hockey team (11-12-year-olds) and has considered factors in the learning environment (chapter 12). Of course she realizes that much practice (chapter 14) will be necessary to improve the skating, shooting, passing, and team play of her players. But she worries that if she talks too much, the players will not have enough time to practice—and the cost of ice rental is, well, really out there! On the other hand, she knows a great deal about the game and wants to share her knowledge with her team. She also wonders about demonstrations for the players. As a former player at the national level, she is confident of her abilities to

demonstrate the skills, and part of her wants the boys to realize that girls *can* play. Brittany is trying to remember something from her coach education program—was it that demonstrations by other children might be as helpful as expert demonstrations? She also remembers learning that demonstrations can be overrated in some situations. Is that really possible? She knows that practices will include verbal instructions and physical demonstrations; a practice that didn't would be rare and odd. She decides to research more so she doesn't talk too much and waste time on ineffective demonstrations. She is curious about how best to use prepractice information to help her players improve their skills, learn how to play the game, and have fun. Hopefully this will result in optimal use of precious practice time on that costly ice.

The purpose

The purpose of this chapter is to explore several prepractice variables that affect performance and learning. Prepractice refers to actions of instructors, therapists, and coaches immediately prior to physical practice rather than more general issues of structuring the environment (chapter 12). These actions include goal setting, demonstrations, verbal instruction, directing attention, and physical guidance. Of course the role of the instructor does not end here. It also includes arranging physical practice (chapter 14) and deciding how to provide feedback during or after physical practice (chapter 15). Somewhat surprisingly, there is little scientific consensus about the role of prepractice information such as demonstrations and verbal instruction in motor learning (Hodges & Franks, 2002).

Goal Setting

Motor learning and self-regulation assume that learners are goal directed. They want to achieve something. As we saw in chapter 12, the purpose of free play and structured play is fun, and as adults we do not want to turn child's play into anything else by inserting goals of achievement. We can modify the environment to present activity challenges and encourage exploration by supporting and interacting with children, but we should allow their natural sense of fun and intrinsic motivation to flourish while they play. In structured practice or deliberate practice, the situation changes and performance improvement becomes a more important factor. In these situations, goal setting is likely to enhance performance and learning.

In practice situations, instructors may have a tendency to encourage students to "do your best." At first glance, this seems sensible, because the instructor knows that a specific goal for the whole class or team (e.g., perform 15 push-ups or 10 throws that hit a target) will result in some students failing and others barely being challenged. **Goal setting** is a self-regulatory skill that allows individuals to monitor progress toward a self-determined goal (Zimmerman, 2000). Instructors and therapists should encourage goal setting because individuals tend to be committed to goals they set for themselves (Schmidt & Wrisberg, 2008). In general, research demonstrates that goals are most effective if they are specific, attainable, challenging, and realistic (Gould, 2006). Goals direct atten-

the bridge to success

tion to important elements of the skill, produce greater effort and persistence, promote new learning strategies, and influence psychological characteristics such as confidence and anxiety (Gould & Chung, 2004).

New slide

There are at least three different types of goals: outcome goals, performance goals, and process goals (Schmidt & Wrisberg, 2008). **Outcome goals** emphasize the results of performance, often in comparison to others—"I want to be first" or "I want to walk without a crutch." Such goals may provide direction to the person, but outcomes are often beyond their control; someone else might win because of outstanding but unexpected performance. **Performance goals** focus on improvement relative to one's own performance, while **process goals** specifically emphasize particular aspects of skill execution. (See table 13.1 for further examples.) Some principles of setting goals include the following:

- Set specific goals.
- Set moderately difficult but realistic goals.
- Set long- and short-term goals.
- Set performance and process, as well as outcome, goals.
- Set practice and competition goals.
- Record goals.
- Develop goal achievement strategies.
- Consider the participant's personality and motivation.
- Foster an individual's goal commitment.
- Provide goal support.
- Provide evaluation and feedback about goals.

Reprinted, by permission, from R.S. Weinberg and D. Gould, 2011, *Foundations of sport and exercise psychology*, 5th ed. (Champaign, IL: Human Kinetics), 349.

Most early research in goal setting compared "do your best" or "give it 100%" to more specific and challenging but achievable goals in industrial settings (e.g., Locke & Latham, 1985). The results showed clearly that the latter type of goals

original research = industrial

TABLE 13.1 Examples of Outcome Goals, Performance Goals, and Process Goals for Different Activities

Activity	Outcome goals	Performance goals	Process goals
Rifle shooting	Finish first in a local shooting competition	Improve bull's-eye percentage from 60% to 70%	Exhale slowly before each trigger squeeze
Water skiing	Qualify for the regional championships	Increase average number of successful buoy passes from four to five	Visually focus on outside of buoys
Volleyball	Win the conference title	Improve blocking percentage from 40% to 50%	Penetrate the plane of the net on each blocking attempt

Reprinted, by permission, from R.A. Schmidt and C.A. Wrisberg, 2008, *Motor learning and performance: A situation-based learning approach*, 4th ed. (Champaign, IL: Human Kinetics), 192.

FIGURE 13.1 Effects of goal setting on learning a shooting task.

Reprinted, by permission, from R.A. Schmidt and T.D. Lee, 2011, *Motor control and learning: A behavioral emphasis*, 5th ed. (Champaign, IL: Human Kinetics), 353. Adapted from B.A. Boyce, 1992, "Effects of assigned versus participant-set goals on skill acquisition and retention of a selected shooting task," *Journal of Teaching in Physical Education* 11(3): 220-234.

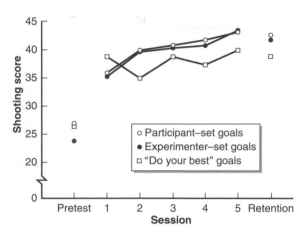

was much superior to the former. Similar comparisons between "do your best" and more specific personal goals have been made in sport and exercise psychology research (see review by Kyllo & Landers, 1995). The findings are similar to those in industrial settings but not quite as dramatic in sport. Schmidt and Lee (2005) speculate that in "do your best" sport situations, people may secretly set their own goals, thus overshadowing the experimenter's manipulations. They also point out that most of the goal-setting research has ignored the difference between performance and learning, with the exception of Boyce (1992). The task was rifle shooting and Boyce used three groups: One was "do your best"; the second was encouraged to set specific but individual goals; and the third was provided with individual goals set by the experimenter and based on previous performance. The results are shown in figure 13.1. The "do your best" group performed better than the other groups only during the first practice session, while the specific goal-setting procedures in the latter two groups were equally effective during performance and retention. It would seem that goal setting has a positive impact on both performance and learning. The goal-setting effects with children are largely unknown, and practitioners might wish to encourage individual goal setting but to check goals periodically to ensure they are realistic. More research is clearly required about development and goal setting.

Demonstrations

Demonstrations, modeling, and observational learning are terms often used interchangeably. These activities are so common in physical activity instruction and therapy that we do not give them much thought. The term demonstration is more closely aligned to motor learning and instruction, while modeling and observational learning are terms more frequently used in the context of social learning and sport psychology. In any case, practitioners often demonstrate a skill such as a forward roll, provide some verbal cues, and then send the class or team off to practice the skill. That a picture is worth a thousand words seems true for learning motor skills. In addition to demonstrations by the instructor, video clips of successful performers and even photos of correct actions may be used (Schmidt & Wrisberg, 2008). Under certain circumstances, demonstrations are effective in teaching motor skills (Hodges & Franks, 2002; McCullagh & Weiss, 2001; Schmidt & Lee, 2005; Scully & Newell, 1985). However, we seldom ask how different task goals or types of task might make demonstrations effective or ineffective, who should perform the demonstration, what the learners are supposed to "see" in the demonstration, or how the demonstration affects learning. We turn to these topics now.

What Do You Think?

1. Pick two activities. Provide examples of outcome goals, performance goals, and process goals. Use table 13.1 as a guide if necessary.

2. It is clear that goal setting is essential to student learning and performance. Would your approach to goal setting differ depending on the (a) task and (b) age of students? Explain.

3. Consider the key principles for goal setting stated on page 279. What are some ways in which you could implement these suggestions? Complete the following table:

Goal-setting principle	Strategies for implementation
Set long- and short-term goals	Discuss with students how to set realistic goals and provide examples. Have students set their own goals. Monitor student progress regularly and help modify goals as necessary.
Record goals	
Foster goal commitment	
Provide support for goal achievement	
Provide evaluation and feedback about goals	
Consider personality and motivation	

Demonstrations and models may serve three functions (Weiss, Ebbeck, & Wiese-Bjornstal, 1993). The first is to *help learners acquire new skills,* such as a forward roll, or new behaviors, such as returning equipment to its proper storage spot. This is the main focus of this section. The second function is to *elicit already learned behaviors*, such as going out for a walk or cheering for your team. The third function is to *reduce avoidance behavior* such as fear by using models that manipulate psychological factors like self-confidence, motivation, and anxiety.

Effectiveness of Demonstrations

A demonstration provides a visual template or model of a desired movement pattern (Hodges & Franks, 2002) and can inform the learner about the nature of the task and its requirements. If a task is very simple and the learner has previous knowledge of the criteria for performance, a demonstration may have no impact (Newell, 1981). "Simple" will depend on the task and the skills of the learner. Tasks such as well-learned dance steps or gymnastics actions might not require a demonstration as individual skills; but if they need to be sequenced in a particular order, a demonstration may effectively convey such cognitive information (Hodges & Franks, 2002).

Whether a demonstration for more complex tasks is effective likely depends on the task goal and what measurements of effectiveness are used. In closed skills, the movement form is often the primary learning goal. In gymnastics, synchronized swimming, diving, and figure skating, how one performs is critical to success. Demonstrations may be effective for acquiring new patterns of coordination since the pattern or technique must be practiced repeatedly until performance is automatic (see table 13.2). A meta-analysis compared results from observational studies that used movement form measures and movement outcome measures (Ashford, Bennett, & Davids, 2006).

Meta-analysis is a mathematical technique that standardizes findings from many studies. As you might imagine, one researcher may use a basketball shooting task while another uses badminton tasks, and it is difficult to combine such studies quantitatively. Meta-analysis transforms the results from different tasks into a standard result called an effect size (ES). The ESs from each study can then be combined to determine an overall effect of the treatment, in this case the ES of the difference between demonstration and practice and practice without demonstration. Combined with statistical significance, the ES provides a quantitative snapshot of treatment effects. Many researchers use Cohen's recommended interpretation of ES: an ES of .80 or higher is a large difference, .50 or higher is a moderate difference, and .20 is a small difference.

In Ashford and colleagues (2006), the form measures were movement dynamics, or how the model performed the task. Outcome measures included accuracy or error scores. A moderately large effect size (.77) was reported for movement form measures; that is, demonstration and practice was more effective than practice without demonstration when measures of movement form were employed. A significant but smaller effect size (.17) resulted with outcome measures. That is, demonstration and practice were still superior to practice without demonstrations, but not to the same degree when assessed with movement technique.

It appears that in the early phase of learning, movement technique is more sensitive to the influence of demonstrations than is the outcome of the movement pattern. To state this simply, initial learning is associated with learning how to assemble the movement pattern, but its effect on outcome is not as obvious. One has to learn something about how to perform before the movement pattern has an effect on the outcome. Movement dynamics were more sensitive to the impact of demonstrations than movement outcomes for serial, continuous, and discrete tasks as well (Ashford et al., 2006). Early in the learning of a new movement, several demonstrations are likely necessary to begin building the template, followed by practice with additional demonstrations thoughtfully interspersed (see Weeks & Anderson, 2000). If the task is an old pattern of coordination and learners are required to perform new parameter characteristics (e.g., faster), demonstrations may be no more effective than other forms of instruction (Magill, 2007).

TABLE 13.2 Effectiveness and Noneffectiveness of Demonstrations

Demonstration may be effective when . . .	Demonstration may not be more effective than other types of information when . . .
• People are acquiring a new pattern of coordination	• The task is simple
• The learner requires a template of the movement pattern	• The learner already knows the task and its requirements
• People are learning a movement sequence	• The "new" task involves a change in parameters
• People are learning strategies and decision making	• The outcome is more important than how the movement is performed
• People are learning to cope with difficult emotional situations	• The outcome is clear and performance feedback is available

Try This

A demonstration should be effective when learners are acquiring a new coordination pattern. Let's see. Pair up with another student and crumple up a piece of paper to throw. One person will demonstrate a throw, and the other person will observe and try to copy the demonstrator. As you learned in chapter 5, a "mature" throw for distance involves a step with the contralateral leg, backward swing of the throwing arm, trunk rotation, lag of the throwing arm, and follow-through. The demonstrator should perform one aspect of the throw in a unique way, for example step with the ipsilateral leg, to demonstrate a new pattern of coordination. After a couple of demonstrations, the other person tries to replicate the new throw. Discuss whether the observer was successful.

With open skills, the movement outcome is often the primary goal, not how it is accomplished. The successful basketball pass to a teammate is the desired outcome, but the movement form of the pass (i.e., how it was executed) is much less important. With many open skills, as discussed in the previous chapter, variability in practice is desirable. There is less need for demonstrations that replicate solutions of others and greater need to emphasize discovering novel tactical solutions. Williams and Hodges (2005) contend that demonstrations may be no more effective than verbal descriptions when the instructor wishes the learners to engage in problem solving, as the outcome is not dependent on the replication of a specific movement pattern or technique. When instructors feel that a demonstration is needed in open skills, it should be combined with the outcome effect. This provides information for learners to use as they problem solve and determine how their actions relate to results. Williams and Hodges also recommend that instructors use verbal instruction expressing the intended outcome of the skill before offering a demonstration (e.g., "Can you pass the basketball from out of bounds to the high post area?"). Demonstration can then be used to guide the learning process.

Hodges and Franks (2002) described several of their motor learning studies involving novel bimanual movements, as might be found in juggling or playing musical instruments. In these situations they conclude that "movement demonstrations and instructions relating to the movement of the limbs convey little useful information in the early stage of acquisition, if information about goal attainment is available through feedback" (p. 805). Thus, if the desired goal outcome is clear and performance feedback is available, demonstrations may not be necessary. Of course, bimanual movements are only one class of movements.

Demonstrations and video presentations may assist in development of strategies and decision making based on perceptual information. Martens, Burwitz, and Zuckerman (1976) used the task of trying to move a ball up an incline while it was on top of two rods by manipulating the distance between the rods. The ball falls into one of eight holes beneath the rods, the most distant hole at the end of the incline being the highest score possible. Two approaches were modeled. A "creep" strategy slowly adjusted the rods, which produced consistent but moderate success. A "ballistic" strategy involved very rapid movement of the rods, which resulted in variable levels of achievement but very high scores when it was successful. Observers tended to replicate the strategy they had observed.

Weeks (1992) argued that most observational research had studied internally paced skills such as locomotor skill sequences or serial arm movements, suggesting that more open, externally paced tasks should shed light on the impact of observation on perceptual processing and decision making in more complex tasks. In a coincident timing task, participants had to displace a barrier at the same time the final light was illuminated on a runway of lights. Three modeling groups were created. The first two groups received modeling that focused on perceptual demands of the task or the motor demands of the task. Perceptual modeling encouraged participants to use 10 observations of the runway lights to assist in timing the arm action to the lights, although their hands had to remain on their knees during the prepractice observations. Motor modeling comprised 10 demonstrations of a person actually hitting the barrier. The third group received both motor and perceptual models, while the fourth group received no prepractice modeling. Groups in perceptual modeling conditions performed better than those in only motor task modeling conditions, which suggested that perceptual demands can be modeled and that they are very important in externally paced activity. Weeks recommended that externally paced tasks such as batting or ground strokes in racket sports include training on perceptual characteristics of ball flight. Thus, demonstrations may help learners focus on relevant perceptual cues and strategies of action.

Another line of research has used videotaped models of children trying to cope with difficult situations (McCullagh & Weiss, 2001; Weiss, McCullagh, Smith, & Berlant, 1998). This represents the third function of modeling noted

284

earlier, reducing avoidance behaviors. One approach is to demonstrate coping models that show negative cognition, affect, and behavior as they perform in difficult or fear-evoking situations like learning to swim. Over repeated trials, the model verbalizes more positive thoughts and also improves in physical performance. For example, statements that change from "I can't do this" to "I can do this" convey a shift from lower to higher self-confidence (Weiss et al., 1998). The model demonstrates how he is learning to cope through problem solving and the impact on his motivation. This has the potential to influence self-confidence and motivation.

Research Notes: Observational Learning and Anxiety

Weiss and colleagues (1998) investigated the impact of observational learning on swimming performance and psychological responses of children who were fearful of swimming. Twenty-four children (average age of 6.2 years) participated. They were matched on age and swim lesson experience and then randomly assigned to one of three model types: control, peer mastery, and peer coping. The control group watched cartoons on days of the swimming lessons, but the cartoons provided no information on swimming. The peer mastery group observed a video of a similar-age peer who was positive in verbalizations and technically correct in swimming. The peer coping group video expressed increasingly positive comments and showed gradual improvement in swimming. Three days of swimming lessons were used, and the researchers evaluated the children's swimming skills, fear of swimming, and swimming self-efficacy, in addition to producing field notes. The coping and mastery groups were superior in swimming performance, were higher in self-efficacy, and showed more change in fear compared to the control group. Coping models had a stronger effect on self-efficacy than mastery models. Thus, such use of modeling may help young learners deal with movements involving some inherent degree of fear and produce change in associated psychological variables.

Wrisberg and Pein (2002) explored self-regulation of the frequency of viewing a demonstration of a badminton long serve by novice university students. One group saw a videotaped model prior to each practice attempt, one group chose when to see the model, and one group never saw the model. The first two groups acquired the correct form of the serve and retained that form better than the group that did not see the model. The group with the option of requesting when to see the video requested it only 9.8% of the time, primarily during the first half of the trials on the first day. This suggests that demonstrations may be most effective for novices early in learning and that self-regulation may be an effective practice for promoting learning. Whether these findings would be the same for children must await further research.

Thoughts, feelings, Actions planned to achieve per S. goals

Performance of Demonstrations

Professionally created videos of top athletes performing the perfect throw or swing create the impression that an expert, or at least a very skilled individual, should be performing the demonstration. This makes sense if the goal is to present the ideal movement pattern that all learners should mimic. Consistent with the formation of a perceptual trace or template to which performance will be compared to detect errors, it is often assumed that more frequent demonstrations by an expert will create stronger blueprints. But the previous chapter *who*

highlighted using variability of practice, promoting problem-solving learning, and questioning if one "gold standard" of movement patterns actually exists. These ideas are at odds with the logic of having all learners mimic one movement pattern and question the necessity of an expert model. In fact, there is some consensus that demonstrations by unskilled individuals may be more effective than those by experts (Darden, 1997; Hodges & Franks, 2002; McCullagh & Weiss, 2001; Magill, 2007). Of course, the learner should have some idea about the movement pattern.

Before conferences — stopped here
F 13

Learning models have been shown to be as effective as expert models and in some cases more effective for learning (e.g., Lee & White, 1990). A learning model is a novice who practices the skill and receives feedback from an instructor or coach. The demonstration is of the model trying to acquire the task, receiving feedback, and then using the feedback to construct the next performance effort. By definition, a learning model demonstrates variability in performance. Learners might identify with the learning model because of similarity in status (both are learning) and realize that the demonstrated skill level is within their reach. It seems that learning can occur from watching others make errors. It is also possible that what is being modeled is not the movement pattern per se, but a process of problem solving. This latter idea was originally put forth by Adams (1986), who argued that the learning model was actively, rather than passively, involved in his own learning and that this would produce performance benefits. If more cognitive effort is expended in acquiring the skill, the chances of significant learning are enhanced. In summary, there are motivational, attention, and learning explanations for the beneficial impact of learning models.

Darden (1997) summarized the detail of expert versus learning model demonstrations (table 13.3). Such learning models could be incorporated into a class through the use of reciprocal teaching or learning groups in which all students are both observers and learning models in a problem-solving activity. Magill (2007) also recommends that a checklist of key aspects of the skill be presented to the pairs or groups to guide observation and feedback to the learner.

TABLE 13.3 Expert Versus Learning Demonstrations

Short-term (expert)	Long-term (learning)
THE MODEL SHOULD REPRESENT . . .	
• High status	• Similar status (peer)
• High-level performance	• Performance just above student's current level
• Repeated, continuous demonstrations	• Varied demonstrations
• Correct performance	• Correct performance plus errors
• Verbal cues with demonstration	• Verbal cues plus instructor feedback with demonstration
• Identification of model's correct technique	• Identification and correction of model's errors
• One correct technique	• Exploration of several task solutions
• Encouragement of mimicry and exact reproduction	• Encouragement of problem solving and thinking

Reprinted, by permission, from G.F. Darden, 1997, "Demonstrating motor skills: Rethinking that expert demonstration," *Journal of Physical Education, Recreation and Dance* 68(6): 31-35.

What Do You Think?

The section has probably made you realize that using demonstrations effectively is much more complex than you previously thought. Describe how you could use demonstrations to teach the following:

- Students who are being introduced to the skill of overhand throw for the first time
- Students who need a review of how to dribble a basketball

Theoretical Explanations of Demonstrations

Thus far we have discussed several demonstration issues: when demonstrations are effective, who should perform the demonstration, and what the learner is viewing. Under some circumstances, demonstrations are very important. But the "when," "who," and "what" questions do not deal with how or why demonstrations are effective. "How" and "why" are theoretical questions. We now look at motor learning, social learning, and ecological theories to see how each explains why demonstrations are helpful to the learner.

Motor Learning Theories

Demonstrations are a part of classic theories of skill acquisition, including the closed-loop theory of motor control (Adams, 1971) and schema theory (Schmidt, 1975b). In Adams' closed-loop theory, a perceptual trace or template of the movement develops with practice. Sensory feedback during subsequent movements can be compared to the perceptual trace to ensure correct execution. An additional memory trace was posited that initiates the movement because the same memory trace could not initiate and evaluate the correctness of a response. Schema theory is an open-loop account of motor control. Not unlike Adams, Schmidt postulated two types of schemas: a recall schema for response production and a recognition schema for response evaluation. If a template of movement already exists (that is, the perceptual trace of Adams and the recall schema of Schmidt), then a demonstration will likely function to refine the template to which feedback during movement execution will be compared (Hodges & Franks, 2002). For example, if a throwing schema exists, the demonstration will provide information about the specific type of throw, force, and direction. If the movement template is not established and is novel, the demonstrations may help learners engage in cognitive processes similar to those that occur in physical practice (Blandin & Proteau, 2000).

The stages of motor learning according to Gentile (1972) and Fitts and Posner (1967) were discussed in chapter 3. Each provides some insight into how movement templates might be established in the early stages. Gentile (1972) refers to early learning as "getting the idea of the movement"; and Fitts and Posner's first stage was termed "cognitive" because the learner attends to cues and feedback to develop an executive program. In both of these theories, a demonstration may present the "idea" of the movement and the "cues" that are necessary for initial learning of the movement skill.

Social Learning Theory

Social learning (Bandura 1986, 1997) theory is perhaps the most detailed account of demonstrations, although "modeling" and "observational learning" are preferred terms. Bandura's original focus was social learning of behaviors rather than motor skills. He contended that people learn most about their social world through observation and that practice is not essential if the behaviors are social or cognitive. This makes sense for simple responses that are already in people's repertoire, for example a sequence of movements. If the movements can already be accomplished, the activity becomes more cognitive than motor (Hodges & Franks, 2002). The demonstration of the sequence might effectively begin the learning process.

Bandura asserts that modeling is information processing with four subprocesses that transfer or code information from the model into a template of correctness to which future movements are compared. The first subprocess is attention to the modeling. (This will be affected by the observer's cognitive capabilities and arousal level.) Attention will also be influenced by characteristics of the modeled event, for example its complexity. If a movement pattern is complex, then the observer should be assisted to focus on relevant cues by verbal directives or alternating good and poor performances. Retention, the second phase, involves reformulating the event into a memory representation. It is assumed to be an abstraction of the event and likely verbal or visual, depending on the task. The third subprocess is production. As McCullagh and Weiss (2001) pointed out, this was not well developed in Bandura's original writings because he was concerned with explaining social behaviors that might be dichotomous, that is, either performed or not. Motor learning specialists are concerned with movement quality, and demonstrations may convey spatial and timing aspects of importance. The final information processing subprocess is motivation, since the individual must be motivated to exhibit the behavior. Reinforcement of observed models or actions by the observer enhances the motivation of the observer to reproduce the action demonstrated. These four processes are developmental in nature; the first three are cognitively oriented while the fourth is motivation oriented (Weiss et al., 1993). Observation learning is therefore expected to improve with age because of critical developmental changes in attention, retention, production, and motivation. *ARP_M*

Ecological Perspectives

As we have discussed in several chapters, practice from this theoretical viewpoint is designed to enable the learner to explore the perceptual–motor landscape and to assemble functional coordination patterns that offer solutions to movement problems. Movement variability is highly valued, and demonstrations that highlight variability rather than one ideal movement pattern should be effective. This theory views perception as direct, and ecological researchers try to determine what information is available and useful for the learner in demonstrations without cognitive interpretations and transformation of information as put forth by Bandura. They place more emphasis on what information is picked up from a demonstration than on how the information should be presented (Hodges & Franks, 2002). It has been proposed that observers are sensitive to the relative motions of movements and that this information can be used to assemble coordination patterns (Scully & Newell, 1985).

Support for the ecological perspective and what information is picked up in a demonstration comes from research using point-light displays

Verbal Cues or Contrast good + poor

(e.g., Williams, 1989). A point-light display is a video showing dots of light that have been placed at a person's joints. Williams provided a point-light display of a throwing motion with dots placed on the wrist, elbow, and shoulder. The observer saw the movement of only the dots, not the arm or ball. Almost 90% of children and adults reported seeing a throwing action after four trials. This research suggests that observers attend to information about the relationships of limb components in the movement pattern. In ecological terms, these relationships are invariant relative motions (Scully & Newell, 1985). Recall from chapter 1 that invariant features include the sequence of action, relative timing, and relative force. The sequence of movements such as rotation of the trunk, the backswing of the arm, and the step with the contralateral foot, followed by forward rotation, was apparently conveyed to the adults and children by the moving dots. Magill (2007) reviewed similar studies of walking patterns in which people distinguished individual gaits on the basis of unique relative motions rather than a single factor such as walking velocity. As he concluded, "We can hypothesize that the invariant relationships in coordinated movement constitute critical information involved in observational learning" (Magill, 2007, p. 311). However, the movements used in most of this research have been rather common and well practiced, such as throwing, walking, and running. It is not yet clear how instructors might help learners focus on the relative motions of skills that are not yet mastered or are very novel, since the perception of the invariant relative motions is likely implicit.

Learning From Demonstrations

What learners see in a demonstration is likely influenced by the nature of the task. In addition, the interpretation will be influenced by the theory behind the research. Schmidt and Lee (2005) suggest that demonstrations can lead to learners' acquiring movement strategies, spatial information, and temporal information. Strategies might include task-specific approaches like the "creeping" and "ballistic" movements described by Martens and colleagues (1976) or throwing a basketball from the foul line with one or two hands. More general problem-solving skills suggested by learning model research might include a student receiving teacher feedback about the front crawl and then saying to herself, "I have to raise my elbow higher during recovery." Modeling of coping strategies led to performance improvement but also to enhancement of psychological function such as self-efficacy. These coping strategies helped the learner acquire a more positive psychological approach.

Spatial information can also be picked up, as shown in a series of studies on learning sign language through modeling (Carroll & Bandura, 1990). Relative motion is also spatial and temporal information about body parts moving in relation to each other or to the environment, and strong evidence suggests that learners are aware of this information (Ashford et al., 2006). Temporal information, that is, about timing of movements, has been demonstrated in a number of studies sometimes described as auditory modeling (Magill, 2007). Think of the instructor who claps his hands, suggesting a skipping motion that young students happily try to imitate. This research presents auditory information about a movement time or rhythm and has led to gains in rhythmic timing of movement sequences as might occur in dance.

Developmental Considerations in Demonstrations

Chapters 7 and 8 dealt with functional constraints such as cognitive functioning, attention, knowledge, self-regulation, and memory. These constraints are developmental in nature, improving with age, experience, and knowledge of the task at hand. Adults, adolescents, and those with sport-specific knowledge are more likely to use self-regulated learning strategies and have access to other capacities that have resulted from years of experience dealing with educational and movement challenges. These functional constraints, coupled with structural constraints, give adults and adolescents an advantage over children when faced with unfamiliar tasks. Experienced observers are more likely to produce closer approximations of a model early in learning. As Ashford, Davids, and Bennett (2007) state, "Adults can adapt existing coordination tendencies but in a way that results in the acquisition of a new coordination pattern suited to the goals of a task" (p. 548). McCullagh and Weiss (2001) provided the corollary that motor skill instruction for children under 12 years of age should facilitate task-relevant attention ("Try not to look at the ball when you are dribbling"), strategies ("Watch me. . . . After I kick the ball to a teammate, I run quickly to a spot where I can receive a pass"), and knowledge ("Let me show you an offside") and that these factors must be considered in observational learning.

McCullagh and Weiss (2001), in a detailed review of studies that shed light on children's ability to benefit from models, underscored the point that effectiveness of models is multifaceted, depending on the age of the observer; how performance is measured; and whether acquisition, retention, or transfer is assessed. We have also discussed that the impact of demonstrations is affected by type of task and task goals. Therefore, developmental generalizations to guide practice are difficult to generate. With young children 4 or 5 years of age, a "show and tell" model can be effective for learning a sequence of movements (Weiss, 1983). "Show and tell" is a demonstration and explanation of what should be done and is helpful for children who do not spontaneously attend to task-relevant cues, such as stepping forward with the foot opposite the throwing arm. It may also use verbal rehearsal strategies for remembering the order of events, such as "arms, legs, glide," for the breaststroke. In an obstacle course task, children were encouraged to use verbal self-instruction by "thinking aloud," that is, saying phrases like "jump and clap" and "jump-jump" that matched the activity they were performing (Weiss, 1983). Older children may benefit from show and tell but not more than from a visual demonstration without suggested rehearsal strategies. With novel tasks requiring new patterns of coordination such as juggling, Meaney (1994) showed that both children and adults benefited from verbal rehearsal and cues combined with a demonstration, whereas adults were capable of improvement from only the visual demonstration. Physical performance by the adults was better than that of the children, and the adults used more strategies. These studies support the premise that the cognitive developmental level of children should be considered with demonstrations, and that children benefit from instruction to focus on relevant cues and to engage in intentional memory strategies.

Wiese-Bjornstal and Weiss (1992) showed that girls as young as 7 to 9 years could watch a demonstration of a softball fast pitch and recognize a correct model from one of four videotaped alternatives, could engage in verbal cues similar to the model, and could show some of the model's form (e.g., stride length, release body angle). Having learners restate the main points about a demonstration and verbal cues following show and tell would be good teaching practice. Increased frequency of observation of the model and more practice resulted in better recognition of correct form and in performance that resembled the model's. Self-regulation and observational learning research also supports the cognitive–developmental changes that occur during childhood and the influence on demonstrations. Older children (aged 11 years) have been shown to request more observations of a model than younger children (aged 8 years) in an attempt to attend to and rehearse a dance sequence (Cadopi, Chatillon, & Baldy, 1995). The older children also used more verbal self-instruction, which is a self-regulated strategy.

 ## Research Notes: Developmental Self-Regulation

Bouffard and Dunn (1993) explored whether developmental differences existed in children's use of self-regulation while they were learning movement sequences of American Sign Language (ASL). They compared children 6 and 7 years to children 9 and 10 years who had unlimited time and unlimited trials of watching a tape with the ASL sequence. The length of the sequence was 1.5 times longer than an estimated memory span for each child. When individual children thought they had learned the sequence, they rang a bell, which signaled the researchers to enter the testing room to watch the child perform the sequence. Thus, this study explored what children do spontaneously in response to a demonstration without any guidance from the teacher. The older children displayed superior recall of the sequences compared to the younger group. In addition, the older children watched the demonstration videos more frequently than the younger ones and used more strategies for learning the sequences, for example, miming the gestures and rehearsing movements. Further, the 9- and 10-year-olds used more instances of language indicating that they monitored their own learning more frequently. It appears that models can assist in self-regulation development and that older children will spontaneously use self-regulation more often than younger children.

A final developmental factor regarding modeling is the tendency for children to focus on task goals in a demonstration rather than movement form. Earlier we stated that movement dynamics (approximation of movement form) are more sensitive to the impact of demonstrations than movement outcomes (outcome performance such as accuracy or time) earlier in skill acquisition for serial, continuous, and discrete tasks (Ashford et al., 2006). It seems that developmental factors affect this generalization. Ashford and colleagues (2007) conducted a meta-analysis of studies that compared children and adults with regard to their awareness of movement dynamics, movement outcome, or both in demonstrations. They analyzed 55 studies. The ES of movement dynamics for adults (.80) was larger than for children (.24) when demonstrations were compared to practice-only conditions. This indicates that adults benefited more than children from demonstration and practice, compared to practice without demonstration, when measures of movement form were employed in the research. In fact, while the ES for the children was positive (.24), it was not significant. The opposite was found for measures of movement outcome, since the ES for adults (−0.02) was negligible but more substantial (.48) for children. In other words, children seem to be assisted more by demonstrations when assessed on measures of movement outcome, thus adding a developmental caveat to the earlier generalization that initial learning is associated with learning how to assemble the movement patterns. Children seem to be more aware of movement outcomes in demonstrations than of movement form compared to adults. Thus, therapists and instructors should feel comfortable using demonstrations with an emphasis on movement outcomes with children. While modeling can facilitate skill acquisition of closed skills, the magnitude of the effect is dependent on age and the measure used to quantify learning. Children can discern and benefit from movement form but have a tendency to focus on movement outcomes. The extent to which instruction can "move" children from movement outcomes to movement form remains unknown; hence teachers and coaches should be sensitive to the natural tendencies of their students and athletes and provide assistance in focusing on movement form if they feel that the youngsters possess the necessary cognitive functioning, attention, knowledge, self-regulation, and memory.

What Do You Think?

Review what you learned in chapter 7 about cognitive functioning, attention, knowledge, self-regulation, and memory. How do these act as constraints for children who are engaging in observation learning? What structural constraints should be considered?

Verbal Instruction

Verbal instruction is a frequent and expected prepractice element often used in conjunction with demonstrations. Verbalization and demonstrations may provide cues that are redundant, but they may also provide different information to learners (McCullagh & Weiss, 2001). Instructions could be in written form such as a task card, but more often they are spoken. Verbal instructions and cues (short phrases like "bend your knees") are assumed to facilitate learning and to establish a safe practice setting. These instructions must be brief. Magill (2007) recommends one or two instructions about what to do because learners will have to remember the instructions and then perform the skill, so the instructor does not want to exceed their attention capacity. This is particularly important for novice learners or children.

Verbal information conveys the nature of task requirements, just as demonstrations do (Lee, Chamberlin, & Hodges, 2001). Examples include the correct and consistent movement form of a closed skill such as a dive, the creation of a smooth sequence of movements in the correct order in learning to stand independently while recovering from an accident, or the movement outcome goal such as a successful pass to a teammate in an open sport. More specifically, Schmidt and Wrisberg (2008) and Schmidt and Lee (2005) indicate that verbal information provides an initial orientation to a new skill, an overall idea or image of a movement, a means of recognizing one's own errors (e.g., checking wrist on a follow-through), details of how to hold an apparatus or implement, where and how to move in a game, cues that are most important (e.g., seams of a baseball), and what results performers should try to achieve (see previous section in this chapter on goal setting). A verbal phrase may simplify a rather complex movement in the tennis serve, such as "Scratch your back with the racket," or reinforce the order of movements, such as "arms, legs, glide" for the breaststroke. Instructors may also promote transfer of related previously learned movements and strategies through verbal means. Feelings that should be expected from a movement can also be conveyed (e.g., "If you are stretching properly you should feel a slight pull in the calf muscle").

Implicit and Explicit Learning

The examples in the previous paragraph underscore the many instances in which clear instructions would appear to be important in skill acquisition. Yet, there is not a great deal of research supporting these common purposes and outcomes of verbal instruction with respect to motor learning beyond specifying the task requirements, for example speed, accuracy, or both; movement form; or movement outcome (Hodges & Franks, 2002; Lee et al., 2001). In fact, research exists that suggests, in some situations, verbal instruction may not be helpful beyond personal practice and may be detrimental to learning. Some of this research deals with **explicit** and **implicit learning**.

Gentile (1998) extended the cognitive learning distinction between explicit and implicit learning to motor learning. "Explicit" refers to conscious awareness of such factors as goal attainment and developing the relationship between the learner and the task. The aim of verbal instructions is to help learners become explicitly aware of some aspects of the skill (e.g., "The goal of this skill is to . . ." or "Hold the ball with your fingers along the stitching"). This is similar to declarative knowledge. Implicit learning is not conscious and likely deals with issues such as force production; for example, the young toddler is offered a tricycle and initially is unable to contract and relax the appropriate muscle groups at the correct time and order, and with the appropriate force, to move the vehicle. He does learn to cycle but is not aware of how he does it. Even adults are unaware of the physical principles that govern bicycle riding or how to explain the tying of shoelaces. Much motor learning is implicit, and knowing mechanical principles is not likely to assist such learning.

Hodges and Franks (2002) propose that tasks with high perceptual–motor demands or complex response requirements would benefit less from explicit instructions. Some support for this comes from a study by Farrow and Abernethy (2002) in which they manipulated the amount of time participants viewed a tennis ball after a serve. The participants were asked to predict whether the ball would fall to their forehand or backhand. The implicit instruction group received no information about the server's action and direction of the ball. The explicit instruction group received specific information through videos, verbal and written information, and feedback during practice trials. Not surprisingly, the explicit group was able to write more rules and strategies that were important for returning serves than the implicit group. The two groups performed equally well in predicting the direction of the tennis ball, but there was an advantage for the implicit group at ball contact, that is, when no ball flight was evident. It seems that the implicit group was using the anticipatory information to predict direction without conscious awareness and without advanced cues.

293

The potential detrimental effect of verbal information was shown by Green and Flowers (1991) in a study in which participants had to manipulate a joystick to catch a "ball" that moved across a monitor. An explicit instruction group received information about expected pathways and their probability. The implicit group received no information other than the goal of the game. During 800 trials, the group who received explicit instruction actually performed more poorly than the implicit group, presumably because the explicit group devoted more attention to remembering the rule and looking for its occurrence so that their performance was disrupted. It seems that instructors should use verbal instructions cautiously when a task has a high degree of perceptual input, as in video games, and involves complex responses such as catching a ball that is thrown fast.

Try This

Create groups of two or three people. We assume all members of the group are able to tie their own shoelaces. It is a common activity that we do regularly, and university students have had many years of practice. Create two columns on a sheet of paper, one labeled "Explicit" and one "Implicit." For the first phase of this activity the group lists explicit information about how to tie shoelaces. This will be a bit of a challenge because you have had so many years of practice with this task. After you generate some explicit knowledge, actually tie your shoelaces a couple of times and see if you can add to the explicit list and begin to identify implicit factors. Select a sport skill and repeat the exercise.

A number of studies have used a ski simulator task to explore explicit and implicit motor learning, as well as discovery learning. The participants' goal is usually to move the platform as far to the left and right as possible for a specified time and with a constant cycle time, for example, for 60 seconds with each cycle taking 3 seconds.

In a study by Wulf and Weigelt (1997), one group—on the basis of previous research on participants who demonstrated high performance—was given explicit instructions to exert force once they moved beyond the center of the simulator platform. The second group was told only the goal of the activity, in this case, to move the platform as far to the left and right as possible for 90 seconds, with each cycle taking 2 seconds. This group was considered a discovery or implicit learning group. On performance and transfer tasks, the discovery group performed better. These individuals apparently learned the technique (exert force once beyond the center) in an implicit manner.

A number of studies have used the ski stimulatory apparatus as well as other complex motor tasks to explore the impact of both demonstrations and verbal instruction compared to discovery learning (see Hodges & Franks, 2002; Lee et al., 2001). In general, the results support the effectiveness of allowing learners to discover how best to achieve task goals. It seems that instructions may interfere with learning if attention is misdirected by either demonstrations or verbal instruction. Of course, this assumes that the task goal is understood and that performance feedback of some form is present in the learning situation. This research has frequently included novice learners, but they have usually been adults rather than children.

Ringenbach and Lantero (2005) extended this line of thinking regarding self-discovery. They asked typically developing children and adults, as well as adults with Down syndrome, to draw circles with both hands. First, in an exploratory phase, participants performed the task in any way they wished. Then the three groups were instructed to draw the circles either symmetrically (in-phase) or asymmetrically (anti-phase). Adults without a disability responded without problems. However the children and the adults with Down syndrome, who had performed symmetrically in the exploratory or self-selected phase, performed less symmetrically when they were requested to perform symmetrically. This demonstrates that even with children and people with an intellectual disability, self-selected or exploratory instructions may be best.

Verbal Cues

Verbal cues are commonly used by coaches, instructors, and therapists. They are brief and concise phrases that direct attention to regulatory conditions in the environment, prompt key skill components (Magill, 2007), or initiate activity. The classic phrase, "Look at the ball" directs attention; "Bend your knees" focuses on a skill component; and "Ready, set, go" prompts activity. Magill (2007) reviewed some of the research supporting verbal cues as a means to direct attention, to guide rehearsal of a skill, to self-prompt while performing, to focus attention while performing, and to enhance the effect of demonstrations. The following are some practical suggestions for using verbal cues (Magill, 2007, p. 327):

Bio r M.L.

Dots on Board

- Cues should be short—one, two, or three words.
- Cues should relate logically to the aspects of the skill the cues are intended to prompt.
- Cues can prompt a sequence of several movements.

Video

- Cues should be limited in number. Cue only the most critical elements of performing the skill.
- Cues can be especially helpful for directing shifts of attention.
- Cues are effective for prompting a distinct rhythmical structure for a sequence of movements.
- Cues must be carefully timed so that they serve as prompts and do not interfere with performance.
- Cues should initially be spoken by the performer.

Reprinted from R.A. Magill, 2007, *Motor learning and control: Concepts and applications,* 8th ed. (New York: McGraw-Hill), 327. © The McGraw-Hill Companies, Inc.

What Do You Think?

1. Choose two skills. Describe how you could effectively implement verbal instruction to facilitate student learning. Provide specific examples of verbal cues.
2. Can you recall instances when an instructor, perhaps even your professor in this course, seemed to go on and on verbally and finally you said, "So that's what you mean!" What made this difficult? Was it simply too much detail, or was the goal of the activity unclear?

Directing Attention and Providing Guidance

One of the uses of verbal cues is directing attention. Previously presented research provided a cautionary note that explicitly directing attention to optimal or correct coordination of the limbs may not facilitate learning and may even be detrimental. How can we assist learners to focus on their bodies or the environment to promote skill acquisition, and what are the developmental implications? As mentioned in chapter 7, one of the concepts of attention is **visually searching** for environmental cues necessary for performance (Magill, 2007; Schmidt & Lee, 2005). Attention may be **broad** or **narrow** and **external** or **internal** (Magill, 2007). Most of us can remember our driver education instructor reminding us to take a broad view of the road, rather than a narrow focus on the center line in order to steer the car. Attention can also be external or internal. Open sports such as ice hockey require the goaltender to assume an external–broad focus as the play develops at the other end of the rink. But as the play descends around his net, a more narrow focus is necessary as well as an internal focus pertaining to personal balance, stability, and readiness to move one way or another. Of course, athletes may be required to switch attention in a matter of seconds or less.

performance or outcome

The internal–external direction of focus is also related to the question of whether it is preferable to focus on one's own movements (internal) or on the intended effects of the movement (external) as one acquires a skill. Should the golfer attend to the backswing and placement of the club head, her forward movements, and follow-through (internal) or simply the contact of the club and ball (external)? Research generally supports the conclusion that learners who focus on the movement effects will perform at a higher level than those who focus on their own movements (Wulf & Prinz, 2001). This is consistent with the positive view of discovery learning and the potential detrimental effects of incorrect attentional focus via demonstrations and verbal instructions regarding coordination patterns. This has been shown on a variety of skills in golfing, basketball, volleyball, soccer, and ski simulation with learners who were beginners. For example, Wulf and Su (2007, Experiment 1) had participants learn a golf "pitch shot" to hit a ball into a circular target. They received a demonstration of the task as well as verbal cues about grip, stance, and posture. Subsequent instructions differed among three groups. The internal focus group was directed to attend to the swinging motion of the arms. The external focus group was directed to the pendulum-like action of the club, while the control group received no-attention focus instructions. The results (figure 13.2) demonstrated the superiority of the external focus group on a retention test, while the internal and no-attention group were similar. It is argued that an external focus promotes more automatic movement control compared to a focus on body movements, which may introduce some awkwardness because automatic control processes are disrupted (Wulf & Prinz, 2001; Wulf & Su, 2007).

FIGURE 13.2

External focus groups performed better in retention tests than the other groups in the Wulf and Su (2007) study.

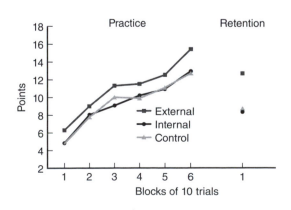

A related study with the ski simulator investigated self-regulation and physical assistance. Physical assistance such as training wheels and spotting belts are used to enhance safety and promote skill acquisition. Wulf and Toole (1999) compared a group who controlled when to use poles to assist with performance on the simulator with a group who had no influence on use of the poles. The self-regulated group was superior on a retention test without poles. This supports the use of physical assistance, as well as self-control over when such assistance is received. Research on providing assistance for children in motor learning does not seem to exist.

The external focus viewpoint is a rather robust finding for novice learners, but children have generally not been involved in these studies. One exception is a dart throwing study with children and adults by Emanuel, Jarus, and Bart (2008). The children were 8.4 to 9.8 years old. Internal instructions focused on movements of the shoulder, arm, and fingers while external instructions focused on the target, the darts, or the flight of the darts. The findings supported the advantage of the external focus instructions for the adults, thus replicating much of the previous research in this area. With the children, the internal and external focus groups were equal with the exception that the internal group was superior on a test of transfer. While more research is necessary to confirm and extend this finding, it seems reasonable that instructors might consider some internal instructions of focus with children.

Visual selective attention refers to directing visual attention to environmental information, often called a visual cue, that helps one prepare and perform an action (Magill, 2007). Important visual cues to guide movements are available in central vision (where the eyes focus) and peripherally. In competitive sport, there is much evidence that experienced or expert performers are better able to attend to the cues than less experienced or novice performers and that they pick up the cues earlier, thus enabling them to anticipate their opponent's movement and prepare their own response. The specific cues are dependent on the situation. Waiting for the serve in tennis, experts actually watched for cues in the few seconds prior to initiation of the serve, particularly focused on the head and shoulder and trunk region (Goulet, Bard, & Fleury, 1989). Experienced players in soccer attended more to the hip region of an opponent in one-on-one situations than less experienced players (Williams & Davids, 1998). Lefebvre and Reid (1998) asked boys and girls aged 6 to 12 years, with and without coordination difficulties, to watch a videotape and predict if the ball thrown by a child would land to the left, to the right, or at the catcher. The older children were more effective predictors with less visual information available; boys were generally more effective than girls; and those without coordination problems were more effective than those with coordination problems. The authors concluded that experience was a significant factor in the development of attention to early cues. Since the cues are quite specific to the activity context, instructors can assist by directing learners' attention to relevant cues as well as providing sufficient practice to use such cues (Magill 2007). Video-based visual search programs have also shown some promise as a teaching tool (e.g., Williams, Ward, Smeeton, & Allen, 2004).

What Do You Think?

Internal focus may be important for transfer of skills among children. As a future teacher or coach, how will you instruct children to use internal focus? Provide specific examples.

Summary

This chapter would provide Brittany, the hockey coach featured in the chapter opening, with some guidance about factors to consider prior to ice hockey practice. Goal setting, demonstrations, verbalizations, and attention directing and physical guidance have been used effectively to promote performance and learning. Demonstrations and verbalizations are advantageous when there is need to explain a task goal, outline a movement sequence, promote the use of strategies, deal with a fearful learning situation, or point out an important cue. If the task goal is movement outcome oriented in a team sport, too many demonstrations and words might detract from problem-solving processing of team tactics. Demonstrations and verbalizations as means to acquire patterns of coordination with closed skills may best be described as overrated, assuming that the task goal is known and performance feedback is available. Implicit learning characterizes much motor learning. Our female hockey coach can feel comfortable using carefully placed demonstrations, sometimes in concert with player demonstrations, and verbal cues to guide action and attention. She was correct in her questions about the potential detrimental impact of too many words and too many expert demonstrations.

Supplemental Activities

1. Some of the suggestions in this chapter might appear contradictory to common practice. For example, research on the impact of demonstrations suggests that they are not as beneficial in as many situations as we might have thought. Interview an experienced and excellent teacher or coach. Determine where your interviewee agrees and disagrees with some of the generalizations in this chapter. Can you resolve the areas of disagreement?

2. Goal setting is so important in many walks of life that the Internet has extensive quotes and images related to goal setting. Locate these and see if they can be matched to outcome goals, performance goals, and process goals. You will also find steps and guides to goal setting. Do these match some of the goal-setting principles discussed in the chapter? Do some of them go beyond the goal-setting principles?

Practice

CHAPTER OBJECTIVES

After reading this chapter, you should be able to

> understand and explain variable and constant practice and the contextual interference effect,

> describe block and random practice by explaining how they are used in instruction,

> explain part and whole practice and their respective challenges for transferring to real-life learning situations,

> describe mental practice and imagery and how they may enhance learning and performance, and

> explain how instructors can mass or distribute practice.

Optimal Practice for Maximal Results

As a new physical therapist, Tawnya knows that she is ready to diagnose and treat many skeletal and muscular problems. But her boss has asked her to teach Philip, a young man, how to walk with new prostheses. He lost both legs just above the knees, and thankfully his legs have healed after the operation. He is eager to get out of the wheelchair he has been using since his operation because prostheses will allow greater mobility than the wheelchair. As a snowboarder in high school, he wonders whether he will be able to enjoy the sport once again. The insurance company has informed Tawnya's clinic of the total number of billing hours, and Tawnya is concerned that unless Philip makes some immediate progress he might slip into a depression. Thus, she wants to maximize her time with him within the total hours available and within the specific sessions that her boss has already established. Tawnya realizes that she has to plan the practice time efficiently. She wonders what practice options are available.

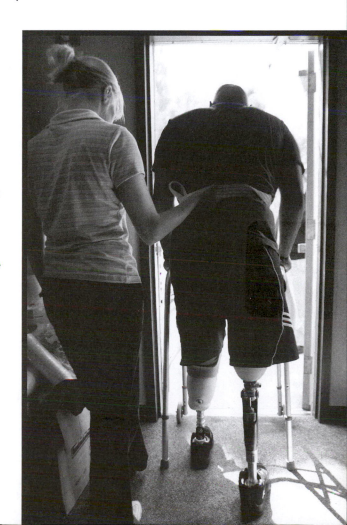

In the present chapter we focus on many types of practice, or how practice can be organized, including variable, constant, random, blocked, part, whole, mental, massed, and distributed practice. That is a lot of different types of practice! The individual learner or instructor or therapist can manipulate these types with the intent to augment learning. This chapter provides the scientific support and discusses issues regarding practice organization that might be relevant to Tawnya. Yet there are variables, such as age, experience, or type of skill, that affect whether or not a particular form of practice actually accelerates learning compared to another.

"One practice variable dwarfs all the others in terms of importance and is so obvious that it need hardly be mentioned at all—practice" (Schmidt & Lee, 2005, p. 322) "If anything is certain in motor learning it is that there is no better, faster, or more efficient way of achieving it than with practice" (Lee, Chamberlin, & Hodges, 2001, p. 136). So, to learn racquetball, downhill skiing, or how to use new prostheses, you need to practice. That is not telling you anything you did not already know. But how much practice is necessary and how practice should be organized are more complicated questions.

Is it just a matter of repeating movements many times to ensure you become skilled, for example practicing walking with prostheses over and over again? If basketball skills of dribbling, shooting, and passing need to be improved, should you focus on one skill for a considerable time before practicing the next skill? What advice can we give the coach who has her soccer team practice fun drills over and over again, only to see the players incapable of executing the skills in a real game?

Research findings relevant to practitioners are sometimes dependent on the type of task involved. When motor learning was in its infancy, simple tasks were often used with which people had little experience. This made much sense because simple tasks could be investigated in controlled laboratories in which only the experimenter and participant interacted. Novel tasks were preferred since researchers did not want their findings affected by previous learning and experience. In fact, early motor learning specialists helped create tasks such as linear positioning, pursuit rotor, coincidence anticipation, and stabilometer tasks. The required responses sometimes included only one degree of freedom or were as simple as pressing a button. Occasionally, an inquisitive young researcher questioned whether the results from controlled laboratory environments could be applied to real environments, for example a physical education class in which one teacher works with 30 students who influence each other and have different experiences with skills to be learned, which are often complex. The practice organization literature therefore has included discussions of findings from laboratories using controlled conditions versus real-life tasks and situations.

Amount of Practice

Practical reasons have restricted the number of motor learning studies using extensive practice, but those conducted have been very insightful. Bryan and Harter (1897, 1899) investigated telegraphic skills over months of practice; Snoddy (1926) required participants to practice a mirror drawing task for 100 days; and Crossman (1959) reported performance changes in cigar rolling over seven years of practice. These studies, among others, have led to a number of general conclusions.

- Early improvement in skill acquisition is generally very large and becomes smaller with additional practice.
- All things being equal, more learning will occur with more practice (power law of practice, Schmidt & Lee, 2005).
- Plateaus in performance may occur during skill acquisition.
- Improved performance, however minute, may be apparent after many years of practice.

As we mentioned in chapter 7, experts often have had 10,000 hours of practice, and a significant portion of those hours occurred under deliberate practice conditions (Ericsson, 2003). Deliberate practice involves activities designed to improve current levels of performance, requiring much effort, but is not necessarily enjoyable. Research has not compared deliberate practice with other forms of extensive practice, and therefore it is difficult to claim that expertise can be achieved only by deliberate practice. Also, athletes have often reported enjoyment under deliberate attempts to improve performance (Deakin & Cobley, 2003). In any case, the amount of practice is a significant factor toward expert performance. While questions of deliberate practice remain, Lee and colleagues (2001) have astutely observed, "The deliberate practice hypothesis does serve to refocus the practitioner's attention onto the importance of practice, rather than 'natural talent' when identifying individuals as potentially future experts" (p. 117). Of course, expert levels of performance may not be a motivating factor for many individuals, either children or adults. They may be motivated to downhill ski so that they can participate with friends and manage a single-diamond hill safely—the desire for competition and to be faster than everyone else is not a factor. One of your authors would be pleased to break 100 in golf, but has no aspirations to challenge Tiger Woods. While the amount of practice required to achieve some personal criterion of success will be influenced by individual goals and motivation, the author should not underestimate the amount of practice that would be required to break 100.

Variable Practice

Variable practice is practice of a skill with several variations of the skill itself or the context of the skill. Three variations of a forehand shot in tennis might include a return at full force because the ball comes directly to your forehand where you are standing, a high lob necessitated because you had to scamper to the back line, and a volley before the ball hits the ground near the net. When these forms of the forehand are practiced in mixed order during a practice period, the practice is called **variable practice** (Schmidt & Wrisberg, 2008). The order of practice (pattern) of the three variations might be BCACBAACBC. The learner may never even use the same shot twice in a row, but certainly the instructor will project the ball to require the three shots to be intermingled during a practice session. If individuals practice the same skill repeatedly, the practice is referred to as **constant practice** (Schmidt & Wrisberg, 2008).

In this case the tennis instructor has the learner repeat many trials of the forceful forehand return with minimal lateral body movement before changing to the lob. The constant practice schedule is more intuitive and the one many of us, as learners, have experienced: a fixed amount of time or number of trials on one skill before moving to the next. This may seem reasonable since concentration on one skill is possible and allows the learner to benefit from feedback and time to refine the movement.

Somewhat surprisingly perhaps, variable practice has actually been shown to be superior to constant practice for learning a wide range of motor skills when a novel variation of the skill is required (Lee et al., 2001; Magill, 2007; Schmidt & Wrisberg, 2008). It is advocated by each of the major models of skill acquisition described in chapter 3, albeit for different reasons (Magill, 2007). Variable practice develops schema and generalized motor programs so that individuals can respond to novel movement situations, according to the cognitive schema perspective of Schmidt (1975b). Such practice provides the necessary variation of regulatory and nonregulatory contexts in Gentile's stages model (1972, 2000). Finally, it provides opportunity to explore and discover the perceptual motor landscape so that learners can assemble functional motor patterns, according to dynamic systems and ecological psychology (Davids, Button, & Bennett, 2008).

Variable practice, or the variability of practice hypothesis, was first postulated by Schmidt (1975b) in the context of generalized motor programs and schema development. When faced with a goal-oriented movement, the person retrieves a generalized motor program from long-term memory and then selects parameters that will dictate how the specific action will be executed (e.g., how forceful, how long). A generalized motor program is largely defined by invariant features, that is, characteristics of the movement that remain constant despite changes in parameters (refer to chapter 1). For example, a throw usually has a stepping action, trunk rotation, arm action, wrist movement, and follow-through (Schmidt & Wrisberg, 2008). Those are the invariant features of the throw and constitute the generalized motor program.

There are many variations of a throw depending on situation factors such as the object (ball or disc) and intended distance of the throw. Variable practice involves variability in the parameters of the movement, not different movements. Different versions or variations of the basketball dribble might include parameters such as different dribbling speeds, height of ball, and player's movement during a dribble. The movement schema is an abstract or general memory representation of a set of rules that connect a person's actions to the parameters needed to produce the outcome (Schmidt & Wrisberg, 2008, and see Schmidt, 1975b, or Schmidt & Lee, 2005, for a more detailed account of schema). For example, in a basketball game context, let us assume that the player's decision, or desired outcome, is to dribble around an opponent rather than shoot or pass. This is achieved by a generalized motor program of dribbling, but with *quickly changing hands so that the ball is on the outside, driving quickly to the left of the opponent, and keeping the ball low*. The variations of the dribble (in italics) are the parameters that can change if the goal and context of the next dribble are different, for example if the player decides to drive to the right because she knows this opponent does not move quickly to that side. Thus a solution to a movement problem involves selecting the correct parameters from a generalized motor program (Schmidt & Wrisberg, 2008).

With practice, the rules or schema are developed and used to determine the parameters required for different versions of a generalized motor program. Practice is variable because different parameters of the movement are included. Over time, the person learns relationships, for example that different intensity and direction of forces generated by the hand produce successful dribbles for different running speeds and heights. Variable practice requires the learner to select new parameters for each movement trial; much less effort is required in constant practice because the same parameters are selected for many trials in a row. Strong schemas enable the individual to select the appropriate parameters in novel contexts.

Much research supports the benefit of variable rather than constant practice when learning is assessed on tests of transfer and retention (Lee et al., 2001). A typical experiment on the variability of practice hypothesis compares variable and constant practice. Using an example from Schmidt and Wrisberg (2008, p. 274), suppose that the movement class is throwing a ball to different distances. Constant practice groups are created, with each group throwing 60 balls at one of the versions of the movement class (e.g., throws of 20, 30, or 40 meters). A variable practice group throws 20 balls at 20 meters, 20 balls at 30 meters, and 20 balls at 40 meters. Thus each group has the same amount of practice, 60 throws. During initial practice, the constant practice groups usually perform better than the variable group. The reason is likely that the constant practice groups are concerned with only one distance and hence one single movement, while the variable practice group is attempting to produce three versions of a movement in an intermingled way. When the groups later switch to a new version of the movement such as a throw of 25 meters, it is usually the variable group that performs better, or at least it performs as well as the constant variable groups.

Thus, the benefits of variable practice may not appear in immediate performance but rather on later tests of transfer and retention. In other words, variable practice may appear to be adversely affecting performance during learning trials, but will ultimately enhance learning (for a reminder of the differences between learning and performance, see chapter 1; to compare retention and transfer, see chapter 4). Variable practice may seem very sensible with open skills since these activities inherently include variability. After all, tennis players try to make it difficult for you to return the ball by hitting it with unexpected direction and force, and those nasty folks called opponents are always trying to prevent you from receiving a pass from your basketball teammate. But even in closed skills, there are benefits from variable practice that might not seem so obvious at the outset. The golfer must perform under different wind conditions and on different fairway layouts, and also under anxiety in competition, and make appropriate decisions, from selection of clubs to how to putt given the layout of the green. The golfer may have a great deal of time to decide on a course of action, but shots must be "parameterized" to the physical and psychological playing conditions.

Moxley (1979) provided an early example of the positive impact of variable practice for children. She asked 6- to 8-year-old children to throw badminton shuttlecocks to a target on the floor. Half the children were required to practice from a constant location (constant practice) and half from four different locations (variable practice). As predicted by schema theory, the variable practice group was more accurate than the constant practice groups on a novel variation of the task. Consistent with schema theory, Green, Whitehead, and Sugden (1995) demonstrated that a variable practice group of 11-year-old girls using four different rackets (tennis, squash, badminton, and short tennis) was superior on an accuracy transfer test to a group who practiced only with a tennis racket and to a group who changed rackets on each block of trials. Neither Moxley nor Green and colleagues investigated children of different ages or experience.

Additional studies with children support the advantage of variable practice in children's learning of motor skills (e.g., Kerr & Booth, 1978; Gerson & Thomas, 1977; Wulf, 1991). However, other studies have provided mixed or minimal support (e.g., Jarus & Goverover, 1999; Pease & Pupnow, 1983; Pigott & Shapiro, 1984; Wrisberg & Mead, 1981). The equivocal nature of these findings caused Yan, Thomas, and Thomas (1998) to conduct a meta-analysis on the variable versus constant practice issue with children. The researchers located 39 effect sizes (ESs) in nine studies that included 272 boys and 336 girls ranging in age from 3 to 11 years. The overall ES between variable and constant practice with regard to transfer to a new task was .28, a relatively small effect. That is,

▶ Try This

In this activity you will compare variable and constant practice on a variation of Moxley's (1979) shuttlecock throwing task. Tape a dollar bill to the wall. Measure distances of 4, 8, and 12 feet (1.2, 2.4, and 3.7 meters). Create groups of six. Three will form the constant practice group and will throw 30 shuttlecocks from 8 feet. The other three will form the variable practice group and throw 10 birds from 4 feet, 10 from 8 feet, and 10 from 12 feet. Count the number of times each individual hits the dollar bill in 30 throws. This number is the performance score. Was there a difference between the constant and variable groups? Now have everyone throw 20 times from 6 feet (1.8 meters; transfer task) and again count the number of dollar hits. This number is the learning score. Was there a difference between constant and variable groups? If not, what is your explanation?

◯ Research Notes: Variable Practice Across Age

Douvis (2005) investigated variable practice on a forehand drive in tennis with 9- and 10-year-old children and 18- and 19-year-old university students. There were 40 males in each group, and no one had experience with tennis prior to the study. Practice sessions were one hour, three times per week, for a total of 18 practice sessions over six weeks. Trained instructors led the practice sessions, providing a warm-up, teaching the technique of the forehand drive, and serving the ball to the participants for 100 return drives per session. There were four practice targets on the far side of net, differing in distance from the participants, as well as a fifth transfer target. Each age category consisted of four experimental groups. Group 1 performed the 100 trials at the transfer target. Group 2 practiced at four targets, 25 trials for each; group 3 practiced 20 trials at each of the five targets; and group 4 executed 100 trials but without a specific target and thus constituted the control group. The transfer test occurred 72 hours following the final practice session at the end of the six weeks and consisted of 60 trials. The older students were superior to the younger students, but variable practice conditions proved superior to constant practice for both groups on a transfer test. That is, groups who practiced with four or five targets were superior to groups who practiced with one or no specific target. These findings support variability of practice.

while variable practice was generally superior, the difference from constant practice was not great. The authors were also interested in the impact of age, type of task (rapid timing vs. slow positioning), and type of movement (simple linear positioning vs. complex or real sport movements such as throwing a beanbag). Their results are shown in figure 14.1. The left figure indicates that age has a strong mediating influence on the advantage of variable practice over constant practice since the effect is smaller for older children. The ES for the younger children (aged 3-5 years) was .80, a large, meaningful difference. The ESs were much lower for the older children. The right figure demonstrates that the transfer benefits of variable practice over constant practice were greater for more ballistic tasks than for slow movements, as well as for more complex real-world movements than for simple movements. One can see that research findings can become quite complex and that generalizations and suggestions for practitioners might depend on age and type of task or movement.

Yan and colleagues (1998) concluded that younger children might benefit more from variable practice than older children. Consistent with the intrinsic dynamics of self-regulation and expertise outlined in chapter 7, the authors suggested that across childhood, youngsters improve in cognitive performance, gather more movement-related knowledge, and effectively use strategies. Thus the older children may have already developed a number of movement schemas, and variable practice therefore has less benefit for them. In contrast, younger children likely have fewer and less well-developed schemas and thus benefit more from variable practice. Overall, the authors concluded that variable practice is better than constant practice for children's motor skill learning; while the magnitude of the effect may be small, practitioners were advised to consider variable practice conditions for children and young athletes.

Yan and colleagues' (1998) results do not mean that variable practice will have no benefit with older elementary school-aged children. The tasks included in Yan and colleagues' study were relatively simple. While they distinguished between simple linear positioning tasks and more complex real-world tasks

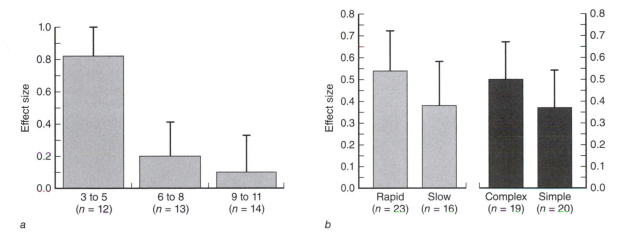

FIGURE 14.1 (a) Variable versus constant practice, weighted means ES and 95% CI (confidence interval) for each group. (b) Variable versus constant practice, weighted means ES and 95% CI for each type of task (rapid vs. slow) and type of movement (simple vs. complex)

such as throwing a beanbag, the latter were likely rather easy for the older children (aged 6-8 and 9-11 years) despite being classified as "complex." With new movements skills in real games and sport, older children may well develop new movement schemas more efficiently with variable practice. In addition, research with children (e.g., Pigott & Shapiro, 1984; Wrisberg & Mead, 1983) has occasionally demonstrated that some combination of variable and constant practice might be most effective. Wrisberg and Mead showed that 6- to 8-year-old children who received six repetitions of a movement speed on a coincident timing task during practice, before moving to additional movement speeds, were more capable on a transfer task than groups who performed completely random or variable practice. There is some agreement that variable practice is likely to be more productive after the learner has some notion of the skill and has moved beyond the "cognitive" phase of Fitts and Posner (1967), or the "getting the idea" notion of Gentile (2000). One does not want to overwhelm the learner with too much variability too early (Boyce, Coker, & Bunker, 2006; Schmidt & Wrisberg, 2008). Of course, consistent with knowledge and expertise perspectives, it is not so much age that is critical when deciding when to introduce variability as it is experience with the task. Boyce and colleagues (2006) recommended several pedagogical practices that should result in variable practice and are outlined in table 14.1.

The original variability of practice hypothesis proposed variability in movement parameters of a single generalized motor program. But what is known about organizing practices when the variability is different movements related to a sport or activity, such as a passing, shooting, and dribbling in soccer? Should a given practice include a mixture of the three skills, much like variable practice, or is it more effective to focus on only one of the skills for a considerable period of time before moving to the next skill? The area dealing with these nuances, known as contextual interference, addresses blocked, random, and serial practice.

TABLE 14.1 Variability of Practice and Pedagogy

Pedagogical method	Explanation and examples
Movement concepts	Bouncing a ball with dominant and nondominant hands or bouncing it slow or fast will result in practice of different parameters.
Challenges	Challenges are task extensions of the current motor program, for example, dribbling the basketball for 30 seconds without looking down at it.
Addition of skills to an existing skill	Dribbling with feet is extended to dribbling, passing, and receiving a ball.
A variety of settings and contexts	Following Gentile's (2000) regulatory conditions, have learners practice skills in a game-like context such as one versus one or small groups. Have learners practice nonregulatory conditions as well, such as a dance performance in front of a class.
Natural variability in open skills	For example, ask grade 3 students to practice catching in pairs, trying to throw directly to their partner. Natural variability of speed and accuracy of throws will be present.

1. Pick two sports. Describe how you would teach these sports using each type of practice.

Sport	Type of practice	Practice session
Overhand throw	Constant	Throw 60 balls 20 meters
	Variable	Throw 20 balls 20 meters Throw 20 balls 40 meters Throw 20 balls 60 meters
	Constant	
	Variable	
	Constant	
	Variable	

2. Recall Makayla (see chapter 1), the 5-year-old girl who attended her first baseball practice. Describe how you would teach her to hit the ball using variable practice and constant practice. Which practice session would likely be most effective? Explain.

3. Choose one skill. Using table 14.1 as a guide, provide examples of how you would use each of these methods to facilitate variable practice.

SKILL	
Method	**Example**
Movement concepts	
Challenges	
Addition of skills to existing skills	
Variety of settings and contexts	
Natural variability in open skills	

Contextual Interference Effect

Battig (1979) introduced the term **contextual interference** to refer to an unexpected research finding on the cognitive task of learning word lists. Contextual interference refers to the "memory and performance disruption (i.e., interference) that results from performing multiple skills or variations of a skill within the context of practice" (Magill, 2007, p. 375). In other words, during practice there is likely to be a negative impact when one is attempting to learn several tasks at the same time, such as a soccer kick, pass, and dribble. Battig also demonstrated a **contextual interference effect**, "the learning benefit resulting from performing multiple skills in a high contextual interference practice schedule" (Magill, 2007, p. 375). Despite creating problems with performance during practice, contextual interference positively influenced learning as measured by retention and transfer.

Contextual interference research often uses blocked, random, and serial practice (Magill, 2007; Schmidt & Wrisberg, 2008; Lee et al., 2001). **Blocked practice** is rehearsal of one skill repeated over a fixed block of time before the learner moves to the next skill. It is similar to constant practice as described in the previous section because one skill is practiced over and over again, as often seen in repeated drills. **Random practice** is a practice sequence in which several skills are mixed in a random order. An attempt is made to avoid rehearsal of the same skill twice in a row. In some ways this is like variable practice, but random practice uses different skills rather than variations of the same skill as in variable practice. The organization of **serial practice** is similar to that of random practice in that various skills are intermingled during practice, but in a fixed format. Table 14.2 shows how these forms of practice might appear across three 30-minute sessions of soccer.

TABLE 14.2   Three Soccer Classes With Three Skills and Three Different Practice Formats

		Class 1	2	3
Blocked practice	30 minutes	All passing	All shooting	All dribbling
Random practice	5 minutes	Dribbling	Passing	Shooting
	5 minutes	Passing	Shooting	Passing
	5 minutes	Dribbling	Shooting	Shooting
	5 minutes	Shooting	Dribbling	Dribbling
	5 minutes	Dribbling	Passing	Dribbling
	5 minutes	Passing	Passing	Shooting
Serial practice	5 minutes	Passing	Passing	Passing
	5 minutes	Dribbling	Dribbling	Dribbling
	5 minutes	Shooting	Shooting	Shooting
	5 minutes	Passing	Passing	Passing
	5 minutes	Dribbling	Dribbling	Dribbling
	5 minutes	Shooting	Shooting	Shooting

Research Notes: Contextual Interference

Shea and Morgan (1979) conducted the first motor learning study that provided evidence of the contextual interference effect. The basic task was to move an arm and grasp a tennis ball and then knock over three of six small wooden barriers as quickly as possible and return the tennis ball to a final rest position. Participants had three different movement patterns through the barriers to learn (skills A, B, C); patterns were illuminated by different-colored lights. Two groups of university-aged students practiced the three different arm and hand movements under blocked or random conditions. The blocked group had 54 practice trials: 18 consecutive trials for skill A, then 18 trials for skill B, then 18 trials for skill C. The random group also had 54 trials to acquire the three skills but practiced them in random order, never performing a skill twice in a row over the 54 trials. As shown in figure 14.2, the blocked group produced quicker movements during the practice phase. To assess learning, the researchers required the participants to perform a retention test, one immediately after practice (10 minutes) and one 10 days later. The retention tests were performed under both blocked and random formats. Figure 14.2 clearly demonstrates that the participants who had practiced under random conditions were now much quicker than those who had practiced with block organization. In fact, the random group maintained the speeds accomplished during acquisition while the blocked group showed very poor performance during randomly ordered retention trials. In line with contextual interference predictions, blocked practice produced faster immediate performance, but random practice produced more learning.

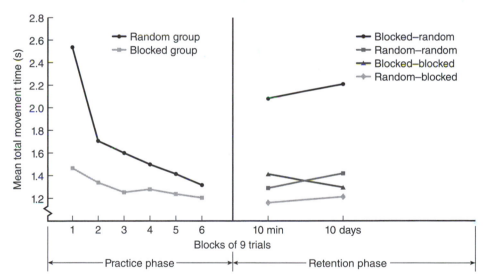

FIGURE 14.2 Performance on movement-speed tasks under random and blocked conditions. The relative amount that the groups learned is indicated by their retention performance at the right.

From J.B. Shea and R.L. Morgan, 1979, "Contextual interference effects on the acquisition, retention, and transfer of a motor skill," *Journal of Experimental Psychology: Human Learning & Memory* 5(2): 179-187. Reprinted by permission of the American Psychological Association.

The contextual interference effect is a paradox, since a random practice schedule can be detrimental during acquisition but have a positive impact on learning. Two main theories have been proposed to explain this paradox (Lee et al., 2001; Magill, 2007; Schmidt & Wrisberg, 2008). The **elaboration and distinctive hypothesis** was proposed by Shea and Morgan (1979).

They suggested that random practice results in more cognitive strategies such as comparing and contrasting movements in working memory. As the person shifts from one skill to the next, the distinct nature of each becomes clearer and more meaningful in long-term memory. This cognitive effort has a deleterious effect during acquisition, but will be advantageous later when learning is assessed. Of course, during blocked practice, individuals are not challenged to compare and contrast skills because they perform many repetitions of the same skill. The second theoretical account, the **forgetting and reconstruction hypothesis**, was proposed by Lee and Magill (1985). They argued that the key explanation for the contextual interference effect was the action planning required for each skill. In random practice, the person must abandon the action plan used on the previous skill because a new one must be constructed. Thus, the action plan is forgotten initially but is renewed each time that particular skill is repeated later during practice. Random practice forces the learner to practice action planning, which is absent in blocked practice. Both the elaboration and distinctive hypothesis and the forgetting and reconstruction hypothesis enjoy research support (Brady, 1998; Magill, 2007); therefore we must wait to see if one emerges as the more effective explanation or if some combination of the two is proposed.

The contextual interference effect is a relatively robust finding based on a great deal of empirical research; practitioners should feel comfortable using random practice in most learning situations. Despite this general statement, though, there are research findings that provide no, or limited, support for the contextual interference effect. Unfortunately, clear and unequivocal guidelines do not exist, which might tell us that skill A under conditions X will not yield the interference effect. More research is needed on this issue. But neither does the research suggest that blocked practice is generally more effective in motor skill acquisition than random practice. When the contextual interference effect fails to enhance learning, the research usually shows a nonsignificant difference between blocked and random practice, not the superiority of blocked practice. A number of mediators have been proposed that complicate the preceding generalization regarding the general benefit of contextual interference. These include age, skill level, type of skill, personality, motivation, and amount of interference.

The contextual interference effect has been investigated with children. Ste-Marie, Clark, Findlay, and Latimer (2004) conducted three studies on handwriting in which 5- to 7-year-old children practiced writing three letters, *h*, *a*, and *y*. This study was unique because it dealt with fine motor skills and very young children. In each study, the blocked condition included 24 practice trials of each letter before moving to the next letter, while the random conditions had 24 practice trials of each letter but in an intermixed sequence. Overall, the findings supported the superiority of the random practice.

Farrow and Maschette (1997) taught the forehand tennis groundstroke to two groups of 26 children 8 to 9 years old and 10 to 12 years old. The blocked group practiced 60 forehands with the preferred hand in one session per week, then 60 forehands with the nonpreferred hand in the next session during the same week. This was continued for six weeks. The random practice group received the same number of trials twice a week, but all sessions included both skills in random fashion. The contextual inference effect was evident for the 10- to 12-year-old children in the retention phase on the preferred hand;

Mix practice → confi → dence

NO

the random group was superior to the blocked group. However, the expected superiority of the blocked group during acquisition was not observed, and interference effects were not evident for the 8- and 9-year-old children.

This mixed pattern of results with children is evident in other studies. Benefits of random practice were found in 6-year-old children in transfer (Edwards, Elliott, & Lee, 1986) and 7-year-old children in retention (Pollock & Lee, 1997), but there were no differences during acquisition practice in either study. The contextual interference hypothesis predicts the superiority of blocked practice during acquisition. Bortoli, Spagolla, and Robazza (2001) demonstrated support for contextual interference in retention of a hurdle run for 8- and 9-year-old children but not for an underhand throw and quintuple jump. Blocked, random, and combined practice schedules were compared in 9-year-old boys and girls with soccer kicking and dribbling skills (Vera, Alvarez, & Medina, 2008). The combined practice group performed best during acquisition trials, but there were no differences on transfer and retention tests. Del Rey, Whitehurst, and Wood (1983) studied 6- to 10-year-old youngsters under random or block practice. Their results are unique in that the blocked group was superior to the random group during acquisition and retention.

Brady (2004) conducted a meta-analysis on the contextual inference effect that provides insight into age as a moderator. He located 139 ESs from 61 studies. The overall ES was .38, that is, across all ages and skills. Three age groups were compared: adults, high school adolescents (grades 9-12), and children. The ESs were .50, .10, and .09, respectively. It appears that despite some research demonstrating the advantage of random practice to motor skill learning in children and youth, the overall effect is quite small indeed. The explanation for the low ES for the children might be similar to that given in the previous discussion of variable and constant practice in children. Young children may be overwhelmed with random practice due to limited information processing capabilities and the complexity of sport skills (Brady, 2004). Newell and McDonald (1992) assert that random practice would have more impact later in the process of learning, and Wulf and Schmidt (1994) suggested that random practice for novices may produce too much variability. In concert with these views, Herbert, Landin, and Solmon (1996) found that low-skilled university students performed forehand and backhand tennis strokes better on a retention test with blocked practice. From a practical viewpoint, it might be wise to use some blocked practice during early stages of learning, regardless of age, before inserting some random practice. On the other hand, even young children might benefit from random practice when they are practicing skills with which they have some experience and knowledge, for example a talented soccer team of 8-year-olds.

Beyond age and skill, the amount of interference might be an important variable when we seek to understand the sometimes equivocal nature of the contextual interference research. Figure 14.3 outlines contextual interference from the perspective of a continuum rather than the two polar opposites of random versus blocked practice. Proteau, Blandin, Alain, and Dorion (1994) demonstrated the superiority of moderate contextual interference over high (random practice) or low (blocked) interference with a barrier knockdown task, and Landin and Hebert (1997) produced similar results with a basketball shooting skill. Pigott and Shapiro (1984) used an underhand toss with children and also found that a moderate contextual interference condition was superior to

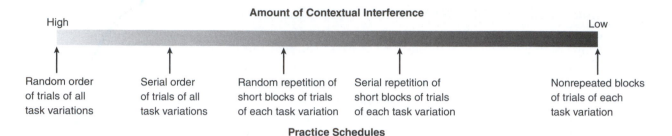

FIGURE 14.3 The amount of contextual interference that is possible in a practice situation is portrayed as a continuum ranging from high to low. Sample variable practice schedules are also presented in terms of how each relates to the amount of contextual interference created by the schedule.

high or low interference. It seems that some repetition of a skill allows learners to make adjustments over a limited number of trials but that moving to another skill may invoke elaboration or action plan reconstruction to optimally benefit from some interference.

Another variable that is entering the random and block discourse is self-regulation. In a recent study there were four groups of participants who learned a task of moving a cursor through a sequence of squares on a monitor as quickly as possible, but stopping at each square long enough to click the mouse button (Keetch & Lee, 2007). One group received blocked practice while a second received random trials. A third group used a self-regulated strategy—a mixture of random or blocked trials determined by the individual. The final group was yoked to the self-determined group, thus receiving the same order as in self-regulation but not deciding individually on the mixture of random or blocked trials. Self-regulation did not provide any special benefits during acquisition, but the self-regulation group was superior to the other groups during retention.

Brady's (2004) meta-analysis also compared contextual interference effects on laboratory tasks and applied or real-world tasks. The EF for laboratory tasks for all ages was a moderate .57, while it was a small .19 for applied research. As shown in another review study, 60% of the studies in applied settings failed to demonstrate contextual interference (Barreiros, Figueiredo, & Godinho, 2007). Reasons for these findings in applied settings may be the complexity of skills in applied compared to laboratory settings, or the fact that students in physical education classes have a wide range of skill level (certainly some were novices in the task studied), or both (Landin & Hebert, 1997). It is also possible that the number of hits or baskets made with applied tasks is too gross a measure to detect differences from findings for laboratory tasks, which can be measured to a millisecond (Goode & Magill, 1986).

Another mediating variable might be motivation and attention (Lee & White, 1990). Random practice necessitates more effort than blocked practice, and therefore tasks that are tedious or lacking in intrinsic interest might profit from contextual interference. A final potential mediator proposed by Brady (1998) might be personality. He reviewed several studies whose results were consistent with the assertion that impulsive persons might particularly benefit from random practice because such practice suppresses impulsivity and the individual adopts a more reflective style.

What Do You Think?

1. Describe, in your own words, the two theories that attempt to explain the contextual interference effect.

2. Choose two sports and indicate how you would teach the skills associated with each using blocked, random, and serial practice.

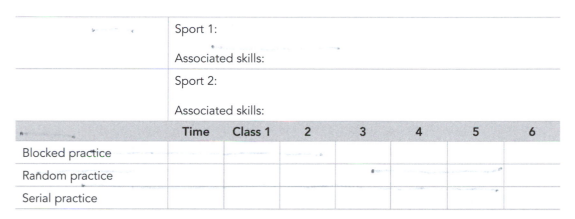

		Sport 1:					
		Associated skills:					
		Sport 2:					
		Associated skills:					
	Time	Class 1	2	3	4	5	6
Blocked practice							
Random practice							
Serial practice							

Practice Specificity

Promoting the advantages of variable and random practice might seem at odds with the concept of specificity of learning described in the section on transfer. Specificity of learning is the idea that practice experiences should reflect the movement components and environmental conditions of the target skill and target context. To state this differently, if we practice to develop skills for game play or individual competition, our practice should resemble the game or competition as much as possible. Specificity of practice is one of the longest-standing principles of human learning (Magill, 2007).

Specificity of practice may have two forms, sensory and motor specificity, and context specificity (Schmidt & Lee, 2005). The idea of sensory and motor specificity has emerged largely from the research of Proteau and colleagues (Proteau, 1992; Proteau, Marteniuk, Girourd, & Dugas, 1987; Soucy & Proteau, 2001). Primarily using aiming tasks such as placing a stylus on a target, they have manipulated the type and amount of feedback using techniques such as occluding vision of either the arm or the target. It is often assumed that over many practice trials, the need for sensory feedback diminishes or changes; for example, the learner depends less on visual feedback as kinesthetic feedback assumes more importance (Schmidt, 1975b). However, Proteau's research challenges this assumption, since findings show that performance deteriorates on a transfer task even following extensive practice if the transfer task includes more or less sensory feedback than in the practice conditions. Proteau (1992) stated, "Withdrawing or adding a significant source of information after a period of practice where it was respectively present or absent results in a deterioration of performance" (p. 96). Thus, if practice included restricted vision, providing more visual information on the transfer task will actually result in poorer, rather than better, performance. It is proposed that this effect of specificity of practice occurs because the learner develops a sensorimotor representation during practice that is disrupted if the "real" game (transfer task) adds or reduces sensory information. Performance will be optimal when the practice conditions match transfer conditions.

This line of thinking was supported in several studies that used a balance beam walking task as reported by Robertson, Tremblay, Anson, and Elliott (2002). The authors challenge some common practice rituals of teachers and coaches that do not match performance conditions. For example, it is fine to direct participants to visual cues on the beam, which should not differ in competition, but probably not to cues on the home gymnasium ceiling or floor, which are most certainly going to be different in competition. They also challenge the coaching practice of talking an athlete through a routine. This added auditory stimulation cannot occur during competition and therefore should be used cautiously during practice. The authors also recommend that therapists in rehabilitation emphasize function- and goal-directed activities rather than isolated muscle actions. Therapists should determine the sources of information required in the functional task and manipulate those in therapy.

Proteau's sensorimotor representation logic can be extended to a broader sense of context specificity. We often hear about the need to practice a task over and over again as if to stamp it into the brain (Schmidt & Wrisberg, 2008). This type of thinking appears to coincide with the thousands of hours of practice that experts report (see chapter 7). Without question, slap shots in hockey, golfing tee shots, and new ways of getting out of bed after an accident are often practiced hundreds of times over only a few weeks. But more than one coach has noted that some players perform wonderfully in practice but cannot perform in the game or competition. One of the difficulties with constant and blocked practice is that the target skill may not be practiced in the target context (Schmidt & Wrisberg, 2008). Dribbling a basketball while walking is simply not the same skill as the dribbling required in a game. In a similar vein, practicing skating in hockey with control of the puck and passing to a teammate might be useful as a quick reminder of some passing or puck control techniques, but ignores the reality that the timing of the pass is often dictated by the positioning of moving opponents and teammates. Athletes must be prepared to produce particular movements in different situations. The target context also refers to such things as elevated anxiety on the first hole of golf compared to the driving range because this is now competition and you want to impress the other players in the foursome. Table 14.3 includes other features of a skill that might be different in the target context and blocked practice.

The specificity of learning idea is to practice in a manner that brings learners as close as possible to the target skill and target context. Practitioners will need to consider the developmental level of the learners (i.e., age and skill) and their motivations (i.e., a team of elite 10-year-olds will be different than a grade 5 class). There will certainly be times when teachers or therapists feel it is appropriate to use constant and blocked practice, but over time they should remember that such practice is unlikely to mimic the target skill and context. As Schmidt and Wrisberg (2008, p. 264) state, "The main point is that many *repetitions* in practice are essential for highly skilled performance—but *repetitiveness* in practice is not effective."

Add

TABLE 14.3 Features of a Skill That Might Be Different in the Target Context and in Blocked Practice

Target context	Blocked practice
Preceded by regular variable conditions	Not preceded by regular variable conditions
Requires the generation of a solution on each attempt	Requires the generation of a solution only on the first attempt
Allows only one chance for success	Allows many chances for success
Same movement not repeated on successive attempts	Same movement repeated on successive attempts
Corrections not allowed on next attempt	Corrections allowed on the next attempt

Reprinted, by permission, from R.A. Schmidt and C.A. Wrisberg, 2008, *Motor learning and performance: A situation-based learning approach*, 4th ed. (Champaign, IL: Human Kinetics), 264.

Part and Whole Practice

382 NOW

Motor skills are often complex and difficult to learn, particularly for children, novices, and others who lack motivation or lack the structural constraints that match the skill. Instructors will be faced with the decision whether to teach a skill as a whole, or to break it into parts and teach these smaller units before combining them into the whole. Skills that overwhelm a learner, elicit some degree of fear, or even pose a real danger will certainly be broken into parts. The key assumption is that practicing one part of a skill will transfer to performing the whole skill (Lee et al., 2001). In fact, whether or not part practice transfers to performance of the whole skill is the ultimate test of its effectiveness (Schmidt & Lee, 2005). Concepts in this area of motor learning research are very dependent on the nature of the task.

The literature on part and whole practice has been advanced by the skill classifications of Naylor and Briggs (1963). They distinguished between task complexity and task organization (Magill, 2007). **Task complexity** refers to the number of parts or components and the amount of attention (information processing demands). Serving a tennis ball, batting a baseball, and performing a dance routine are complex skills because they demand much attention and have many components. Low-complexity skills have few components and require little processing, such as picking up a ball or walking. Of course, whether a task is complex is also dependent on the experience of the individual with that task. **Task organization** deals with the relationships among the components of a skill. The layup in basketball is a skill with a high level of organization because the parts are interdependent in terms of time and space. Other examples are juggling, ski racing, and the golf drive. The time and space performance characteristics of one part are dependent on the characteristics of the part performed just prior to it. If part A is not performed well, part B cannot be performed well, and so on. Tasks with a low level of task organization are those in which performance of each component is relatively independent. For example, a folk dance has many components, but each task is more or less independent of the one preceding it; I can perform the dance even though I am a bit shaky with the gallop at one point in the dance.

Task organization

[handwritten: Reverse = part]

[handwritten: ↓ complexity | ↑ Organization — Whole (interdepency)]

It is often recommended that if the skill is low in complexity and high in organization, the better practice choice is the whole task because high interdependency of the parts makes it difficult to practice parts outside the whole skill context. On the other hand, if skills are high in complexity and low in organization, then part practice can be effective because the interdependence of the parts is not critical and part practice can reduce the information processing demands (Magill, 2007). Teachers and coaches must therefore analyze tasks to judge their complexity and organization.

❓ What Do You Think?

Think of three tasks in each of the four quadrants shown. Tasks could be high in both complexity and organization, high in neither, high in complexity but low in organization, or low in complexity but high in organization.

		TASK ORGANIZATION	
		High	**Low**
Task complexity	High		
	Low		

[handwritten left margin: Continuous — High Complex]
[handwritten: High Org   Low Org Interdepence]
[handwritten: Discrete Low complex.]
[handwritten: High attention Gymnastics]
[handwritten: RAPID Discrete Skills batting - part]

As you performed this challenge, you might have realized that some skills are not easily categorized as high or low. There may be some intermediate level of both organization and complexity, and thus the general guidelines for high organization–low complexity and low organization–high complexity may be difficult to follow. And did you identify any skills that were both low or both high on each factor? The skill classification of continuous, discrete, and serial skills may help here. Continuous skills are usually high in complexity but may be either high or low in organization; however, more often they are also high in organization because of the interdependence of the parts (Magill, 2007). Discrete skills may be low in complexity from the viewpoint of number of parts, but some will still demand a great deal of attention. Schmidt and Wrisberg (2008) make the point that rapid discrete skills such as a bat swing or bimanual skills such as the toss and swing of a tennis serve might be the least likely candidates for part practice. They argue that such skills can be broken down into parts, but that the parts are quite arbitrary and practicing them in isolation contributes little to whole-task performance, the ultimate goal. For example, practicing the backswing of a golf shot by itself produces different dynamics than in the whole swing because you stop at the end of the backswing. Serial skills will have levels of organization that depend on the skill but often are high in complexity because of the number of skills.

Lee and colleagues (2001) have also argued that despite the challenge of learning highly interdependent parts (high organization), the research literature does not generally demonstrate instances of negative transfer from part practice; rather some benefits of part learning are usually described. In other words, if a task has high organization but would overwhelm and discourage a learner, some form of part practice might be absolutely necessary. The issue becomes which part practice technique should be used. Four different part practice techniques have been proposed: fractionation, segmentation, simplification, and attention cueing (Lee et al., 2001; Magill, 2007).

Fractionation

Fractionation is part practice that separates parts of an action that normally are executed simultaneously; for example, swimming instructors often have part practice drills for either the arms or legs in a given stroke. This seems to work because the arms and legs perform different movements, and instructors frequently move back and forth between the part and the whole. However, breaking a symmetric movement like that of the arms of the breaststroke down into drills for each arm is likely counterproductive since the arms perform the same movement and the task is high in organization.

Lee and colleagues (2001) have reviewed the fractionation studies and found that those with video games, tapping, tracking, and bimanual aiming tasks have usually shown part practice to be ineffective as a means to promote positive transfer to the whole task. This is likely due to the high degree of coordination and interdependence among the parts. With bimanual sport skills such as the side stroke in swimming or the tennis serve, the evidence is mixed, with some support for both part and whole practice (Magill, 2007). If asymmetric bimanual tasks must be broken down, it is likely that practice with the limb that has the more difficult and complex task should come first. Bimanual rhythmical tapping tasks as used in music are likely best learned with whole practice, but part practice has shown some effectiveness in piano when rhythm and melody are separated (Lee et al., 2001).

Segmentation

Segmentation is also known as progressive part practice. In this form of practice the task is segmented into distinct parts, usually along the dimension of time. For example, a specific folk dance may be segmented into five distinct steps. In pure part practice, the five steps would be practiced separately and then all parts gathered together into the whole task of the folk dance. Progressive part practice involves practice of first part alone and then the second part alone, but then the first and second together. In this manner the whole task is achieved through progressive practice of larger versions of the whole task.

Progressive part practice can be achieved by either forward or backward chaining. Forward chaining is the practice of the parts in their timed order; part one, parts one and two, and so on. Learning the folk dance with forward chaining gradually assembles the actual whole dance. Backward chaining is practice in the reverse order, starting with the end part. With some tasks this might be desirable because the learner accomplishes the end goal at the beginning of practice, which may be a strong motivational factor. For example, backward chaining of the basketball layup begins with the shot, then proceeds to the step–shot combination, the dribble–two step–shot combination, and so on for several dribbles (Lee et al., 2001). Backward chaining has been demonstrated to be most effective when the end point of the chain is accuracy, as in the layup (Lee et al., 2001). Forward chaining is more effective in tasks such as the folk dance in which each segment contributes equally to the overall task goal.

Magill (2007) points out that progressive part practice takes advantage of both part and whole practice methods. Part practice reduces attention demands of the whole task so that the learner can concentrate on one specific aspect. Building toward the whole has the advantage of coordination of the parts that may have some degree of interdependence.

Simplification

Simplification is practice of an easier version of the task, a pedagogical principle that teachers have been using for decades. Magill (2007) describes six ways in which skills can be simplified:

- Reduce object difficulty (e.g., juggle with scarves, catch a larger ball, or bat with a large plastic bat).
- Reduce attention demands (e.g., provide physical assistance such as support in gymnastics).
- Reduce speed.
- Add auditory cues (e.g., a clapping that dictates a skipping action).
- Sequence skill progressions (e.g., hit baseballs from a tee, then a pitching machine, and later a pitcher; also lead-up games in general).
- Use simulators (e.g., rebounders in basketball) and virtual reality.

While simplification is common practice, the research support is rather limited (Lee et al., 2001). If simplification creates a new task or changes the dynamics of the task dramatically, then part practice may not be effective. Mane, Adams, and Donchin (1989; as cited by Lee et al., 2001) manipulated the speed of a video game. A slower speed transferred positively to the performance of the game at regular speed, but there was a limit. At some point, the reduced speed was ineffective, presumably because the game became quite a different one.

Attention Cueing

Attention cueing is not strictly a part practice method because the whole skill is performed. However, the performer directs attention to a specific part of the whole, for example the backswing of the slap shot in hockey or the elbow on the recovery of the crawl stroke. Attention research supports the fact that selective focus can be achieved (Lee et al., 2001).

``/14

  What Do You Think?

Choose your favorite sport or frequent therapeutic activity. Try to provide specific examples of how you could implement each part practice technique.

SPORT OR ACTIVITY	
Practice techniques	**Example**
Fractionation	
Segmentation	
Simplification	
Attention cueing	

Mental Practice and Imagery

It may surprise you to learn that just thinking about certain aspects of a skill can have performance and learning benefits (Lee et al., 2001; Magill, 2007; Schmidt & Wrisberg, 2008). **Mental practice** is cognitive rehearsal of a physical skill without overt physical movements (Magill, 2007). **Imagery** is a form of mental practice that involves a visual or kinesthetic representation of one's own performance. These forms of practice should be considered when physical practice is inconvenient or impractical. In general, mental practice is used to aid skill acquisition, while imagery usually serves a performance preparation role.

Mental practice has a rather long history and usually involves rehearsing procedural or symbolic aspects of the skill. Rehearsing procedures could follow the actual sequences of a series of movements in therapy or in a gymnastic or dance routine. Rehearsal might also be related to response selection procedures such as technique for the arm action of a swimming stroke, or a decision-making strategy such as "If my opponent backs away, I will keep the puck and drive to the net" (recall discussion of procedural knowledge in chapter 7).

practice —

= race strategy
pool shot
golf shots

Symbolic aspects include mental rehearsal to remember to follow through when throwing a ball. Mental practice research usually compares mental practice conditions to a physical practice condition and a no-practice condition. Some studies have incorporated experimental conditions combining physical and mental practice. With regard to learning the physical skill, the results typically demonstrate that ==mental practice is better than no practice but certainly not as effective as physical practice==. The latter is hardly surprising given all that we have said about physical practice in this chapter.

Some studies have shown that a combination of physical and mental practice is almost as effective as physical practice alone (e.g., Hird, Landers, Thomas, & Horan, 1991; Kolb, Ellis, & Roenker, 1992). Combined groups may have almost half the physical practice that physical practice groups do. Magill (2007) explained these findings from a cognitive problem-solving perspective. During mental practice, learners are engaged in cognitive practice strategies that normally are used during physical practice but can be effectively developed during mental practice as well. From a developmental perspective, the review of mental practice studies conducted many years ago by Feltz and Landers (1983) showed that ==mental practice was effective regardless of the skill level==.

Mental imagery is frequently used as athletes prepare for performance. Divers mentally view themselves rotating, twisting, and opening prior to the actual dive. Table 14.4 describes five types of imagery in physical skill performance. Martin, Moritz, and Hall (1999) concluded that there is "tentative support" in the research literature for imagery as a preparation for competition strategy. Moreover, imagery is effective for high-performance athletes and beginners.

Magill (2007) describes three generally accepted hypotheses that explain why mental practice and imagery are effective. A neuromuscular hypothesis links

TABLE 14.4   Five Types of Imagery Related to Motor Skill Performance

Imagery type	Description and example
Motivational	
Specific	Imagery that represents specific goals and goal-orienting behaviors, for example winning a medal for first place, receiving congratulations for a specific accomplishment
General mastery	Imagery that represents effective coping and mastery of challenging situations, for example being confident, being focused
General arousal	Imagery that represents feelings of relaxation, stress, arousal, and anxiety in a situation, for example being relaxed prior to an event
Cognitive	
Specific	Imagery of performing specific skills, for example, performing a golf shot, walking down a flight of stairs
General	Imagery of strategies related to an event, for example a strategy to overcome full-court press in basketball, a strategy to organize items for cooking a meal

Adapted, by permission, from K.A. Martin, S.E. Moritz, and C.R. Hall, 1999, "Imagery use in sport: A literature review and applied model," *The Sport Psychologist* 13(3): 245-268.

mental practice of an action such as bending the elbow to electromyographic (EMG) activity in the muscles responsible for the bending. This may facilitate neuromotor pathways involved in learning. The brain activity hypothesis comes from brain scan results indicating that motor pathways activated during imagining an action are similar to those activated during actual performance (Jeannerod, 1999). The third explanation is the cognitive hypothesis, which asserts that the first stage of motor learning involves a high degree of cognitive activity regarding the task as individuals struggle with performance-related questions.

What Do You Think?

You just learned that mental practice has performance and learning benefits. How could you incorporate mental practice into instructional or therapeutic settings? When would be the most appropriate times to encourage the use mental practice in each of these settings? Explain.

Distribution of Practice

Is it better for learning to have fewer but longer practice sessions or shorter but more sessions? Distribution of practice refers to the amount of practice during each period and the amount of rest between practice sessions in order to ensure optimal learning of motor skills (Magill, 2007). This body of knowledge usually compares schedules of practice called **massed and distributed**. Massed practice involves longer practice sessions with many practice trials during the time period. This is contrasted to distributed practice, which has fewer practice trials in shorter practice sessions. Massed practice schedules will have fewer practice sessions than distributed practice. When the time between trials is a focus, massed practice will have minimal or short rest periods while distributed practice will have longer rest intervals.

Many educational, recreational, and rehabilitation situations have specified practice times, and practitioners have little flexibility in allotting practice time. For example, teachers know the number of days during the week on which a given class will have physical education, and youth soccer teams are often allotted the practice fields in a predetermined fashion. As Magill (2007) points out, little research addresses the optimal number and length of practice sessions, but in general, researchers recommend more frequent and shorter sessions as would occur in distributed practice. This recommendation is supported by three hypotheses: Massed practice may result in more physical fatigue compared to distributed practice, may reduce cognitive effort compared to distributed practice, and provides less time for the memory representation of the motor skill to be consolidated.

A recent study by Dail and Christina (2004) supports distributed practice for novice golfers. The task was a golf putt, and each participant had 240 trials. A mass practice schedule group performed all the trials on one day, with a short break after each block of 10 trials, while the distributed group had 60 trials on each of four consecutive days. At the end of the 240 trials, 24 hours later, and seven days later, the distributed group putted better than the massed group.

Try This

Let's compare mass versus distributed practice for a throwing task using the nondominant hand. The throw will be an underhand toss of a badminton shuttlecock to an archery target of concentric circles 10 feet (3 meters) from the thrower. A direct hit in the center will score 5 points, one in the next circle will score 4 points, and so on. Establish a group of six. Three will throw under massed conditions, three under distributed conditions. The mass practice participants will throw 40 times in succession. Record the scores from the 40 trials. The distributed group will throw in 4 sessions by 10 blocks with 2 minutes between blocks. Again, record the scores from the 40 trials. Compare the mass and distributed groups. Did you find differences that are consistent with the suggestion in the next paragraph?

Most of the research on distributed practice has investigated the length of the intertrial interval, that is, the rest time between trials (Magill, 2007). Reviews of this literature point to the importance of the type of task. Continuous skills are learned better with distributed schedules of practice than massed, while the reverse is true with discrete skills. Thus, swimming, dancing, and skiing would benefit from distributed practice, while hitting a golf ball or baseball can be learned effectively under massed practice.

What Do You Think?

You just learned about distributed and massed practice. Fill in the table by indicating whether the skills can likely be taught more effectively under distributed or massed practice conditions.

Skill	Massed practice	Distributed practice
Dancing		
Long jump		
Chest pass		
Riding a bicycle		
Skipping rope		

Summary

Physical practice is by far the most important factor in learning motor skills. And Tawnya now realizes that the ultimate goal of "practice" is to perform the skill outside the therapeutic practice venue, for activities of daily living, recreation, or competition. To some extent, the amount of practice will depend on the goals and aspirations of the learner. The research evidence suggests that a great deal of practice will be necessary as higher levels of performance are sought. Will Tawnya's client be satisfied when he is able to walk to the store, or might he aspire to becoming a Paralympian? How to organize and schedule practice sessions so that individuals can reach their goals was the focus of this chapter. We explored variable, constant, random, blocked, part, whole, mental, mass, and distributed practice and attempted to describe the best practice conditions. However, sometimes the research is incomplete, and the results are controversial or equivocal. While we would like to have offered simple summary statements on exactly how therapists, teachers, and coaches should organize their practices, learning motor skills is simply too complex and is influenced by a host of factors beyond practice schedules. So we highlighted the moderating factors available from the research; these include age, level of skill, type of task (laboratory or real world), type of skill, motivation, attention, and personality.

Supplemental Activities

1. Biographies of highly skilled athletes and musicians often speak to the issue of practice. Select a person you admire or would like to know more about, and read his or her biography. What are the reflections about practice?

2. Locate an experienced therapist you know and ask for an interview about practice. Does this person distinguish among the many types of practice discussed in this chapter? Does he or she see instances of the contextual interference effect? Does he or she use mental imagery?

Detecting and Correcting Errors

CHAPTER OBJECTIVES

After reading this chapter, you should be able to

> explain why extrinsic feedback is an essential component of motor skill acquisition,

> provide examples of various types of extrinsic feedback,

> identify the main functions of extrinsic feedback,

> understand various feedback schedules including when and how to use them,

> describe the factors that should be considered in order to effectively provide feedback, and

> explain the temporal components of feedback and how the timing of the provision of feedback following a performance attempt affects motor learning.

What Am I Doing Wrong?

Bridgette is learning the overhand serve in volleyball and is having a difficult time hitting the ball over the net. She has tried tossing the ball higher, then closer, then farther, but she cannot seem to get the ball over the net. Her focus then shifts to the force of her swing. She thinks perhaps her problem is that she is not generating enough force, or that she is hitting the ball too early or too late. Soon Bridgette becomes quite frustrated and begins losing interest and motivation.

Without any feedback on her form, Bridgette has a difficult time improving her serves. She does not have enough experience with overhand serving to know what she is doing correctly or incorrectly, so she does not know which aspects she should change and which aspects she should maintain. The provision of appropriate feedback is critical when one is learning a new motor skill, especially complex motor skills. Feedback is quite possibly just as important, if not more important, for injured individuals who are trying to reacquire motor skills, whether they are sport-specific skills, such as making sharp cuts on the basketball court following an anterior cruciate ligament tear, or relevant life skills, such as relearning how to walk, write, or even brush one's teeth. Injured individuals often have to either relearn a motor skill or learn a new or modified motor skill (Sabari, 2001). In occupational and physical therapy, it is critical for the therapist to understand how to provide feedback effectively to maximize the patient's learning. When practitioners are providing feedback to facilitate motor learning, regardless of the situation (e.g., whether people are unskilled learners, are learning a new motor skill, or are recovering from injury or illness), they must consider the type, frequency, and timing of the provision of feedback. This chapter examines each of these and discusses some common myths about the delivery of feedback. The type, accuracy, and frequency of feedback most often delivered in athletic or clinical settings are not optimal (Seidentop & Tannehill, 2000).

Feedback

The two main types of feedback are intrinsic feedback, feedback derived from sensory systems, and extrinsic feedback, feedback provided by external sources. Effective extrinsic feedback is an essential component of clinical, educational, or athletic programs. The only variable more important than extrinsic feedback in learning a motor skill is practice (Bilodeau, 1966). Let's take a closer look at these two types of feedback, with much of our focus on extrinsic feedback.

Intrinsic Feedback

The production of the task itself generates feedback, termed **intrinsic feedback**. Intrinsic feedback includes any feedback received through the sensory systems, including vision, proprioception, and audition. A basketball player who takes a 3-point shot receives information from each of these sensory systems with regard to the shot. The player feels the release of the shot and the force with which he made the shot (proprioceptive intrinsic feedback). He sees the trajectory of the ball and whether it hits the rim, hits the backboard, or is "nothing but net" (visual intrinsic feedback), and hears it hit the rim or ideally hears the swoosh of the ball through the net (auditory intrinsic feedback). A skilled basketball player often knows if he is going to make the shot long before the shot even approaches the net. Intrinsic feedback can also be supplemented by coaches, instructors, peers, or equipment.

Extrinsic Feedback

Feedback that is supplemental to the intrinsic sources of feedback is termed **extrinsic feedback**. Any feedback provided by an instructor, trainer, therapist, coach, or even a friend is extrinsic feedback. A fitness trainer who tells her client that her reps are too fast, or a fencing coach instructing his student to lunge more when striking, is giving extrinsic feedback. Equipment such as a stopwatch, a heart rate monitor, or a video replay of a movement also provides a type of extrinsic feedback.

Providing appropriate feedback is one of the most important responsibilities of an instructor. There are many important considerations for effective extrinsic feedback, such as determining the most appropriate type, precision, and frequency of feedback, as well as when to schedule the presentation of feedback. Extrinsic feedback can enable quicker learning and enhance retention while also increasing learner motivation. Learners who cannot detect their own errors may spend countless hours trying different techniques, which would not be necessary if they received a simple tip from an instructor who had observed their attempts. In trying to learn the volleyball serve, Bridget progressed very slowly because she did not know which aspects of her movement pattern were correct and which were incorrect.

Extrinsic feedback is pivotal in rehabilitation settings as well. Patients with perceptual or cognitive deficits may only be able to use limited intrinsic feedback (Flinn & Radomski, 2002). They may rely on extrinsic feedback to even understand how they are performing because they cannot accurately feel the movement or see the outcome.

Extrinsic feedback can be provided in many forms. Most simply, extrinsic feedback can be provided verbally or nonverbally. Nonverbal forms of extrinsic feedback can come, for example, from a buzzer that sounds following poor performances or a stopwatch that displays a race time. Extrinsic feedback can be provided either during the movement, **concurrent feedback**, or following the completion of the movement, **terminal feedback**. A 1-mile race time is terminal feedback. However, running splits, race times during set intervals of a particular distance (e.g., quarter mile, half mile, three-quarters mile), are examples of concurrent feedback because the runner is receiving information about his or her pace *during* the run.

Verbal Forms of Feedback

When we think about feedback, we generally think about verbal feedback. We often think of a coach providing feedback in terms of what athletes did incorrectly (e.g., "You did not throw the shot put with a whipping motion"), or how they can perform better the next time (e.g., "You need to hit down on the golf ball, not up to carry the ball"), or the outcome of the performance ("You jumped 19 feet, 2 inches in your last long jump attempt"). Verbal feedback provides **knowledge of results (KR)** or **knowledge of performance (KP)**. These give learners feedback regarding the outcome (KR) and the quality of their performance (KP).

Knowledge of results is terminal feedback that describes the outcome of the movement, for example, a gymnastics score, the distance of a punt, the score on a sit and reach test, or the speed of a pitch. Knowledge of performance provides specific feedback about the quality of the movement production. This type of feedback informs the learner about the components of the movement pattern that led to the outcome. An instructor could tell learners that they need to shift their weight more, use more force with the follow-through, or use more torso rotation when throwing. Most instructors or clinicians emphasize the outcome of the performance (KR) while failing to provide appropriate constructive feedback regarding the movement production (KP) (Fishman & Tobey, 1978). Outcome-based feedback is often inadequate in guiding the learner to perform the skill correctly (Newell & Walter, 1981; Kernodle & Carlton, 1992; Janelle, Barba, Frehlich, Tennant, & Cauraugh, 1997).

What Do You Think?

Label each of the following examples as either KR or KP.

- *KP* You are releasing the ball too early.
- *KR* You just missed the target by 2 inches.
- *KP* Your plant foot landed 3 inches over the take-off board.
- *KR* You just cut 2 seconds off your mile.
- *KP* You are not bending at the knees enough.
- *KP* You need to straighten your back when you bring the weight down.

There are two types of knowledge of performance: descriptive feedback and prescriptive feedback. **Descriptive feedback**, as the name implies, *describes* the movement pattern. This type of feedback is useful for explaining to learners what they are doing incorrectly. One of the most common errors in golf is an exaggerated twist of the backswing. It is an incorrect assumption that a greater twist of the backswing will help them generate more force. An instructor could provide learners with descriptive feedback by describing this exaggerated twist.

Prescriptive feedback provides suggestions to correct the error. An instructor could tell the novice golfer, "By exaggerating your twist, you will not be able to stay in the same swing plane, which will be very difficult to compensate for. You need to maintain perfect posture and swing fluidly. This will help you to maintain contact with the ball and avoid twisting too far on the backswing." The appropriate type of feedback depends on the skill level of the learner. Novice learners need more prescriptive feedback than skilled performers because they have not learned how to correct errors yet. Regardless of skill level, a combination of both descriptive and prescriptive feedback is the most effective. When given both types of KP, learners begin to associate the causes of an error with the appropriate corrections.

What Do You Think?

Label each of the following examples of feedback statements as descriptive or prescriptive feedback.

- You are decelerating the club through the ball.
- Plant your foot more to the right.
- Follow through at the release.
- You are stopping too abruptly.
- You are using too much force at the backswing.
- You need to use more elbow flexion.

Try This

Form pairs. Each pair will need two different-colored pens (or markers or pencils), a piece of paper, and a blindfold. One student will be the participant while the other student is the experimenter, providing feedback. On the piece of paper, the experimenter draws a basketball hoop and a stick figure of a person about to shoot the basketball. The participant then puts on the blindfold and draws a line from the hands of the stick figure to the hoop using a typical basketball shot trajectory, completing this 10 times with no feedback and without looking at the picture. The participant remains blindfolded throughout the entire experiment and will need assistance from the experimenter to get the pen to the starting point after each attempt. For a second group of trials, the participant uses a different-colored pen and completes the same task 10 times, but during these trials, the experimenter provides the participant with feedback after each attempt. When you are finished, switch roles with your partner and complete the activity again.

- Compare your results after receiving KR versus no KR.
- How detailed was the feedback you and your partner provided?
- Do you think this may have affected your results during the KR trials?
- What other factors do you think may have affected your results for each condition?

Nonverbal Forms of Feedback

Although we often think of feedback as verbal, most individuals have used many forms of nonverbal feedback. Nonverbal feedback can include auditory feedback, such as buzzers or a metronome, or visual feedback, such as pictures or videos. Many other devices can be used for feedback as well. Nonverbal forms of feedback can include sounds consequent to the movement, buzzing noises to indicate the end of a period, or feedback received from the use of equipment. Consequent sounds can include the differing sounds of a racquetball hitting the wall. These sounds can provide the player with information regarding the speed of the ball's movement and even the trajectory. Consequent sounds can also provide information about the rhythm of a movement. For some motor skills, such as Double Dutch jump rope, the rhythm of the movement is crucial.

Equipment   Feedback can be provided from a wide variety of equipment. Equipment can be used to monitor performance; for example, radar guns monitor the speed of a pitch, and stopwatches provide running splits. Perhaps more teaching aids have been developed to improve the golf swing than for any other motor skill, such as helping to eliminate swaying and lunging and facilitating proper impact. Equipment is also critical for therapists, who need specific devices to assist with walking, regaining balance, or increasing strength.

Biofeedback   **Biofeedback** is extrinsic feedback that provides concurrent information related to the activity of physiological processes (Magill, 2007). This information is provided to shape behavior during performance. One of the most commonly used forms of biofeedback is the heart rate monitor. Heart rate monitors, readily available at department or sporting goods stores, continuously display an individual's current heart rate. Heart rate monitors help people adjust their intensity levels throughout a workout based on their heart rates. Blood pressure monitors and chronometers are other sources that provide biofeedback. Blood pressures may be continuously monitored for individuals with cardiovascular problems. Chronometers have been developed to assist swimmers by providing them with real-time, nonverbal biofeedback without interfering with their performance (Pèrez, Liana, Brizuela, & Encarnación, 2009). It is particularly difficult to provide feedback during water sports due to the swimming pool environment. Chronometers have been found to be beneficial for improving swim times while also allowing the instructor to focus on other aspects of the swimming performance or on other swimmers.

Biofeedback is also commonly used in rehabilitation settings. Feedback can be provided for muscular activation and joint angle excursions. By viewing electromyographic (EMG) biofeedback, patients have increased voluntary activation in particular muscle groups (Brucker & Bulaeva, 1996) and relearned how to walk following a stroke by changing walking patterns (Colborne, Olney, & Griffin, 1993; Intiso, Santilli, Grasso, Rossi, & Caruso, 1994). Biofeedback devices can improve postural control and gait, particularly in patients with pathologies that impair their vestibular, visual, or somatosensory information (Dozza, Wall, Peterka, Chiari, & Horak, 2007; Easton, Greene, DiZio, & Lackner, 1998; Wall & Kentala, 2005). Unfortunately, these benefits are generally lost once the biofeedback is removed; thus the use of these devices should be limited so that learners do not become over reliant on the feedback.

Visual Feedback   Visual feedback, which can be very beneficial during the learning process, can take the form of visual displays of kinetic or kinematic feedback. Kinetic and kinematic feedback are types of knowledge of performance, providing information in addition to intrinsic feedback (Schmidt & Young, 1991), and have been shown to be more effective than knowledge of results (Newell & Carlton, 1987; Schmidt & Lee, 2005).

Kinematic feedback provides information on the observable aspects of the movement, such as the space–time properties of a performance, and can be very beneficial during the learning process. The most commonly used forms of kinematic feedback are pictures, illustrations, and video replays of limb position, velocity, or acceleration (figure 15.1). For example, illustrating the aiming trajectory of the rifle barrel, an essential aspect of shooting performance (Konttinen, Lyytinen, & Viitasalo, 1998), provides information on the movement of the barrel and is supplemental to intrinsic sources of feedback (Mononen, Viitasalo, Konttinen, & Era, 2003). **Kinetic feedback** provides information on the underlying processes of the movement such as force. Graphs illustrating force–time curves for a motor skill have been found useful for such actions as learning how to jump out of starting blocks and the trigger squeeze and release for rifle shooters. Learners can see whether they need more or less force and learn the appropriate timing in relation to the amount of force required.

For kinematic feedback to benefit the acquisition and retention of motor skills, it must provide additional feedback to the feedback regarding goal achievement (KR) (Young & Schmidt, 1992). The goal for most motor skills is to induce a change in the environment through a particular movement or set of movements, such as batting in baseball. It is easy to separate the movement patterns in batting (kinematics of the swing) from the goal outcome (where the ball was directed and landed, KR), so learners of skills like these are likely to benefit from kinematic feedback. For other tasks, such as gymnastics, dance, or figure skating, the information provided on the movement production and the goal achievement would be the same (Newell, Quinn, Sparrow, & Walter,

FIGURE 15.1   This is an example of how a series of photographs can provide kinematic feedback. These photographs of a golf swing illustrate the changing form and the correct alignment of the body relative to the club throughout the swing.

1983). It is not that the movement *affects* the goal achievement; rather, the movement pattern *is* the goal achievement. For these tasks, the kinematics of the movement and the goal achievement cannot be separated.

The most effective kinematic patterns are generally known for most sporting activities, and kinematic feedback is very commonly provided to learners to optimize their movement patterns. The provision of feedback on some kinematic variables is more beneficial to learning than on others. The most appropriate feedback is on kinematic variables that are motor skill specific, but feedback on spatial characteristics (positional information) tends to be more effective for learning than feedback on temporal aspects (Young & Schmidt, 1992). It is probably easier for learners to visualize where to place and move body parts and equipment, such as a racket, than to understand the timing of the movement, as this is more abstract and harder to conceptualize.

Research Notes: Let's Play Ball!

To examine the influence of the type of feedback provided on performance and retention, Young and Schmidt (1992) had 60 college students strike a ball with a bat. The goal was to strike the ball to propel it as far as possible. Although people can use multiple possible movement patterns to strike a ball, they will achieve optimal performance if the bat has a high velocity at the coincidence point and if the trajectory of the bat is appropriate in relation to the ball. Participants performed the task 100 times over two days and completed a retention test on the third day. Feedback was provided on four kinematic variables, and each variable improved during acquisition. However, feedback on only one of these variables, mean reversal position information, improved learning. Although feedback on the other variables influenced performance during acquisition (short-term effects), it did not have long-term learning effects. Feedback that provided spatial information conferred a more permanent benefit than feedback providing temporal information. The authors concluded that feedback on a kinematic variable may influence performance and still not necessarily benefit learning.

Video Feedback   Learners may think that they are performing a particular task correctly until they see for themselves via pictures or a video. Although video feedback can be quite useful, practitioners must consider several factors when using videos, such as the time period during which the video is presented, the skill level of the learner, and whether the video is supplemented with additional feedback from the instructor.

Video feedback is more useful when it is provided over an extended period of time. Because this type of feedback provides so much information, learners need time to be able to fully benefit from its use. The longer time period also gives learners more opportunities to practice the motor skill. Research studies have shown that video feedback used for less than five weeks resulted in no improved performance (Rose & Christina, 2006).

Providing video feedback without cueing the learner to specific aspects of the movement is also ineffective, especially the novice learner, and may actually be detrimental (Kernodle & Carlton, 1992). This is likely because video feedback provides "too much information." Video feedback is not effective for learners who do not understand what they should be looking for in the video or how to interpret this information (Coker, 2009). Skilled performers, on the other hand, know what key aspects of the movement pattern they need to focus on and can benefit from viewing videotapes of their performance with little to no supplementation.

Minimally, novices should be given attention-directed cues (Newell & Walter, 1981) when they view videos. Because novices have little experience with performing the movement pattern correctly, they may become overwhelmed with all of the information available on the video. **Attention-directed cues** are cues that direct attention to the most important aspects of the movement pattern. For instance, a juggler may be instructed to focus on the height of the toss, a golfer to focus on the position of the club during the backswing, and a soccer player to focus on the plant foot position. The benefits of attention-directing cues are not limited to novice performers. Highly skilled athletes have also benefited from the addition of these cues when viewing videotapes (Menickelli, Landin, Grisham, & Hebert, 2000).

Although attention-directed cues have been found to improve performance following video feedback, attention-focusing cues provide the greatest benefit (Kernodle & Carlton, 1992). **Attention-focusing cues** are cues that not only direct the learner's attention to specific aspects of the movement pattern but also include error correction suggestions. For instance, rather than simply directing the juggler's attention to the toss, the instructor could inform the learner that she needs to make tosses that peak between the shoulder and the head. The golf instructor could inform novice golfers that they need to avoid overswinging the club because they will lose control of it, preventing them from staying in the same plane of motion. A soccer coach could inform novice players that the position of the plant foot is critical to soccer dribbling. The position of the plant allows for the direction and control of the dribble. Refer to table 15.1 for an example of an attention-focusing and attention-directed protocol.

TABLE 15.1   Examples of Attention-Focusing and Attention-Directed Protocol (Suggested Corrections) for Throwing Form

Attention-focusing protocol	Attention-directed protocol
1. Focus on the initial position of the body.	1a. Align your body so that the right shoulder faces the target area. 1b. Place your feet close together, parallel to each other, and at a 90-degree angle to the target area.
2. Focus on the initial movement of the trunk.	2. Rotate the hips 15 to 20 degrees from right to left during the initial phase of the throw.

3. Focus on the left arm during the preparatory phase of the left arm swing.	3. Begin the arm backswing with initiation of the right foot stride.
	  a. Keep the left arm relatively straight during the backswing.
	  b. During the backswing, raise the left arm until even with the shoulder.
	  c. At the end of the backswing, flex the elbow and allow the hand and ball to drop down behind the back.

4. Focus on the right foot during the throwing phase.	4. Stride forward with the right foot toward the target area.

Reprinted with permission from *Research Quarterly for Exercise and Sport*, Vol. 68, No. 4, 269-279, Copyright 1997 by the American Alliance for Health, Physical Education, Recreation and Dance, 1990 Association Drive, Reston, VA 20191.

 Research Notes: Who Can Throw the Best Sponge Balls?

Kernodle and Carlton (1992) illustrated the benefits of supplementing video feedback in a study that examined video feedback on performances of participants who threw sponge balls at a target with their eyes closed. Participants were separated into four groups: One group was provided only KR (distance the ball was thrown, no video); one group was provided only KP (video); one group viewed the video and received attention-directing cues ("Focus on the hips during the throwing phase"); and another group viewed the video and received attention-focused cues ("Rotate the hips from left to right during the throwing phase"). While all groups started at approximately the same level, the greatest gains in performances were seen in the group that received the attention-focusing cues (videotape + correcting cues). Significant benefits were also found for the attention-directed cues (videotape + attention cues) over the KR-only and KP-only (video) groups. No significant differences were found between the KR-only and KP-only groups, indicating that providing video feedback without attention-focusing or attention-directing cues provides no more benefit than simply providing KR (e.g., "You threw the ball 35 feet"). Videotapes should be extrinsic by an instructor who can direct learners' attention to the most important cues and describe how they can correct their errors.

 What Do You Think?

1. What are some advantages to using videos?
2. What are some disadvantages?
3. Video feedback is most effective for learners at what level of skill?
4. When is using video feedback least effective?

Video Feedback Learning Stages Four stages have been described for learners who are introduced to video feedback: (1) shock, (2) error detection, (3) error correction, and (4) independence (table 15.2; Darden, 1999). When learners are introduced to video feedback, they are often more focused on their visual appearance than on their movement patterns or performance. Because of this preoccupation with irrelevant factors (overall appearance rather than movement patterns), this stage has been termed the **shock stage**. Darden stated that until learners have adjusted to viewing themselves on video, further instruction is ineffective. During stage 2, the **error detection stage**, instructors should supplement the video feedback with attention-focusing cues. This is especially important for novice learners who may not know what the task-relevant cues for the motor skill are and may be focusing on irrelevant cues. These cues will enable the learners to begin to critically analyze their performance and prepare them to detect and correct their errors. Learners who are able to identify their errors and may understand the cause of an error have advanced to stage 3, the **error correction stage**. During this stage, learners are developing error correction strategies. With learners in this stage, the instructor's role in this stage is to focus on problem-solving skills. **Independence** is the final video feedback learning stage. Learners who reach this stage require minimal to no video supplementation by an instructor. Skilled performers know exactly what to look for when viewing the videos and are able to identify and correct their errors.

TABLE 15.2 Video Feedback Learning Stages

Stage	Learner characteristics	Instructor's role
Shock	Learners are preoccupied with appearance.	• Allow learner to become familiar with viewing videos. • Hold off on further instruction until learner is ready.
Error detection	• Learners critically observe performance. • They identify some performance errors.	• Distinguish relevant and irrelevant cues. • Provide attention-focusing cues.
Error correction	• Learners can now identify what the errors are. • They know the cause of errors. • Learners focus upon learning how to correct for the identified errors.	Encourage problem solving.
Independence	• Learners detect and correct errors. • They have little to no dependence on instructor.	• Little or no supplemental role. • Provide encouragement.

Research Notes: Using Video Feedback in Practical Settings

Roberts and Brown (2008) described how to best use video feedback to assist in aquatic instruction. An intermediate swim class met twice per week for 50-minute sessions. The first day of class was an orientation session in which students were informed of all of the skills and expectations but did not enter the pool. The students' current skill levels were assessed during the second session. Instructors demonstrated the skills and then video recorded the students using digital cameras and underwater cam sticks. Following the completion of each skill, the students viewed their performances at poolside while the instructor provided attention-directed cues. Students then practiced the skill again and often showed immediate improvement. One student said, "The video REALLY did help. I'm doing things in my underwater swim that I am totally not aware of! I had no idea that I flutter kicked some and my kick is kinda tilted towards the side."

Student performances were also contrasted with videos of skilled demonstrations. Using video editing software, the researchers were able to show the two videos together, allowing the students to compare their performances with those of the model. They were encouraged to watch these videos as much as they liked. It is key for instructors to remember the importance of including attention or correcting cues (or both) with videos. Instructors can also provide this additional feedback through written questions, giving students another opportunity to reflect on their performances (Herbert & Landin, 1997). Reflection is an important component in improving error correction capabilities. In this example, five to eight online questions were combined with the videos for each skill using an online questioning tool (Webassign). This allowed students to critique their own skills as guided by the questions. This video feedback model saved instructor time while also enhancing student learning and decreasing learning time. Students of all levels have benefitted from this type of video technology (Roberts & Brown, 2008).

Importance of Studying Feedback

There are three main functions of extrinsic feedback: information, motivation, and reinforcement (figure 15.2). Feedback that provides information can give learners an understanding of how they are moving, what they are doing correctly

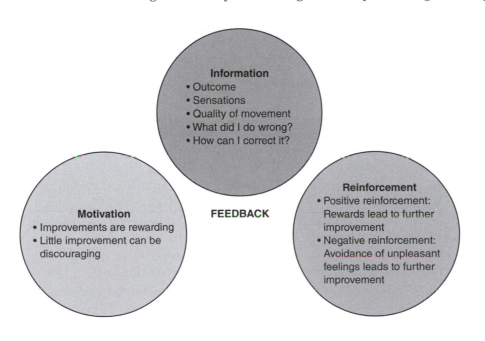

FIGURE 15.2 Extrinsic feedback has three main functions: (1) guiding the learner to better performances, (2) providing an incentive to motivate the learner; and (3) reinforcing the movement.

or incorrectly, and how they can correct errors. This information can guide the learner to more successful performances. Feedback as information to correct performance errors includes the performance outcome (knowledge of results), sensations produced by the movement (intrinsic feedback), information about the nature of errors (descriptive), and suggestions on how to correct errors (prescriptive feedback). For example, a pole vaulter will receive information about his movement from multiple sources. He will see the outcome of the vault, hear the pole make contact with the vaulting box and hear it fall if it hits too hard, feel if he pulled his body up and around the bar or if he hit the bar, and likely know the outcome before he is even near the bar. These are all types of intrinsic feedback. The pole vaulter may also receive extrinsic feedback from a coach or a teammate that describes his form or provides corrective information.

Feedback also functions to motivate learners. When learners receive feedback on their movement performances, they can compare it with their performance goals. Learners who are progressively improving are receiving feedback that they are moving closer and closer to their goals. Improved performance is very rewarding and provides learners with an incentive to continue practicing so that they can achieve further success. Conversely, if learners see little improvement or are actually getting worse, they will probably become frustrated with the task, like Bridgette in the opening scenario in this chapter. Frustrated learners are likely to decrease their effort toward improving or even to quit. To help increase motivation, instructors can provide more feedback on correct aspects of the performance attempts than on errors to help reduce some of the frustration learners may be experiencing.

The third function of feedback is reinforcement. **Reinforcement** occurs when the feedback following a performance attempt increases the probability of similar performance attempts in the future. Feedback can provide positive and negative reinforcement. **Positive reinforcement** following a performance attempt can be rewarding. This reward is intended to increase the likelihood that successful attempts will occur more consistently, but must be provided immediately following the performance attempt to be beneficial. Positive reinforcement can be given verbally through compliments or praise. Short positive phrases such as "Great job on the backswing" or "You're getting there! You can do it!" can help motivate the learners to continue their efforts. These phrases should be used sparingly and only when they are deserved. If a learner is having very little success, the instructor should find at least some aspect of the movement pattern, however small, to praise. Nonverbal gestures can also provide positive reinforcement, such as a smile, a thumbs up, or a pat on the back.

For extrinsic feedback to be an effective positive reinforcement, it must be *perceived* as a reward by the learner (Rose & Christina, 2006). For example, a coach may increase the intensity or duration of practice for an athlete because he perceives the athlete to be capable of improving to the next level. If the coach does not explain the reason behind the change, the athlete may perceive the added workload as a punishment. Similarly, a coach may switch an athlete's position because of the player's well-rounded athleticism. However, the athlete may interpret the change as suggesting her inability to play her position well rather than her enhanced capabilities at multiple positions.

Feedback that evokes unpleasant feelings that the learner will want to avoid at all costs is **negative reinforcement**. Negative reinforcement can be derived simply from embarrassment over a poor performance, such as a missed shot, a poor throw, or a missed catch. A hurdler with a knee injury may avoid hitting the hurdle with his trail leg at all costs to avoid the pain. An inexperienced driver learning how to drive a manual transmission may initially cause the car to jump or stall. The embarrassment this causes can serve as negative reinforcement, strengthening the desired movement (Coker, 2009). Golf teaching aids can provide negative reinforcement to eliminate lunging. To be effective, the aid must be placed just ahead of the lead leg. When swinging, the learner should stay behind the pad through impact of the ball. If the pad has been hit (negative reinforcement), you are moving ahead of the ball. You want to avoid hitting the pad (incorrect movement), so the correct movement is reinforced.

Another common negative reinforcer is the buzzing sound in a car indicating that your seat belt is not fastened. Fastening your seatbelt is negatively reinforced because you do not want to hear the annoying buzzing noise (Gredler, 1992). To decrease the length of a step for a batter, a coach could place a wooden barrier on the ground (Rose & Christina, 2006) such that the batter's foot contacts the barrier if she takes too long a step. Shorter steps (correct movement) would be reinforced because the batter would want to avoid making contact with the barrier (negative reinforcer).

What Do You Think?

Describe two examples of using negative reinforcement for one or more motor skills of your choice. How effective do you think each of these methods would be? Explain your answers.

Providing Effective Feedback

Instructors and clinicians often spend much time preparing the learning situation by properly setting up the environment, setting goals, and designing the practice sessions, but they do not effectively provide feedback. Important factors in the effective provision of feedback include the frequency of feedback, the timing of provision of feedback, and scheduling feedback.

Corrective or Error-Based Feedback

When providing feedback, instructors must determine whether to provide feedback on the correct aspects of the movement pattern or on the learner's errors. The effectiveness of error versus corrective feedback is largely dependent on the learner's skill level, motivation, and interest. For novices, feedback focused on the error can be very effective. This helps guide the learner to the correct movement patterns. Learners who are not very motivated toward or interested in the activity would benefit more from feedback on the correct aspects of the movement pattern. This feedback will serve to encourage learners to continue their efforts by confirming their progress (Coker, 2009).

In general, it is optimal to provide feedback on *both* the error and correct components of the movement. The sandwich approach (figure 15.3) is a recommended strategy for providing feedback on both error and correct components

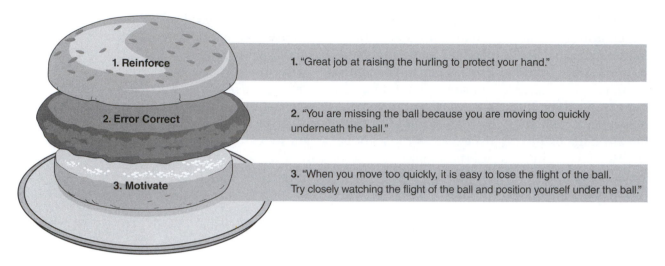

FIGURE 15.3 The sandwich approach to providing error feedback.

(Fischman & Oxendine, 2001). In the sandwich, the bread is praise and constructive criticism is the meat. Initially, instructors praise the learner's strengths to reinforce correct performance (e.g., "Good! You kept your eye on the ball, and you had good timing"). Improvements are then suggested based on the learner's errors ("Next time, spread your feet a little wider"). The instructor concludes with motivational information, encouraging the learner by discussing the benefits of correcting the error (e.g., "Spreading your feet wider will help your balance").

What Do You Think?

1. Using the sandwich approach, change the following statement: "You messed it up again! How many times do I have to tell you to follow through? You never listen!" You can choose any motor skill for which following through is a key component in the movement. Be sure to add something that the learner did correctly and discuss the benefits of following through.

2. Devise a feedback example using a motor skill of your choice using the sandwich approach. Describe how each step will benefit the learner.

Feedback Frequency

Traditionally, researchers thought that the more frequently feedback was provided following performance attempts, the greater the gains in learning (Thorndike, 1931). This line of thinking developed because performance tends to increase more and at a faster rate when extrinsic feedback is given most or all of the time. However, current research has indicated that too much feedback is detrimental to learning (Salmoni, Schmidt, & Walter, 1984). The **guidance hypothesis** asserts that the benefits of high-frequency KR can be deceiving because learners will generally perform better initially than if they received lower-frequency KR (Salmoni et al., 1984; Winstein, Pohl, & Lewthwaite, 1994). Unfortunately, these effects are only temporary. Learners become overly dependent on the extrinsic feedback, often relying more on the extrinsic feedback than on their own sensory sources of feedback. This promotes passive learning, such that the learner does not develop the critical problem-solving skills necessary for performing the motor skill without the guidance of the extrinsic feedback. On the other hand, learners who receive extrinsic feedback at a lower frequency become much more active in the process. They reflect on and evaluate their movements. This active process helps them to perform the motor skill without the provision of feedback.

Feedback Precision

Knowing the appropriate level of precision of feedback is an important consideration. It is important to adjust the precision based on the skill level of the learner. Feedback should be less precise for beginners. When learners are introduced to a task, they are simply trying to obtain a broad understanding of the movement pattern. More general instructions can be more effective during this stage. As learners progress from the cognitive stage to the associative stage, their focus shifts to refining the task. At this time, more precise feedback is more meaningful.

When feedback is given only when performance is outside a particular range, it is referred to as **bandwidth feedback**. For example, a long snapper may receive feedback only when his snap exceeds a range of correctness, such as above the chin or below the knees of the kicker; a volleyball player may receive feedback only when her toss is not between her shoulder and a foot in front of the shoulder; or a long jumper receives feedback on his take-off only when his foot lands more than 3 inches behind the line. The learner knows that if he does not receive feedback, he has performed to a satisfactory level. With this method, the absence of feedback provides positive reinforcement and can be motivational. Bandwidth feedback eliminates the provision of too much feedback because learners receive feedback only when they are outside a predefined "range of correctness." Bandwidth feedback has been found to promote significantly more retention than both high- and low-frequency KR (Lai & Shea, 1999; Lee & Carnahan, 1990; Sherwood, 1988). These benefits may result from the fact that this strategy inherently involves a fading schedule (Schmidt, 1991). Novice performers require more feedback because they are performing outside of the satisfactory range much more often. With practice and increased consistency of movement, learners perform more and more in the satisfactory range, so they receive progressively less and less feedback. Choosing an appropriate bandwidth is an important consideration for the instructor. Depending on the task, it may be more effective to have a larger bandwidth for beginners. As learners progress, the bandwidth can be slowly decreased. The goal is to provide the most feedback initially, but the task should not be so challenging that the learner does not achieve any success or see much progress. Tasks that are perceived as too challenging can cause learners to quickly lose motivation or interest in the activity.

Feedback Schedules

It is important to note that not only is too much KR detrimental; not enough KR during the initial stages of learning is also detrimental (figure 15.4).

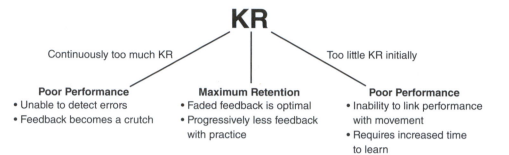

FIGURE 15.4

Negative outcomes can result from continuously providing KR or not providing enough KR.

When very little KR is provided for novices, learners are not receiving the guidance they need to be able to perform the movement pattern. Beginners do not yet know what they are doing correctly or incorrectly and may spend significant amounts of time trying new strategies. Learners who do not receive enough KR during these initial stages require significantly more time to improve and may even lose motivation or interest during the process.

Although research has determined that the traditional "the more, the better" concept about providing KR is not valid, no optimal reduced feedback schedule has been found to be most effective. In this section we discuss several reduced-frequency feedback schedules. The appropriateness of each schedule depends on the complexity and duration of the task and the intrinsic factors of the learner.

Faded Feedback

Winstein and Schmidt (1990) developed a feedback schedule in which the amount of feedback is based on the skill level of the learner, appropriately termed **faded feedback**. Beginners receive high-frequency feedback to help guide their movements and reinforce the correct aspects of their movements. A beginner should be receiving 80% to 100% relative frequency of KR depending on the complexity and duration of the motor skill. **Relative frequency of KR** is the percentage of performance attempts in which KR is provided. To calculate relative frequency KR, the number of trials with KR, which is termed **absolute frequency of KR**, is divided by the total number of trials. This number is then multiplied by 100%. For example, if a gymnast receives feedback following four out of eight vaults, then the absolute frequency is 4 attempts and the relative frequency is 50%, because she received feedback 50% of the time. As learners improve, the relative frequency of KR should be progressively reduced. This feedback schedule should be tailored to the individual and should not be reduced until the learner has reached a certain level of proficiency.

 What Do You Think?

1. Calculate the relative frequency of KR when the absolute frequency of KR is 10 trials and the total number of trials is 40 trials.

2. Calculate the absolute frequency of KR for a relative frequency of 80% and a total number of trials of 60.

3. Calculate the total number of trials for an absolute frequency of five trials and a relative frequency of 50%.

Summary Feedback

Summary feedback is feedback following a set number of performance attempts. The instructor summarizes each performance attempt. For example, a gymnast could complete her entire floor routine; then the coach would provide feedback regarding each of the moves. Similarly, a learner could perform a set number of attempts for a discrete skill, such as shooting a foul shot or throwing a shot put, before receiving summary feedback. Videos are also a source of summary feedback. Learners can watch a video following the completion of a series of moves and preferably receive attention-directed feedback regarding their performance attempts. The number of performance attempts appropriate for a motor skill would be dependent on task complexity and duration (Swinnen, 1996). Fewer trials should be summarized with longer or more complex motor skills.

Average Feedback

Average feedback is very similar to summary feedback in the sense that both occur following a set number of performance attempts. However, rather than providing feedback on every attempt or movement, the practitioner discusses only the average performance error(s) or the essence of the performances with the learner. Summary and average feedback also differ with respect to the amount provided. Average feedback provides less, more focused feedback than summary feedback. Summary feedback and average feedback have been found to be equally effective (Weeks & Sherwood, 1994), but average feedback may be more appealing to practitioners. Given the demands and time constraints imposed on most instructors, clinicians, or coaches, it is unlikely that they can devote attention to many individual performance attempts for one learner and provide specific feedback on each individual attempt. Instead, it is more practical to provide a description of the quality of the overall performances (average feedback). This is also advantageous to learners because they are less likely to become overwhelmed with too much information.

Learner-Regulated Feedback

All of the feedback schedules we have considered are designed and implemented by the practitioner. Over approximately the past decade, a newer feedback schedule has been the focus of many research studies, termed **learner-regulated feedback**. With learner-regulated feedback schedules, the learner is in control of the provision of feedback, deciding after which trials and how often to receive extrinsic feedback. Shifting the control on the provision of feedback from the instructor to the learner resulted in increased learning even in comparison to matched participants who received feedback during the same performance attempts as the learner-regulated groups (Chiviacowsky, Wulf, Laroque de Medeiros, Kaefer, & Wally, 2008). The only difference between the groups was that one group decided *when* they would receive feedback. The possible benefits to learner-regulated feedback include (1) an increased active role, providing learners with increased cognitive processing of the movement and the feedback (Wulf, Clauss, Shea, & Whitacre, 2001), and (2) increased motivation (Chiviacowsky & Wulf, 2007). The frequency with which learners request feedback is largely dependent on their characteristics, including skill level and age, as well as characteristics of the task such as complexity and duration. As previously discussed, beginners require more feedback until they obtain a certain level of proficiency. More feedback is also required for more complex tasks and tasks that are longer in duration.

Research Notes: Do Children Require More or Less Feedback?

Chiviacowsky and colleagues (2008) investigated the effectiveness of learner-regulated feedback in 10-year-old children, comparing the frequency of their requests for feedback with their learning. The investigators also sought to determine whether children would choose the "optimal" frequency of feedback. Previously, it had been found that children who requested feedback (learner-regulated group) learned the task more effectively than a group who received feedback on the same schedule but did not control when they received the feedback (Chiviacowsky & Wulf, 2006). On the basis of the results, participants were separated into two groups, a more KR group (requested 39.3% KR on average) and a less KR group (requested 8.4% KR on average). The more KR group showed enhanced learning in comparison to the less KR group. The authors suggested several potential reasons why children require more feedback than adults. First, children have less movement experience, so learning new motor skills is more challenging. Children also have shorter attention spans and a reduced ability to process information in comparison to adults (Lambert & Bard, 2005). Processing speed increases from age 3 years to adolescence (Lambert & Bard, 2005), so children require more time to process information than adults.

These results indicate that although children significantly benefit from learner-regulated feedback (Chiviacowsky & Wulf, 2006), they may not always choose an optimal frequency. Because of their limited movement experiences, attentional capacities, and slower processing speeds, children require more frequent feedback than adults. Learner-regulated feedback may be the most optimal feedback schedule for children if the movement educator devises the instructions so as to encourage children to request more feedback for more difficult tasks, since children have a tendency to request feedback at a lower than optimal rate (Chiviacowsky et al., 2008).

Extrinsic Feedback Timing

Another critical issue is the timing of the provision of extrinsic feedback (figure 15.5). In other words, when is it most appropriate to provide extrinsic feedback? Many instructors and clinicians assume that feedback is most effective immediately following a performance attempt. Although one might expect immediate feedback to be most beneficial because it allows learners to link the performance with the outcome or quality of the movement before their memory of the movement production fades, immediate feedback actually prevents learners from reflecting on the movement. Just as the provision of high-frequency KR (i.e., 80-100% relative KR) eliminates active processing, feedback provided too soon following a performance attempt promotes passive learning. The learner will become reliant on the feedback and will not develop the critical problem-solving skills necessary for performing the motor skill without the guidance of the extrinsic feedback.

The time period between one performance attempt and the next is termed **interresponse interval**. This time period is broken down into two other temporal intervals, feedback delay interval and postfeedback delay interval—the amount of time between the first attempt and the provision of feedback, and the time between the provision of feedback and the second attempt, respectively. In the following sections we examine these intervals further, as their duration has important implications for learning.

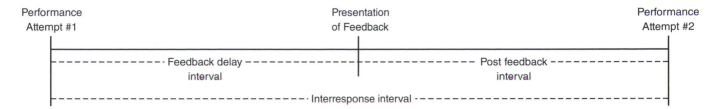

FIGURE 15.5 Timing components for the presentation of extrinsic feedback.

Adapted from C. Coker, *Motor Learning and Control for Practitioners*, Second Edition, p. 261. Copyright © 2009 by Holcomb Hathaway, Publishers (Scottsdale, AZ). Used with permission.

Feedback Delay Interval

Researchers have examined the timing of feedback to determine the most effective time lapse between the completion of a performance attempt and the provision of KR. The period of time between the completion of an attempt and the presentation of feedback is termed the **feedback delay interval**. The length of the feedback delay interval is a critical component in the presentation of extrinsic feedback. If the feedback delay interval is too long, then memory of the movement production will be decreased due to forgetting. On the other hand, if the feedback delay interval is too short, the learner will not have time to engage in the necessary cognitive operations for learning error detection and correction strategies (Salmoni et al., 1984; Swinnen, Schmidt, Nicholson, & Shapiro, 1990).

The key question is, how long should instructors and clinicians wait before providing extrinsic feedback? The feedback delay interval does not need to be lengthy. It simply needs to be long enough that learners can process and evaluate their own intrinsic feedback. Learners need to think about how the movement felt, how they performed, what errors they may have made, and how to correct them. Even just a few seconds can be long enough for the learner to do this thinking about the movement. However, research has indicated that longer delays do not adversely affect learning (Bilodeau & Bilodeau, 1958). Although it is less likely that a longer feedback delay interval will negatively affect learning compared to the provision of immediate extrinsic feedback (a very small feedback delay interval), motor forgetting can occur during this time, which makes it more difficult for learners to link their performance with the extrinsic feedback.

Now let's assume you have chosen a feedback delay interval of 5 seconds. How do you know that your learners are reflecting during this period of time and not simply waiting for your feedback? The truth is that you don't know, unless you ask. Prompting learners to self-reflect and evaluate their performances during this break leads to increased retention (Swinnen et al., 1990). To promote self-evaluation following a performance attempt, the instructor should ask the learner directed questions. The questions could be general, such as "How do you think you did?" or "What do you think you did wrong [or correct] during that attempt?" He could follow up on answers by asking. "How did you come to the conclusion that [a particular aspect of the movement] was correct [or incorrect]?" or "What about that movement was incorrect?" or "How could you correct that mistake?"

Self-evaluation is a learned strategy and will take time for learners to develop. It may be more effective to ask specific questions, especially with beginners, since they will likely not know the causes of their errors or how to correct them. For example, an instructor could ask leading questions, such as "Do you think you followed through the release of the ball?" or "Where did you make contact with the ball? Was it the correct location?" As learners develop better self-evaluation strategies and improve their performance, the questions can become more general. Eventually the learner will be able to self-evaluate with little to no help from the instructor.

Postfeedback Interval

The time period between the presentation of the extrinsic feedback and the learner's subsequent performance attempt is called the **postfeedback interval**. Similarly to what has been found with the feedback delay interval, if this time interval is too short, learning is negatively affected (Gallagher & Thomas, 1980). Learners need sufficient time to be able to process the information provided through extrinsic feedback and plan how they are going to perform their next attempt (Rose & Christina, 2006). The appropriate length of the postfeedback interval depends on the age of the learner, with children requiring longer postfeedback intervals (Barclay & Newell, 1980). As previously mentioned, children have greater processing limitations than adults. Increased postfeedback intervals allow young learners more time to develop the error detection and correction mechanism that is necessary for learning motor skills.

To facilitate cognitive processing during the postfeedback interval, the instructor can ask learners how they are going to execute the next attempt, or more specifically what they are going to do differently in comparison to the previous attempt. By encouraging learners to further process this information, the instructor can check how well they understand their performance errors and the effectiveness of the feedback.

Misconceptions Associated With Feedback

Now that you've looked at various provisions of feedback, it's important that you also understand some misconceptions about feedback. Table 15.3 outlines three common misconceptions associated with the provision of feedback and provides best practices for each misconception.

TABLE 15.3 Misconceptions About and Best Practices for Extrinsic Feedback

Misconceptions	Best practices
• *More is better:* The more feedback provided, the better the learning.	• Fade the amount of feedback provided.
• The *faster the better:* Providing feedback immediately following the performance attempt is most effective.	• Allow processing time after the performance attempt *and* after the provision of feedback.
• *Increased precision is better:* Decreasing the bandwidth is more effective.	• Fade the bandwidth (expect progressively better performances as skill level increases).

What Do You Think?

1. Is giving extrinsic feedback always a good idea?
2. What are the benefits of extrinsic feedback?
3. When *might* extrinsic feedback not be needed?
4. When *might* extrinsic feedback enhance skill acquisition?
5. When can extrinsic feedback be counterproductive, that is, hinder skill acquisition?
6. Counter the misconceptions listed in table 15.3. Explain why each is a misconception.

Summary

Feedback is one of the most important factors in skill acquisition, second only to practice. Feedback helps guide the performer toward executing the proper movement pattern, motivates the learner, and reinforces successful performances. Feedback received via the sensory systems is considered intrinsic feedback, while feedback that has been given in addition to sensory sources is extrinsic feedback. There are many types of extrinsic feedback. The two main forms are knowledge of results (performance outcome) and knowledge of performance (quality of the movement pattern). Knowledge of performance can be descriptive or prescriptive, but the provision of both is most effective.

Novice learners require more extrinsic feedback than skilled learners. Feedback during the initial stages of learning can help decrease learning time by helping the learner to link a successful performance with the movement pattern produced. As a learner progresses, the amount of feedback provided should decrease, also known as faded feedback. Practitioners can accomplish this by progressively providing less relative KR or by providing bandwidth KR, as more skilled learners will be performing within the bandwidth progressively more and more and therefore receiving less feedback. Learner-regulated KR is also very effective, especially in adults. Learners generally ask for KR only when they actually need the feedback, so they are not receiving too much and feel a greater sense of control over the learning situation.

The importance of appropriate extrinsic feedback cannot be emphasized enough. More often than not, movement educators provide extrinsic feedback too frequently or too soon, without realizing the negative effects this has over both the short and the long term in relation to retention. Just as practice should be designed around the individual and the task, feedback should be individualized to the learner and the task.

Supplemental Activities

1. You will experience six different feedback schedules and identify the one that appeals to you. You will record your scores, but you may find other reasons for preferring one schedule over another apart from better performance scores. As soon as you and your partner complete one KR schedule, you are to start another. Your task is the same for all the KR schedules. Sit on the floor 10

feet (3 meters) away from a target while blindfolded. You will toss a ball to the target 20 times per feedback schedule. Your partner will record your score for all trials and will retrieve the ball (Scoring is as follows; starting at the bull's-eye and moving out: 9, 7, 5, 3, 1 with a score of 0 if it does not hit the target). The task and total number of trials (20 per schedule) is the same for each KR practice schedule; only the frequency and form of KR vary. The six schedules of KR are (1) relative frequency 100%, (2) relative frequency 25%, (3) summary KR; (4) average KR, (5) bandwidth KR, and 6) learner-regulated KR.

- Relative frequency 100%: After every trial, your partner will announce the score as well as record it.

- Relative frequency 25%: You will receive KR for only four trials instead of 20 trials. At the end of every fifth trial, your partner will announce the score only for that particular trial. Your partner will record all trials.

- Summary KR: A drawing of a target face with the outcome or result for five tosses will be shown to you after every fifth trial. Each outcome can be numbered so you can see where each toss hit the target.

- Average KR: The numerical average (sum of the values of the scores divided by the number of scores) is calculated after five trials and then given to you.

- Bandwidth KR: You are only told your score if it was outside the bandwidth of the inner two circles. You will not receive any other information regarding your performance if it is in the inner two circles.

- Learner-regulated KR: Your partner will provide you with your score only when you ask for it. Your partner should note the times you ask for feedback.

- *Note:* The numerical score is recorded on every trial.

Questions
- Which feedback schedule did you perform the best?
- Which feedback schedule did you prefer regardless of your performance? Explain why.
- Calculate your absolute and relative frequency for the learner-regulated KR condition.
- Which feedback schedule would be most appropriate for a beginner? Explain your answer.
- Which feedback schedule would be most appropriate for a skilled performer? Explain your answer.

2. Feedback schedules. If you were teaching an individual a new motor skill, how would you incorporate feedback into your program? Provide a progression of feedback instruction from the initial instruction to skill refinement. You could design this feedback schedule for any motor skill, from learning striking skills in a child to relearning how to walk following an injury in an adult. Describe the motor skill you are teaching and the characteristics of the learner. Be sure to also include a timeline for this progression.

1. RELATIVE FREQUENCY 100%
SCORE GIVEN ON EVERY TRIAL
BLOCKS OF TRIALS

1	2	3	4
1 ____	6 ____	11 ____	16 ____
2 ____	7 ____	12 ____	17 ____
3 ____	8 ____	13 ____	18 ____
4 ____	9 ____	14 ____	19 ____
5 ____	10 ____	15 ____	20 ____

_____

2. RELATIVE FREQUENCY 25%
SCORE GIVEN ON EVERY FIFTH TRIAL
BLOCKS OF TRIALS

1	2	3	4
1 ____	6 ____	11 ____	16 ____
2 ____	7 ____	12 ____	17 ____
3 ____	8 ____	13 ____	18 ____
4 ____	9 ____	14 ____	19 ____
5 ____	10 ____	15 ____	20 ____

Average _____

3. SUMMARY KR
SCORE GIVEN FOR EVERY TRIAL
AFTER EVERY FIFTH TRIAL
BLOCKS OF TRAILS

1	2	3	4
1 ____	6 ____	11 ____	16 ____
2 ____	7 ____	12 ____	17 ____
3 ____	8 ____	13 ____	18 ____
4 ____	9 ____	14 ____	19 ____
5 ____	10 ____	15 ____	20 ____

_____

4. AVERAGE KR
AVERAGE SCORE GIVEN
AFTER EVERY FIFTH TRIAL
BLOCKS OF TRIALS

1	2	3	4
1 ____	6 ____	11 ____	16 ____
2 ____	7 ____	12 ____	17 ____
3 ____	8 ____	13 ____	18 ____
4 ____	9 ____	14 ____	19 ____
5 ____	10 ____	15 ____	20 ____

Average _____

5. BANDWIDTH KR
FEEDBACK IS ONLY GIVEN WHEN THE
SCORE IS A 5 OR BELOW.
BLOCKS OF TRIALS

1	2	3	4
1 ____	6 ____	11 ____	16 ____
2 ____	7 ____	12 ____	17 ____
3 ____	8 ____	13 ____	18 ____
4 ____	9 ____	14 ____	19 ____
5 ____	10 ____	15 ____	20 ____

_____

6. LEARNER-REGULATED KR
SCORE GIVEN WHEN REQUESTED
MARK AN X FOR EACH TRIAL IN WHICH
FEEDBACK WAS REQUESTED.

1	2	3	4
1 ____	6 ____	11 ____	16 ____
2 ____	7 ____	12 ____	17 ____
3 ____	8 ____	13 ____	18 ____
4 ____	9 ____	14 ____	19 ____
5 ____	10 ____	15 ____	20 ____

Average _____

Scores From Summary KR

Mark the actual location of each attempt, numbering them 1 through 5. Use a separate target illustration for each block of five attempts.

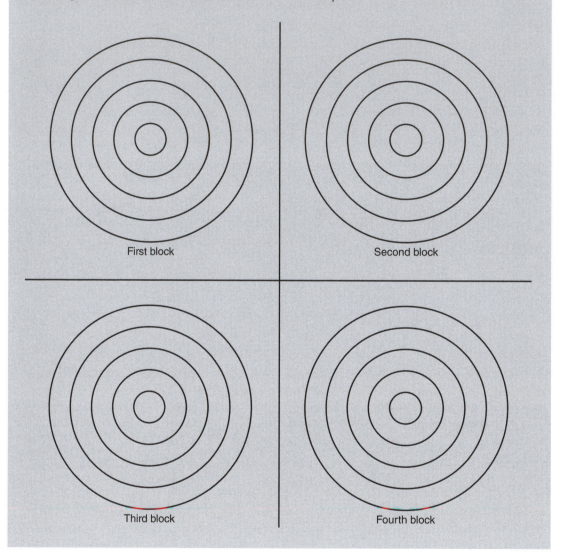

First block

Second block

Third block

Fourth block

CONCLUSION: DEVISING A PLAN

This conclusion ties together the many concepts discussed throughout this book to help the reader devise a plan for motor skill acquisition. Designing an appropriate plan is the most critical component in promoting skill acquisition and often the most complex part of the process. Before practitioners implement any motor program plan, they must conduct a full assessment of the learner, the task, and the environment—the "who" (learner), the "what" (task), and the "where" (environment). After this assessment, they can appropriately individualize a program for the learner by establishing the practice and feedback methods. This conclusion deals with each of these areas and then provides case study examples to give readers the opportunity to practice designing appropriate programs.

Constraints

Constraints, which are the boundaries that limit movement possibilities, influence everything that we do (refer back to chapter 1). The distance we can jump is limited by our structural constraints, including variables such as height, weight, strength, and number of fast-twitch muscle fibers, and functional constraints such as motivation, interest, and attention. Although it is very difficult to alter individual constraints, at least on a short-term basis, movement educators can manipulate the task and the environment to allow learners to move more proficiently.

By manipulating constraints, an instructor can induce both short- and long-term performance changes. Learners who are attempting a motor skill that is too complex may give up before they are ever able to obtain success. Small children rarely learn how to play baseball with an adult-sized baseball and bat. The bat would be far too heavy and long for them to swing successfully. A good test for finding an appropriate bat for a child is to have the child hold the bat out at shoulder length. If the child cannot hold the bat out for 20 seconds, then the bat is too heavy for him. Environmental constraints are also often manipulated to increase success for children learning how to bat. The most common method is to use a stationary ball sitting on a tee. The formerly open environment has become much more predictable for the child with the temporal component of the swing eliminated. Functional constraints can also impair an individual's performance. Adults who have a fear of the water may never learn how to swim until they feel comfortable in an aquatic setting. They may need several lessons just to get used to being in the water without even attempting the basics of swimming.

Often there are many ways in which the environment can be adapted to enhance performance. Children may perform poorly at shooting baskets or catching balls in an environment with poor lighting or when the walls and the balls are a similar color. Practitioners could improve children's performances simply by using balls with vibrant colors, increasing the ambient lighting, or placing white paper on the walls. The surface of support can also have a strong influence on performance. Think about the importance of playing a game of golf on a well-groomed golf course or running on a rubber versus a cinder track. For rehabilitation settings, the environment should be designed so that it is as similar to real-world settings as possible to maximize transfer when patients leave the facility.

The learning task should also be designed around the learner. The goals and the rules of a task constrain the movement patterns performed by the learner. For example, if the rules of basketball were changed such that only two dribbles were allowed, the pace of the game would likely decrease as players could no longer make a fast break. When teaching novices, the goal of the learning session should be on the process of the movement rather than the movement product, or outcome (e.g., how far the ball is thrown), so that the focus is on the learner's form. To encourage children to focus on form, the goal of the task could be to throw at a target on the wall rather than to throw as far as they can. A focus on the process rather than the product of the movement is not only important in sport and physical education, but also for rehabilitation settings. When teaching an individual how to walk following a severe injury or stroke, physical therapists should encourage patients to focus on increased independence with their steps rather than increased number of steps or distance traveled.

Using developmentally appropriate equipment is also a very important factor in designing the learning task. Equipment should be appropriate to the structural constraints of the learner. Smaller balls are easier to throw because they fit better into smaller hands. However, larger, lighter balls are easier to catch. Nets should be lowered for tennis, and rackets should have a larger surface area to allow for increased success. Therapists use many devices and equipment during their interventions. Clinicians must adapt the equipment according to their patients' individual constraints, such as their size and the type of injury. Therapists can also inform patients of appropriate and inexpensive equipment that they can use at home such as medicine balls, balance boards, and exercise peddlers. The following section examines the *who*, *what*, *where*, *when*, and *how* of designing appropriate programs.

Devising a Plan

Devising an appropriate plan may be one of the most challenging elements of teaching a motor skill, but it is the most critical component. Designing appropriate programs requires a full assessment of the learner's characteristics, the task, and the environmental context prior to planning and scheduling practice (table 1). Practice sessions that are individualized for learners are most effective, providing them with optimal chances for short- and long-term success. You will want to use all of the material in this book to help you develop an optimal program. It is essential that you examine the characteristics of the learner, including both functional and structural constraints, in order to design the most effective program. It is perhaps equally important to fully analyze the task and the environmental context, as certain practice designs, schedules, instructional strategies, and feedback schedules are more or less appropriate dependent on the motor skill and the environment. A full assessment of the learner, task, and environment enables the movement educator to devise an individualized and developmentally appropriate program for learners.

TABLE 1 Checklist for Designing Appropriate Programs

Who? Learner characteristics	What? Task analysis	Where? Environmental context
Age of learner	Nature of the skill	Recreation
Number of learners	• Discrete	Competition
Structural constraints	• Serial	Rehabilitation
• Size of learner	• Continuous	Fitness
• Physical limitations	Precision of the skill	Conditions of the environment
Functional constraints	• Fine motor skill	• Varying surface
• Motivation	• Gross motor skill	• Varying weather conditions
• Attention	Predictability of the skill	• Controlled conditions
• Skill level	• Open skill	
• Arousal level	• Closed skill	
Goals	Pace	
• Performance goals	• Externally paced	
• Outcome goals	• Internally paced	
• Process goals		

When? Distribution of practice	How? Presentation	Feedback
Massed	Verbal instructions	Type of feedback
Distributed	Demonstrations	• KR or KP
Scheduling practice	Guidance	• Descriptive or prescriptive
	Practice	• Terminal or concurrent
	• Part versus whole practice	• Kinetic or kinematic
	• Mental practice	Feedback schedules
	• Variability of practice	• Summary KR
		• Average KR
		• Bandwidth KR
		• Learner-regulated KR
		• Faded KR
		Frequency of feedback
		Timing of feedback

Who: Learner Characteristics

The first step in designing appropriate programs is examining the learner's characteristics. Movement educators should have a solid understanding of their learners' functional characteristics (e.g., motivation, attentional capacity, skill level) and structural characteristics (e.g., height, weight, physical impairments). Are you instructing one learner or patient, a group or a class, or a sport team? Are the learners young or old? Are you teaching learners of various ages? What are the learners' movement experiences? How motivated are the learners? It is also important to set specific individual goals for your learners. Is the goal to teach a skill that is new to the learner, or are you varying a skill that the learner can already perform? The approach to teaching a novel skill would be very different than varying a skill that is familiar to the learner.

What: Analyzing the Task

The second step in planning a program is analyzing the task. Effective programs are specifically designed for the type of task and the learner's characteristics. The type of motor skill should be determined, including the nature of the task (discrete, serial, continuous), the predictability of the environment (open or closed), the pace of the skill (externally or internally paced), and the precision of the skill (fine or gross). The key elements and the purpose of the task should be determined as well.

Where: Environmental Context

Practitioners should also examine the environment before designing programs, including the environmental location, conditions, and context. For some sports, such as golf, tennis, or football, the environmental conditions can vary greatly. Golf performance can be strongly affected by the course or the current weather conditions. The surface of a tennis court can vary from grass to clay to asphalt. Football can be played indoors or outdoors and on artificial turf or grass. Other sports or games are performed in very similar settings. For instance, National Collegiate Athletic Association or National Basketball Association basketball is always played indoors on a hard wooden floor. However, a pickup game of basketball can be played indoors or outdoors.

Therapists must also consider the environmental context, such as the surface of the floor, the steepness of a slope, and the number of external distractions. A therapist working with an infant's gross motor milestones (e.g., crawling, creeping, or walking) should expect different movement patterns when placing the infant on a hard surface such as a wood floor versus soft flooring such as carpet. The hard flooring may encourage walking because it is less comfortable to crawl or creep on, or it may discourage walking if it is slippery.

The context of performing the motor skill may vary as well. The context often depends on the goals of the learner. Some learners want to learn a motor skill or game solely for recreational purposes, while others want to play competitively. Some motor skills may be practiced in a clinical setting for rehabilitation but are intended for functional purposes and to be performed at home. Some motor skills or activities can be performed alone (e.g., hiking or weightlifting), while others require additional players (e.g., ballroom dance or field hockey).

The environment in which the motor skill is practiced can be manipulated as the learner progresses. Beginners should first learn a motor skill in a more controlled environment that will allow them more opportunities for success. For open skills, the environment should become progressively less predictable as the learner improves. Closed skills with intertrial variability should also be practiced in variable environments. For instance, golfers would not limit their practice to only one green or even only one golf course. They would likely practice on all 9 or 18 holes, and probably would not limit themselves by always playing on the same course. They would also practice during various weather conditions. Interventions used by clinicians should provide patients with varied treatments to prepare them to function in diverse settings that they will encounter outside of the medical clinic.

When: Distribution of Practice

After, and only after, having examined the learner's characteristics, analyzing the task, and assessing the environment, should the practitioner begin to design the practice schedules. The focus should be on individualizing practice. Unfortunately, the "when" of practice planning is often dictated by the amount of time available for instruction or the length of the season. In clinical situations, the amount of time is often set by the insurer or HMO, often restricting the overall time available for instruction and practice. Practitioners should take time constraints, combined with the type of task and the learner's characteristics, into consideration when determining the number and length of practice sessions. If little time is available and the learner is motivated and capable, the instructor may opt for massed practice. Clinicians need to especially consider the safety implications of massing practice, which can cause more harm than good for patients who do not yet have the strength to undergo such intense therapy.

How: Skill Presentation and Feedback Provision

The "how" of program development includes decisions on skill presentation, practice design, and the provision of feedback. Instructors must decide how they will present the motor skill depending on characteristics of the learner, including the person's learning style, motivation, attention, skill level, and capabilities; the task; and the environmental context. Practice design factors include whether to instruct the skill in its entirety (whole practice) or to break it down (part practice), the level of contextual interference (constant, blocked, repeated blocked, or random practice), and the amount of physical and mental practice.

One aspect that is often overlooked in the design of motor skill programs is the provision of feedback. As discussed in chapter 15, augmented feedback is the most important factor in the acquisition of motor skills second to practice. Many factors are involved in providing effective feedback, including what type of feedback (KR, KP, visual, verbal, descriptive, prescriptive, etc.), how much feedback to provide (learner regulated, summary, average), and when to provide feedback (length of feedback delay interval). Feedback that is provided too soon or too frequently blocks the processing of sensory information, impairing error correction capabilities.

Case Studies

This section presents six case studies. For each case study, develop an appropriate program (figure 1). Begin by examining the learner *(who)* and describing the task *(what)* and the environmental context *(where)*. After you have fully assessed these constraints, determine how you can manipulate the task and environmental constraints to assist the learner *(when* and *how)*. Describe how these constraints will interact with one another and why they will be effective in improving the learner's performance. After reading through the first case study example (which we have worked out for you), choose two of the remaining case studies and assess the learner, task, and environmental constraints, and design an appropriate program. Use the checklist on table 1 as a guide.

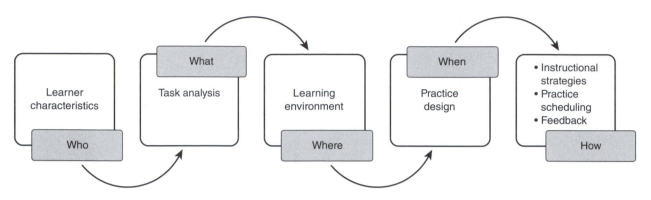

FIGURE 1 Model for designing appropriate programs.

Case Study 1: Getting to the Next Level of Competition

Xavier is a 17-year-old competitive varsity soccer player. He has been playing soccer at some level since the age of 5 years. Xavier is very skilled and very motivated to continue to improve his skills. Currently Xavier is in his senior year of high school and is hoping to continue playing at the Division I level. Although he is highly motivated, Xavier's performance has reached a plateau and even declined somewhat during his senior year. How can you, as his coach, continue to push Xavier to improve? What are the learner's characteristics? Analyze the task. What is the environmental context in this situation? How would you design and schedule Xavier's practice schedules with the goal of breaking out of this plateau? How could you manipulate the task, the environment, or both?

Assessing the Constraints

Xavier is a very motivated and skilled soccer player with a lot of experience. It appears that Xavier may be becoming frustrated with his lack of improvement. It is essential to maintain Xavier's current level of motivation so that he can not only maintain his performance level but improve to the next level to play Division I soccer. Soccer requires both continuous (soccer dribbling) and discrete motor skills, is played in an unpredictable environment (open skill), and is externally paced. Xavier is playing in a competitive environmental context with varying weather conditions and playing surfaces (indoor and outdoor soccer).

Designing an Appropriate Program

Because Xavier is a highly skilled, physically fit, and motivated soccer player, massed practice would be most beneficial for him. Massed practice would help prepare him for competitive situations and would help keep his motivation high. Because Xavier is highly skilled, it is unlikely that he will derive much benefit from added verbal instructions, demonstrations, or guidance. Part practice would not be beneficial either unless he was trying to eliminate a bad habit, which does not appear to be the problem. It is possible that Xavier does not incorporate mental practice into his practice sessions. Doing so could help reduce his frustration, keep his arousal levels in check, and prepare him for competitions. Highly variable practice would also be most effective for him since he is a skilled soccer player. Because Xavier is a skilled competitive player, he should not receive too much feedback. He is likely able to detect and correct for his errors, so learner-regulated feedback should be used to avoid the provision of unwanted feedback. It would also be helpful to ask Xavier to explain why he may have made certain errors (subjective estimations). This will force him to attend to his intrinsic feedback. It may also be useful to video Xavier's performances from multiple angles and have him explain his errors. His subjective estimations should be followed up with attention-focusing cues. As Xavier approaches competitions that may involve Division I scouts, the coach should focus on keeping Xavier's motivation up and his arousal at appropriate levels. His arousal levels should not be so high that he misses relevant stimuli, or so low that he can't maintain focus.

Case Study 2: Motivating the Unmotivated

You are a physical education teacher in a middle school. Teaching middle school students always has its challenges, but this year you have a particularly unmotivated class. You have taught various sports and games, including net and wall games, invasion sports, and individual sports, none of which interested this particular group. What can you do to increase their interest level in physical education class? Provide a specific example of a sport, game, or motor skill. Describe how you would manipulate the task and environment with the goal of motivating the students to want to participate.

Case Study 3: Relearning How to Walk

Matthew is an 18-year-old student-athlete. He was the captain of his football, basketball, and baseball teams, leading each of them into the playoffs for multiple years and even two state championships. He was a "superathlete" until he was severely injured in a car accident in which he fractured his spine in the lumbar region. Matthew's focus quickly changed from leading his teams to victory to relearning how to function without the use of his legs. As Matthew's physical therapist, describe how you would design a program to help Matthew relearn how to walk. Keep in mind that relearning basic functional activities can be quite frustrating, especially when the loss of function has occurred so quickly. Describe some activities you would use to help him relearn how to transport himself from one place to another. How would you keep Matthew motivated?

Case Study 4: Making Positive Changes

Hilary is a 79-year-old widow. She is overweight and has arthritis in her knees. Hilary has not exercised much in the past and is intimidated at fitness facilities. However, she has decided that she does want to make some positive changes in her lifestyle, so she has asked you to be her personal trainer. How would you design an exercise program for Hilary?

Case Study 5: Various Skill Levels

You have volunteered to coach a soccer team for children aged 5 to 8 years. As you know, children vary greatly between the ages of 5 and 8 years. Some of the players have already played on a soccer team for three years while others are new to the sport. Not only do the children vary widely in their skill level, but you also notice a wide variability in other individual constraints, including structural (height, weight) and functional (motivation level, attentiveness) constraints. Some of the children are quite confident in their abilities, while others are intimidated by the stronger, taller, and faster players. How can you, as the coach, challenge the skilled players while also maintaining the interest of the younger, less skilled players? How would you design practices so that all players are participating and challenged without being overwhelmed?

Case Study 6: Inclusive Activities

You are teaching a sixth grade physical education unit on basketball. In one of your classes, you have a student, Victoria, who is blind. Victoria has recently moved to your school district and has few movement experiences, in part because her former physical education teacher excluded her from many of the activities. How can you modify the task and the environment to include Victoria while also maintaining the involvement and interest of the rest of the class?

Summary

To promote retention and positive transfer, programs must be designed specifically for the individual. Designing appropriate programs is a very time-consuming and complex task but is essential for optimizing skill acquisition. Once a movement educator has devised a program, it is fairly easy to implement or manipulate it by changing task demands. The first step in developing a program is to examine the constraints, including the learner's characteristics, the task, and the environmental context. Only after the constraints have been assessed can the program be created. As a current or future movement educator, you must always keep these three constraints in mind when designing any program or manipulating any task.

GLOSSARY

abilities—Genetically predetermined characteristics, including such things as agility, coordination, strength, and flexibility.

absolute frequency of KR—The number of trials with KR.

absolute retention—The learner's performance immediately following the retention interval.

accommodation—The process that enables the eye to adjust and focus, producing a clearer image.

action slip—An error in the sequence or order of an action due to a momentary error in the specifics of the task.

activity theory—Social theory on aging; suggests that adults who maintain social interactions and active lives can not only maintain their life satisfaction, but may even increase it.

adaptability—The capability to make movement adjustments to fit the changing demands of the task and environmental conditions.

affordances—The action possibilities of the environment and task in relation to the perceiver's own capabilities.

age grading—Decreasing physical activity levels based on age.

ageism—Stereotyping of an individual on the basis of the person's age.

aging—A process or group of processes occurring in living organisms that with the passage of time lead to a loss of adaptability, functional impairment, and eventually death.

amotivation—Lack of any motivation, present when an individual does not see any relationship between outcomes and actions.

anxiety—An emotional response to perceived threat; can involve cognitive concerns or physiological reactions.

arousal—A general state of activation or excitability of an individual.

arterio–venous oxygen difference—The difference in oxygen content between arterial and venous blood.

associative stage—The second stage in Fitts and Posner's learning model, in which the goal of the task has shifted from learning how to solve the movement problem to refining the movement.

attentional capacity—The amount of information that an individual can process at any given period of time.

attention-directed cues—Cues that direct attention to the most important aspects of the movement pattern.

attention-focusing cues—Cues that not only direct the learner's attention to specific aspects of the movement pattern but also include error-correcting suggestions.

attractors—Preferred state of stability toward which a system spontaneously shifts (dynamic systems theory).

auditory figure–ground perception—The ability to ignore background noise while attending to particular sounds such as holding a conversation.

automaticity—The capability to perform a skill with essentially no conscious attention devoted to the production of the movement pattern.

autonomous—Referring to engaging in a task by free will, without external influence from others; autonomy is one of three basic needs according to self-determination theory.

autonomous stage—The third and final stage in Fitts and Posner's learning model, in which the performer is at the highest level of motor skill proficiency.

average feedback—A feedback schedule in which only the average performance error(s), or the essence of the performances, is discussed with the learner.

awareness talks—One of the strategies in Hellison's model; students are reminded about the levels of responsibility explicitly discussed and posted in the learning environment.

Bandura's social cognitive theory—Theory asserting that self-efficacy determines (1) if an individual is even going to attempt a task; (2) how persistent an individual will be amid challenges; and (3) with reference to an exercise program, the final outcome, successful maintenance of the program or failure to adhere to the program.

bandwidth feedback—A feedback schedule in which feedback is given only when performance is outside a particular range.

biofeedback—Extrinsic feedback that provides concurrent kinematic information related to the activity of physiological processes.

biological aging—The physiological adaptations that occur within the body due to the passage of time.

blocked practice—A practice sequence in which one skill is repeated over a fixed amount of time before learners move to the next skill. This is usually contrasted to random practice, which includes different skills intermingled during a designed time period.

body awareness—A sense of the body in space, including the ability to locate body parts, knowing the movement of body parts, and knowing how to efficiently move body parts.

body orientation—Classified as either body transport, as during a basketball layup or triple jump, or body stability, as in archery shooting.

body proportions—The relationship of one body part size to another.

body scaled—Referring to making decisions about the size and mass of equipment relative to the person's body.

broad attention—Using a wide focus when visually searching for environmental cues critical to performance.

capability—An individual's potential, such as skilled behavior, that can be present if the conditions are favorable.

central limited capacity—A theory of attention suggesting that human attention is limited because the central nervous system does not have endless space to process information.

central-resource capacity theory—A theory of attention suggesting that information process-ing capacity is able to expand depending on conditions related to the individual, task, and situation.

cephalocaudal—Proceeding from the head to distal structures; development begins with the head, and distal structures grow more slowly.

cerebral palsy—A neuromuscular disorder that negatively affects coordination; typically, external factors prevent optimal brain development.

choice reaction time—Time to react on a task with multiple stimuli.

chronological age—The number of years an individual has been alive since birth.

closed skills—Motor skills that are performed in a stable environment in which objects are also stationary.

coarticulation—Simultaneous movements that occur in sequential tasks.

cognitive interference—A decrement of performance as a result of exceeding one's attentional capacity due to a limitation in central capacity.

cognitive plasticity—The structural changes that occur in the organization of the brain as a result of experience.

cognitive skills—The skills that enable a performer to make decisions and problem solve, including intellectual skills.

cognitive stage—Fitts and Posner's first stage. The learner's main goal is to understand the basic components of the motor skill movement pattern.

commitment stage—Stage 2 of Kirschenbaum's self-regulation process, in which the individual commits to making the sacrifices necessary to persevere through the process of making a change.

compensation period—A period from Clark's mountain of motor development; an adaptation to the environment as a result of an injury or due to declines resulting from aging.

competent—Referring to realization of success in a given domain; competence is one of three basic needs according to self-determination theory.

competitive environment—An environment in which individuals or teams compete against each other. Performance expectations and social pressures are high.

component approach—The perspective that components of the body (e.g., for throwing, the torso, arms, and legs) develop, potentially, at different rates; contrasts with whole body assessment.

concrete operations—Piaget's third stage (ages 7-11) of intellectual development in which children develop logical thinking that is restricted to events or things experienced, seen, or heard.

concurrent feedback—Feedback received during the production of the movement.

conservation of liquids—Piaget's experiment demonstrating that, unlike that of adults, children's logic is based on one dimension.

constant practice—Very similar to blocked practice because one skill is repeated for a fixed amount of time or number of trials before learners move to the next skill. This is usually contrasted to variable practice, which includes variations of specific skill intermingled during a designed time period.

constraints—Boundaries that limit an individual's movement capabilities.

constraints model—Model of behavior asserting that coordination is developed by changing constraints imposed by the interaction of the organism with the environment.

context-specific motor skills period—Refinement of fundamental motor patterns to movements specific for sports or other movement forms from Clark's mountain of motor development.

contextual interference—The memory and performance disruption that results from performing multiple skills or variations of a skill within the context of practice. This disruption has a negative impact when people are attempting to learn several tasks at the same time.

contextual interference effect—The learning benefit resulting from performance of multiple skills in a high contextual interference practice schedule.

continuous motor skills—Motor skills that do not have a clearly defined beginning or ending

point. These motor skills are longer in duration and the mover is in constant motion.

contrast sensitivity—The amount of contrast necessary to discriminate between an image and its background.

control—Manipulation of movements so as to meet the demands of the task.

control parameters—Variables that induce a shift from the current attractor state to a new attractor state.

cooperative play—Play in which children strive to achieve the same goal.

coordination—Constraining the number of degrees of freedom in order to decrease the complexity of the movement task, producing a movement pattern, and achieving some task goal.

coordinative structures—Structures that occur when the degrees of freedom become incorporated into larger functional units of action to preserve a certain posture or movement.

counseling time—One of the strategies in Hellison's model; time is devoted to discussion of problems identified by the teacher or students.

cue-utilization hypothesis—Hypothesis that the level of arousal influences attentional focus.

decision making—Making a selection from a variety of choices knowing the consequences of the choice.

declarative knowledge—Factual and conceptual information about knowledge stored in memory.

declarative memory—Memories that are consciously available through recollection or recall, including both episodic and semantic memory.

degrees of freedom—(1) The number of independent elements that must be constrained in order to produce coordinated motion. (2) The number of functional units that are required to solve a movement problem.

deliberate play—Activities in which some rules are established and monitored by children or adults.

deliberate practice—Activities designed to improve current levels of performance, requiring much effort and not necessarily enjoyable.

depth perception—The ability to see in three dimensions.

descriptive feedback—Feedback that describes the nature of a performance error.

developmental taxonomy—A framework for grouping motor skills into themes when one is teaching fundamental motor skills.

difference score—A measure of relative retention calculated by subtracting the absolute retention score from the last score during the acquisition phase (original learning).

discrete motor skill—A motor skill for which the beginning and end points of the movement are clearly defined.

disengagement theory—Social theory on aging that asserts it is important for older adults to separate themselves from society in order for them to maintain their integrity through accepting their changing status and physical decline.

distance curve—The extent of growth in terms of height and weight.

distributed practice—Practice that typically involves a shorter session with fewer practice trials and longer rest intervals.

divided attention—The ability to attend to more than one sensory input at the same time.

dizygotic—Referring to twins who develop from two separate ova and therefore share no more genes than typical siblings.

dual-task paradigm—Procedure used in attention research that requires participants to perform two tasks simultaneously.

dynamic systems theory—Perspective that discusses the interplay of the environment, task, and individual on skilled movement. Movement is the result of a self-organization of many systems owing to interactions across these constraints.

dynamic visual acuity—The ability to distinguish moving objects.

ecological psychology perspective—Motor development or learning perspective that rejects the hierarchical view of the brain as the ultimate controller of movement. This perspective stresses the role of the environment as it interacts with the individual to produce fluid movement.

ecological task analysis model—A method of analyzing movement performance that accounts for individual differences by manipulating the environment and task on a progression of complexity, allowing learners to increase their level of complexity on one or more levels of a skill at a time.

egocentric—The inability to view the world from a perspective other than one's own.

ego-involved climate—Climate that encourages participants to improve their skills to outperform others. Success is defined in comparison to other people in the group or some idealized model.

elaboration and distinctive hypothesis—Idea that random practice results in the use of cognitive strategies. When learners shift from one skill to another, the distinct nature of each strategy becomes clearer and more meaningful in long-term memory. This cognitive effort has a deleterious effect during skill acquisition but is beneficial to skill learning.

emotional display rules—Socially defined circumstances in which emotions should or should not be expressed.

emulation—Zimmerman's second level of the development of self-regulation; adoption of a model's style of skill rather than imitation of exact response components.

endocrine system—A body system that controls the hormones of body tissue.

environmental constraints—Constraints that are external to the mover.

environmental management stage—Stage 4 of Kirschenbaum's self-regulation process, in which adults prepare strategies to deal with potential environmental or social barriers that may prevent them from attaining their goals.

environmentalism perspective—Perspective that assumes that it is not heredity that molds the maturational process; rather, maturation occurs as humans are nurtured by their environment.

episodic memory—Memories that are associated with personal experiences and are related to a specific period in time; the ability to remember personal events.

error correction stage—Stage 3 of the video learning stages, characterized by learners' ability to identify their errors and in some cases understand the cause of errors.

error detection stage—Stage 2 of the video learning stages; occurs when learners are comfortable with viewing their performances. Attention-focused cues should be used to assist learners in detecting their errors during this stage.

execution stage—Stage 3 of Kirschenbaum's self-regulation process, the active stage of behavioral change. During this stage the individual develops self-expectancies for success through goal setting.

exercise–aging cycle—A cycle that begins when adults decrease their involvement in physical activity, which results in increased body fat and decreased physical abilities and leads to lowered self-esteem and increased stress and anxiety. These psychological changes often cause people to further reduce their involvement in physical activity, which leads to physiological decline.

exercise economy—The oxygen cost to exercise at a particular velocity.

expert performance—Superior athletic performance over an extended period.

explicit learning—Conscious awareness of learning a task.

external attention—Focus on the intended effects of movements.

external imagery—A type of visualization in which the person sees images from an outside vantage point, not his own, as he were an observer watching himself.

external locus of control—The belief that an individual's actions do not affect the environment and that events happen by chance.

externally paced tasks—Motor skills that are paced by an object or person external to the mover.

extrinsic feedback—Feedback that comes from an external source; additional to sensory information.

extrinsically motivated behaviors—Behaviors engaged in as a means to an end and not for their own sake.

faded feedback—A feedback schedule in which the amount of feedback provided is based on the skill level of the learner, with beginners receiving high-frequency feedback initially and progressively less feedback with improvement.

fast-twitch fiber—A type of muscle fiber that has a quick contraction–relaxation cycle and is well suited for short-duration, high-intensity activities such as sprinting or powerlifting.

feedback delay interval—The period of time between the completion of a performance attempt and the presentation of feedback.

fielding games—Team games in which the contest begins with one team occupying positions throughout the field (the fielders), with one player who throws the ball (pitcher) toward a player on the opposing team.

figure–ground perception—Distinguishing an object from its surroundings.

fine motor skills—Skills in which smaller muscle groups perform with accuracy and control.

fixation—The focusing of visual attention on an object.

Fleishman's taxonomy—A classification system for motor skills that identifies the underlying motor abilities necessary to perform successfully.

forethought—A phase of Zimmerman's (2000) cyclical model of self-regulation. This phase involves planning an action and consists of task analysis and self-motivation beliefs.

forgetting and reconstruction hypothesis—Hypothesis suggesting that the key to understanding the contextual interference effect is to consider the action planning required for each skill. Random practice forces learners to practice action planning, as they must reconstruct a new action plan each time they learn a new skill.

formal operations—Piaget's fourth stage (ages 11+) of intellectual development, in which children develop logical thinking.

frailty—A condition in which an individual exhibits severe limitations in mobility, strength, balance, and endurance, resulting from weak and highly fatigable muscles often due to a long-term inactive lifestyle.

free play—Activities engaged in exclusively for intrinsic reasons, often during infancy and early childhood.

functional constraints—Individual constraints imposed by psychological variables such as motivation, arousal, and intellect.

fundamental motor patterns—Basic movements such as throwing, catching, hopping, and jumping that form a base for more complex sport-specific movement patterns.

fundamental motor skills—The basic skills that provide the foundation for activities that require much more complicated sport-specific motor skills.

fundamental movement skills—Basic movements such as twisting, bending, throwing, catching, hopping, and jumping that form a base for more complex, sport-specific movement patterns.

game—Any form of playful competition whose outcome is determined by physical skill, strategy, or chance, employed singly or in combination.

game experience—Knowing about a sport (i.e., processing declarative knowledge) without necessarily knowing how to perform the sport (i.e., processing procedural knowledge).

generalization stage—Stage 5 of Kirschenbaum's self-regulation process, in which individuals focus on sustaining their efforts for long periods of time.

generalized motor program (GMP)—A representation of a pattern of movements that are modifiable to produce a movement outcome; enables the production of skilled movement in the information processing approach.

general motor ability—The early hypothesis that there is only one motor ability.

getting the idea of the movement stage—Gentile's first stage of learning, similar to Fitts and Posner's cognitive stage of learning. During this stage the learner has two main goals: to understand the movement coordination required to perform the movement task and to determine the regulatory and nonregulatory conditions of the movement.

goal setting—A self-regulatory skill that allows individuals to monitor progress toward a self-determined goal. Goals should be specific, attainable, challenging, and realistic.

gross motor skills—Skills in which large muscle groups produce the movement, such as the quadriceps, hamstrings, and gluteus maximus during a kick; these tend to be much larger and less precise movements.

group meeting—One of the strategies in Hellison's model; encourages discussion of what constitutes self-control and responsibility and establishment of self-control rules.

guidance hypothesis—A hypothesis on the provision of feedback; asserts that the benefits of high-frequency KR can be deceiving because learners tend to perform better initially than if they received lower-frequency KR.

hands-off practitioner—Role of teachers and coaches consistent with dynamic systems theory. The hands-off practitioner incorporates problem solving, self-discovery, and self-regulation into the learning environment, allowing greater opportunity for each learner to find appropriate personal motor patterns within practice.

heritability—A statistic that can be calculated to estimate genetic influences in producing differences among individuals.

hyperplasia—An increase in the number of muscle units such as muscle fibers or neurons.

hypertrophy—An increase in the relative size or volume of an individual unit such as muscle fibers of neurons.

identical elements theory—A theory on transfer; asserts that the amount and direction of transfer are dependent on the number of identical elements between two motor skills.

imagery—A form of mental practice that involves a visual or kinesthetic representation of performance; the visualization or cognitive rehearsal of a movement.

implicit learning—Learning without consciousness.

incidental attention—Attentional focus is shifted onto some unexpected sensory information, such as a telephone ringing or someone calling one's name.

independence stage—The final stage of the video feedback learning stages. Learners who reach this stage require minimal to no video supplementation by an instructor.

individual constraints—Boundaries imposed by the organism itself. *Also see* structural and functional constraints.

individual decision making—One of the strategies in Hellison's model; students are encouraged to be in control of their own actions and decisions.

information processing approach—One of the theoretical constructs of motor behavior; proposes that the brain receives, processes, and interprets information in order to send signals to produce skilled coordinated movements, similar to how a computer functions.

instructional environment—Closed and supportive environments with ample instruction, feedback, and encouragement for students to explore their movement options.

intentional attention—Attentional focus on selected sensory information by choice, such as maintaining a conversation.

interference—A limitation on performance as a result of exceeding one's attentional capacity.

internal attention—Focus on one's own movements.

internal imagery—A form of visualization in which images are viewed from one's own vantage point, as if with one's own eyes.

internal locus of control—The belief that an individual's actions affect the environment.

interresponse interval—The time period between one performance attempt and the next performance attempt.

intertrial variability—The amount of change that occurs between trials, with a trial being a practice attempt.

intrinsically motivated behaviors—Behaviors that provide pleasure and satisfaction from participation in the absence of material rewards or constraints.

intrinsic feedback—Response-produced information that is received from sensory sources before, during, and after the production of a movement.

intrinsic motivation—Motivation that comes from within the individual; behaviors are performed for personal interest and enjoyment.

invariant features—Variables that cannot be modified from one attempt to another attempt (include sequence of movements, relative force, and relative timing).

invasion games—Games in which players are divided into two opposing teams separated by sides on the playing field.

inverted-U principle of arousal—Idea that arousal and performance are related such that optimal performance is seen at a moderate level of arousal.

investment years—Years characterized by achieving elite levels of performance. The main focus is strategic, competitive, and skill development within a context of deliberate practice directed and assisted by a coach.

kinematic feedback—Feedback on the observable aspects of the movement, such as the space–time properties of a performance; can be very beneficial during the learning process.

kinetic feedback—Feedback on the underlying processes of the movement such as force.

knowing—An individual's base of knowledge.

knowing about knowing—Knowledge of how our personal memory functions; also known as metamemory or metacognition.

knowing how to know—The use of control processes and strategies for deliberate learning.

knowledge of performance (KP)—Feedback that provides information about the specific characteristics of the movement pattern produced.

knowledge of results (KR)—Terminal feedback that describes the outcome of the movement.

kyphosis—Curvature of the upper spine; can be the result of years of poor posture, weak back muscles, senile osteoporosis, and osteoarthritis of the vertebrae.

lactate threshold—The exercise intensity at which blood lactate begins to accumulate significantly above the baseline levels in the bloodstream.

learner-regulated feedback—A feedback schedule in which the learner is in control of the provision of feedback, deciding after which trials and how often to receive extrinsic feedback.

learning model—A model who demonstrates variability in performance. In physical education, this usually refers to a novice who practices the skill and receives feedback from an instructor. Learners likely identify with the learning model because of similarity in status or as a result of watching the model engage in the problem-solving process.

Legg-Calvé-Perthes—An irritation of the femur where it inserts in the hip.

linear curve—A performance curve that indicates a direct relationship between the performance measure and time.

locomotor skills—(1) Gross motor skills in which the goal of the movement is body transport. (2) Movement skills that transport an individual from one place to another place.

locus of control—Individuals' perception of their influence on the environment.

long-term memory—A permanent store for information.

manipulative skills—(1) Fine motor skills in which the goal of the movement is object control. (2) Movement skills that involve giving force to an object or receiving force from an object. Examples include overarm and underarm throwing, rolling, striking, kicking, catching, and trapping. *Also see* object control skills.

massed practice—Longer practice sessions with many practice trials.

mastery climate—Climate that encourages participants to improve their skills and judge success by a positive change in individual performance.

maturation—The fixed transitions or order of progression that enables a person to progress to higher levels of function.

maturational perspective—Perspective that development occurs as a function of nature; assumes that maturation occurs as a result of genetic or internal factors.

meaningfulness—The degree to which a new movement relates to previous movements or knowledge.

memory—The ability to recall things from experience.

mental practice—A cognitive rehearsal of a physical skill without overt physical movements.

metacognitive knowledge—A higher level of declarative knowledge that includes a self-awareness of strengths and weaknesses.

metacognitive skill—A higher level of procedural knowledge that is particularly important in selecting and planning goal-directed learning.

monozygotic—Referring to twins who develop from a single fertilized ovum and therefore have identical genotypes.

motivation—A set of reasons or personal drive that pushes an individual to achieve a particular goal or outcome.

motor behavior—An umbrella term for the fields of motor development, motor learning, and motor control.

motor control—Field of study that investigates the neural, physical, and behavioral aspects of human movement.

motor development—Field of study that examines the products and underlying processes of motor behavior changes across the life span.

motor learning—Field of study examining the processes involved in the acquisition of a motor skill and the variables that enhance or inhibit an individual's capability to perform a motor skill.

motor skill—A voluntary goal-oriented movement that is learned or relearned and requires the use of the limbs.

multiple resource theories—Perspectives of attention suggesting that humans have several attention mechanisms (such as modalities, stages of information processing, and codes of processing information), each with a limited capacity.

narrow attention—Use of a limited focus during visually searching for environmental cues critical to performance.

negatively accelerating curve—A performance curve that illustrates a very rapid initial rate of improvement followed by a gradual reduction in the rate of improvement.

negative reinforcement—Feedback that elicits unpleasant feelings that the learner will want to avoid.

negative transfer—Hindrance to performance because of the performance of another motor skill.

net or **wall games**—Sports in which the object of play is to serve or return the ball strategically so that the opponent is unable to sustain the play of the ball.

neural plasticity—The ability of the brain to change function as a result of either damage or experience.

neurofibrillary tangles—Neural fibers that are twisting together.

nonlinear pedagogy—The foundation of instruction based on dynamic systems. Practitioners promote problem solving, discovery learning, and self-regulation.

nonregulatory conditions—Factors, unrelated to the movement task, that can distract the learner from important relevant cues, preventing skillful performances.

nonself-determined extrinsic motivation—Motivation toward a behavior based on avoiding immediate negative consequences.

novel movements—New movements never before practiced; trademark of exceptional sport performers.

object control skills—Movement skills that involve giving force to an object or receiving force from an object. Examples include overarm and underarm throwing, rolling, striking, kicking, catching, and trapping. *Also see* manipulative skills.

object permanence—An awareness that an object exists even if removed from vision.

observation—Zimmerman's first level of the development of self-regulation; includes witnessing skills of peers or older children or hearing about them from others.

ontogeny—Level of development occurring over the life span of one individual.

open skills—Motor skills performed in an ever-changing environment, in which objects, people, and events are constantly varying.

Osgood-Schlatter—A disruption in growth of the upper shinbone where the patella tendon attaches.

osteoarthritis—A very common degenerative joint disease affecting approximately 80% of adults over the age of 65 years which can cause pain and stiffness in the joint.

osteoporosis—A crippling disease resulting from low bone mass and poor structural bone quality, that increases the threat of bone fractures.

outcome goals—Goals that focus on the results of performance in comparison to others.

parallel play—Playing alongside peers but not really interacting.

parameters—Features that can be modified during the execution of a movement pattern (including muscle selection, overall force, and overall duration).

peak bone mass—The highest bone mass acquired prior to the age of 30 years.

peak height velocity—The period during adolescence in which gain in height is fastest.

perceived competence—An individual's sense of skill and capability in a specific domain.

percentage score—A measure of relative retention calculated by dividing the difference score by the change in the original learning and then multiplying by 100%. This score is interpreted as the percentage of performance that was lost (or gained) following the retention interval.

percentile—A relative rank or position on a scale; the percent of a distribution that is equal to or below that position.

perceptual narrowing—A progressive reduction in attentional focus with increased levels of arousal.

perceptual skills—Skills that involve interpreting and integrating sensory information to determine the best movement outcome.

performance—The act of executing a motor skill.

performance control—A phase in Zimmerman's (2000) cyclical model of self-regulation. This phase involves self-control and self-observation.

performance goals—Goals that focus on improvement relative to one's own performance.

performance improvement—Increase in the overall performance outcome.

peripheral vision—Vision outside of the center of gaze.

personal attributes—Qualities in an individual that influence the development of a social role. One of the major elements of the sport socialization process.

personal performance games—Games in which individuals attempt to outperform their opponents, their personal best performance measures, or both.

phase shift—The change in a state that causes a shift or reorganization to a new attractor state.

phylogeny—The evolutionary development of the history of a species, which can occur over many hundreds and thousands of years.

physical environmental constraints—External conditions that can aid or hinder movement patterns; examples include weather, temperature, lighting, floor surface, step height, and so on.

physical growth—An increase in body size or in individual parts that occurs through maturation.

pituitary—A gland that secretes hormones responsible for skeletal growth.

positively accelerating curve—Performance curve that illustrates only small gains initially but an increasing rate of improvement with every practice session.

positive reinforcement—Feedback following the completion of a movement that promotes the reoccurrence of the same movement pattern.

positive transfer—Enhanced learning of a motor skill because of the performance of another motor skill.

postfeedback interval—The time period between the presentation of extrinsic feedback and the learner's subsequent performance attempt.

posttest—A test conducted at the end of the practice sessions.

power law of practice—Mathematical law describing a negatively accelerating rate of performance improvement.

practice environment—An instructor-controlled learning environment with emphasis on proper execution of specific skills under increasingly more demanding space and time constraints.

preadapted period—The mountain of motor development period in which infants start interacting with the environment by engaging in phylogenetic motor behaviors such as sitting up, standing, crawling, and walking.

prenatal period—The mountain of motor development period consisting of the last two trimesters of pregnancy with much movement of the fetus in the womb.

preoperational thought—Piaget's second stage of intellectual development, characterized by symbolic but egocentric thinking.

presbycusis—Age-related hearing loss.

prescriptive feedback—Feedback that provides suggestions to correct the performance error.

pretest—A test conducted prior to the practice sessions.

primary memory—Information that is actively available in short-term memory.

primary rules—The rules that characterize the play of the game and how the game is won.

primary task—The main skill on which an individual focuses in a dual-task paradigm.

problem identification stage—Stage 1 of Kirschenbaum's self-regulation process. During this stage, adults identify the problem and must decide whether the change is possible and worth the effort.

procedural knowledge—Knowledge of how to do something; this type of knowledge underlies an action and includes anticipation and prediction, decision-making, and response selection aspects of information processing.

procedural memories—Memories about how to perform a particular task.

process—Focus on the underlying mechanisms of change.

process goals—Goals that focus on particular aspects of skill execution.

product—Focus on the outcome of performance.

proximodistal—In relation to development, referring to earlier advancement of the trunk than of the limbs.

qualitative—Subjective, as opposed to quantitative (measured).

quantitative—Objective, given a numerical value; for example, how high, how far, how fast.

random practice—A practice sequence in which several different skills are mixed in a random order. Rehearsal of the same skill twice in a row is avoided.

rate limiter—A control parameter that limits or hinders performance.

rate of change—The speed at which a variable changes over time.

recall—Retrieval of long-term memories with very few cues, requiring much conscious effort.

recognition—Retrieval of long-term memories, requiring both conscious and unconscious processes, with the help of environmental support.

reflection time—One of the strategies in Hellison's model; occurs at the end of each lesson. Students contemplate what went well or not so well in the session, which may involve writing in a personal journal, completing checklists, and engaging in discussion with others.

reflexive period—The mountain of motor development period following birth and lasting two weeks as the newborn is adjusting to sensory changes such as bright lights and sounds.

regulatory conditions—Environmental factors specifying movement characteristics necessary for a particular motor skill or sport.

reinforcement—A benefit of feedback that occurs when the feedback increases the probability of similar performance attempts in the future.

related—Referring to a connectedness with other people; one of three basic needs in self-determination theory.

relative frequency of KR—The percentage of performance attempts for which KR is provided.

retention interval—The amount of time between the last practice session or posttest and the retention test.

retention savings score—A measurement of the amount of time required to return to a given level of performance as compared to the time required to reach this level during the original practice sessions.

retention test—A performance test given following a break from practice.

retinal disparity—Differences in the two retinal images produced by the eyes due to the different positions of the eyes in the head.

sampling years—Years characterized by exposure to many fundamental motor skills and a wide range of sports with an emphasis on fun and excitement.

schema—An abstract or general memory representation of a set of rules that connect a person's actions to the parameters needed to produce an outcome.

schemes—Structures developed by children for thoughts and action, resulting from actively constructing understandings of the world based on their experience.

secondary rules—Rules that can be modified without changing the nature of the game.

secondary task—A skill an individual focuses on after attending to the primary skill.

selective attention—The ability to focus on selected sensory information while ignoring irrelevant information.

self-control—Zimmerman's third level in the development of self-regulation; the use of personal strategies as a planned and self-monitored process.

self-determination—A theory of motivation (Deci & Ryan, 1985) proposing that the basic needs of competence, autonomy, and relatedness drive individuals to action.

self-determined extrinsic motivation—Motivation based on extrinsic reasons.

self-efficacy—(1) Belief in personal capabilities to successfully execute action required to achieve identified goals. (2) The belief that one can successfully perform a desired behavior given various instrumental barriers.

self-esteem—A self-evaluation of individual competency, successfulness, and worthiness.

self-motivation beliefs—The perceived value of an activity for an individual, the degree of intrinsic interest in the activity, the degree of self-efficacy or belief that one is capable of achieving the goal, and outcome expectation or awareness of what benefits will occur if the goal is attained.

self-observation—Process that guides personal progress toward a goal, particularly self-recording.

self-organization—The system's ability to change states or acquire a new structure or pattern of movement.

self-paced tasks—Motor tasks that begin when initiated by the mover and as such can be initiated when the mover chooses, as in golf, bowling, or archery.

self-reflection—A phase of Zimmerman's (2000) cyclical model of self-regulation. This phase involves reflecting on the success of an action and consists of self-judgment and self-reaction.

self-regulation—(1) "Self-generated thoughts, feelings, and actions that are planned and cyclically adapted to the attainment of personal goals" (Zimmerman, 2000, p. 14), or informally, the ability to practice and play without formal instruction. (2) A complex process whereby athletes or exercisers engage in voluntary goal-directed behaviors over time and context by initiating, monitoring, sustaining, and achieving certain thoughts, feelings, and behaviors (Weiss, 2004, p. 385).

semantic memory—The ability to remember general knowledge built from life experiences and learning.

senile plaques—Masses that form on the outside of neurons and have been related to memory loss.

sensorimotor period—Piaget's first stage of intellectual development (ages 0-2), in which children coordinate sensory experience and movement to act upon the world and generate knowledge.

serial motor skills—Motor skills that include a series of discrete skills that must occur in a specific sequence.

serial order problem—Motor control issue that pertains to the sequencing and timing of movement behaviors.

serial practice—A practice sequence in which different skills performed are in a mixed order but in a fixed format.

shock stage—Stage 1 of the video learning stages. Learners are often more focused on their visual appearance than on their movement patterns or performance.

short-term memory—The capacity for holding a small amount of information in memory for a short period of time.

sigmoid curve—An S-shaped pattern of change, for example for height and weight.

simple reaction time—Time to react on a task with only one stimulus.

single-channel filter theories—Attention perspectives that propose serial processing of tasks and the occurrence of a bottleneck at some point in information processing, a point at which the system can process only one task at a time.

skill—An individual's capacity to perform a task proficiently.

skillful—Referring to an individual who has achieved a criterion of excellence for a particular motor skill and is capable of performing at a high level the majority of the time.

skillfulness period—The period at the peak of the mountain of motor development in which a learner has acquired a high level of skill proficiency. This period does not separate between levels of performance, such as college or professional athletes.

skills—Learned abilities to bring about predetermined results with maximum certainty, often with minimum outlay of time, energy, or both.

slow-twitch fiber—A type of muscle fiber that has a slower contraction–relaxation cycle than fast-twitch fibers and is best suited for endurance activities such as long-distance running or swimming.

socializing agents—(1) Individuals who affect an individual's adherence to a healthy lifestyle including physical activity. (2) Individuals who influence the development of someone's social role, such as parents, teachers, and coaches. One of the major elements of the socialization process.

social situations—Contexts in which socialization takes place, such as school and home. One of the major elements of the socialization process.

sociocultural environmental constraints—Constraints imposed by social and cultural norms and pressures.

spatial awareness—Awareness of the size of the body and the position of the body in relationship to others and external objects.

specializing years—Years during which people spend significant time on one or two sporting activities. Development of skill takes on a higher priority than during the sampling years, but fun remains a critical component of this phase.

specificity hypothesis—The hypothesis by Henry that specific abilities exist that are necessary to perform each motor skill proficiently.

spoonerism—A speech error of mixing speech sound positions in words, named after Professor William Spooner for his speech errors.

S-shaped curve—A performance curve indicating that initial learning occurred at a positively accelerating rate for a period of time and then continued to increase at a negatively accelerating rate.

stability—The ability to maintain body position against forces of gravity, which may include other circumstances that increase the difficulty of the task.

stability skills—Movements around the axis of the body such as bending, stretching, swinging, swaying, pushing, pulling, turning, and twisting; done with little or no movement of the base of support.

static visual acuity—The ability to clearly see an image that is stationary; commonly assessed using the Snellen eye chart.

storage problem—A problem with the idea of memory programming; if movements were stored in memory as simple motor programs, there would be almost unlimited variations of movements to be stored.

stroke volume—The volume of blood that is pumped through one ventricle during one contraction.

structural constraints—Individual constraints imposed by physical characteristics such as gender, height, weight, and body makeup.

structural interference—Interference that occurs as a result of a physical structure.

structured practice—Activities in which skill performance assumes a higher priority than in deliberate play.

subjective organization—Arrangement of information into memorable parts.

summary feedback—A schedule in which feedback is provided on all attempts following a set number of performance attempts.

synapses—Gaps between two nerve cells in which a nerve impulse is transmitted.

tactics—Organized actions by individuals, pairs, or groups to acquire an advantage over an opponent.

target games—Games in which the performer competes without direct body contact or physical confrontation during the competition.

task analysis—Setting of personal goals of achievement and general strategies for how to achieve those goals.

task complexity—The number of parts or components of a skill and the amount of attention required to complete the skill.

task constraints—Constraints imposed by the task itself, including the goals of the movement, rules, and equipment.

task organization—The relationships among the components of a skill.

taxonomies—Classifications of objects or events according to a common scheme.

terminal feedback—Feedback that is received following the production of the movement.

theory of planned behavior (TBA)—Theory that attitudes toward a behavior are dependent on two factors: (1) the belief that the behavior will produce a specified outcome and (2) the individual's desire to attain the specified outcome.

thyroid—A gland that secretes hormones responsible for skeletal growth.

traditional task analysis—A method of analyzing movement performance by comparing the movement pattern to a correct model.

transfer-appropriate processing theory—Theory on transfer asserting that movements or games requiring similar cognitive processing can positively transfer.

transfer of learning—The effect of a previous movement experience on performance in another task.

transfer tests—Tests that measure the adaptability between the practiced motor skill and a different, but related, motor skill or performance situation.

variable practice—A practice sequence in which several variations of the same skill occur in a mixed order.

velocity curve—A curve that describes change per unit time, such as height (centimeters/year).

verbal cues—Brief and concise phrases used by teachers and coaches to direct attention to regulatory conditions in the environment, prompt key skill components, or initiate activity.

verbal labels—Words used to describe a part of a skill to improve memory.

vertigo—A balance disorder that can vary from dizziness and vomiting to difficulties with standing and walking.

visual acuity—Sharpness of vision.

visual imagery—Images stimulated by memory.

visually searching—An aspect of attention that involves detecting environmental cues necessary for performance.

visual search—The act of directing attention toward important cues in the environment.

visuomotor coordination—The ability to visually track a moving object and guide the body, the limbs, or both to intercept the object.

volitional control—A phase of Zimmerman's (2000) cyclical model of self-regulation; self-regulation strategies such as self-control or self-observation that can be applied during learning or performance.

warm-up decrement—A reduction in performance due to a period of inactivity.

whole body approach—The perspective that the entire body (e.g., for throwing, the torso, arms, and legs) develops at the same rate; contrasts with component assessment.

working memory—(1) Information in short-term memory that can be manipulated. (2) The structure within which memory control processes work to transfer information to long-term memory.

zero transfer—Lack of effect of a previous movement experience on performance in another task.

Abernethy, B. (1991). Visual search strategies and decision-making in sport. *International Journal of Sport Psychology, 22,* 189-210.

Abernethy, B., Maxwell, J.P., Masters, R.S.W., Van der Kamp, J., & Jackson, R.C. (2007). Attentional processes in skill learning and expert performance. In G. Tenenbaum & R.C. Eklund (Eds.), *Handbook of sport psychology* (3rd ed., pp. 245-263). Hoboken, NJ: Wiley.

Abourezk, T. (1989). The effects of regular aerobic exercise on short-term memory efficiency in the older adult. In A.C. Ostrow (Ed.), *Aging and motor behavior* (pp. 105-113). Indianapolis: Benchmark Press.

Adams, D.L. (1999). Develop better motor skill progressions with Gentile's taxonomy of tasks. *Journal of Physical Education, Recreation and Dance, 70*(8), 35.

Adams, J.A. (1971). A closed-loop theory of motor learning. *Journal of Motor Behavior, 3,* 111-150.

Adams, J.A. (1986). Use of the model's knowledge of results to increase the observer's performance. *Journal of Human Movement Studies, 12,* 89-98.

Adams, R., & Dijkstra, S. (1966). Short-term memory for motor responses. *Journal of Experimental Psychology, 71,* 314-318.

Adolph, K.E. (1997). Learning in the development of infant locomotion. *Monographs of the Society for Research in Child Development, 62*(3, Serial No. 251).

Adolph, K.E., Eppler, M.A., & Gibson, E.J. (1993). Crawling versus walking infants' perception of affordances for locomotion over sloping surfaces. *Child Development, 64*(4): 1158-1174.

Adolph, K.E., Vereijken, B., & Shrout, P.E. (2003). What changes in infant walking and why. *Child Development, 74,* 475-497.

Adrian, M.J., & Cooper, J.M. (1995). *Biomechanics of human movement* (2nd ed.). Indianapolis: Benchmark Press.

Ajzen, I. (1985). From intentions to actions: A theory of planned behaviour. In J. Kuhl & J. Beckman (Eds.), *Action control: From cognition to behavior* (pp. 11-39). Heidelberg: Springer.

Akima, H., Kano, Y., Enomoto, Y., et al. (2001). Muscle function in 164 men and women aged 20-84 years. *Medicine and Science in Sports and Exercise, 33,* 220-226.

Almond, L. (1986). Primary and secondary rules. In R. Thorpe, D. Bunker, & L. Almond (Eds.), *Rethinking games teaching* (pp. 38-40). Loughborough: University of Technology, Loughborough.

Anderson, J.R. (1993). *Rules of mind.* Hillsdale, NJ: Erlbaum.

Argyle, M., & Kendon, A. (1967). The experimental analysis of social performance. In L. Berkowitz (Ed.), *Advances in experimental social psychology.* New York: Academic Press.

Arutyunyan, G.A., Gurfinkel, V.S., & Mirskii, M.L. (1968). Study of taking aim at a target. *Biophysics, 13,* 536-538.

Arutyunyan, G.A., Gurfinkel, V.S., & Mirskii, M.L. (1969). The organization of movements in human execution of a task involving exactness of post. *Biophysics, 14,* 1162-1167.

Asher, J.J. (1964). Vision and audition in language learning. *Perceptual and Motor Skills, 19,* 255-300.

Ashford, K., Bennett, S.J., & Davids, K. (2006). Observational modeling effects for movement dynamics and movement outcome measures across differing task constraints: A meta-analysis. *Journal of Motor Behavior, 38,* 185-205.

Ashford, K., Davids, K., & Bennett, S.J. (2007). Developmental effects influencing observational modeling: A meta-analysis. *Journal of Sports Sciences, 25,* 547-558.

Atkinson, R.C., & Shiffrin, R.M. (1968). Human memory: A proposed system and its control processes. In K.W. Spence & J.T. Spence (Eds.), *The psychology of learning and motivation: Advances in research and theory* (vol. 2, pp. 89-197). New York: Academic Press.

Baddeley, A.D. (1986). *Working memory.* New York: Oxford University Press.

Baddeley, A.D. (1995). Working memory. In M.S. Gazzaniga (Ed.), *The cognitive neurosciences* (pp. 755-764). Cambridge, MA: MIT Press.

Baker, J., & Davids, K. (2007). Introduction. *International Journal of Sport Psychology, 38,* 1-3.

Bandura, A. (1986). *Social foundations of thought and action: A social cognitive theory.* Englewood Cliffs, NJ: Prentice-Hall.

Bandura, A. (1997). *Self-efficacy: The exercise of control.* New York: Freeman.

Barclay, C.R., & Newell, K.M. (1980). Children's processing of information in motor skill acquisition. *Journal of Experimental Child Psychology, 30,* 98-108.

Barreiros, J., Figueiredo, T., & Godinho, G. (2007). The contextual interference effect in applied settings. *European Physical Education Review, 13,* 195-208.

Bassey, E.J., Fiatarone, M.A., O'Neill, E.F., Kelly, M., Evans, W.J., & Lipsitz, L.A. (1992). Leg extensor power and functional performance in very old men and women. *Clinical Science, 82,* 321-327.

Battig, W.F. (1979). The flexibility of human memory. In L.S. Cermak & F.I.M. Craik (Eds.), *Levels of processing in human memory* (pp. 23-44). Hillsdale, NJ: Erlbaum.

Bayley, N. (1935). The development of motor abilities during the first three years. *Monographs of the Society for Research in Child Development,* 1, 1.

Beak, S., Davids, K., & Bennett, S.J. (2000). One size fits all? Sensitivity to moment of inertia information from tennis rackets in children and adults. In S.J. Haake & A. Coe (Eds.), *Tennis science and technology* (pp. 109-118). London: Blackwell.

Bebko, J.M., Demark, J.L., Im-Bolter, N., & MacKewn, A. (2005). Transfer, control, and automatic processing in a complex motor task: An examination of bounce juggling. *Journal of Motor Behavior, 37,* 465-474.

Beilock, S.L., Bertenthal, B.I., McCoy, A.M., & Carr, T.H. (2004). Haste does not always make waste: Expertise, direction of attention, and speed versus accuracy in performing sensorimotor skills. *Psychonomic Bulletin & Review, 11*(2), 373-379.

Belsky, J.K. (1984). *The psychology of aging.* Monterey, CA: Brooks/Cole.

Benham, T., & Heston, M. (1989). Memory retrieval in the adult population. In A.C. Ostrow (Ed.), *Aging and motor behavior* (pp. 87-104). Indianapolis: Benchmark Press.

Berger, B.G., & Hecht, L.M. (1989). Exercise, aging, and psychological well-being: The mind-body question. In A.C. Ostrow (Ed.), *Aging and motor behavior.* Indianapolis: Benchmark Press.

Berger, B.G., & McInman, A. (1993). Exercise and the quality of life. In R.N. Singer, M. Murphy, & L.K. Tennant (Eds.), *Handbook of research on sport psychology.* New York: Macmillan.

Bernstein, N. (1967). *The co-ordination and regulation of movement.* London: Pergamon Press.

Bherer, L., Kramer, A.F., & Peterson, M.S. (2008). Transfer effects in task-set cost and dual-task cost after dual-task training in older and younger adults: Further evidence for cognitive plasticity in attentional control in late adulthood. *Experimental Aging Research, 34,* 188-219.

Bickmore, T.W., Caruso, L., Clough-Gorr, K., & Heeren, T. (2005). "It's just like you talk to a friend" relational agents for older adults. *Interacting with Computers, 17,* 711-735.

Biddle, S., Fox, K., & Boutcher, S. (2000). *Physical activity and psychological well-being.* London: Routledge.

Bilodeau, E.A., & Bilodeau, I.M. (1958). Variable frequency of knowledge of results and the learning of a simple skill. *Journal of Experimental Psychology, 55,* 379-383.

Bilodeau, I.M. (1966). Information feedback. In E.A. Bilodeau (Ed.), *Acquisition of skill* (pp. 225-296). New York: Academic Press.

Blandin, Y., & Proteau, L. (2000). On the cognitive basis of observational learning: Development of mechanisms for the detection and correction of errors. *Quarterly Journal of Experimental Psychology, 53A,* 846-867.

Bloom, B.S. (Ed.). (1985). *Developing talent in young people.* New York: Ballantine.

Bogin, B. (1998, February). The tall and the short of it. *Discover,* 40-44.

Bonds, A.G. (1980). The relationship between self-concept and locus of control and patterns of eating, exercise, and social participation in older adults. *Dissertation Abstracts International, 41*(4), 1397A.

Bortoli, L., Spagolla, G., & Robazza, C. (2001). Variability effects on retention of a motor skill in elementary school children. *Perceptual and Motor Skills, 93,* 51-63.

Bouchard, C., An, P., Rice, T., Skinner, J.S., Wilmore, J.H., Gagnon, J., Perusse, L., Leon, A.S., & Rao, D.C. (1999). Familial aggregation of VO2 max response to exercise training: Results from the HERITAGE family study. *Journal of Applied Physiology, 87,* 1003-1008.

Bouffard, M., & Dunn, J.G.H. (1993). Children's self-regulated learning of movement sequences. *Research Quarterly for Exercise and Sport, 64,* 393-403.

Boyce, B.A. (1992). Effects of assigned versus participant-set goals on skill acquisition and retention of a selected shooting task. *Journal of Teaching in Physical Education, 11,* 220-234.

Boyce, B.A., Coker, C.A., & Bunker, L. (2006). Implications for variability of practice from pedagogy and motor learning perspectives: Finding a common ground. *Quest, 58,* 330-343.

Brace, D.K. (1927). *Measuring motor ability.* New York: A.S. Barnes.

Brady, F. (1998). A theoretical and empirical review of the contextual interference effect and the learning of motor skills. *Quest, 50,* 266-293.

Brady, F. (2004). Contextual interference: A meta-analytic study. *Perceptual and Motor Skills, 99,* 116-126.

Bransford, J.D., Franks, J.J., Morris, C.D., & Stein, B.S. (1979). Some general constraints on learning and memory research. In L.S. Cermak & F.I.M. Craik (Eds.), *Levels of processing in human memory* (pp. 331-354). Hillsdale, NJ: Erlbaum.

Braver, E.R., & Trempel, R.E. (2003). Are older drivers at higher risk of involvement in crashes resulting in deaths or nonfatal injuries among their passengers or other road users? *American Journal of Epidemiology, 157,* S50.

Brown, A.L. (1975). The development of memory: Knowing, knowing about knowing, and knowing how to know. In H.W. Reese (Ed.), *Advances in child development and behavior* (vol. 10). New York: Academic Press.

Brown, A.L. (1978). Knowing when, where, and how to remember: A problem of metacognition. In R. Glaser (Ed.), *Advances in instructional psychology.* Hillsdale, NJ: Erlbaum.

Brucker, B.S., & Bulaeva, N.V. (1996). Biofeedback effect on electromyographic responses in patients with spinal cord injury. *Archives of Physical Medicine and Rehabilitation, 77,* 133-137.

Bryan, W.L., & Harter, N. (1897). Studies in the physiology and psychology of telegraphic language. *Psychological Review, 4,* 27-53.

Bryan, W.L., & Harter, N. (1899). Studies on the telegraphic language. *Psychological Review, 6,* 345-375.

Bunker, B., & Thorpe, R. (1986). The curriculum model. In R. Thorpe, D. Bunker, & L. Almond (Eds.), *Rethinking games teaching* (pp. 7-10). Loughborough: University of Technology, Loughborough.

Butler, J., Griffin, L., Lombardo, B., & Nastasi, R. (Eds.). (2003). *Teaching games for understanding in physical education and sport: An international perspective* (pp. 1-224). Reston, VA: National Association of Sport and Physical Education.

Butler, R.J., Crowell, H.P., & Davis, I.M. (2003). Lower extremity stiffness: Implications for performance and injury. *Clinical Biomechanics, 18,* 511-517.

Butterfield, S.A., & Loovis, E.M. (1993). Influence of age, sex, balance and sport participation on development of throwing by children in grades K–6. *Perceptual and Motor Skills, 76,* 459-464.

Button, C., MacLeod, M., Sanders, R., & Coleman, S. (2003). Examining movement variability in the basketball free-throw action at different levels. *Research Quarterly for Exercise and Sport, 74*(3), 257-269.

Cadopi, M., Chatillon, J.F., & Baldy, R. (1995). Representation and performance: Reproduction of form and quality of movement in dance by eight- and 11-year-old novices. *British Journal of Psychology, 86,* 217-225.

Calvo-Merino, B., Glaser, D.E., Grezes, J., Passingham, R.E., & Haggard, P. (2005). Action observation and acquired motor skills: An fMRI study with expert dancers. *Cerebral Cortex, 15,* 1243-1249.

Caprara, G.V., Pastorelli, C., & Weiner, B. (1997). Linkages between causal ascriptions, emotion, and behavior. *International Journal of Behavioral Development, 20,* 153-162.

Carroll, W.R., & Bandura, A. (1990). Representational guidance of action production in observational learning: A causal analysis. *Journal of Motor Behavior, 22,* 85-97.

Castro, C., Martínez, C., & Tornay, F.J. (2005). Vehicle distance estimations in nighttime driving: A real-setting study. *Transportation Research Report Part F: Traffic Psychology and Behavior, 8*(1): 31-45.

Centers for Disease Control and Prevention. (n.d.). Data 2010: *The Healthy People 2010* Database 2008. U.S. Physical Activity Statistics [Electronic Version]. www.cdc.gov/nccdphp/dnpa/physical/stats/.

Chase, W.G., & Simon, H.A. (1973). Perception in chess. *Cognitive Psychology, 4,* 55-81.

Chen, H.H., Liu, Y.T., Mayer-Kress, G., & Newell, K.M. (1995). Learning the pedalo locomotion task. *Journal of Motor Behavior, 37,* 247-256.

Chi, M.T.H. (1978). Knowledge structures and memory development. In R.S. Siegler (Ed.), *Children's thinking: What develops?* (pp. 73-105). Hillsdale, NJ: Erlbaum.

Chi, M.T.H. (1981). Knowledge development and memory performance. In M.P. Friedman, J.P. Das, & N. O'Connor (Eds.), *Intelligence and learning* (pp. 221-229). New York: Plenum Press.

Chiviacowsky, S., & Wulf, G. (2005). Self-controlled feedback is effective if it is based on the learner's performance. *Research Quarterly for Exercise and Sport, 76,* 42-48.

Chiviacowsky, S., & Wulf, G. (2006). Self-controlled feedback: Does it enhance learning because performers get feedback when they need it? *Research Quarterly for Exercise and Sport, 73,* 408-415.

Chiviacowsky, S., & Wulf, G. (2007). Feedback after good trials enhances learning. *Research Quarterly for Exercise and Sport, 78,* 40-47.

Chiviacowsky, S., Wulf, G., de Medeiros, F.L., Kaefer, A., & Tani, G. (2008). Learning benefits of self-controlled knowledge of results in 10-year-old children. *Research Quarterly for Exercise and Sport, 79,* 405-410.

Chiviacowsky, S., Wulf, G., Laroque de Medeiros, F., Kaefer, A., & Wally, R. (2008). Self-controlled feedback in 10-year-old children: Higher feedback frequencies enhance learning. *Research Quarterly for Exercise and Sport, 79*(1), 122-127.

Chogahara, M., O'Brien Cousins, S., & Wankel, L.M. (1998). Social influences on physical activity in older adults: A review. *Journal of Aging and Physical Activity, 6*(1), 1-17.

Clark, J.E. (2007). On the problem of motor skill development. *Journal of Physical Education, Recreation and Dance, 78*(5), 39-44.

Clark, J.E., & Metcalf, J.M. (2002). The mountain of motor development: A metaphor. In J.E. Clark & J.H. Humphrey (Eds.), *Motor development: Research and reviews* (vol. 2, pp. 163-190). Reston, VA: National Association for Sport and Physical Education.

Clark, J.E., & Whitall, J. (1989). What is motor development? The lessons of history. *Quest, 41,* 183-202.

Clark, J.E., Phillips, S.J., & Peterson, R. (1989). Developmental stability in jumping. *Developmental Psychology, 25,* 929-935.

Clarke, H.H. (1975). Joint and body range of movement. *Physical Fitness Research Digest, 5,* 16-18.

Cleary, T.J., & Zimmerman, B.J. (2001). Self-regulation differences during athletic practice by experts, non-experts and novices. *Journal of Applied Sport Psychology, 13,* 185-206.

Coggan, A.R., Spina, R.J., King, D.S., et al. (1992). Skeletal muscle adaptation to endurance training in 60- to 70-year old men and women. *Journal of Applied Physiology, 72*(5), 1780-1786.

Cohen, R.G., & Rosenbaum, D.A. (2004). Where objects are grasped reveals how grasps are planned: Generation and recall of motor plans. *Experimental Brain Research, 157,* 486-495.

Coker, C.A. (2003). *Motor learning and control for practitioners.* New York: McGraw-Hill.

Coker, C.A. (2009). *Motor learning and control for practitioners* (2nd ed.). Scottsdale, AZ: Holcomb Hathaway.

Colborne, G.R., Olney, S.J., & Griffin, M.P. (1993). Feedback of ankle joint angle and soleus electromyography in the rehabilitation of hemiplegic gait. *Archives of Physical Medicine and Rehabilitation, 74*(10), 1100-1106.

Cole, K.J., Rotella, D.L., & Harper, J.G. (1999). Mechanisms for age-related changes of fingertip forces during precision gripping and lifting in adults. *Journal of Neuroscience, 19,* 3228-3247.

Collier, D.H. (2005). Instructional strategies for adapted physical education. In J.P. Winnick (Ed.), *Adapted physical education and sport* (4th ed., pp. 109-130). Champaign, IL: Human Kinetics.

Comfort, A. (1979). *Aging, the biology of senescence* (2nd ed.). New York: Holt, Rinehart, Winston.

Cook, V.J. (1997). L2 users and English spelling. *Journal of Multilingual and Multicultural Development, 18,* 474-488.

Corso, J.F. (1987). Sensory-perceptual processes and aging. *Annual Review of Gerontology and Geriatrics, 7,* 29-55.

Côté, J. (1999). The influence of the family in the development of talent in sport. *Sport Psychologist, 13,* 395-417.

Côté, J ., Baker, J., & Abernethy, B. (2003). From play to practice: A developmental framework for acquisition of expertise in team sports. In J.L. Starkes & K.A. Ericsson (Eds.), *Expert performance in sports* (89-113). Champaign, IL: Human Kinetics.

Craik, F.I.M. (1986). A functional account of age differences in memory. In F. Flix & H. Hagendorf

(Eds.), *Human memory and cognitive capabilities, mechanisms, and performance* (pp. 409-422). Amsterdam: Elsevier, North-Holland.

Crain, W.C. (1985). *Theories of development: Concepts and applications* (2nd ed.). Englewood Cliffs, NJ: Prentice-Hall.

Crews, D.J., Lochbaum, M.R., & Karoly, P. (2000). Self-regulation: Concepts, methods and strategies in sport and exercise. In R.N. Singer, H.A. Hausenblas, & C.M. Janelle (Eds.), *Handbook of sport psychology* (2nd ed., pp. 566-581). New York: Wiley.

Crocker, P.R.E., Hoar, S.D., McDonough, M.H., Kowaski, K.C., & Niefer, C.B. (2004). Emotional experiences in youth sport. In M.R. Weiss (Ed.), *Developmental sport and exercise psychology: A lifespan perspective* (pp. 197-221). Morgantown, WV: Fitness Information Technology.

Crossman, E.R.F.W. (1959). Theory of acquisition of speed-skill. *Ergonomics, 2,* 153-166.

Dacey, M., Baltzell, A., & Zalchkowsky, L. (2008). Older adults' intrinsic and extrinsic motivation toward physical activity. *American Journal of Health Behavior, 32*(5), 570-582.

Dail, T.K., & Christina, R.W. (2004). Distribution of practice and metacognition in learning long-term retention of a discrete motor task. *Research Quarterly for Exercise and Sport, 75,* 148-160.

Darden, G.F. (1997). Demonstrating motor skills: Rethinking that expert demonstration. *Journal of Physical Education, Recreation and Dance, 68*(6), 31-35.

Darden, G.F. (1999). Videotape feedback for student learning and performance: A learning stages approach. *Journal of Physical Education, Recreation and Dance, 70*(9), 40-45, 62.

Darwin, C. (1859). *On the origin of species by means of natural selection, or the preservation of favoured races in the struggle for life* (1st ed.). London: John Murray.

Darwin, C. (1871). *The descent of man, and selection in relation to sex* (1st ed.). London: John Murray.

Darwin, C. (1872). *The origin of species by means of natural selection, or the preservation of favoured races in the struggle for life* (6th ed.). London: John Murray.

Davids, K., & Baker, J. (2007). Genes, environment and sport performance: Why the nature-nurture dualism is no longer relevant. *Sports Medicine, 37,* 961-980.

Davids, K., Button, C., & Bennett, S. (2008). *Dynamics of skill acquisition: A constraints-led approach*. Champaign, IL: Human Kinetics.

Davis, W.E., & Burton, A.W. (1991). Ecological task analysis: Translating movement behavior theory into practice. *Adapted Physical Activity Quarterly, 8,* 154-177.

Deakin, J.M., & Cobley, S. (2003). A search for deliberate practice: An examination of the practice environments in figure skating and volleyball. In J.L. Starkes & K.A. Ericsson (Eds.), *Expert performance in sports* (pp. 115-135). Champaign, IL: Human Kinetics.

Deci, E.L., & Flaste, R. (1995). *Why we do what we do: The dynamics of personal autonomy*. New York: Putnam.

Deci, E.L., & Ryan, R.M. (1985). *Intrinsic motivation and self-determination in human behavior*. New York: Plenum Press.

Deci, E.L., & Ryan, R.M. (2000). The "what" and "why" of goal pursuits: Human needs and the self-determination of behavior. *Psychological Inquiry, 11,* 227-268.

Deci, E.L., Koestner, R., & Ryan, R.M. (1999). A meta-analytic review of experiments examining the effects of intrinsic rewards on intrinsic motivation. *Psychological Bulletin, 125*(6), 627-668.

Deci, E.L., Koestner, R., & Ryan, R.M. (2000). Extrinsic rewards and intrinsic motivation in education: Reconsidered once again. *Review of Educational Research, 71*(1), 1-27.

Deford, F. (1980, July 14). A match goes down in history. *Sports Illustrated.*

Del Rey, P., Whitehurst, M., & Wood, J. (1983). Effects of experience and contextual interference on learning and transfer. *Perceptual and Motor Skills, 56,* 581-582.

Dempsey, J.A., & Seals, D.R. (1995). Aging, exercise and cardiopulmonary function. In D.R. Lamb, C.V Gisolfi, & E. Nadel (Eds.), *Perspectives in exercise science and sports medicine: Vol. 8. Exercise in older adults* (pp. 237-297). Indianapolis: Benchmark Press.

DeOreo, K., & Keogh, J. (1980). Performance of fundamental motor tasks. In C.B. Corbin (Ed.), *A textbook of motor development* (2nd ed., pp. 76-91). Dubuque, IA: Brown.

DeStefano, F., Coulehan, J., & Wiant, M. (1979). Blood pressure survey on the navajo indian reservation. *American Journal of Epidemiology, 109*(3), 335-345.

Dewey, J. (1916). *Democracy in education.* New York: Macmillan.

DiPietro, L., Williamson, D.F., Caspersen, C.J., & Eaker, E. (1993). The descriptive epidemiology of selected physical activities and body weight among adults trying to lose weight: The Behavioral Risk Factor Surveillance System Survey, 1989. *International Journal of Obesity, 17,* 69-76.

Dishman, R.K. (1994). *Advances in exercise adherence.* Champaign, IL: Human Kinetics.

Dishman, R.K., Sallis, J.F., & Orenstein, D.O. (1985). The determinants of physical activity and exercise. *Public Health Reports, 100,* 158-171.

Dixon, R.A., Kurzman, D., & Friesen, I.C. (1993). Handwriting performance in younger and older adults: Age, familiarity, and practice effects. *Psychological Aging, 8,* 360-370.

Donato, A.J., Tench, K., Glueck, D.H., Seals, D.R., Eskurza, I., & Tanaka, H. (2003). Declines in physiological functional capacity with age: A longitudinal study in peak swimming performance. *Journal of Applied Physiology, 94*(2), 764-769.

Donorfio, L.K.M., Mohyde, M., Coughlin, J., & D'Ambrosio, L. (2008). A qualitative exploration of self-regulation behaviors among older drivers. *Journal of Aging and Social Policy, 20*(3), 323-339.

Douvis, S.J. (2005). Variable practice in learning the forehand drive in tennis. *Perceptual and Motor Skills, 101,* 531-545.

Dozza, M., Wall III, C., Peterka, R.J., Chiari, L., & Horak, F.B. (2007). Effects of practicing tandem gait with and without vibrotactile biofeedback in subjects with unilateral vestibular loss. *Journal of Vestibular Research, 17,* 195-204.

Duffy, L.J., Ericsson, K.A., & Baluch, B. (2007). In search of the loci for sex differences in throwing: The effects of physical size and differential recruitment rates on high levels of dart performance. *Research Quarterly for Exercise and Sport, 78*(2), 71-79.

Easterbrook, J.A. (1959). The effect of emotion on cue utilization and the organization of behavior. *Psychological Review, 66,* 183-201.

Easton, R.D., Greene, A.J., DiZio, P., & Lackner, J.R. (1998). Auditory cues for orientation and postural control in sighted and congenitally blind people. *Experimental Brain Research, 118,* 541-550.

Eckert, H. (1987). *Motor development.* Indianapolis: Benchmark Press.

Edwards, J.M., Elliott, D., & Lee, T.D. (1986). Contextual interference effects during skill acquisition and transfer in Down's syndrome adolescents. *Adapted Physical Activity Quarterly, 3,* 250-258.

Eimas, P.D. (1975). Auditory and phonetic coding of the cues for speech: Discrimination of the [r-l] distinction by young infants. *Perception & Psychophysics, 18,* 341-347.

Eimer, M., Nattkemper, D., Schröger, E., & Prinz, W. (1996). Involuntary attention. In O. Neumann & A.F. Sanders (Eds.), *Handbook of perception and action. Vol. 3: Attention* (pp. 155-184). San Diego: Academic Press.

Elble, R.J. (1997). Changes in gait with normal aging. In J.C. Masdeu, L. Sudarsky, & L. Wolfson (Eds.), *Gait disorders of aging. Falls and therapeutic strategies* (pp. 93-106). Philadelphia: Lippincott-Raven.

Emanuel, M., Jarus, T., & Bart, O. (2008). Effect of focus of attention and age on motor acquisition, retention, and transfer: A randomized trial. *Physical Therapy, 88,* 251-260.

Ennis, C. (1992). Reconceptualizing learning as a dynamical system. *Journal of Curriculum and Supervision, 7*(2), 115-130.

Ericsson, K.A. (2003). Development of elite performance and deliberate practice: An update from the perspective of the expert performance approach. In J.L. Starkes & K.A. Ericsson (Eds.), *Expert performance in sports* (pp. 49-83). Champaign, IL: Human Kinetics.

Ericsson, K.A. (2007). Deliberate practice and the modifiability of body and mind: Toward a science of the structure and acquisition of expert and elite performance. *International Journal of Sport Psychology, 38,* 109-123.

Erikson, E. (1980). *Identity and the life cycle.* New York: Norton.

Erikson, E.H. (1963). *Childhood and society* (2nd ed.). New York: Norton.

Eskurza, I., Donato, A.J., Moreau, K.L., Seals, D.R., & Tanaka, H. (2002). Changes in maximal aerobic capacity with age in endurance-trained women: 7 year follow-up. *Journal of Applied Physiology, 92,* 2303-2308.

Evans, S.L., Davy, P., Stevenson, E.T., & Seals, D.R. (1995). Physiological determinants of 10-km performance in highly trained female runners of different ages. *Journal of Applied Physiology, 78,* 1931-1941.

Fagan, J.W., & Rovee Collier, C. (1983). Memory retrieval: A time-locked process in infancy. *Science, 222*(4630), 1349-1351.

Fagard, R., Thijs, L., & Amery, A. (1993). Age and the hemodynamic response to posture and to exercise.

American Journal of Geriatric Cardiology, 2(2), 23-30.

Farrow, D., & Abernethy, B. (2002). Can anticipatory skills be learned through implicit video-based perceptual training? *Journal of Sports Sciences, 20,* 471-485.

Farrow, D., & Maschette, W. (1997). The effects of contextual interference on children learning forehand tennis groundstrokes. *Journal of Human Movement Studies 33,* 47-67.

Faulkner, J.A., & Brooks, S.V. (1995). Muscle fatigue in old animals. Unique aspects of fatigue in elderly humans. *Advancements in Experimental Medicine and Biology, 384,* 471-480.

Faulkner, J.A., Larkin, L.M., Claflin, D.R., & Brooks, S.V. (2007). Age-related changes in the structure and function of skeletal muscles. *Clinical and Experimental Pharmacology and Physiology, 34,* 1091-1096.

Fazzi, E., Lanners, J., Ferrari-Ginevra, O., Achille, C., Luparia, A., Signorini, S., & Lanzi, G. (2002). Gross motor development and reach on sound as critical tools for the development of the blind child. *Brain and Development, 24,* 269-275.

Feltz, D.L., & Landers, D.M. (1983). The effects of mental practice on motor skill learning and performance: A meta-analysis. *Journal of Sport Psychology, 5,* 25-57.

Feltz, D.L., Short, S.E., & Sullivan, P.J. (2008). *Self-efficacy in sport.* Champaign, IL: Human Kinetics.

Fiatarone, M., Marks, E.C., Ryan, N.D., Meredith, C.N., Lipsitz, L.A., & Evans, W.J. (1990). High intensity strength training in nonagenarians: Effects on skeletal muscle. *Journal of the American Medical Association, 263*(22), 3029-3039.

Figueredo, L. (2006). Using the known to chart the unknown: A review of first-language influence on the development of English-as-a second-language spelling skill. *Reading and Writing, 19,* 873-905.

Finkelstein, J.S., Lee, M.L., Sowers, M., Ettinger, B., Neer, R.M., Kelsey, J.L., Cauley, J.A., Huang, M.H., & Greendale, G.A. (2002). Ethnic variation in bone density in premenopausal and early perimenopausal women: Effects of anthropometric and lifestyle factors. *Journal of Clinical Endocrinology and Metabolism, 87,* 3057-3067.

Fischman, M.F., & Oxendine, J.B. (2001). Motor skill learning for effective coaching and performance. In J.M. Williams (Ed.), *Applied sport psychology: Personal growth to peak performance* (pp. 13-28). Mountain View, CA: Mayfield.

Fishman, S., & Tobey, C. (1978). Augmented feedback. In W.G. Anderson & G.T. Barrette (Eds.), What's going on in gym: Descriptive studies of physical education classes [Monograph]. *Motor Skills: Theory Into Practice, 1,* 51-62.

Fitts, P., & Posner, M.I. (1967). *Human performance.* Belmont, CA: Brooks/Cole.

Flanagan, E.P., & Harrison, A.J. (2007). Muscle dynamics differences between legs in healthy adults. *Journal of Strength and Conditioning Research, 21,* 67-72.

Fleishman, E.A. (1962). The description and prediction of perceptual motor skill learning. In R. Glasser (Ed.), *Training research and education* (pp. 137-175). Pittsburgh: University of Pittsburgh Press.

Fleishman, E.A. (1964). *The structure and measurement of physical fitness.* Englewood Cliffs, NJ: Prentice-Hall.

Flinn, N.A., & Radomski, M.V. (2002). Learning. In C.A. Trombly & M.V. Radomski (Eds.), *Occupational therapy for physical dysfunction* (5th ed., pp. 283-297). Baltimore: Lippincott Williams & Wilkins.

Fox, P.W., Hershberger, S.L., & Bouchard, T.J. (1996). Genetic and environmental contributions to the acquisition of motor skill. *Nature, 384,* 356-358.

Fredricks, J.A., & Eccles, J.S. (2004). Parental influences on youth involvement in sports. In M.R. Weiss (Ed.), *Developmental sport and exercise psychology: A lifespan perspective* (pp. 145-164). Morgantown, WV: Fitness Information Technology.

French, K.E., & Thomas, J.R. (1987). The relation of knowledge to children's basketball performance. *Journal of Sport Psychology, 9,* 15-32.

French, K.E., Spurgeon, J.H., & Nevett, M.E. (1995). Expert-novice differences in cognitive and skill execution components of youth baseball performance. *Research Quarterly for Exercise and Sport, 66,* 194-201.

Fried, L.P., Storer, D.J., King, D.E., & Lodder, F. (1991). Diagnosis of illness presentations in the elderly. *Journal of the American Geriatric Society, 39,* 117-123.

Gabbard, C.P. (2004). *Lifelong motor development* (4th ed.). San Francisco: Benjamin Cummings.

Gabbard, C.P. (2008). *Lifelong motor development* (5th ed.). San Francisco: Benjamin Cummings.

Gallagher, J.D., & Thomas, J.R. (1980). Effects of varying post-KR intervals upon children's motor performance. *Journal of Motor Behavior, 12,* 41-46.

Gallagher, J.D., & Thomas, J.R. (1984). Rehearsal strategy effects on developmental differences for recall of a movement series. *Research Quarterly for Exercise and Sport, 55,* 123-128.

Gallahue, D., & Cleland-Donnelley, F. (2003). *Developmental physical education for today's children* (4th ed.). Champaign, IL: Human Kinetics.

Gallahue, D.L., & Ozmun, J.C. (2005). *Understanding motor development: Infants, children, adolescents, adults* (6th ed.). Boston: McGraw-Hill.

Garzia, R., & Trick, L. (1992). Vision in the 90's: The aging eye. *Journal of Optometric Vision Development, 23*(1), 4-41.

Geladas, N., Koskolou, M., & Klissouras, V. (2007). Nature or nurture: Not an either-or question. *International Journal of Sport Psychology, 38,* 124-134.

Gentile, A.M. (1972). A working model of skill acquisition with application to teaching. *Quest, 17,* 3-23.

Gentile, A.M. (1987). Skill acquisition: Action, movement and neuromotor processes. In J.H. Carr, R.B. Shepherd, J. Gordon, A.M. Gentile, & J.M. Held (Eds.), *Movement science: Foundations for physical therapy in rehabilitation* (pp. 93-154). Rockville, MD: Aspen.

Gentile, A.M. (1998). Implicit and explicit processes during acquisition of functional skills. *Scandinavian Journal of Occupational Therapy, 5,* 7-16.

Gentile, A.M. (2000). Skill acquisition: Action, movement and neuromotor processes. In J.H. Carr & R.B. Shepherd (Eds.), *Movement science: Foundations for physical therapy in rehabilitation* (2nd ed., pp. 111-187). Rockville, MD: Aspen.

Gerson, R.F., & Thomas, J.R. (1977). Schema theory and practice variability within a neo-Piagetian framework. *Journal of Motor Behavior, 2,* 127-134.

Gesell, A. (1928). *Infancy and human growth.* New York: Macmillan.

Gesell, A. (1954). The ontogenesis of infant behavior. In L. Carmichael (Ed.), *Manual of child psychology* (2nd ed.). New York: Wiley.

Gibson, J.J. (1966). *The senses considered as perceptual systems.* Boston: Houghton Mifflin.

Gibson, J.J. (1977). The theory of affordances. In R. Shaw & J. Bransford (Eds.), *Perceiving, acting and knowing: Toward an ecological psychology.* Hillsdale, NJ: Erlbaum.

Gibson, J.J. (1979). *The ecological approach to visual perception.* Boston: Houghton Mifflin.

Ginsburg, H., & Opper, S. (1969). *Piaget's theory of intellectual development: An introduction.* Englewood Cliffs, NJ: Prentice-Hall.

Gollnick, P.D., Timson, B.F., Moore, R.L., & Riedy, M. (1981). Muscle enlargement and number of fibers in skeletal muscles of rats. *Journal of Applied Physiology, 50,* 936-943.

Goode, S., & Magill, R.A. (1986). Contextual interference effects in learning three badminton serves. *Research Quarterly for Exercise and Sport, 57,* 308-314.

Goodpaster, B.H., Park, S.W., Harris, T.B., et al. (2006). The loss of skeletal muscle strength, mass, and quality in older adults: The health, aging and body composition study. *Journals of Gerontology: Biological Sciences and Medical Sciences, 61,* 1059-1064.

Gould, D. (2006). Goal setting for peak performance. In J.M. Williams (Ed.), *Applied sport psychology: Personal growth to peak performance* (pp. 240-259). New York: McGraw-Hill.

Gould, D., & Chung, Y. (2004). Self-regulation skills in young, middle, and older adulthood. In M. Weiss (Ed.), *Developmental sport and exercise psychology: A lifespan perspective* (pp. 383-402). Morgantown, WV: Fitness Information Technology.

Gould, D., Feltz, D., & Weiss, M.R. (1985). Motives for competing in competitive youth swimming. *International Journal of Sport Psychology, 16,* 126-140.

Goulet, C., Bard, C., & Fleury, M. (1989). Expertise differences in preparing to return a tennis serve: A visual information processing approach. *Journal of Sport and Exercise Psychology, 11,* 382-398.

Gredler, M.E. (1992). Educational games and simulations: A technology in search of (research) paradigm. *Handbook of research of technology and communications* (pp. 521-538). New York: Simon & Schuster Macmillan.

Green, D.P., Whitehead., J., & Sugden, D.A. (1995). Practice variability and transfer of a racket skill. *Perceptual and Motor Skills, 81,* 1275-1281.

Green, T.D., & Flowers, J.H. (1991). Implicit versus explicit learning processes in probabilistic, continuous fine-motor catching task. *Journal of Motor Behavior, 23,* 293-300.

Grehaigne, J.F., Godbout, P., & Bouthier, D. (2001). The teaching and learning in decision making in team sports. *Quest, 53,* 59-76.

Griffin, L.L., Brooker, R., & Patton, K. (2005). Working towards legitimacy: Two decades of teaching for understanding. *Physical Education and Sport Pedagogy, 10,* 213-223.

Guralnik, J.M., & Simonsick, E.M. (1993). Physical disability in older Americans [Special issue]. *Journal of Gerontology, 48,* 3-10.

Gutteridge, M.V. (1939). A study of motor achievements of young children. *Archives of Psychology, 244,* 1-178.

Hagberg, J.M. (1988). Effect of exercise and training on older men and women with essential hypertension. In W.W. Spirduso & H.M. Eckert (Eds.), *The academy papers: Physical activity and aging* (pp. 187-191). Champaign IL: Human Kinetics.

Halverson, L.E. (1970). Research in motor development. Implications for program in early childhood education. Paper presented at the Midwest Association for Health, Physical Education and Recreation, Chicago.

Halverson, L.E., & Williams, K. (1985). Developmental sequences for hopping over distance: A prelongitudinal screening. *Research Quarterly for Exercise and Sport, 56,* 37-44.

Halverson, L.E., Roberton, M.A., & Landendorfer, S. (1982). Development of the overarm throw: Movement and ball velocity changes by seventh grade. *Research Quarterly for Exercise and Sport, 53,* 198-205.

Harter, S. (1978). Effectance motivation reconsidered: Toward a developmental model. *Human Development, 21,* 34-64.

Harter, S. (1981). A new self-report scale of intrinsic versus extrinsic orientation in the classroom: Motivational and informational components. *Developmental Psychology, 17,* 300-312.

Harter, S. (1999). *The construction of self: A developmental perspective.* New York: Guilford.

Haubenstricker, J., Wisner, D., Seefeldt, V., & Branta, C. (1997). Gender differences and mixed longitudinal norms on selected motor skills for children and youth. *Journal of Sport and Exercise Psychology: NASPSPA Abstracts, 19,* S63. (6) Haubenstricker, J.L., Branta, C.F., & Seefeldt, V.D. (1983). Standards of performance for throwing and catching. Paper presented at the annual conference of the North American Society for Psychology of Sport and Physical Activity, Asilomar, CA.

Haubenstricker, J.L., Seefeldt, V., Fountain, C., & Sapp, M. (1981). Preliminary validation of a developmental sequence for the standing long jump. Paper presented at the annual convention of the American Alliance for Health, Physical Education, Recreation and Dance, Chicago.

Haubenstricker, J.L., Seefeldt, V.D., & Branta, C.F. (1983, April). Preliminary validation of a developmental sequence for the standing long jump. Paper presented at the meeting of the American Alliance for Health, Physical Education, Recreation and Dance, Houston, TX.

Hausenblas, H.A., Carron, A.V., & Mack, D.E. (1997). Application of the theories of reasoned action and planned behavior to exercise behavior: A meta-analysis. *Journal of Sport and Exercise Psychology, 19,* 36-51.

Haywood, K.M., & Getchell, N. (2005). *Life span motor development* (4th ed.). Champaign, IL: Human Kinetics.

Haywood, K.M., & Getchell, N. (2009). *Life span motor development* (5th ed.). Champaign, IL: Human Kinetics.

Hellison, D. (1995). *Teaching responsibility through physical activity.* Champaign, IL: Human Kinetics.

Hellison, D. (2003). *Teaching responsibility through physical activity* (2nd ed.). Champaign, IL: Human Kinetics.

Henderlong, J., & Lepper, M.R. (2002). The effects of praise on children's intrinsic motivation: A review and synthesis. *Psychological Bulletin, 128*(5), 774-795.

Henry, F.M. (1968). Specificity vs. generality in learning motor skills. In R.C. Brown & G.S. Kenyon (eds.), *Classical studies on physical activity* (pp. 331-340). Englewood Cliffs, NJ: Prentice-Hall.

Henry, F.M., & Rogers, D.E. (1960). Increased response latency for complicated movements and the "memory drum" theory of neuromotor reaction. *Research Quarterly, 31,* 448-458.

Herbert, E., & Landin, D. (1997). Videotape feedback in skill acquisition. Paper presented at Southern District AAHPERD conference, New Orleans.

Herbert, E.P., Landin, D., & Solmon, M.A. (1996). Practice schedule effects on the performance and learning of low- and high-skilled students: An applied study. *Research Quarterly for Exercise and Sport, 67,* 52-58.

Hess, T.M., Follett, K.J., & McGee, K.A. (1998). Aging and impression formation: The impact of processing skills and goals. *Journals of Gerontology: Psychological Sciences and Social Sciences, 53B,* 175-187.

Hick, W.E. (1952). On the rate of gain of information. *Quarterly Journal of Experimental Psychology, 4,* 11-26.

Hill, A.V. (1925). The physiological basis of athletic records. *Lancet, 209*(2), 483-486.

Hird, J.S., Landers, D.M., Thomas, J.R., & Horan, J.J. (1991). Physical practice is superior to mental practice in enhancing cognitive and motor task performance. *Journal of Sport and Exercise Psychology, 13,* 281-293.

Hodges, N., & Franks, I.M. (2002). Modelling coaching practice: The role and demonstration. *Journal of Sports Sciences, 20,* 793-811.

Holt, L., Strean, W.B., & Bengoechea, E.G. (2002). Expanding the teaching games for understanding model: New avenues for future research and practice. *Journal of Teaching in Physical Education, 21*(2), 162-176.

Honeybourne, J. (2006). *Acquiring skill in sport: An introduction.* London: Routledge.

Hoover, J.H., & Wade, M. (1985). Motor learning theory and mentally retarded individuals: A historical review. *Adapted Physical Activity Quarterly, 2,* 228-252.

Hopper, T., & Bell, R. (1999). Games classification system: Teaching strategic understanding and tactical awareness. *California Association for Health, Physical Education, Recreation and Dance, 66*(4): 14-19.

Horn, T.S. (1987). The influence of teacher-coach behavior on the psychological development of children. In D. Gould & M.R. Weiss (Eds.), *Advances in pediatric sport science: Volume 2, Behavioral issues* (pp. 121-142). Champaign, IL: Human Kinetics.

Horn, T.S., & Hasbrook, C.A. (1986). *The sport competence information scale.* Oxford, OH: Miami University.

Howe, M.J.A., Davidson, J.W., & Sloboda, J.A. (1998). Innate talents: Reality or myth? *Behavioral and Brain Sciences, 21,* 399-442.

Hyde, T.E., & Gengenbach, M.S. (2007). *Conservative management of sports injuries* (2nd ed., p. 845). Sudbury, MA: Jones & Bartlett.

Ille, A., & Cadopi, M. (1999). Memory for movement sequences in gymnastics: Effects of age and skill level. *Journal of Motor Behavior, 31,* 290-300.

Intiso, D., Santilli, V., Grasso, M.G., Rossi, R., & Caruso, I. (1994). Rehabilitation of walking with electromyographic biofeedback in drop-foot after stroke. *Stroke, 25,* 1189-1192.

Jagacinski, R.J., Greenberg, N., & Liao, M.J. (1997). Tempo, rhythm, and aging in golf. *Journal of Motor Behavior, 29*(2), 159-173.

Janelle, C.M., & Hillman, C.H. (2003). Expert performance in sport: Current perspectives and critical issues. In J.L. Starkes & K.A. Ericsson (Eds.), *Expert performance in sports* (pp. 19-47). Champaign, IL: Human Kinetics.

Janelle, C.M., Barba, D.A., Frehlich, S.G., Tennant, L.K., & Cauraugh, J.H. (1997). Maximizing performance feedback effectiveness through videotape replay and a self-controlled learning environment. *Research Quarterly for Exercise and Sport, 68*(4), 269-279.

Jarus, T., & Goverover, Y. (1999). Effects of contextual interference and age on acquisition, retention, and transfer of motor skill. *Perceptual and Motor Skills, 88,* 437-447.

Jeannerod, M. (1999). To act or not to act: Perspectives on the representation of actions. *Quarterly Journal of Experimental Psychology, 52A*(1), 1-29.

Jette, A., & Branch, L. (1992). A ten-year follow-up of driving patterns among community-dwelling elderly. *Human Factors, 34,* 25-31.

Jette, A.M., Rooks, D., Lachman, M., et al. (1998). Home-based resistance training: Predictors of participation and adherence. *Gerontologist, 38*(4), 412-421.

Johnson, E.E. (2003). Transportation mobility and older drivers. *Journal of Gerontological Nursing, 29*(4), 34-41.

Joyner, M.J. (1993). Physiological limiting factors and distance running: Influence of gender and age on record performances. *Exercise and Sport Science Reviews, 21,* 103-133.

Kahneman, D. (1973). *Attention and effort.* Englewood Cliffs, NJ: Prentice-Hall.

Kannel, W., Sorlie, P., & Gordon, T. (1980). Labile hypertension: A faulty concept? The Framingham Study. *Circulation, 61*(6), 1183-1187.

Kasch, F.W., Wallace, J.P., Van Camp, S.P., & Verity, L. (1988). A longitudinal study of cardiovascular stability in active men aged 45-65 years. *Physician and SportsMedicine, 16*(1): 117-126.

Keele, S.W. (1973). *Attention and human performance.* Pacific Palisades, CA: Goodyear.

Keetch, K.M., & Lee, T.D. (2007). The effect of self-regulated and experimenter-imposed practice schedules on motor learning for tasks of varying difficulty. *Research Quarterly for Exercise and Sport, 78,* 476-486.

Kellman, P.J., & Arterberry, M.E. (1998). *The cradle of knowledge: Development of perception in infancy.* Cambridge, MA: MIT Press.

Kenshalo, D.R. (1977). Age changes in touch, vibration, temperature, kinesthesis, and pain sensitivity. In J.E. Birren & K.W. Schaie (Eds.), *Handbook of the psychology of aging* (pp. 562-579). New York: Van Nostrand Reinhold.

Keogh, J., & Sugden, D. (1985). *Movement skill development.* New York: Macmillan.

Kernodle, M.W., & Carlton, L.G. (1992). Information feedback and the learning of multiple-degree-of-freedom activities. *Journal of Motor Behavior, 24*(2), 187-196.

Kerr, R., & Booth, B. (1978). Specific and varied practice of motor skill. *Perceptual and Motor Skills, 46*, 395-401.

Kilpatrick, M., Hebert, E., & Jacobsen, D. (2002). Physical activity motivation: A practitioner's guide to self-determination theory. *Journal of Physical Education, Recreation and Dance, 73*, 36-41.

Kirschenbaum, D.S. (1984). Self-regulation and sport psychology: Nurturing and emerging symbiosis. *Journal of Sport Psychology, 6*, 159-183.

Kirschenbaum, D.S. (1987). Self-regulation of sport performance. *Medicine and Science in Sports and Exercise, 19*, S106-S113.

Kitsantas, A., & Zimmerman, B.J. (1998). Self-regulation of motoric learning: A strategic cycle view. *Journal of Applied Sport Psychology, 10*, 220-239.

Kitsantas, A., & Zimmerman, B.J. (2002). Comparing self-regulatory processes among novice, non-expert, and expert volleyball players: A microanalytic study. *Journal of Applied Sport Psychology, 14*, 91-105.

Klinger, A., Masataka, T., Adrian, M., & Smith, E. (1980). Temporal and spatial characteristics of movement patterns of women over 60. Paper presented at the National Conference of the American Alliance for Health, Physical Education, Recreation and Dance, Detroit.

Klissouras, V., Geladas, N., & Koskolou, M. (2007). Nature prevails over nurture. *International Journal of Sport Psychology, 38*, 35-67.

Knapp, B. (1963). *Skill in sport.* London: Routledge & Kegan Paul.

Ko, Y.G., Challis, J.H., & Newell, K.M. (2003). Learning to coordinate redundant degrees of freedom in a dynamic balance task. *Human Movement Science, 22*, 47-66.

Kolh, R.M., Ellis, S.D., & Roenker, D.L. (1992). Alternating actual and imagery practice: Preliminary theoretical considerations. *Research Quarterly for Exercise and Sport, 63*, 162-170.

Konttinen, N., Lyytinen, H., & Viitasalo, J. (1998). Rifle-balancing in precision shooting: Behavioral aspects and psychophysiological implication. *Scandinavian Journal of Medicine and Science in Sports, 8*, 78-83.

Kourtessis, T., & Reid, G. (1997). Knowledge and skill of ball catching in children with cerebral palsy and other physical disabilities. *Adapted Physical Activity Quarterly, 14*, 24-42.

Krogman, W.M. (1972). *Child growth.* Ann Arbor, MI: University of Michigan Press.

Kugler, P.N., Kelso, J.A.S., & Turvey, M.T. (1982). On the control and coordination of naturally developing systems. In J.A.S. Kelso & J.E. Clark (Eds.), *The development of movement control and coordination* (pp. 5-78). New York: Wiley.

Kuhl, P.K., Williams, K.A., Lacerda, F., Stevens, K.N., & Lindblom, B. (1992). Language experience alters phonetic perception in infants by 6 months of age. *Science, 255*, 606-608.

Kyllo, L.B., & Landers, D.M. (1995). Goal setting in sport and exercise: A research synthesis to resolve the controversy. *Journal of Sport and Exercise Psychology, 17*, 117-137.

Lai, Q., & Shea, C.H. (1999). Bandwidth knowledge of results enhances generalized motor program learning. *Research Quarterly for Exercise and Sport, 70*, 79-83.

Lambert, J., & Bard, C. (2005). Acquisition of visuomanual skills and improvement of information processing capacities in 6-to-10-year-old children performing a 2D pointing task. *Neuroscience Letters, 377*, 1-6.

Landin, D., & Hebert, E.P. (1997). A comparison of three practice schedules along the contextual interference continuum. *Research Quarterly for Exercise and Sport, 68*, 357-361.

Lashley, K.S. (1951). The problem of serial order in behavior. In L.A. Jeffress (Ed.), *Cerebral mechanisms in behavior* (pp. 112-131). New York: Wiley.

Leavitt, J.L. (1979). Cognitive demands of skating and stick handling in ice hockey. *Canadian Journal of Applied Sport Science, 4*, 46-55.

Lee, T.D., & Carnahan, H. (1990). Bandwidth knowledge of results and motor learning. *Quarterly Journal of Experimental Psychology, 42*, 777-789.

Lee, T.D., & Magill, R.A. (1985). Can forgetting facilitate skill acquisition? In D. Goodman, R.B. Wilberg, & I.M. Franks (Eds.), *Differing perspectives on memory, learning and control* (pp. 3-22). Amsterdam: North-Holland.

Lee, T.D., & White, M.A. (1990). Influence of an unskilled model's practice schedule on observational learning. *Human Movement Science, 9*, 349-367.

Lee, T.D., Chamberlin, C.J., & Hodges, N. (2001). Practice. In R.N. Singer, H.A. Hausenblas, & C.M. Janelle (Eds.), *Handbook of sport psychology* (2nd ed., pp. 115-143). New York: Wiley.

Lefebvre, C., & Reid, G. (1998). Prediction in ball catching by children with and without a developmental coordination disorder. *Adapted Physical Activity Quarterly, 15,* 299-315.

Leme, S., & Shambes, G. (1978). Immature throwing patterns in normal adult women. *Journal of Human Movement Studies, 4,* 85-93.

Lexell, J. (1995). Human aging, muscle mass, and fiber type composition. *Journals of Gerontology: Biological Sciences and Medical Sciences, 50* (Special Issue): 11-16.

Lexell, J., Taylor, C.C., & Sjostrom, M. (1988). What is the cause of the ageing atrophy? Total number, size and proportion of different fiber types studied in whole vastus lateralis muscle from 15- to 83-year old men. *Journal of Neurological Science, 84,* 275-294.

Lloyd, M., Reid, G., & Bouffard, M. (2006). Self-regulation of sport-specific and educational problem solving tasks by boys with and without DCD. *Adapted Physical Activity Quarterly, 23,* 370-389.

Locke, E.A., & Latham, G.P. (1985). The application of goal setting to sports. *Sport Psychology Today, 7,* 205-222.

Locke, E.A., & Latham, G.P. (1990). *A theory of goal setting and task performance.* Englewood Cliffs, NJ: Prentice-Hall.

Lowrey, G.H. (1986). *Growth and development of children.* Chicago: Year Book Medical.

Loy, J. (1968). The nature of sport: A definitional effort. *Quest, 10,* 1-15.

Luo, L., & Craik, F.I.M. (2008). Aging and memory: A cognitive approach. *La Revue canadienne de psychiatrie, 53*(6), 346-353.

Luria, A.R. (1966). *Higher cortical functions in man.* New York: Basic Books.

Lustig, C., & Meck, W.H. (2001). Paying attention to time as one gets older. *Psychological Science, 12*(6), 478-484.

Lustig, C., Hasher, L., & Tonev, S.T. (2001). Inhibitory control over the present and the past. *European Journal of Cognitive Psychology, 13,* 107-122.

Määttä, S., Pääkkönnen, A., Saavalainen, P., & Partanen, J. (2005). Selective attention event-related potential effects from auditory novel stimuli in children and adults. *Clinical Neurophysiology, 116,* 129-141.

Magill, R.A. (2007). *Motor learning and control: Concepts and applications* (8th ed.). New York: McGraw-Hill.

Malina, R.M. (1978). Growth of muscle tissue and muscle mass. In F. Faulkner & J.M. Tanner (Eds.), *Human growth: A comprehensive treatise.* New York: Plenum Press.

Malina, R.M. (1989). Growth and maturation: Normal variation and the effects of training. In C.V. Gisolfi and D.R. Lamb (Eds.), *Perspectives in exercise science and sports medicine, volume II: Youth, exercise, and sport.* Indianapolis, IN: Benchmark Press.

Malina, R.M., & Bouchard, C. (1991). *Growth, maturation, and physical activity.* Champaign, IL: Human Kinetics.

Malina, R.M., Bouchard, C., & Bar-Or, O. (2004). *Growth, maturation, and physical activity* (2nd ed.). Champaign, IL: Human Kinetics.

Malina, R.M. Bouchard, C., & Beunen, G. (1988). Human growth: Selected aspects of current research on well-nourished children. *Annual Review of Anthropology, 17,* 187-219.

Marisi, D.Q. (1977). Genetic and extragenetic variance in motor performance. *Acta Genetica Medica, 26,* 3-4.

Marshall, J.D., & Bouffard, M. (1994). Obesity and movement competency in children. *Adapted Physical Activity Quarterly, 11,* 297-305.

Marshall, J.D., & Bouffard, M. (1997). The effects of quality daily physical education on movement competency in obese versus nonobese children. *Adapted Physical Activity Quarterly, 14,* 222-237.

Marshall, S.C. (2008). The role of reduced fitness to drive due to medical impairments in explaining crashes involving older drivers. *Traffic Injury Prevention, 9,* 291-298.

Marteniuk, R.G. (1976). *Information processing in motor skills.* New York: Holt, Rinehart & Winston.

Martens, R., Burwitz, L., & Zuckerman, J. (1976). Modeling effects on motor performance. *Research Quarterly, 47,* 277-291.

Martin, K.A., Moritz, S.A., & Hall, C.R. (1999). Imagery use in sport: A literature review and applied model. *Sport Psychologist, 13,* 245-268.

McArdle, W., Katch, F., & Katch, V. (2001). *Exercise physiology: Energy, nutrition, and human performance* (5th ed.). Philadelphia: Lippincott Williams & Wilkins.

McAuley, E. (1992). The role of efficacy cognitions in the prediction of exercise behaviour in middle aged adults. *Journal of Behavioral Medicine, 15,* 65-88.

McCaskill, C.L., & Wellman, B.L. (1938). A study of common motor achievements at the pre-school ages. *Child Development, 9,* 141.

McCleneghan, B.A., & Gallahue, D.L. (1978). *Fundamental movement: Observation and assessment.* Philadelphia: Saunders.

McCullagh, P., & Weiss, M.R. (2001). Modeling: Considerations for motor skill performance and psychological responses. In R.N. Singer, H.A. Hausenblas, & C.M. Janelle (Eds.), *Handbook of sport psychology* (2nd ed., pp. 205-238). New York: Wiley.

McGraw, M. (1935). *Growth: A study of Johnny and Jimmy.* New York: Appleton-Century-Crofts.

McGraw, M.B. (1940). Signals of growth. *Child Study, 18,* 8-10.

McGraw, M.B. (1969). *The neuromuscular maturation of the human infant.* New York: Hafner. (Original work published in 1945)

McKiddie, B., & Maynard, I.W. (1997). Perceived competence of school children in physical education. *Journal of Teaching in Physical Education, 16,* 324-339.

McPherson, S.L., & Kernodle, M.W. (2003). Tactics, the neglected attribute of expertise. In J.L. Starkes & K.A. Ericsson (Eds.), *Expert performance in sports* (pp. 137-167). Champaign, IL: Human Kinetics.

Meaney, K.S. (1994). Developmental modeling effects on the acquisition, retention, and transfer of a novel motor task. *Research Quarterly for Exercise and Sport, 65,* 31-39.

Meltzer, D.E. (1994). Age dependence of Olympic weightlifting ability. *Medicine and Science in Sports and Exercise, 26*(8), 1053-1067.

Menickelli, J., Landin, D., Grisham, W., & Hebert, E. (2000). The effects of videotape feedback with augmented cues on the performances and thought processes of skilled gymnasts. *Journal of Sport Pedagogy, 6,* 56-72.

Michaels, C.F., & Carello, C. (1981). *Direct perception.* Englewood Cliffs, NJ: Prentice-Hall.

Michels, T.C., & Kugler, J.P. (1988). Predicting exercise in older Americans: Using the theory of planned behavior. *Military Medicine, 16*(8), 524-529.

Mihalik, B.J., O'Leary, J.T., Mcguire, F.A., & Dottavio, F.D. (1989). Sports involvement across the life span: Expansion and contraction of sports activities. *Research Quarterly for Exercise and Sport, 60*(4), 396-398.

Miller, G.A. (1956). The magical number seven plus or minus two: Some limits on our capacity for processing information. *Psychological Review, 63,* 81-97.

Millodot, M. (1977). The influence of age on the sensitivity of the cornea. *Investigative Ophthalmology & Visual Science, 16*(3), 240-242.

Mitchell, S., & Oslin, J. (2007). Ecological task analysis in games teaching: The tactical games model. In W. Davis & G. Broadhead (Eds.), *An ecological approach to human movement: Linking theory, research and practice.* Champaign, IL: Human Kinetics.

Mokdad, A., Serdula, M., Dietz, W., Bowman, B., Marks, J., & Koplan, J. (1999). The spread of the obesity epidemic in the United States, 1991-1998. *Journal of the American Medical Association, 282,* 1519-1522.

Molander, B., & Bäckman, L. (1989). Age differences in heart rate patterns during concentration in a precision sport: Implications for attentional functioning. *Journal of Gerontology: Psychological Sciences, 44,* P80-P87.

Molander, B., & Bäckman, L. (1994). Attention and performance in miniature golf across the life span. *Journal of Gerontology: Psychological Sciences, 49*(2), P35-P41.

Mononen, K., Viitasalo, J.T., Konttinen, N., & Era, P. (2003). The effects of augmented kinematic feedback on motor skill learning in rifle shooting. *Journal of Sports Sciences, 21,* 867-876.

Morgan, D.W., & Craig, M. (1992). Physiological aspects of running economy. *Medicine and Science in Sports and Exercise, 24,* 456-461.

Morris, G.S. (1980). *Elementary physical education: Toward inclusion.* Salt Lake City: Brighton.

Morris, L. (2001). Going through a bad spell: What the spelling errors of young ESL learners reveal about their grammatical knowledge. *Canadian Modern Language Review, 58,* 273-286.

Mosston, M., & Ashworth, S. (2002). *Teaching physical education* (5th ed.). Boston: Benjamin Cummings.

Mount, J. (1996). Effect of practice of a throwing skill in one body position on performance of the skill in an alternate position. *Perceptual and Motor Skills, 83,* 723-732.

Moxley, S.E. (1979). Schema: The variability of practice hypothesis. *Journal of Motor Behavior, 2,* 65-70.

Murray, M.P., Kory, R.C., & Sepic, B.C. (1970). Walking patterns of normal women. *Archives of Physical Medicine and Rehabilitation, 51,* 637-650.

National Highway Traffic Safety Administration. (2000). *Traffic safety facts 2000. National Center for Statistics and Analysis, Research and Development.* Overview DOT HS 809 329. Washington, DC: National Highway Traffic Safety Administration.

National Institutes of Health. (2007). Osteoporosis and Related Bone Diseases National Resource Center. www.osteo.org.

Naylor, J.C., & Briggs, G.E. (1963). Effects of task complexity and task organization on the relative efficiency of part and whole training methods. *Journal of Experimental Psychology, 65,* 217-224.

Nelson, C.J. (1981). Locomotor patterns of women over 57. Unpublished master's thesis, Washington State University, Pullman.

Neuman, A.C., & Hochberg, I. (1983). Children's perception of speech in reverberation. *Journal of the Acoustical Society of America, 73,* 2145-2149.

Neumann, O. (1984). On controlled and automatic processes. In W. Prinz & A. Sanders (Eds.), *Cognition and motor processes* (pp. 225-295). New York: Springer.

Newell, K.M. (1981). Skill learning. In D. Holding (Ed.), *Human skills* (pp. 203-226). New York: Wiley.

Newell, K.M. (1984). Physical constraints to development of motor skills. In J.R. Thomas (Ed.), *Motor development during childhood and adolescence* (pp. 105-120). Minneapolis: Burgess.

Newell, K.M. (1986). Constraints on the development of coordination. In M.G. Wade & H.T.A Whiting (Eds.), *Motor development in children: Aspects of coordination and control* (pp. 341-360). Dordrecht, The Netherlands: Martinus Nijhoff.

Newell, K.M., & Carlton, M.J. (1987). Augmented information feedback and the acquisition of isometric tasks. *Journal of Motor Behavior, 19,* 4-12.

Newell, K.M., & McDonald, P.V. (1992). Searching for solutions to the coordination function: Learning as exploratory behavior. *Advances in Psychology, 87,* 517-532.

Newell, K.M., & Rosenbloom, P.S. (1981). Mechanisms of skill acquisition and the law of practice. In J.R. Anderson (Ed.), *Cognitive skills and their acquisition* (pp. 1-55). Hillsdale, NJ: Erlbaum.

Newell, K.M., & van Emmerik, R.E.A. (1989). The acquisition of coordination: Preliminary analysis of learning to write. *Human Movement Science, 8,* 17-32.

Newell, K.M., & Walter, C.B. (1981). Kinematic and kinetic parameters as information feedback in motor skill acquisition. *Journal of Human Movement Studies, 7,* 235-254.

Newell, K.M., Kugler, P.N., van Emmerik, R.E.A., & McDonald, P.V. (1989). Search strategies and the acquisition of coordination. In S.A. Wallace (Ed.), *Perspectives on the coordination of movement* (pp. 85-122). Amsterdam: North-Holland.

Newell, K.M., Quinn, J.T. Jr., Sparrow, W.A., & Walter, C.B. (1983). Kinematic information feedback for learning a simple rapid response. *Human Movement Science, 2,* 255-270.

Nicholls, J.G. (1989). *The competitive ethos and democratic education.* Cambridge, MA: Harvard University Press.

Niinimaa, V., & Shephard, R.J. (1978). Training and exercise conductance in the elderly. II. The cardiovascular system. *Journal of Gerontology, 35,* 672-682.

Nillsson, B.E., & Westlin, N.E. (1971). Bone density in athletes. *Clinical Orthopaedics, 77,* 179-182.

Ntoumanis, N. (2001). A self-determination approach to the understanding of motivation in physical education. *British Journal of Educational Psychology, 71,* 225-242.

Ornstein, P.A., & Naus, M.J. (1978). Rehearsal processes in children's memory. In P.A. Ornstein (Ed.), *Memory development in children.* Hillsdale, NJ: Erlbaum.

Owsley, C., & Ball, K. (1993). Assessing visual function in the older driver. *Clinics in Geriatric Medicine, 9*(2), 389-401.

Paterson, D.H., Cunningham, D.A., & Babcock, M.A. (1989). Oxygen kinetics in the elderly. In G.D. Swanson, F.S. Grodins, & R.L. Hughson (Eds.), *Respiratory control: A modelling perspective* (pp. 171-178). New York: Plenum Press.

Payne, G.V., & Isaacs, L.D. (2008). *Human life motor development: A lifespan approach* (7th ed.). New York: McGraw-Hill.

Pease, D.G., & Pupnow, A.A. (1983). Effects of varying force production in practice schedules of children learning a discrete motor task. *Perceptual and Motor Skills, 57,* 275-282.

Pèrez, P., Liana, S., Brizuela, G., & Encarnación, A. (2009). Effects of three feedback conditions on aerobic swim speeds. *Journal of Sports Science and Medicine, 8,* 30-36.

Petlichkoff, L.M. (2004). Self-regulation skills for children and adolescents. In M.R. Weiss (Ed.), *Developmental sport and exercise psychology: A lifespan perspective* (pp. 269-288). Morgantown, WV: Fitness Information Technology.

Piek, J.P. (2006). *Infant motor development.* Champaign, IL: Human Kinetics.

Pigott, R.E., & Shapiro, D.C. (1984). Motor schema: The structure of the variability session. *Research Quarterly for Exercise and Sport, 55,* 41-45.

Polit, A., & Bizzi, E. (1978). Processes controlling arm movements in monkeys. *Science, 201*(4362), 1235-1237.

Pollock, B.J., & Lee, T.D. (1997). Dissociated contextual interference effects in children and adults. *Perceptual and Motor Skills, 84,* 851-858.

Poole, C., Miller, S.A., & Booth Church, E. (2006). Ages & stages: All about body awareness. *Early Childhood Today.* www2.scholastic.com/browse/article.jsp?id=10573.

Proffitt, D.R., Bhalla, M., Gossweiler, R., & Midgett, K. (1995). Perceiving geographical slant. *Psychonomic Bulletin & Review, 2,* 409-428.

Proteau, L. (1992). On the specificity of learning and the role of visual information for movement control. In L. Proteau & D. Elliott (Eds.), *Vision and motor control* (pp. 67-103). Amsterdam: North Holland.

Proteau, L., Blandin, Y., Alain, C., & Dorion, A. (1994). The effects of the amount and variability of practice on the learning of a multi-segmented motor task. *Acta Psychologia (Amst), 85,* 61-74.

Proteau, L., Marteniuk, R.G., Girourd, Y., & Dugas, C. (1987). On the type of information used to control and learn an aiming movement after moderate and extensive training. *Human Movement Science, 6,* 181-199.

Ranganathan, V.K., Siemionow, V., Sahgal, V., Liu, J.Z., & Yue, G.H. (2001). Skilled finger movement exercise improves hand function. *Journal of Gerontology A: Biological Science and Medical Science, 56,* M518-522.

Ratey, J.J. (2001). *A user's guide to the brain: Perception, attention, and the four theaters of the brain.* New York: Vintage Books.

Rehling, S.L. (1996). Longitudinal differences in overarm throwing velocity and qualitative throwing techniques of elementary boys and girls. Unpublished doctoral dissertation, Arizona State University, Tucson.

Reid, G. (1980a). Overt and covert rehearsal in short-term motor memory of mentally retarded and nonretarded persons. *American Journal of Mental Deficiency, 85,* 69-77.

Reid, G. (1980b). The effects of memory strategy instruction in short term motor memory of the mentally retarded. *Journal of Motor Behavior, 112,* 221-227.

Reider, B. (2008). Live long and prosper. *American Journal of Sports Medicine, 36*(3), 441-442.

Rhodes, R.E., Martin, A.D., Taunton, J.E., Rhodes, E.C., Donnelly, M., & Elliot, J. (1999). Factors associated with exercise adherence among older adults: An individual perspective. *Sports Medicine, 28*(6), 397-411.

Ribadi, H., Rider, R., & Toole, T. (1987). Comparison of static and dynamic balance in congenitally blind, sighted, and sighted blindfolded adolescents. *Physical Activity Quarterly. 4,* 220-225.

Ries, W. (1994). The determination of biological age. In A.K. Balin (Ed.), *Practical handbook of biologic age determination* (pp. 173-180). Boca Raton, FL: CRC Press.

Ringenbach, S.D.R., & Lantero, D.A. (2005). Bimanual coordination preferences in adults with Down syndrome. *Adapted Physical Activity Quarterly, 22,* 83-98.

Rink, J. (1998). Teaching concepts and content-specific pedagogy. In *Teaching physical education for learning* (pp. 281-292). Boston: McGraw-Hill.

Roberton, M.A. (1977). Stability of stage categorizations across trials: Implications for the "stage theory" of overarm throw development. *Journal of Human Movement Studies, 3,* 49-59.

Roberton, M.A., & Halverson, L.E. (1984). *Developing children: Their changing movement.* Philadelphia: Lea & Febiger.

Roberton, M.A., & Konczak, J. (2001). Predicting children's overarm throw ball velocities from their developmental levels in throwing. *Research Quarterly for Exercise and Sport, 72,* 91-103.

Roberts, T., & Brown, L. (2008). Learn more in less time: Fundamental aquatic skill acquisition via video technology. *Strategies, 21,* 20-31.

Robertson, S.D., Tremblay, L., Anson, J.G., & Elliott, D. (2002). Learning to cross a balance beam: Implications for teachers, coaches and therapists. In K. Davids, G. Savelsbergh, S. Bennett, & J. van der Kamps (Eds.), *Dynamic interception actions in sport: Current research and practical applications* (pp. 109-125). London: Taylor and Francis.

Rode, A., Shephard, R.J., Vloshinsky, P.E., & Kuksis, A. (1995). Plasma fatty acid profiles of Canadian Inuit and Siberian nGanasan. *Arctic Medical Research, 54,* 10-20.

Rook, K.S. (2000). The evolution of social relationships in later adulthood. In S.H. Qualls & N. Abeles

(Eds.), *Psychology and the aging revolution.* Washington, DC: American Psychological Association.

Rose, D.J., & Christina, R.W. (2006). *A multilevel approach to the study of motor control and learning* (2nd ed.). San Francisco: Pearson Benjamin Cummings.

Rosenbaum, D.A. (2010). *Human motor control* (2nd ed.). Amsterdam: Academic Press.

Rosenblum, S., & Werner, P. (2005). Assessing the handwriting process in healthy elderly persons using a computerized system. *Aging Clinical and Experimental Research, 18*(5), 433-439.

Rovee Collier, C.K., Sullivan, M.W., Enright, M., Lucas, D., & Fagen, J.W. (1980). Reactivation of infant memory. *Science, 208*(4448), 1159-1161.

Rumelhart, D.E., & Norman, D.A. (1982). Simulating a skilled typist: A study of skilled cognitive-motor performance. *Cognitive Science, 6,* 1-36.

Runion, B., Roberton, M.A., & Langendorfer, S.J. (2003). Forceful overarm throwing: A comparison of two cohorts measured 20 years apart. *Research Quarterly for Exercise and Sport, 74,* 334-330.

Ryan, R.M., & Deci, E.L. (2000). Self-determination theory and the facilitation of intrinsic motivation, social development, and well-being. *American Psychologist, 55,* 68-78.

Sabari, J.S. (2001). Teaching activities in occupation therapy. In L.W. Pedretti & M.B. Early (Eds.), *Occupational therapy: Practice skills for physical dysfunction* (5th ed., pp. 83-90). Philadelphia: Mosby.

Sachs, C., Hamberger, B., & Kaijser, L. (1985). Cardiovascular responses and plasma catecholamines in old age. *Clinical Physiology, 5,* 239-249.

Salmoni, A.W., Schmidt, R.A., & Walter, C.B. (1984). Knowledge of results and motor learning: A review and critical appraisal. *Psychological Bulletin, 95,* 355-386.

Savelsbergh, G., Davids, K., van der Kamp, J., & Bennett, J. (2003). *Development of movement coordination in children: Applications in the field of ergonomics, health sciences and sport.* New York: Routledge.

Sawner, K., & LaVigne, J. (1992). *Brunnstrom's movement therapy in hemiplegia: A neurophysiological approach* (2nd ed.). Philadelphia: Lippincott.

Saxon, S.V., Etten, M.J., & Perkins, E.A. (2010). *Physical change & aging: A guide for the helping professions* (5th ed.). New York: Springer.

Schaie, K.W., & Willis, S.L. (1991). *Adult development and aging* (3rd ed.). New York: Harper Collins.

Schieber, F. (1992). Aging and the senses. In J.E. Birren, R.B. Sloane, & G.D. Cohen (Eds.), *Handbook of mental health and aging* (2nd ed., pp. 252-306). San Diego: Academic Press.

Schmidt, R.A. (1975a). *Motor skills.* New York: Harper & Row.

Schmidt, R.A. (1975b). The schema theory of discrete motor skill learning. *Psychological Review, 82,* 225-260.

Schmidt, R.A. (1991). Frequent augmented feedback can degrade learning: Evidence and interpretations. In G.E. Stelmach & J. Requin (Eds.), *Tutorials in motor neuroscience* (pp. 59-75). Norwell, MA: Kluwer Academic.

Schmidt, R.A., & Lee, T.D. (2005). *Motor control and learning: A behavioral emphasis* (4th ed.). Champaign, IL: Human Kinetics.

Schmidt, R.A., & Wrisberg, C.A. (2008). *Motor learning and performance: A situation-based learning approach* (4th ed.). Champaign, IL: Human Kinetics.

Schmidt, R.A., & Young, D.E. (1991). Methodology for motor learning: A paradigm for kinematic feedback. *Journal of Motor Behavior, 23,* 13-24.

Schrauf, M., Wist, E.R., & Ehrenstein, W.H. (1999). Development of dynamic vision based on motion contrast. *Experimental Brain Research, 124,* 469-473.

Schultheis, L. (1991). The mechanical control system of bone in weightless spaceflight and in aging. *Experimental Gerontology, 26,* 203-214.

Schulz, R., & Curnow, C. (1988). Peak performance and age among superathletes: Track and field, swimming, baseball, tennis, and golf. *Journal of Gerontology, 43*(5), 113-120.

Schwartz, R. (1990). Body fat distribution in healthy young and older men. *Journal of Gerontology, 46*(6), 181-185.

Scully, D.M., & Newell, K.M. (1985). Observational learning and the acquisition of motor skills: Towards a visual perception perspective. *Journal of Human Movement Studies, 11,* 169-186.

Seefeldt, V., & Haubenstricker, J. (1975). Developmental sequence of kicking (rev. ed.). Unpublished research, Michigan State University, East Lansing.

Seefeldt, V., & Haubenstricker, J. (1976). Developmental sequences of fundamental movement skills. Unpublished research, Michigan State University, East Lansing.

Seidentop, D., & Tannehill, D. (2000). *Developing teaching skills in physical education* (4th ed.). Mountain View, CA: Mayfield.

Seligman, M. (1975). *Helplessness: On depression, development, and death.* San Francisco: Freeman.

Shaffer, D. (1999). *Developmental psychology: Childhood and adolescence* (5th ed.). Pacific Grove, CA: Brookes/Cole.

Shank, M.D., & Haywood, K.M. (1987). Eye movements while viewing a baseball pitch. *Perceptual and Motor Skills, 64,* 1191-1197.

Shea, J.B., & Morgan, R.L. (1979). Contextual interference effects on the acquisition, retention, and transfer of a motor skill. *Journal of Experimental Psychology: Human Learning and Memory, 5,* 179-187.

Shephard, R.J. (1991). Fitness and aging. In C. Blais (Ed.), *Aging into the twenty-first century* (pp. 22-35). Downsview, Ontario: Captus University.

Shephard, R.J. (1993). *Health and aerobic fitness.* Champaign, IL: Human Kinetics.

Shephard, R.J. (1994). Determinants of exercise in people aged 65 years and older. In R.K. Dishman (Ed.), *Advances in exercise adherence* (pp. 343-360). Champaign, IL: Human Kinetics.

Shephard, R.J. (1997). *Aging, physical activity, and health.* Champaign, IL: Human Kinetics.

Shephard, R.J. (1998). Aging and exercise. In T.D. Fahey (Ed.), *Encyclopedia of sports medicine and science.* Internet Society for Sport Science. http://sportsci.org.

Sherwood, D.E. (1988). Effect of bandwidth knowledge of results on movement consistency. *Perceptual and Motor Skills, 66,* 535-542.

Shiffman, L.M. (1992). Effects of aging on adult hand function. *American Journal of Occupational Therapy, 46,* 785-792.

Shirley, M.M. (1931). *The first two years: A study of twenty-five babies. Vol. 1: Postural and locomotor development.* Minneapolis: University of Minnesota Press.

Siedentop, D. (2007). *Introduction to physical education, fitness, and sport* (6th ed.). Boston: McGraw-Hill.

Siedentop, D., & Tannehill, D. (2000). *Developing teaching skills in physical education.* Mountain View, CA: Mayfield.

Singer, R.N. (2002). Preperformance state, routines, and automaticity: What does it take to realize expertise in self-paced events? *Journal of Sport and Exercise Psychology, 24,* 359-375.

Snoddy, G.S. (1926). Learning and stability: A psychophysical analysis of a case of motor learning with clinical applications. *Journal of Applied Psychology, 10,* 1-36.

Snowdon, D.A. (2003). Healthy aging and dementia: Findings from the nun study. *Annals of Internal Medicine, 139*(5), 450-454.

Soberlak, P., & Côtè, J. (2003). The developmental activities of elite ice hockey players. *Journal of Applied Sport Psychology, 15,* 41-49.

Soucy, M-C., & Proteau, L. (2001). Development of multiple movement representations with practice: Specificity versus flexibility. *Journal of Motor Behavior, 33,* 243-254.

Sparrow, W.A. (1992). Measuring changes in coordination and control. In J.J. Summers (Ed.) *Approaches to the study of motor control and learning* (pp. 147-162). Amsterdam; New York: North-Holland.

Sparrow, W.A., & Newell, K.M. (1994). Energy expenditure and motor performance relationships in humans learning a motor task. *Psychophysiology, 31,* 338-346.

Spirduso, W.W., Francis, K.L., & MacRae, P.G. (2005). *Physical dimensions of aging* (2nd ed.). Champaign, IL: Human Kinetics.

Starkes, J.L., & Allard, F. (1991). Motor-skill experts in sports, dance, and other domains. In K.A. Ericsson & J. Smith (Eds.), *Towards a general theory of expertise: Prospects and limits* (pp. 126-152). Cambridge: Cambridge University Press.

Starkes, J.L., & Ericsson, K.A. (Eds.). (2003). *Expert performance in sports.* Champaign, IL: Human Kinetics.

Starkes, J.L., Deakin, J.M., Lindley, S., & Crisp, F. (1987). Motor versus verbal recall of ballet sequences by young expert dancers. *Journal of Sport Psychology, 9,* 222-230.

Steffen, T.M., Hacker, T.A., & Mollinger, L. (2002). Age and gender-related test performance in community-dwelling elderly people: Six-minute walk test, Berg balance scale, timed up & go test, and gait speeds. *Physical Therapy, 82*(2), 128-137.

Ste-Marie, D. (2003). Expertise in sport judges and referees: Circumventing information processing limitations. In J.L. Starkes & K.A. Ericsson (Eds.), *Expert performance in sports* (19-47). Champaign, IL: Human Kinetics.

Ste-Marie, D.M., Clark, S.E., Findlay, L.C., & Latimer, A.E. (2004). High levels of contextual interference influence handwriting skill writing acquisition. *Journal of Motor Behavior, 36,* 115-126.

Stephens, T., & Craig, C.L. (1990). *The well-being of Canadians: Highlights of the 1988 Campbell's Soup Survey.* Ottawa: Canadian Fitness and Lifestyle Research Institute.

Sugden, D.A. (1978). Visual motor short term memory in educationally subnormal boys. *British Journal of Educational Psychology, 48,* 330-339.

Sutherland, D. (1997). The development of mature gait. *Gait and Posture 6,* 163-170.

Svänborg, A., Eden, S., & Mellstrom, D. (1991). Metabolic changes in aging as predictors of disease: The Swedish experience. In D.K. Ingram, G.T. Baker, & N.W. Shock (Eds.), *The potential for nutritional modulation of aging* (pp. 81-90). Trumbull, CT: Food & Nutrition Press.

Swinnen, P.S. (1996). Information feedback for motor skill learning: A review. In H.N. Zelaznik (Ed.), *Advances in motor learning and control* (pp. 37-66). Champaign, IL: Human Kinetics.

Swinnen, P.S., Schmidt, R.A., Nicholson, D.E., & Shapiro, D.C. (1990). Information feedback for skill acquisition: Instantaneous knowledge of results degrades learning. *Journal of Experimental Psychology: Learning, Memory and Cognition, 16,* 706-716.

Talvoć, M., Hodžić, M., Bajramović, I., Jelešković, E., & Alić, H. (2009). Influence of the motor and functional abilities to the efficiency of football techniques elements performance. *Homo Sporticus, 11*(1): 41-44.

Tanaka, H., & Seals, D.R. (2003). Dynamic exercise performance in Masters athletes: Insight into the effects of primary human aging on physiological functional capacity. *Journal of Applied Physiology, 95,* 2152-2162.

Tanner, J.M., Whitehouse, R.H., & Takaishi, M. (1966). Standards from birth to maturity for height, weight, height velocity and weight velocity in British children. *Archives of Disease in Childhood, 41,* 613-635.

Tate, C., Hyek, M., & Taffet, G. (1994). Mechanisms for the response of cardiac muscle to physical activity in old age. *Medicine and Science in Sports and Exercise, 26*(5), 561-567.

Tauer, J.M., & Harackiewicz, J.M. (2004). The effects of cooperation and competition on intrinsic motivation and performance. *Journal of Personality and Social Psychology, 86,* 849-861.

Thapa, P., Gideon, P., Fought, R., Kormicki, M., & Ray, W. (1994). Comparison of clinical and biomechanical measures of balance and mobility in elderly nursing home residents. *Journal of the American Geriatrics Society, 42,* 493-500.

Thelen, E. (1995). Motor development: A new synthesis. *American Psychologist, 50*(2), 79-95.

Thelen, E., & Smith, L.B. (1994). *A dynamic processes approach to development of cognition and action.* Cambridge, MA: MIT Press/Bradford.

Thelen, E., & Ulrich, B.D. (1991). Hidden skills: A dynamic systems analysis of treadmill stepping during the first year. *Monographs of the Society for Research in Child Development, 56,* (1, Serial No. 223).

Thelen, E., Fisher, D.M., Ridley-Johnson, R., & Griffin, N.J. (1982). Effects of body build and arousal on newborn infant stepping. *Developmental Psychobiology, 15*(5), 447-453.

Thelen, E., Ulrich, B.D., & Jensen, J.L. (1989). The developmental origins of locomotion. In M.H. Woolacott & A. Shumway-Cook (Eds.), *Development of posture and gait across the lifespan* (pp. 25-47). Columbia, SC: University of South Carolina Press.

Thomas, J.R., Thomas, K.T., & Gallagher, J.D. (1993). Developmental considerations in skill acquisition. In R.N. Singer, M. Murphey, & L.K. Tennant (Eds.), *Handbook of research on sport psychology* (pp. 73-105). New York: Macmillan.

Thomas, W.H., Sorensen, K.L., & Abby. L.T. (2006). Locus of control at work: A meta-analysis. *Journal of Organizational Behavior, 27,* 1057-1087.

Thorndike, E.L. (1914). *Educational psychology.* New York: Columbia University.

Thorndike, E.L. (1931). *Human learning.* New York: Century.

Thorpe, R., Bunker, D., & Almond, L. (1986). *Rethinking games teaching.* Loughborough: University of Technology, Loughborough.

Timiras, P.S. (1972). *Developmental physiology and aging.* New York: Macmillan.

Tseng, M.H., & Cermak, S.A. (1993). The influence of ergonomic factors and perceptual-motor abilities on handwriting performance. *American Journal of Occupational Therapy, 47,* 919-926.

Tulving, E. (1985). How many memory systems are there? *American Psychologist, 40,* 385-398.

Tulving, E. (2002), Episodic memory: From mind to brain. *Annual Review of Psychology, 53,* 1-25.

Turvey, M.T. (1990). Coordination. *American Psychologist, 45*(8), 938-953.

U.S. Department of Health and Human Services. (2008). *2008 physical activity guidelines for Americans: Be active, healthy, and happy!* Washington, DC: U.S. Department of Health and Human Services.

U.S. National Center for Health Statistics. (1981). Basic data from wave I of the National Survey of Personal Health Practices and Consequences: United States, 1979. *Vital and Health Statistics, Series 15, Nos. 1 and 2.* Hyattsville, MD: U.S. Department of Health and Human Services.

Ulrich, B.D., Ulrich, D.A., & Collier, D.H. (1992). Alternating stepping patterns: Hidden abilities of 11-month-old infants with Down syndrome. *Developmental Medicine and Child Neurology, 34,* 233-239.

Ulrich, D.A., Ulrich, B.D., Angulo-Kinzler, R.M., & Yun, J. (2001). Treadmill training of infants with down syndrome: Evidence-based developmental outcomes. *Pediatrics, 108,* 84-91.

Vallerand, R.J. (1997). Toward a hierarchical model of intrinsic and extrinsic motivation. In M.P. Zanna (Ed.), *Advances in experimental social psychology: Vol. 2* (pp. 271-360). New York: Academic Press.

Vallerand, R.J. (2007). Intrinsic and extrinsic motivation in sport and physical activity: A review and a look at the future. In G. Tenenbaum & E. Eklund (Eds.), *Handbook of sport psychology* (3rd ed., pp. 49-83). New York: Wiley.

Valois, P., Shephard, R.J., & Godin, G. (1986). Relationship of habit and perceived physical ability to exercise behavior. *Perceptual and Motor Skills, 62,* 811-817.

Van Norman, K. (1995). *Exercise programming for older adults.* Champaign, IL: Human Kinetics.

Vera, J.G., Alvarez, J.C., & Medina, M.M. (2008). Effects of different practice conditions on acquisition, retention, and transfer of soccer skills by 9 year old school children. *Perceptual and Motor Skills, 106,* 447-460.

Vereijken, B. (1991). The dynamics of skill acquisition. Unpublished doctoral dissertation. Free University, Amsterdam.

Vereijken, B., van Emmerik, R.E.A., Whiting, H.T.A., & Newell, K.M. (1992). Free(z)ing degrees of freedom in skill acquisition. *Journal of Motor Behavior, 24*(1), 133-142.

Verhaeghen, P., Steitz, W.D., Sliwinski, M.J., & Cerella, J. (2003). Aging and dual-task performance: A meta-analysis, *Psychology and Aging, 18,* 443-460.

Vickers, J.N. (2007). *Perception, cognition, and decision training.* Champaign, IL: Human Kinetics.

Visser, J., & Geuze, R.H. (2000). Kinaesthetic acuity in adolescent boys: A longitudinal study. *Developmental Medicine & Child Neurology, 42,* 93-96.

Voss, D.E., Ionta, M.K., & Myers, B.J. (1985). *Proprioceptive neuromuscular facilitation* (3rd ed.). Philadelphia: Harper & Row.

Vouloumanos, A., & Werker, J.F. (2004). Turned to the signal: The privileged status of speech for young infants. *Developmental Status, 7,* 270-276.

Wall, A.E., McClements, J., Bouffard, M., Findlay, H., & Taylor, J. (1985). A knowledge-based approach to motor development: Implications for the physically awkward. *Adapted Physical Activity Quarterly, 2,* 21-42.

Wall, A.E., Reid, G., & Harvey, W.J. (2007). Interface of the KB and ETA approaches. In W.E. Davis & G.D. Broadhead (Eds.), *Ecological task analysis and movement* (pp. 259-277). Champaign, IL: Human Kinetics.

Wall III, C., & Kentala, E. (2005). Control of sway using vibrotactile feedback of body tilt in patients with moderate and severe postural control deficits. *Journal of Vestibular Research, 15,* 313-325.

Wang, L. (2008). The kinetics and stiffness characteristics of the lower extremity in older adults during vertical jumping. *Journal of Sports Science and Medicine, 7,* 379-386.

Warren, W.H. Jr. (1984). Perceiving affordances: Visual guidance of stair climbing. *Journal of Experimental Psychology: Human Perception and Performance, 10,* 683-703.

Waschall, S.B., & Kernis, M.H. (1996). Level and stability of self-esteem as predictors of children's intrinsic motivation and reactions to anger. *Personality and Social Psychology Bulletin, 22,* 4-13.

Wattam-Bell, J. (1996). Visual motion processing in one month old infants: Habituation experiments. *Vision Research, 36,* 1679-1685.

Weale, R. (1963). New light on old eyes. *Nature, 198,* 944-946.

Weeks, D.L. (1992). A comparison of modeling modalities in the observational learning of an externally paced skill. *Research Quarterly for Exercise and Sport, 63,* 373-380.

Weeks, D.L., & Anderson, L.P. (2000). The interaction of observational learning with overt practice: Effects on motor learning. *Acta Psychologica, 104,* 259-271.

Weeks, D.L., & Sherwood, D.E. (1994). A comparison of knowledge of results scheduling methods for promoting motor skill acquisition and retention. *Research Quarterly for Exercise and Sport, 65*(2), 136-142.

Weinberg, R.S., & Gould, D. (2003). *Foundations of sport and exercise psychology* (3rd ed.). Champaign, IL: Human Kinetics.

Weiner, B. (1985). An attribution theory of achievement motivation and emotion. *Psychological Review, 92,* 548-573.

Weiss, M.R. (1983). Modeling and motor performance: A developmental perspective. *Research Quarterly for Exercise and Sport, 54,* 190-197.

Weiss, M.R. (2004). *Developmental sport and exercise psychology: A lifespan perspective.* Morgantown, WV: Fitness Information Technology.

Weiss, M.R., & Stuntz, C.P. (2004). A little friendly competition: Peer relationships and psychosocial development in youth sport and physical activity contexts. In M.R. Weiss (Ed.), *Developmental sport and exercise psychology: A lifespan perspective* (pp. 165-196). Morgantown, WV: Fitness Information Technology.

Weiss, M.R., & Williams, L. (2004). The why of youth sport involvement: A developmental perspective on motivational processes. In M.R. Weiss (Ed.), *Developmental sport and exercise psychology: A lifespan perspective* (pp. 223-268). Morgantown, WV: Fitness Information Technology.

Weiss, M.R., Ebbeck, V., & Wiese-Bjornstal, D.M. (1993). Developmental and psychological factors related to children's observational learning of physical skills. *Pediatric Exercise Science, 5,* 301-317.

Weiss, M.R., McCullagh, P., Smith, A.L., & Berlant, A.R. (1998). Observational learning and the fearful child: Influence of peer models on swimming skill performance and psychological responses. *Research Quarterly for Exercise and Sport, 69,* 380-394.

Werner, P., & Almond, L. (1990). Models of games education. *Journal of Physical Education, Recreation and Dance, 61*(4), 23-27.

Werner, P., Thorpe, R., & Bunker, D. (1996). Teaching games for understanding: The evolution of a model. *Journal of Physical Education, Recreation and Dance, 67*(1), 28-33.

Weymouth, F. (1960). Comments on "dynamic myopia." *American Journal of Optometry and Archives of American Academy of Optometry, 37,* 148-150.

Whitall, J. (2003). Development of locomotor coordination and control in children. In G. Savelsbergh, K. Davids, J. Van der Kamp, & S. Bennett. (2003). *Development of movement co-ordination in children: Applications in the field of ergonomics, health sciences and sport* (pp. 251-270). New York: Routledge.

White, R.W. (1959). Motivation reconsidered: The concept of competence. *Psychological Review, 66,* 297-330.

Wickens, C.D. (1980). The structure of processing resources. In R. Nickerson (Ed.), *Attention and performance VII* (pp. 239-257). Hillsdale, NJ: Erlbaum.

Wickens, C.D. (1992). *Engineering psychology and human performance* (2nd ed.). New York: HarperCollins.

Wickens, C.D., & and Benel, D.C.R. (1982). The development of time-sharing skills. In J.A.S. Kelso & J.E. Clark (Eds.), *The development of movement control and coordination* (pp. 253-272). New York: Wiley.

Wickstrom, R.L. (1983). *Fundamental motor patterns* (3rd ed.). Philadelphia: Lea & Febiger.

Wiese-Bjornstal, D.M., & Weiss, M.R. (1992). Modeling effects on children's form kinematics, performance outcome, and cognitive recognition of a sport skill: An integrated perspective. *Research Quarterly for Exercise and Sport, 63,* 67-75.

Wilcox, S., & Storandt, M. (1996). Relations among age, exercise, and psychological variables in a community sample of women. *Health Psychology, 15*(2), 110-113.

Wild, M. (1938). The behavior pattern of throwing and some observations concerning its course of development in children. *Research Quarterly, 9*(3), 20.

Williams, A.M., & Davids, K. (1998). Visual search strategy, selective attention, and expertise in soccer. *Research Quarterly for Exercise and Sport, 69,* 127-135.

Williams, A.M., & Hodges, N.J. (2005). Practice, instruction and skill acquisition in soccer: Challenging tradition. *Journal of Sports Sciences, 23,* 637-650.

Williams, A.M., Ward, P., Smeeton, N.J., & Allen, D. (2004). Developing anticipation skills in tennis using on-court instruction: Perception versus perception and action. *Journal of Applied Sport Psychology, 16,* 350-360.

Williams, H.G. (1983). *Perceptual and motor development.* Englewood Cliffs, NJ: Prentice-Hall.

Williams, J.G. (1989). Visual demonstrations and movement production: Effects of timing variations in a model's action. *Perceptual and Motor Skills, 68,* 891-896.

Williams, J.M., & Leffingwell, T.R. (1996). Cognitive strategies in sport and exercise psychology. In J.L. Van Raalte & B.W. Brewer (Eds.), *Exploring sport and exercise psychology* (pp. 51-73). Washington, DC: American Psychological Association.

Williams, K., Haywood, K., & VanSant, A. (1990). Characteristics of older adult throwers. In J.E. Clark & J. Humphrey (Eds.), *Advances in motor development research* (vol. 3, pp. 29-44). New York: AMS Press.

Williams, K., Haywood, K., & VanSant, A. (1991). Throwing patterns of older adults: A follow-up investigation. *International Journal of Aging and Human Development, 33*(4), 279-294.

Williams, K., Haywood, K., & VanSant, A. (1998). Changes in throwing by older adults: A longitudinal investigation. *Research Quarterly for Exercise and Sport, 66*(1), 1-10.

Williams, M., & Davids, K. (1995). Declarative knowledge in sport: A by-product of experience or a characteristic of expertise? *Journal of Sport and Exercise Psychology, 17,* 259-275.

Willmott, M. (1986). The effect of vinyl floor surface and carpeted floor surface upon walking in elderly hospital inpatients. *Age and Ageing, 15,* 119-120.

Wilmore, J.H., & Costill, D.L. (1994). *Physiology of sport and exercise.* Champaign, IL: Human Kinetics.

Wilson, T.M., & Tanaka, H. (2000). Meta-analysis of the age-associated decline in maximal aerobic capacity in men: Relation to training status. *American Journal of Physiology, Heart and Circulatory Physiology, 278,* H829-H834.

Winstein, C.J., & Schmidt, R.A. (1990). Reduced frequency of knowledge of results enhances motor skill learning. *Journal of Experimental Psychology: Learning, Memory, and Cognition, 16,* 677-691.

Winstein, C.J., Pohl, P.S., & Lewthwaite, R. (1994). Effects of physical guidance and knowledge of results on motor learning: Support for the guidance hypothesis. *Research Quarterly for Exercise and Sport, 65,* 316-323.

Winter, D.A., Patla, A.E., Frank, J.S., & Walt, S.E. (1990). Biomechanical walking pattern changes in the fit and healthy elderly. *Physical Therapy, 70,* 340-347.

Winther, K.T., & Thomas, J.R. (1981). Developmental differences in children's labeling of movement. *Journal of Motor Behavior, 13,* 77-90.

Wright, V.J., & Perricelli, B.C. (2008). Age-related rates of decline in performance among elite senior athletes. *American Journal of Sports Medicine, 36*(3), 443-450.

Wrisberg, C.A., & Mead, B.J. (1981). Anticipation of coincidence in children: A test of schema theory. *Perceptual and Motor Skills, 52,* 599-606.

Wrisberg, C.A., & Mead, B.J. (1983). Developing coincident timing skill in children: A comparison of training methods. *Research Quarterly for Exercise and Sport, 54,* 67-74.

Wrisberg, C.A., & Pein, R.L. (2002). Note of learners' control of the frequency of model presentation during skill acquisition. *Perceptual and Motor Skills, 94,* 792-794.

Wulf, G. (1991). The effect of type of practice on motor learning in children. *Applied Cognitive Psychology, 5,* 123-134.

Wulf, G., & Prinz, W. (2001). Directing attention to movement effects enhances learning: A review. *Psychonomic Bulletin & Review, 8,* 648-660.

Wulf, G., & Schimdt, R.A. (1994). Feedback-induced variability and the learning of generalized motor programs. *Journal of Motor Behavior, 26,* 348-361.

Wulf, G., & Su, J. (2007). An external focus of attention enhances golf shot accuracy in beginners and experts. *Research Quarterly for Exercise and Sport, 78,* 384-389.

Wulf, G., & Toole, T. (1999). Physical assistance devices in complex motor skill learning: Benefits of a self-controlled practice schedule. *Research Quarterly for Exercise and Sport, 70,* 265-272.

Wulf, G., & Weigelt, C. (1997). Instructions about physical principles in learning a complex skill: To tell or not to tell. . . . *Research Quarterly for Exercise and Sport, 68,* 362-367.

Wulf, G., Clauss, A., Shea, C.H., & Whitacre, C. (2001). Benefits of self-control in dyad practice. *Research Quarterly for Exercise and Sport, 72,* 299-303.

Yan, J.H., Thomas, J.R., & Thomas, K.T. (1998). Children's age moderates the effect of practice variability: A quantitative review. *Research Quarterly for Exercise and Sport, 69,* 210-215.

Yerkes, R.M., & Dodson, J.D. (1908). The relation of strength of stimulus to rapidity of habit-formation. *Journal of Comparative Neurology and Psychology, 18,* 459-482.

Young, D.E., & Schmidt, R.A. (1992). Augmented kinematic feedback for motor learning. *Journal of Motor Behavior, 24,* 261-273.

Zanone, P.G., & Kelso, J.A.S. (1994). The coordination dynamics of learning: Theoretical structure and experimental agenda. In S. Swinnen, H. Heuer, J. Massion, & P. Casaer (Eds.), *Interlimb coordination: Neural, dynamical, and cognitive constraints* (pp. 461-490). San Diego: Academic Press.

Zelinski, E.M., & Kennison, R.F. (2001). The Long Beach Longitudinal Study: Evaluation of longitudinal effects of aging on memory and cognition. *Home Health Care Services Quarterly, 19*(3), 45-55.

Zerzawy, R. (1987). Hämodynamische Reaktionen unter verschiedenen Belastungsformen [Hemodynamic reactions to different types of work]. In R. Rost & F. Webering (Eds.), *Kardiology im Sport [Cardiology in sport].* Cologne: German Sports Medicine Federation.

Zimmerman, B.J. (2000). Attaining self-regulation: A social cognitive perspective. In M. Boekaerts, P.R. Pintrich, & M. Zeidner (Eds.), *Handbook of self-regulation* (pp. 13-39). San Diego: Academic Press.

Zimmerman, B.J., & Kitsantas, A. (1997). Developmental phases in self-regulation: Shifting from process goals to outcome goals. *Journal of Educational Psychology, 89,* 29-36.

Zimmerman, B.J., & Kitsantas, A. (1999). Acquiring writing revision skill: Shifting from process to outcome self-regulatory goals. *Journal of Educational Psychology, 91,* 241-250.

Zinsser, N., Bunker, L.K., & Williams, J.M. (2001). Cognitive techniques for building confidence and enhancing performance. In J.M. Williams (Ed.), *Applied sport psychology: Personal growth to peak performance* (4th ed., pp. 284-311). Mountain View, CA: Mayfield.

Note: The italicized *f* and *t* following page numbers refer to figures and tables, respectively.

(*l* to *r*) Greg Reid, Pamela Haibach, and Douglas Collier. Photo is courtesy of the authors.

Pamela S. Haibach, PhD, is associate professor in the department of kinesiology, sport studies, and physical education at the College at Brockport, State University of New York. She is also coordinator of the kinesiology major and the study abroad programs for four majors in the kinesiology, sport studies, and physical education department at the College at Brockport.

Her teaching and research, including descriptive and intervention studies, focuses on performance, learning, postural control, and balance. Her research has spanned from children to older adults, including developing individuals, individuals with disabilities, and other special populations. Haibach earned her doctorate in kinesiology (2005) with an emphasis in motor behavior from Pennsylvania State University under the advisement of Dr. Karl M. Newell.

Haibach is president of the National Association for Sport and Physical Education's (NASPE) Motor Development and Learning Academy and a member of the International Federation of Adapted Physical Activity (IFAPA); American Alliance for Health, Physical Education, Recreation and Dance (AAHPERD); International Society of Motor Control (ISMC); and the North American Society for the Psychology of Sport and Physical Activity (NASPSPA). Active in her community, Haibach serves as a board member for the Brockport Child Development Center, co-chair of the Parent

Teacher Association at the Brockport Central School District (Barclay), and co-advisor for the College at Brockport Lions Club, which fundraises for CampAbilities, an on-campus sport camp for children and adolescents with visual impairments.

In her free time, Haibach enjoys fitness-related activities, ballroom dancing, boating, cross-country skiing, and water sports. She and her husband, Jeff, and two children, Tristan and Makayla, reside in Brockport, New York. As both a researcher and a mother, she enjoys experiencing the growth and development of her two young children.

Greg Reid, PhD, is a professor in the department of kinesiology and physical education at McGill University in Montreal, Quebec. A former elementary school physical education teacher and long-time youth coach in ice hockey and baseball, Reid obtained his graduate education in adapted physical activity, motor learning, and special education. As a teacher and researcher, Reid maintains a strong focus on theory-to-practice applications. Reid has taught motor development since 1986 and has conducted research since 1978 in the areas of performance, learning, and development spanning from children to older adults and including the study of individuals with and without disabilities.

In addition to his teaching and research, Reid supervises the practicum experiences of undergraduates teaching individuals with disabilities. He is also a former undergraduate program director and chair of the department of kinesiology and physical education at McGill University.

Reid is a member of the International Federation of Adapted Physical Activity (IFAPA); American Alliance for Health, Physical Education, Recreation and Dance (AAHPERD); and the Council for Exceptional Children (CEC). In 1997 he received the G. Lawrence Rarick Research Award from AAHPERD's National Consortium for Physical Education and Recreation for Individuals with Disabilities. He was elected an international member of the American Academy of Kinesiology and Physical Education in 1999.

Reid and his wife, Carol, reside in Ste-Adele, Quebec. They have two grown sons, Drew and Tyler. In his free time he enjoys hiking, bicycling, cross-country and downhill skiing, and reading novels. He is also currently enjoying the motor development and learning accomplishments of his grandson, Jacob Liam Reid.

Douglas H. Collier, PhD, is associate professor in the department of kinesiology, sport studies, and physical education as well as the co-coordinator of the teacher certification major at the College at Brockport, State University of New York. Collier was a delegate to the Jasper talks (1985), a significant policy workshop that became the catalyst to Collier's career-long interest in motor development. For the past three decades, his research agenda has examined, with an emphasis on theory to practice, various facets of motor development that pertain to the education of typically developing children and those with identifiable disabilities. Collier has presented his research at multiple national and international conferences concerned with the study of motor development and pedagogy.

Over the course of his 18-year career in higher education, Collier has served in multiple leadership positions at local, state, and national levels. Currently he is a member of the North American Federation of Adapted Physical Activity (NAFAPA); American Alliance for Health, Physical Education, Recreation and Dance (AAHPERD); and the North American Society for the Psychology of Sport and Physical Activity (NASPSPA).

Collier holds a doctorate in human performance from Indiana University (1993), where he studied under the advisement of Drs. Dale Ulrich, Beverly Ulrich, and Esther Thelen. In his free time, Collier enjoys racket sports, photography, and canoeing. He and his wife, Christine, reside in Brockport, New York. They have two grown daughters, Robin and Shannon.